MAR 16 1990

D1225193

1812: NAPOLEON'S RUSSIAN CAMPAIGN

1812: Napoleon's Russian Campaign

by

Richard K. Riehn

McGRAW-HILL PUBLISHING COMPANY
New York   St. Louis   San Francisco   Bogotá
Hamburg   Madrid   Mexico   Milan
Montreal   Paris   São Paulo   Tokyo   Toronto

Copyright © 1990 by Richard K. Riehn. All rights reserved. Printed in the United States of America. Except as permitted under the Copyright Act of 1976, no part of this publication may be reproduced or distributed in any form or by any means or stored in a data base or retrieval system without the prior written permission of the publisher.

1 2 3 4 5 6 7 8 9 DOC   DOC 9 5 4 3 2 1 0

ISBN 0-07-052731-8

Library of Congress Cataloging-in-Publication Data

Riehn, Richard K., 1928–
   1812 : Napoleon's Russian campaign / Richard K. Riehn.
     p.   cm.
   Includes bibliographical references.
   ISBN 0-07-052731-8
   1. Napoleonic Wars, 1800–1814—Campaigns/Soviet Union.
2. France.   Armée—History—Napoleonic Wars, 1800–1814.   3. Soviet
Union—History, Military—1801–1917.   4. Napoleon I, Emperor of the
French, 1769–1821—Military leadership.   I. Title.   II. Title:
Napoleon's Russian campaign.
DC235.R43   1990

Quality Printing and Binding by:
R.R. DONNELLY & SONS COMPANY
1009 Sloan Street
Crawfordsville, IN 47933 U.S.A.

To my friends Andrew Zaremba, who struck the spark, and Peter Wacker, whose untiring efforts made this possible, and to the memory of Major Freiherr von der Osten-Sacken und von Rhein, whose work presents the foundation of this campaign narrative.

Contents

I: PRELUDE

II: THE MILITARY BACKGROUND

APPENDICES

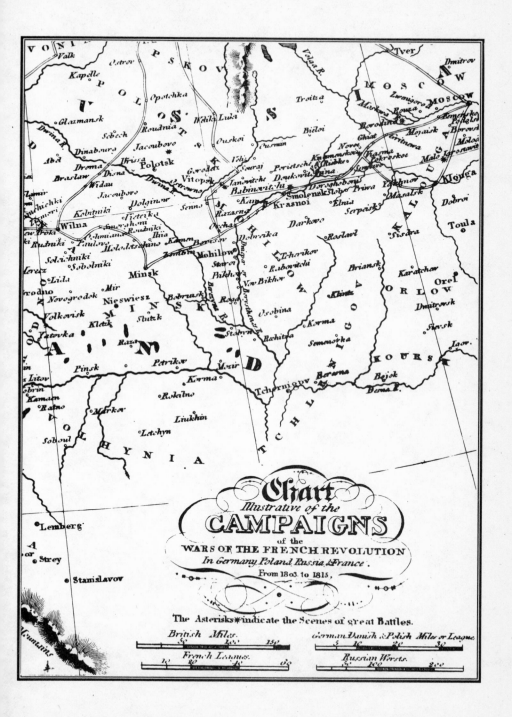

Chart Illustrative of the CAMPAIGNS of the WARS OF THE FRENCH REVOLUTION In Germany, Poland, Russia, & France. From 1803 to 1815.

The Asterisks indicate the Scenes of great Battles.

British Miles.

German Danish & Polish Miles or League.

French Leagues.

Russian Wersts.

I
Prelude

1. Prologue

The events of the French Revolution and the Napoleonic era aroused the passions of Europe every bit as much as did the two world wars of our own century. Collectively, they set into motion forces of nationalism and patriotism that would reverberate into modern times. And as long as veterans of the Napoleonic wars continued to survive in large numbers, the memories of those momentous times colored the thinking of every European nation.

Until the wars of the second half of the nineteenth century furnished new grist for the mills of military history, the Napoleonic wars represented virtually the sole subject for research and study in every western military establishment. This pervasive interest was bound to generate an unusually rich literature, albeit of quite uneven content. Half of the nineteenth century passed before all the documents relating to those events were deposited in the archives, and nearly the entire century ran its course before the first objective assessments were made of the characters and events of that period of *Sturm und Drang*. It is understandable that, especially in France, the study of the Napoleonic campaigns remained for a long time the central object of military and historical dissertation.

"I will write the history of your deeds." These words of the departing emperor inspired many of the companions of his glory to emulate his example, and the years of misfortune, from 1812 to 1815, offered an especially rich soil for narrative. It seemed a patriotic undertaking to write accounts that would restore to French arms the luster which had become tarnished in defeat. Chroniclers rendered dazzling descriptions of the years of ascendancy and explained away the defeats suffered from 1812 onward with allusions to treason, defection, incompetence, and chance, not to mention the weather in 1812.

The *Memorial de St. Helene*, the *History of the Consulate and the Empire* by Thiers, and the works of Pelet, Fain, Norvious, Bourienne, Sarazin, Segur, Vaudancourt, Marbot, and many others succeeded in keeping alive among the French the memories of the great times of world supremacy and also in formulating the Napoleonic legend. Even in our own time, modern works such as the *West Point Atlas of the Napoleonic Wars*[1] have perpetuated those traditions. In general, however, these works often failed to depict some of the realities with historical fidelity.

It was not until the defeat of 1870 that the French looked backward in earnest in a search for the principles Napoleon had formulated, principles which seemed to have gotten lost. This gave rise to a new style of general staff–sponsored military historical study and resulted in some outstanding works; they will probably never be improved upon because the mechanisms which produced them no longer exist.[2] Among the writers of these works, the French and Germans were easily the most prolific. They offered both a framework and a background against which thousands upon thousands of detailed studies in books and periodicals, as well as personal narratives in memoirs, diaries, and journals, could be used and evaluated by academicians and special-interest groups alike.

In 1908, Kircheisen,[3] who attempted to put together a bibliography of the Napoleonic era, estimated that more than 200,000 books, articles, and essays had been devoted to the military history of the era alone. Although this might not appear all that impressive to modern eyes, which have seen as many as 70,000 titles published in a single year, this was a staggering number in 1908. Howard[4] estimates that another 20,000 studies on the topic have been added since.

The Napoleonic era, however, was not simply one of conquests and military events. It also witnessed, on a grand scale, the rise of nationalism and a direct confrontation between national and dynastic interests. Ultimately, the wave of French nationalism set into motion by the French Revolution begot a nationalistic response from the rest of Europe. And even though this remained largely latent in Napoleon's time, it nevertheless cast long shadows across events from 1812 onward. Napoleonic Europe was every bit as complex as modern-day Europe, and the French empire was enmeshed in

a net of particularist interests which must be understood if the events themselves are to make sense.

Napoleon was riding the crest of a wave of French nationalism unleashed
by the revolution, but he had harnessed it and given it direction. He had,
to put it in the simplest terms, replaced republican nationalism with his
own dynastic interests, even as a flock of other, minor dynasts was riding
on his coattails. These dynasts, in their turn, regarded the nationalistic force
as a danger to their own particularist interests, even as they began to feel
its pressures stirring among their own people.

Yet the Napoleon who constantly appealed to the forces of French nationalism thought he could also effectively suppress similar stirrings toward
a national identity in the rest of Europe. However, by the time the Russian
campaign had run its course in 1812, the princes of the Rhine Confederation
had cause to look toward their own futures with some apprehension. The
Napoleonic alliance still offered security of a sort, but the common man
was becoming as weary of the continuing military demands as were the
French themselves. What would become of the princes if Napoleon was to
fall from power? The response, when it came from dynastic Europe beyond
Napoleon's orbit, and against him, had distinctly nationalistic overtones,
even though it continued to be dominated by dynastic interests. Thus, the
Grand Alliance of 1813, binding together the three main characters—
Hapsburg, Romanov, and Hohenzollern—still furnishes an object lesson
about the difficulties attending allied undertakings of any sort.

The Austrian emperor, apprehensive about nationalistic stirrings in his
own polyglot state, carefully avoided anything that might arouse or give
vent to the passions of his people. He was even reluctant to raise a strong
militia because this would have, in effect, armed the nation. Instead, he
conducted an old-fashioned cabinet war in true dynastic fashion, with all
its limited objectives, thereby contributing more than a little to the anemic
pursuit of the 1813 campaign. His war aims went no further than a con-
tainment of Napoleon behind the Rhine.

The Russian tsar, on the other hand, once he saw the means at hand,
was prepared to settle for nothing less than Napoleon's downfall. Still, his
was not the national war nineteenth-century historiography tended to make
of it. Even modern Soviet historians were rather lukewarm on the subject
until its specter was resurrected during World War II to foster a holdout
mentality against the invading Germans.

The Prussian king, too, was not enthusiastic about a national war, but
like it or not, he got one. The independent action of one of his generals at
the close of Napoleon's Russian campaign had already compromised him in
that regard, and the mood of the nation prevented him from repudiating

the event. His proclamation of 1813 merely put an official stamp on an issue that had already been taken out of his hands.

In Spain, a homogeneous population had expressed its will against French tyranny as the French had during their own earlier revolution. In the Rhine Confederation, however, realpolitik continued to keep rising anti-French sentiments in check for a while. Still, even here the fabric was decidedly uneven and not easily reduced to a common denominator.

Beyond this circle stood mercantile Britain, which waged what was largely a war in defense of its economic interests, and Sweden, which lent its services for the possession of Norway.

Thus, the student of history, in search of a leitmotiv, is bound to have a difficult time. Even though there were no neutrals anywhere, there was also little clash of ideologies. The conflict was one of interests, and these ran at cross-purposes everywhere. Given this general background—with so many players and pawns in the game, with so many perspectives from which even the simplest of events might be viewed—there can be little wonder that this era spawned nearly a quarter of a million books and articles. Such an abundance can well result in confusing, as much as enlightening, the issues.

For the British, the view of the Napoleonic wars is dominated by Wellington, the Peninsula, and Waterloo, not to mention Nelson and Trafalgar; for the Austrians, by Archduke Charles and Aspern; for the Prussians, by Bluecher, the Katzbach, and Belle Alliance (the Prussian name for Waterloo); and for the Russians, by Kutuzov, Borodino, and the Beresina. Nor were the lesser actors on the Napoleonic stage lacking their share of heroes. The era produced them in wholesale fashion, their magnitude varying only with the viewer's perspective. In France, the names of Napoleon's marshals became inextricably bound up with the glorious milestones that were Austerlitz, Jena, and Friedland.

Last, but far from least, is the overwhelming image of Napoleon himself, bringing into sharp focus all the encumbrances of romance and legend. Here, the problem for the historian is exacerbated by the fact that Napoleon the general, Napoleon the statesman, and Napoleon the emperor all represented different facets of Napoleon the man. Of these, only Napoleon the general, one of the great captains of all time, had the stature to gain a unanimous positive vote. Yet the genius of Napoleon the soldier, wrapped in romance and legend, is so overpowering that it constantly cuts across the image of the other Napoleons, frequently obscuring the underlying realities.

But if the whole of the Napoleonic era thus offers a rich palette from which the historian may extrapolate an endless variety of views, then the events of the 1812 Russian campaign offer an equally rich microcosm of their own. In a campaign that lasted only 5 months and 21 days, the mightiest army the world had ever seen was all but totally destroyed. For a long time, the Russian winter was allowed to bear the brunt of the blame for this monumental failure, and this was entirely understandable. Even though the killing frost did not descend until the very end, when the campaign had for long been a failure and the remnants of the Grand Army were in full retreat, the freezing cold was the last and most profound impression the survivors brought away with them.

The idea of the winter and the suffering it had heaped upon the shoulders of the human wreckage fleeing back into Poland at once took hold of the imagination of an astounded Europe, which was unable to think of a better explanation for the disaster that had overtaken the Grand Army. The severity of the Russian winter was eagerly seized upon by the French and by Napoleon himself to explain away the awesome failure. Thus, the legend of Napoleonic invincibility was kept alive, and the glory of French arms remained unblemished. Only God and the elements were stronger. But the "Sun of Austerlitz" no longer shone quite so brightly.

The bill for Napoleon's Russian debacle would be presented in 1813. Attempting to bring down the Russians by means which had, by 1812, become conventional for Napoleon, he had simply overreached himself. However, the story of how he had set his sights too far ahead did not begin with the mobilization for his march into Russia. Nor did it begin when the first Grand Army crossed the Rhine in 1805. By then, Napoleon had long made himself the instrument of French policies which reached back, far beyond the French Revolution, into the times of Richelieu and the Thirty Years' War.

NOTES

1. Esposito, V. J., and Elting, J. R. A *Military History and Atlas of the Napoleonic Wars* (popularly known as the *West Point Atlas of the Napoleonic Wars*). New York, 1965.
2. With the coming of the atomic age, the study of military history fell out of favor in many military establishments. Particularly in the U.S. armed services, the fields of business administration, corporate management, and computer sciences were deemed of greater importance than the military arts and sciences. For an interesting view on the subject, see "Musket and Quill," by Col. L. J. Matthews, in *Military Review*, vol. 16, no. 1, Fort Leavenworth, 1981.
3. Kircheisen, F. M. *Bibliographie des Napoleonischen Zeitalters*. Berlin, 1908–1912.
4. Horward, D. D., ed. *Napoleonic Military History. A Bibliography*. London, 1986.

2. Napoleonic Europe: The Years of Ascendancy

When the energy released by the French Revolution (1789–1792) spilled into neighboring countries, France's centuries-old dynastic struggle with Austria and England flared up again. At first, the European powers adopted a wait-and-see attitude toward the events in France. Louis XIV had made few friends for France, and his successors had done little to improve relations with their neighbors. As a result, no one was greatly perturbed by the humbling of the Bourbons. The established order of European institutions did not appear to be threatened (although its upset was only a question of time). The incarceration of a king, however, and the eventual threat of his execution did shake dynastic Europe to its very foundations. Thus, when the threatened execution became a reality, a reaction from the European powers was inevitable, and it demanded some sort of unified action. Even so, the First Coalition formed against the French republic in February 1792, involving virtually all of France's neighbors, did little more than exert political pressure against the Paris government.

But Paris itself was a political battlefield. When the internal struggle for power threatened the continuing existence of the republican government, the discovery of an enemy without offered an excellent means for subduing the enemy within. France declared war against Austria in April 1792. This marked the beginning of nearly a decade of war, fought by the French republic against two coalitions of the European community. These coalitions had been formed largely on British initiative and were heavily reliant upon British subsidies. Bound together by a complicated patchwork of alliances, treaties, and accommodations, the military images of these coalitions were as varied as the political backgrounds that had brought them into existence. But time would prove Austria and Britain to be the mainsprings that drove the contest onward, even though the cast of characters would change virtually from one campaign to the next.

Against this background of military events, an internal political contest was raging within the young French republic. In its course, a succession of men stepped into the power vacuum created time and again by plots, counterplots, and the paranoia of the Terror, their careers, like shooting stars, flaring brightly and then becoming extinct almost as quickly as they had appeared.

In the midst of these upheavals, a young artillery captain named Napoleon Bonaparte appeared on the scene during the siege of Toulon, a Mediterranean harbor the British had occupied at the invitation of French royalists. At once recognizing the weakest point in the enemy's defenses, he advanced a scheme designed to bring the siege to a speedy conclusion. When he met with resistance, he promptly went over the heads of his superiors. His plan was a brilliant success. Toulon fell and the British lost their foothold on French soil. This affair gave Napoleon's military career a quick boost. Raised to the rank of a temporary major during the siege operations, he was made a brigadier general as soon as a warrant could be obtained from Paris.

But these were the days when France was full of hopeful young men like Napoleon who had leaped through the ranks and up the ladder of command far in advance of their years. Still, Napoleon had gained the attention of important men on the Committee of Public Safety in Paris, men such as Paul Barras and Lazare Carnot (the latter would eventually reorganize the armies of the republic). Recalled to Paris in 1795, Napoleon declined to accept a command in the Vendée, in western France, where royalists were in revolt. He sensed that chasing a bunch of rebellious peasants, even if they were royalists, would hardly enhance his newly won reputation or advance his ambitions. They were, after all, Frenchmen.

Soon, however, he was to do something worse. In October of that same year he confronted one of the most powerful forces of the revolution, the Paris mob, and gave it his celebrated "whiff of grapeshot."

With Prussia and Spain dropping out of the First Coalition against France in 1795 and the British beyond the reach of the land-bound French armies, only the Austrians remained in the field to carry on the fight. Since Napoleon's intervention against the Paris mob had invested him with a certain political coloring, the Directorate thought it wise to send this potentially dangerous young man off somewhere, before he developed a taste for political power. The sideshow in Italy, where the Austrians still maintained an army, was thought to be the perfect place. Surely, Jourdan and Moreau would settle with the Austrian main forces, operating north of the Alps, in Germany. But that was not to be the case.

Firing up a ragtag army that was down on its heels, living a hand-to-mouth existence because Paris had very little to give, Napoleon now had the opportunity to put into effect his own ideas on how to run a campaign. The comparatively small army of Italy was just the right sort of instrument on which he could cut his teeth. Within one year both Austria and the rest of Europe learned two things about Napoleon: the way he conducted a campaign and the sort of treaties he imposed.

The decision fell in Italy—not, as expected, in Germany. The Treaty of Campo Formio, concluded in October 1797, took the Austrians out of the war. Napoleon conducted the negotiations as though he had done this sort of thing all his life. The price was high. Hapsburg Austria and Bourbon France may have been at swords' points for centuries, but it was now Napoleon and republican France that would incur the wrath of Austria.

On the whole, the French republic had done very well against the First Coalition arrayed against it. Prussia had already renounced its claims against all territories west of the Rhine. Austria was forced to cede possession of Wallonia (the Austrian Netherlands), known today as Belgium. At the same time, recognition of the former United Provinces of the Netherlands, now styled the Batavian Republic, as a "sister republic" of France was forced through.

In northern Italy, Napoleon had added materially to these gains with the establishment of yet another dependency, the so-called Cisalpine Republic, patched together from several Italian principalities. In addition to this, Venice was forced to yield the Ionian Islands, thus affording France a naval base at the doorstep to the Adriatic Sea.

Napoleon was given a hero's reception when he returned to Paris in December 1797, even though the Directorate viewed him with an even greater sense of foreboding than before. Thus, when he advanced his project for an invasion of Egypt, which was to be the first step toward opening an overland route to India, the very heart of British economic power, it was eagerly accepted. The Egyptian adventure turned out to be a fiasco. For once, Napoleon had miscalculated, and he got his first real lesson about British seapower. In Egypt, he faced the possibility of being stranded on the wrong side of the Mediterranean, which proved to be a place ruled by the British navy. The situation could have easily been Napoleon's undoing, but his luck continued to hold. (He had felt that a lucky star was guiding his fortunes; now he could well start believing in it in earnest.) Departing Egypt on August 24, 1799, he landed in France on October 9, after being becalmed on the Egyptian coast for a couple of weeks. Fortunately, the doldrums had also immobilized the British scouts and raiders that were cruising everywhere.

Arriving in Paris on October 15, Napoleon once again found the government in a state of ferment. It was time to take an active hand in the nation's political affairs. In a game that anyone seemed to be able to play, he now decided to become a player himself, rather than remain the pawn of men he didn't respect. When he made his first concrete political moves, he fully justified the suspicions of the Directorate, which had twice deliberately sent him off to distant parts. The final result of these moves was the new Constitution of the Year VIII, enacted in December 1799, which also made Napoleon the first consul of France.

However, the Austrians had not gone away. Predictably, the Treaty of Campo Formio had been little better than a truce. It was spring 1800, and the Austrians were on the march again both to the north and to the south of the Alps. Napoleon, who now had a choice, opted to seek the decision in the Italian theater of operations. It had served him well before, and it would do so again. Arriving in Italy, he restored the erstwhile Cisalpine Republic, now called the Italian Republic, and marched on to Marengo, the most controversial of his victories. This might have spelled an end to yet another coalition war, but British subsidies kept the Austrians fighting. It was left to Moreau, who commanded in Germany, to put an end to it with his victory at Hohenlinden on December 3, 1800. This led to the Treaty of Luneville in February 1801, and it made Moreau the hero in the eyes of a war-weary French public. The turn of events was an embarrassment to Napoleon and probably gave rise to his lifelong campaign to make of Marengo something it had never been: one of his greatest, if not the greatest, of his victories. (It was not until 1804 that Napoleon was finally able to rid himself of Moreau's embarrassing presence, when the latter was implicated in a royalist plot.)

Meanwhile, the British, also wearying of the war that they had been carrying on single-handedly since the Austrians had bowed out, made peace at Amiens in March 1802. It was not to be a lasting peace, but Napoleon used this breathing spell to set about refining all the skills the republican armies had gained in their long series of campaigns. In addition, Napoleon the statesman saw to the territorial expansion of France. Piedmont and the Swiss canton of Wallis were annexed, along with the island of Elba. His failure, however, to negotiate a trade agreement with the British and their refusal to return the island of Malta soon created new tensions. At the same time, the French colonial adventures in the Caribbean were failing. Thus, by 1803, the storm clouds began to gather again.

If money was the root of all evil and Britain used so much of it to keep the enemies of France in the field, then, Napoleon reasoned, why not strike at the very roots of these subsidies by shutting down the markets of British commerce? The Egyptian failure had, for the time being, ruled out any possibility of conducting overland expeditions against India. But if it was possible to close Continental ports to British traders, this might strike a serious blow at them even as it might (and indeed did) stimulate French commerce. Unfortunately, closing the ports would involve a long, drawn-out methodical process that was not at all to Napoleon's liking. It might do as a last resort, but meanwhile, more direct action might offer a quicker solution.

This situation gave rise to the military encampments along the English Channel, where the bulk of French combat forces was massed to train for an invasion of the British Isles. Nelson's victory over the combined French and Spanish fleets at Trafalgar in October 1805 rendered any such invasion plans useless. But the time the army had spent in the Channel encampments had been highly beneficial for its state of training, reaching a level it was never to achieve again in years to come. The Austrians and Russians would be the first to feel the brunt of this new French military machine. But before this happened, Napoleon had another surprise in store for his adversaries.

Coaxing the senate into proclaiming him emperor in May 1804, Napoleon now entered the dynastic club of European monarchs. Perhaps the French were tiring of the shaggy-haired Jacobins, perhaps they were beginning to miss some of the old pomp and circumstance, even if they would not welcome a return of all the old evils. Perhaps somber airs were out of step with the newly found power and prestige of the republic. As it was, a plebiscite showed that the nation approved of the appointment with a landslide response.

On December 2, 1804, Napoleon placed Charlemagne's crown, commandeered from Aachen, onto his own head. In doing so, he finally realized an old dream whose reality had been denied to all the French monarchs who had gone before, but he also placed his foot squarely into an area that had for long been a traditional Hapsburg preserve. The Hapsburgs were, after all, the legitimate successors to the Holy Roman Empire. The Austrians received another jolt when, in May 1805, Napoleon placed the Lombard crown of Italy on his head, made himself king of Italy, and installed his stepson, Eugene Beauharnais, as viceroy.

On his way back to France in July, he also picked up Genoa in passing. The Napoleonic game of imperial monopoly was gaining momentum even as the enmity of Austria deepened. Again, he had put his foot into yet another Austrian preserve, and no one in Vienna believed, even for a moment, that the Austrians had seen the last of this French parvenu. Thus, before the year was out, the Austrians were in the field again, reacting to what they justly perceived to be a "clear and present danger."

Under the leadership of the younger Pitt, who had returned to office in April 1804, Britain had succeeded in resurrecting what was now called the Third Coalition. The self-made Carolingian emperor and Italian king had gone too far. That the Austrians would come out fighting again was to be expected. Russian intervention was secured because Napoleon's sphere of influence had also drawn dangerously close to Russian interests in the Balkans.

Napoleon was ready. The army of England had been training long enough by the Channel coast. It was time to use it.

In a lightning campaign during the closing months of 1805, Napoleon took the first and most important step toward the realization of his goals when he trounced the Austrians and Russians at Austerlitz. This "Sun of Austerlitz" was to beam warmly upon his intention to finally give shape to his idea of the "Three Germanies," an idea rooted deeply in the past.

The military histories have frequently bypassed the question of how a nation professing liberty, equality, and brotherhood, which had rid itself of one dynasty and risen to its own defense against intervention from outside dynastic reactions, could undergo an apparently seamless metamorphosis into a conquest society. Likewise, many studies fail to address how Napoleon, in the name of dynastic interests, not only could continue a trend that had begun long ago in Bourbon France and had been picked up again by the revolutionary governments but also could now carry it to a conclusion by himself. Fiedler, a German military historian, summarizes the part the republic played in this when he points out: "After the era of enlightenment had already awakened ideas of a national identity among all the Europeans, the [French] revolution permeated its own nation with the belief that it was the vanguard of the achievements of civilization for all mankind."[1]

The Terror, however, and the excesses committed by the republican *soldateska* were not well received beyond the French borders. To the contrary, the tangible aspects of all this "liberty, equality and fraternity," quite apart from the official dynastic reaction, had elicited a popular negative response as well. "As a result," Fiedler goes on, "this ideological universalism changed into an egotistical nationalism. The republic, enforced by the democratic left, was no longer content with securing against the outside the victory that had been won within but embarked upon the road to conquest in order to enhance the ideological substance of the revolution with territorial gain."[2]

This explains how the cooperation of the masses—who had just risen to the cries of *"la partie est en danger!"*—was for the first time secured in wars of aggression. But it does not explain why the main thrust of this aggression turned east, toward the Rhine River and Germany.

When Danton, one of the leaders of the revolution, declared at the beginning of 1793 that nature had fixed France's boundaries on the Rhine and that "no power on Earth shall keep us from our goal," he was expressing an idea that had its roots deep in Bourbon dynastic thinking. A strong case may be made for the fact that precisely this kind of dynastic ambition left several European provinces, from the Alsace in the west to West Prussia and the Baltic Provinces in the east and various points in between, on the wrong side of ethnic and national boundaries, creating problems that have militated right into modern times.

In 1629, Cardinal Richelieu had already drawn up his well-known memorandum delineating the necessity for French intervention in German affairs. Thus, when Napoleon declared to a Prussian negotiator, "I shall play the part which Richelieu assigned to France,"[3] he was simply expressing a policy that had been prevalent in France over the previous two centuries. Oman, the eminent British historian, commented that one of the curious aspects of German history was that the Hapsburgs consistently failed to summon the combined might of the German empire to put an end, once and for all, to the constant French aggressions against its western territories.[4] The revolution had not even interrupted, much less derailed, the dynastic objectives of the *ancien regime*. Thus, when Napoleon announced on another occasion that "the annihilation of the German nationality was an essential feature of his policy, he was again merely reducing to a phrase what had been the essence of French policy since Richelieu."

Just as Richelieu, and even some before his time, had always found helpmates among the south German princes, who had made fishing in the particularist backwaters of the Thirty Years' War so profitable for France, so too did Napoleon find rich and fertile soil for intervention. These German princes, according to Barraclough, worked their principalities like a landlord works his farm.[5] They regarded the idea of a national identity among their subjects and those of neighboring states as a danger to their own particular interests, because it would ultimately strengthen the political cohesion of the Holy Roman Empire and weaken their own independence. In short, any nationalistic stirrings smacked of Hapsburg domination. Prussia was, at this point, still far away from even entering into the equation. Thus, with Napoleon apparently restraining a general surge toward nationalism by returning France to the dynastic fold (even if he was a parvenu), the German princes not only saw in him a release from Hapsburg apron strings but thought that exchanging domination from Vienna for that from Paris would guarantee the independence they craved.

The immediate result of the Austrian defeat in 1805 and the flooding of south Germany with French troops was the creation of the Rhine Confederation, headed by Napoleon as its protector. With the exception of Frederick of Wuerttemberg, who did not relent until French troops inundated his capital city, all the south German princes flocked willingly into Napoleon's embrace.

At this point, Napoleon had already gone a giant step beyond Richelieu's fondest dreams. But the edifice of Napoleon's grand design would not be complete until Prussia was brought down and Saxony and northern Germany were brought into the fold. Then the creation of the three Germanies would be an accomplished fact: All that was not Austria or Prussia would be the Rhine Confederation. The first two would counterbalance and neutralize each other, and the latter would be wholly in Napoleon's hands. Germany would thus be effectively removed as a threat to Napoleonic ambitions.

The Treaty of Pressburg, which had officially ended the war of 1805 against Austria, was signed on December 26. It did not put an end to the Third Coalition, but it added Istria and Dalmatia to the kingdom of Italy and ceded the Tyrol to the Bavarians, a gift that was to spell more trouble than good for the latter. The Tyroleans, after five centuries under the Austrian crown, did not take kindly to being handed over to the Bavarians.

More importantly, however, the war had finally put an end to the old Roman empire and had made possible the creation of the Rhine Confederation, which became official with the signing of a treaty on July 12, 1806. With the Holy Roman Empire passing from the scene, Austria was now forced to recognize the rulers of Bavaria and Wuerttemberg as kings, even as those of Baden and Hesse-Darmstadt were elevated to the rank of grand dukes. They, as well as others in the new Rhine Confederation, were rewarded with territorial gains as well, with the sequestration of church territories providing a major medium of exchange.

Even as all of this was in progress, Napoleon had sent Massena, probably the ablest of his marshals, to settle with Naples. The Neapolitan Bourbon army, however, promptly fled to Sicily and safety behind the wooden ramparts of the British fleet.

At about the same time, the Batavian Republic saw itself elevated from the status of "sister republic" to that of a kingdom for one of the imperial brothers, Louis Bonaparte. Not only did an empire have no use for such "sisters," but tying up the Netherlands in proper dynastic fashion also provided Napoleon with better insight into Dutch ledgers.

The Austerlitz campaign had left the Russians suitably chastised but far from defeated. Nor did the Prussians keep Napoleon waiting any longer. Put off at first by the Austro-Russian defeat at Austerlitz, they now suddenly decided to take on Napoleon all by themselves. They joined the coalition in 1806, and instead of hanging back and waiting for the Russians to come up, they boldly marched forward, right into the jaws of disaster. Jena and Auerstaedt became the milestones of their defeat, which was to furnish the grist for the mills of controversy over the relative merits of the old linear order and the new column tactics.

In a headlong pursuit of the Prussians which sent Napoleon and his Grand Army east, all the way to the Vistula, the emperor suddenly saw himself brought up short for the first time by conditions which proved to be beyond even his control. He was reminded in no uncertain terms that there were limits to how long and how well an army could support itself from the land. A more skilled opponent could easily have landed him in serious trouble.

In Poland, the emperor met the Russians again, but the engagement was not another Austerlitz. Instead, at Eylau, Napoleon ended up on the wrong side of a thrashing, and the victory he claimed stood on no more solid ground than his possession of the battlefield. To add some spice to the soup, a relatively small Prussian detachment (the main army had already been beaten) had taken a decisive hand in the battle.

Friedland, the battle fought on June 14, 1807, put an end to the war. There was no question about who won this one. Napoleon did. But for the Grand Army, the overall cost of the 1806 and 1807 campaigns had been dear, cutting deeply into the substance which had made the army of 1805 the best Napoleon had ever commanded. Russian losses had been heavy as well, but the Russians were standing on their own doorstep. Indeed, the scope of Napoleon's operations had again expanded to such a point that he would have been hard-pressed to field a sufficiently powerful army against the Russians in Poland if the newly gained troops of the Rhine Confederation had not undertaken the lion's share of secondary but necessary tasks.

Napoleon had won, but he had not been able to deliver a knockout blow. Although Prussia had been overrun and was totally at his mercy, he had beaten only a Russian army. Behind it still stood the whole of Russia, which, as far as Napoleon was concerned, would remain totally beyond reach for some time to come.

Thus, when Napoleon made peace with the Russians at Tilsit, he was not in a position to wring as much from them as he had from his previous adversaries. All he could really do for the time being was put a good face on things and seek to further his ends by heaping flattery upon the Russian tsar by pretending friendship and admiration for him. It was, of course, not difficult to dazzle Alexander's vanity, and the tsar easily succumbed to the overtures of his imperial "brother" or "cousin." It is doubtful that Napoleon's motives were anything but opportunistic, yet the price paid for this "friendship" was far too high for a man who had become thoroughly accustomed to having his way. Not only was Napoleon forced to moderate his intentions toward Prussia, but he also had to abandon Finland and Turkey to Russian interests. Of course, he didn't think that Alexander would benefit all that much from the possession of Finland, since that was sure to incur the enmity of Sweden. And there was always the possibility of doing something indirectly by retarding the advance of Russian interests in the Balkans.

As for the Prussians, they had no bargaining power whatever. Thus, they did not come away nearly so well, even though Napoleon probably had not yet made up his mind about their ultimate disposition. Still, it is fairly certain that the idea he expressed to Metternich, the Austrian plenipotentiary, during negotiations in 1813—that the Hohenzollerns might be given a duchy along the Vistula—hadn't occurred to him on the spur of the moment. At the same time, however, Napoleon did not neglect the idea of driving a wedge between the Russo-Prussian relationship by presenting Alexander with a small portion of the territories Prussia had been forced to cede.

Tilsit represented a pivotal point in Napoleon's ascendancy. Many see it as both the beginning and the high-water mark of the "friendship" between Napoleon and Alexander. Some also think, not without justification, that Tilsit saw Napoleon at the very apex of his power. Even though his march would continue unchecked for some time, the difficulties would begin to mount and nothing would ever be as easy in the future as it had been during the previous three years.

Napoleon may have been forced by the Austrians and Russians to shelve his project for the invasion of Britain in 1805, but Nelson's stunning victory at Trafalgar finally put an end to the plan. The time for the economic assault, even if it was only a second-best approach, appeared to have come. The unqualified success of the Prussian campaign of 1806 would furnish an even better starting position for what had until now been only an imperfect attempt. Napoleon had already issued a decree from Berlin on October 21, 1806, proclaiming the Continental blockade, but the effort was somewhat premature. His military success against the Russians in 1807, however, coupled with his unquestionable personal diplomatic triumph over Alexander, offered the possibility of making it a reality at last. With a compliant Russia and a defeated Prussia, the entire Baltic could now be fitted into the system. All that remained was to bring Sweden and Denmark into line.

One of the immediate results of Alexander's agreement to join the blockade was the British preemptive strike at Copenhagen and the Danish fleet; this drove the Danes into the Continental system before the year 1807 had run its course. Another year passed before the Russians, after wresting Finland away from Sweden, pressed the Swedes into joining the blockade as well. The Treaty of Fredrikshamn, ratified in Paris in 1809, ensured Swedish cooperation through the promise of returning Anterior Pommerania to the Swedes as compensation. With this agreement, Napoleon's string of successes radiating from the Treaty of Tilsit were just about played out.

In the interests of bringing the events in northern Europe to a temporary conclusion in an uninterrupted sequence, events taking place on the opposite end of the Continent have been bypassed. It is now necessary to return to them.

Even while the tones of his friendship for Alexander continued to hit high notes, Napoleon knew that the Russian question had merely been shelved, not by any means settled. Meanwhile, the Iberian Peninsula had to be integrated into the blockade if it was to become effective.

King John of Portugal, who had maintained close relations of long standing with Britain, had balked at joining the blockade. This at once prompted Napoleon to dispose of him. In October 1807, he concluded an agreement with Spain to divide Portugal between them, provided French troops had permission to cross Spanish territory to eject the House of Braganza. John VI fled to Brazil, and Napoleon declared him deposed.

But Napoleon had not yet finished. Next to feel the ax were the Spanish themselves. Talleyrand was still in Berlin, sorting out the affairs of the Prussians and letting them know just how much their defeat was going to cost them, when Napoleon advised him that he meant to dispose of the Spanish Bourbons as well. This was yet another act that could hardly endear the French emperor to the rest of dynastic Europe. Even those who still basked in the sunshine of his friendship must have come to the realization that they no longer ruled by divine right, or even by the will of their people, but by Napoleon's permission alone.

Although the wars of the previous centuries had been dominated by ideological struggles, the seventeenth century had already been marked by the beginning of struggles for naked power and territorial aggrandizement, led by France, the first nation-state of Europe. Still, even the Age of Reason subscribed to certain universal ideas, tacitly accepted by all. Princes and monarchs, scrambling for power and domination, fought what have been termed "cabinet wars" with clearly defined and limited objectives; they settled their scores with the exchange of this or that border province. It would not have done for either the Bourbons or the Hapsburgs to eliminate each other outright. The princes, great or small, all ruled by "divine right"—at least, they believed they did. Thus, they might seek to curb each others' power and influence, but they would hardly question each others' right to exist. To do so would have placed one's own legitimacy in question and disturbed the established order. Thus, Napoleon's high-handed monopoly game did not fail to shock the European dynastic club, no matter on which side of the fence one stood.

While his "friends" experienced a certain unease over this cold wind blowing through their audience chambers, the Spanish venture was a miscalculation for Napoleon on yet another score. Disposing of the Bourbons had been simple enough, but unlike the case in politically fragmented Germany, in Spain a red-hot wave of fierce nationalism struck at the French. For the first time, Napoleon was faced with a situation for which even he had no ready-made solution.

Until then, Napoleon had waged war against regular military establishments that, even under the best of circumstances, had found it difficult to replace themselves. Now he was faced with a national insurrection by a politically and religiously united people in a country ideal for guerrilla war. Indeed, it is the Spanish tongue that has invested this style of warfare with its universal cognomen: The term "guerrilla" is a diminutive of the Spanish *guerra*, meaning "little" or "minor" war.

Today, with the benefit of hindsight and with present-day experiences of this kind of resistance, we know that Napoleon could not possibly have succeeded where even modern military establishments armed with twentieth-century technology have failed—especially not while the forces of the resistance had outside help. And this the British provided. As it was, the French columns marching into Spain in 1807 and 1808 were not those of the glorious Grand Army, which had never tasted defeat. They were, for the most part, an ad hoc collection of immobile cadre and depot battalions, hastily filled up with raw recruits.

Eventually, Napoleon was forced to put in a personal appearance in Spain with parts of the Grand Army. In order to do this with a reasonable degree of safety, however, he first had to reassure himself about the tsar's continued cooperation. This was especially important since it was no longer a secret that the Austrians were making a spectacular recovery and that their military establishment was being modernized under the leadership of Archduke Charles, the Austrian emperor's brother. They were obviously arming for another round.

Again, the friendship of the tsar demanded a price on the diplomatic front. It would be necessary, for the time being, to give the Russians a free hand in their advances along the lower Danube. This, at least, was the tenor of the meeting at Erfurt, which was to shore up the Treaty of Tilsit once more.

Napoleon found no laurels in Spain. The British expeditionary force, the only suitable objective for the Grand Army, successfully avoided a lethal confrontation. As a result, Napoleon decided that the further conduct of operations in Spain could be handed back to his subordinates. It was time to return to France and see to the security of the throne, which appeared imperiled by succession plotters. He foiled them easily enough, but new laurels were needed to shore up the flagging interest and support of the French nation. Again, the Austrians obliged.

The hawks among the Austrians, burning to avenge their grievances against Napoleon, pushed Archduke Charles into yet another attempt to take the measure of the French, even though he thought the time was not yet ripe. Napoleon was hardly surprised by these events, even if their timing was most inopportune. He wasted no time in reconstituting the Grand Army, which was called the Army of Germany this time because there was now also an Army of Spain. But this was merely a passing technicality.

The Austrians stood alone. The hoped-for insurrection in Germany never materialized, except for some sporadic events.

That the recently Bavarianized Tyroleans would rise against their new masters was to be expected. They still considered themselves Austrians, and their country was going to war. Their leader, Andreas Hofer, was to die in front of an Italian firing squad at Mantua.

In Prussia, Major von Schill took his regiment of hussars into the field without permission in the hope of sparking a general insurrection. He died on a street pavement in Stralsund under the guns of Dutch and Danish troops. His head was severed from his grossly mutilated body and sent to Jerome Bonaparte in Kassel as a trophy, and eleven of his officers fell before a firing squad of Nassauers in Wesel.

A free corps of Brunswickers, raised by their deposed and exiled duke, found itself isolated in southern Germany and succeeded in making a dash across the face of the country all the way to the North Sea, where the men were rescued by the British. One could hardly have arranged a more striking symbolism for the German impotence born of disunity.

As for the archduke and his Austrians, he managed to do something no one else had done before: He handed Napoleon a clear-cut check at Aspern/

Essling. A few weeks later, at Wagram, Napoleon redressed the balance, but decidedly not in the grand style of the past. And no one knew this better than Napoleon himself. The Austrians of 1809 were nothing like those of 1805.

The 1809 campaign marked the beginning of a developing pattern. Napoleon was—and would continue to be—the greatest captain of his time, but the days when he could simply roll over the opposition were passing. Even as the quality of his own armies was being diluted by the continuing demands placed upon them, the opposition was learning to cope. But if Napoleon took any notice of this at all, he was far too confident in his own abilities to give these matters more than a passing thought. Still, Wagram held no fond memories for him.

Despite the Erfurt agreements, Napoleon had gotten little satisfaction from Alexander, other than keeping Prussia dormant, in his role as a go-between. But the Prussian king, who would still exhibit considerable reluctance to join in the fray in 1813, would hardly have stirred so much as a finger in 1809. Indeed, the main reason for Alexander to have entered into any agreements with Napoleon had been his desire to keep a hand in the game in order to forestall any more calamities on the scale of the Spanish Bourbons. If Napoleon had looked upon the domination of Germany as a focal point of his objectives, the tsar was no less interested. It could hardly be in Russia's interests to see either the Hapsburg or the Hohenzollern monarchy plowed under in the style of what had happened in Spain and Portugal.

Even so, Napoleon appeared to do everything in his power to deepen Alexander's growing suspicions and dismay. And even if he did notice Alexander's reactions, he probably didn't care very much anyway. A Napoleon could only march to the sound of his own drums.

Because of its defeat in 1809, Austria now had to part with its Illyrian provinces of Goerz, Istria, Carinthia, and Carinola. Napoleon's mastery over Italy was complete.

Included in the Austrian treaty was a clause that would hand Western Galicia, with its 1.3 million inhabitants, over to the grand duchy of Warsaw. Such an enlargement of the Polish state, sitting right on the Russian doorstep, was totally unacceptable to the Russians. Thus, even if many historians claim that the relationship between Napoleon and Tsar Alexander had begun to cool soon after its high point at Tilsit, this last bit of Napoleonic horse trading definitely marked the end of the honeymoon and put the final stamp upon Alexander's growing disenchantment. The air of Franco-Russian relations was becoming downright frigid.

NOTES

1. Fiedler, Siegfried. *Grundriss der Militaer und Kriegsgeschichte.* Vol. 2. Munich, 1976.
2. Fiedler.
3. Barraclough, G. *The Origins of Modern Germany.* New York, 1963.
4. Oman, Sir Charles. *A History of War in the Sixteenth Century.* London, 1937.
5. Barraclough.

3. Europe from 1810

Even in our own time, wars occasionally come as a surprise, though people paying close attention to the media can usually read the signs in advance. In 1810, only townsfolk got to see newspapers regularly; the rural population received most of its news by word of mouth. Thus, the commoner had little occasion to take note of the sharper tones entering into the diplomatic exchanges between Russia and France.

Nor were the diplomats, much less the *militaires* of the lesser powers, all that well informed. For example, even while campaign plans were being submitted in St. Petersburg for the tsar's consideration in 1810, Funck, a Saxon general, had no idea why the Saxon army was concentrating on the right bank of the Elbe in May 1811. While the orders had come from Dresden, he knew very well that they had originated in Paris. Were the Saxons to attack the Prussians with 20,000 men? Hardly. Some thought that they might be there just to frighten them. But that, too, was ruled out as being ludicrous.

If the events of 1809 had already caused Alexander to become suspicious of what might be coming his way, those of 1810 did nothing to lessen his apprehensions. Napoleon had gone right on playing his game of imperial monopoly. One by one, virtually every European ruling house had been offered the choice of compliance or oblivion. Not one was secure from his grasp. Even Napoleon's royal brother had to vacate the Dutch throne when his kingdom was incorporated into metropolitan France. And with the stroke of a pen at Fontainbleau, the entire German North Sea coast was annexed and also incorporated into metropolitan France.

This last move was ostensibly part of the further tightening of the Continental blockade. Still, without so much as a "by your leave," the neo-Franks of other sequestered territories were now joined by a sizable block from the German lowlands. Napoleon's mastery of Europe appeared complete. Only Spain and Russia remained as unresolved problems. Spain was already living up to its reputation as the festering sore in the side of Napoleon's empire, and the Treaty of Tilsit was beginning to look more and more like what it had always been beneath the surface: a truce rather than a settlement of the Russian situation.

All this proved problematic for Napoleon's objectives toward the least accessible of his adversaries, the British. If the blockade was ever to become really effective, the British expeditionary force supporting the Spanish insurrection would have to be ejected from the Iberian Peninsula. For the moment, however, the British posed no immediate threat. The Russian matter appeared more serious.

The Russians were economically far too dependent upon foreign trade to permit the French emperor to continue inserting his hand so deeply into their affairs. Russia was rich in natural resources but had poorly developed industries. Thus, the Continental blockade was choking the flow of foreign exchange the country required in order to obtain the needed manufactured goods. All other considerations aside, the Russians could hardly continue to participate in Napoleon's power game without courting severe economic depression. The situation was driven by more than merely Alexander's loss of interest in being Napoleon's man.

There was little the French emperor could do for the moment to counter such a defection except, of course, to introduce sharper tones into the diplomatic exchanges. At the same time, the situation lent renewed currency to Napoleon's old idea of hitting the British where it would really hurt: India. But apart from all the logistical problems that the overland trek would involve, directing such a crippling blow against the motherlode of British commerce would require the willing cooperation of a compliant Russia. It meant seizing the overland routes to India, ejecting the British from the Iberian Peninsula, and closing the Strait of Gibraltar—a tall order, even for Napoleon.

For the moment, however, these actions were all abstractions. Still, Napoleon perceived himself to be in an invincible position. Who was to stand against him? To the emperor, what happened today, tomorrow, or the day after was up to him and him alone—all the others could do was react to his initiative. As always, however, the realities were more complex and subject to a multitude of secondary influences.

At first, Napoleon had sought to achieve Russian cooperation through an alliance by marriage. But when Alexander had dawdled over Napoleon's suit for the hand of his sister, Napoleon had promptly turned to the Austrians and married the daughter of the Austrian emperor. If he thought that this marriage might at last offer security from that quarter, however, he had miscalculated. In a day and age when the bartered bride had become a common medium of dynastic exchange, the Hapsburgs could no longer be appeased, much less bought, by such a marriage of convenience. Besides, the proposed transfer of Western Galicia into Polish hands ran contrary to both Austrian and Russian interests.

Such an enlargement of the territories of the grand duchy of Warsaw bore all the earmarks of a French staging area in the eyes of anyone who cared to look. It was time for the Russians to draw up plans for the campaign that was sure to come. Napoleon was quite aware of these undercurrents but hardly concerned. If the Russians chose to go after him, all the better. The time of being content with mastery over only half of Europe was coming to an end, especially since things in Spain were at last beginning to look promising.

At Tilsit, Napoleon had suffered from what Clausewitz would later term the "crisis of victory." Although he had overrun Prussia, he had merely handed yet another defeat to a Russian army and lacked the means of achieving more. His military machine had been in dire need of repair, and the inadequacy of his logistics had been driven home to him in no uncertain terms. The victors were going hungry. But he had spent the years since 1807 profitably. The military power he now held in his hands seemed greater than ever before, and he was still arming.

But the Russians were wide awake to the threat now. The Treaty of Vienna in 1809 may have come as a rude shock, but French intrigues in the Balkans were no longer a secret either. Thus, when Napoleon again reached into Germany, incorporating the estuaries of the Ems, Weser, and Elbe rivers into the French empire during December 1810, Alexander became convinced that a peaceful coexistence with a predator of Napoleon's stripe would be impossible. As if to hammer home this point to Alexander, Napoleon sequestered the duchy of Oldenburg, its duke an uncle by marriage to Alexander himself. When the latter attempted to intercede, Napoleon offered payment but refused to give up the duchy. These were no longer matters of statesmanship. In those days, Napoleon simply took what he wanted and invoked the law of might makes right whenever it suited him.

Yet Napoleon could certainly resort to grace and charm whenever he was of a mind to do so. Thus, it is easy to understand how Alexander, at least for a while, could have come under the spell of the French emperor's flattery, which was even further enhanced by the glittering aura of success that surrounded Napoleon in 1807.

By 1810, however, an intense dislike for the man and all that he represented had taken hold of the Russian tsar. This feeling was actively nurtured by those around him, Russians as well as men like von Stein, a Hanoverian in the Prussian service, and Pozzo di Borgo, a Corsican who served the Hapsburgs. Eventually, this dislike would turn into an irreconcilable enmity. For the moment, however, Alexander contented himself by answering Napoleon with tit for tat.

On December 31, 1810, he officially declared Russia to be no longer bound by the Continental blockade, thereby reopening a gap larger than the one Napoleon had just closed. Alexander's action was more than a reaction to Russia's own needs; it was an open act of defiance. Moreover, with it came the demand that Napoleon renounce all attempts to fully restore the Polish state. The gloves had come off.

This left Napoleon in something of a quandary that rested squarely with the Polish question. If and when he was ready to settle with the Russians, Polish cooperation would be all important. His adversaries had not been deceived on that score. Poland was indeed to be his staging area, and in return for this cooperation, the Poles expected nothing less than the reconstitution of their state.

Even in retrospect, it is still not clear what Napoleon's real intentions toward Poland were. Nor does there seem to be a consensus on what the Poles expected. From the looks of it, they were to exchange their current nominal ruler, the king of Saxony, for Jerome, Napoleon's brother. But the latter, upon arriving in Poland on the eve of the Russian campaign, wasn't at all sure that, in the exchange of his present kingdom of Westphalia for Poland, he was getting the best of the bargain. To his wife, Katharina, he wrote on May 31, 1812 that he thought Westphalia was worth more than Poland. Nor was Katharina eager to exchange her residence in Kassel for one in Warsaw. At the same time, the grand duke of Wuerzburg also turned up as a possible candidate for the Polish crown, while in 1813 Napoleon suggested to Metternich that he figured on giving the Prussian Hohenzollerns a duchy along the Vistula in exchange for their own territories, as already mentioned. Thus, it appears questionable that independence and self-rule for the Poles would have come from Napoleon any more than it would from Austria, Prussia, or Russia. National stirrings had no place in the Napoleonic design for empire, and that, for better or worse, did not exclude the Poles.

Thus, Napoleon did not respond to Alexander's demand to renounce any attempts to restore the Polish state. He could afford neither to accept conditions nor to make concessions. He—who had changed the face of Europe, who had disposed of established dynasties like so much excess baggage—had to remain on a forward course. He had enemies everywhere. As soon as the sails of his ship of state lost the wind, he stood in danger of foundering on the reefs which lurked just beneath the surface, both at home and abroad. It was, however, not yet time for war. Neither Alexander nor Napoleon was ready. Instead, a diplomatic feud ensued.

Napoleon, of course, understood that a showdown by force of arms with the Russians on their home ground would be anything but easy. But while his actions over the previous several years had caused the failure of his efforts to secure Russian cooperation by diplomatic means, he still hoped that his military reputation might suffice to bring them around anyway. Unfortunately, the Russians were justly suspicious of what might lie beyond any sort of political compromise or accommodation with Napoleon.

The thought advanced in a recent work[1] that much of what happened in 1812 came down simply to the personal relationships between the two principal players, Napoleon and Alexander, and that the two might have settled matters personally, man to man, makes light of the realities. Of course Alexander might have relented, but only at the expense of Russian sovereignty. Of course Napoleon might have backed away, but when did he ever? Both men suffered from insecurities that were deeply rooted in their respective environments. That is, none of the events that transpired in the direct relationships between France and Russia took place in a political vacuum. Napoleon had leaped up the ladder of military command and made what we would today call a lateral entry into the European dynastic club, and the tsar of all the Russians had literally stepped over the corpse of his assassinated father to take on what was surely the most dangerous job in dynastic Europe (his father, after all, was not the only tsar whose reign was terminated in such fashion whenever the establishment was displeased).

Neither man was free from the political demands of his own environment. Napoleon could keep his throne secure only as long as he justified his existence in the eyes of the French nation by remaining a winner, and he could also feel the eyes of a dozen European capitals on his back. And Alexander? He might have been born to legitimate rule, but he could not afford to do anything that might cause sensitive Russian egos to look small in the eyes of western Europe. Thus, without even entering into questions of moral justification, it is clear that each man, despite all the power he wielded, found himself impelled to follow a relatively limited course of action.

*   *   *

Even as this direct confrontation between Russia and the French empire was building, seemingly unrelated events were being played out elsewhere. Eventually, these would synergistically add up to a whole greater than the sum of its parts in the effect the events were to exercise upon the war of 1812. One of these situations involved Sweden.

As late as January 1812, Napoleon drove the Swedes into the arms of Russia with his occupation of Swedish Pommerania. Ostensibly, this was a punishment for Sweden's more or less open disregard for the Continental blockade.

Napoleon's relations with Prince Bernadotte, once a political rival in Paris, had never been cordial. Indeed, Napoleon had been anything but pleased when the Swedes selected this erstwhile French marshal to succeed their childless king. But what had come as an unexpected and rather nasty surprise was the sudden backbone Bernadotte now exhibited. The new Swedish crown prince, no matter what else he might have been, was nobody's fool. He was a man not well understood by his times, and most of the bad press he received in both France and nineteenth-century Germany was quite undeserved. To read his character, one had to look deeply into his background.

Personally brave and a commanding figure, capable of winning the loyalty of those around him, he had both the intellect and some of the qualities of which leaders are made. Unfortunately, these traits were marred by the fact that he became excessively cautious whenever he found himself in command, faced with making important decisions. This defect had already enabled Napoleon to step right past him and seize power in France, even though Bernadotte had been politically better connected. His indecision had also cast long shadows over his military career, both as a corps commander and in 1813 as an army commander.

One of the by-products of the Treaty of Tilsit had been a renewal of the old struggle between Sweden and Russia for the Baltic. In February 1808, Alexander had declared war against Sweden, ostensibly because its king, Gustav IX, one of Napoleon's confirmed enemies, had refused to join the Continental blockade. The real issue, however, was the possession of Finland. The Russians had wanted it, and Napoleon had given his consent, no doubt hoping that they would have a difficult time of it. But the war was over in a comparatively short time, and the Treaty of Fredrikshamn, already mentioned, left Finland in Russian hands.

Perhaps it was the cautious Bernadotte who decided to let matters concerning Finland rest. Certainly, both his sharp intellect and the fact that he was not a native Swede enabled him to take a dispassionate long-term view. Realizing that the Russians considered Finland vital to their own security, he desisted from pursuing its recovery. It would have been an unequal struggle that Sweden could have sustained only with outside help and at the expense of its own independence of action. However, in renouncing all Swedish claims upon Finland in favor of Russia, he also directly contradicted the aspirations of his newly adopted nation. Doing so took courage, more than Napoleon thought he possessed, but perhaps the stakes had for once been high enough for even Bernadotte to take a firm, albeit unpopular, stand.

In a treaty concluded on March 24, 1812, Russia and Sweden mutually recognized their respective possessions. Russia also promised to compensate Sweden for the loss of Finland by lending military support to wrest Norway from the Danish crown. Obviously, Sweden could not participate in the war everyone now knew was coming. But Alexander had the double security of knowing that no potential threats would materialize on his northern flank and that the tens of thousands of troops thereby freed would be available for use against the impending French invasion.

In another sideshow on the extreme opposite flank, things were going awry as well. French intrigues with the Turks to impede the furtherance of Russian interests in the Balkans had been temporarily suspended on Napoleon's own initiative in the wake of the Erfurt accords in 1808. The British had been quick to intercede in the diplomatic void this created; as a result, Russia and Turkey concluded the Treaty of Bucharest on May 28, 1812, suspending hostilities on the Turkish front, even as the Grand Army was massing in Poland. Thus, at least for the time being, the Turks were out of the picture as well, freeing even more Russian troops.

Napoleon still held the military initiative, but he was not mastering the developing political situation. He had been counting on simultaneous diversionary actions on both Russian flanks, from Sweden in the north and Turkey in the south. But his rigidness with Bernadotte and his inattention to the Turks had spoiled the broth. The Russians could now focus their full resources on the coming showdown. The Swedish and Turkish failures would cost Napoleon dearly. But he was to learn of these events only after his Russian campaign was already under way.

A Russian treaty with the Spanish government-in-exile, concluded on July 20, ensured only moral support and was plainly a paper tiger. But a promised subsidy to Russia of £700,000 from Britain was decidedly tangible. Still, Russia would have to throw everything against the coming assault, as the adversary looked strong enough in June 1812 to turn the world upside down.

The power potential of the resources at Napoleon's command was of a magnitude not seen in the west since the days of the Roman empire. From the Atlantic coast, the English Channel, and the North Sea to the banks of the Tiber in Italy, the French empire comprised 310,000 square miles with about 42 million inhabitants.[2] Added to this must be the rest of Italy, with the exceptions of Sicily and Sardinia. Then there were the Rhine Confederation and the grand duchy of Warsaw, with another 17.5 million inhabitants, as well as Switzerland, Illyria, and Denmark-Norway. Even Austria, with more than 20 million people, and Prussia with a population of about 5 million—after the Treaty of Tilsit—were forced to do yeoman service, because they had no other choice.

Still, there were clouds on Napoleon's horizon. The war in Spain had again taken a turn for the worse, and no end appeared in sight. Nor had the Austrians given up on getting back at Napoleon. Although there was an Austrian auxiliary corps in the Grand Army, it wasn't to do Napoleon as much good as it might have. Throughout the campaign, the Austrians never lost touch with the Russian court. Moreover, by the terms of a secret agreement between Vienna and St. Petersburg, the Austrians would not strengthen their corps beyond the numbers originally demanded by Napoleon. (Thus, contrary to the belief widely held until modern times, Schwarzenberg's lackadaisical conduct of operations was not entirely due to his own anemic qualities as a commander. Napoleon's suspicions, on the other hand, stood on firm ground.)

In northern Germany, especially in Prussia, the relentless economic pressure and continued exactions by the French had literally ruined the existence of hundreds of thousands. The oppression generated a smoldering resentment that needed but a spark to flare into an open conflagration.

Nor was the situation in the Rhine Confederation on all that much of an even keel. The princes might still be firmly in Napoleon's corner, but their people were also wearying of the continued material demands that supported Napoleon's endless ventures.

Even France, after 20 years of unabated war, was beginning to show signs of fatigue. Not only were French finances in dire shape despite the incessant milking of both the allied and the vanquished, but the population was showing increased resistance toward renewed military service. There were as yet no draft cards to burn, but the prevailing attitudes were not unlike those of our own Vietnam era, which were serious enough to contribute to the halting of the Vietnam venture. For the French nation, the days of a "clear and present danger" had long passed. Not only were Napoleon's republican and royalist opponents becoming restive again, but even some of his followers were beginning to despair of ever seeing the return of a lasting peace. Despite the glitter and glory of the empire and a tightfisted police regiment, the roots of the Napoleonic regime had not yet sunken all that deeply. Only the Polish nation looked forward to the coming war with great expectations. It was going to be their war, with nothing less than the restoration of the Polish state at stake.

None of these storm clouds, however, threatened to burst unless the Russian venture failed and Napoleon's juggernaut was seriously damaged. But Napoleon did not believe for an instant that this was even within the realm of possibility. He had already beaten the Russians twice, and he was certain he could do it again. Nor did Napoleon envision a fight to the finish. As in the past, he expected that the Russians would come forward to meet him. Then, with his usual quick, sharp hammer strokes, he would bend Alexander to his will.

That he would be able to make a quick end of the Russians was the first and most serious delusion to which Napoleon would succumb. He had become far too contemptuous of his adversaries and far too accustomed to easily imposing his will on others. Still, his contempt would not have been all that misplaced had the campaign simply been a matter of dealing with the Russian army. However, it was not the Russian army that would turn out to be his sternest and most relentless opponent. The real challenge would come from different quarters.

In an extensive dissertation on critique, Clausewitz states that while one might certainly judge an event by its outcome, the event can be justly critiqued only on the basis of information that was available at the time, not with the benefit of hindsight. Thus, a judgment of Napoleon's actions with respect to the Russian campaign may be made only on the basis of matters that ought to have governed Napoleon's thinking as he contemplated the excursion into the vast expanses of Russia.

In 1812, Russia could already be considered a most dangerous opponent in a defensive war that would enable the country to bring all its natural resources to bear. At that time, European Russia had a homogeneous population of about 34 million people, and they saw the tsar as both their political and their spiritual head. As in Spain, any foreign penetration would raise the specter of a national war, mobilizing the resources of the people. Although the country did not offer the type of natural terrain that would facilitate a guerrilla war such as that in Spain, the vast Russian expanses, once they were brought into play, could literally swallow up an army of half a million men. In addition, the vast forested areas, sparsely populated tracts, and poor network of roads added difficulties for any invader that could easily be exploited by the defender.

Certainly, these implications were crystal clear to so seasoned a campaigner as Napoleon. This is probably why, up to the very last, he had

avoided the final break with Alexander, hoping to gain his ends by intimi-
dation and with a minimum of military engagement.

Still, to the Napoleon of 1812, such moments of insight and doubt came
ever less frequently and, perhaps, only fleetingly. Having become expert at
pulling the wool over his opponents' eyes, he was increasingly doing so to
himself. Thus, the pragmatic and empirical soldier, the master of his trade
and one of the greatest captains of all time, ended up failing to draw upon
the lessons he had already learned. This failure would prove to be his fatal
error. He closed his eyes to the fact that just as the guerrilla war in Spain
offered no ready solution, so too a war in Russia—with the possibility that
the Russians might conduct a fighting retreat and carry on an endless
resistance—could eventually wear down an attacker's strength. (He had
already experienced this in Poland during the winter of 1806–1807.)

Certainly, Napoleon's power potential was staggering. The only question
was whether that power was sufficiently well organized and controlled to
enable national wars to be conducted on two fronts. If Emperor Napoleon
could not furnish General Napoleon with the necessary means, the venture
was doomed and Russia would not be conquered.

NOTES

1. Cate, Curtis. *The War of the Two Emperors*. New York, 1985.
2. See Appendix I.

4. The Gathering Storm

RUSSIAN PLANS

Napoleon had not yet annexed the German lowlands when, in the fall of 1810, the Russians already saw the storm clouds on the horizon and began to work up proposals about how a French attack might be best met. It was a game with many players—Russians and foreigners, with and without qualifications—submitting all sorts of plans, some possible and others impossible. Of all the plans, only four merit discussion, since they collectively contained not only the elements that would influence the actual conduct of operations at the outset of the campaign but also some important indications about how the operations would continue afterward. The four plans were advanced by General Barclay de Tolly, the Russian minister of war; General Ernst von Phull, the tsar's military adviser; Count d'Allonville, a French émigré; and Count Ludwig von Wolzogen, latter-day adjutant to the tsar.

The plans submitted by Wolzogen in October 1810 and by d'Allonville in January 1811 (the latter laboriously attempting to take note of every conceivable and inconceivable contingency) held in common the idea that the war should be dragged out and prolonged. This was because the state of France's finances did not permit an extended struggle and because Napoleon desired a rapid conclusion of the war in the interests of keeping his reputation of invincibility and omnipotence intact. Deviating from Wolzogen, however, d'Allonville wanted to open the war with a quick offensive toward the Oder. Since Napoleon had not yet finished arming for the oncoming campaign, d'Allonville thought there would be sufficient time to disarm the Poles and drag the Prussians into the war. Then, as soon as Napoleon brought his superior forces eastward from their main staging areas along the Rhine and in the German lowlands, a systematic fighting retreat could be made. Both Wolzogen and d'Allonville agreed that a decisive confrontation with Napoleon was to be avoided and that a scorched-earth policy and guerrilla operations were to go hand in hand with this retreat, thereby making it difficult for the invader to subsist off the land.

D'Allonville further assumed that the thrust of Napoleon's attack would be aimed at Moscow, the spiritual capital of Russia, which he felt should be covered by the retreating Russian army. Wolzogen disagreed. He wanted to see the formation of two separate armies with diverging lines of retreat. The armies would cooperate with each other so that if one came under attack, it would operate defensively while the other switched to the offense. (This idea was to reemerge in full bloom in 1813.) The suggested objective of Wolzogen's retreat was a fortress or fortified encampment. He had proposed Riga, Drissa, Bobruisk, and Kiev as likely points for such a scheme. The major flaw in this plan was that it did not envision continuing operations beyond the Dvina, Beresina, and Dnieper rivers, thus eschewing the utilization of the vast Russian expanses to effect a fragmentation and dispersal of the enemy's forces. Moreover, it left the most likely direction of the attack, Moscow, without a stronghold.

While both the tsar and General Barclay were suitably impressed by Wolzogen's and d'Allonville's plans, Barclay and Phull had already worked up proposals of their own. Together all the plans bore eloquent testimony to how little the essence of Napoleonic warfare was understood in the Russian high command.

Barclay saw the oncoming campaign simply as an extension of the campaign of 1807. Neither he nor Phull had the vaguest notion about the means Napoleon was gathering or about the grandiose scale on which the decisive events would be played out. Like Wolzogen and d'Allonville, Barclay and Phull did not even consider the possibility of carrying the war beyond the lines of the Dvina, Beresina, and Dnieper. Notwithstanding his consideration of a retreat into the Russian interior during the 1807 campaign, Barclay had either drifted away from this mode of thinking or, far more likely, had never envisioned that the coming campaign would occur on such a grand scale. Indeed, such a retreat would have hardly been necessary in 1807, when Napoleon had already found it difficult to maintain himself in Poland

and when an advance even to the often-mentioned three-river line would have been out of the question without further extensive logistical preparations.

Barclay's plan, drawn up near the end of 1810, saw the operations area divided in two by the Pripet Marshes and assumed that the enemy's main objectives were on both sides of the marshes. Thus, he proposed the formation of two armies to cover these areas, with the northern army having a special flanking corps; an intermediary corps was to link the two main forces. The war was to begin with a short offensive thrust into enemy territory to ravage the borderlands, thereby impeding the enemy's attack. Faced by superior forces, both main forces were to retreat to cover their respective areas. The tsar, however, apprehensive about his great adversary, wanted to take the offensive only in the event Napoleon opened his attack with the destruction of Prussia. Alexander stood his ground on this even when Barclay renewed his proposal in the summer of 1811, pointing to Wellington's success with a scorched-earth policy in Portugal.

Unable to sell the idea of what might today be called a "forward defense," Barclay and Phull, the former "enlightened" by the latter, now proposed to cover the western border provinces with a flanking position on the basis of the "lines of operation" thesis once advanced by von Buelow, a famous Prussian theorist. This had called for such a position to be taken on Prussian territory, which, however, was presently officially neutral. Instead, Barclay and Phull insisted that this position be taken on Russian territory, in the area of Szaly. But this would result in the loss of whatever forces were placed there, since the enemy would simply back them up against the Baltic.

Phull, at least at the beginning, thought Svenciany, due east of Kovno, offered a good position. But he saw the actual defense line, where the enemy was to be stopped, along the three-river line as well. With this in mind, Phull presented the tsar with his own plan in the spring of 1812. The "Drissa" plan, as it is known, was in some parts reminiscent of Wolzogen's original proposal, but it was altered several times before ending up, roughly, in the form described here.

Assuming that Napoleon's main force would cross the Niemen not at Kovno but at Grodno (Phull had no doubts whatever about this), from whence he could turn either toward Vilna or Minsk, he was to be faced by an army in either of these directions. In the former direction, which Phull deemed Napoleon's most likely choice, he would be met by an army of 120,000 men; in the latter, by an army of only 80,000 men. If the attack went in the direction of Vilna, the larger army was then to be concentrated and led back into the fortified camp of Drissa, which could defend both the

Sebesh-St. Petersburg and the Vitebsk-Moscow roads. Phull believed that the mere existence of this camp, modeled vaguely on Frederick the Great's encampment at Bunzelwitz, from whence he had succeeded in keeping the vastly superior Austrians in check in 1761, would suffice to paralyze the enemy's operations.

If the camp induced the enemy to split its forces, the Russian army should break out and fall upon whatever detachments the enemy had left to cover the camp. If the enemy failed to split its forces, the enemy should be prompted to do so by having the right flanking corps operate against those forces. Phull thought it likely that the enemy would have already split its forces even before arriving in front of Drissa, in order to facilitate obtaining subsistence from the land. Thus, as the enemy's main force ground itself down against the Russian main army in and around the Drissa camp, the second Russian army and the Cossacks were to operate against its flanks and rear. In the event the enemy directed its main attack against the second army, that army was to withdraw to Bobruisk.

This plan, which was accepted by the tsar, contained none of the elements that were to give the Russians such unexpected and extraordinary success later on: the desire to unite the two western armies in undamaged condition; the continuous contact with the southern provinces, which contained the heart of Russian resources; the utilization of the Russian interior to precipitate the dispersal of the enemy's forces; and the attempt to prolong operations until the onset of winter.

The adoption of Phull's plan (of which Barclay was not immediately informed) and the fact that the location of the magazines envisioned operations only within the boundaries of the three-river line offer clear proof that Alexander's often-quoted remark that he would "make no peace, even if he was pushed back all the way to Kazan," was merely a figure of speech to underline his resolution, not his intent.

The Phull plan did not, and indeed could not, make any mention of the Danube Army or the Finnish Corps, since these did not become available for consideration until after operations had gotten under way. There were, nevertheless, expansive plans for their employment at that time. However, since none of these plans were ever implemented because of the totally changing situation, they need be only briefly outlined as follows: The Finnish Corps was to support the Swedes in their conquest of Norway. Having accomplished this, they were to continue acting together to create a diversion in northern Germany. The Danube Army was even expected to carry operations into northern Italy.

This is where matters stood for a time, as the two adversaries slowly moved toward a final confrontation.

FRENCH PREPARATIONS

The differences in the *modus operandi* of the Russians and of the French or, rather, of Napoleon, for the French had very little to do with this, clearly indicate that Napoleon was the aggressor on the political as well as the military front. The Russians, in response to the situation, saw themselves in an entirely defensive posture, in which they attempted to develop contingency plans to meet virtually every conceivable move Napoleon might make against them. The French emperor clearly held the initiative. But one would seek in vain for a similar theoretical engagement on Napoleon's part. He had no need for this. Had he been asked, he would have probably replied: "I will pretend an attack against Moscow on a front sufficiently broad to carry it out in earnest. And when the Russians come to me, I will pin them and then we will see how it goes. Once I have destroyed their army, I will dictate a peace."

This is not to say that there were no preparations being made in the Napoleonic camp. But these were concerned wholly with bringing the French formations earmarked for the campaign up to operational strength, seeing to the mobilization of the allied contingents, formulating the organization and deployment of the Grand Army, and preparing for its logistical support. At the same time, action continued to proceed on the diplomatic front.

The levies of 1810 and 1811 were sending a steady flow of replacements to the unit cadres already in Germany. Even though the call-up of the class of 1812 was supposed to flesh out the units remaining behind, most of the men were sucked into the reserve and replacement formations for the Grand Army. At the same time, most of the regiments assigned to the Grand Army were ordered to form extra field battalions.

In the beginning of 1811, troop movements were starting to get under way all over Germany. In time-honored fashion, the troops themselves, going this way and that, had little if any idea of what was afoot. This emerges from the speculations made by many diarists. Unlike the authors of memoirs, who wrote long after the fact but occasionally claimed a foreknowledge of events, the diarists jotted down the events and their thoughts about them as they occurred. The newspapers of the time, too, had nothing to say about an impending Russian campaign.

Among the first to march eastward were a number of battalions from the Rhine Confederation, sent to reinforce the garrisons of Danzig and various other places. Most thought they were being sent to guard the Baltic coast, where they were to enforce the Continental blockade because the Prussians could not be relied upon to do this with sufficient zeal. The first French march battalions moved forward to fill up and reinforce the garrisons of the Prussian fortresses, which had remained in French hands ever since the war of 1806.

The actual mobilization orders for the Rhine Confederation contingents did not go out until December 11, 1811, around which time the other allies were informed as well. The treaties obligating the Austrians and Prussians to furnish contingents were not concluded until early in 1812, but these were mere formalities, settling the final details. The Army of Spain was also called upon to furnish some of its sorely needed veteran cadres, including the Vistula Legion, which was called home to provide more backbone for the rapidly expanding Polish army.

THE SAXONS

First to leave their garrisons and to mass in the field were the Saxons. With the exception of the Regiment Gardes du Corps and the artillery, which remained behind in Dresden for the time being, the entire Saxon army assembled to the east of the Elbe during March 1811. Massed in the area of Grossenhain-Torgau-Luebben, only the regiments normally billeted there remained in their peacetime quarters. The war was, as yet, an entire year in the future.

Tactically, this was of great value to the Saxons, because not only the individual units but also entire brigades could be exercised. Lacking anything else to do, they set about this with a vengeance. The cavalry especially had a splendid opportunity to make use of the barren plains in the area. As a result, the Saxon military machine, at least, was well oiled.

This arrangement, however, had a dark side as well. Since the troops had left their garrisons in campaign order, they had not been allowed to take along anything that could not be fitted into the packs of the infantry or the cantle packs of the cavalry. Thus, every man had to wear his best issue every day. And this, thanks to the shameless corruption of the quartermaster services, was to have repercussions well after the campaign had gotten under way. (When the army finally marched into Russia a year later, it carried on its wagons an entire new issue of uniforms that were to be given out in June, right around the time the campaign got under way. But the gentlemen of the supply services, in a conspiracy reaching all the way back to Dresden and the ministries, decided to withhold the uniforms until some of the expected campaign losses set in; the redundant uniforms could then be saved and resold to the treasury the following year. However, this clever plan came to naught. Alternating periods of heavy rains and tropical heat right at the start of the campaign caused the uniforms to mildew and rot, so none were fit to be used. Thus, when the Saxons marched to war in worn-out uniforms, it was not because their king or the treasury had not provided for a proper new issue. This corruption was a cancer that beset every military establishment whose size was large enough to make accountancy difficult to oversee. Napoleon's military was to suffer from this as well, on a correspondingly larger scale. But this was still in the future. There were other, more immediate problems.)

With about 20,000 troops concentrated into a relatively small area for nearly an entire year, the resources of the surrounding countryside were soon exhausted. Food prices rose so sharply that the rank and file was soon reduced to a diet consisting mainly of bread and water, because their meager pay did not allow more and because there were as yet no magazines from which they could be provisioned. The bulk of the army had been mobilized and placed on operational status even as it was expected to continue its subsistence on a peacetime footing. Funck,[1] a Saxon general, states bitingly that at the same time, it was seen fit to continue docking the soldiers' pay for the forced purchase of such parade-dress fripperies as pompons and plumes, procured on the initiative of the individual unit commanders. The cavalry was especially hard hit. Even though it was issued hard fodder (oats), only monetary allowances were given for the purchase of hay or straw. As with the foodstuffs, the allowances were totally out of step with the inflationary prices.

Officers, up to the rank of captain, were each allowed only two packhorses. At the same time, however, they were expressly ordered to carry along the unnecessary luxuries of full gala-dress uniforms. Infantry officers were allowed to stow their kits on the battalion baggage wagons. All in all, this microcosm was a dress rehearsal of the difficulties the Grand Army as a whole was to suffer. Even while some Saxon districts, stripped of their garrisons, complained over the loss of a market for their produce, the districts to the right of the Elbe were cleaned out. As for the endless wagon columns streaming into the area of concentration, only the contractors, commissariat, and innkeepers benefited from them. The soldiers went hungry. Funck was of the opinion that the entire quartermaster administration was not unhappy over the mountains of paperwork all this unnecessary movement of supplies created, as it wonderfully muddled the already murky waters even further.

As to the purpose of this massive concentration of the Saxons, no one was certain. A corps of 20,000 men stood ready to commence a campaign, but everyone was keenly aware of the fact that it stood alone. The Bavarians were still at home and the nearest French troop concentrations, apart from various garrisons, stood all the way downriver around Hamburg, the main French depot on German soil. The prevailing view was that the Saxon concentration was just another bit of Napoleon's political chicanery, intended to worry the Prussians. But even that view made no sense, because everyone knew that Prussian officers, in and out of uniform, were constantly coursing about the Saxon encampments, even while the Russian and Prussian ambassadors leisurely viewed all that was going on from a front-row seat in Dresden.

"If Napoleon merely intended to worry the Prussians," observed Funck, "he could have easily accomplished this in a manner far less costly to the army and the country by extending the Saxon cantonments to include the Wittenberg district as well as the Upper and Lower Lausitz,"[2] thereby easing the density of the concentration without impairing its operational effectiveness.

In this fashion, the year 1811 ran its course. While the Saxons sat, the allies began to mobilize. Some of Napoleon's veteran cadres set out on a long march that would take them all the way from sunny Spain to Moscow, with a return trip across plains where the freezing temperatures (as low as $-27°$ Reaumur, about $-29°F$, recorded in Vilna on December 7, 1812) and bitter winds were as deadly as canister fire and grapeshot.

1812: A YEAR OF UNBIDDEN GUESTS

For Napoleon, the new year broke on a note of great expectations. His military machine was now grinding toward the ultimate objective of making him the undisputed master of the European continent. Inwardly, he must have thrilled at the prospect of wielding an army whose likes not even he had seen before.

It was, however, not so much the traffic created by the massive troop movements that was apt to draw the attention of the civilians in the countryside as it was the ubiquitous sight of the agents of the commissariat. Combing through the farms, they were buying up (on credit, of course) grain, which was then moved to collecting points and mills, from whence mile-long wagon trains were heading in unending streams toward the depots in the army's future assembly areas.

By the time the winter snows were turning into spring rains, the troops began to move in earnest. The diarists rarely fail to praise the hospitality of the Germans, who took the weary soldiers into their homes and provided coffee so that they might warm limbs stiffened by cold and rain. Many managed to fill their canteens with more potent liquids, designed to keep up their spirits on the march.

These early birds, however, were the lucky ones. As the traffic increased and more and more troops began to pass long the same roads and crowd into the same areas, the days of milk and honey were dwindling fast. Still, few complained about their passage through the fertile German provinces. But all, especially the Germans from the Rhine Confederation, noted the drastic change when, marching eastward, they crossed into Prussian territory. "Quiet," "distant," "sullen," "openly hostile," and "angry" are the adjectives used most often in the diaries to describe the mood of the population there.

In Pommerania, the old-Prussian air became downright oppressive. A young lieutenant from the Regiment Dukes of Saxony avoided Frederick's Square in Stettin: "I didn't want to walk past Old Fritz's statue standing there," he explained, "because of the accusing stare he gave me." Wuerttembergers, who ran into an old Prussian parson to the east of the Oder, got a sermon as well. The parson warned: "There are too many of you. The Russians will let you in. And when you weaken, you will do battle with cold and hunger. And then the Russians will begin to fight!" The French themselves often got more than an earful. Even though few of them understood German, they could hardly fail to notice the hostility. Things worsened when the French began requisitioning horses from the farms, 67,000 of them in Prussia alone, along with thousands of men summarily commandeered as teamsters.

By the time the bulk of the army had passed east into Poland, reserves and march battalions coming through Prussian territory frequently were subjected to more than mere verbal abuse. In East Prussia, brawls erupted everywhere. Major Horadam, who commanded one of the battalions from Frankfurt on the Main, was a veteran from the Spanish peninsula, where he had learned to read the signs. He commented, "All that is missing here are the mountains to make guerillas." Thus, minor hostilities were already under way even before the Grand Army had crossed the Russian frontier.

Poland experienced its share of troubles as well when the bulk of the army began to concentrate there and remained in place for several weeks. The grand duchy of Warsaw was not by any means a rich country. The Poles, enthusiastic about the coming war, which held for them the promise of the reconstitution of Poland, had dug deeply into their meager resources to raise an army of astonishing proportions. Now, the Napoleonic juggernaut came rolling in, swallowing up both their army and their country. The conditions the Grand Army witnessed in Poland filled many, no matter from which part of Europe they hailed, with a sense of foreboding even before they set foot on Russian soil.

Only the officers, who generally found quarters in the manor houses, still found some of the amenities to which they were accustomed. For the rank and file, the privations of war were already descending with full force. Living conditions in Poland were depressing; the poverty was oppressive.

Thus, the countryside was stripped bare and frictions quickly ensued. Especially for the Wuerttembergers, a series of incidents set an ominous tone for the future.

According to the official report of General Woellwarth, in command of the Wuerttemberg cavalry, the magazines established on Polish territory had been closed to the cavalry from the start. Moreover, his troops were passing through an area in which no preparations whatever had been made for their arrival and through which others had already passed before. It was well known to Woellwarth's men that the Polish peasantry had precious little surplus food and forage and that they had already been forced to give up most of what they had to stock the French magazines. Only the noble estates and manors still possessed the means to supply the troops passing through. These, Woellwarth states emphatically, rarely condescended to hand over anything, even against properly executed receipts, and the local prefects, who were supposed to act as go-betweens, deliberately made themselves scarce.

On reaching the Vistula, the Wuerttemberg cavalry was ordered to halt and sent into cantonments in an area already depleted. Again, the magazines were closed to the cavalry. Woellwarth sent the French official from the commissariat (*intendance*, in French) who was assigned to him to the nearest magazine on several occasions, only to have him return empty-handed, with the explanation that the contents of the magazine were reserved for the Guard Corps and French troops passing through. Again, the troops were forced to fend for themselves.

This set the stage for Marshal Ney's order, issued from Thorn, that on the emperor's orders enough livestock was to be requisitioned in the cavalry cantonments and the areas immediately to their rear to supply the entire Wuerttemberg division with meat for 20 days—about 800 cattle. The order also demanded that this be accomplished by June 2, at which time the division would be expected to march, that is, within 48 hours.

The commissioners were sent out at once to get in touch with the local prefects, but none of these worthy gentlemen were to be found. They had all gone off to pay their respects to the emperor, who was expected to pass through on his way to Thorn. Not that these prefects didn't know what was afoot. They had already declared, even before the order was issued, that they would be unable to assist and that they would leave their districts to the discretion of the troops.

For a time, it appeared as though Napoleon already had a quarrel with the Wuerttembergers. A general, representing himself as one of the emperor's adjutants, appeared at Woellwarth's headquarters on May 27, just prior to the issue of Ney's order, and presented a complaint about the Wuerttembergers that he claimed was from Napoleon, who was still in Dresden. When Woellwarth followed up on the matter, it turned out that the "adjutant" was no adjutant at all, but General Kraczinsky, the commander of the Polish lancers of the guard, who were standing nearby. Woellwarth doesn't say so in his report, but it seems that the local gentry had heard about Ney's order even before it was issued and had appealed to the Polish general, who happened to be nearby, to set up some impediments against its execution. (A later confrontation between Woellwarth and Kraczinsky became heated when Murat, who would command the French cavalry reserve in the coming campaign, arrived unexpectedly at the very moment of Woellwarth's departure. According to the latter, Kraczinksy at once ran up to Murat's coach to complain about the Wuerttembergers.)

When Ney's order arrived, it seems that the Wuerttembergers, many of whom were of peasant stock themselves, knew exactly where to find 800 cattle in a short time. They left the peasants alone and went straight to the manor houses and noble estates, turning up what was needed in far less time than expected. In the ensuing hue and cry, no one came to Woellwarth, who held the requisition order issued by Ney. Instead, everybody looked to Kraczinsky, even as Napoleon himself approached Thorn and ran head-on into a horde of complaining landowners, who accused the Wuerttembergers of looting and robbery.

To make matters worse, in another, unrelated incident, a fistfight broke out between Wuerttembergers and French light infantrymen over an argument about some wagons. It must have ended badly for the French, because Ney demanded that the Wuerttembergers involved be court-martialed.

None of this was, in itself, unusual; similar incidents took place all over the assembly area. But Napoleon, making what can only be described as a grandstand play to impress the Poles, decided to make an issue of the purloined cows (an issue which Segur was to immortalize, with all its inaccuracies, in his often-quoted memoirs). Even worse, however, was the fact that Napoleon apparently believed his own propaganda. This was a bad start for the Wuerttembergers. During the early weeks of the campaign, Napoleon was to target them with his pique by assigning them the worst march positions in the rear of the army's columns.

But Napoleon was far from being the only master of "doublespeak." Another piece of jabberwocky on the subject of requisitioning and foraging came from Colonel Langenau, Reynier's Saxon chief of staff in VII (Saxon) Corps. Calling all the adjutants of this corps to the headquarters at Radom, he declared: "The regimental or battalion commander who lets his command go without adequate food and forage for so much as a single day, will be at once relieved of his command and sent home because of incompetence.

How each obtains what he needs is his own affair. However, every excess will be punished and the brigadiers are especially held responsible."[3] This came at a time when the taking of so much as a single bale of hay at once raised cries of thievery and robbery! But there were brighter sides as well.

Funck states that when the Saxon corps arrived in the Lublin area, everything was in exemplary order. The local prefect, Prince Jablonovski, was everywhere, seeing to everything and assisted by an excellent staff. Unfortunately, when Funck reported to Reynier how perfectly the prefect had organized everything, he unwittingly did the man a great disservice, because the French general at once threw all of Jablonovski's efforts out the window, just as he had done in Radom, where the local authorities had also gone to extraordinary lengths to see that everyone was well served. Everything had to be done over again, not because it was necessary but because Reynier wanted it that way. What had been collected at one place had to be taken to another, and from there to someplace else, and the only result was that the troops were kept waiting for supplies that had been depoted correctly in the first place. Funck attributes this irrational behavior to the fact that Reynier allowed no initiative on the part of anyone and always insisted on regulating everything with his own despotic orders, more often than not made in total ignorance of the situation.

When Reynier arrived to take command of the Saxons in March 1812, he was already highly unpopular with them. This went back to the days in 1809 when he commanded the Saxons for the first time, taking over from Bernadotte, who had maintained far better relations with his foreign subordinates. In making one soldier's assessment of another, Funck, who campaigned twice under Reynier as a general officer, offers a more intimate view of this strange man than the platitudes normally found in the capsule biographies. He describes Reynier as being a pragmatic soldier who possessed all the instincts that make a first-class combat commander. Still, Funck did not think that Reynier had even one of all the other talents necessary to run the affairs of an army.

Napoleon once described Reynier as a man of talent but one who was better fitted (as a combat officer) to handle an army of 20,000 or 30,000 men than to command one of 5,000 or 6,000. Funck offers the key to this apparent contradiction when he states that Reynier could hardly drill a battalion and was totally lacking in matters relating to drill and elementary tactics. He had a stutter. This, no doubt, had caused this man, described by Funck as educated and widely read, with an extraordinary talent for languages (which he could read but dared not speak), to firmly turn his back on these things during his formative years as an officer. The aftermath of the revolution had taken him through the lower ranks in a breeze, without this fundamental shortcoming ever rising to the surface. Thus, he who could not deploy a battalion, much less a brigade, nevertheless showed an adept hand at handling larger formations and had experienced seventeen campaigns as a general officer to hone this natural talent. He had developed a keen sense of divining the enemy's intentions even during the opening moves of an action.

From his physical infirmity, however, radiated other handicaps which militated against him in his role as a commanding general. In time-honored fashion, he had learned to cope with his speech impediment by speaking in a soft, singsong manner with often indistinct enunciations, which made it difficult to understand what he was saying, particularly for those whose native tongue was not French. Because of this, Reynier shut himself away from those around him with a remote, aloof, and brusque manner and cultivated the habit of firing off verbal orders and then turning away before anyone had the opportunity to comment or ask questions. His bearing was stiff, but not commanding, and he was suspicious of everyone around him. Abhoring anything relating to military formalities, discipline, administration, or elementary tactics, he felt at home only with the artillery. He knew nothing about cavalry and wasted it senselessly. But that, according to Funck, was a shortcoming he shared with many French generals.

Napoleon, of course, was quite aware of the fact that Reynier was less than popular with the Saxons. But he also knew that Reynier was a better general than most of his marshals and that he did not have a surfeit of such men, capable of independent command. The same was true of St. Cyr, who was soon to take command of VI (Bavarian) Corps. He, too, was unpopular with the foreign troops placed in his charge, but they were to help him win his marshal's baton before the Russian campaign had run its course.

THE RUSSIANS CONCENTRATE

As the Grand Army at last caught up to the Saxons and was converging on Poland, the Russians were putting Phull's plan into action as soon as the tsar arrived at supreme headquarters in Vilna on April 22. Orders were issued at once to prepare the field fortifications at Drissa, but time had grown too short to turn Dunaburg into a fortress capable of supporting the Drissa encampment as Phull had envisioned.

At this time, the First Western Army under Barclay already stood assembled with its main force around Vilna; its right wing, under Wittgenstein, near Keidany; and its left (the intermediary corps of Barclay's plan), under Doctorov, near Lida. Bagration and the Second Western Army (also in accordance with Barclay's original plan) still stood near Lutzk in Volhynia. It was forced to hang back this far because the staging area of the French forces still ran along the entire length of the Vistula, affording as yet no hint as to the direction their advance would take.

When an enemy offensive in the southerly direction of Shitomir and Kiev was no longer thought likely, there was no reason why this Second Army should not be shifted into the area of Volkovisk, which would satisfy Phull's plan. This was done in May.

When this move was accomplished, Bagration's army was substantially weakened because he had to leave behind a considerable number of troops to form the Third (Reserve) Army under Tormassov. The reserves that had originally been earmarked for this purpose were slow in arriving, and Alexander, despite Austrian assurances, still thought it necessary to keep a watchful eye in the direction of Austria. Tormassov's instructions were simple: "to observe the Austrian border and to withdraw in the face of an attack by superior forces."

These measures immediately disturbed the equal or near equal strength the two western armies were supposed to have in Phull's plan. In order to restore the balance, at least partially, Doctorov's intermediary corps was to join Bagration instead of Barclay. It was the general opinion at supreme headquarters that Barclay would still have sufficient strength to defend Drissa even without Doctorov. This may explain why Doctorov's corps, whose role had become redundant when the Second Army was brought closer to the First, had not already joined Barclay at this time.

Barclay, however, was not at all agreeable to Phull's plan when he heard of it. Not only was he reluctant to give up his own plan, but he was prepared to act on his own judgment and initiative, should this become necessary. Just how he wanted to see operations run emerged from an instruction he sent to St. Priest, Bagration's adviser; it had been worked up at the beginning of the year, when the Second Army stood near Lutzk. This instruction still concerned itself primarily with an offensive into Poland and then dealt with the contingencies if the enemy's main force turned against either of the western armies, the right flanking corps or Doctorov's intermediary corps. In such an event, whichever army was under attack was to withdraw, respectively, to Drissa, Bobruisk, Riga, or Kiev. At the same time, the others, not under direct attack, were to take vigorous offensive action: Barclay himself possibly against the enemy's flank and rear, Bagration into Poland. Despite the fact that the tsar was more than ever against an offensive when the conclusion of the Franco-Austrian alliance became known, Barclay continued to hope for one and was diametrically opposed to Phull's ideas of retreating.

Barclay, however, was not the only one who didn't care for Phull's ideas. All the ranking officers in the army registered their disapproval as soon as the ideas became known. Everyone thought the challenge could be met and complained about the proposed retreat and the great distance between the two western armies. A large party, including the currently unemployed Benningsen, who had been in command of the army in 1807, was now joined by Barclay and demanded that a battle be offered at Vilna.

Other plans, some of them rather adventurous, were submitted to the tsar by a horde of dilettantes, including the duke of Wuerttemberg, a close relative; Count Armfeldt, a diplomat; Paulucci, an Italian marquis and an accomplished spinner of intrigues; and young Count Chernishev, an adjutant; to name but a few. They all clamored to be heard.

The growing resistance against Phull's plan soon changed into plots to bring him down, creating a state of confusion at supreme headquarters. As a result of this, Alexander's confidence in Phull was visibly shaken, even though none of the others at headquarters were able to come up with any convincing counterproposals that didn't involve an offensive of some sort. Consequently, Phull's plan remained in place. But his proposal that the Second Army and Corps Doctorov be sent back toward Minsk (that is, toward the defensive line) even before commencement of hostilities, was refused. This would have gone against Barclay's own offensive plans, which he continued to carry in his pocket. It would also have widened the gap between the two armies. To Phull's even greater distress, the parties who wanted to see the two western armies united were beginning to gain the upper hand.

In the midst of all this, news arrived that the French were beginning to move away from the Vistula and toward the Niemen, which at that time marked Russia's western border. It was also learned that Napoleon himself had arrived in Koenigsberg on June 12. The time for planning and arguing was past. This was reality. The French emperor was taking command of the juggernaut massing at the Russian doorstep. But who was to take command against him?

The leading candidates were Generals Mikhail Iillarionovich Golenish-chev-Kutuzov and Levin August Benningsen. Both had already been beaten by Napoleon. Not even his subsequent success against the Turks could let Kutuzov forget his defeat at Austerlitz. On the other hand, Benningsen was a German. A contrary character, he was given to intrigue and was widely unpopular among the Russians as one of the murderers of Tsar Paul, Alexander's father.

Kutuzov, aging and ailing, had just been relieved of his command of the Danube Army by the tsar because it was thought he had deliberately delayed the peace negotiations with the Turks in order to make Alexander more compliant to Napoleon's demands. This was not because he was Napoleon's man but because he did not think that the Russian army could stand up to the emperor. Kutuzov reasoned that a military defeat at the hands of Napoleon would have more dire consequences than a political accommodation with him.

In the meanwhile, the tsar decided to assume command himself. After the defeats of 1805 and 1807, Alexander had lost confidence in his own military abilities. By 1813, he had learned enough to be able to make some sound military judgments. After fumbling at the Battle of Dresden by reinforcing Schwarzenberg's indecisiveness with his own, he inserted a decisive hand in the events leading to the Battle of Kulm. Early in October 1813, when the allies and Napoleon were groping toward each other, Alexander gave Schwarzenberg a lecture on how operations should be run, bluntly asking him why the cavalry, which ought to be in front of the army, was trailing a day's march to its rear.

Historians love to berate Alexander for his interference in military matters, and with regard to 1805 and 1807, they are right. His vanity had led him astray. But those were the years of his apprenticeship. The journeyman one may observe in 1813 was only just emerging during the closing stages of the 1812 campaign. It would be foolish to assume that a man, virtually any man, as close as he was to the decisions being made, and the results that ensued from them, should have learned nothing at all. Yet the reputation of the imperial dilettante, garnered in 1805 and 1807, sufficed to pigeonhole Alexander as a meddler. And such his reputation remained, especially in the eyes of military historians.

Still, it is quite true that early in 1812 his apprenticeship in military matters had not yet been completed. Thus, it did not help at all when, at the very beginning of the campaign, the plans of his military mentor, Phull, turned out to be a fiasco. It would have hardly been possible for Alexander to make a worse choice than Phull, who was a theoretician of the worst sort with some remarkably curious ideas about war. Clausewitz said that he knew of no other ranking personage who would lose his head quite so quickly as would Phull. But Alexander was not by any means alone in his error of judgment. There were others, in Russia and elsewhere, who also thought highly of Phull. Certainly, as a theoretician, skilled at the art of discourse and dissemblage, Phull was bound to be uncommonly persuasive in convincing Alexander.

Exasperated and, once again, unsure of himself, Alexander gave up and decided to leave the running of the war in the hands of the generals. Unfortunately (or fortunately, in terms of the ultimate outcome), he failed to specify who was to be in command when he departed from supreme headquarters. Thus, it devolved upon Mikhail Bogdanovich, Count Barclay de Tolly to take the helm by default, but this was easier said than done. From the start, Barclay's authority had been undermined by the tsar's presence at supreme headquarters, even though most of the tsar's orders had passed through Barclay's hands in his capacity as minister of war. Now, the general stepped into the vacuum left by the tsar's departure without being specifically ordered to do so.

Barclay was a capable officer, personally brave and cool-headed, but he lacked the abilities needed to handle the tasks of a supreme commander. This was exacerbated by the fact that his long-time chief of staff, General Count Yermolov, was not the sort of man who could give him sound military advice. At the same time, Colonel von Toll, his quartermaster general and a man of considerable talent, could gain no more influence over Barclay than anyone else.

Moreover, Barclay's cold and unbending personality prevented him from overcoming the difficulties posed by the fact that he was not a Slav and thus was a thorn in the eye of ethnic Russians. His distant and brusque manner alienated him even further from those around him. Far worse, both Bagration and Tormassov, two full-blooded Russians, were his seniors in the service. Of these, the gallant Bagration, popular throughout the army, was an aggressive fighter, but far better suited to leading an advance guard than running the affairs of an entire army.

With the crisis still unresolved, Napoleon's arrival in Koenigsberg found the Russian army deployed as follows:

- *Imperial headquarters:* at Vilna.

- *First Western Army, under Barclay:* 104,250 men, 7000 Cossacks, 558 guns

    The right, under Wittgenstein: I Corps near Keidany
    The center: II, III, and IV Corps at Orsziszki, Novi-Troki, and Olkieniki; I and II Cavalry Corps at Vilkomir and Smorgoni; V (Guard) Corps at Svenciany
    The left, under Doctorov: VI Corps and III Cavalry Corps at Lida
    The Cossack Corps, under Platov: at Grodno

- *Second Western Army, under Bagration:* 33,000 men, 4000 Cossacks, 216 guns

    The main force: VII and VIII Corps and IV Cavalry Corps assembled around Volkovisk by 20 June

> The Cossacks pushing forward in the direction of Bialystok
> 27th Infantry Division (another 8000 men) approaching Vileyka

- *Third (Reserve) Army, under Tormassov*: 38,000 men, 4000 Cossacks, 164 guns
  Still concentrating, with its main force around Lutzk and Sacken's corps in southern Volhynia.

Thus, as of June 20, 1812—when the news of Napoleon's arrival in Koenigsberg was received at supreme headquarters—the Russian field forces amounted to 183,250 men, 15,000 Cossacks, and 938 guns.

NAPOLEON DEPLOYS

By the end of May, Napoleon had deployed the Grand Army along the Vistula. In all, 449,000 men with 1146 guns were ready to open the campaign, more than twice what the Russians could muster at that time. The positions were as follows:

> I (Davout), II (Oudinot), and III (Ney) Corps stood along the lower Vistula, between Thorn and Elbing, with the Guard Corps (Mortier) still approaching.
> IV (Eugene) and VI (St. Cyr) Corps stood near Plozk.
> V (Poniatowski) Corps was near Warsaw.
> VII (Reynier) and VIII (Vandamme) Corps were further upriver.
> The Austrian Auxiliary Corps stood near Lemberg.
> X (Macdonald) Corps, with the Prussians, stood at Koenigsberg in East Prussia.

Napoleon had deliberately deployed on so broad a front in order to keep the Russians up in the air about the true direction of his attack and induce them to spread their forces as well.

To ensure that they were properly deceived, Schwarzenberg was to circulate the rumor among the Russians that 100,000 Austrians were massing at Lemberg. However, in view of the fact that the Austrians and Russians had never lost contact, it is doubtful that this had any effect at all, even though Alexander had positioned an observation corps to watch the Austrian frontier. This latter corps was more of an insurance policy than an expression of the idea that real trouble might develop there. That none was expected is proven by the fact that Bagration's Second Army was moved closer to Barclay and away from the Austrian frontier before the end of May.

At that time, Napoleon was still in Dresden, where he held court over his vassals in a glittering levee that was to signal unity to all. His arrival at Posen, in the staging area, on May 30 signaled the start of the army's movement away from the Vistula and toward Niemen, which formed the border between Poland and Russia. He arrived in Koenigsberg on June 12.

Napoleon had studied every bit of printed material to be found on the Russian theater of operations. A Russian general staff map of western Russia had been obtained and passed on to the topographical section, where it was copied, with all the cyrillic characters translated, and distributed to all the general commands. Of course, all the roads, be they proper highways or mere trails, looked alike on this map. Indeed, most turned out to be little better than what one would today call country lanes or forest paths. Still, agents had been busy collecting all sorts of data, so Napoleon had become reasonably well informed about general conditions in the operations area.

He was also informed in some detail about Barclay's army, which had been assumed to be standing near Vilna with nearly 150,000 men. But he still thought Bagration's army numbered 100,000 men, because he had not yet learned that it had been split and that only part of it was marching via Brest-Litovsk to join Barclay. Nor had he yet learned that Bagration had been replaced by Tormassov in Volhynia and that a new army was forming around him and the troops left behind.

This was the situation in which Napoleon made his original plan of operations. His main force was to pass around the enemy's right and push the enemy to the south, that is, in the very direction of its richest resources, in order to clear the road to Moscow. Recognizing that Moscow was both the national and spiritual capital of Russia, Napoleon had thus made it the objective of his operations. It was there, at the very latest, that he would make peace. He had prepared his great successes of 1800, 1805, 1806, and 1807 with this same kind of movement, enveloping the enemy with the bulk of his forces. But certainly, he hoped to accomplish most of the long march to Moscow after he had effectively destroyed the Russian army's capacity to resist.

Accordingly, the second week in June saw his forces concentrating in distinct groupings that were to be reflective of the tasks to which they would be set:

Napoleon himself, with the Guard, I, II, and III Army Corps and I and II Cavalry Corps, including headquarters (222,400 men and 652 guns) massed between Koenigsberg and Goldap in East Prussia.

Echeloned to the right rear was Eugene, the viceroy of Italy, with IV and VI Corps and III Cavalry Corps (80,600 men and 178 guns) around Rastenburg.

Still further to the right and rear was Jerome, the king of Westphalia, with V, VII, and VIII Corps and IV Cavalry Corps (79,400 men and 192 guns) near Warsaw.

Macdonald's X Corps (32,500 men and 84 guns), intended to operate on the army's extreme left flank along the Baltic, was still around Tilsit.

Schwarzenberg and the Austrians (34,100 men and 60 guns) were around Lublin.

While Napoleon himself was to envelop the enemy right, Eugene was to pin the Russians in front. At the same time, Eugene was to cover Napoleon's own right against a Russian offensive and support Jerome, in case the latter was attacked on the far side of the Narev. Overestimating Russian initiative, Napoleon was convinced that such an attack by the Second Western Army would probably come from the central area of the Bug River.

In the meanwhile, Napoleon's agents and informers brought news to Koenigsberg of some changes that had taken place on the other side since the end of May. The picture unfolding now placed Bagration in the area of Volkovisk and had Barclay's forces stretched out from Lida to Keidany, with his reserves near Svenciany. Napoleon also learned that field fortifications were being thrown up at Dunaburg and Drissa, that only Cossacks stood between the two western armies, and that only weak forces stood in Volhynia under Tormassov and Kamensky.

This gave him a better picture of the enemy's intentions and made it clear that, in view of the Russians' apparent concentration toward their own right, it might be difficult to get that flank. On the other hand, the Russians' greatly extended position invited a breakthrough at some point with concentrated force, similar to his opening gambits in 1796, 1808, and 1809. With this in mind, Napoleon decided to cross the Niemen near Kovno with his main force and make straight for Vilna, right in the center of Barclay's area of deployment.

Eugene, echeloned to the right rear, was to move toward Seiny. Still covering Napoleon's own right and forestalling the possibility of a Russian offensive via Olita or Grodno with a thrust of his own, he would also be widening the gap between the two Russian armies.

Jerome had a dual mission along the Narev. On the one hand, he was to make the Russians believe that he would be conducting a joint offensive with the Austrians via Lublin; it was hoped that this would induce the Russians to separate their armies even further. On the other hand, Napoleon still expected a Russian attack. If Jerome could draw the attack upon himself, then Eugene could thrust into the Russians' flank, with Napoleon sweeping into their rear via Vilna.

Soon, however, Napoleon began to think an attack by the Russian Second Army was unlikely, unless it came soon. On June 16 Jerome was advised that if the emperor should succeed in isolating that army, then Jerome would be able to attack simultaneously with Napoleon. On the 21st, however, the emperor advised Jerome that he would probably draw him in toward Grodno with his entire army. This move would shift the center of gravity of Napoleon's operations onto a more northerly course, pointing to a crossing of the Niemen by the central army group at Kovno.

Crossing at Kovno was favored for several reasons. The locale was ideal. Not only did the bend of the river in that area project it into the Russian positions, but its confluence with the Vilia at that point would offer control of both banks of the latter. This was quite important, since Napoleon expected to use that river to bring supplies by water as far as Vilna.

There was as yet no plan; that would come as the situation developed. Napoleon's intention, however, aimed in the following direction: He would hold back his right echelon while his strong left broke through the Russian right wing. That way, he could place himself across the lines of communication of the Russian center and left.

This idea has met with the approval of most critics. It may, however, be fairly asked if it would not have been better to do the opposite, that is, to take the right shoulder forward and, instead of trying to separate Bagration from Barclay, push the former into the latter and then pin both against the Drissa. This would have made all the more sense once Napoleon learned that the enemy intended to retreat in that direction anyway. He would then have only had to help them along. This, however, would have required that Jerome's army group be substantially reinforced and deployed much further south than Grodno so that it might get around Bagration on the upper Niemen. Napoleon's great numerical superiority made this entirely possible, indeed virtually imperative. As it was, his operations base was entirely too narrow for a hostile penetration beyond Smolensk.

Had Napoleon thus succeeded in pushing both western armies against the Drissa, he would have separated them from their communications with the southern and central provinces of the Russian empire, the seats of its greatest resources, and opened the road to Moscow as well. Furthermore, given Napoleon's great numerical superiority, had he been able to bring the two Russian armies to battle, the outcome could have hardly been in doubt. Indeed, their destruction would have been a distinct possibility, thereby knocking out the core of the entire Russian force then available for a defense.

Nor would there have been much of a refuge for the armies thus defeated, and the road to St. Petersburg would have been open to the French as well. With a single stroke, the two western armies would have seen themselves boxed into a corner and cut off from the vast expanses of the Russian empire. This would have been the sort of move one might expect from Napoleon, who had always reached for the "brass ring" instead of aiming at partial successes. It will forever remain an open question whether Alexander, despite his personal aversion to Napoleon, might have faltered and whether his resolution to resist might have dissipated had Napoleon successfully carried out such a maneuver.

This kind of success, which would have shunted aside the bulk of the Russian combat forces, might have made it impossible for the Russians to make the kind of retreat they ultimately did, a retreat apparently without a finite limit or objective. In addition, this retreating "strategy" of the Russians, if it may even be called that, had been forced upon them by Napoleon's attempt to keep them separate in the first place.

Thus, Napoleon's attempt to repeat his masterpiece of 1796, when he had succeeded in placing himself between the Austrians and Piedmontese in northern Italy (if he even thought of this analogy), was a mistake under the entirely different spacial conditions of the Russian theater. This was so especially because Napoleon's reputation (which had not yet come into existence in 1796) and his great numerical superiority would naturally force his opponents to be cautious and prevent them from facing him with anything less than their united forces.

Of course, had Napoleon opted to go the route of pushing the two Russian armies northward and into each other, he would have been required to make a substantial rearrangement in his deployment. Additionally, the poor and sparsely populated country along the upper Niemen, extensively wooded and covered by swamps, would have presented considerable difficulties for the movement of masses. These, however, were not insurmountable obstacles.

That Napoleon did not choose this alternative may have been due largely to the reasons already noted. First, he thought Alexander lacked the moral fiber to conduct a drawn-out war, which would surely take place if the expanses of Russia were brought into play. He still believed that all he needed to bring Alexander to his knees were some decisive military strokes or, as a last resort, the capture of Moscow. Added to this must be the fact that this would be the first time the vastness of the Russian empire would be brought into play in its full extent. Just as the Russians themselves had as yet no idea of the advantages offered by their own country, so too did Napoleon underestimate its inherent dangers. He thought these could be minimized by the very size of his army, which he obviously considered too large to be swallowed up by the terrain.

By this point, Napoleon had too often been able to impose his will upon others and had consistently been able to bend circumstances to suit his objectives. In doing so, he had often made the difficult seem far easier than it had actually been. His successes had made him succumb to the great field marshal's most dangerous illusions: underestimating the opposition and seeing things as he wanted them to be, not as they were.

Thus, for the first time Napoleon the general had lost the eye for what was possible, something that Napoleon the statesman had lost long before. In Spain, the general had demonstrated this ability for the last time, when he saw at once that he could leave the conclusion of that war to his lieutenants; the statesman had already lost it when he thought that getting rid of the Portuguese Braganzas and the Spanish Bourbons would suffice to make him the master of the Peninsula. Indeed, he had already lost it when, by decreeing the Continental blockade, he thought he could subordinate the economic interests of the whole of Europe to his own.

In Russia, there could be no question of leaving matters in the hands of subordinates in the event of a national insurrection or a drawn-out war. There, he had put himself and his reputation for omnipotence on the line, and that made his errors all the more dangerous. Of these, underestimation of his adversary, the Russian tsar, was the first error. Underestimation of the difficulties the operations area would pose was the second. And from these two sprang the third, a faulty operations concept, if not a plan, that was to turn the entire campaign into a failure.

NOTES

1. Brabant, A. *In Russland und in Sachsen, 1812–1815.* Dresden, 1930. Uncensored material from Funck's papers, which were declassified only after Saxony became a republic after World War I.
2. Ibid.
3. The conditions under which Charles XII of Sweden had marched to Poltava were so different that no valid conclusions could have been drawn from this.

II
The Military Background

5. The French Military Establishment

BACKGROUND

The army Napoleon inherited when he became first consul in December 1799 was essentially the creation of Lazare Carnot's reforms. Even though the latter had labored mightily to eliminate the chaotic conditions caused by the erratic and often nonsensical measures of the republican government, the army was still a long way from what Napoleon wanted it to be.

Napoleon's first concrete step was to ensure a steady flow of replacements for the army. The new law, which was to be strictly enforced, called for an annual draft of 30,000 recruits. This would replace the old random calls made until then on an as-needed basis. And, of course, the drafts would be made whether or not the country was at war.

The idea of grouping the combat elements of the French army into divisions consisting of infantry, cavalry, and artillery went back to the royal ordinance of July 28, 1778. An administrative rather than a tactical-operational measure, this had required extensive dislocations among the garrisons all over France and a complete restructuring of the administration. As a result, the process had been nowhere near completion when the revolution swept the country in 1789.

It was left to Carnot's reforms of 1793 and 1794 to finally establish the division, composed of the three combat arms, even though there did not as yet exist a corresponding doctrine for its tactical employment. Indeed, in the years following, it was found that this measure resulted in the cavalry being fragmented into too many small detachments, so it was taken out of the divisions to form larger formations of its own. The infantry divisions, however, retained their artillery. By 1805, a cavalry brigade had been given to each army corps. With the growth of the Grand Army, entire cavalry divisions were eventually assigned to the army corps, ideally at the ratio of three infantry divisions to one of cavalry. Everything in excess of these requirements was massed into the cavalry reserve. These measures, of course, went hand in hand with the development of doctrines that had changed the divisional unit from an administrative to a tactical entity.

In Italy, Napoleon had already experimented with the idea of grouping divisions, by twos and threes, as needed, into army corps, which were to be commanded by lieutenant generals. When the latest Austrian war was brought to a successful conclusion with the Treaty of Luneville in February 1801, the first consul was able to devote himself in earnest to the reshaping of the army. The as yet unsettled Egyptian question and the continuing naval war by Britain gave Napoleon the opportunity to enlarge the army again.

During the Austrian war, the army had made do with an annual draft call of 30,000 recruits. Now the draft was doubled, with 30,000 being called twice every year, for an annual total of 60,000 men. Thus, between May 1802 and May 1805, no fewer than 210,000 men were called to the colors, even though the army had been fighting only a sit-down war.

The bulk of this additional manpower went into the invasion force gathering in the encampments along the English Channel. Styled the *Armee d'Angleterre*, it was to become the proving ground for the new divisional and corps organizations and the only real basic training facility on a grand scale the French military establishment would ever experience.[1] Although Nelson's victory at Trafalgar in October 1805 put an end to all pretense of invading the British Isles, the years in the encampments along the Channel coast would put their stamp on the Grand Army yet to be.

On the left flank, at Brest, Augerau was in charge. The main force was deployed along the Pas de Calais, with Ney in charge of the camps around Etapes-Montreuil, Soult around Boulogne-Ambleteuse, and Davout in Oost-ende-Dunkirk. On the right flank was Marmont's group at Utrecht. Along with Mortier's force, which had stood in the Nymwegen-Breda area until it was sent off to occupy Hanover in 1803, these would eventually become the Grand Army of 1805.

Even though the techniques of embarkation and debarkation stood high on the training agenda for a while, the troops in these encampments did experience a considerable amount of brigade, division, and even corps drills.

Typically, however, this period failed to produce anything in the way of standard directives, much less a new field manual. Napoleon, who had neither the background nor much interest in matters relating to elementary tactics, was content to leave such matters to his subordinates. He did, on occasion, issue a general directive and eventually effected a reorganization of the infrastructure of the infantry battalions, which was designed to affect tactical employment and limit the number of skirmishers to be deployed under normal circumstances. But that came later. On the whole, the army continued to operate on the basis of empirical experience, with the last of the old royal army's regulations (published in 1791) being invoked only for the most basic evolutions, and even then only with uneven frequency, depending upon who was the man in charge. Thus, the standards and training methods along the Channel coast differed from one encampment to the next. As was to be expected, Marmont's, Soult's, and Davout's troops drilled often; those under Ney, for example, not nearly so much.

On the most fundamental level, however, this massing of the bulk of the army's combat elements in the Channel camps did provide Napoleon with the welcome opportunity to isolate these men from the republican influences of the civil population. In this way, the army could be whipped into shape, disciplined and reinfused with the older ideas of soldierly professionalism.

In this the commanders succeeded, even though the results would be something of a mixed blessing. The soldiers' years of isolation, first in their native country and later as conquerors in Germany, had given rise to what Morvan[2] termed the *miles gloriosus* (the glorious soldier), a subject often greeted with silence by the romantics. Nevertheless, it was real. (By 1808, when elements of the Grand Army marched across France on their way to Spain, the villages and townships in their path were dismayed, some apparently even petitioning the authorities to reroute the marching columns to avoid their districts.)

By 1803, the new organizations as established in the Channel encampments were extended to cover the entire French military establishment, which became the Imperial Army when Napoleon took the emperor's crown for himself in 1804. In the same year, most of his lieutenants, who had been in command of the Channel encampments, were among those who received their marshal's batons. But even if this Army of England was fated never to cross the English Channel, it was to make history in 1805, when the Austrians appeared in the field for yet another contest with the French. By then, this organization of several years' standing was ready to face its first test on the battlefield.

In the course of their training, the formations of each encampment had become accustomed to functioning as operational entities. Thus, despite the fact that they were of quite unequal size, Napoleon did not tamper with this arrangement by shifting some of their constituent elements around, simply in the interests of achieving uniformity. Far more interested in preserving their identity and the established relationships with their respective commanders, he left them intact. The unequal size of the different army corps that resulted from this was to remain a characteristic throughout the Napoleonic era. Their size was as much a reflection of the emperor's confidence in the military abilities of the men he placed in charge of them as it was of the tasks to which they would be put.

In this way, the Armee d'Angleterre, when mobilized for the war of 1805, became the Grand Army. Its constituent army corps, entirely due to the circumstance of the sequence in which they had originally been placed, were identified by Roman numerals. Commencing on the right with Bernadotte (who had replaced Mortier), whose troops became I Corps, the numbering proceeded in counterclockwise fashion, across the Channel front, to Augerau on the left, whose troops now formed VII Corps.

Henceforth, the Grand Army and its numbered army corps would remain the first string, the starting team of the French military establishment. Whenever it took to the field, it would always be commanded by Napoleon himself. Over the years, the Grand Army was to grow from one campaign to the next, not only through the growth of its French constituents but mainly through the inclusion of increasing numbers of foreign troops. Although the Grand Army of 1809 was officially termed the Army of Germany, because there was also an Army of Spain, this was a mere technicality. In 1812, it became the Grand Army again, and would remain so in 1813 as well.

The Grand Army was only a *part* of the French military establishment. The two were not identical. This is a point that should be understood, particularly by American readers, who, with the example of the Grand Army of the Republic in mind, tend to see the two bodies as one and the same.

The Grand Army of 1805, as yet quite a national army, was the best Napoleon ever commanded, not only because it had had years of training along the Channel coast but also because it contained the largest cadre of veterans, both officers and rank and file. Half the generals had already held commissioned rank in the royal army. Indeed, three-fifths of the staff officers (the modern-day equivalents of the field grades—majors to colonels) and about half of all the officers had seen service in the old army, even if very few had held commissions. All but the youngest officers (about 600) and about half the rank and file had campaigned before.

However, even the victories of Austerlitz, Jena, Auerstaedt, and Friedland, not to mention the battering at Eylau, had torn huge gaps into the ranks of the Grand Army's cadre. At the same time, the ongoing expansions of the Guard Corps, as well as the creation of numerous new line formations, constantly diluted the remaining cadres even further. This process of dilution proceeded at a faster pace than did the creation of new veterans by successive campaigns. Things got even worse when, from 1808 onward, a great number of provisional units had to be formed and the depots were stripped for the Spanish venture, which would become a constant drain, regardless of what transpired elsewhere.

Thus, by 1812, there was already a shortage of good regimental officers, even though the ranks of the sergeants had been combed over and over and the National Guard had been raided to find suitable lieutenants. At the same time, there was an ever-growing resistance against the incessant drafts; this was despite the fact that, given the size of the French population, these demands were not excessive.

In economic terms, the Grand Army, the most powerful and effective military instrument of the empire, had also cost the least. From the time it crossed the Rhine in October 1805 until it was expelled from Germany in December 1813, its upkeep had rested on the backs of the German principalities, friend and foe alike. Even Napoleon's brother Jerome, the king of Westphalia, complained bitterly about having to keep up remittances to the French treasury while he was forced to support French garrisons fully as large as the army he had been ordered to maintain as his contribution to the Rhine Confederation.[3]

Although the material costs of the Grand Army imposed only a negligible burden upon the French nation, matters stood differently when it came to the human costs of the French military establishment as a whole. By September 1807, that is, in the 2 years following the outbreak of the Austrian war, another 420,000 men had been called up, as the annual draft had been raised to 80,000 men. To accommodate this, the draft age had been lowered from 20 years and 4 months to 18 years and 6 months. Such a draft was not by any means insupportable for a nation numbering about 29 million in 1806. However, numerous exemptions and the purchase of substitutes by those who were drafted had narrowed the draft base, and the rising cost of substitutes (which came hand in hand with the increased drafts) hit the middle class right where it hurt the most—in the pocketbook. Then as later, in France as elsewhere, the bourgeoisie was as quickly inclined to complain about the costs of the military as it was disinclined to serve.

During our own Vietnam era, one could observe the massive flight of the sons of the well-to-do into colleges and universities to escape the draft. When, some years later an attempt was made to merely reinstitute draft registration, one could again observe the well-dressed scions of the bourgeoisie, attended by batteries of lawyers, appearing in front of television cameras in protest. It was no different in Napoleonic France. Even the popular rising of 1813 in Prussia saw strong elements of middle-class youth resisting entry into the army. Special Jaeger volunteer units had to be created to make military service palatable for them.

Most importantly, however, just as the American nation of the Vietnam era perceived neither a "clear and present danger" nor itself as a "nation in arms"—the Vietnam war was, after all, an old-fashioned cabinet war—so did the French nation no longer view itself as being under attack. And among those who continued to support Napoleon's imperial ventures, many continued to do so only as long as things went well and added to the glories of France. Thus, as the draft calls went on through 1808, 1809, and 1810 and were increased to 120,000 in 1811 and 1812, and as the demands placed upon the National Guard to do yeoman service continued to rise, the number of *refractaires* (draft dodgers) also rose.

For years, there had existed in France a phenomenon that Morvan, quoted earlier, described as the *armee roulante*. It consisted of hordes of soldiers traveling back and forth across France with improper travel orders. That is to say, the travel orders were genuine, but the men to whom they had been originally issued had exchanged them along the way for the orders of men going in a different direction. In this fashion, they would course back and forth without ever arriving at their destinations.

By 1812, when the army was being beefed up even further, thousands of these illegal travelers, along with other draft dodgers, were picked up in dragnets specially set up for this purpose and were stuffed into penal regiments such as the Regiment de Re and de Walcheren. No fewer than five regiments were formed in this fashion; they eventually became the 131st, 132nd, and 133rd Line Regiments and the 35th and 36th Light. Also included in these were some Spanish and Portuguese prisoners of war, as well as French soldiers who had ended up in the stockades for sundry reasons. Most of these troops ended up in the Grand Army of 1812. Funck,[4] who met with some of them in Russia, found their appearance less than reassuring and had serious doubts concerning their military value.

The total French military establishment at the foundation of the Grand Army of 1812 numbered about 800,000 men.[5] Of these, about 220,000 men were committed in the Spanish theater of operations,[6] which also involved an additional 30,000 allied Italian, German, and Spanish troops.

Remaining behind in France and Italy were, according to Napoleon's own calculations, about 413,000 men.[7] This number, however, was based on the organizational, or "paper," strength of the units involved. The line battalions remaining behind in the garrisons generally consisted of weak cadres, since the 1812 drafts, which had been originally earmarked to bring these units up to strength, had, whenever possible, been funneled straight into the mobile reserves of the Grand Army (the single battalions assigned to IX and XI Corps). In addition, the cohorts of the National Guard showed large deficits as well. The actual number of troops not committed either in Spain or with the Grand Army most likely did not exceed 275,000 men.

None of these figures include the foreign troops in French pay (which appear in the detailed listing of the French military establishment in Appendix II). These foreign troops should not be confused with those of the Rhine Confederation or Italy.

Thus, the overall strength of about 800,000 men must be seen as reflecting a "present" strength, because the organizational, that is, the planned, strength had all the units been up to par would have run close to 1.2 million men.

THE GRAND ARMY

The French

The Grand Army of 1812, including the few replacements that were brought up after operations got under way, consisted of the following French units (see Appendix V for a detailed order of battle):

  4 regiments of the Old Guard

11 regiments of the Young Guard, the guard cavalry, honor guards, and the guard artillery

51 infantry regiments (line and light regiments combined), consisting of 39 old and 7 neo-French, as well as 5 regiments without numbers[8]

62 single battalions (some composite, but most from regiments in Spain that were, for the greatest part, grouped into provisional regiments in Augerau's XI Corps and Victor's IX Corps)

49 cavalry regiments

  8 individual squadrons (drawn from dragoon regiments in Spain)

100 artillery companies
13 artillery train battalions

The total figures are:

	Battalions	Squadrons	Artillery Companies	Artillery Train Battalions
The guard	34	24	15	2
The line	269	204	100	13
Total	303	228	115	15

Added to these must be:

13 pontoon companies
28 sapper companies
 6 miner companies
17 army train battalions

According to the organizational tables, the number of these troops should have come to about 380,000 men. Their present strength, however, did not come to more than 325,000 men at the outset of the campaign.

The foreign troops in French pay must also be included:

4 Swiss regiments, totaling 11 battalions
1 Battalion Neufchatel
4 regiments of the Vistula Legion, with 12 battalions
3 Portuguese regiments, with 6 battalions
1 Spanish infantry regiment
1 Spanish engineer battalion, totaling, with the infantry regiment, 3
   battalions

In total, the 33 battalions comprised 22,000 men.

With regard to the French troops in the Grand Army, it should be noted that they consisted largely of conscripts. Many of them were young and poorly trained and in no way prepared for the hardships of any campaign, let alone one as difficult as the Russian campaign promised to be.

The Allied Contingents

On the whole, the allied contingents have received a mixed press from writers steeped in the Napoleonic romance. However, their services were certainly appreciated by almost all French military historians. Indeed, men like Marshals Victor and Mortier spoke well of them, particularly of the German troops they commanded. Even so, apologists have often struck condescending notes and, by rote, consider them to have been only second best to the national French troops.

Of course, whenever Napoleon needed a spanking boy and some allies were handy, they would provide a ready-made scapegoat (as, for example, in the incident with the Wuerttembergers in Poland, in which Ney and the French commissariat were actually the perpetrators). Napoleon, as was to be expected, was quite insensitive toward matters concerning the pride of others. On more than one occasion, when addressing the troops, he would extol the virtues of the French soldiers above all others, even as troops from the allied contingents stood within earshot. However, some historians have pointed out that, Napoleon, not being a Frenchman himself, took a rather detached and somewhat cynical view of his own adopted nation, so why should he be sensitive toward others'?

Certainly, the princes in his retinue, especially those of the Rhine Confederation, shared his views in this direction. The revolution was history, and the people, as in the days of the old regimes, had once again become the objects rather than the partners of government. The only change was that they now got at least some lip service. However, the more omnipotent the French empire grew, the broader the contact of French troops with friend and foe alike, and the more Napoleon talked, the more the commoner was made aware that he was not French. Even if, as stated earlier, Napoleon had made it an object of his policy to destroy the German identity, the results were militating in the opposite direction.

Still, the evidence as it emerges from hundreds of diaries kept by Napoleon's German veterans (of which many found their way into print) is mixed, to say the least. Their evaluations, based on the sociological backgrounds of the writers alone, invites a study in itself. However, even a cursory survey yields some general trends.

First, there were the regular soldiers, who lived in a tight little world of their own. They found it easy to admire and, indeed, be part of Napoleon's winning ways. In particular, they liked the easygoing way in which the French conducted their day-to-day affairs and the relatively loose discipline. It was by far preferable to the tight discipline and "spit and polish" generally experienced in their own armies.

An excellent case in point is furnished by Karl Schehl,[9] a neo-Frank (a cognomen often applied to the inhabitants of annexed territories), who enlisted as a boy musician with the French 2nd Carabinier Regiment just prior to its departure for the Russian campaign. Life as a boy bandsman, what few months of it he experienced, was pleasant indeed. But his words become shrill when he devotes the last chapter of his memoirs to the comparatively harsh life in the Prussian horse artillery, where he found himself when his home territory became Prussian again after the war.

The reactions of the recruits, who suddenly found themselves in the army, appear to have been conditioned largely by their civilian backgrounds. Certainly, unpropertied individuals, stableboys, grooms, day laborers and so on, whether from town or country, were apt to find military life, French or otherwise, easier than what they had left behind. But men from such social backgrounds rarely wrote memoirs.

The great bulk of the written materials comes from men of middle- and upper-class backgrounds, and here, attitudes were more complex. These men were, on the whole, well educated and well read and thus better informed; among them, the ideals of the revolution had found broad, if generally tacit, acceptance. But there were also many who realized that the revolution was history. They could see that whatever the revolution might have wrought in France, what had actually come their way was something different altogether. Much of this, however, was colored again by how well things were being run at home.

At the same time, the aftershocks of the Reformation and the Thirty Years' War had not yet fully abated, and the German nation was religiously divided like no other in Europe. Thus, the Protestant north was generally slower in accepting things French than was the Catholic south.

But these were ideological undercurrents. Day-to-day relationships were part of the real world. And in that sphere, as the years passed, many of the better-educated scions of the bourgeoisie, and certainly some of the high-ranking officers in the army, were beginning to weary of the offhanded and frequently high-handed treatment accorded them by the French in general. While it was easy to follow, even to worship, a Napoleon, particularly for a military man, it was not nearly so easy to constantly submit to the airs of far lesser men. Worst of all was the constant economic pressure that was exerted to finance Napoleon's schemes. It knew no boundaries and affected friend and erstwhile foe alike. Nowhere was the change wrought by prolonged contact with the French more starkly drawn than in Prussia.

In 1806, the Prussian civilian population had stood aside politely while the French emperor struck a mortal blow at their own king's army. Even if the Prussians did not openly approve of the coming of the French, they certainly regarded them with open interest. It took them no more than a couple of years to realize that their country had become just another cow to be milked by Napoleon. Their king, Frederick William III, had been no Frederick the Great. If they had felt themselves bound to the idea of Prussia, it had been to the state and its institutions, not to this king.

By 1812, the Prussian nation had done an about-face. The king had become a partner in his people's suffering. While Napoleon had not incurred the enmity of the Prussian nation by waging war against its king, it had become hostile when he became its master by remote control. Thus, he had achieved by 1812 what he had failed to do in 1806. The rising of the Prussian nation in 1813 was something Frederick William could have never accomplished by decree. Only Napoleon could take the credit for that.

Thus, in Prussia and elsewhere, Napoleon had gathered allies and subjects, but he had made very few friends. This, of course, was reflected in the allied military contingents.

The vast majority of the allied soldiers, just like their French counterparts, marched and fought for the same reasons that they had before—and would again, after Napoleon was gone: because they were soldiers, because they were ordered to, and because that's what soldiers are expected to do. At the same time, however, the allied soldiers had sworn allegiance to more than a dozen different colors, and their sovereigns were tied to Napoleon's coattails for reasons that were largely remote and obscure, reasons that were barely if at all understood by the majority of the rank and file. This was not so with the officers, who were on the whole very much aware of the world around them.

Thus, the idea of a common cause, and even more so the objective of the coming campaign, was meaningless to most of the allied rank and file. Moreover, the veteran soldiers of all ranks—and they were still numerous among the allied contingents—had serious misgivings about a Russian war. As is generally the case, only the young and inexperienced, which included many of the junior officers, thought they were heading for a great and glorious adventure.

Still, regardless of a soldier's personal outlook, whenever Napoleon put in a personal appearance, his charisma never failed to elicit shouts of "*Vive l'empereur.*" Nor were these insincere. Napoleon's personal presence exerted a powerful magnetism. But the popular historians who take delight in rendering glowing and romantic recitals of such occasions also fail to note that these expressions of enthusiasm were but manifestations of the moment. They would wane after the first missed meal, rarely survive the first bad bivouac, and vanish in a puff of smoke when the first cannonball tore through a formation.

This outline does not represent an exhaustive study of the complexities that went into the attitudes and the morale of the allied contingents. But what held true for the Germans as a whole also held for most of the others, especially the Neapolitans. Only the Poles entered into the war with their eyes wide open and their expectations running at a fever pitch.

That is not to say that the foreign troops in the Grand Army of 1812 did not perform well. However, Napoleon's desire to step onto the stage with an overwhelming force had seen to it that the foreign contingents also contained many raw troops. Still, on average, the foreign troops of the Grand Army contained larger veteran cadres and thus had a higher performance standard. In general, they were among the last to relinquish the bonds of order and discipline, and most did so only after all else around them had already fallen apart.

Nevertheless, the ingredients of internal strife were present from the start. It was reflected mainly in the often-strained relationships with the French commanders and especially with the French commissariat. The problems ran the gamut from passive resistance to open confrontation.

As to the individual allied contingents, these varied greatly in size and composition. They ranged from entirely Polish, Saxon, Bavarian, and Westphalian corps—of which only the Poles were commanded by a native son —to Italian and Wuerttembergian divisions, as well as brigades and individual regiments appended to various major formations. The Poles and Germans provided an uncommonly large proportion of cavalry formations, many of which had been split away from their own forces and dispersed throughout the Grand Army.

The allied contingents are discussed individually in the following sections.

The Poles The largest single national contingent among the foreign troops was the Poles. Against the promised reconstitution of their state, most Poles went to extraordinary lengths to accommodate the Grand Army passing through their territories. In addition, the Poles raised some 75,000 soldiers, not counting the Vistula Legion or the lancers in the Imperial Guard. None went into the war with more enthusiasm. It was going to be their war, and they followed the emperor's colors willingly. In number, they were second only to the French, unless the various German contingents are taken collectively.

Even though the grand duchy of Warsaw was impoverished, it raised the highest percentage of troops in proportion to its population. This brought on so rapid an expansion that the Poles had to be regarded as a conscript army, not dissimilar to the French in this respect. The situation was exacerbated by the fact that, like Russia, Poland lacked a broadly based middle class, so the army forever suffered from a chronic shortage of good noncoms.

As everywhere else, the march into and out of Russia cleaned house: Only the fittest survived. Thus, the decimated remnants, particularly those of the Polish cavalry, who were familiar with the country, climate, and language, became the safe-conduct of what was left of the main army group. They served with distinction at Smolensk and Borodino and played a major role in making the crossing of the Beresina possible.

The Lithuanians, about 12,000 strong, were added to the Polish army. These troops, however, had been formed only after the campaign was under way. Thus, their military value was dubious.

Not counting these latter formations, the Polish army numbered 54 battalions and 62 squadrons.

The Italians This 30,000-man contingent, organized into 18 battalions and 16 squadrons, was largely made up of veteran troops. Indeed, its cadre mainly consisted of old-time republicans, who had been with the colors since revolutionary times. National pride and esprit de corps ran exceptionally high in these formations, and their commander in chief, Eugene, was very popular with the rank and file.

In the course of the campaign, the Italians performed extremely well at Malo-Jaroslavets, where they suffered heavy losses. Their decimated remnants, however, were still counted among the combat-worthy and stood, once more, in the firing line at the Beresina.

The Neapolitans About 11,000 Neapolitans formed the bulk of the 33rd Division, under Detres, which came up quite late in the campaign with Augerau's XI Corps. Unfortunately, these men from the sunny south of Italy did not in any way measure up to their cousins from the north. Nor did they take kindly to the Russian winter. Numbering 11 battalions and 5 squadrons, the cadres of this respectable force had already given the Bourbons no joy, had fought against the French in 1806, and had no love for Napoleon. Their desertion rate exceeded even that of the Spaniards.

The Neapolitans did not penetrate deeply into Russia; they melted away without having fought in any major action. When they came upon the shattered remnants of the retreating Grand Army, its sight was apparently more than they could bear.

Napoleon selected the Neapolitan Horse Guard to form part of his escort when he left the army behind to speed on to Paris. The Neapolitans lost all their horses long before the emperor's retinue reached the Rhine.

The Westphalians   Westphalia was one of Napoleon's artificial creations. Formed after the Treaty of Tilsit in 1807, the kingdom included various German territories, among them Brunswick, parts of Hanover, Hesse-Kassel, and the bishoprics of Paderborn, Hildesheim, and Magdeburg. The Westphalians, by this time termed neo-Franks by their fellow Germans, held their new king, Jerome, in little esteem.

On the whole, the Westphalian contingent of 24,000 men in 22 battalions and 21 squadrons consisted of good soldiers with a numerous veteran cadre. Still, they were lacking any kind of national cohesion beyond being collectively referred to as Westphalians.

Jerome was not entirely lacking in military talents, as he had shown in more modest circumstances in 1806. But he was in command of his corps only during the opening stages of the campaign; he left in July to return to Westphalia. Thereafter, the corps passed in quick succession first to Tharreau and then to Junot. This was a serious mistake. The latter, one of Napoleon's oldest friends, was by 1812 an alcoholic in an advanced state of mental decay. He was no longer fit to command troops. As a result, Westphalian performance fell far short of its potential.

The Bavarians   This, the largest of the Rhine Confederation contingents, numbered some 30,000 men in 30 battalions and 24 squadrons, nearly 90 percent of the entire Bavarian field army. Of these, about 5000 men, or one-sixth, were recruits from the Tyrol, which had only recently become part of Bavaria and which had just risen in a bloody insurrection in 1809.

These men cared about neither the Bavarian king nor Napoleon. Their hero was Andreas Hofer, the rebel leader who had fallen before a firing squad at Mantua. Thus, the Tyrolean recruits harbored strong resentments against both the French and the Bavarians, a situation that did not bode well for the Bavarian corps. The veterans among the Bavarians had their own share of misgivings. They had already participated in the campaign of 1806–1807 and thus had a good idea of what to expect.

As a result, desertion, while not the highest in the army, was nevertheless the highest among the German contingents. Coupled with a rising tide of disillusionment with the Napoleonic cause was the adverse effect exercised upon the Bavarians by their French commander, Gouvion St. Cyr.

The Bavarian corps was positioned in the left flank of the main army group and thus did not take part in the advance on Moscow. Instead, it was burned out in a series of grinding actions around Polotsk, a pestilentious, fever-ridden tract of land that has become known as the Bavarian grave. During the final stage of the retreat, the Bavarian corps disappeared virtually without a trace.

The Saxons   About 22,000 strong, in 24 battalions and 32 squadrons, the Saxons ranked with the best troops in the campaign. Their commander, Reynier, was highly unpopular with the Saxons and strongly prejudiced against the Germans, but he was also a man of frustrated ambitions. He had commanded a division in Egypt, only to see other men, junior to him, advance to the highest rank in the army.

Although the choice of Reynier to command the Saxons again in 1812 might have been questionable, the Saxon contingent suffered even worse from internal troubles. These ranged from the ambitious Thielemann, who managed to have his cavalry brigade detached from the Saxon corps and thus left it critically short of cavalry, to a profiteering cabal that reached all the way from Langenau, Reynier's Saxon chief of staff, back to Dresden and the ministries. The scheme about the issue of the uniforms, mentioned earlier, was only part of an entire network of machinations designed to defraud their own king and country. As a result of these problems, the Saxons did not do as well as they might have in the campaign.

This corps, part of the southern flanking force, never advanced beyond Volhynia. Thus, it avoided sharing in the disastrous disintegration of the Grand Army. The Saxon corps did its duty, but not one iota more. However, Thielemann's brigade, the Saxon cuirassiers, often described as being "the most beautiful heavy cavalry in the Grand Army," had its day of glory at Borodino with the taking of the Raievsky redoubt.

The Wuerttembergers   This veteran contingent of 14,000 men, organized into 14 battalions and 16 squadrons, formed a division in Ney's III Corps. They rendered excellent service even though they were not enthusiastic about Napoleon or the campaign. Hard-nosed professionals, they performed with distinction in every action up to the Battle of Borodino.

The unfortunate incident in Poland that, incidentally, also served to discredit Ney has already been discussed in some detail. As a result of the accusations, the Wuerttembergers drew the worst assignments and positions in the order of march. By August, the contingent had dwindled to no more than 4000 effectives. Coupled with this were losses from several engagements around Smolensk between August 14 and 19 and the Battle of Borodino on September 7. On November 29, Napoleon took note of about thirty Wuerttembergers who were still in marching formation.

This brings up the last three of the German contingents that were at least of brigade size, those from Baden, Berg, and Hesse. They were in many ways the cream of the crop—and not merely of the foreign contingents.

The Badeners   This force of 7000 men in 7 battalions and 4 squadrons is generally regarded as having been the best of the German contingents. All were excellent soldiers who performed well even though they hardly had the opportunity to enter into combat as an integrated unit. Their battalions were scattered all over; the grenadier battalion was assigned to watch over Napoleon's war chest.

The remnants of the Baden Field Brigade did get to see their day at the Beresina, where they stood shoulder to shoulder with the last and toughest of the Poles and some of the other "poor country cousins" in a legendary rear-guard action.

The Bergers   The grand duchy of Berg furnished 7000 men in 7 battalions and 4 squadrons. Of these, all the infantry was in IX Corps, while the lancer regiment was attached to the guard cavalry.

The Bergers, all good professionals, many of them ex-Prussians from Cleve, shared all the bloody actions at the Beresina with the Poles and the Badeners. Even at Kovno, when all had fallen apart, the Bergers still marched with their colors.

The Hessians   These were not the sons of the Hessians who had been brought across the Atlantic during the American Revolution; they would have been found mostly among the Westphalians. This contingent came from Hesse-Darmstadt, and all were old-style professionals in the eighteenth-century mold. Numbering 5000 men in 6 battalions and 3 squadrons, their excellence was attested to by the fact that one regiment was attached to the Young Guard while another served at imperial headquarters.

As such, the Hessians were engaged only during the retreat. At that time, in the ranks of the guards, they performed with distinction at Krasnoi under the personal command of their young hereditary prince.

Together, the contingents discussed above accounted for more than three-quarters of the foreign troops. There were also a few small contingents from other areas, as follows:

Wuerzburg	3 battalions
Mecklenburg	3 battalions
Frankfurt	3 battalions
Saxon duchies	7 battalions

The Prussians   In addition to these there was a Prussian contingent of about 20,000 men in 20 battalions and 24 squadrons. Of these, one hussar regiment was attached to I Cavalry Corps and one lancer regiment to II Cavalry Corps. Two artillery companies were attached to the Guard Corps.

The entire Prussian contingent consisted of well-trained professionals who performed well. They formed the bulk of Macdonald's X Corps on the northern flank. Following the debacle of the central army group, their commander, Yorck, played a pivotal role in the events that would eventually force Frederick William's hand.

The Austrians   The Austrian Auxiliary Corps of about 30,000 men consisted of 32 battalions and 50 squadrons.

Prince Schwarzenberg, who was in command, was under the constraints of secret agreements between Vienna and St. Petersburg, as already noted. Thus, Napoleon who had received little help from the Russians in his 1809 war against Austria, now got just as little help from the Austrians against Russia. Was it due to duplicity? Self-interest? Self-preservation? Any of these motives may be cited as the cause, depending entirely upon the viewer's perspective.

The Austrian contingent was also composed of veteran troops and was capable of doing far more than it did.

The Organization of the Foreign Contingents

The internal structure of most of the foreign contingents had long been assimilated into the French model by 1812. However, the Austrians continued to use their light infantry in the old way, while the Prussians obtained their skirmishers from the third rank.

Several of the contingents had grenadier battalions, which were elites obtained in the same fashion as those in the French infantry. That is, they replenished themselves from the line and did not directly introduce recruits into their ranks. Other military establishments also had elite light infantry formations, like the French *voltigeurs*. However, several establishments maintained entire such battalions, whereas the French did not maintain them above the company level, the so-called French voltigeur regiments of the Young Guard notwithstanding.

Some, such as the Saxons and Westphalians, had regimental artillery, which Napoleon had reintroduced into the French army before the start of the 1809 campaign. While the infantry battalions throughout the Grand Army, French and foreign alike, generally numbered from about 650 to more than 800 men, the complements of the foreign cavalry squadrons ran considerably less than those of the French, normally from about 125 to 150 sabers each.

In addition to the French troops and the foreign troops in French pay, the allied contingents provided 272 battalions and 262 squadrons, comprising about 278,000 men.

Replacements

The assembly of the foreign contingents had placed heavy burdens upon the allied military establishments, leaving behind in most cases little more than weak depots with untrained recruits. Thus, very few replacements could follow the mobile units. The great majority of those from the allied contingents who did were Poles. This was because of the Poles' belief that the war was their war, and also because of their country's proximity to the operations area, which made it possible for such a second effort to become effective. Toward the end of the year, about 7500 replacements, mostly Bavarians and Westphalians, did become available. But none got even as far as the Russian border.

Austria and Prussia were both capable of sending substantial replacements, but neither was remotely inclined to do so unless pressed. However, by the time the issue had become acute, Napoleon's scramble for sheer survival had already begun. The Austrians did eventually send 5 battalions and 6 squadrons, totaling 5800 men, toward the end of October. These, however, were merely intended to keep Schwarzenberg's corps up to strength by replacing some of his formations, because the Austrians did not use march battalions, which were intended to be broken up and distributed upon arrival. They, too, never reached the area of operations.

There were manpower reserves elsewhere as well, such as in Naples. But these were so far from the scene of the action that they no longer mattered once the Grand Army began its retreat.

On the other hand, the 14,000 troops raised in Lithuania were formed into 16 battalions and 22 squadrons. Except for five of the squadrons, which were raised to become a third lancer regiment in the guards, and thus taken into French pay, all these units were considered part of the Polish army. But here, too, the time element was such that these troops had little military value.

SUMMARY

To recapitulate, the Grand Army marching into Russia, as well as all the units organically assigned to it (including the reserves already mobile and under way when the campaign started) totaled:

	Battalions	Squadrons	Men (approx.)
French forces	303	228	325,000
French auxiliaries	33		22,000
Allies	272	262	278,000
Total	608	490	625,000

In the course of the campaign, these troops were joined by march formations—French, Polish, and Lithuanian troops—totaling another 60,000 men. This number included, at best, 30,000 French other than those already accounted for above. These were, in the main, conscripts who had been earmarked for the cavalry but who, unlike the case in the infantry, could not be directly introduced into the line units without prior formal training.

In terms of the combat arms, the total included:

    522,300 infantry
     94,000 cavalry
     47,000 artillery
     21,500 train troops, etc.
    684,800 men (with 1302 field guns and 130 siege guns)

With the exception of the Imperial Guard Corps, these were formed into 10 army corps (to which the reserves were later added as XI Corps) and 4 cavalry corps. The details of their respective compositions are presented in Appendix V.

The artillery was generally distributed so that, in addition to the regimental artillery, every infantry division also had its own horse battery and foot battery, while corps had another two foot batteries at its disposal. The Guard Corps had a powerful artillery reserve. In the cavalry corps, the cuirassier divisions each had two batteries, the remainder generally only one.

Of all these troops, the Guard Corps and all but IX and XI Corps were intended to be first-line troops. Their total strength at the crossing of the Niemen came to:

    368,400 infantry and artillery
     80,600 cavalry and horse artillery
    449,000 men (with 1146 guns)

At the start of the campaign, Marshal Victor's IX Corps remained behind in Prussia. However, by July 4 it was ordered to divide itself in the manner shown in the order of battle in Appendix V and to follow the army into Russia. The 1st Reserve Division was also temporarily assigned to this corps and soon followed in several echelons, to be broken up and divided once it arrived at the front.

The troops remaining behind were designated XI Corps, and command was given to Marshal Augerau. The Neapolitan division continued to remain in Prussia and northern Germany but eventually joined the corps. Another two divisions from this corps ultimately joined the field army as well.

The first of these, Division Durutte, is of interest because it contained the penal regiments mentioned earlier, along with the hapless Wuerzburgers, who could hardly have relished this assignment. Most likely, they fulfilled the role of field gendarmes for General Durutte, because they could probably be relied upon to deal much more harshly with the *refractaires*, should the occasion demand it, than would another French unit. Also, the bad example of the troublesome units would not be quite so contagious for a foreign unit as it would be for another unit composed of their own countrymen.

The second division sent forward was Loison's, known as *le division princiere* because it contained the contingents from the small German duchies in addition to one Saxon regiment and the so-called Erfurt Brigade, made up of the erstwhile garrison of that town.

Morand's French-Saxon brigade was detached and remained in Stralsund, while 2 battalions and 5 squadrons of Neapolitans were attached in its stead. They arrived in Vilna between October 21 and 23 and soon got the opportunity to relieve the Baden troops of their rear-guard duties.

Added to all these must be the march formations, generally said to have totaled 80,000 men. But that figure includes the 1st Reserve Division, so about 68,000 would be more correct. This includes some 4200 Poles from the Vistula Legion, attached to the guard; more Wuerttembergers of III Corps, who came from Danzig but went only as far as Minsk; more Westphalians of VIII Corps, who had remained behind in Pillau and joined their contingent only shortly before the retreat began; the 5800 Austrian replacements already mentioned; approximately 44,000 march troops, among them 26,000 French and 9000 Poles (among the latter were three newly formed battalions, which became the garrison of Smolensk); and, finally, the 14,000 troops raised in Lithuania.

Thus, the total strength of the reinforcements that reached the Grand Army in the course of the campaign was:

141,200 men (with 96 guns)
<u>21,500</u> men (with 130 guns, the trains, and the siege park
     intended to invest Riga)
162,700 men (with 226 guns)

This brings the total number of troops who eventually crossed the Russian border in the course of the campaign to approximately 612,000 men, with 1242 field pieces and 130 siege guns.

Added to this number must be about 25,000 civilians: officials accompanying the army, their staffs, and the grooms and servants of imperial headquarters and the higher-ranking officers. There was an even larger number of horse handlers and grooms who had been summarily commandeered, more often than not by force. Finally, there were about 184,000 army horses and another 150,000 requisitioned horses (67,000 from Prussia alone) that hauled the army's supplies.

This somewhat lengthly exercise in military bookkeeping explains why so many different numbers appear in the literature on the subject. Although most of the numbers are usually correct, they are sometimes not sufficiently qualified.

In this discussion of men and matériel, it is important to note that the French artillery had to face special problems during the Russian campaign.

In general, the draft teams were far too light, especially since only four draft horses were allowed for each 6-pounder and six horses for each 12-pounder, as well as their respective ammunition caissons, which were almost as heavy as the guns. This might have sufficed for comparatively short hauls on the generally well surfaced and properly drained roads in central Europe. However, for the Russian campaign, the guns and caissons had to be taken clear across Germany and Poland just to reach the staging areas between the Vistula and the Niemen. As a result, the horses were worn out by the time the Niemen was reached, even though the campaign was only just getting under way. This occasioned losses among the artillery as well as the army train horses at an explosive rate as soon as the army entered Lithuania. There, the road network, if it may even be called that, consisted mainly of little better than wagon tracks and forest paths, which had been improved only in the immediate vicinity of such major towns as Kovno, Vilna, and Vitebsk. To make matters worse, alternating spells of heavy downpours and tropical heat quickly turned the roads into a wagoner's nightmare.

The matériel of the artillery was very good. However, the proportion of heavy guns was far too small. The reintroduction of the regimental guns had not only caused far too much fragmentation but also introduced a large number of light calibers as well.

In an effort to stiffen the firepower of the infantry, Napoleon had returned to the old system of assigning gun sections directly to the regiments or, rather, the brigades, even though the sections were known as the "regimental" guns. These sections, however, required greater mobility, since they were intended to operate up front, with the infantry, and thus their guns had to be light enough to be manhandled whenever the situation demanded it. Even though there was sufficient ordnance in the depots, there were not enough artillery personnel, much less the necessary draft teams, available to have both a regimental artillery and an undiminished field artillery. As a result, many 6- and 12-pound guns were left behind, while a great many old 3- and 4-pounders, no longer considered standard, were dusted off and pressed back into service.

An excellent example of how this affected the weight of the artillery is furnished by a status report of the artillery in the central army group (including VIII Corps) as of October 7. It reads as follows:

> 58 12-pounders
> 264 6-Pounders
> 32 4-pounders (with the Young Guard)
> 122 3-pounders (regimental guns)
> 10 6-inch, 4-line howitzers
> <u>119</u> 6-inch, 6-line howitzers
> 605 field pieces

On the plus side was the fact that all the artillery equipment was uniformly of Griebeauval design, which offered the well-known advantage of maximum caliber at minimum weight. However, the French artillery still had not introduced the crucial standardization of wheels, which had long been a part of Liechtenstein's reforms of the Austrian artillery. This standardization made the wheels of all the artillery's gun carriages, limbers, and caissons freely interchangeable. Instead, even the purpose-built French vehicle park still included at least twenty different sizes and types of wheels —a severe handicap when the deeply rutted column roads in Lithuania began to take their toll.

Finally, a summation of the Grand Army in national or ethnic terms indicates that not half, as is commonly stated, but only about a third of the force Napoleon took into Russia actually consisted of French troops:

300,000 French	(including the neo-Franks of the annexed territories, Dutch, Germans, Belgians, and Italians, who constituted nearly a third of this number, or about 100,000)
190,000 Germans	(i.e., 40,000 Austrians, 23,000 Prussians, 30,000 Bavarians, 23,000 Saxons, 21,000 Westphalians, 15,000 Wuerttembergers, 6000 Badensians, 5000 Hessians, 5000 Bergers, 13,000 from the small principalities, and 9000 Swiss)
90,000 Poles and Lithuanians	(including the Vistula Legion)
32,000 Italians, Illyrians, Spaniards, and Portuguese	

From this alone, it can be seen why Napoleon could boast to Metternich in 1813 that the Russian campaign had cost few French lives.

After the departure of the troops mentioned above, 73,000 men and 60 guns remained behind in Prussia and adjoining territories. There were also 6 cohorts of National Guard, about 3300 men, around Bremen, which was, at that time, part of metropolitan France.

This includes the remainder of XI Corps, plus a few weak detachments, as well as the artillery troops in the Prussian fortresses and Danzig, which were not included in the above calculations. It also includes about 27,000 men, mostly French, from all corps: Some were in hospitals, some were detached, but large numbers were stragglers, including thousands of French cavalry troopers who had lost their horses even before they reached the Niemen!

NOTES

1. Freytag-Loringhoven, H. von. "Die Armeen des Ersten Kaiserreichs." In *Truppenfuehrung und Heereskunde*. Berlin, 2/1908.
2. Morvan, J. *Capitaine M. Tixier. Le Soldat Imperial (1800–1814)*. Paris, 1904. 2 vols.
3. Kleinschmidt, A. *Geschichte des Koenigreichs Westfalen*. Gotha, 1893.

4. Brabant, p. 167.
5. See Appendix II.
6. See Appendix III.
7. See Appendix IV.
8. The "correspondence" lists only 49 regiments, apparently not including two composite regiments in Victor's corps, the bulk of which had remained behind in France. Thiers and most French historians list only the 36 old French regiments in I, II, III, and IV Corps.
9. Schehl, C. *Vom Rhein zur Moskwa, 1812.* Repr. Krefeld, 1957.

6. The Russian Army

BACKGROUND

The debut of the new and reformed Russian army in the Battle of Narva had not been auspicious. However, by 1709 the Swedish king, Charles XII, had been lured deeply into Russia, where his army, deprived of its supply trains, met with an ignominious end in the Battle of Poltava. It might have been a dress rehearsal for meeting with the invader who was to come a century later. But even though Napoleon was to meet with a similar end, the Russians seemed to have difficulty remembering the nature of their earlier success until circumstances forced it upon them.

About midway between these two events, the Russian army had also faced the Prussian firing lines of Frederick the Great's army, defeating one of his generals and handing him both his most costly victory and most costly defeat, at Zorndorf and Kunersdorf. The latter, however, might not have happened, had Frederick left well enough alone.

Both the Swedish and the Seven Years' War were marked by characteristics that ought to have given Napoleon cause for concern. And perhaps they did. Both wars firmly established the remarkable tenacity of the Russian soldier. Although he was generally described as uneducated and unimaginative, these very factors contributed to the Russian soldier's almost infinite capacity to endure and to be virtually immune to the so-called impressions of war—a fact that powerfully illustrated Napoleon's oft-quoted maxim that, "In war, the moral relates to the physical as three to one."

In 1799, during the War of the Second Coalition, Massena's republican soldiers were rudely reminded of the Russians' apparent inability to understand they were beaten before they had been physically knocked down. Thinking they had the Russians bottled up in one of the Swiss canyons, the French were severely shocked when, instead of laying down their arms, the Russians closed ranks and with their heads bent low and bayonets leveled, the walls of the canyon echoing their shouts of "urrah," they sent the French republicans scrambling up the slopes to get out of their way.

In the centuries past and, indeed, even in the present century, the Russians may have lacked the tactical agility of their western adversaries, but the latter have generally agreed that the Russians were as tough an opponent as one could ever hope not to meet.

The new Russian army that emerged from a backward medievalism occasioned by some two centuries of Mongol domination was essentially the creation of Peter the Great. The tireless reformer, better known to the west for his hands-on effort to become a shipwright and for the building of a Russian fleet, began the reconstruction of the army long before his eyes fastened upon the sea.

No doubt, this Peter, as a young prince, set an example for Frederick William of Prussia, who formed his grooms and servants at the royal Wusterhausen estate into a toy regiment. From this beginning sprang the Giant Grenadier Battalion, which, far from being the foible an amused Europe thought it to be, became the training school of the army. Peter had similarly cut his teeth with such apparent child's play when he formed his Potjeshne. What was tested in play went into the making of the two premier regiments of the Russian army, the Preobrashensky and Semenovsky, named after the towns in which they were garrisoned.

In his attempts not only to reform but also to accelerate the pace of the reforms, Peter reached beyond the borders of Russia to find all the special talents that were in short supply at home, and this included soldiers. As a result, a great many itinerant officers—and they were numerous in those days—found ready employment in Russia. Many among them were Germans, who would soon predominate when they were joined by the numerous Baltic Germans who would become national, if not ethnic, Russians. They were to play an important role in the Russian army right up into our own century, even while they continued to be a thorn in the eye of every proud ethnic Russian aristocrat. This created a perpetual dichotomy within the Russian army, pitting the ethnic Russians against the national Russians—foreigners, who were mostly Germans. Interestingly, despite all the smoke, despite all the cabals, these foreigners remained and continued to penetrate into the highest ranks simply because they were better educated. In his introduction to the reprint of Stein's *History of the Russian Army*,[1] Ellfeldt, one of the best modern experts on the subject, points out that even in 1881, when Germans constituted only 1.1 percent of the Russian population, they held 41 percent of the higher commands in the Russian army.

Against this background of perpetual strife between the German-speaking foreigners and ethnic Russians, the army's re-Prussianization under Tsar Paul, who reigned from November 6, 1796 to March 11, 1801 (when he was assassinated), has occupied the minds of many modern historians. Much of what they have to say bears a tinge of the polemic. Thus, in the effort to show some sort of cause-and-effect relationship, some historians have left many of their readers uncertain as to whether the mental disturbances from which Tsar Paul suffered were the result of his fascination with Frederick's Prussian army or, conversely, whether it was his mental infirmity that caused this fascination.

Paul, however, did turn back the clock. When he ascended the throne, instead of appointing a commission to see to whatever reforms might be in order, as had been done by his predecessors, he threw himself into the task personally. And his military instincts were certainly those of a "gaiter-button" mentality: He was a martinet, very much given over to outward appearances. (This streak, incidentally, remained alive in the Russian army right into modern times. Entire formations were matched by the soldiers' height, their hair color, whether or not they wore mustaches, etc.) Paul's reforms, however, were very much the result of his own perceptions. While he temporarily changed the outward appearances of the Russian army, he also initiated some accomplishments of a more lasting value.

The Russian artillery was reformed into an integrated organization that was ahead of its time. Another step forward came with the institution of twelve inspections (or divisions), which bore the names of their garrison districts. Even though this arrangement, like the initial French division system, was modeled on the Prussian inspection system established by Frederick the Great, the Russians originally labeled them "divisions," then briefly reverted to the term "inspections," and finally renamed them "divisions" again, on the French model. As in France and Prussia, these divisions were not of uniform composition and were entirely of an administrative nature. That is, in the field the army still deployed in the fashion of the linear era.

Under Alexander, who ascended the throne on March 11, 1801, the army entered into a phase of constant expansion and changes, wrought to a large degree in response to events taking place in the west. Even though the storm clouds loomed ever larger on the horizon, Russia, by virtue of its remoteness from the rest of Europe, was able to reform its military establishment gradually. It could even absorb the shocks of two failed campaigns and still retain full sovereignty. In addition, Russia's vast manpower resources and hinterland were such that the country could never be deprived of either by being overrun or effectively occupied. At the same time, an effective attack against Russia would require a buildup that could hardly escape notice.

When Alexander came to power in 1801, the army numbered 405,659 men. Adding to this the Cossack army of about 100,000 men and another 65,000 or so in the military orphanages and cadet training facilities (including about 25,000 of the usual miscellanea attaching itself to any military establishment), the total came to about 595,000 men. Impressive though this number may seem, its magnitude dwindles when viewed in terms of the military commitments of the Russian empire, which encompassed an area stretching from Finland in the north to Turkey, the Black Sea, and Persia in the south and from the western frontiers to the Siberian and Orenburg lines facing Inner Asia.

Alexander armed twice during his reign. In the first instance, a more conventional mobilization, he geared up for his initial confrontation with Napoleon, which added 25,815 men in 1803, 28,721 men in 1805, and another 60,756 in 1806 to the military establishment. The second, and far more expansive, mobilization—on the scale of a national war—got under way in 1810. Even so, it would not be possible to match the forces Napoleon would field against Russia in 1812. (See Appendix VI for the composition of the Russian military establishment in 1812.)

MOBILIZATION

To reinforce the army, once hostilities had gotten under way in 1812, the formation of a militia was ordered in the central and northern government districts. Although it was designed to have a complement of 270,000 men, this number was never actually reached. Stein cites 223,361, without giving an exact date. Since nothing had been prepared for the gathering of such masses—no cadre, no arms or accoutrements—they remained no more than bands, armed mostly with pikes, and were used mainly to support the guerrilla war throughout 1812. It was not until the summer of 1813 that they started to become useful for the conduct of military operations. The only exceptions to this were the militias of St. Petersburg and Novgorod, along with some of the militia Cossack regiments, which had become more or less usable by the end of September and the beginning of October.

Still, the numbers of the total Russian mobilization when hostilities got under way, as cited by the Russian statistician Shuravski, are impressive:

	Men
Active army, with the Guard, in 1810	516,770
New regiments raised in 1811 and 1812	113,275
Reserves raised from reserve and depot battalions	185,000
Total active army	815,045
Garrison troops	63,279
Irregular troops	100,000
Various auxiliaries	10,000
Entire militia	330,000
Total	503,279
Grand total	1,318,324

But these numbers require qualification. Otherwise, it would be difficult to explain how only one-fourth of these men were available immediately to face Napoleon's onslaught and no more than a third were committed by the end of the campaign.

Of all the troops listed in Appendix VI, only the Guard, the cuirassiers, 16 infantry divisions, 6 cavalry divisions, 36 Cossack regiments, and the artillery attached to these formations were available for the defense of the western frontiers. All of these formations were considerably under strength.

The infantry regiments were able to take only two of their three battalions into the field. One battalion, the 2nd by ordinal number, transferred all its able bodies into the other two, so that they might at least be brought up to an average strength of 500 men each. The 2nd (now reserve) Battalions were to remain behind in a second line and be filled up with recruits. But they also had to give up their grenadier companies, which were amalgamated into 31 battalions, of which 8 remained with their respective divisions and the others were formed into two United Grenadier Divisions and one brigade. Similarly, each cavalry regiment took only 4 squadrons (the 10 squadron regiments took 8), which brought the field squadrons up to an average of about 125 horses. The reserve squadrons remaining behind took in recruits and drafted horses. All the troops that thus became available were formed into three armies (see Appendix VII) of quite unequal size.

Each corps was to include 2 infantry divisions and 1 light cavalry regiment. However, two of the corps each had a cuirassier division instead of a light cavalry regiment. The remainder of the cavalry formed very weak cavalry corps. Shortly before the Battle of Borodino, however, the cavalry corps were reinforced when the light cavalry regiments were detached from the infantry corps and reassigned. The two cuirassier divisions were also united to form another cavalry corps. All the corps gave up the greater part of their artillery to strengthen the reserve artillery, which had been rather weak.

The average strength of the infantry and cavalry corps was about 15,000 and 3000 men, respectively. The total Russian mobilization can be summarized as follows:

- *The First Western Army*, under Barclay de Tolly, consisted of I, II, III, IV, V (Guard), and VI Infantry Corps and I, II, and III Cavalry Corps. In 150 battalions, 132 squadrons, 18 Cossack regiments and 49 batteries, it numbered 104,250 men and 7000 Cossacks, with 558 guns.

- *The Second Western Army*, under Bagration, consisted of VII and VIII Infantry Corps and IV Cavalry Corps. In 46 battalions, 52 squadrons, 9 Cossack regiments, and 18 batteries, it numbered 33,000 men and 4000 Cossacks, with 216 guns. [Originally, this army was to be considerably stronger. However, nearly half the troops designated for its formation had to be given to the Third (Reserve) Army, since it had proved impossible to man the latter entirely with reserve troops, as was originally planned.]

- *The Third (Reserve) Army*, under Cavalry General Tormassov, consisted of 2 infantry and 1 cavalry corps, with another corps formed entirely of reserve troops. These corps had no numbers but bore the names of their commanders. In 54 battalions, 76 squadrons, 9 Cossack regiments, and 14 batteries, it numbered 38,000 men and 4,000 Cossacks, with 164 guns.

Thus, the total forces deployed in the first line came to 250 battalions, 260 squadrons, 36 Cossack regiments, and 81 batteries, comprising 175,250 men and 15,000 Cossacks, with 938 guns.

These troops, however, could count on being substantially reinforced in the course of the campaign. First, the Second Western Army was joined on July 3 by the newly formed 27th Infantry Division (12 battalions, 8000 men, but no artillery), coming from the direction of Moscow. Next, and most importantly, the Peace of Bucharest, concluded at the last moment with the Turks, freed the Danube Army under Vice Admiral Tshitshagov. In 4 infantry and 2 cavalry divisions, that army numbered 53,000 men, with 240 guns, at that time. Of these, 34,000 men joined the Third (Reserve) Army on September 21 by the River Styx. They were soon followed by another 7000 men and yet a few thousand more in December. Of the 13th Infantry Division (16 battalions, 2 batteries, 8000 men), which was still in southern Russia when the war started, 4000 men arrived in Volhynia simultaneously with the Danube Army and another 1200 arrived shortly thereafter.

Another detachment at the disposition of the first line was the Finnish Corps under Lieutenant General Steinheil. It consisted of 3 infantry divisions and 2 dragoon regiments, totaling 30,000 men, with 84 guns. Originally earmarked for a joint operation with the Swedish army against Denmark (for the Swedish possession of Norway), the greater part of this corps (18,000 men, with 72 guns) was brought into the operations area along the Dvina by September.

Finally, there remained in the second line one marine regiment, several Cossack regiments, and a few batteries—4000 men in all—as well as the aforementioned 2nd Battalions and the 9th and 10th Squadrons. In all the 87 battalions and 54 squadrons comprised about 34,000 men. These formed into two reserve corps and also provided the garrisons for the fortresses in the operations area and various other detachments. Of these two corps, I Reserve Corps, under Moeller-Sakomelsky, stood at the Dvina. With its headquarters in Toropez, it was used to reinforce the First Western Army and Wittgenstein's corps, which would be detached from it. The other corps, II Reserve Corps, under Oertel, stood near Mozyr by the Pripet. It would remain independent until the end of the campaign.

In summation, the total forces in the second line came to 251 battalions, 128 squadrons, 21 Cossack regiments, and 36⅓ batteries, numbering 137,000 men (including about 8000 Cossacks), with approximately 434 guns. Of these, about 105,000 men were actually available for the defense against the invasion.

In the third line were the 36 recruit depots, which contained the men called up in the fall of 1811. (Added to these would be the draft calls of July 13 and August 16, 1812.) These recruits were used to form 4th Battalions for the infantry regiments and 6th and 11th Squadrons for the cavalry regiments, as well as the depot artillery brigades. Since the army received 89,000 replacements from this source (and probably more), of which 8,000 did not arrive in time, the total number of replacements (apart from a few cadres and three battalions) was probably about 95,000 men.

Of the militias, which were not actually called up until July, only about

15,000 men from St. Petersburg and Novgorod were more or less ready to be used as already noted. As a temporary measure, another 16,000 militiamen from the Moscow and Smolensk districts were placed into the third ranks of the field battalions, which were heavily depleted after the Battle of Borodino. However, the idea that most of these men were armed only with pikes must be taken with a grain of salt. Similar legends about the Prussian Landwehr in 1813 enjoyed long-standing currency. Reviews of the primary sources have consistently failed to support the assertions that men so armed appeared in the ranks of mobile field battalions.

Another 7000 men, volunteers and militia cavalry, found employment as irregular cavalry. Of another volunteer group, about 4000 in all, only a fraction were used in 1812, during the defense of Riga.

Finally, the Cossacks provided 24,000 men (10,000 from the Don alone). Most of them were available by the beginning of October and all but a few went into action.

In all, the manpower of the third line came to about 161,000 men, of which about 133,000 actually took part in the defense.

Thus, the grand total of all the forces in the first, second, and third lines was 488,000 men, of which about 428,000 gradually came into action against the Grand Army. This bottom line, however, includes more than 80,000 Cossacks and militiamen, as well as about 20,000 men who garrisoned the fortresses in the operations area.

The troops in the Asian border territories and the garrison and local troops in the interior do not come under consideration here, because they were needed where they were. Also not included are the remaining militiamen, who did not become mobile before the end of the campaign. According to some sources, the former numbered about 130,000 to 140,000, the latter about 230,000 to 240,000, which seems too high.

A comparison of these numbers with those quoted by Shuravski, which are cited in Stein,[2] reveals glaring inconsistencies (not dissimilar to Napoleon's own calculations of how many troops he was leaving behind in France). First off, Shuravski's calculations were based on financial records, and the budget, of course, assumed that the army was at full strength. However, by reviewing the details of the mobilization noted above, the source of these inconsistencies becomes obvious.

As shown in Appendix VI, the complement of an infantry battalion was 738 men and that of a cavalry squadron was 159 men. However, in order to mobilize two field battalions from each regiment, a third had to be stripped down to cadre just to bring the other two to an average strength of 500 men, which still represented only about two-thirds of the plan strength. Similar conditions prevailed in the cavalry. This means that the "present" strength of the army prior to mobilization amounted to no more than about half of the 630,000 men shown for the active army by Shuravski. In this fashion, the numbers cited by Shuravski may be reconciled with those shown by Bogdanovich and others.

SUMMARY

All things considered, the Russian army of 1812 was a good one, enhanced by its uniform national fabric and organizational structure. An important advantage it enjoyed over its adversary was the matter of replacements, both in relative and absolute terms. These went a long way toward redressing the great imbalance of numbers that existed during the opening stages of the campaign.

Uneducated and of simple peasant stock, the Russian soldier had little imagination that might run away with him in touchy situations. But he was also brave, obedient, and frugal, and he was fighting on his own ground. This explains why the army, despite the disheartening retreats and even after the dreadful bloodletting of Borodino, never lost its poise or relinquished its combat-readiness. Therein reposes the reason for the success of the campaign. Even when sorely pushed, the army never fell apart.

The mass of the Russian officers were regarded as being crude by their western counterparts. With the exception of the guards officers, who came from the high Russian aristocracy—some of whose members also found their way into the more distinguished cavalry regiments—the majority of the officers were relatively uneducated. This alone explains why the foreigners were not to be pushed aside, no matter what the personal feelings of the ethnic Russians. As it did with the Poles, the absence of a broadly founded middle class made it difficult for the Russian army to obtain an adequate corps of noncommissioned officers.

The cavalry was well founded and, if well led, could perform outstandingly. At that time, the Cossacks were still entirely irregulars and were not counted upon in a formal battle, but they were quite effective in the conduct of guerrilla warfare. Despite the frequently disparaging remarks made about them by many diarists of the time, they were highly efficient against foragers and stragglers. More than anything else, they created among the retreating enemy troops an aura of apprehension and even outright fear about becoming isolated and caught. On balance, the Cossacks probably did more direct and indirect damage to the Grand Army than did the regular Russian army. Most of the bad press they received at the hands of numerous survivors of the campaign (criticism that perpetuated itself in future writings) was the product of the frustration they caused by being forever elusive and just beyond reach.

The Cossacks also provided good outpost and security services for the army, though they left much to be desired in matters relating to reconnaissance. They generally failed to report promptly and accurately, and there were numerous instances in 1812 and 1813 when they captured the baggage of various headquarters but failed to recognize and pass on important documents.

Generally very good was the artillery, which was well equipped and quite mobile despite the fact that most of its guns were of heavy caliber. At the same time, it was better concentrated than that of the French, which had been fragmented by the reinstitution of the regimental artillery.

A great encumbrance, on the other hand, was the excessive size of the regimental trains and baggage, which also brought large numbers of noncombatants into the army. These, more than anything else, were responsible for the clumsy movements of the Russians.

All things considered, however, the Russian army on the eve of Napoleon's invasion was a serviceable army. Properly led, its potential could have easily exceeded its actual accomplishments in 1812, as the army was to prove handsomely in 1813.

NOTES

1. Stein, F. von. *Geschichte des Russischen Heeres*. Repr. Krefeld, 1975.
2. Ibid., p. 305.

7. The New Ways of War

The new ways of war unleashed by the French Revolution and the concomitant rise of column and skirmishing tactics have produced a mountain of literature, much of it of quite uneven content. This is especially true in matters relating to minor or elementary tactics, the combat methods employed up front, on the firing line. Even during the immediate postwar years, when the events of the Napoleonic era became the primary subject of historical studies in every western military establishment, the focus was mainly on the great captain's strategic and operational concepts. Matters relating to elementary tactics were, to the soldier-historians, so obvious, commonplace, and familiar that they hardly merited mention in the dissertations produced.

This was further exacerbated by the fact that elementary tactics, by their very nature, are highly transcendental. Although rapid advances in technology have enforced one change after another since the last third of the nineteenth century, ultimately changing the face of battle altogether, the pace of change was much slower in earlier times. Still, the 150 years from about 1700 to the middle of the nineteenth century—marked by the dominance of the smoothbore, muzzle-loading fusil—were to witness their share of changes on the elementary tactical level. Thus, by the time the men who had witnessed the combats of the Napoleonic wars had passed from the scene, so had many of the elementary tactics that had been an inextricable part of those combats. The military events of the era were no longer current and topical, and how soldiers equipped with muzzle-loading, smoothbore muskets might have operated on the firing line became a matter of purely academic interest.

Another part of the problem is the fact that elementary tactics continue to be the eminent domain of the fighting soldier and the junior officer who leads him in combat. In a game played out on the firing line, where friend and foe are often separated by no more than a few hundred paces of no-man's land, such soldiers share a front-row view in an arena where the truth is made up of 99 percent empirical experience and where academicians tend to show the theorist in his worst light. As a result, when the subject of elementary tactics did come up for an airing in post-Napoleonic times, academicians generally played the role of ideologues (e.g., Gore Vidal) or theorists (e.g., Siegfried Fiedler) who tended to intellectualize the practical. This, in turn, gave rise to some amateurish notions that were rooted in a general lack of knowledge about practical details, which also gave Schwarz cause to complain in his massive work on eight centuries of infantry tactics.[1] Some of these notions even found an echo in the works of military men (e.g., Fiedler again) who ought to have known better.

Thus, researchers must peel away layer after layer of apocrypha, even in some original source materials, to arrive at a semblance of the elementary tactics as seen and experienced on the Napoleonic battlefields. The diarists generally jotted down their impressions in telegraphic style. They had neither time nor room for belaboring the obvious. Thus, it is only on rare occasions that a diarist includes a remark that might have a bearing on the subject.

Most misleading can be the memoirs, often written years, even decades, after the events described. Here, the memories of old campaigners, colored by the passage of time, display a marked tendency to describe the actions they had witnessed as they ought to have gone rather than as they actually went. Skirmishing actions often become pitched firefights, giving the impression of deployed firing lines blazing away at each other at point-blank range. General advances of the masses are usually described in phrases such as "The battalion advanced against the enemy with leveled bayonets." Such statements are factual enough in themselves, but they don't tell what happened next. Thus, they generally leave the reader with the impression that the advances culminated in pitched hand-to-hand combats, which, in fact, almost never took place. Even the memoirs of general officers generally yield very little on the subject of elementary tactics. These were, after all, the responsibility of the lower command echelons.

This leaves the best, albeit rarest, of primary sources: the after-action reports of company and field grade officers. These no-nonsense narratives are extremely difficult to find. Most of the originals have been lost. A few can still be found in secondary sources, notably in regimental histories published during the first half of the nineteenth century, but these works are almost as rare as the original reports themselves.

This, of course, raises the question of just how important elementary tactics are within the larger framework of combat techniques. The answer to this is that they are nothing less than crucial. Many historians, especially military men, are of the opinion that when the reins started to slip from Napoleon's hands, the problem began on the elementary tactical level, where things failed to go as expected with increasing frequency.

It appears sheer heresy to say that even Napoleon, the great master of the battlefield, did not exercise nearly as much tactical control over his battles as cultists and romantics would have us believe. The image of the commander in chief, standing atop a hill in magnificent isolation, manipulating the army at his feet like so many puppets on strings, is overwhelming. But it is also largely a mirage. The commander in chief might set the tasks for his corps and division commanders, but it was left to the brigadiers to actually carry them out up front. They were the men who made the final dispositions of their combat elements and who decided in precisely what fashion a given objective was to be attained. And it was the success or failure of their endeavors that would eventually ripple up the chain of command.

The commanders, in their turn, could order measures to exploit, redress, or counter, but the fate of their orders would also be determined by the men up front. No matter how brilliant an operational or major tactical concept was, it would achieve nothing if the attacker (or defender) failed to impose his will upon the enemy on the firing line. Thus, it would probably be accurate to say that while a commander in chief could win or lose campaigns, his direct influence could not nearly so often win or lose battles.

The commander in chief was responsible for the condition of the army, its morale and state of training, its organization and its channels of command. He could direct its movements, concentrate his forces in the right place at the right time, institute strategic or operational moves, and determine how many reserves to hold back and how to use them when the opportunity or need presented itself. All of this was no mean task. But it could do no more than give victory a better-than-even chance. After all was said and done, it was up front, on the firing line, where success or failure was determined, and it was there that chance played its strongest hand.

In an attempt to avoid this inescapable element of chance, the era preceding the French Revolution had sought to reduce war to a science, in which everything could be calculated and predicted beforehand. It was believed that maneuvering and the control of strategic lines of points would afford sufficient leverage to eliminate the need for direct confrontations in battles that were as chancy as they were costly.

Tolstoy carried these ideas to the extreme when he maintained that battles revolve around the individual confrontations between thousands of men, organized into hundreds of formations, commanded by dozens of generals. He thought that battles are basically unintelligible to those who take part in them because the individual's horizon is limited to what he can see, which is but a fragment of the whole. Thus, he concluded, generals delude themselves when they claim that they can control the uncontrollable and predict the unpredictable, because the events are generated by so many disparate elements. This had the ring of the extreme to those in search of theorems and maxims. But Tolstoy's remarks bear more than a grain of truth, as any living soldier who has ever participated in a major battle will readily attest.

What was it, then, about the wars of republican and imperial France that was new? Certainly not the stratagems so dear to the theorists: the operations on interior lines and across lines of communications, the flankings, the envelopments or breakthroughs, which are so often invoked by historians in their attempts to get to the bottom of Napoleon's formula for success. Although these were an integral part of the emperor's military tool kit and he demonstrated his ability to use every one of them time and again, they were not by any stretch of the imagination something new.

What was new, quite apart from Napoleon's natural and acquired talents, was the infrastructure of the military machine born of the revolution, which made it possible for him to exploit these talents to their fullest extent. During the years of Napoleon's ascendancy, the backbone of this infrastructure rested squarely upon a concomitant system of elementary tactics for which the opposition had no immediate answer.

Before these elementary tactics can be properly evaluated, something must first be known of the old approach so that the impact of the new may be better understood.

THE PROCESS OF TACTICAL EVOLUTION

Throughout military history, firepower and offensive power have stood in an inverse relationship. From bow to musket, as the proportion of missile weapons increased, the resultant combat forms became increasingly static. Indeed, until the advent of modern technology, only the Asian horse archer had ever succeeded in effectively combining firepower and movement. (The devastating effect of this combination can be readily measured by the impact of the Mongols when they came west during the thirteenth century.)

In ancient times, the Greeks and early Romans relied upon the speed and boldness of their attack to carry cold steel to the enemy. During the more advanced stages of their evolution, the Roman legions resorted to a slower, more grinding mode of combat, obtaining missile support virtually at the point of contact, when the rear ranks hurled their pila over the heads of the front ranks. However, while the Greeks were able to run down the static Persian foot archers with the speed and boldness of their attack, the Romans, despite all their military successes, never developed an effective answer to the mobile horse archer. The marriage between firepower and mobility continued to remain the exclusive domain of the horse archer.

In fifteenth-century Europe, the bold advance with bare steel again reigned supreme. The swift charge of the Swiss pike squares was all but unstoppable, until the immobile artillery, still in its infancy, was able to reach out far enough with shot of sufficient weight to inflict crippling losses on the deep formations of pikemen before it was overrun.

The English or Welsh foot archer, for all the potential destructiveness of his longbow, could no more take the field unsupported by infantry than could the artillery. His unquestionable firepower could only defend or support the attack of others who were equipped for close combat. Still, the rate of fire the archer could develop might have easily enabled him to come forward with an attack carried with bare steel, once an appropriate tactic was developed. However, as long as the bow remained a viable weapon, archers were forever in short supply. Years of conditioning and practice were required to produce an archer capable of making effective use of a heavy war bow.

As a result, the course of tactical evolution was soon driven in another direction. Firearms, even though they were still quite primitive and unhandy, offered a better alternative because a man could easily be taught to use one effectively in no time at all. Before long, as the quality of firearms and the methods of their construction improved, it was found that, unlike the situation with the archers, money could buy as many arquebusiers and musketeers as one could afford. Supply had found the means to meet demand.

At first, these new firearms were decidedly inferior to the bow, the early matchlocks being cumbersome affairs. Fired by inserting a burning slow-burning match into an open firing pan, they had to be handled with considerable care lest the charge be set off accidentally. This made for a slow rate of fire and left the musketeer virtually helpless during the comparatively long time it took to reload his musket. Two rounds a minute was tops under ideal conditions. A skilled archer could let six, eight, or even more shafts fly during the same time, and probably with greater accuracy at anything above a hundred paces. Thus, if even the foot archer had forever stood in grave danger of being run down by a determined attack, then the musketeer was fair game indeed. His weapon was no more than an expensive club between firings. These intervals of danger could be minimized only if a formation of musketeers was divided into several groups that fired in rotation. Ultimately, as the number of musketeers grew, they formed into companies of 60 to 100 men, commonly ranked six to eight deep. Firing by alternating ranks, about half were expected to be loaded and ready at all times, representing the fire reserve, while the remainder either were firing or were at various stages of reloading. This meant that fewer muskets were fired at any given time, but it guaranteed an available fire reserve during moments of crisis. This arrangement, by itself, was not enough to keep the cavalry at arm's length. For that, it was necessary to have the pikemen standing by in case the modest firepower of the musketeers failed to turn back a cavalry attack.

If the musketeers made any offensive movement at all, it was slow and easily disturbed. The complicated business of loading, firing, and defiling through the ranks was cumbersome and worked best when the formations remained in place. Intended for striking from a distance, the musketeer was as yet imperfectly equipped to offer direct contact with the enemy, whether offensively or defensively. For that, the pikes were still needed; they could not abandon their charges at any time.

Thus, the pikes, still splendid offensive weapons, were tied to the muskets, whose numbers nevertheless grew rapidly as ever more firepower was sought. With the static element of the infantry constantly proliferating in this fashion, the history of the Thirty Years' War already recorded very few instances of infantry actually entering into combat against other infantry. As during medieval times, the footsoldier had virtually reverted to his role of furnishing a breakwater against the cavalry.

Toward the end of the seventeenth century, this situation changed drastically with the confluence of improved firing mechanisms and prewrapped paper cartridges, which speeded up the loading process. This made it possible to reduce the depth of the musketeer formations down to six or even five ranks, since the quickened pace of reloading demanded less of a fire reserve. And it was the advent of the bayonet that finally consigned the pike to oblivion. Thus equipped, the new musketeer formations were now on their own. (They were actually armed with the new flintlock fusil, which quickly acquired the cognomen of its heavier precursor.) Thus, the early eighteenth century saw the infantry entering into an era of pure fire tactics. The bayonet made it possible to resist cavalry, and the musketeer no longer found it necessary to put down his firearm and reach for his sword when entering into close combat with other infantrymen.

The interior ballistics of the smoothbore musket, however, were such that individually aimed fire at distances greater than 100 paces was virtually useless. Since the ball was slightly smaller than the diameter of the bore, it would flutter when propelled forward by the powder charge, bouncing in random fashion against the inside of the barrel; the last contact before the ball left the muzzle would determine the actual direction of its flight. As a result, the shotgun effect of the volley was intended to achieve what individual fire could not.

At the same time, the process of loading and firing had improved to such an extent that the musketeer formations were again flattened out—first into four ranks and then three—to increase the frontage and make it possible to bring all the muskets to bear without the need of defiling through the ranks. The shallow depth of these new linear formations demanded fast loading if an adequate fire reserve was to be maintained. This was facilitated by the new fashion of retaining so-called standing armies during peacetime; these were populated by professional soldiers and could be subjected to considerable amounts of drill.

Even though the Prussian model of rapid-fire drill was to capture the imagination of succeeding generations, and fast guns were considered the acme of perfection, quick fire was not by any means the only difficulty facing the military establishments of the era of linear tactics. Actually, there were four problems:

1. Training the individual soldier to a high standard of proficiency with his musket

2. Designing the infrastructure of the battalion (now the basic tactical unit) for the purposes of both deployment and fire control

3. Finding the best means for moving these battalions, now deployed in long, thin lines, forward in the face of enemy fire

4. Developing the best means of deploying an entire army into a linear battle order

All this had been worked out fairly well by the turn of the eighteenth century. The common soldier was sufficiently proficient in the use of his musket to deliver what was demanded of him. For the purposes of movement, the battalion had been vertically divided into divisions, platoons, and even sections so that it might march in division, platoon, or section fronts. In the proximity of the enemy, this was done with sufficient intervals so that a front could be formed simply by having the subdivisions make a simultaneous left turn.

An army deploying in this fashion was said to be executing a parallel march. This had to be conducted at some distance from the enemy's front, if the enemy was already deployed; lest he disturb one's own deployment at a critical time. Of course, the enemy had to be to the left of one's direction of march. If circumstances placed him to the right, then the order of march had to be inverted so that the right guide (he was the pivot and point of dress upon whom every formation and every movement hinged) as well as the first company would end up on the right, where they belonged, even when a right turn was made. This was of great importance throughout the era of formal mass tactics, because this was the way soldiers trained and it was considered imperative that a soldier should stand in his accustomed place, especially in combat. Thus, the order of battle was predetermined even as an army assembled for a campaign, and that order was never lightly disturbed afterward.

If the army was to deploy with a parallel march to the left or right, two columns, one for each echelon, were sufficient. The cavalry, generally deployed on the flanks, might form columns of its own. If the march went against the center of the enemy's deployed line, then four infantry columns were required. Once the heads of these columns, marching side by side, reached the expected line of departure, the two on the left, marching in inverted order, would turn left to form the left wing while the two on the right, marching in regular order, would form the right.

This brief discussion has not explored all the options, but it should suffice to explain how complicated and tricky the linear order was and how much training was required to execute even the relatively simplest movements.

Up to this point, there was generally little difference between the way things were done in one army and another. The exception was fire control: An entire book could be devoted to the many ways that this was handled by the French, British, Austrians, and Prussians. Without going into tedious detail, the various methods of fire control might be summarized as follows:

The battalion was divided vertically, as was done for the purposes of marching and deploying, but it was also divided horizontally, that is, by ranks. Thus, a constant rate of fire was obtained not only by having the vertical subdivisions, that is, the divisions and platoons, alternate with each other but also by alternating fire by ranks within any or all of these for-

mations. It was notably the Prussians and the British who eventually eschewed fire by ranks and leaned, instead, in the direction of platoon fire.
That is, ultimately deployed in three ranks, the entire platoon would deliver
its salvo at once, alternating with the platoons to the left and right in
accordance with various schemes.

The difficulty came when this fire, whatever the means of control, was
to be brought forward offensively. A formation could hardly fire and move
at the same time. What was generally done was that after having fired once
or twice, the formation reloaded, took several steps forward, realigned, fired,
and then moved on again. In this fashion, one or both lines would gradually
grope their way forward until the range closed to the point where casualties
really began to mount and one side or the other decided that enough was
enough. The British, for example, had their platoons in the battalion front
grouped into "fires," that is, first, second, and third, with each consisting
of two or three platoons spaced across the front. Thus, whenever a "fire"
had delivered its volley, the battalion would advance, then halt for the
second fire, and so on.

This was the general fashion in which all armies of the linear era fought.
However, there were a multitude of different firing systems (which have
gone unmentioned here) because the tacticians of that era sought to develop
a specific type for each and every tactical eventuality that might arise in an
action.

It was left to the "royal corporal," Frederick William I of Prussia, and
his drillmaster, Prince Leopold von Dessau, to recognize that the true potential firepower of the fusil, still a new weapon, had not yet been achieved.
In finding a way to achieve that potential, these men also found the means
of elevating their state, which was then of a third-rate magnitude at best,
into the forefront of the European power game.

Quality over quantity was the guiding principle of their reforms. Prussia
was a poor country. It could not hope to match the states around it musket
for musket. Thus, the chase began. Drill saw to it that the Prussian musketeers could shoot faster than their potential adversaries. In the interests
of this, the hickory ramrod, which broke too easily, was replaced with one
made of iron. An extra inch or so of barrel gave the Prussian musket greater
hitting power and an improved effective range. And while the rest of Europe
made the "royal corporal's" mania for tall soldiers and his giant Potsdam
Grenadiers as much the objects of hate and derision as the butts of jokes,
the front ranks of his musketeer battalions quietly filled with men who were
on average, between 5 feet 8 and 5 feet 10 inches tall. This was not a
common sight in European armies, where many men under 5 feet 5 inches
stood in the front.

Of course, these tall soldiers with their longer arm spans found it that much easier to handle the muzzle-loading muskets, thus further accommodating the demands for speed and more speed. Soon, they could fire three times a minute on command. Indeed, during the years from 1745 to 1763, when the Prussian army underwent the most rigorous and hard-nosed combat training (devoid of all the baroque parade-ground artifice), properly trained Prussian musketeers were expected to fire off six rounds a minute, firing at will. The best of them would even manage to get the seventh round rammed down the bore.

Historians and even military men have frequently taken umbrage with these claims, labeling them "exaggerations." Today, however, such claims need no longer rely on contentions made a couple of centuries ago. There are literally thousands of experienced modern muzzle-loader shooters, notably in the American North South Skirmishers Association, who dismiss these objections made by men ignorant of the workings of the muzzle loader. They don't think that three rounds a minute on command is an exaggeration, and many say that six rounds, firing at will, are entirely within reach.

However, quick fire was not the only new wrinkle in the Prussian system. It was the new platoon fire that finally struck a balance between fire and motion. That is, once the Prussian battalion was ordered to commence firing, the platoons stepped off at the "slow march," starting a steady sequence of forward movement that was interrupted only by the brief halt to fire before starting up again. (One may still observe such a slow march being performed by the British Brigade of Foot Guards during the annual Queen's Birthday Parade in London, when the colors are trooped.) Divided into eight platoons, the battalions front had the platoons fire off, starting from both flanks inward in the rotation of 1-8-2-7-3-6-4-5 and then starting over again with 1-8 until halted. The lieutenants in charge of the platoons would see to it that they were always one command behind the platoon preceding them in the rotation.

Obviously, such a fire-control system required an extraordinary amount of drill. Even though this platoon fire worked well on the parade ground (to the consternation of visiting foreign militaries), it appears to have gone well on the battlefield only during the battles of the First and Second, as well as the opening stage of the Third, Silesian Wars. It eventually fell into disfavor.

There was another, even more telling reason why the Prussians practically abandoned platoon fire in all but the elite guard and grenadier formations. It had frequently resulted in what has occasionally been called "the lieutenants' battle." Platoon fire on the left and right made it problematic for a lieutenant in charge of a platoon to listen for the platoon on the other side of the battalion front, which was to cue him. The situation became altogether impossible under battlefield conditions. The fire of the battalion guns, usually two in every interval between the battalions, as well as incoming fire from the other side, raised a cacophony that soon made a shambles of the orderly firing sequence.

This is what Berenhorst,[2] a well-known Prussian critic of the Frederician army, had in mind when he said, "Once or twice around, then it was every man for himself." And that is exactly what happened when the officers and noncoms were being knocked out of action. The result was "battlefire!" A dirty word in the Prussian dictionary, it meant firing at will.

This, of course, didn't hurt firepower at all. The individual rate of fire probably even increased, and the thousandfold rote of repetition probably still caused every man to continue taking his three long paces forward before he leveled his musket to fire. That is, battlefire didn't even halt the forward progress of the Prussian firing lines until the range became quite close. What made battlefire a dirty word was that it spelled the loss of fire control; and with this came the loss of tactical control.

This was a problem even when the lieutenants were still around, conducting the fight of their platoons. Even in the best of times, once the lieutenants and their platoons had taken the bit, it was next to impossible to get them to stop firing and make a bayonet attack. Instead of an orderly chain of command, working from the top down, it generally became a matter of fifty or more platoons, each fighting its own battle. This was the "lieutenants' battle."

Frederick dealt with this problem by replacing the platoon fire with the so-called general discharge, the battalion volley. It was much less complicated and even the less well trained replacements could still manage three volleys per minute. Most importantly, however, fire control had been taken out of the lieutenants' hands and moved up to the battalion.

Yet, for all this business of firepower, Frederick himself stated on several occasions that the real task of the infantry was to close quickly and to push the enemy from the ground on which he stood. Once this was done, the enemy's formation was broken and the rest would follow as a matter of course. Frederick saw in firepower not so much a means of doing physical damage to the enemy—even though this could be real enough—but rather a means of causing disruption, confusion, and disorganization and of easing his own infantry's way in going the last 300 paces.

Directly linked to firepower was yet another problem involved with the linear order: Once a firing line was engaged, there was little chance to disengage it in orderly fashion. The lines were difficult to move forward and even more difficult to move to the rear, even though old Field Marshal

Lehwald made a textbook demonstration of such a difficult tactical maneuver against the Russians at Gross Jaegersdorf (on July 30, 1757). This is why the predetermined point and direction of attack were so important in linear tactics—and totally unlike the Napoleonic style, which would generally open on a probing note to determine where the center of gravity might develop to greatest advantage. In the linear battle, the all-out attack came right up front in head-through-the-wall fashion. Like a bullet fired from a gun, there was little chance to alter the line's thrust, once it had been committed.

The second line in the linear battle order was not a reserve in the modern sense. It was generally composed of second-string regiments and more of a fire reserve than a tactical reserve, even though Frederick might have used his well-drilled battalions in the latter fashion. He had shifted the emphasis, however, from fire control to rapid deployment, and he had trained his army to do this in the direction of its march.

Actually, the latter-day French assault column, formed on the center, was a microcosm of what Frederick might do with an entire army. Thus, with the proper arrangement of his columns, they could head straight for the enemy line, fanning out from the center (or from one flank, in the manner of the latter-day column of divisions).

Characteristically, these new wrinkles in Frederick's bag of tricks were an addition to, rather than a replacement for, the old ways. Thus, his celebrated victory at Leuthen with the so-called oblique order was entirely a result of local circumstances. Beginning with an old-fashioned parallel march, which set up a frontal attack in echelon, that is, with each battalion stepping off 50 paces after the one to its right, it became an oblique attack only after each of the battalions made a slight wheeling movement to its left in the course of its advance. With the lever thus applied to the left wing of the Austrian battle array, a stunning victory was gained over an opponent at least twice as strong.

All of this, of course, has a deceptively simple ring to it, but any officer who has ever maneuvered masses of men, even on the comparatively benevolent confines of a parade ground, will appreciate the amount of drill and coordination that had to go into pulling off such maneuvers, and then over uneven terrain and under fire! (The plains that the linear battle is said to have sought were not exactly parade grounds.) Ideally, all this was to happen so fast that even if the enemy finally saw it coming, he would have little chance to react effectively.

The grand success at Leuthen was to implant itself firmly into the minds of future generations of Prussian officers. It reached a point where both the oblique and the echelon attacks came to be regarded as a panacea that would serve for all occasions. Old Fritz himself had never quite seen it that way.

From the foregoing, it becomes self-evident that the column, which was to dominate the next stage of tactical evolution, was not by any means something new. Everyone used it during the linear era. In a tactical sense, however, it was regarded as nothing more than a means of moving troops and deploying them into the linear order.

Still, many people who were theoretically and practically engaged in matters of warfare, including men such as the Mareshal de Saxe and Folard, had long pondered the use of the column as an offensive weapon. They envisioned bringing it forward into the small-arms fire zone in the manner of a battering ram to pierce the thin firing lines. Frederick himself was aware of this. The very sight of these thin lines begged for such an offensive.

However, the column lacked the firepower needed to go up against a deployed firing line, and Frederick's own experiences with attempts to bring his infantry forward without musketry certainly caused him to shy away from such methods. Also, some historians think they see an example of Folard's *grande colonne* in the primary sources describing the attempted French advance at Rossbach. This, too, must have set a bad example for the Prussian king.

Be this as it may, the time for the offensive use of the column had not yet come. When its time did finally arrive, the tactic was employed far more as a child of necessity than as a product of planned evolution. As the human resources changed, so the face of battle had to alter its appearance.

IDEALS AND REALITIES

Although the foregoing touched mainly on the technical aspects of linear tactics, some of the problems attending linear combat methods have been raised. They were seldom discussed because they did not conform to the ideals. Theoreticians, in quest of theorems, frequently intellectualized the ideals and were prone to eschew the realities because they generally tended to complicate matters. Thus, Berenhorst's remarks about battlefire, even though they were admittedly overcritical—and notwithstanding the fact that other militaires as well, admitted that platoon fire inevitably degenerated into battlefire—were not happily received by many. In this, the theoreticians were reinforced by the contemporary military publications, which were generally reticent on the subject; if they mentioned it at all, it was only in passing remarks because the subject was considered an aberration. Official after-action reports deliberately suppressed any mention of it. The bottom line of all this, of course, is that there was a great deal more battlefire in Frederician battles than is commonly admitted.

This is neither new nor unusual. Homer is held to have tampered with the primary source material available to him (but lost to posterity) to bring it into line with his own notions of what was, to him, the classical age. Archaeological findings fail to support him on many details. Historians, too, have not always paid attention to what was actually set down by the original chroniclers; they often saw not what was actually said but what they only thought was said. (For example, the questions raised by some modern historians about Isokrates' account of the Battle of Dipaea (in Archidamus) are themselves open to question.)[3] Thus, the detailed study of every era of military history is beset by its own problems, some of them already contained in the original source materials, others created by posterity.

In more modern times, the great Frederick himself threw up some smoke screens when he admonished his infantry to "move in quickly on the enemy, put a volley into his ribs at twenty paces and charge home with the bayonet." Call it wishful thinking, an ideal, or whatever—it never quite came to pass that way. When he did give way to this idea and ordered the infantry to drive its attack home at the quick march, without bothering to fire, the attempt caused some of his best soldiers to be literally blown away by the platoons. Ideals and realities never got on well together.

Even the Napoleonic era was rife with false images and idealistic conceptions. This was despite the widespread literacy among combatants of all ranks, which resulted in a plethora of personal narratives (notably absent in earlier times). Nowhere is this more evident than in the arguments raised over the relative merits of the column and the line. There can be no question whatever that even during the peak of the Napoleonic era, the line never lost its place in the scheme of things.

The only way the infantry could maximize its firepower was by deploying into line. At the same time, it was self-evident that anything done to shorten the front of the infantry battalion in the interests of increased maneuverability was done at the expense of its inherent firepower. An effort was made to compensate for this by using skirmishers and by resorting to the mixed order, that is, by deploying a mixture of columns and lines into the front, thereby retaining the advantages of both.

It is, however, on the issue of how the battalions deployed into line came into action, that the imagery of the ideal persistently cuts across the realities. Thus, the *ordre mixte* is a fact of life, but it is difficult to find a narrative from the opponents of either the republican or Imperial armies that speaks of the advance of deployed French firing lines.

Lynn, in his work on the motivation and tactics in the army of revolutionary France, 1791–1794,[4] compiled an outstanding list of references citing examples of the use of the line in combat. They are gleaned from the French War Archives and other official sources, as well as some memoirs of participants. His listing documents the use of the line on no fewer than fifty-five occasions. Of these, however, only seven instances point toward an offensive use of the line, and two of these are doubtful or confusing. Moreover, these examples largely represent a record of tactical failure rather than of success. The remaining instances indicate the use of deployed lines on defense (thirteen examples), on defense in retreat (seven examples), on defense during the passage of defiles (two examples), as a waiting or preliminary formation (seventeen examples), in support of light infantry (six examples), and, finally, as receiving or covering positions on the march (three examples).

Even the great confrontations with the Prussians at Jena and Auerstaedt in 1806 yield very few mentions of an offensive use of the line by the French. Often-cited examples are those of the 105th French Line and 16th Light Regiment at Jena, as well as the 111th Line at Auerstaedt. But the general narratives give a somewhat different picture. They usually speak of the advance of the columns as soon as the combined effect of the *tirailleur* (skirmishing) fire and the French artillery caused the Prussian lines to waver. This, too, points toward the static and defensive, rather than offensive, use of deployed battalions. But then again, the harassing effect of the well-planned and well-executed skirmishing actions, the smoke screen they laid down, and the effective use of a strong artillery obviated the offensive use of the line until the constant decline of the training standards of the infantry gradually caused it to fall into disuse. As the rank and file eventually lost the knack of deploying and advancing under fire, there was also a decrease in the number of officers who had experienced the handling of deployed battalions in training or on the battlefield. If the echelon attack had become the panacea for all occasions in the minds of the Prussians, then the column soon became the pervasive cure-all for the French.

Certainly, the new tactics took the battles out of the plains, which the linear order had sought, and put them into more richly structured terrain. With equal certainty, this brought on a correspondingly rich variety of combat situations. But was Oman, the noted British military historian and chronicler of Wellington's peninsular campaigns, really as far off the mark about the French penchant for column attacks as Elting,[5] one of the best American connoisseurs of the Napoleonic armies, believes? And did General Bugeaud's often-cited description of how such a column attack would materialize represent an isolated incident or a general modus operandi? These are crucial questions that are not easily answered out of hand but must be approached one step at a time.

In the end, the great confrontations, the battles, always came down to the same old question: How well did the attacker get through the small-arms fire zone? Even today, the "last 300 meters" is a concept that looms large in the rifleman's world, despite the fact that it lies deeply buried beneath the counts of the tanks, guns, aircraft, and other hardware that are so dear to the modern military analysts because they make good copy. Major English, in his work on infantry,[6] observes that while there is copious literature on the supporting combat arms and their nuts and bolts, next to nothing is to be found on the infantry. Thus, the surfacing of a term such as the "last 300 meters" must have come as an all-but-forgotten reminder to military readers, except, of course, former riflemen.

The last 300 meters roughly describes the zone in which the other rifleman's fire becomes effective, the area where combat indeed becomes a personal matter between men. Every soldier who survived the ordeal of coming out of the trenches in 1916 to charge into no-man's land knew exactly what that zone was. And all the supporting weaponry that has been developed since then can ultimately be said to have been designed for one purpose: to ease the rifleman's way in going the last 300 meters.

During the eighteenth century, the small-arms fire zone was generally regarded as covering about 250 to 300 paces. This was the maximum range at which the musket was thought to be effective. That is, with the musket barrel leveled horizontally, the ball would strike the ground at a distance of about 200 to 250 paces when fired with a normal powder charge. Of course, a musket ball would carry much farther than that. If the ground was hard, the ball would bounce or ricochet and, in two or three bounds, reach about 400 to 500 paces. If the musket was aimed high, the ball, flying in an arc, could reach a distance of 1000 paces or even more. The practical effects at such distances were considered questionable—and rightfully so. The modern assault rifle can also shoot a great deal farther than 300 meters, but at that range, a man makes a small target. Even a firing line appears to be composed of dwarfs.

What is nevertheless surprising is that the small-arms zone has not changed all that much over the past two centuries. Certainly, the difference between 300 paces and 300 meters bears no relationship whatever to the comparative quantum leap from the smoothbore musket to the modern rifle. However, even though time has not appreciably changed the depth of the small-arms fire zone, the conditions under which the infantry was expected to cross it have altered drastically.

RUNNING: A TACTICAL PROBLEM

Throughout the era of formal mass tactics, running had no place in the military dictionary unless it described something the enemy was doing when trying to get away. The need to maintain order in the ranks was so over-powering that even deployments from column into line or from the line back into column were conducted at a walk, lest formation be lost. Only the skirmisher, operating out of ranks, was allowed to adjust his movements to the needs of the situation.

But the self-preservation instinct provided, and always will provide, a powerful incentive to run from danger. Nobody, including the soldier, is immune to this. And it is on this issue that the ideals consistently faced the most determined assaults of reality.

In the military, discipline and peer pressure have always provided pow-erful tools for steeling the soldier's resolve to stick it out. These, however, were not by any means sufficient in themselves, unless backed by combat forms and the rote of their practice, which aim to equip the fighting man with methods designed to minimize the dangers of combat and reinforce his self-confidence. For this reason, definitions of tactics—and they have been numerous—generally stress two objectives: (1) practicing combat forms that provide for the maximum use of one's own arsenal and (2) protecting the soldier as much as possible against the impressions of combat, that is min-imizing the effects of the enemy's efforts. In an offensive situation, these ideas appear contradictory, almost to the point of mutual exclusion. Still, throughout history, every military establishment employing a rationalized system of combat has sought to come to grips with this contradiction, each in its own fashion.

In modern times, we see the rifleman attempting to cross open ground under fire, either by creeping along on his belly, making use of whatever low cover may be available, or by dashing from one cover to the next, pursuing an erratic course. Such elementary techniques offer the rifleman a temporary haven of relative safety and enable him to recharge his psychic batteries, to steel himself for the moment when he might again break cover to make his next move under extreme mental stress.

This is indeed elementary. Everyone knows that a small target is more difficult to hit than a large one and that a stationary target is easier to hit than a moving one. Only a fool would stand up and amble across open ground under fire. Yet this is precisely what the military establishments of the eighteenth century expected their infantry to do in order to accommodate the requirements of linear tactics. That is, the infantry was expected to literally waltz downrange at an ambling cadence of about 45 paces per minute as, densely ranked and elbow to elbow, they went up against the enemy's deployed firing lines.

Although the mass conscriptions of the Napoleonic era made the replacement of a good musket a more difficult proposition than finding a warm body to carry it, the linear era tended to husband its human resources more carefully. This may again sound contradictory. But the eighteenth century saw no way out of the dilemma posed by linear tactics, which was extremely wasteful of the carefully trained manpower the system demanded. Even though defense was better than offense, if the attacker meant to move forward and carry the fight to the enemy, then he had to accept the cost. And, whether attack or defense, the linear battle was so costly that eventually it was thought better to achieve success without having any battles at all. But that was a theory that never achieved any lasting results. Still, the idea had its adherents. Even Frederick the Great endured constant criticism from his younger brother, Prince Henry, a master strategist himself, who accused him of "battling, battling, constantly battling!"

Obviously, defense was the stronger form of combat, and he who could stand and await another's attack held the high card. It requires no great military expertise to realize that a firing line which remained in place could throw more lead than one which was trying to combine its fire with movement. Thus, despite all the improved methods for fire control, in the end it always came down to the same thing: At some point, the attacker had to face the music. And he had to do it standing or walking upright, in effective range, because there was no way in which a musket could be properly loaded by a kneeling man, much less by one lying on the ground. Russian roulette offered far better odds, as may readily be calculated from the battle casualties linear armies were forced to accept over and over.

The interior ballistics of the smoothbore musket caused the ball to pursue an erratic course, so individually aimed fire was considered useless and the shotgun effect of the volley was relied upon. This meant that the men had to stand together, elbow to elbow, three ranks deep at least, to accommodate both firepower and fire reserve. If they were to do this effectively, there had to be order in the ranks. The military, in effect, attempted to turn ordinary men into duelists without extending to them the social status and morale that fortified the sense of honor of the aristocrats, who engaged in such practices. Instead, it was thought that discipline, dressage, and more discipline were the only viable means of instilling in the ordinary man something that ran totally contrary to his instinct for self-preservation. In an era in which the common man was the object rather than the partner of his government and in which the army was the king's rather than the nation's, one could hardly rely on lofty emotions to fortify the soldier's response. This was especially so in times that still saw substantial numbers of itinerant adventurers in the ranks of all the armies.

Thus, the draconic discipline that characterized the linear era (not by any means in Prussia alone) was deliberately designed to make taking on one's own establishment a more difficult and dangerous proposition than facing the enemy. The individual accounted for nothing. Frederick himself gave voice to this when he said, "That I should live is not important, but that I should serve is!" Thus, if the militaires of the old regimes thought a well-trained musketeer was important and worthy of preservation, this was so because he represented a valuable property and a considerable investment in time and money, not because of humane considerations.

As a result, the ideals of the time saw armies of peasant soldiers (mostly farmhands, stableboys, grooms, etc.—certainly not propertied landowners) in the ranks, commanded by the younger sons of the aristocracy, who would not inherit and thus largely saw in military service the last justification for their estate. Thus, the rank and file, composed of men who had been accustomed to obeying orders from the time they were old enough to understand them, was commanded by men who had been just as accustomed to giving them. This practice, according to Vagts,[7] prevailed in the British army right into modern times.

For all that, moving forward the thin firing lines of the linear era remained a serious problem. Once the range shortened to anything under 250 paces, that is, when the troops entered the small-arms fire zone, life became precarious. The difficulties of maintaining order in the ranks and keeping the men from breaking into a trot—whether forward, to get it over with in a hurry, or to the rear, to get out—increased with every step. Sooner or later, these difficulties became overwhelming.

As a result, life in the small-arms fire zone was short, even during the best of times. Once the masses came forward, it was only a matter of 2, 3, or 4 minutes, before the decision came. By then, either the attacker had gained the ascendancy, if he was still coming on, or he knew it was time to get out and let the other fellows have a go at it, if the defender still held his ground. This is a point generally lost in the narratives of battles, especially during the Napoleonic era (in which these problems continued to remain operative). During that period, the sustained action of skirmishers, fighting dispersed and from cover, and the advance of the masses are generally melded together, giving rise to totally false images.

Once the masses came into the effective range of massed musketry, casualties mounted at an explosive rate, as was witnessed over and over again during the linear era. If the false image of a sustained firefight under such circumstances were pursued to a logical conclusion, then two deployed firing lines would have quickly reduced each other to thin skirmishing lines, while a column attempting to face a line would have ensured its own destruction.

The issue of how strong defensive musketry might have been remains generally distorted by the layman's vision of the muzzle-loading musket's technical limitations. To modern man, long accustomed to repeating and automatic firearms, one, two, or even three rounds per minute is nothing to write home about. However, once one comes to grips with the idea of 500 or 600 men, packed into a front of about 200 paces, able to throw anywhere from 1000 to 2000 rounds per minute, then the image alters drastically, even in the eyes of a modern soldier. This approaches the cyclic rate of modern machine guns and exceeds the effective rate of most.

As to the relative accuracy of two such disparate instruments as the musketeer battalion and the machine gun, surely many veterans can recall seeing the effect of a burst from a modern machine gun sprayed all over the side of a barn. Only in the movies do these guns stitch the rounds as neatly as a sewing machine.

But this relates only to the effects of a single deployed musketeer battalion. One Austrian officer likened the Prussian musketry at Mollwitz (in 1741) to an unceasing thunder. Von Angeli, a noted Austrian historian, presents an even more graphic eyewitness account in his description of the action around Baumersdorf (July 5, 1809), a focal point of the Battle of Wagram. His narrative states: "One exchanged musketry at very close range. The enormous din, as wave upon wave of musketry constantly erupted, and the even greater iron rattle of 20,000 muskets (ramrods) being worked in such close proximity, is completely beyond the imagination. Everything, even the thunder of the numerous cannon, seemed insignificant amid the raging storm of the so-called smallarms."[8] Elsewhere, an Austrian regimental padre stated that a battery standing on the flank of his regiment could not even be heard during the climax of the small-arms fire storm.

It was over in minutes. Even though Napoleon had made haste in preparing for the assault to exploit an apparent weakness in the Austrian line, to the accompaniment of the skirmishers and artillery of both sides it had taken more than an hour. But the assault by the masses, once it came, was over in no time at all. Assault columns came in, faltered, and fell back, even as others coming up renewed the attack, only to be beaten off as well. Still other columns never even got up to the last 300 paces. The attempts of some to deploy into line under fire turned into a shambles.

Skirmishers, grimly hanging on, covering the withdrawal of the shattered columns, prolonged the action, or at least the impression of it. But the main event was over until the next effort, by other brigades, by other divisions, was made. It would not be on that day, because the sun was setting. All the while, artillery, well handled on both sides, offensively and defensively, played the part of the great spoiler. For the masses, life in the small-arms fire zone was short, and this must be understood if the tactical imagery of the era dominated by the muzzle-loading musket is to make sense.

Ever since the Seven Years' War, the Austrians had increasingly relied on the battalion guns (placed in the intervals of the infantry battalions) to lend an ever more effective hand. Attacking infantry had no answer against grape and canister at 300 paces, unless it could bring its own guns along to take on the enemy's gunners. Thus, if the Austrian gunners "stuck to their guns," as they did at Kolin and Prague, the oncoming infantry lines had little chance of driving home their assaults. However, if the gunners lost their nerve, as they did on other occasions, then the Austrian infantry had equally little chance to cope with Prussian musketry.

Even when things went well, the sternest discipline and quick fire could do no more than delay the inevitable point of dissolution for perhaps another minute or two. These, of course, could be crucial and enough to turn a bloody mess into a success. However, during the linear era, which sought to deliver its Sunday punch up front, it was the elite, the best men, who were the first to bleed white (whereas Napoleonic warfare tended to save them for last). They might succeed by the boldness and resolution of their attacks, but when that wasn't enough, they would tend to hang in just long enough in moments of crisis to suffer crippling losses.

This brought on a decline in the quality of the Prussian infantry similar to what the Napoleonic armies would experience later, except that in Frederick's time it came much faster because of the more limited human resources involved. On the other hand, this decline was compensated for by the meteoric rise of the Prussian cavalry in the hands of brilliant training masters such as Zieten and Seydlitz, and this occurred at a time when the fusil had already made the traditional cavalry charge problematic, to say the least. Napoleon was not to benefit from such a phenomenon. He lacked both the raw materials and the cavalry commanders to make it happen on a sufficiently broad scale. As a result, when his infantry went on a downward spiral, the cavalry preceded it at an even faster rate.

Thus, the linear era perceived the peak of its perfection in the ability to bring deployed firing lines forward into the small-arms fire zone in perfect order and in total response to command. That was the ideal, but it was only rarely achieved. Of course, this was to be accomplished at the stately cadence of about 45 short paces per minute, which was deemed best for bringing the lines forward in good order. This caused Bleckwenn[9] to characterize these affairs as "ballets accompanied by fireworks." His obvious sarcasm is lost only on those who fail to realize how deadly the linear battles were for the infantry, who sweated under powdered wigs, pipe clay, and uniforms that were as uncomfortable as they were spectacular.

The next era, rocked by great political upheavals, was to find new solutions to old military problems, even if it was not able to entirely divest itself of the old.

FROM HORDE TO COLUMN TACTICS

When the revolution erupted in France, the French royal army was demolished from within almost as effectively as the political institutions of the old order. Not only did it lose the vast majority of its officers in the wake of the terror, but even the rank and file walked away from the colors in large numbers. By the time the eyes of the republican government once again looked upon the army as a means of national defense, rather than as one of the objects of the revolution, the army had become but a shadow of its former existence. However, even then, it continued to be viewed with suspicion. Rather than bringing it back up to strength, the decree of January 28, 1791, ordered the formation of the National Volunteer Battalions.

Unlike the old regular regiments, who still wore the Bourbon white, these new volunteer battalions were to be dressed in blue coats, so that no true republican would find it difficult to tell them apart. Eventually, the new "blue" battalions were integrated into the line in the course of the first reorganization at the planned ratio of one white and two blue battalions per regiment. These, however, were known as demi- or half-brigades; the very term "regiment" had become reactionary. By then, the old "white" army had been allowed to disintegrate to such an extent that it was no longer possible to give each of the new half-brigades one of the remaining white battalions.

The great depletion of the old (white) regiments, quite apart from the effects of the revolution itself, had been further exacerbated when many of the rank and file who had remained eventually decided to escape the more rigid disciplinary standards still prevailing in the old white battalions by transferring to the volunteers. Not only was life there more pleasant, but promotions also came quickly to anyone who could boast of some previous military experience.

Of course, constant efforts were made to bring the new volunteer battalions into some sort of order. Like all else, they encompassed both a good and a bad side. On the one hand, the first call for volunteers had brought a new breed of soldier to the colors, men filled with a kind of zeal and devotion to a cause that had been all but unknown in the armies of the *ancien regime*. Their spirit might have produced excellent material for a real reconstitution of the army. On the other hand, the efforts to rebuild the army were severely hampered by the continuing attitude of the republican government, in which hysteria prevailed over anything that was even vaguely reminiscent of the old order—in particular, the army, the instrument of the old order's power.

Arriving in the field to defend the young republic against the armies of an alarmed dynastic Europe, the blue volunteer battalions exhibited no lack of courage, spirit, and devotion to their cause. But when they attempted to deploy for action in the manner of the old order, to meet the enemy on his own terms, the results were generally pathetic and occasionally disastrous. Yet fight they did, as well as they could. Even if their tactics failed, the sheer volume of their numbers certainly had a sobering effect on the rank and file of the other side.

Of course, there was no way in which these new republicans could be subjected to the kind of harsh discipline that had been the trademark of the old linear system, at least not so long as the revolution was still a going concern. In his own perceptions, the common man had just participated in a revolution to rid himself of precisely such things. There were those in authority who thought that a good republican could beat the stuffing out of a blockheaded soldier of the old regime any day. Thus, the medium of discipline, drill, and more discipline and drill, so necessary to the linear order, was light-years away. Also, the rank and file was no longer disposed to render the sort of unquestioning obedience that had been a major operative ingredient of the old ways.

However, while the linear order provided insurmountable difficulties for the new republican armies, the column, not new by any means, offered workable solutions. Teaching the new recruits to form up and march in column formations was easy enough (relatively, of course). So was the deployment into line. But when attempts were made to move these lines forward in an offensive movement, everything fell apart in short order. Dissolving into long, dense skirmishing lines, the men at once sought whatever cover was to be found and started a standing firefight at distances considerably greater than the 300 paces regarded as the outside line of optimum effect for the musket. However, in places where some sort of cover facilitated a closer approach, the skirmishers would work their way in and fire with correspondingly good effect.

Something could be made of this situation if the columns waiting in the second line could be brought forward quickly under the cover of the smoke

screen laid down by the skirmishers. The advance could capitalize on whatever confusion the most forward elements might have caused in the enemy
line. Unfortunately, more often than not, an extended firefight would gradually suck in the columns of the second line, with or without the consent
of their commanders—an unthinkable state of affairs in an army of old-style
regulars. Eventually, dense swarms (or hordes) would feel emboldened to
make a run at the enemy's deployed lines. But there, the neophytes of the
new order would run up against a line drawn by the fire discipline of the
old order. Crossing this line was not easy—not then, not later.

Even General Bugeaud's often-recited description of a French column
attack in Spain continues to bear testimony to this reality. There, Wellington
unpacked an old method of dealing with frontal assaults (the Austrians had
already done this successfully against the Prussians), and the real surprise is
that the French obliged him so often, even if they did not always do so. At
the same time, Napoleon himself was to learn at Wagram in 1809 that
frontal assaults against deployed firing lines were adventures fraught with
frustration.

At this point, it is appropriate to ask what the difference was between
a column attack and a horde attack. Who cared, as long as both came
forward with equal resolution? But here again, the same forces were at work
as those that had already caused the Prussians to frown at battlefire. A unit
in orderly formation was still an instrument in the hands of its officers and
noncoms. That is, the officers on the flanks and the noncoms in the closing
rank of each successive company in the battalion column would take notice
at once if a man hung back or attempted to leave the ranks. However, once
the column took the bit and the trotting began, the first thing to fall apart
was the formation. Ranks became intermingled; oversight and control were
lost. This, in its turn, brought other things into play.

Not every man was a natural-born hero; not every individual was equally
psyched (or pumped) up for the occasion. Thus, some would hang back as
soon as the opportunity presented itself. However, even all those who were
psychologically up to the occasion were not made of the same stuff. A 25-
pound pack jumping around on a trotting man's back, a 10-pound ammunition pouch and attached paraphernalia bouncing on his right hip, a hanger
(short sword) on his left hip, and a 10-pound musket in his hands would
cause the breath of many a soldier to run short after only about 50 paces.
If the run went to 100 or more paces, especially over uneven ground or,
worse yet, up an incline, things began to get serious. Thus, even those who
were still bravely going forward were being spread apart, if for no other
reason than the fact that some were stronger, fitter, and better runners than

others. This was a problem even for cavalry charges ridden on entirely sound horses.

At some point, some men would fire off their muskets. Those in front might halt to level their weapons; others, in the rear, would simply fire them off into the air in acts of defiance. Inevitably, there came that point when the hardiest souls in front would suddenly find themselves within hailing distance of a deployed firing line, which was waiting with muskets loaded and ready. And the better the fire discipline of the waiting line, the longer the officers in command could wait before ordering fire. The shorter the range, the more devastating the effect of the volley when it came.

The sight of such a firing line, suddenly up close, could make the most intrepid front-runner feel very much like a man standing alone in the middle of a football field in an empty stadium. It would cause many men to stop short, and the rest of the upcoming mass of winded men would telescope into each other, suddenly creating a confused press in which a well-timed volley could create havoc. Often, such a volley would be no more than a send-off, fired into a crowd that was already falling back.

This was an ideal situation in the eyes of the defender. Yet it occurred in endless variety on hundreds of occasions when the infantry masses clashed, during the times of both the republic and the empire.

From the start, it was the skirmishers' mission to ease the columns' way into the small-arms fire zone. By dint of circumstances, these skirmishing actions, preceding the formal attack, loomed large in French tactics. Indeed, it had been the tactical ineptitude of the republican volunteer battalions that had brought them onto the battlefield in wholesale fashion.

But once the French learned how to control this preparatory phase of the action better and how to keep the masses from being sucked into action prematurely, their tactical successes began to assume more definite shape. Above all, they learned to take the action out of the open country, which favored linear tactics, and carry it into more richly structured terrain. The landscapes of northern Italy and the Dutch lowlands, dissected by hedges and fences, provided ideal proving grounds. This did not happen all at once, however, and the performance of various republican armies remained quite uneven for some time. It was only during the consulate, when the bulk of the French combat forces were subjected to a considerable amount of formal training, much of it aimed at tighter control of the skirmishing action, that a dramatic improvement began to manifest itself.

The skirmishers, preceding the columns and fighting in open order, made use of whatever cover presented itself but were elusive targets even when in the open. They became expert at harassing the enemy and causing confusion as well as casualties. During the wars of the republic, this system worked reasonably well, but not well enough to cause the opponents of the young republic to have any serious doubts about their own military capacities.

However, once the flaws were worked out of the modus operandi of the old republican armies during the encampments along the English Channel, the world was in for a stunning surprise. The French had learned to maximize the combination of the masses with the preparatory action of the skirmishers, even as the artillery came into action with powerful batteries to take a direct hand as well.

Since the Seven Years' War, the artillery had played an ever more decisive role and the battalion guns, firing canister at ranges under 600 paces, did more damage than the musketry, unless the attacker brought his own guns along. By that time, the Austrians had developed the tactic of awaiting the Prussian attacks on high ground; half a century later, Wellington employed the same tactic against the French in the Peninsula. Ascending even the gentlest of slopes turned the manhandled battalion guns into deadweight, so the Prussian infantry generally ended up going it alone over the last several hundred paces.

By Napoleonic times, much of the preparatory artillery fire was being handled by what used to be the position artillery; the French were deploying ever stronger batteries, because neither the skirmishers nor the columns had any real firepower of their own. Even though other reasons have been cited for their abandonment of the battalion guns in favor of deploying batteries (not the least of which was that artillery was better handled by artillerymen than by infantry officers), the French now customarily sent their battalions to operate in terrain that made taking the guns along highly problematic anyway.

Still, a defensive line holding the high ground continued to present problems even for the new artillery formations because it was never easy to unlimber the guns on a slope to give close support to infantry going uphill. The last noteworthy example underlining this difficulty occurred when Napoleon's guards attacked Wellington's center at Waterloo in 1815.

It has become conventional to say that Napoleon reintroduced the battalion guns (now called the regimental artillery) in 1809 because the infantry had lost its firepower. But that explanation does not really address the heart of the problem. It appears more realistic to say that the Napoleonic infantry, even the celebrated Grand Army of 1805, never had any real firepower—at least, not in terms of what the linear era understood firepower to be. Thus, some thought should be given to the idea that the Austerlitz campaign of 1805 and the Prussian war of 1806–1807, which had placed the reins into Napoleon's hands, had also taken the cover off the new and refined French tactical system. The element of surprise had gone out of its modus operandi.

The Austrians, the British, the Prussians, and the Russians had all been beaten in their initial encounters with the new French army. The only difference was that the British and Russians had somewhere to run, whereas the Austrians and Prussians, whose countries were overrun, did not. But all of them, without exception, proved tougher the second time around. Their infantry was no longer apt to be rattled by what had once been the unfamiliar, and the French infantry was to find them a more difficult proposition all the way around. The Russians offered a glimpse of this in 1807, and even the remaining Prussians made a much better showing than they had in the campaign of the previous year. In 1809, the Austrians dealt a reverse at Aspern (Lobau), and Napoleon had no fond memories of his victory at Wagram. And in the peninsula, Wellington, the first to take the field after the initial round of defeats, had already found a way of dealing with the French mode of operations.

Seeking the high ground in a defensive posture, as the Austrians had already done against Frederick, Wellington avoided the effects of French artillery preparations by having his firing lines step back from the crest. When they finally did come a few paces forward to meet the French assault columns with musketry, their elevated position generally offered them good insight into their field of fire, notwithstanding the skirmishers' smoke screen. Indeed, on the face of a slope, it probably did more to obscure the attacker's than the defender's vision.

But the most important change was that Napoleon's opponents now also began to deploy skirmishers of their own. The immediate effect of this was twofold: First, it tended to keep both sides' skirmishers at arm's length, thereby reducing the damage and confusion wrought on the massed formations in their rear. Second, the potential damage of the skirmishers was further impaired by the circumstance that, in addition to being kept at a greater distance, they now also expended at least part of their energy sniping at each other.

General Bugeaud's graphic account of a French column assault has been repeated many times.[10] Stripped of its enshrouding verbiage, the essential description reads: "Very soon we got nearer, crying 'Vive l'empereur! En avant! A la bayonette!' Shakos were raised on the muzzles of our muskets (!), the column began to double (!), the ranks got into confusion (!), the agitation produced a tumult (!), shots were fired as we advanced (!)." This covers, in a nutshell, just about everything said on the subject so far. A lack of discipline had caused the columns to break into a run, even when they were not under direct fire; muskets were fired off; formation was lost; column became horde—back to the hard days.

The British historians Oman and Fortescue believe French commanders did this deliberately because they did not think their men were capable of deploying into this line once they came into the small-arms fire zone and they thought that to do so before reaching the zone would be useless, since the firing lines could not be brought forward in good order. Commandant Colin and Hillaire Belloc, French historians, claim that launching the columns in this fashion was the result of errors in judgment. They point out that many surviving battle orders stress the need to deploy into line before contact is made with the enemy and that the commanders merely attempted to bring their columns in too close before this was ordered.

The historians are probably all correct in their assertions. The latter are merely attempting to explain that which was already implicit in the contentions of the former. Deployment was indeed possible, but the movement of the resulting firing lines was problematic in the extreme. The only difference between the British and French views is that while the British claim that the columns were run in deliberately, the French claim that deployment was delayed until it was too late. Both probably occurred with sufficient frequency to prevent either being labeled right or wrong. The fact is that the movement of deployed firing lines remained as much an illusion for the Imperial French armies as it had been for the republicans. Such maneuvers could be achieved only with the sort of drill no French army—not the republic's, not the empire's—had known since the days of the *ancien regime*. Thus, even when a deployment was effected, what would happen to the columns would happen faster yet to a line. There was never sufficient dressage, except in a few elite formations, that could effectively overcome this.

Even if the troops had such capacities on the battalion level, where would the brigadiers, capable of handling a deployed front of several battalions, come from? Once Napoleon's string of military adventures got under way, the army had all it could do to put an unending stream of replacements through basic training and battalion drill. Where does one hear of the French army conducting maneuvers and brigade drills? Even Davout's efforts to institute regimental training schools after the 1809 campaign remained stillborn when the preparations for the Russian campaign occasioned renewed expansions and dislocations of formations. Indeed, the opportunity for the Saxons to engage in brigade drills, when they were taken out of their quarters and concentrated in the field in 1811, was so unusual that Funck made special mention of it at considerable length. There is no mention of such large-scale maneuvers ever being conducted by the French army between campaigns after the Channel encampments. Moreover, the great majority of the generation of brigadiers who might have participated in such exercises between 1801 and 1805 no longer stood at the same posts in 1809. And the notion that any brigadier could effect such evolutions simply by giving the appropriate commands, without his—or the troops under his command—ever having benefited from the opportunity to practice on the drill field, must be relegated to the realm of fantasy.

Thus, one sees Marcognet's battalions deploying into line at Waterloo, and, from all accounts they did this reasonably well. Even the advance appears to have been orderly. Significantly, however, the formation resulting from this was a white elephant that hearkened back to Folard's idea of the *grande colonne*: The deployed battalions were not placed abreast in a line but, instead, were stacked up in a column of such proportions that it had virtually no room for maneuver.

The road from horde to column tactics was a rocky one, but several distinct phases do emerge from the mountain of confusing and often contradictory sources.

During the first phase, massive swarms of skirmishers dominated the scene. But they had difficulty in consolidating whatever gains they made because there were usually only a few, mostly white battalions still in column formation who might have accomplished this.

The second phase was characterized by a considerable reduction of the skirmishers, as command gradually succeeded in maintaining better control of the troops. This, in its turn, increased the number of supporting columns still in hand. These were generally deployed in two lines, checkerboard fashion, with the second line on the intervals of the first. Ideally, these intervals were to be sufficient to allow the columns to deploy into line without causing any to be squeezed out.

The third phase was largely the result of the long encampments on the English Channel front. By then, the elite companies of each battalion were, by designation, charged with all manners of service detached from the column, and this included skirmishing. At this stage, the effective combination of the skirmishers and the columns proved a fatal combination for the military establishments of the old order.

With speed of movement an essential factor of these new tactical forms, the injunction against running, a dominant factor throughout the era of formal mass tactics, had been somewhat accommodated by the *pas de charge*. This was done at a cadence of between 132 and 140 paces per minute, as opposed to the deployment march, which was done at about 100 cadence, or the advancing pace of the old linear order, which was done at around 45. Sometime during the first decade of the nineteenth century, the quick march, at about 109 paces, came into use in Prussia and elsewhere. This comes close to the modern 114 cadence as practiced in the U.S. Army today.

The final phase of the tactical infrastructure of the battalion came in 1808, when the effectiveness of the French army was already beginning to pass its peak. At that time, the battalions were organized into four fusilier companies, each nearly twice the size of the old companies, with the elite companies (grenadiers and voltigeurs) similarly enlarged. This released a large number of company officers and noncoms for new formations and gave formal expression to the idea that no more than a third of the battalion should normally be dissolved for skirmishing actions. This, of course, represented the norm; right up to the end, the French infantry exhibited a remarkable flexibility on the use of the skirmishers.

The 1808 reorganization also spelled the end for the specialized nature of the light infantry regiments, which had been dispersed throughout the infantry divisions to provide the bulk of light infantry duties (i.e., anything not associated with service in the battle line, which, of course, included skirmishing). Although they continued to maintain their light infantry traditions, these regiments were not singled out for special replacements.

Thus, the infantry battalion became a self-contained tactical entity, capable of conducting all forms of infantry combat with its own resources. This was the theory. In practice, the considerable tactical skills and initiative displayed by the French infantry and its lower command echelons, as long as their standards remained up to par, permitted an infinite variety on the basic themes to fit any imaginable situation. Incessant campaigning and repeated expansions, however, diluted the substance and gave rise to increasingly uneven performances.

Further impairing the effects of the French skirmishers from 1808 onward was the fact that their opponents were beginning to deploy skirmishers of their own, with the results already mentioned earlier. Still, the French continued to maintain an edge mainly because they tended to deploy their skirmishers quicker and in greater numbers than did their opponents.

At the same time, the idea of a standard infantry, capable of all forms of combat, was making progress, particularly in the Prussian army, where the skirmishers, instead of forming separate units, stood in the third rank throughout all the companies in the battalion. In this way, the rank and file was in more or less constant elbow contact with the elites, whose presence set the example for the rest. This arrangement also helped prevent the constant drain of the best men out of the companies, a problem that continuously impaired the effectiveness of the French fusilier companies, especially when the French infantry entered into its period of decline.

For once, however, it appears that Napoleon took a cue from his adversaries. The French had continued to deploy in three ranks until the eve of the Battle of Leipzig, when, on October 13, 1813, the emperor ordered Berthier to issue the following order:

> Include in the army order that as of this day the emperor orders the entire infantry of the army to form up in two ranks instead of three, in that His majesty regards the fire and the bayonets of the third rank useless. When the battalions form up in closed columns of divisions this two rank formation will offer six ranks and three firing lines [the elite companies obviously included in this two company front formation], this is sufficient and has the additional advantage that the battalion frontage will be increased by a third. An additional advantage is that, coming on the eve of a battle, the enemy as yet unaware of this will estimate the army before him to be a third stronger than it actually is.[11]

The language of this order implies that a deployed firing line no longer figured in Napoleon's tactical thinking. Indeed, except for initial deployment or a defensive posture, the *ordre mixte*, so dear to the theorists, had become as much an illusion for Napoleon as platoon fire had become for Frederick after Kolin and Prague. Only veteran units that had escaped the drains of incessant campaigns might still hope to execute any movements at all in line formation. In this respect, the schematics of battle deployments seen so often in Napoleonic literature can be highly misleading.

That Morand, for example, would have been able to produce two battalions capable of advancing in line formation in the action against the great redoubt at Borodino in 1812 is doubtful in the extreme, given the general condition of I Corps. Yet this is precisely what is implied in the schematics showing the deployments for this battle. It is far more likely that these battalions were deployed in a line intended to dissolve into strong skirmishing lines. This is not only a more sensible mode for an attack against breastworks but also a more plausible one under the circumstances. The great depletion of the French battalions at that stage of the Russian campaign made it more practical to entirely dissolve a few battalions for such purposes than to weaken all of them further by detaching the remaining elites from the columns.

The schematics for Macdonald's giant hollow square at Wagram indicate that it was headed by two echelons, each consisting of four battalions deployed in line abreast. One must wonder if the lumbering advance of this behemoth was not largely occasioned by the difficulties encountered in bringing the deployed infantry battalions forward in reasonably good order.

Thus, the line, the mixed order, and the deployment schematics were merely recommendations of how units might be employed to interact and support each other to maximum effect. In practice, it usually happened quite differently and was subject to all sorts of factors, not the least of which was the terrain.

But this flexibility was the very backbone of the new system. It offered the artful commander a far greater range of options than was ever possible in the linear era. Experience and formal training could be helpful, but they were not necessarily essential at the higher levels of command, which called for a different set of skills. Is there a better example than Napoleon himself? But they could also be the undoing of excellent combat commanders who had made enviable reputations for themselves at the lower levels of command. Thus, most of Napoleon's marshals were capable combat commanders, but very few showed any aptitude for holding independent command. On the other hand, some of his best general officers never achieved that rank.

On the whole, however, even though Napoleon's top soldiers were entirely self-made men, those who had a formal background in military education generally came off best. Still, his veteran officers were practical men, seasoned by years of campaigning, who had largely thrown away the old books, even if they were too busy to write new ones. (No new drill manual was produced during Napoleon's reign.)

But this was the very crux of the new system of war. The discussion so far has focused on mechanics, but these new mechanics were extraordinarily important, because the linear system of warfare could not possibly have produced a Napoleon. However, while they became the wheels of the Napoleonic juggernaut, they were neither the engine that drove it nor the column that steered it. And this is what had lulled the opponents of the French republic into a false sense of security. They had seen the wheels and even the parts of the engine and adjudged them good but not overwhelming. During the years from 1801 to 1805, however, Napoleon had assembled all the parts of the engine and tuned it to perfection. What he then unveiled during the Austerlitz campaign in 1805 was good enough to simply roll over the opposition.

Obviously, the new system was not the result of a planned evolution, from theory to practice, but the sum total of a vast amount of experience gained by many men at various levels of command. By the time Napoleon came to the fore, there were entire platoons, even companies, of such men who had survived the hard school of the revolutionary wars. And these men were to be as indispensable to Napoleon as the new system was.

During the days of the linear order, the field army had been a unitary entity, and the great majority of the officers who had commanded its constituents had been reduced to the role of mere mechanics. Their jobs entailed nothing more than seeing to it that the parts of the military machine entrusted to their care were well greased and functioned smoothly. Their powers of decision on the battlefield had been next to nil. The linear system had reduced them to simple conduits for the transmission of orders from above. With the exception of the hussars, even a cavalry officer had to reach general rank before he was ever called upon to make an independent decision. It was not that these men lacked the intelligence or capacity to make decisions. Rather, the demands of the system had bred it out of them. Thus, it was not merely the rank and file that had been reduced to an unthinking automaton. The officers had been subjected to the same influences.

As a result, when the junior officers were confronted with what were to them unorthodox combat forms, they tended to find themselves either unsure about what to do or hesitant to act without orders. At the same time, the senior officers, mostly hide-bound traditionalists, realized too late that their excessive reliance upon the old methods had been misplaced. This, of course, communicated itself at once to the rank and file, causing them to lose confidence in their officers.

Thus, there had been moments even at Jena and Auerstaedt, where the Prussian firing lines had advanced briskly, brushing the skirmishers aside, as expected, as they confronted the French masses and inflicted heavy casualties, only to find themselves unsupported at the critical moment. This was despite the fact that their commanders had sent virtually all their light troops (the fusilier battalions) off on all sorts of detached assignments, mainly because the commanders had either failed to understand their proper use or resented their presence because they had been too long removed from the authority of the line officers. These were the moments when the linear system, deprived of the services of the light troops that should have been available on the firing line, had failed to provide the means to exploit a local success, even while the new order found the means to redress the setback.

The monumental failure of the Prussian army at Jena and Auerstaedt in 1806 continues to serve as the textbook example of the confrontation between the old and the new. But the failure was due far less to a disparity between tactical systems than it was to the inability of its commanders to realistically foresee the implications of the new tactical system to their fullest extent. And the frantic, last-minute attempts to bring the Prussian army closer to the new system could not penetrate the heads of generals who had grown old in the service, deeply immersed in the ruts of the past.

.   .   .

In the new system of war, each battalion, each brigade—every tactical unit—was an articulated fighting entity that could change its shape and the direction of its attack virtually at will. Most importantly, these constituent units of the new order were in the hands of tactically self-reliant officers who knew how to make use of this flexibility and how to use their own judgment in adapting themselves to whatever a situation demanded. It is impossible to overemphasize this point. Here, the tools and the craft had gone into the shaping of each other. These men were the motor that drove the wheels of the new tactical system. Collectively, they embodied a potential that merely awaited a Napoleon to maximize it.

This, then, brings up Napoleon and the role he was destined to play. Although generations of historians have analyzed his campaigns, they have come up with little more than what others had already done before him. Nor does a classification of his battles into envelopments, breakthroughs, or whatever offer anything new or revolutionary. Instead, one might look at the *way* in which he did what others had already done before. And here, the matter of style—not of what but of how one does something—so often invoked in Prussian military thinking, rises to the fore at once.

That Napoleon was an artillery officer is an accident of history, but the style of warfare he developed from this background certainly is not. He did very little to advance tactics or the grammar of war except to occasionally alter a detail here or there. He left these things to his lieutenants, who were already experienced in such matters. Yet he changed the face of war despite the fact that he had very few tactical skills.

Trained in the artillery sciences, he had a keen grasp of the principles of physics and the concepts of energy and force. No one understood better than he the relationships of mass, time, and distance that went into the creation of energy. This much emerges clearly from his methods of conducting a campaign or a battle.

The French army, as it emerged from the crucibles of the revolutionary wars, with its modular structure in the hands of capable and experienced soldiers, was perfectly suited to the talents of Napoleon. Large armies broken into units of manageable proportions could be moved quickly along separate roads and swiftly concentrated with forced marches to accommodate the requirements of distance, time, and mass, creating his own brand of energetic warfare. But this concept of force and energy did not end with a rapid concentration on the battlefield.

Napoleon might arrive with a set of ideas in mind, but generally a concrete plan would take shape only after he saw what was developing on the field itself, what his probing attacks revealed, or what mistakes the enemy was making or had already made. Once his plan developed, Napoleon's understanding of the concepts of energy and force would erupt again. Massive batteries, massive infantry columns, and, on occasion, massive cavalry columns would hurl cannonballs, both real and figurative. Just as a cannonball could breach a wall by the concentration of great energy and force onto a small area, so did Napoleon emulate its effects by managing to create rapid concentrations of force at his chosen point of attack, achieving local superiority even if he did not enjoy the overall advantage in numbers. At his best, Napoleon would handle his reserves like an enterprising captain might handle a horse battery during moments of crisis and decision. Of course, things might occasionally not work out as planned. Enveloping forces might be delayed or go astray. Things up front might not go as expected. But as long as Napoleon held the wind gauge, the very momentum of the new system and the energy he breathed into it would ride roughshod over obstacles.

But this was only one side of Napoleon: the general. There was also Napoleon the leader of men, who had an excellent, seat-of-the-pants understanding of troop psychology, even if neither the term nor the discipline had yet come into being. He could step down into the rank and file and move freely among the common soldiers, making eye contact and drawing them into conversations, which would take on a continued life as they were repeated around the campfires. After he became emperor, he deliberately eschewed the trappings of rank. It may hardly be claimed that this affectation originated with him, but it worked; it endeared le petit tondu all the more to his soldiers. Collectively, this was all part of the stuff that had, time and again, made it possible for him to ask more of the troops than could be expected—and get it.

There can be little doubt that the new system of war would have eventually forced the European monarchies into a reappraisal of the old order. But the fact that this came about in such precipitate fashion was due entirely to Napoleon, the master gunner, and the concepts of force and energy he applied to this new system.

Yet, for all this, these new ways of war exercised little control over the ultimate outcome of the 1812 campaign, even though the Russians probably possessed fewer skills than any of Napoleon's other adversaries. Instead, it was Napoleon's own failure to foresee the difficulties the Russian theater of operations might offer and to adapt his success formula to these conditions that caused the great captain to stumble. Thus, the failure of logistics, which stood at the root of the greater failure, may not be entirely placed at the feet of the clumsy supply services, and much less may it be blamed on the winter.

NOTES

1. Schwarz, Herbert. *Gefechtsformen der Infanterie in Europa durch 800 Jahre.* 2nd ed. Munich, 1977. 2 vols.
2. Berenhorst, von. *Betrachtungen ueber die Kriegskunst.* I, 205. *Aphorismen.* Leipzig, 1805.
3. Delbrueck, Hans. *History of the Art of War.* I, 61. Westport, 1975.
4. Lynn, John A. *The Bayonets of the Republic.* Urbana and Chicago, 1984.
5. Elting, John R. *Swords around a Throne.* New York, 1988.
6. English, John A. *On Infantry.* New York, 1981.
7. Vagts, Alfred. *A History of Militarism.* New York, 1959.
8. Angeli, Moritz von. *Erzherzog Karl als Feldherr und Heeresorganisator.* Vienna and Leipzig, 1896–1898. 5 vols.
9. Bleckwenn, Hans. *Brandenburg-Preussens Heer 1640–1807.* Osnabrueck, 1978.
10. Quoted in Chandler, D. G. *The Campaigns of Napoleon.* New York, 1966.
11. Quoted in Friederich, R. *Geschichte des Herbstfeldzuges 1813.* II, 352. Berlin, 1904. 3 vols.

THE ANATOMY OF COLUMN TACTICS

The column first appeared in the firing lines during the last decade of the eighteenth century. From that time until well past the Napoleonic era, its presence on the battlefield was so ubiquitous that a general knowledge of its structure and of how it might actually operate in combat is essential to an understanding of the military events of those times. In order to give the reader a better "feel" of what the columns were all about, they are rendered here in terms of the men who gave them shape and substance, rather than as the blocks and diagrams that are generally found in descriptions of the various tactical evolutions.

Thus, the illustrations accompanying this analysis have been drawn to scale and reflect an accurate head count, according to the tables of organization, as it existed in terms of the 1808 reorganization of the French infantry and as it cast itself down in the 1812 regulations of the Prussian army. The placement of the charges, that is, the officers and noncoms, is in accordance with the 1791 regulations (the last published in France before the onset of the revolutionary and Napoleonic wars) which continued to remain in force, especially in matters relating to such details. Indeed, the only drill manual ever published during the Napoleonic era was the one produced for the Westphalian army; while reflective of prevailing doctrine, the manual was still strongly based on the old 1791 regulations.

During the early stages of column tactics, it was customary to form the "column divisions." That is, the 8 companies of the battalion (each with about 90 men in 30 files) were formed up in the following order:

2nd company	1st company
4th company	3rd company
6th company	5th company
8th company	7th company

Two companies constituted a division, and the name stuck, even after the companies became as large as the erstwhile divisions. Hence, the so-called division column had a 2-company front and later a 2-platoon or 2-section front. In this "column of divisions," the first company, standing on the right flank, constituted the stationary pivot, or point of dress. When the grenadier company, which might be tacked onto the column anywhere, was joined by the voltigeur company, the two could be added to the battalion column in any imaginable fashion, to the front, sides, or rear.

It is in the matter of the stationary point, or pivot, in which the division column differed from the so-called assault column. When a battalion ranked in a column of divisions deployed into the line formation, all the rearward companies moved to the left and entered the line to the left of the stationary 1st company. Thus, they ended up in their ordinal sequence, from the 1st company on the right flank to the 8th on the left.

The "assault column"—which already appears as the *colonne centrale*" (in Marechal de camp Dampierre's narrative) during the very first victory of republican arms at Jemappes (November 6, 1792)—had a difficult time establishing itself, despite the fact that it was far more practical for deployment into line. As its name implies, it was formed on the center in the following scheme:

5th company	4th company
6th company	3rd company
7th company	2nd company
8th company	1st company

With this arrangement, the distance the rearmost elements had to travel for a deployment into line was just about halved. That is, the 5th and 4th companies were now the pivot, or stationary element, with the rear elements attaching themselves to the right and left.

The reorganization of 1808, which saw the reduction of the number of companies on the one hand and the increased size of the remaining companies on the other, hardly affected the appearance of the assault column. That is, setting aside for the moment the grenadier and voltigeur companies, the remaining eight fusilier companies had been reduced to four, but each now consisted of two platoons, each nearly the size of the old companies. The new assault column had the following internal structure:

1/fusilier 4	Color	2/fusilier 3
2/fusilier 4	section	1/fusilier 3
1/fusilier 5		2/fusilier 2
2/fusilier 5		1/fusilier 2
1/voltigeur 6		2/grenadier 1
2/voltigeur 6		1/grenadier 1

In this arrangement, shown in **Figure 1**, each platoon or half-company had 2 corporals and 73 fusiliers (grenadiers or voltigeurs) in the ranks, resulting in 25 files, or a 25-man front. All other charges either stood on the flanks or formed the so-called closing, that is, the fourth rank. The battalion commander and the adjutant were the only mounted officers in the infantry battalion. Thus, the platoon front

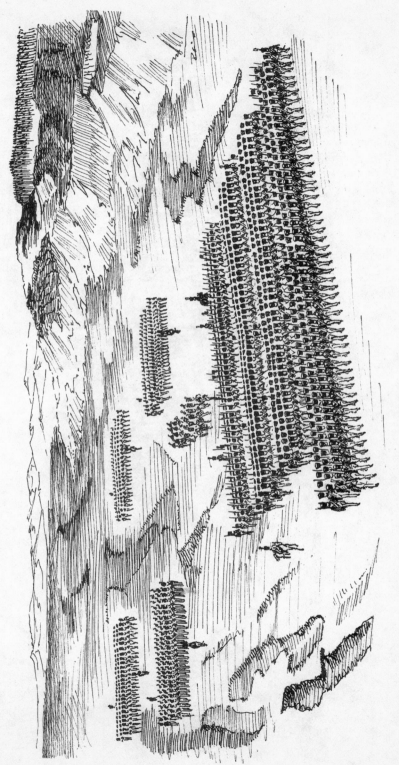

Figure 1

Figure 2

was 25 files and the company's was about 54 files, counting the officers and noncoms on the flanks.

The small group behind the center consisted of the drummers and, if present, the band. Figure 1 also illustrates the special case of the color section being present. After 1808, there was only one color per regiment, regardless of the number of battalions in the regiment. This section was inserted in front, between the platoons of the 3rd and 4th fusilier companies, so that the flanks of these leading formations extended somewhat beyond those of the rearward formations. The color sections generally included the eagle bearer, 2 eagle guards, and the 6 farrier corporals of the battalion (one from each company).

The Prussian Assault Column

The outward appearance of the Prussian column, shown in open order in **Figure 2**, hardly differed from that of the French column. However, the Prussian rearward echelons did not close behind the color section, so the two half-battalions appear quite distinctly.

In the Prussian front, the platoons were slightly larger, with 84 musketeers forming 28 files. However, with the exception of a single noncom on the outer flank of their respective plátoons, all the other officers and noncoms formed the 4th (closing) rank. In Figure 1, showing the French column in closed order, these can be seen only at the rear of the column, but in the open order in Figure 2 they are clearly visible.

There were three mounted officers in the Prussian battalion: the battalion commander, the adjutant, and the "Schuetzen Captain," whose mount was led behind the battalion until the skirmishers were called out. And this brings up the fundamental difference between the French and Prussian columns: While the French kept their elites in separate companies, which constantly drained the fusilier companies of their best men, the Prussians had their elites form the third rank of their line companies (a system that has often been misunderstood by critics).

In either system, the skirmishers always had to be appropriately deployed before they could be used, so there were no inherent disadvantages in one system or the other. The clear advantage of the Prussian system, however, was that the companies were not deprived of their best men—veterans and men of superior ability. This was advantageous not only because the posture of the elite would rub off on the rest of the company in the day-to-day grind of the service but also because the company, if detached for whatever reason, would continue to benefit from having these men still in the ranks.

When the bugle called upon the skirmishers to form up, the third ranks would simply make a right- and left-face, respectively, and file out to the flanks. There, they formed up, looking no different from the French column, as may be readily seen in *Figure 3*. The Schuetzen Captain has mounted his horse, and the battalion, its companies now of only two ranks, have formed in closed order.

Figure 4 illustrates the gradual deployment of the skirmishers in front of the Prussian column, with their supporting sections and platoons. At this stage, the French looked no different, but they were generally more aggressive in deploying their skirmishers in full strength at a faster rate.

The Russians generally deployed their jaeger platoon at the right front of the column in the 1st company position. However, even at full strength, the Russian skirmishers had no more than about a quarter of the strength of their opposite numbers in the French or Prussian battalions.

The trend toward a standard infantry, skilled at all forms of combat, had been emerging since 1808, when the French light infantry regiments became such in name only. Throughout the Napoleonic era, the French would occasionally dissolve entire battalions into open order, whenever the tactical situation called for it.

Finally, at Gross Goerschen (Luetzen), when the Prussians unexpectedly ran into Ney, they did not bother calling out the skirmishers but simply sent the leading companies of the columns forward.

A new tactical element came near the close of the Napoelonic era with the institution of the column with a 2-division front. It has generally been assumed that this arrangement came into use only during the postwar era, but the general order issued by Napoleon on the eve of the Battle of Leipzig contradicts this. According to the order, the battalion deployed in the following manner:

2/fusilier 4	1/fusilier 4	2/fusilier 3	1/fusilier 3
2/fusilier 5	1/fusilier 5	2/fusilier 2	1/fusilier 2
2/voltigeur 6	1/voltigeur 6	2/grenadier 1	1/grenadier 1

This increased the fire front without entirely yielding the maneuverability of the column or taking on the difficulties of moving a line. At the same time, Napoleon ordered the companies to deploy in two instead of three ranks, which is how he arrived at the increased frontage with three firing lines.

All the illustrations presented here assume that the battalions were at their full organizational or planned strength. In practice, however, the battalions rarely appeared in the field with their complements up to par. From the day the troops left their quarters, operational noncombat losses would occur, due to illness, fatigue, or

Figure 3

Figure 4

accidents. The number of such losses varied in direct proportion to the difficulties of the march, the distances covered in the daily stages, and the weather. Consequently, the strength of the battalion columns diminished even before they came under enemy fire on a day of combat. Generally, the columns were considered fully functional as long as they did not fall much below 60 percent of full strength. The Russians in 1813 continued with battalions numbering no more than 250 men. Once units reached such levels of depletion, amalgamation, that is, joining two or more battalions together, was the answer.

As the illustrations clearly indicate, a shortage of 100 or 200 men in a battalion would hardly be noticeable to an observer standing at ground level. That is, it would require careful study for an uneducated observer to notice that a few files were missing in the front and that the third ranks of the individual companies were rather thin. That this is true is supported by the fact that unskilled observers, throughout history, have shown a marked tendency to overestimate what they were seeing. So much, then, for the all-important "impressions of war," the psychological factor.

This discussion has presented a broad outline of the anatomy of the column and its function at the elementary tactical level. Although the exact numbers and details might have varied from one military establishment to the next, these specifics did not matter a great deal in the practical aspects of tactics. The differences between a 700-man and a 900-man battalion pertained mainly to how long a battalion might retain its operational effectiveness on campaign before it reached critical mass, that is, before its functions in combat became seriously impaired.

The French and Prussian columns were selected for comparison primarily because the Prussian system, emerging from the reforms after the debacle of 1806, is generally regarded as the best distillation of the Napoleonic experience, just as the Prussian 1812 manual has been pronounced the best to emerge from the Napoleonic wars.

8. Logistics

The wisdom of the observation that an army marches on its stomach is timeless. A corollary of this axiom is the symbiotic relationship that exists between the soldier's stomach and his readiness to respond to discipline. Even though this link between logistics—the science of providing the soldier with his needs—and discipline is self-evident, it may be argued that it was especially close in the French revolutionary armies and the Napoleonic military machine that sprang from them. Indeed, they were so closely interwoven that it is hardly possible to discuss one without the other.

Much has been made of how the armies of the old order had been tied to their magazines, and how the Napoleonic armies, released from these umbilical cords, were free to course across the countryside at will. And certainly, this appears confirmed by a string of successes which, beginning with the campaigns of Pichegru and Jourdan in 1794, had also carried Napoleon from one victory to the next with a freedom of movement and speed that prevented his opponents from regaining their feet for a second effort.

It must, however, be kept in mind that these successes came during a military interregnum in which the old was put to the test by the new and found wanting. Thus, the relative ineptitude of Napoleon's opponents and the technical shortcomings of their military establishments played a far greater role in his early victory marches than did new ideas about logistics. And even though logistics certainly played their part, the overall successes of his campaigns also gave rise to a dangerously false sense of security in the French commissariat that would eventually have dire consequences. Of course, Napoleon's own style of warfare, which generally banked on muddling through somehow on the sheer momentum of his operations, contributed to this as well.

It has been noted from time to time that Napoleon, coming from the artillery, often exhibited a disregard for the infantry's capacities, frequently demanding marches that would drive it to the limits and, occasionally, beyond. As long as his armies contained large numbers of veterans, their conditioning, coupled with Napoleon's drive, could carry the rest along. But when the conscripts began to outnumber the veterans by a large margin and when the momentum stabbed into a vacuum, Napoleon's manner of driving the troops turned back on him. This, in a nutshell, was to be the story of 1812. (In 1813, as well, his young conscripts would fill the hospitals by the tens of thousands. Both campaigns produced some of the highest operational noncombat losses on record.)

However, even if all was glitter and glory on the surface of Napoleon's unchecked march during the years of his ascendancy, the winter of 1806–1807 flashed the first warning—and the danger came with the lack of adequate logistics. It was then and there when Napoleon realized that if logistical troubles ever became linked to operational problems at the same time, things could get serious, even for him.

As it was, these early campaigns, in which everyone managed to get by one way or another—with copious use of field expedients and a lot of help from the enemy—had a debilitating and eventually disastrous effect upon the generals, the army administration, and the commissariat. Even as Napoleon finally strove to create an efficiently functioning system of army trains, the administration and commissariat had become lulled into a false sense of security. The experiences gained in the agriculturally rich Dutch Lowlands and the German provinces had accustomed them to the idea that the need to survive would force the troops to see to their own necessities and that, come what may, their ingenuity would enable them to succeed. It had always worked before, and the moments of crisis, if and when they arose, had always passed as quickly as they had come. A campaign had yet to fail because the army ran short of supplies. All this gave rise to a *laissez-faire* attitude that would eventually result in outright incompetence, further exacerbated by the ever-present corruption.

It was to be an inept supply administration, marching to the sound of a different drummer and totally lacking an orderly system of distribution (even when supplies were available) that became a direct and totally un-necessary cause of the loss of thousands upon thousands of troops during the

Russian campaign and a major contributory cause of the dissolution of the Grand Army. This dissolution was already in an advanced stage even before the army had fought any major actions.

It remains to be seen, however, how these shortcomings at the top manifested themselves at the bottom, in the rank and file of the army.

The fact that the soldier constantly had to see to his own needs consistently weakened the bonds of an already lax discipline both in the French republican and Imperial armies. The revolutionary battle cry of "liberty, equality, and fraternity" had already become deeply etched into the consciousness of the old republican soldiers, who became the veteran cadre of the new Imperial Army. They were bound to transmit much of this and more to new generations of conscripts, who, themselves, came from a population that had not yet forgotten these tenets.

Not even a staunch disciplinarian like Davout, one of Napoleon's most capable marshals, ever succeeded in eradicating these attitudes from his own commands. They had become part of the customs and traditions, and a particularly beloved part at that. And, as modern soldiers still learn during their indoctrination, customs and traditions have greater staying power than regulations. A regulation may be amended or abolished with the stroke of a pen, but customs and traditions have a way of perpetuating themselves, assuming a life of their own.

Indeed, the times when it was thought that the true "republican spirit" was a superior substitute for discipline and training were not all that distant in the past. One minister of war, Bouchotte, thought to see the real enemies of the revolution among the aristocrats of the old officer corps in particular and all officers in general. He deemed it necessary to "protect" the young republicans against their influence and authority!

His was not by any means a lone voice. Platoons of watchdogs, *commissaires* (the forerunners of the infamous Soviet Kommissars of our own time), were out in the army, looking over the shoulders of every officer. It was often a case of damned if you do and damned if you don't for the commissioned defenders of the republic. At times, they were forced to walk a tightrope, with the guillotine beckoning from all sides. On the one hand, extreme punishment was threatened if an officer exerted too much discipline upon his charges, and, on the other, a directory gone wild also saw treason behind every military failure at the front.

Eventually, Carnot's reforms made inroads into the worst of this nonsense, although he did this at considerable risk to his own person. At least, he began to replace some of the worst republicanisms, often bordering on sheer lunacy, with the concepts of duty, discipline, and competence. But he could only begin what Napoleon was still trying to finish in the Army of England when it massed in the Channel encampments. However, even after the worst excesses were curbed and were replaced with sensible laws, the relationships between the common folk and the established authorities, as well as those between the common soldier and his officers, would never again be quite the same.

Of even greater and more lasting effect, because they fell right into line with the necessities and realities of the incessant wars fought by republican France, were the resolutions by the Committee of Public Welfare with regard to the upkeep of the army. Because the government was perpetually out of money, it was decreed that the war should support the war. That is, the republican armies were ordered to see to their own upkeep in the occupied enemy territories.

If this idea was a child born of necessity, then typically republican zeal again went far beyond reason with its exhortations, which branded any moderation exercised in this respect to be not merely disobedience but downright treason, endangering ultimate victory. The enemies of the revolution were to be punished not merely militarily but economically as well. This heralded a return to practices that bore more than passing resemblance to the lawless *soldateska* of the Thirty Years' War. It was here where the making of Morvan's[1] *miles gloriosus* began. Typically, much of this kind of "provisioning" was conducted in ad hoc fashion, every man for himself, and continued even after more organized forms of "contributions" were exercised from the top. Every general officer and the vast majority of staff officers, not to mention tens of thousands of veterans from the ranks, had participated in this evolution and had carried its memory over into the Army of England and the Grand Army of 1805. A custom had become tradition, and the borderline between foraging and looting had become all but indistinct.

This, then, represented the dark side of the relationship between logistics and discipline in the French armies of the Napoleonic era. And nothing that radiated from this dark side was good. It would be an injustice to say that every French soldier gave himself over freely to these practices, but the restraints controlling the "run of the herd" had become seriously weakened. Eventually, these ad hoc "requisitioning" habits were officially discouraged, because the troops had fallen into the even worse habit of summarily absenting themselves from their formations whenever nothing was to be found immediately at hand.

Thus, as early as 1805, when Davout sought Napoleon's permission to resort to execution by firing squads in an attempt to curb the worst offenses, the object of his ire was not so much the looting as it was the fact that an astonishing number of his troops had gone off on unauthorized "foraging" expeditions. A similar request made by him in 1812 was unenforceable because, as Morvan asserts, it would have required the shooting of a quarter of the army. Thus, these conditions were regretted and were even militated against on occasion, but in the end they were accepted as being unavoidable. Indeed, the Prussians were fond of saying that Napoleon could hardly insist that his men should not loot when he was himself a thief on the grandest scale imaginable.

It would, of course, be incorrect to take Morvan's portrait of the dark side as being representative of the sum total of the imperial soldier. At the same time, however, his discussion of these matters must not be dismissed as the contention of a single individual. Rather, he was one of the few who were willing to speak of things which the chroniclers of Napoleon's glories preferred to sweep under the rug or which they merely touched upon in passing. These were, after all, characteristics that cast their shadows across the entire body of Continental literature produced outside France on the subject of the Napoleonic era, though they could find no echo in the romances of those subscribing to the Napoleonic legend.

It is an inescapable truth that from the time the French armies crossed the frontiers of France into neighboring countries, they began to incur debits in the name of foraging, requisitioning, and contribution. Payment for these would be extracted at every step along the way of the long retreat that began in Moscow during October 1812 and ended in Paris in March 1814.

SUPPLY SYSTEMS

The change from the old linear order to the new system of war was not so much a replacement of the old by the new as it was a shift in emphasis, in which the old never lost its value. Similarly, it was learned that while the new system of foraging worked well in the short run, it became fraught with danger in the long unless it was combined with the old magazine system. Unfortunately for Napoleon's armies, the tactical and operational solutions regarding how to employ the new masses effectively in the field came faster than those regarding how to keep them well fed.

Napoleon himself wasted little time in recognizing the problem. But whereas his genius was forever focused on the battlefield, his style of personally running everything could not possibly oversee the correct execution of his ideas in what might be termed the fringe areas of his immediate concerns. The supply services especially—which were not an object of his constant scrutiny—would have required a man of initiative and ability at

the helm. But none such was available. Thus, despite Napoleon's considerable efforts, the French supply services never even remotely approached
the standards of the army's combat forces.

Of course, modern analysts are of the opinion that, by modern standards,
all such efforts were actually doomed from the start. The scope of Napoleon's
operations and the magnitude of his forces had raced ahead of their time
and had thus become an anachronism. To keep forces of several hundred
thousand men, hundreds of miles distant from their bases, adequately supplied was patently impossible until the advent of the telegraph and railroads.

As matters stood, neither horse-drawn transport nor the roads over which
such transport was to travel were up to the task—unless water transport
could lend extensive support. In Continental Europe, however, most rivers
run on a north-south axis, while almost all of Napoleon's operations ran
east-west. Thus, the Danube, for example, was able to render excellent and
timely service during Napoleon's 1809 campaign, but that was the exception
rather than the rule. The Baltic might have furnished access to the estuaries
of all the rivers running south to north, but even coastal traffic was running
the gauntlet under the guns of the British navy.

The idea of letting armies support themselves off the land was born as much
of necessity as of expediency. It has been often said that this was possible
only with the new kind of politically reliable republican soldier the French
revolution had wrought. But this is merely a half-truth and, as such, beguiling
for the casual observer.

The armies of the old order always included large numbers of "professional
volunteers" who would habitually drift from one engagement to the next.
The rate of their drifting was governed not so much by the duration of their
enlistment contracts as by the opportunity to terminate these unilaterally.
That is, given half a chance, they would go "over the hill" just as soon as
they collected and spent their hand money. They would then move on to
another army and start the process all over again. In eighteenth-century
Europe, with its numerous military establishments, such practices became
an industry in their own right.

This was a cancer that affected all the armies of eighteenth-century
Europe, and Strachan[2] offers some illuminating statistics that are not generally found together in one place. He notes that one out of every four
soldiers deserted from the French army during the Wars of the Spanish
Succession and 70,000 more during the Seven Years' War. At the same
time, the Russians lost 80,000 men in the same fashion and the Austrians
62,000. Of course, the beckoning enlistment bonuses weren't the only in-

ducement. An oncoming war or battle, bad officers or noncoms, bad food, bad anything might cause a man to run. And the proximity of protective mountains, forests, or borders always offered a strong inducement. At the same time, it must be understood that desertion was rampant mainly and particularly among the international professionals, who had already become footloose. If an indigenous peasant-soldier engaged in desertion, he would be cut off from home and family because his action would soon become known in his native canton or district.

Given such circumstances, letting men go off on foraging expeditions would have amounted to an open invitation to run, even for many who ordinarily would not have dared to even think about it. To prevent this from happening, once the army went into the field, it was kept in formation. Thus, the eighteenth-century soldier marched, camped, ate, slept, fought, and occasionally died in formation. It was an effective way of keeping track of everybody. And this meant that the army had to be provisioned from magazines.

Of course, in the eighteenth century the army's supplies were obtained as much through foraging and requisitioning as they were through purchase. That's how many of the forward magazines were stocked. However, whether by requisition or free purchase, such matters were generally handled through the intermediary offices of agents and contractors, not in the ad hoc, free-for-all fashion that became the custom of the French armies during the revolution.

Thus, the full truth about the revolutionary armies requires noting that even though they might have been politically reliable, they were themselves anything but free from desertion. Quite the contrary. Even the shortfall between the levies and the number who actually reported to the colors set new heights. However, unlike the carefully trained soldier of the old order, these raw new soldiers had become just about the cheapest commodity for war. The mass levies had seen to that. Thus, it might be added that it was not simply the high-toned phrase of "political reliability" that afforded the republican soldier greater freedom of movement. As ever, the realities were more complex than that.

Still, even with the new system, it was found that unless the divisions marched along separate roads and at a reasonably fast pace, foraging alone was no longer practicable. As soon as the presence of the enemy forced the concentration of masses and as soon as the rate of advance slowed, the immediate countryside was quickly stripped bare and the foragers were forced to course ever further afield in search of provender.

In this respect, the population density and the extent to which the country was cultivated also played an important role. A generally accepted rule was that a density of about ninety inhabitants to the square mile was necessary to support a large army passing through. Still, an army's size remained limited by its rate of movement. If it moved too slowly or remained in place too long, the countryside would soon be stripped bare. The proximity of large towns and cities was, of course, helpful, since such population centers already had mechanisms for the gathering of food in place. But it was soon learned that even in well-populated areas it was a good idea to send about 8 days' worth of rations after the army as soon as it departed. Even the revolutionary armies, as soon as they ventured far afield, were forced to establish forward magazines.

How massive the task of supplying an army in the field was is illustrated by the following example: To make an army of about 250,000 men with 100,000 horses entirely self-sufficient would require about 4000 wagonloads of supplies per day. This daily wagon requirement would increase with each day's march as the army distanced itself from its magazines, even as the draft animals necessary to haul these supplies would themselves consume more and more of what was being brought forward. Indeed, the feed and fodder to keep the 100,000 horses moving would amount to about twenty (!!) times the weight of the flour for the bread rations of the 250,000 men.

This points out the central concern in the movement of large armies reliant on horse-drawn transport. Even in our own time, the weight of the fuel necessary to keep the supply columns moving remains a primary factor of logistics. In the nineteenth century, the term "horsepower" was still taken quite literally, and acquiring the necessary feed and fodder for the animals was even more difficult than feeding the troops. It was next to impossible to haul sufficient quantities of green fodder, hay, straw, and oats. As a result, the cavalry, artillery, and trains always relied heavily on the resources of the country through which they passed. And this, then, illuminates another problem.

By its very nature, the cavalry was in a much better position to course far afield in search of feed and fodder. Not so the artillery. Road-bound, it was heavily dependent upon whatever was within ready reach. However, by the time the supply trains came up in the wake of the army, the roadside would be stripped and every nearby barn emptied. Thus, if the cavalry began to suffer shortages, the artillery was already worse off and the trains were in dire straits. They would be the first to suffer, and this would hit the infantry hardest. As a result, the combat elements were always eager to lay their hands on whatever transport they could find for their own, exclusive use. In 1805, they even commandeered the wagons of the commissariat and prevented them from returning to fetch new loads.

Under Napoleon, there never existed a supply system as we know it today, fixed by regulations and uniform general orders binding throughout the army. Instead, in the course of numerous campaigns, a general method had developed that took the place of an orderly system. It varied from one place to the next and could never divest itself of an ad hoc character that altered with time and circumstances. From time to time, the commanding generals would issue supply directives, but it was usually left to the lower echelons to fend for themselves.

When planning his operations, Napoleon generally paid close attention to matters involving time and distance. But when it came to logistics, he frequently tended to skate over the details, trusting in his ability to drive the infantry hard. And he got away with it as long as the troops held up. At other times, he would keep his intentions secret and would issue his orders so late that the commissariat couldn't respond in time even when conditions were favorable. Still, he expected that his orders would be carried out, or, at least, he pretended that they would be. This, in turn, undermined the confidence his subordinate commanders had in his logistic measures.

The campaign of 1805, conducted with the best army Napoleon ever commanded, culminated in the grand victory at Austerlitz. But even as the "Sun of Austerlitz" beamed brightly, its glare tended to wash away the shadows cast by what was to be a dress rehearsal for things to come. Referring to October 6, 1805, Fezensac wrote in his *Souvenirs Militaires*:[3] "Thus the first day of bivouac was also the first day on which looting was done." On the 16th, before Ulm, not a picket, not a sentry remained at his post. In the streaming rain, the men simply sought shelter and many remained there. Life behind the lines and beyond supervision was thought to be more comfortable by an astonishing number of men. On October 11, Davout had requested permission to place a few of these *marodeurs* in front of a firing squad, to make an example of them.

Napoleon, then as later, was quite aware of these disorders. However, despite the occasional attempt to raise the standards of discipline, he considered them to be embedded in the army's modus operandi and preferred to regard them as occasional lapses and an inevitable by-product of war. Indeed, war has often been regarded as the great spoiler of armies, then this certainly held true for those of Napoleon.

THE ORGANIZATION OF THE ARMY TRAINS

During the Austrian war of 1805 the movement of supplies for the army had been in the hands of a civilian contractor, the Breidt Company. That is to say, this company had been contracted to furnish the draft teams and drivers necessary to haul the wagons that were to be supplied by the depots. These wagons, however, ended up being largely nonexistent. As a result, even though it appears that Breidt adhered to its part of the bargain, only 163 wagons were available, which were formed into six brigades instead of the thirty originally planned. As a result, about 1000 wagons had to be requisitioned from the farms in the Alsace. This took time, and November came around before the first wagonloads reached the army.

Under these conditions, the order that each corps was to carry four rations of bread and another four of rusk (zwieback) could not be carried out. Thus, as soon as the troops crossed the Rhine, foraging began in earnest, even while the army was still in friendly territory. The first discordant notes in foreign relations were already being struck even as the Grand Army began its triumphal march. When Marmont, in charge of II Corps, complained about the situation, the emperor replied on October 11: "In all of his reports, General Marmont speaks to me only of his supply difficulties. I repeat for him: In the expeditionary and invasion war the emperor wages, there are no magazines and it is up to the commanding generals to obtain their provender from the territories through which they pass."[4]

In the further course of the Ulm-Austerlitz campaign, there followed alternating periods of abundance and privation. As was to be expected, without a guiding hand, more was wasted than was actually used during periods of plenty. That wastage would have gone a long way toward alleviating the lean times.

Even before Napoleon reached Ulm, and despite what he had told Marmont, it was abundantly clear to him that an army of 200,000 men, even in the best of circumstances, could not maintain a hand-to-mouth existence for any length of time. Thus, on October 24, 1805, he wrote to the commissary general of the army: "Until now we have marched without magazines. Circumstances have forced us to do so. Here, the season was extraordinarily advantageous to us; however, although we are continuously victorious and found potatoes on the fields, we constantly suffered from great want. During a season when no produce is to be found on the fields or if we were to sustain but a few reverses, the lack of magazines would have the direst consequences."[5]

In the wake of the experiences of 1805, the emperor was more circumspect when he set out to campaign against the Prussians in 1806. Apart from having 10 days' rations ready on the upper reaches of the Main River, the assembly area of the army, he also accorded two supply wagons to each infantry battalion and cavalry regiment. The remaining wagons of the Breidt Company, about 200 in number, were to remain at the disposition of the army commissariat. The artillery, of course, had no problems in this respect, because it had ample room to off-load its food supplies onto the gun limbers and battery wagons, as long as the horses were well fed and the roads reasonably good.

Between the batteries and the corps artillery parks, the estimated maximum ammunition supply for a day of battle was carried, with a like quantity held in reserve in the grand park of the army. Here, the reserves of infantry ammunition were kept as well, along with all sorts of spare parts for the artillery equipment. In 1806, the grand park numbered 400 vehicles. This number, however, was subject to constant change and grew as the size of the Grand Army increased. In Russia, there were to be more than five times as many.

If the trains were large, then the baggage hauled along by the officers, from the marshals on down, also increased with every campaign, assuming enormous proportions by 1812. On campaign, from one year to the next, every officer, within the limits of his means (and in whatever way he could improve upon these whenever the opportunity presented itself), attempted to carry along as many of the comforts and luxuries of home as the pecking order permitted. In 1806, only one wagon was allowed for the officers' baggage of each infantry battalion and cavalry regiment. However, this limit existed only on paper and not at all in the brigade, division, and corps staffs. As one campaign followed the next, the limits placed upon the officers' baggage were increasingly honored in the breach, and the unofficial baggage train grew from year to year.

On the whole, however, the Grand Army was considerably better off in 1806 than it had been in 1805. Particularly after Jena and Auerstaedt, with the corps separating widely and marching fast in pursuit of the Prussians, all went well until the Vistula was reached. There, things rapidly went from bad to worse.

The French had gone into winter quarters there, but the Russians gave no rest until after the Battle of Eylau had been fought. Then, even though he could claim a victory when the Russians withdrew, Napoleon was himself forced to withdraw behind the Passarge River to go into winter quarters for a second time. Even at the outset of this winter campaign in East Prussia, Napoleon had admitted, "Conditions have forced me to return to the magazine system."[6] And on March 12, 1807, he wrote: "At the moment, the fate of Europe and all further calculations depend upon the question of food. If only I have bread, it will be child's play to beat the Russians."[7]

Operations in eastern Europe had brought about a complete breakdown of the Breidt Company's services. One might reasonably ask how it could not have failed. However, as on other occasions, when Napoleon needed a scapegoat, he did not look too far to find one: "It is not easy to find something worse than the transports of the Breidt Company."[8] Somewhat later, he says of the same company: "It consists of a pack of charlatans who do nothing; better to have none than such people."[9] He might have also looked to the administration and the commissariat, but he was constantly at war with them as well. However, as it was, the experience in eastern Europe spelled the end for civilian contractors. On March 26, 1807, Napoleon issued the orders that would militarize the transport services of the army.

Utilizing the material of the Breidt Company to start with, he ordered the formation of eight train battalions. Each of these was to have 140 wagons, organized into four companies. By 1811, the number of battalions had already risen to thirteen, even as the battalions themselves had been enlarged to include six companies with more than 200 wagons between them. However, even with Napoleon's resources, putting these battalions onto wheels was far more difficult than putting them on paper. Most of the original equipment of the Breidt Company had already followed the army from the Vistula all the way to Spain, and the wear and tear of incessant service continuously caused critical losses of both horses and wagons.

Despite the existence of the train battalions, the new war against Austria in 1809 again posed difficulties. Coming at an inopportune time, no more than 300 wagons were available, and these could load only a 2-day supply of bread for 150,000 men. Campaigning in southern Germany, however, for once had the advantage of having some waterways flowing in the right direction. Thus, the Danube and Lech made it possible to move massive quantities of supplies by water into forward magazines, sufficient to sustain 200,000 men for 2 months. To this end, marine labor companies and sailors, totaling about 2500 men, were hurried into southern Germany to conduct the barge traffic along the Danube.

With the experience of 1807 in mind, Napoleon went to considerable lengths to secure his expedition into Russia in 1812, even though he did not, at any time, envision a rapid penetration all the way to Moscow (notwithstanding some statements to this effect, which are occasionally quoted). To Davout he wrote: "The result of all of my movements will concentrate 400,000 in one place. Then there will be nothing to be expected from the land and one must be self-sufficient."[10]

With this in mind, the Guard and the first four corps, which were made up mostly of French divisions, were each to be served by their own train battalion. In all, these were to carry 34,000 hundredweight (cwt)[11] of flour on 1740 wagons, of which about 1500 were drawn by four-horse teams. Two battalions were equipped with 1200 wagons of special light construction to facilitate their movement over poor roads. These had a further capacity of 12,000 cwt. Two ox-drawn battalions with 600 wagons also had a capacity of 12,000 cwt. Since the corps thus equipped numbered about 240,000 men, this would provide a 25-day supply of bread.

When this supply is added to the 4 days' rations the troops were to carry, there was bread on hand for 29 days. In addition, the draft oxen in the two above-noted battalions were intended to become a fresh meat source once the supplies they hauled were consumed. Unfortunately, these animals, who had never been accustomed to traveling farther than from the barn to a field or pasture, dropped dead long before their wagons ever reached the troops for whom they were intended.

In all, once the army went beyond the Niemen, a total of seventeen French train battalions with about 6000 vehicles were able to carry a 40-day supply. This, and whatever the army could obtain by foraging, was deemed sufficient by Napoleon to cover the operation.

But these were merely the military preparations. As already noted, about 150,000 draft horses were commandeered in Germany, along with about 25,000 civilian horse handlers and an indeterminate number of wagons. Some of the drivers were turned loose after a hundred miles or so, others had escaped long before then, and some, along with all the horses and wagons, were never heard from again.

Backing these mobile supplies were well-stocked magazines in Warsaw, Modlin, Thorn, Bromberg, Marienburg, Elbing, and Danzig. Of these, the one at Thorn contained 100,000 cwt of flour, while the one at Danzig had 300,000 cwt. A bakery installed in Thorn could bake 60,000 bread rations a day, and in Danzig 2 million portions of rusk were kept ready to be sent by water along the Baltic coast and from there up the Niemen.

In the operations area, Vilna was to be the main magazine because it was linked to the Baltic by water. Two large water transports were made ready; they included not only victuals but also bridging and siege equipment. As a result of the dry summer, however, the Vilia, the final link in the chain of waterways, was navigable only as far as Kovno, so there still remained an overland trek of 65 miles.

The emperor had thus gone to considerable lengths to secure adequate supplies for the army. In view of the massive number of horses necessary to keep this juggernaut moving, the opening of the campaign was delayed until June, when it was thought that there would be a sufficiency of grass. However, nothing was to go as planned, because Napoleon had failed to take into account conditions that were totally different from what he had known so far.

To begin with, heavy rains turned what were but poor tracks in the best of times into bottomless mires, which exhausted the horses right from the start. The wet green fodder, unripened grain, and half-rotten straw from the thatch roofs didn't do them any good either. The results were every sort of sickness, ranging from diarrhea to constipation. Worst of all was the bloating caused by the wet green fodder. If the horses were still strong enough, running them hard for a while would fix them up again. However, if they didn't have the strength anymore, their intestines would burst. Bavarian Staff-Auditor Stubenrauch saw hundreds of such horse cadavers, with their burst stomachs and intestines, lying around the bridges of Pilony. And the diaries of other Bavarians resound to the stench of 1600 such cadavers around Vilna. The diarists had good cause to remember, because their bivouacs were within smelling distance of this grisly scene.

As a result, the most advanced magazine in the operations area during the attacking phase was Vilna. Beyond that point, the army was on its own. The farther it marched beyond Vilna, the more illusory became the idea that a shuttle transport system might keep the army supplied in the sparsely populated expanses of Russia. In the wake of forced marches, the organic train battalions quickly lost touch with the formations they were supposed to provision. Even the baggage was generally late in reaching the bivouacs. Not even during the approach marches through Prussia and Poland were the troops properly supplied. In an effort to keep the rearward magazines filled, the commissaires constantly remanded the troops to forward magazines that had not even been established yet.

During the retreat, when the magazines, by then well stocked, might have facilitated the survival of thousands of men, the absence of an orderly and flexible distribution system exacerbated the problems of what was left of the army. An inept administration, on top of everything else, not informed of the oncoming retreat, had also done nothing to collect supplies from the relatively untouched areas to both sides of the Smolensk-Moscow road. Even when the Cossacks moved in on the rearward lines of communication, the administrators did nothing and even allowed the trains, gathered in the area around Smolensk, to fall into their hands. Finally, no attempts were made to make the supplies that were on hand accessible, nor was anything forward to meet the returning army, even after its approach became known.

Unfortunately, the bulk of the troops passing through were stragglers; they had no officers to duly execute the *bon en regle* that was demanded against the issue of supplies. Thus, the officials in charge of the magazines stubbornly stuck to regulations despite the sight of men dying in the streets. The blame for this idiotic behavior, however, cannot simply be laid at the feet of the magazine administrators. The situation stemmed from the abysmal lapse on the part of the French high command and from its total failure to exert a strong hand. It was business as usual: "Every man for himself."

This does not, by any means, exonerate the hordes of marauders who had absented themselves from their units and were now collecting along the line of retreat. But it did result in the loss of additional thousands of men who might have again become soldiers at some time in the future, when they would be sorely needed. The greatest irony of all was that the supplies the commissariat denied to its own men either were destroyed or ended up in the hands of the Russians, who inherited 4 million rations in Vilna alone!

A discussion of the supply services would not be complete without making mention of the pervasive corruption at the highest levels of the administration. This was not an exclusively French problem, but it was here where both the best and the worst existed side by side. Napoleon's own correspondence is shot through with complaints, running over the entire course of his reign.

Nor would it be correct to assume that corruption was a condition merely characteristic of the Napoleonic era. Ever since ancient Rome, the upkeep of the armed forces represented the largest single line item of the budget. This put large amounts of cash into circulation, which attracts dishonesty as honey attracts bears. The Roman emperors had already complained about this. In many places, collecting taxes, carrying them to central collecting points, and disbursing them to their designated purposes was like attempting to carry water in a sieve.

Not even our own nation has been immune to this. During the American Civil War, sharp Yankee traders considered fleecing the government to be a legitimate business pursuit. Even though the methods might vary, from "Five Percent Myers" of World War II infamy to the more recent scandals involving major defense contractors, the end effect has always been the same: The nation, the soldier, and, ultimately, the taxpayer got less than their money's worth.

Whereas today's shaving of points is a very sophisticated business, it must be understood that the Napoleonic era didn't have any of those simple tools such as carbon paper, stencils, or, for that matter, typewriters. Everything was written by hand. Copies were executed by hand as well, which made it possible to alter documents virtually at will. Batteries of scribes, for the greatest part as unthinking as a typewriter, simply copied whatever was placed before them. And when the originals disappeared, who could tell the difference?

But if the story of the administration and the supply services during the Russian campaign is dismal, there is one story about a small cog in the machinery of the Napoleonic military Juggernaut that stands out like a beacon. A train officer from Baden, one Lieutenant Hammes, departing from Karlsruhe in July with a convoy of forty-one wagons loaded with supplies, accomplished what appeared to be a miracle at the time. Successfully bringing every one of his wagons over a trek of more than 1100 miles, from the Rhine to the Beresina, he had prevailed where many others had failed. Making his way over impossible roads and preserving his charges against marauders from the ranks of both friend and foe, he found his destination, the Baden Field Brigade, on the eve of the Battle of the Beresina. Well shod and fed, the Badeners were the envy of their intrepid companions, the Poles and Swiss, who all fought a legendary stand there.

With a hundred more like him—a small number, when compared to the size of the Grand Army—the rank and file surely would have fared better, to say the least. Certainly, the central army group would have returned to the Niemen in far better shape than it did.

RUSSIAN LOGISTICS

The Russians had also prepared for the oncoming confrontation. Since theirs was a defensive posture and the war was expected to be carried to them, they could avail themselves of fifteen already existing collecting points.[12] Still, new magazines were established along the roads leading from the Niemen to St. Petersburg, Moscow, and Kiev.[13] These, however, were concentrated in the western border districts, since no one expected the deep penetration into Russian territory that would eventually take place. In a very short time, about 1.2 million hektoliters[14] of flour, a like quantity of grits, and about 1.6 million hektoliters of oats were collected there, with more arriving constantly.

In addition, reserve magazines were established along the expected routes of operations at intervals of about an 8 days' march. These were too far apart, and the quantities gathered in any one place were too large. As a result, the precipitous French advance prevented all but a small portion of these supplies from being saved. The French managed to lay their hands on some, but most ended up being destroyed. Thus, the Russians were to suffer some shortages as well, but these were generally short-lived and not nearly so severe as those suffered by the French.

Not only Napoleon was plagued by an inept and corrupt commissariat; Alexander fared no better. However, although the Russians had their horror stories as well, theirs did not result in a failed campaign.

The Russians also had to help themselves with requisitioning, but unlike the case with the French, this was not done in an ad hoc fashion by letting the troops take matters into their own hands. And, certainly, they were at an undeniable advantage, operating on home territory.

In order to keep the army well supplied with ammunition, fifty-eight reserve parks were deployed in three successive lines. Of these, the first was the so-called mobile line, which included twenty parks stretching in a line from Dunaburg, via Bobruisk, to Kiev. Each was to be equipped with 534 horses and the necessary wagons. The second line, reaching from Pskov, via Smolensk, to Briansk, had nineteen depots, where laboratory commands from the artillery prepared cartridges. Finally, a third line, reaching from Novgorod to Kaluga, also included nineteen parks, where the bulk materials for the production of ammunition were collected. These second and third lines had no transport of their own but were to requisition what they needed locally.

According to a report completed by the inspector of artillery, bearing a dateline of July 22, 1812, the three depot lines held 296,000 artillery cartouches, 44 million rounds of small-arms ammunition, and a total of 17,500 cwt of powder. Another 102,940 cwt were stored in the other parts of the empire, and a further 18,000 cwt were prepared during the summer.

In this fashion, the two protagonists of the approaching drama had prepared for what was to come. Each had worked out his own plans, attempting to take into account all possible eventualities. And, as is usually the case in massive undertakings such as this promised to be, an unexpected sequence of events took charge. As action and reaction took the reins out of the hands of the main actors, nothing came to pass as planned, thus lending renewed emphasis to the Clausewitzian dictum that "as soon as the first shot is fired, all plans come to naught."

NOTES

1. Morvan.
2. Strachan, H. *European Armies and the Conduct of War*. London, 1983.
3. Montesquiou-Fezensac, R. *Souvenirs Militaires de 1804 a 1814*. Paris, 1863.

4. Alombert, P. C., and Colin, J. *La Campagne de 1805 en Allemagne, III.* Paris, 1902–1908. 6 vols.
5. Napoleon I. Correspondence. XI, No. 9245.
6. Ibid., XIV, No. 11,767.
7. Ibid., No. 12,015.
8. Ibid., No. 11,945.
9. Ibid., No. 12,178.
10. Osten-Sacken, von. *Der Feldzug von 1812.* Berlin, 1901.
11. 1 cwt = 110.25 lb avdp. = 100 lbs metric.
12. Vilna, Svenciany, Koltyniani, Grodno, Zlonim, Zlusk, Pinsk, Mozyr, Brest, Kovel, Lutzk, Dubno, Sasslavl, Staro-Konstantinovo, and Ostrog.
13. Riga, Dunaburg, Drissa, Sebesh, Velish, Bobruisk, Rogatshov, Shitomir, Kiev, Novgorod, Veliki-Luki, Kaluga, Trubcheosk, and Ssossmiza.
14. 1 hektoliter = approx. 106 quarts, or about 3 bushels.

III

The Advance

9. Crossing the Niemen

Preparing for the advance toward the Niemen, the French army had assembled in its initial staging areas stretching along the Vistula for some 300 miles. However, advancing toward the Russian frontier, the different army groups began to take on more distinct shape as they gradually concentrated in the direction of the river that marked the border between Poland and Russia. This concentration was largely achieved by June 21, when Napoleon, accompanied by the duty squadrons from the guard cavalry, arrived in Vilkoviezki.

By the 23rd, on the eve of the river crossing that would mark the official start of the war, the Grand Army had reached the following positions:

Napoleon's own army group was between Kovno and Pilviszki.
Eugene's army group was around Kalvaria; III Corps, at Mariampol, was about to leave Eugene to join Napoleon's group.
Jerome was near Novgorod, with his VII Corps near Pultusk.
Macdonald, with X Corps, was at Tilsit.
Schwarzenberg's Austrians were near Siedlice.

All the forces contained in this initial deployment came to about 449,000 men, with 1146 guns. Against these, the Russians could muster only about 183,000 men and 15,000 Cossacks, with 938 guns.

159

.   .   .

With Kovno, on the Russian side of the Niemen, marking the point where the central army group was to cross the river, the small village of Alexioten, on the Polish side of the Niemen, became the focal point toward which all of the army's constituent parts moved. By June 23, on the eve of the crossing, the Guard and Davout's I Corps were in place, with Oudinot's II Corps and Murat's reserve cavalry close at hand. Ney's III Corps, which had originally been scheduled to cross the Niemen a bit farther south, at Prenn, was ordered to close up to the central army group so that it would not be isolated in the event of an immediate counterattack by the Russians.

It is difficult for the modern observer to conjure an image of more than 120,000 men, with tens of thousands of horses, thousands of wagons, and dozens of artillery batteries, all concentrated into an area of only a few square miles. And these numbers merely encompass the forces immediately at hand for the crossing at Alexioten. It had already been a major feat on the part of Marshal Berthier and his staff to bring all these troops across Germany and into Poland, ending up in the right places at the right time. But that had been the comparatively easy part, since the constituent elements of the Grand Army had moved in relatively small units along many different roads. From here on in, everything would be much more difficult. Now it became a matter of assembling and moving entire army corps. The casual observer might well think that this was done simply by having the men gather up their belongings, fall into ranks, and then follow the order "Right face! Forward March!" Nothing could be further from the truth.

It took time to gather the troops from their bivouacs and billets (if they had any) and form up the battalions; assemble the brigades and divisions, with their organic artillery and baggage trains in place; and then to have all step off in their designated order of march. But all this merely set the stage for the march, which was yet to begin.

It is one thing for an individual or even a small group to accomplish a 15-mile hike in about 6 or 7 hours, allowing for a midday rest and about a 10-minute break every hour or two. For a division or an entire army corps, a 15-mile march was a long day's work, because the picture changed completely when long marching columns stepped onto the road, with wagons and artillery in their midst. A bad section of road, a narrow point, a balking horse, a frozen or broken wagon wheel, a broken axle—these and an extensive catalog of other potential mishaps could create obstacles and bottlenecks: Traffic would back up as the formations telescoped into each other, and the resulting stop-and-go pace was far more debilitating for man and horse than was a long but uninhibited march. And then, of course, the weather exercised its influence as well.

During the eighteenth century and the era of linear tactics, it had been customary for an army to conduct its operational marches by breaking the battalions off into platoon fronts. That is, about twenty to twenty-five men marched abreast. With the intervals between the platoons closed, the column was relatively short. Only when the troops came into the proximity of the enemy's forces were the intervals between the platoons opened sufficiently so that the battalions could make a front simply by having the platoons execute a simultaneous right or left turn to form the line. Passing over bridges or through towns, the platoons could be further broken off into sections or half-sections to negotiate any bottlenecks that presented themselves.

Unlike more modern practice, in which the troops simply form into three ranks, make a right face, and march off in the desired direction, the linear order broke the front into increments of whatever width was deemed appropriate and then stacked these like a deck of playing cards. Marches conducted on such broad fronts were possible in eighteenth-century Europe because the roads were actually quite wide by modern standards. That is, the original tracks made by wagon traffic had gradually widened as, particularly after heavy rains, subsequent traffic simply passed around bad spots in the road, thus adding a few feet here and a few more there. However, as villages grew into towns and towns into cities, the increasing commercial traffic brought about a constantly growing network of improved roads. Provision was made for proper drainage of the roadbeds, which had been given foundations of stone, sand, and gravel. An immediate result of this was that the roads became narrower, generally providing for the comfortable passing of two-way traffic at low speed. A well-traveled main road might have three lanes. Even today, as soon as one ventures away from the superhighways, the dimensions of many of these roads are still clearly marked by the trees that had been planted along their sides to protect them against the elements.

Thus, by the times of the Napoleonic wars, there were few roads left that could accommodate marches conducted with platoon fronts. Of course, it was possible to march cross-country, or, as was frequently done, to leave the road to the wagons and guns and have the infantry march alongside. But this was at all times a field expedient, hard on the feet and shoes of the infantry. Only those who have long fallen out of the custom of making long overland marches make light of this reality.

In Russia, these problems were magnified not merely by the extremes of weather conditions the troops experienced but also by the fact that much of Lithuania was heavily wooded and the roads shown on the maps were, in reality, little better than wagon tracks, often so narrow that a wagon had to pull up to the side to let another pass. Under such conditions, a Napoleonic infantry division of about 10,000 men, with man, horse, gun, and wagon, formed a column about 3 to 4 miles long. However, even if a man walking by himself might cover 3 miles in an hour, an entire division, for all the reasons stated above, would take much more than an hour to file past a given point along the road. This is what the French called the *découlement* (the runoff; from *découler*: to flow or to stream), that is, the time required for a formation to defile past a given point or, for that matter, to vacate a bivouac or campsite. And this involved only a single division.

Davout's I Corps in 1812 numbered five such divisions, which included a total of about 70,000 men—more than the entire army the Austrians had put into the field during the Battle of Leuthen in 1757. However, the presence of five divisions multiplied the problems just outlined by more than a factor of five. When several strong marches were strung together, the problems could multiply exponentially, especially if the pace was forced and the columns were kept on the road to extend the marching stages beyond the norm of about 15 miles per day.

In terms of the *découlement*, Davout's five divisions actually formed a column longer than an ordinary day's march. His leading division would arrive at its objective even before his last division would leave the previous night's bivouac. But this did not necessarily afford the rearward elements several extra hours of rest before commencing their day's march. Instead, they would have spent most of their day packed and saddled up, waiting to be moved from one place to the next, inching their way closer to the designated road, before they would actually start off to complete their day's marching stage (unless two or more columns were to march simultaneously along different roads). This, in addition to other problems encountered on the march (such as foraging along roads where others had passed before) was another major reason why the rearward positions in the marching order were always undesirable. Such problems, however, were still another day or two in the future when Napoleon's central army group concentrated across from Kovno for the crossing of the Niemen.

With the points (military parlance for the leading elements) of his own army group held back and out of sight from the opposite river bank, Napoleon exchanged the gray overcoat he usually wore for a Polish hussar's cloak and rode along the Niemen to make a personal reconnaissance and to finalize the exact locations where the bridges were to be laid down. On this occasion a fleeing hare caused Napoleon's horse to shy and throw him. This incident and the thunderstorm of the next day furnished grist for the mills of the superstitious. Even though Napoleon laughed off both events, we will never know how he, a firm believer in his own "lucky star," really felt about them.

With the bridge sites selected, the construction of three pontoon bridges began after nightfall near the village of Alexioten, across from Kovno. A company of engineers was sent across to prepare the opposite bank; two companies of infantry covered the bridgeheads. The job was completed in about 3 hours, and Morand's division from I Corps went across at once, followed soon by the rest of Davout's I Corps and Murat with the reserve cavalry.

They found no resistance. The few Cossack detachments that had been in the area withdrew in the direction of Vilna. Thus, Napoleon spent the early morning hours reviewing the defile of his troops as their columns rolled toward the bridges with their customary shouts of "*Vive l'empereur*" and "*Vive Napoleon.*"

The emperor had pitched his tent on a piece of high ground that afforded a fairly good oversight of the area where the marching columns drew together as they headed for the three bridges, which could be seen in the near distance. It is often said that he held a review of his army group from there, but this was impossible because the columns rolled by hour after hour. He did come out from time to time, however, to watch them going by; on occasion, he would sally forth to review one or another formation as it was drawn up awaiting its turn for the crossing.

Still, it was an event of much pomp and circumstance, which found its echo in the press of the times. Expressions such as "streams of lava" described the endless columns winding toward and away from the bridges, and the columns of cuirassiers with their burnished breastplates were likened to "perambulating citadels." Seen from the distance, the sight was impressive, but up close, there was neither pomp nor glamour.

Lieutenant von Brandt, a latter-day Prussian general, but at the time a member of a Polish regiment, painted a vivid picture of some of the scenes.[1] The baggage wagons had been pulled out of the columns that were drawn up for a muster and review by the emperor, so every brigade and division must have assembled a sizable vehicle park of its own. Of course, it was not a formal parade. The idea was to get the army across the river. As the columns rolled past the spot where the emperor stood, all the participants tried to make a brave show of it. At the same time, however, everyone wanted to get across the bridges ahead of everyone else, and this resulted in unbelievable confusion at the bridgeheads. The army gendarmes did their best to keep order, but to little avail as they met with resistance and outright disobedience. Everybody tried to pull rank on everybody else.

Major crises arose whenever baggage columns arrived at the bridges. Heated arguments would ensue with the artillery officers, stationed by every bridge, who naturally claimed precedence over the wagons when it came to crossing the river. The officers of the infantry and cavalry columns, of course, were loathe to see themselves separated from their baggage trains, as this meant the trains would not arrive in the bivouacs until long after nightfall, at best. Some might even take a day or two to catch up. If the brigadier or, perhaps, even the division commander was present, things would be settled quickly. If he had gone ahead, matters would be settled by whoever's column was closest and ready to roll.

Meanwhile, the great press of densely packed columns, expanding and contracting in the endless stop-and-go movement, brought tempers to a boiling point—until rain cooled them down again. A hussar from the 2nd (Prussian) Combined Regiment in Nansouty's I Cavalry Corps described another scene:

> Our corps was drawn up and ready to be reviewed by the emperor, before commencing its march. Both, however, were delayed by a thunderstorm, whose coming had gone altogether unnoticed in the bustle of preparing for the crossing. Suddenly, the thunder cracked and the rain came down in sheets. We quickly wrapped ourselves into our overcoats and patiently waited for the end of the torrent.
>
> The coincidence of this with the first important undertaking of the war did not fail to stir the superstitions of the common soldiers. Nor were the officers entirely immune. Whispers quickly passed through the ranks. "This is a bad sign!" "Few will return!"
>
> This mood was fittingly interrupted by the trumpeters' choirs of the French cuirassier regiments. Defying the storm, they sounded lively tunes and blaring fanfares. One could hardly conceive of a more fitting use of military music.
>
> But it was the sight of the enormous masses rolling toward the bridges and away from them on the other bank which restored the spirits even of the doubters.[2]

"And the scene after nightfall," relates a French soldier, "was even more impressive, the glimmer of a thousand campfires illuminating the sky creating impressions upon the mind, which could not possibly be matched by what the eye could see in daylight."[3]

NOTES

1. Brandt, H. von. *Aus dem Leben des Generals Heinrich v. B.* Berlin, 1868.
2. "Fragmente zur Geschichte des Feldzuges 1812." In *Militaer Wochenblaetter.* Berlin, 1839–1840.
3. Pouget, Baron de. *Souvenirs de Guerre.* Paris, 1895.

10. The Road to Vilna

By the 25th, Napoleon's army group had completed its crossing of the Niemen, and the heads of Ney's columns were arriving at the bridges. Further north, Macdonald also crossed on the same day. Eugene would soon follow further upriver, near Pilony, but Jerome would not make his crossing until June 28 at Grodno.

Murat went on at once with the cavalry reserve to scour the countryside, while the rest of the central army group sorted itself out again. But by the 26th Napoleon was on his way. Vilna was only 70 miles away, and one of the Russian armies was known to be there.

With Murat and the reserve cavalry up front, Napoleon, with the Guard and I Corps, took the main road to Vilna. The rain had given way to the sun again, but it was burning hot. Napoleon was in a hurry, so the troops were driven along in dense columns at a forced pace. His points arrived in Vilna on the 28th, having covered the 70-mile march in 2 days.

Ney and III Corps took the road to Suterva, which followed the left bank of the Vilia. Oudinot, who had been reinforced by Cuirassier Division Doumerc from III Cavalry Corps, marched in two columns along the other side of the river, toward Bobty and Ianovo. He was to try to cut off Wittgenstein, who was known to be somewhere around Keidany. Macdonald, with X Corps, was to support this move by heading toward Rossieny so that he might drive Wittgenstein into Oudinot's arms. But Macdonald took too much time and had too far to go; all everyone got out of this maneuver was the exercise. And the unrelenting heat was worse than the rain had been.

Napoleon no longer expected the Russians to make an early offensive. So on the 24th, the day of the crossing, orders had been sent to Jerome stating that he was to attach himself to Bagration. The latter, according to a report from Schwarzenberg, had been marching toward Vilna since June 17. He was to accomplish the order by marching to Grodno with three of his corps, while Reynier's VII (Saxon) Corps was to march to Bialystok via Brok and Tykoczin.

At the Russian headquarters in Vilna, galloping couriers had already brought news of Napoleon's crossing by the evening of the 24th. Before the night was out, orders were sent to Bagration and Platov to make an immediate offensive, while First Army was ordered to withdraw into the Sokol-Svenciany-Kobylniki line. Each corps was to get there quickly by its own individual route. Only III and IV Infantry Corps, coming, respectively, from Novi-Troki and Olkieniki, were to assemble at Vilna.

Alexander left Vilna on the 26th, thereby giving Barclay a free hand. However, the two last-mentioned corps left him with only about 25,000 men in hand, since the rear guard of IV Infantry Corps (4 battalions, 8 squadrons, 1 Cossack regiment, and 1 battery) under Dorochov could no longer come to Vilna directly but had to evade in the direction of Olszani and Woloczin. Napoleon's surprise had been complete.

Right up to the end, Barclay had hoped to fight a battle at Vilna. Even at this late stage, the thought of offering some kind of resistance there briefly flashed through his mind, but the idea was hopeless. His patrols were already informing him that Napoleon was approaching by forced marches, so he ordered that the magazines be set on fire and that the Vilia bridges be dismantled. He began his own retreat toward Niemenczin during the early morning hours of the 28th, even as the points of the French cavalry were approaching.

On the extreme Russian right, Wittgenstein had reached Perkele on the same day, thereby eluding the danger posed by Macdonald's and Oudinot's approaches. But it had been close: His rear guard, supported by elements from I Cavalry Corps, which had stood near Vilkomir, had become embroiled with Oudinot's advance guard. In a lively action near Develtovo, the French cavalry quickly learned that it would face a difficult task in dealing with the Russian cavalry—and the campaign was only beginning.

On the whole, First Army had made a good getaway. Only on the Russian left, where Doctorov had VI Infantry and III Cavalry Corps, did a precarious situation develop. Late in receiving news of the opening of hostilities, Doctorov had not concentrated his VI Infantry Corps around Olszani until the 27th. From there, he marched off in the direction of Djunaszev. This was the same direction taken by Pahlen's III Cavalry Corps, which had stood in an advanced position forward of Lida but was now marching toward Lebioda.

Alexander had been in Svenciany since the 26th. Even though the signs had been visible everywhere that the war was about to begin and even though the direction of the enemy's attack was no longer a secret, both still came as a surprise at imperial headquarters. Everyone was troubled over Doctorov's exposed position and wondered whether or not Bagration had actually advanced to attack, but no one seemed to know what orders should be issued. The campaign was only two days old when the first orders deviating from the original plan were issued. Platov was to be sent to Lida and on to Smorgoni, while Barclay was directed to order Bagration back to Minsk, via Slonim—something Phull had wanted to do earlier. On the 28th, however, these orders were changed again.

Since the occupation of Vilna was not yet known about in Svenciany, it was deduced from Macdonald's and Oudinot's movements that the main French force had turned against the Russian right. As a result, in order to save time, orders were sent directly to Bagration—and repeated 2 days later—sending him toward Vileyka, via Bielitza or Novogrodok, where he would be closer to Barclay. A later communication indicates that this was not done with the object of uniting the two western armies but, rather, with the notion of enabling them to have "the center of the empire at their backs." To this day, no one is quite clear what this was supposed to mean, but the nebulous phrase does illustrate the sort of muddle-headed thinking that prevailed in the Russian headquarters at that time.

Ney's occupation of Suterva further strengthened the opinions held at imperial headquarters, despite Barclay's report that Napoleon had entered Vilna. Such a lack of clarity and resolution was bound to make a bad impression on the entire army.

Thus, as Barclay made his retreat, the French entered Vilna on the 28th after a light skirmish. It was still morning when Napoleon made his formal entry into the town.

The march into Lithuania had gone through a barren and heavily wooded countryside that offered even less forage than that in Poland. Two forced marches from the Niemen had exacerbated the supply situation, which had already gone from bad to worse even upon arrival at the Niemen, as the distances to the rearward supply bases had steadily increased (not that anything could have caught up with an army making forced marches).

Most debilitating had been the constant stop-and-go and the resultant press as the columns telescoped into each other. The thunderstorm at the crossing was followed by other downpours, turning the tracks—some diarists claim that there were no roads as such in Lithuania—into bottomless mires. Wagon wheels sank into mud up to the hubs; horses dropped from exhaustion; men lost their boots. Stalled wagons soon became obstacles, forcing the troops to make their way around them and halting other wagons and the artillery columns. Then came the sun, which would bake the deep ruts into canyons of concrete, where horses would break their legs and wagons their wheels. Lieutenant Mertens, from Wuerttemberg, who was with Ney's III Corps, gives this account:

> Until Ianovo [a town north of the Kovno-Vilna road], the heat was oppressive and the dust stifling. In the afternoon, the thunder would roll and we were drenched to the skin.
>
> On 28 June, the rains settled in and the first order of the day was to build some huts. Our exertions on this and the days following were the reason for the outbreaks of dysentery and influenza, which soon ran through the ranks without let-up and thinned them more effectively than enemy shot.
>
> The rain held on through the 29th and left us in dire straits. On the 30th, we left our swamp-camp at the crack of dawn and on the 1st of July, many more men and horses fell victim to the mud. On the 3rd, the sun greeted us again, but the dysentery raged so badly that several hundred sick had to be brought to Maliaty, where a field hospital had been hastily established.

Mertens kept his diary with typical Teutonic efficiency, never failing to mention the date, time, place, and weather when he made his entries. Thus, we know that thunderstorms again erupted on July 6 and that by the 9th the heat and humidity had again reached oppressive magnitudes, interspersed with torrential downpours. The weather remained gruesome for several more days, and men were beginning to die from sunstroke and heat prostration.

Indeed, the crown prince of Wuerttemberg reported to his father that from July 15 to 29, twenty-one men had died in the bivouacs. But he never got to sign the report himself, because the dysentery felled him as well, as it would the general who took over command from him. The entry on July 18 reads: "The entire camp reeked of peppermint and Hofmann's drops, which stuck in our noses like the stench of cadavers."

Things were no better in the Bavarian corps, where apothecary Gras-mann reports 129 sick on July 8, 200 on the following day, and 345 by 13 July. Under these circumstances, even the more disciplined Germans were beginning to leave men behind in large numbers.

But it was not merely the sick who were being left behind. Deserters were beginning to leave their formations in even greater numbers, looting everything they could lay their hands on, terrorizing the population, and thus stoking its anger against the French and their allies. The men from the Illyrian and Portuguese formations had already deserted in wholesale fashion, just as great numbers of Spaniards had found refuge among the Roman Catholics of Silesia. This was all the more alarming since the attitudes of the Lithuanians were to play a considerable part in the fate of the Grand Army.[1]

The Lithuanians were of a somewhat more sober disposition than the easily inflammable Poles. Still, many members of the Lithuanian-Polish nobility had pitched in right up to the end in the fervent hope of recon-stituting Greater Poland. But the common people, who stood quite removed from all such political considerations, had no head for these grandiose ideas. They were outraged by the devastation caused by the Grand Army, which had descended upon them like a swarm of locusts. "Nowhere an inhabitant," complained Brandt, the Polish officer, on the 27th, just 2 days after the crossing of the Niemen. "A nearby village had disappeared almost entirely. The troops arriving ahead of us had dismantled it to satisfy the needs for their bivouac." However, the official requisitioning details did not treat the civilians any better. Things were already worse than they had ever been in Poland. Thus, by the time Vilna was reached, the estimated losses of the Grand Army from all causes already added up to about 25,000 men.

Even more alarming was the condition of the French cavalry. Not only were the Poles and Germans far more effective than the French at keeping their mounts fit for service, but the French light cavalry was hopelessly outclassed by the Russians, even when the former enjoyed numerical su-periority. The reconnaissance patrols Murat sent forward learned the hard truth of this on the very first day after the Niemen had been crossed.

For this reason, Napoleon, who didn't want to see his cavalry run down or exposed to unnecessary losses, had an order issued from Vilna on June 29 that prohibited the sending forward of weak detachments over long distances—"*de toute petite groupe isolee*"—and in terrain that could not be overseen. If it became necessary to do so, then the cavalry was to have an infantry backup. This, of course, drastically curtailed the reconnaissance activities of the cavalry and curbed its initiative. Such a restriction became even more troublesome later, when it grew increasingly difficult to get civilian informers in Russia and when much of the information obtained from them about the Russian armies turned out to be false or outdated.

The wedge Napoleon had driven forward was intended to separate the two Russian armies. However, he had no idea to what extent he had succeeded. The blame for this rested squarely with the French cavalry, which had plainly not been up to the task of maintaining contact with the enemy to observe his movements. Setting aside the guard cavalry and the cavalry divisions in the army corps, Murat had 30,000 horsemen under his command. Yet, despite this crushing superiority, contact with the enemy, hardly won, had been lost again. As a result, Napoleon thought Barclay's First Army was safe and in retreat toward the Dvina, and he was still uncertain about Bagration. Thus, he halted at Vilna with the Guard.

In order to obtain some clarity and possibly widen the gap between the two Russian armies, he sent two strong columns forward. Murat, with the Infantry Divisions Friant and Gudin of I Corps, Nansouty's I Cavalry Corps (minus Cuirassier Division Valence), and Montbrun's cavalry corps, was sent in the direction of Niemenczin. Davout, with the remainder of his corps (Infantry Divisions Morand, Desaix, and Compans and two light cavalry brigades), the Guard Lancer Brigade Colbert, and Cuirassier Division Valence (from I Cavalry Corps), was to go toward Michaliszki and Oszmiana.

At the same time, Ney was ordered to cross to the right bank of the Vilia near Suterva and march toward Maliaty so that he might support either Murat or Oudinot. He arrived there on July 2. But the marches in torrential downpours, which extended over the whole of Lithuania during those days, had taken a heavy toll of his troops, as already noted. Worst of all, Ney had been forced to leave behind most of his artillery, as the guns were hopelessly mired and the horses, their numbers diminishing by the hour, were too weak to pull them out.

As if forgotten, Eugene had spent all this time standing in place at Pilony, on the left bank of the Niemen. He finally crossed near Prenn on June 30. Of Jerome's army group, which had been spurred on by Napoleon, VII (Saxon) Corps was on its way to Bialystok, while the remaining three corps were marching toward Grodno. The cavalry points arrived at Grodno on the 29th, but the infantry was still a long way off.

On July 1, Murat reached Niemenczin and Davout had Morand's division in Michaliszki. The remainder of Davout's troops were in Oszmiana, where his light cavalry had a brush with parts of Doctorov's III Russian Cavalry Corps, which was on its way to Djunaszev. This renewed contact with the

Russians gave Napoleon news of Doctorov's march, but he thought Doctorov was Bagration, with Jerome on his heels. He should have known better, since the distances involved made this practically impossible.

Napoleon acted at once on this news. On the morning of July 1, he ordered Davout, reinforced with Grouchy's III Cavalry Corps (minus Division Doumerc) to move into the enemy's flank via Oszmiana. At the same time, Nansouty's cavalry corps (minus Division Valence) was to march to Michaliszki, where it was to join Division Morand of Davout's corps, which was already there, to block the march of the reported column.

Napoleon realized his error the very next day, July 2, when he learned of the identity of the column. But he still had no news of Bagration and thought that he had to be farther away than Doctorov. And that brought his intent to isolate and destroy Bagration to the fore again.

Davout was to take the troops he had in hand at Oszmiana and march toward Minsk. There, he was to receive Bagration, who would be driven toward him by Jerome. In addition to the troops he already had, the Polish Vistula Legion was now assigned to him as well, so Davout had a force of about 43,000 men.[2] Eugene, who was sharply reprimanded for dawdling at Pilony, was ordered to make haste as well and get to Novi-Troki. From there, he was to go on to Oszmiana, replacing Davout and thus also taking a hand in cutting off Bagration.

This was exactly the kind of maneuver at which Macdonald and Oudinot had already failed on the left wing against Wittgenstein.

On the Russian side, the various corps of First Army reached their designated line by July 1. They rested on the 2nd, on which day Doctorov's corps and Pahlen's cavalry arrived as well. Doctorov had already made a forced march from Djunaszev to Svir, succeeding, not without sacrifices, in staying ahead of Nansouty, of whose approach he had learned only at the very last moment.

Despite the fact that the opening of hostilities had surprised the Russians in their far-flung positions, all the corps of First Army had succeeded in evading the threat of being isolated and run over and were now concentrated in their designated line. Only a detachment under Dorochov and Platov's Cossacks (11 Cossack regiments and 1 Cossack battery, totaling 4500 men, with 12 guns) had failed to make the connection, going toward Bagration instead. Platov had been late in receiving the orders of the 26th and 27th; as a consequence, he had not left Grodno until the 29th, heading in the direction of Lida.

As already noted, Bagration had concentrated his army around Volkovisk by June 20. Still waiting for permission to make a thrust in the direction of

Warsaw, he had received news of Napoleon's advance and the order to operate against his flank quite late. Completely in the dark, he had stood fast at Volkovisk until June 28, when he received Barclay's order of the 27th, initiated by the tsar on the 26th, to withdraw to Minsk. He marched at once, reaching Zelva by the 30th. There, the order sent to him directly from imperial headquarters arrived, sending him to Vileyka, either by way of Bielitza or Novogrodok.

The negative aftereffects of these conflicting orders have already been discussed. That is, Bagration was loathe to sublimate himself to Barclay's command from the start, and he now readily assumed that Barclay was entirely responsible for all the confusion. The original orders, calling upon him to make an offensive into Poland, had been properly amended by those issued through Barclay's headquarters on the 27th. But these last orders had gone over Barclay's head (without his knowledge) and, as a result, stood in conflict with the last orders received by Second Army. Thus, Bagration's reaction was inevitable.

Marching via Slonim over bottomless roads (the rains had set in there as well by the 29th), Bagration reached Novogrodok by July 3. There he was joined by the 27th Infantry Division, freshly arrived from Moscow. On the 4th, he reached Nikolaiev, his designated crossing point of the Niemen. Parts of his army had already made the difficult crossing and were entering the forests and swamps between the upper Niemen and Vileyka when Platov's Cossacks reported that Wisznev was already held by Davout. At the same time, other reports warned of the approach of additional forces from the directions of Grodno and Zelva. Bagration at once did an about-face, reaching Koreliczy on July 5 and Mir on the 6th. If Platov and Dorochov could delay the enemy at Voloczin, he could make it to Minsk.

Platov, who had gone from Lida to Voloczin to join Dorochov, who was on his way to Kamen, learned of Davout's approach in Ivie. Since Dorochov had reached Voloczin ahead of him, Platov followed Bagration toward Koreliczy. Dorochov, who had also been directed to Minsk by Bagration, succeeded in getting there by means of an extraordinary forced march from Kamen.

There can be no doubt that Bagration would have ended up in an extremely difficult position at Nikolaiev had Jerome been on his heels, as Napoleon had ordered. However, due to Jerome's rearward starting position, which was entirely in accordance with Napoleon's own dispositions, the points of Jerome's cavalry did not reach Grodno until June 29, with its mass arriving on the next day. His infantry, on the other hand, did not make it until July 3, by which time VII Corps had reached Bialystok.

The tropical heat, followed by the heavy rains, which began on the 27th in that area, combined with the atrocious supply situation, had already precipitated heavy losses in men and horses in this army group as well. Funck relates that, due to the bad roads, the trains were generally a day's march to the rear. Even when they did manage to catch up to the troops, they would generally not arrive in the bivouacs until the small hours of the morning. By now, V and VIII Corps alone had lost 9000 men between them—one-sixth of their strength. And these are the lowest estimates! Even the Polish cavalry in V Corps, mostly green formations as well, had lost about 1000 horses. Given these circumstances, Napoleon's summons notwithstanding, Jerome thought it necessary to halt at Grodno to allow his army to rest and reassemble. He did not send Latour-Maubourg's cavalry off to Novogrodok until July 4, followed by the infantry on the 6th. Also on the 6th, Bagration was already marching from Koreliczy to Mir. And the sun was burning again.

Around this time, the tensions between Jerome and General Vandamme, a capable officer, broke out into the open. Jerome had been resentful of what he considered Vandamme's interference, which was supposedly based on Napoleon's authority. The emperor had assigned Vandamme to VIII Corps and Jerome's army group so that Jerome might avail himself of the general's experience. However, as was Napoleon's custom, he had failed to define a clear pecking order.

Now, Jerome relieved Vandamme of his command over VIII Corps and handed it to Tharreau, the French senior division commander in the corps. Both Jerome and Vandamme dispatched officers to Napoleon to present their grievances. Meanwhile, Vandamme continued to accompany the army as far as Bielitza, claiming that it was beyond Jerome's competence to relieve him of his command. Jerome wrote to his queen: "I had to relieve Vandamme of his command because he was guilty of various things, looted, stole and passed out slaps and kicks to everyone. . . . His name elicits unbelievable hate around the countryside and the inhabitants are incredibly terrified of him."[3] General Ochs, a Westphalian in command of 24th Division, paints a different picture. He says that VIII Corps had good relations with Vandamme and respected his military skills and that his insistence on an iron discipline was paired with a great deal of solicitude for the welfare of the troops.[4]

As is usually the case, there was probably some truth on both sides. Vandamme did look after his troops. That is the mark of the good soldier he was. On the other hand, Vandamme had incurred the wrath of the

German citizenry with some of his draconic measures during his tenure in Hamburg. When he was captured at Kulm in 1813, only the intercession of some officers prevented him from getting a beating at the hands of the Russian soldiers who had captured him. So there was some fire beneath the smoke.

Because he wanted to prevent an open break with his brother at the moment, Napoleon upheld Jerome's authority and sent Vandamme home. This was entirely a military choice, rather than a display of brotherly affection. Given the well-known intransigence and independent-mindedness of the marshals in their dealings with each other, Napoleon thought it was more expedient at the time to replace a corps commander than to attempt to find a man who could replace Jerome and command the army group. However, his choice of Junot who arrived on July 30 to take over VIII Corps from Tharreau's temporary command was a bad error that was to have its consequences at Smolensk.

Napoleon was angry with Jerome, but this anger did not have its source in the incident with Vandamme. It had been brewing for a long time, much of it rooted in the emperor's disapproval of his younger brother's frivolous nature. Admittedly, Jerome might have been oversolicitous toward his troops—perhaps one day's rest instead of two would have sufficed, perhaps he should have marched on, as Bagration had done—but it was completely impossible for him to reach Koreliczy with sufficient force to block Bagration. The place was more than 100 miles away.

Napoleon, however, still did not have a clear insight into the true situation because he was not accurately informed of all the main actors' respective positions. He was highly indignant about his brother's extended delay at Grodno and had Berthier, his chief of staff, tell Jerome so in no uncertain terms on July 6. In order to put more unity and some life into the action, he had Jerome placed under Davout's command on the next day. In Napoleon's time-honored fashion, the order was for the moment secret; of course, Jerome was not informed of this either.

While these events were being played out in the central and southern army groups, Schwarzenberg's Austrians, who represented the right flank of the Grand Army, had crossed the Bug near Drohiczyn on July 3 and reached Pruzany. Their light troops spread out all the way to the Muchavetz and Pina, capturing a large stockpile of supplies in Pinsk.

As for Bagration, his army had reached Mir on July 6, as already noted. When Dorochov reported to him there that Davout was closing in on Minsk, he changed his direction again, going to Bobruisk via Slutzk. Uniting with

Dorochov on the 7th at Novi-Sverzen, he assembled his entire army, now more than 45,000 men,[5] around Niesvicz on the 8th and remained there on the 9th and 10th, because his own troops were as desperately in need of a rest as were the French.

On July 8, Platov's rear guard brushed off an attack by Polish light cavalry at Koreliczy and stayed around Mir. There, his cavalry laid an ambush on the 9th in which a Polish lancer brigade of IV Cavalry Corps was severely mauled. Substantially reinforced, the French came back on the 10th to hand the Russians a beating. Instead, they suffered another thrashing by Platov, who, on this occasion, was himself supported by Russian regular cavalry.

In the meanwhile, Davout had arrived at Minsk on July 8, but he had driven his troops too hard. The blistering heat, which had set in again on the 6th, and the supply situation that attended every forced march had reduced his force, originally more than 40,000, to less than 30,000 men. The Vistula Legion and Colbert's lancer brigade had not yet caught up. On top of all else, the troops that made it to Minsk were in such a state of disarray that it took Davout, the stern disciplinarian, 3 days to restore order. He had to bring all his authority to bear to prevent further mass desertions and excesses. In view of this situation and his numerical weakness, Davout considered himself incapable of confronting Bagration before Jerome came up.

Under these circumstances, Bagration might possibly have succeeded in breaking through at Minsk. (Later, Alexander reprimanded him for having failed to make the attempt. Many feel the reprimand was justified, but this view can be upheld only with the benefit of hindsight.) But Bagration was in a very difficult situation, and neither he nor Davout had been given the opportunity to study each other's morning reports. Thus, Davout thought Bagration had 60,000 men, while the latter thought Davout had 70,000, with more behind him, about whom he was no better informed. Because of the presence of strong French cavalry, which was actually far ahead of Davout's infantry columns, Bagration could hardly know that Davout had merely reached the Slonim–Novogrodok line by the 10th, especially since the Cossacks and the Russian line cavalry did not do well at reconnaissance themselves.

Moreover, he thought Davout's columns were the French main force; this was a significant factor in Bagration's continuing course of operations. The constant stream of amendments to his original orders had already shaken Bagration's faith in Barclay's conduct of the campaign. Now he believed that Napoleon's main force was coming after him, and he saw himself left in the lurch by Barclay's ineptitude. He even thought all Russia had been betrayed, and he saw salvation only in Barclay's recall. The result of this was a highly charged relationship between the two army commanders, in which Bagration carried out Barclay's orders reluctantly and, at that, only partially.

Alexander was not the only one dissatisfied with the poor results of the operations so far. Napoleon also had no cause to be happy with the results achieved against Bagration, and he laid all the blame on Jerome. The drama between the two imperial brothers was brought to a conclusion only a week later when, on July 16, Jerome left the army.

Du Casse[6] says that Napoleon had already used harsh words on July 10 and gave Jerome permission to go home, but Jerome wouldn't hear of it. At the same time, the communiqués between the observers in the diplomatic corps with the Grand Army and the princes of the Rhine Confederation and Prussia were buzzing with Vandamme's intrigues on the one hand and Poniatowski's and Reynier's complaints about Jerome on the other.

On July 13, Jerome sent one of his adjutants to Davout to confer with him on the imminent junction of their forces. On the evening of the 14th, Jerome was thunderstruck when the adjutant returned and reported that Davout, handing over a copy of Napoleon's secret order of the 6th, had informed him curtly that he was now in command of the entire right wing.

Historians who have specialized in researches on the two main characters of this sideshow have different views of the incident. However, Kleinschmidt's[7] contradiction of Mazade,[8] who makes claims for Davout's tactful handling of the situation, may certainly be upheld on the basis of corollary information. That Davout and Jerome had no liking for each other went back to the days when Davout was in charge of the French troops garrisoned in Westphalia. Furthermore, when Napoleon was unhappy with Davout's performance during the days of Minsk, Davout gladly absolved himself of any responsibility for the failure to catch and stop Bagration by implying that it had all been Jerome's fault.

Still, Davout must have had misgivings about Jerome's possible reaction, as well as about the fact that he had revealed Napoleon's secret orders prematurely, since their content was not to become known or effective until all the corps of the right wing were assembled. Furthermore, there was always the possibility that if Jerome felt greatly affronted, this feeling might transplant itself to Napoleon by proxy. Therefore, Davout wrote a very civil letter to Jerome on the 15th, informing him of Napoleon's orders in obviously more courteous terms than he had used with his adjutant. But Jerome marched off anyway.

His departure was no loss to the army. Jerome did not have the talents to play the role of a commander in chief, nor was he a good subordinate. Indeed, his appointment to so important a post had been entirely due to Napoleon's chronic lack of men who had both the necessary talents and the proper stature in front of their peers. In Napoleon's absence, the marshals were prone to bicker, and the emperor was very much aware of this state of affairs. For this reason, men like Murat, Eugene, and Jerome, by virtue of their connection to the imperial family, were time and again called upon to fill posts of independent command, even though the army had men better fitted for such tasks. Still, the treatment meted out to Jerome by Napoleon was unjust.

As the reader can see from this (and will see from other incidents yet to come), the Russians were not alone in suffering from internal frictions that threatened to interfere with operations.

While the operations of his reinforced right wing were in progress, Napoleon remained in Vilna with his center, content with having his left wing stay in touch with Barclay.

The campaign itself was barely 2 weeks old, but already the conditions of the Russian theater of operations were taking their toll. From the start, the troops had been forced to march in dense columns, over bad roads, through poor and almost arid country. Poorly supplied even before the campaign had actually gotten under way, most of the men had already consumed the 4 days' iron ration they carried in reserve for days when the supply columns failed to catch up with them. As a result, hungry and thirsty men had been pushed into making extraordinary marches in weather that could only make things worse. Starting between the 27th and the 29th of June, depending on the location of the different army groups, thunderstorms, followed by torrential downpours, had extended all over Lithuania; they lasted until about July 5, when tropical heat set in (the exact dates again varying with the different locations). The heat was to last until the second half of August.

Already, thousands upon thousands of stragglers floated in the wake of the army. Most of them wouldn't turn up again until the retreat got under way. Many more thousands populated the field hospitals, from whence very few would ever be returned to duty. Many had already died from the heat, exhaustion, and disease. Even Mortier, whose Young Guard was better taken care of than the line, let alone the foreign troops, wrote home that several of his men had died from starvation on the way to Vilna.

Things were even worse with the draft teams, which were so important to the army. Not in the best condition even by the time they had arrived at the Niemen, the cadavers of 10,000 horses already littered the road from there to Vilna. The artillery, in particular, since its teams were too light to begin with, had left behind thousands. Even though horses had been taken from the army trains to keep the artillery rolling, eighty guns were left behind in Vilna.[9]

When Napoleon reached Vilna on June 28, he halted there to organize a provisional government, to turn the town into an advanced base, and to harness the military resources of the country. His lieutenants were sent off in all directions to find the enemy and clarify the situation. In the making of these arrangements, Napoleon committed a fatal error.

On June 26, the Polish Diet had convened in Warsaw and, amid the cheers of an enthusiastic crowd, had proclaimed itself the General Confederation of All Poland and had declared the union between Poland and Lithuania. Napoleon's recognition of this might have stirred the enthusiasm of the Poles even further, bringing in yet larger numbers of volunteers. Even though the Treaty of Vienna contained a clause obligating Austria to cede Galicia in exchange for the Illyrian provinces in the event Greater Poland was reconstituted, Napoleon hedged. His attitude put a noticeable damper on Polish enthusiasm.

Napoleon was in a quandary. He still believed that Alexander would come to heel after the first decisive blows were struck. However, despite this self-delusion, he did not think that Alexander would ever hold still for handing Lithuania over to the Poles.

The Prussian Osten-Sacken presents the problem in a deliciously Clausewitzian manner that is sure to exercise the passions of modern ideologues because it revolves around the great military theorist's contention that war is a continuation of politics by different means and that political objectives must govern all military objectives. Unfortunately, the good Clausewitz failed to provide posterity with a surefire formula for how to distinguish a political from a military objective. This has misled many modern historians into citing some curious examples in support of Clausewitz's theorem.

According to Osten-Sacken, the task that Napoleon the head of state posed for Napoleon the commander in chief of the army, that is, the overthrow of Russia, was difficult enough as it was. He goes on to maintain that Napoleon committed an error when the statesman prevented his general from utilizing as important a means as the unreserved cooperation of the Poles. Once the war had begun, the first order of business was to win. And in order to win, every means had to be employed. All else could be settled later. Thus, Osten-Sacken maintained, one error begot the next.

One might well ask, Was defeating Alexander a political or merely a military objective? Indeed, was the political objective to defeat him or to appease him? At Tilsit, in 1807, Napoleon had accomplished both because the situation had arisen out of a military standoff. Napoleon's eye, at that time still undimmed by self-delusion, had clearly perceived the limits of what was obtainable. But the stakes had changed. Napoleon's reluctance to commit himself on the Polish issue is all the more ironic since, in 1812, it became obvious that the future of Polish aspirations was apparently in Alexander's, not Napoleon's, hands.

Meanwhile, Barclay continued his retreat in the direction of the camp at Drissa. When Ney appeared at Maliaty and Murat made contact with the rear guard, it seemed unwise to stay in the Sokol-Svenciany-Kobylniki line, where the entire army had stood assembled by July 2, with Doctorov's arrival.

Barclay was now convinced that a battle at Svenciany was out of the question and that, instead, the junction of his and Bagration's armies had to be the first order of business. On the following 2 days, the retreat was therefore carried to the far side of the Disna. Phull thought this was being done too slowly. All that remained on the southern bank of the Disna was Ostermann-Tolstoy,[10] with IV Infantry and II Cavalry Corps. Imperial headquarters had moved to Vidzy on July 3. It was there, at Vidzy, on the evening of July 4, that an incident occurred that would finally discredit Phull and shake the tsar's confidence in him to the very breaking point.

A report had just been received indicating that strong enemy forces were threatening to envelop the left wing of the army. This at once gave rise to the fear that the Guard Corps and Doctorov might become isolated and be beaten. Alexander had Phull asked for his opinion, but that worthy gentleman completely lost his head. Literally running around in a circle, he ranted on that Barclay had precipitated the entire dangerous situation because he had been too slow to retreat. Having no idea what to do next, Phull then announced that since his advice had not been followed from the start, he would now wash his hands of the entire business.

Clausewitz, who was present at imperial headquarters, advised that the orders given to the Guard and Doctorov not be changed. He was of the opinion that the report that had so alarmed everybody was erroneous. Subsequent events were to prove him correct.

The retreat was continued on the 5th, and Murat's advance guard, which had arrived in Svenciany on the 4th, ran into the Russian rear guard on the next day. This brought on a lively action around the village of Koczergiszki, which ended with the Russians withdrawing across the Disna.

The 4th was also a red-letter day for the Prussian hussars. Surely, the Prussians were anything but enthusiastic about Napoleon or his cause. Still, the action furnishes an excellent example of how soldiers, once their professional pride is placed on the line, will rise to an occasion even if doing so is against their own convictions. The 2nd Combined Hussars had been split away from their contingent serving with Macdonald and been assigned to Nansouty's I Cavalry Corps, part of Murat's advance guard on the 4th.

When the heads of the French cavalry columns approached the Disna, the Russians set fire to the bridge at Kosziany and withdrew to the village on the other side of the river. There, they dismounted their carabiniers, who barricaded themselves and prepared a defense. It was the job of the French cavalry to force a crossing over a narrow ford running alongside the burning bridge and to drive the Russians from the village.

The 16th (French) Chasseurs, who attempted to do just that, lost their composure when they came under the fire of the Russian skirmishers; they flooded back in disorder, claiming that it was impossible to get into the village. Now it was the Prussians' turn. They made a good crossing, only to be driven back into the river by a sudden charge of Russian hussars, armed with lances. Major von Zieten at once ordered the trumpeter to signal "Front!" The command was obeyed. In the ensuing melee, the Russians were beaten; following on their heels, the Prussians broke into the opening of the barricades, through which the Russians had come, and cut down the dismounted Russian defenders. Tearing through the village, they came out on the other side and ran into a dismounted Russian regiment of dragoons, which was completely dispersed. One Prussian was killed and twenty-four were wounded. The Russian losses ran to over 100 men. It was the first occasion during the campaign in which the Russian cavalry was actually bested in combat. This notwithstanding claims to the contrary by the romancers who see nothing but an unbroken string of successes for the French cavalry, based on no more solid ground than the fact that the Russians, fighting rear-guard delaying actions, generally broke off the engagements whenever the time was ripe.

The Russian retreat continued without further difficulties. Wittgenstein marched via Braslav to Druia, where he crossed the Dvina on July 10. The main column went via Leonpol, with the different corps arriving one by one in the fortified camp of Drissa between the 9th and 11th of July. Doctorov came via Stary Kriuky. While the corps of the main column were to occupy the camp itself, Wittgenstein and Doctorov were to extend the position on the opposite, the right, bank of the Dvina. Because of the extraordinary heat, more than 90°F, the Russians made their final marches during the moonlit nights, letting the troops rest during the day.

Murat followed slowly and did not reach Zamosza, where Nansouty had been directed as well, until the 13th. While Murat remained there with the three infantry divisions of I Corps, Nansouty's cavalry was sent forward to Czerk and Montbrun's II Cavalry Corps went toward Druia. Ney reached Drisviaty on the same day. Oudinot had gotten as far as Sokol on the 12th and went on, reaching Dunaburg by the 13th. There, he made an anemic attack against the 3000-man garrison defending the place, but he was beaten off. He then proceeded upriver on the 14th to get closer to Murat. Napoleon had not sanctioned Oudinot's try for Dunaburg, because this would have removed him too far from the army. He now placed both Oudinot and Ney under Murat's command for the next phase of operations.

On the extreme northern flank, Macdonald had remained in Rosieny for a spell after failing in his attempt against Wittgenstein and had pushed a few columns into Courland. He then advanced the Prussian division to Szavly, while Grandjean's division advanced against Smigli, where Macdonald himself arrived on the 14th.

It seems as though there was some sort of telepathy that linked the two combined Prussian hussar regiments, because on the very day of the crossing of the Disna, where the 2nd Regiment had shown a kind of performance that hearkened back to the days of Frederick the Great, the 1st Regiment, the famed "Death's Heads," mounted a commando-type operation that might have come right out of the script of an adventure movie.

At Poniewicz, some 50 miles south of Bauske, there was a Russian magazine known to be prepared for instant destruction. The fuses were laid and ready to be fired. Guarding it were forty Cossacks, a company of veterans, about 120 men, and a few regular soldiers. The hussars were sent to make a try for it. Lieutenant Raven, appropriately known as "Wild Raven," took an advance party of fifty hussars and marched some 30 miles ahead of the regiment. About 12 miles from his destination, Raven took his detachment off the road and went cross-country to avoid sentries and patrols. When his troopers arrived at Poniewicz, they quietly dismounted and overcame the sentries guarding the fuses without alarming the rest of the garrison.

While the fuses were being rendered harmless, it was learned that almost all the Cossacks were in the local tavern. Raven quickly had the place surrounded while he and a handful of hussars dismounted and entered the tavern. His demand that the Cossacks surrender was happily refuted as sabers flew from their scabbards. Another irony. Decades ago, Frederick the Great had complained about the regiment's predilection for dueling and had sent a tough new commanding officer to help them mend their ways. Quite obviously, Frederick's injunction against dueling had gone only skin deep because a new generation of "Death's Heads" now entered into a free-for-all. The tavern resounded to the clank of steel on steel, punctuated by some pistol shots. Not waiting for the rest of their detachment, "Wild Raven" and his *bon sabreurs* threw themselves into the fight and methodically cut the Cossacks down to size. The saber fight raged through the tavern and ended in the wine cellar, where the last of the Cossacks were finally cornered.

Word of this action immediately got around and became the subject of one of the patriotic picture postcards of the times.[11] As for "Wild Raven," he is said to have become the very first officer to receive the cross of the Legion of Honor during the Russian campaign.

Macdonald's main mission now was to cover the Niemen, which had become the water artery for the movement of supplies to the army. At the same time, he was to keep the garrison of Riga in check and to threaten a crossing of the Dvina in order to engage Barclay's attention. Eventually, he was to reduce Riga. Napoleon put great store in having this accomplished, because he wanted this strong point on the lower Dvina to anchor his right flank.

During the interim, Napoleon ordered Eugene and St. Cyr's Bavarians into the gap left by Davout's advance against Minsk; they were to form a reserve for Murat's columns moving toward Drissa and to form a link with Jerome's army group in the south. Eugene's IV (Italian) Corps reached Dveniki on the 10th after making a difficult lateral march over secondary tracks in a country where the main roads were often secondary themselves. This again took a terrible toll of the horses. St. Cyr and his VI (Bavarian) Corps had a comparatively easy time of it. They halted at Anusziszki while the Guard remained behind in Vilna with Napoleon. By July 6, the emperor had formulated the plan described below.

Barclay was to be held in front with demonstration by Murat, Oudinot, and Ney. Meanwhile, Napoleon himself, with the Guard and the two corps under Eugene—who was to be joined by Davout and Jerome, once Bagration was either eliminated or shunted too far south to take a hand—would advance toward Polotsk or Vitebsk. This would envelop Barclay's left flank and cut him off from both St. Petersburg and Moscow, this bringing on the final decision. It was toward this end that Napoleon had given Davout command of his own as well as Jerome's forces. (Of course, Davout had also not been informed that Jerome was in ignorance of this.) But Napoleon did not want this important movement to be set up in his absence. He therefore postponed carrying out his plan, because he thought he should remain in

Vilna until some sort of decision had fallen against Bagration. While his halt at Vilna, during the first few days, was justified by the condition of his army and his desire to see what developed against Bagration, his interests demanded that he follow Barclay sooner rather than later to deliver a decisive stroke.

Napoleon could not possibly expect Barclay to remain in happy ignorance of the danger he was in. Instead, the emperor should have done everything in his power to push Barclay and stay ahead of him. He knew very well that even without Davout and Jerome he was strong enough to deliver a crushing blow against the Russian main force, no matter what the cost. Thus, his faulty plan of operations, which awaited the outcome of what was but a subsidiary operation, resulted in another error. On the 9th, Napoleon realized that his plan was foiled when he learned that Bagration had fallen back to Bobruisk, and he finally decided to send forward to the Dvina the forces he had held back at Vilna.

The Young Guard marched at once, reaching Glubkoye by the 14th. The next day, Eugene marched, reaching Smorgoni on the 12th; he stayed there until the 14th and then moved on to Dokszitzi. For the time being, the troops of the Old Guard continued to remain in Vilna, where they were joined by the Bavarians, until they too departed on the 14th to join the Young Guard at Glubkoye. Once again, the entire army was advancing. But Napoleon's inactivity at Vilna had cost valuable time that could not be regained.

On the right wing, Davout, who by now had also taken charge of Jerome's army group, was directed toward Mohilev. But he was minus Reynier's VII (Saxon) Corps, which had been ordered back on the 11th to cover Poland and the right flank. This was done to free the Austrians, who had nearly twice his strength, for operations closer to the center of the action. Napoleon had become distrustful of the Austrians; he thought he would be able to keep a better eye on them by bringing them into the game. He had also learned that another Russian army was assembling around Lutzk under Tormassov (it was, in fact, completed by the 14th), but he did not think that this could involve any important forces.

The end of Napoleon's stay in Vilna, which represented the first interruption of the general advance, also defines the first phase of the campaign. The results obtained thus far had to be entirely unsatisfactory. Even though many military writers consider Napoleon's campaign a success up to this point, one must ask why. Because he had not been effectively opposed? Because he held a sizable chunk of Russian territory? Napoleon had hoped to open his offensive with a crushing blow to scatter his opposition and destroy Wittgenstein and Bagration, but he had been disappointed in all his aims. With the expenditure of considerable energy, he had merely succeeded in preventing the juncture of the two Russian armies—and only temporarily at that. This was actually a negative result. It would have been better if he had allowed the two to unite and face him as early as possible.

With his operations plan already a failure, the only possibility in the immediate offing was that he might still deliver a crushing blow against Barclay. Infinitely more troublesome had to be the fact that this theater of operations obviously presented severe obstacles to his usual method of conducting a campaign—fast marches and concentrated masses. If he closed his mind to these realities and did not intend to alter his methods to suit them, then he was bound to ruin his army and defeat himself.

The scene in the wake of the Grand Army was even less reassuring than the state of operations. By the end of July, the central army group under Napoleon was already down by about 65,000 men and the corps under Davout by over 30,000. More than 50,000 marauding deserters had spread themselves out across Lithuania alone. Many had congregated into bands, taking over the country manors of the nobility and even entire villages. Some were well organized and far more efficient than when they had been with the colors. They set out pickets against friend and foe alike and made travel along the lines of communication troublesome for the train columns and dangerous for individuals.

Thus, across the entire rear areas of the Grand Army there already ensued a struggle that can only be described as an out-and-out guerrilla war. The local peasantry, army detachments, and these bands of outlaws were pitted against each other in a free-for-all that knew no allegiances. And not many more weeks would pass before the Cossacks joined the action.

NOTES

1. Holzhausen, P. *Die Deutschen in Russland, 1812.* Berlin, 1912.
2. At the beginning of the campaign, these troops numbered as follows:

	Men
First Army corps	31,000
Grouchy's two divisions and Div. Valence	10,000

	Men
Vistula Legion (Div. Claparede)	7,000
Guard Lancer Brig. Colbert	1,700
Total	49,700

The Mecklenburg regiment of Division Compans had been left behind in Kovno (and would soon move to Vilna) and a substantial number of men were already missing from the ranks, so the total came to only 43,000 men.

3. Letter from Grodno, dated July 5, 1812. Cited in Du Casse, A. *Les Rois Freres de Napoleon.* Paris, 1883.
4. Cited from Ochs's unpublished papers in Kleinschmidt, A. *Geschicte des Koenigreichs Westfalen,* p. 507. Gotha, 1893.
5. At the beginning of the campaign, Bagration's troops numbered as follows:

	Men	Guns
Second Western Army	37,000	216
27th Inf. Div. (still coming up)	8,000	
Dorochov's detachment, inc. Cossacks	3,500	12
Platov's Cossacks	4,500	12
Total	53,000	240

Although the Russians, too, had suffered their share of losses from the great exertions, theirs were far fewer than those of the French, due to the better discipline of their troops. Bogdanovich puts the number of their troops at only 40,000, which seems too low.

6. Du Casse.
7. Kleinschmidt.
8. Mazade, Comte de., ed. *Correspondance du Mareshal Davout, 1801–1815.* Paris, 1885. 4 vols. Cited from Vol. III, by Kleinschmidt.
9. Thiers, in *History of the Consulate and the Empire,* Paris, 1834–1835, states that during the advance from the Niemen to the Dnieper, the Guard was forced to leave 100 guns behind. The number of those left behind by the rest of the corps was smaller—probably because they had fewer pieces of heavy caliber.
10. He assumed command of IV Infantry Corps due to Shuvalov's illness.
11. Pelet-Narbonne, G. von. *Geschichte der Brandenburg-Preussischen Reiterei.* II, 33. Berlin, 1905. 2 vols.

11. Drissa and Beyond

The fortified encampment of Drissa was to be the jewel of Phull's plan. The camp, established in a position covering both the St. Petersburg and Moscow roads, would offer the enemy few options, none of them good—so insisted Phull. Napoleon could not simply bypass the camp, because that would leave the Russian army astride his line of communications. If he left a covering force to contain the troops in the camp and advanced with the rest of his army, he would split his forces and run the risk of their piecemeal defeat. Should Napoleon decide to make an all-out assault against the camp, his columns would be shattered in front of its earthen ramparts.

That Napoleon's intelligence services would fail him in Russia is understandable. But what of the Russians? They had sources all over Europe, especially in Austria and Prussia, the latter being one of the major staging areas of the French assault. Although it is quite true that Phull's plan took concrete shape only during the early months of 1812, when the Grand Army was still assembling in Poland, the Russians should have been better informed than they were. It seems that they were still thinking in terms of the forces Napoleon had assembled in 1807 instead of the forces that were coming their way now.

At first, Alexander had been prepared to go along with Phull's Drissa plan. However, over the previous several weeks his confidence in his military adviser had been severely shaken. Just about all the top-ranking men in the army had pointed out the strategic disadvantages of the position at Drissa, particularly the fact that the forces deployed in the camp could easily be bypassed and bottled up there, notwithstanding Phull's contention that this was an unacceptable option for Napoleon.

Now, one of the tsar's senior adjutants, Colonel Michaud, a capable engineer officer, informed Alexander that the camp fortifications were not of state-of-the-art design. The faulty layout of the redoubts meant that they weren't even mutually supporting. Nor were the redoubts themselves much good. Their profiles were too low. There were other technical shortcomings as well. Worst of all was the field of fire the redoubts offered. In several places, wooded terrain came far too close allowing the enemy a covered approach. The inside of the camp also left more than a little to be desired. There, deeply cut ground would impede the internal movement of reserves from one threatened spot to another. Just above and below the camp were fords that would facilitate an easy crossing of the river by enemy forces. Directly in back of the camp flowed the deeply bedded Dvina, across which three bridges had been laid. The bridges were covered by bridgeheads that were too small, poorly situated, and not even completed. Indeed, in the event of a precipitate evacuation of the camp, the bridges would pose greater difficulties for friend than for foe. The Bunzelwitz Phull had in mind could have easily become a Pirna, the place where an entire Prussian corps was captured during the Seven Years' War. Alexander could see all this for himself, and he envisioned Phull's plan collapsing like a house of cards. He was by now fully aware that it would be impossible to face the French in the open field unless the two western armies were united.

Meanwhile, Barclay had learned from an adjutant that Napoleon was attempting to drive a wedge between him and Bagration. This bore the earmarks of an envelopment of his left flank. As a result, Alexander now gave Barclay permission to withdraw to Vitebsk, where Bagration was to join him. Orders were sent off to Bagration at once, directing him to effect this junction via Mohilev. This put an end to Phull's plan. The effort to unite the two western armies would lead both of them deeply into the Russian interior. This was to lend a new and, in the end, decisive character to the entire campaign. The urgency of the situation, as it was then perceived, also put an end to all the far-flung secondary operations. The Army of the Danube, freed by the Peace of Bucharest, was ordered to Volhynia as soon as the sultan ratified the treaty, which he did on July 15. There would be no offensive into Italy, as had been projected in some of the earlier plans.

A few weeks later, at a meeting in Abo that was held on August 27 to 31, Russian agreements with Sweden were finalized and Bernadotte consented to the recall of the Russian forces that were to have supported his campaign against the Danes in Norway. This made it possible to bring the bulk of the Finnish Corps to the Dvina.

Other measures now became necessary as well. Some 10,000 reservists had already arrived in Drissa, far fewer than had been expected. Wintzingerode was ordered to gather the best of what was available in the recruit depots to form a reserve corps around Smolensk. This was to include 17 battalions, 8 squadrons, and 4 artillery companies. Similar orders went to Miloradovitch, then the governor of Kiev. He was to form another reserve corps at Kaluga, numbering 54 battalions, 26 squadrons, and 14 artillery companies. These were to become the nucleus of a large reserve army to be formed from the militia. In order to replenish the recruit depots after this, a draft was ordered on July 13 calling upon the western provinces to furnish five men out of every 500 souls.

Barclay abandoned the Drissa camp and crossed the Dvina on the 14th, leaving behind Wittgenstein, who was reinforced to about 25,000 men. This left First Army with little more than 82,000 men.[1] These departed on the 16th, making a rather leisurely march toward Vitebsk via Polotsk. Wittgenstein, now also in charge of the 3000-man garrison of Dunaburg under General Hamen, was to cover the road to St. Petersburg from a position between Druia and Drissa. These measures put an end to the central idea of Phull's plan of making the fortified camp at Drissa a focal point of the Russian defense against the invasion.

Alexander's self-confidence, which had not been all that strong to begin with, was now at a low ebb. Any confidence there may have been had vanished with the demise of Phull's plan, so the tsar decided to leave the army and go to Moscow. From there he could direct whatever further measures were to be undertaken in defense of the empire. Some sources claim that he was gently induced to leave so that the generals could get on with their business.

Unfortunately, he neglected to name a commander in chief to direct the overall effort against Napoleon. Therefore, actual command devolved upon Barclay in his capacity as the minister of war. When Alexander left the army from Polotsk on July 18, he warned Barclay to see to the preservation of the army since Russia had no other. But, failing to take with him all the soothsayers and hangers-on, he left Barclay saddled with their continued presence at headquarters, which greatly added to the latter's difficulties.

Alexander arrived in Moscow on July 24, and he stayed there for a week before returning to St. Peterburg. From Moscow, the orders were issued for the raising of the militia in the central and northern provinces. The proclamation of a national war and the circulation of Alexander's resolve to make no peace as long as a single enemy soldier stood on Russian soil found their expected echo throughout the empire.

However, the raising of the militia and the goodwill everywhere proved insufficient. Large numbers had been gathered, but the general lack of preparation promised little hope for an effective reinforcement of the army. Not only was it a problem to arm and equip these men, but there was no cadre to turn these masses into combat-worthy formations. Thus, the job fell back to the army itself when a general conscription was ordered on August 16, that would bring recruits into the army depots to replace the losses sustained by the field army.

For the time being, First Army continued its retreat. Leaving Polotsk on July 20, it headed toward Vitebsk along the right bank of the Dvina. For a time, Barclay had considered crossing the river at Budhilovo, to reach Bagration via Senno and Orsza, with the idea of operating against Davout. Reportedly, he abandoned this idea because of a lack of magazines between the Dvina and the Dnieper. Had he marched at a faster pace from the start, such an undertaking might have been successful. But by now, the time had passed.

On the 23rd, First Army reached Vitebsk where its two columns were reunited. Before the day was out, III, IV, and V Infantry Corps and I Cavalry Corps returned to the left bank of the Dvina and took a position behind the Luczessa, one of its tributaries, along the road to Beszenkoviczi, while the rest of the army was still approaching. Its total strength was barely 82,000 men. Barclay had vacated Drissa none too soon. Napoleon might have caught up with him there and put him into a very difficult position. Indeed, it was due to fortuitous circumstances that Barclay even got to Vitebsk ahead of the French.

First, however, it is necessary to review the events transpiring around the Second Army and Bagration. He was last observed at Niesvicz, where his entire army had assembled with the exception of Platov's Cossacks, who had been left at Mir. The army had rested at Niesvicz between the 8th and 10th, while Platov fought the successful cavalry engagements of the 9th and 10th which were mentioned earlier.

At that time, Davout was in Minsk; from there he sent forward a strong detachment under Pajol (1 infantry and 1 cavalry regiment) as far as Igumen. Meanwhile, Jerome had reached the area of Novogrodok with V and VIII Corps and reached Slonim with VII Corps.

Bagration continued his retreat on the evening of July 10, reaching Slutzk on the 13th. There, he learned that the enemy was already at Sviszlocz. This impelled him to hurry, and he speedily covered the 100 miles to Bobruisk with five forced marches, arriving there on the 18th. Along the way, his rearmost elements had again been molested by the points of the French advance on the 13th. This called for some discouragement by the Russians to slow up the French. Once more, Platov turned around and fought another cavalry action near Romanovo on the 14th, and again Latour-Maubourg's cavalry corps was turned back with help from Vassilchikov's regular cavalry.

When, on July 9, Napoleon issued his detailed plans for an offensive against Barclay, the latter was thought to be concentrating at Drissa and ready to make a fight there. Davout was to shift to the north, in the direction of Borisov and Orsza, while Jerome, supported by Schwarzenberg, was to stay on top of Bagration. By July 11, Napoleon decided to send Davout as far east as Kochanov. From there Davout could operate either northward, in the direction of Vitebsk, toward Orsza, which was just a short march to the northeast, or southward toward Mohilev. Reynier and his Saxons, who had gotten as far as Stoloviczy, were now ordered to turn around and go back to Slonim to operate independently, covering Warsaw against Tormassov's army, which was known to be assembling to the south of the Pripet Marshes. With Reynier thus taking over the chore of covering the extreme right of the army, Schwarzenberg was to march across his rear and insert himself into the advance closer to the center.

But by July 13, Davout had received orders to march east toward Mohilev, while Grouchy's III Cavalry Corps was to go northeast to Kochanov and from there on to Babinoviczi to form a link with the main army group. At that time, both Grouchy and Colbert's Lancer Brigade of the Guard would pass back into the control of the main army. It was around this time when Davout thought he saw a chance to strike a decisive blow against Bagration. Davout had left Minsk on June 13, leaving one of his regiments behind temporarily to garrison the city, which was earmarked to become a major forward depot. That regiment was to be relieved by a march regiment coming up from the rear. Pajol's detachment was left in Igumen to keep an eye on the direction of Bobruisk.

Davout reached Mohilev from Igumen on July 20 and took the place after a light skirmish with the lone garrison battalion stationed there. He came upon a veritable bonanza of supplies, which the Russians had failed to destroy in the confusion, but this windfall was negated by the fact that the march from Minsk to Mohilev had again caused heavy losses in men and horses. Grouchy's III Cavalry Corps, on its march toward Kochanov, took Borisov on the 15th, ejecting its defending force, three weak garrison battalions under Colonel Gresser, who had then also gone off in the direction of Mohilev.

Bagration reached Bobruisk on July 18. There, on the following day, he met Prince Volkonski, another of Alexander's adjutants, who carried the dispatch mentioned earlier that ordered Bagration to seek a junction with the First Army via Mohilev and Orsza. In order to reach Mohilev ahead of Davout, Bagration sent General Raievsky forward on the same day with VII Infantry Corps and parts of IV Cavalry Corps under Sievers. The rest of the army followed on the next day, along with the Bobruisk garrison of six reserve battalions, which were incorporated into the army. By the 21st, Raievsky had gotten as far as Staroi-Bichov, and from there he sent his cavalry forward to check out Mohilev. They were in the nick of time to receive Gresser's detachment of the three reserve battalions Grouchy had ejected from Borisov. Also heading for Mohilev, but from a more northerly direction, these battalions now had Davout's cavalry hot on their heels. But instead of catching up to Gresser, Davout's cavalry got yet another unpleasant surprise when it encountered Sievers's horsemen and was chased back to Mohilev with substantial losses. All of this made it patently clear that the French were already in Mohilev.

Davout, no longer certain that he had the strength to overcome Bagration, was nevertheless convinced that he must block his path or at least make an attempt to do so, even though he had no more than 17,000 men[2] at best, and had no expectation for any timely reinforcements. Finding no suitable position at Mohilev, he went a short distance south toward the village of Saltanovka (Saltaitka), where he found an excellent position behind a tributary of the Dnieper, which provided an anchor for his left flank.

Bagration ordered Raievsky[3] to attack this position on the 23rd. Since both forces were fairly evenly matched, Raievsky could not drive Davout out. All that the Russians could do was withdraw in the direction of Dashkova. Davout made only a feeble pretense at a pursuit, because he knew that Bagration was somewhere behind Raievsky and had no desire to encounter his superior force. Davout was also aware that he had lost more than had his opponents. That it had been a stiff fight is attested to by the casualties: about 2500 Russians and 3400 French. For the latter, this amounted to about 20 percent of the troops.

During the night of July 23–24, Bagration concentrated his entire force, including Platov's and Dorochov's detachments, so he now had more than 40,000 men. However, despite his superior numbers, he—reluctantly—did not renew his attack on the next day. He had his orders from the emperor, and they directed him to join Barclay.

Some of the other reasons occasionally advanced for Bagration's failure to go after Davout must be dismissed as nonsensical, nothwithstanding Alexander's censure for not going right through Davout. Indeed, Bagration might have even welcomed finding his road to First Army blocked after an unsuccessful attack, because the desire to elude Barclay's authority continued to remain uppermost in his mind. He had already entertained the idea to march into the Ukraine, where he wanted to raise recruits to reinforce his army so that he might operate against the flank and rear of the French.

Barclay must have sensed Bagration's reluctance to join him when he sent Wolzogen, one of his adjutants, to confer with Bagration. It took all of Wolzogen's powers of persuasion and a pointed reference to Alexander's orders to keep Bagration from embarking on his own adventurous plans. In any event, Bagration withdrew to Staroi-Bichov, crossed the Dnieper there, and marched via Mstislavl to Smolensk, where he arrived on August 3. Platov and Dorochov, who had already crossed at Vorkolabov, joined First Army via Dubrovna and Liuboviczi.

Given the weakness of his forces, Davout had to be glad that Bagration did not renew his attack on the next day; he could not even think of pursuing him across the Dnieper. However, the weakness of his forces cannot be blamed on Jerome's actions and the turmoil caused by Jerome's departure from the army; much less can it be said that things would have turned out differently if Napoleon had allowed Davout to take all five, instead of just three, of his divisions in I Corps for his excursion against Bagration. These are fruitless speculations for apologists; they could be carried on endlessly. After all, it could also be said that if Bagration had not been forced to give up a large part of his Second Army to form a reserve army, the situation would have gone differently again.

Davout remained in place at Mohilev until Poniatowski came up on the 28th. Then, anticipating Napoleon's order, he marched upriver to a point across from Dubrovna, where he crossed the Dnieper on August 2 and had his troops go into cantonments on the left bank. At that time, the Westphalians under Junot, who had arrived to take charge of VIII Corps on July 30, stood in Orsza. Finally, IV Cavalry Corps under Latour-Maubourg arrived in Mohilev on August 5, coming from Glusk via Berezino. However, he and Division Dombrowski of V Corps, which was attached to him, were sent to Rohaczev at once. They arrived there on August 9 to observe Bobruisk and the Russian Corps Oertel, which was standing along the Pripet near Mozyr. These moves finally put an end to the attempts to isolate and destroy Bagration's Second Army, as the forces that had been earmarked for this purpose were positioned to support Napoleon's operations against Barclay in the center.

While the events just described were transpiring on the right wing of the army, Napoleon went after Barclay with his center and left. As already noted, the emperor's plan, formulated around the 6th, aimed at having Murat pin Barclay frontally at Drissa, so that Napoleon himself could take his center toward Vitebsk or Polotsk, thereby enveloping Barclay's left flank and cutting him off from St. Petersburg and Moscow. This plan had been set into motion on July 9, when the forces of the center, held back at Vilna, began their march toward the Dvina in the direction of Beszenkoviczi, where the river changes its course from a southwesterly to a northwesterly direction.

Napoleon departed from Vilna during the night of July 16–17, leaving Maret and the entire diplomatic staff behind. Appointed the emperor's deputy, Maret was empowered to issue orders even to the generals left in charge of the communications areas in the wake of the army. Actually, by the time he left Vilna, Napoleon had given up on the idea of catching Barclay at Drissa and was ready to settle for driving him toward St. Petersburg while Davout pushed Bagration across the Dnieper. He still entertained the hope of keeping the two Russian armies apart. With regard to his plans, this had so far been the sole positive result of the entire campaign.

At the very moment he left Vilna, however, Napoleon received news of an incident that had involved Sebastiani's division of II Cavalry Corps, which had arrived in Druia on July 14. There, during the dawn hours of the 15th, Wittgenstein's cavalry, crossing the Dvina during the night, had fallen upon Sebastiani's bivouacs. A French and a Polish hussar regiment caught the brunt of the attack and suffered heavy losses before the Wuerttembergers could come to their aid. Sebastiani had been forced to draw back to Slobodka. This incident renewed Napoleon's hope that Barclay might make an offensive after all, and the emperor took measures at once to meet such an attack with strong forces. The corps that had already advanced beyond Svenciany were halted, while the others were ordered to come up fast. On the 17th, when he learned that the Russian cavalry had withdrawn across the Dvina again, Napoleon recognized his error, and the army resumed its advance on the 18th.

On that same day, in Glubkoye, Napoleon received news that Barclay had abandoned the camp at Drissa and marched off in the direction of Polotsk. This made the time Napoleon had lost all the more regrettable. There was only a small hope that he might get to Vitebsk ahead of the

Russians, unless Barclay would do the unlikely and make an attack via Beszenkoviczi. On the right, Eugene, now joined by the Bavarian cavalry, had gotten only as far as Dokszitzi by the 18th; he was given a spur by Napoleon. In the center, the Guard, which had already been reunited at Glubkoye on the 16th, was followed at a distance by St. Cyr. On the left, Murat with I[4] and III Army Corps and I and II Cavalry Corps had gone from Zamosza to Disna, from whence he had sent Montbrun to reconnoiter the opposite banks of the Dvina on the 20th. Murat then followed to Beszenkoviczi. To Murat's left, Oudinot's II Corps had been directed to Drissa, which it reached on the 22nd. There, Oudinot's troops had the unwelcome task of undoing what the Russians had wrought. After the earthworks there had been leveled, Oudinot went on to Disna as well.

On the 23rd, the points of Eugene's IV Corps reached Beszenkoviczi, situated on the western bank of the Luczessa (actually, its south side at this bend of the river), and drove out some Russian light troops there. On the next day, the rest of the corps arrived with Murat's cavalry reserve. When patrols reported that Russians could be seen marching on the other side of the Luczessa, Eugene sent a light cavalry brigade to ford the river at once and ordered that a bridge be laid down. This was just finished when Napoleon arrived and joined the pursuit. He rode with them for 2 hours until it was ascertained that the Russian army had already gone past and that the force ahead was merely Doctorov's corps. When Napoleon returned, he sent Montbrun's cavalry across the river to conduct the pursuit, while Murat was ordered to take Nansouty's corps toward Vitebsk along the left bank of the Dvina.

By evening and all through the night, the entire central army group was massing at Beszenkoviczi. Only Oudinot and St. Cyr were still coming up. On the 25th, the entire army advanced in a single column. At its head marched Murat with Nansouty's cavalry, followed by Eugene, then the Guard and I Corps, with Ney's III Corps bringing up the rear. The Wuerttembergers were at the tail end.

Since the 23rd, the main force of the Russian First Army had stood behind the Luczessa at Vitebsk. Its assembly had been completed by the 24th, with only Doctorov and Pahlen still coming up. Because of a false report that Bagration had already seized Mohilev, Barclay thought that the junction of the two armies was secured. Still underestimating the strength of the French, he now considered a joint offensive with Bagration. However, he soon discovered his error—about Bagration, that is—and decided to wait at Vitebsk for the arrival of supply columns from Velish before moving on via Orsza to link with the Second Army. To prepare for this movement, he sent a detachment under Tutshkov III[5] ahead toward Babinoviczi on the

24th. On the next day, orders went to Bagration, in the name of the tsar, to make an advance against the enemy's right.

In order to delay the French advance, Barclay sent Ostermann forward on the 24th with IV Infantry Corps,[6] reinforced with some cavalry. Toward Beszenkoviczi, the French cavalry points were encountered and driven back while Ostermann took a position near Ostrovno. There, a lively engagement ensued on the 25th between Ostermann and Murat's advance guard, consisting of Division Delzons of IV Corps and Nansouty's cavalry.[7]

Of course, the cavalry had been the first to arrive on the scene and Murat, his blood up, was impatiently awaiting the arrival of the infantry, for better or worse, because the Russian advance troops stood under the cover of brush and trees. An hour passed before some Italian light infantry arrived on the double. Although worn-out, they were hounded into the attack at once, but they could make no headway until some artillery arrived on the scene. Then, the Russians were slowly pushed back to a point where it was possible for the arriving infantry masses to deploy on the open ground.

Unexpectedly, one of the Italian infantry regiments was in trouble. Two Russian guns, unnoticed by the edge of a stand of trees, had opened fire and found the range, landing several well-placed hits. The infantry was already severely shaken when Russian dragoons swept around the trees and into the breaking infantry, doing a great deal of damage. Suddenly, the entire wing was in danger. Murat's time had come at last. Placing himself in front of the nearest cavalry regiment, the 9th Lancers, he led them in a wild charge that restored the action and forced Ostermann to withdraw to Kakuvaczino, where he was received by Division Konovnitzyn from III Infantry Corps.

The advance of the French army made Barclay's march to Babinoviczi impossible. Instead, he now intended to fight a battle in the Vitebsk position. With this in mind, an order was sent to Bagration to make haste toward Orsza and prevent the enemy from going past that point toward Smolensk and thus into Barclay's rear.

Barclay's army, after the detachment of Tutshkov's column and the combat losses of the 25th, barely came to more than 75,000 men. Since Napoleon had more than 135,000,[8] Barclay could have hardly escaped a terrible beating. Apparently, Barclay had permitted himself to become influenced by the aggressive mood of the army, as well as by the strutters and posers who continued to clutter his headquarters, because the position at Vitebsk was not even a good one.

Now, however, it was necessary to concentrate the army, but since Doctorov and Pahlen still had not come up, Barclay needed to gain yet another day, July 25. Therefore, Konovnitzyn, with a newly formed rear guard,[9] was ordered to impede the enemy's progress on that day as much as he could. In this fashion, the events of the previous day were repeated. Step by step, from one position to the next, Konovnitzyn succeeded in holding up the French advance troops all day until, toward evening, General Tutshkov I received him with the rest of III Infantry Corps near Dobreika. During the night, both Tutshkov and Ostermann crossed the Luczessa and returned to the main position, while Doctorov and Pahlen also came in from the other side of the river.

It was a stroke of good fortune for both Barclay and Russia when, during the same night, Bagration's dispatch arrived, reporting that he had been unable to break through at Mohilev because Davout was there in force and that he would have to evade him by going farther to the right. This information robbed Barclay of the hope that the Orsza-Smolensk road would be covered, and it gave him as good an excuse as any for not making a stand against Napoleon at this time, notwithstanding the clamoring of all the saber rattlers at his headquarters. Still, Yermolov, Barclay's chief of staff, pressed for a war council, at which it was decided, not without opposition, to continue the retreat. In view of the enemy's presence, however, this was easier said than done. It would be necessary to deceive the French into believing that the army intended to stand and fight. Toward this end, the army was ordered to remain in place until midday on the 27th. Meanwhile, an advance guard under Pahlen[10] was sent across the Luczessa during the night. It was to make a step-by-step defense of the forefield to keep the French away from the main position.

The ruse worked well beyond expectations. Napoleon was busy throughout the 27th, preparing for the battle he had so ardently sought. For this reason, the action by the French advance guard[11] was not strongly pursued, even though Division Broussier from IV Corps had been drawn into the action as well. As a result, Pahlen was able to maintain himself much longer than expected, so the retreat did not begin until after 4 p.m., when the army departed in three columns. The cavalry remained behind long enough to receive Pahlen and, once disengaged, broke up into three rear guards, one for each of the columns that had gone before. This put an end to the delaying action. In 3 days of fighting, the Russians had lost 3500 men; the French losses were probably the same.

Doctorov's column arrived in Smolensk on July 31; the remaining columns arrived the next day, after rejoining at Porietchie. Platov also reached

Smolensk before nightfall. Thus, the First Army was in Smolensk a day before Bagration, who arrived on the 2nd and was followed by his Second Army on August 3.

Napoleon's attempt to keep the two armies separated was now a complete failure. He had wasted July 27 waiting for the rest of his army to arrive. With the exception of IV Corps, which had come only as far as Uszacz, the army's advance had been delayed by the fact that the corps were marching in a single column from Beszenkoviczi rather than advancing by different routes that would converge on their objective.

It is justifiable to speculate about why Napoleon had not made straight for the Vitebsk-Smolensk road via Senno once he learned that the Russians had left Drissa, which meant he had little chance of catching up with them at Vitebsk. Going straight for the Smolensk road, he might have blocked them there after keeping Murat on their heels. Yet he failed to do this even after he should have realized that it was as much in the interests of the Russians to avoid a battle as it was in his to force one. Worse, he had fallen victim to a fairly plump ruse, and he was unable to make up his mind to attack with the corps he had in hand while there was still time. The risk involved was hardly unacceptable in view of the forces he had. Just as his subordinates had failed in his play against Bagration, so had Napoleon himself failed to take on Barclay. He had been angry with his subordinates over the former and blamed them for their failure, even though it had been largely the result of his asking too much of them. He now had even better reason to be angry with himself. He could have avoided his own failure, but he had not done all that was possible because, at the decisive moment, he had lacked resolution. His hesitation had prevented him from having the battle he so desperately wanted, and it saved the Russian army.

When the departure of the Russians became known on the morning of the 28th, the French immediately advanced to Vitebsk. Since not a trace of the Russians was found there, Murat was sent toward Agapanovszina and Ney toward Rudnia. When Murat ran into the Russian rear guard, Eugene, who had at first followed Ney, was sent after Murat. Because Napoleon now thought he had the entire Russian army before him, he also pulled up the Guard. The situation was clarified on the next day, when it was learned that the Russians had not crossed the Dvina but had gone to Smolensk. Napoleon then gave up the pursuit and returned to Vitebsk.

The extreme heat—the mercury hit 95°F on July 28—and the great supply difficulties made it necessary to interrupt operations again. Kovno was 250 miles to the rear, and the magazines along the Vistula were twice that distance. In addition, the supply columns in the wake of the army were unable to stay in touch. Worst of all was the shortage of water along the march routes. Due to the parching heat, the groundwater level had receded; the wells that were found soon yielded little better than liquefied mud, which the men strained through cloth and drank anyway. This gave rise to all sorts of intestinal disorders. The surgeon general of the Wuerttembergers, Schuntter, described the bivouacs of the 25th Division as looking like hospitals. Suicides were being reported all over the army.

Entire villages were going up in flames, which, in view of the disorder prevailing everywhere, was not at all surprising. In the droughtlike conditions, even a single spark would set the thatched roofs of the cottages ablaze. Captain Borcke, a Westphalian with Jerome's corps, explained that this was not generally done on purpose but occurred because the great need drove the men to carelessness. As a result, every hour, single buildings went up in flames that, more often than not, turned entire villages and even sizable towns into blazing infernos. The causes were often innocuous: Here, men, who had obtained some flour, overheated an oven in the attempt to bake their own bread; there, a small fire lit under a beehive to get at the honey was left unattended. These were the sorts of things that often brought on disaster. [12]

On the other hand, one hears stories from the cavalry, which was often far afield from the column roads, reminiscing about roasted chicken, beefsteaks, and omelets. But these were the exceptions. On the whole, the march route of the army led through a barren wasteland, made worse by the actions of both friends and foe. Not a little of this damage was, of course, perpetrated by the Russians themselves, as they gradually implemented their scorched-earth policy. This was done in the deliberate effort not only to destroy the sources for subsistence but also to incite the hatred of the Russian peasantry, who were abandoning their land in droves, with entire communities seeking refuge in the forests. In the hot and dry weather, the Cossacks would set entire abandoned villages ablaze simply by firing a pistol at a thatched roof at short range. On the whole, privations had reached a point where even the members of the Guard, who were always accorded preferential treatment and were the first to receive supplies, looted the abandoned buildings of Vitebsk.

As a result, Napoleon had Berthier write on July 29 that "unless the enemy forces other measures, the army is to have a rest of 7 or 8 days, in order to establish magazines." Of course, in the apologists' opinion Napoleon halted operations at Vitebsk partly because he finally wanted to make it possible for Barclay and Bagration to unite and he believed the halt might embolden them to accept a battle. If this was indeed so, then his decision came at a time when he was no longer able to prevent the junction of their forces anyway, and it was made after the initial attempts to keep them apart had taken far too great a toll of his forces.

At that time, Oudinot's II Corps stood in the area of Polotsk, facing Wittgenstein and a great deal of trouble. From there, on August 4, the marshal sent a plea for help, which caused Napoleon to divert St. Cyr's VI (Bavarian) Corps[13] to his assistance.

The results of the campaign thus far not only were unsatisfactory but had to give reason for grave concern. Not a single blow had been landed on the enemy. Instead, as will be seen, Napoleon's detachments under Oudinot and Reynier had even been handed setbacks. Napoleon's sole success so far had been the occupation of a large but poor patch of enemy territory, for which he had paid an exorbitant price. Despite the fact that most of the troops had yet to lay eyes on the enemy's main force, the army had already lost 130,000 men and 80,000 horses. Oudinot's, Ney's,[14] and St. Cyr's corps, as well as the reserve cavalry and the divisions of I Corps with Davout, had suffered the most. In particular, the shrinkage of the cavalry in the main and in Davout's army groups, from 62,147 to 38,722, must have been adversely felt in so large a theater of operations.

The reasons for this frightening meltdown of the army rested in part with the army itself and in part with Napoleon, who had not paid·sufficient heed to the difficulties the country would offer. The poor discipline of the troops—partly resentful, partly youthful and inexperienced—has already been noted, as has the poor performance of the commissariat. The lion's share of the blame for the deterioration of the army belongs to the commissariat, however, because even when it functioned, it did so inadequately and incorrectly.

Given the poverty of the country, the oppressive heat, the forced marches conducted with great masses, and the daily bivouacs in areas that had little water, much of it bad or deliberately spoiled, the troops were bound to become doubly sensitive to the lack of proper supplies. Sicknesses of epidemic proportions hit everywhere, especially in VI Corps. Men fell by the thousands, and so did the horses, who were lacking feed as well. Other thousands absented themselves from the army to find sustenance wherever it was to be had, and when they did find it, they had little desire to return to the misery prevailing along the column roads. As already noted, more than 50,000 stragglers drifted around in Lithuania alone. Napoleon had even authorized the nobility there to use their serfs to round up as many stragglers as possible and to hand them over to the nearest garrisons.

Thus, a halt was indeed necessary, especially since the area around Vitebsk was only marginally better cultivated than the country left behind. However, as Napoleon informed Berthier on the 29th, the halt was to be of short duration, only long enough to allow stragglers and the convoys to catch up. The emperor was resolved to continue his advance as relentlessly as before. Despite the cost of the campaign so far, it still had not occurred to him that his method of campaigning was out of place in this theater of war and that it was, in fact, the most important source of his losses. Yet given the thinly populated expanses of Russia and the prevailing means of communication, success, if it was to be had at all, could come only through a systematic conduct of the war.

Just as the exploitation of the country's resources would require much time, given the distances involved, so would the securing of these require a step-by-step advance, establishing new operations bases because no territory could be left behind with its resources not secured. This kind of warfare, however, was totally alien to Napoleon's style. Worst of all, he still thought the means he had at hand were sufficient to free himself from such considerations. Thus, all the care he expended in the attempt to regulate his rearward communications and the flow of supplies would remain fruitless, because he had left untouched the roots of the problem.

NOTES

1. At the beginning of operations, the First Western Army numbered 150 battalions, 132 squadrons, 18 Cossack regiments, and 49 batteries, comprising 104,250 men and 7000 Cossacks, with 558 guns. Added in Drissa were 19 battalions and 20 squadrons, totaling 9917 men. Absent at this time were:

   Dorochov's detachment: 4 battalions, 8 squadrons, 2 Cossack regiments, 1 battery—about 3500 men, 12 guns

   Platov's Cossacks: 11 Cossack regiments, 1 battery—4500 men, 12 guns

   Detached to Riga: 1 Cossack regiment, 1 battery—600 men, 12 guns

   The losses incurred so far came to about 5000 men.

   Wittgenstein's corps, reinforced with reserves, numbered 36 battalions, 31 squadrons, 1 Cossack regiment, and 9 batteries, totaling about 25,000 men, with 108 guns. Additional reserve formations arriving at Drissa (11 battalions and 5 squadrons) were broken up and distributed to the line formations. Thus, the army, when it departed from Drissa, numbered 82,500 men, with 414 guns, in 118 battalions, 108 squadrons, 3 Cossack regiments, and 37 batteries. This figure includes about 1200 Cossacks.

2. Of the troops directly under Davout's orders on the day of the action at Mohilev, the Vistula Legion, Light Cavalry Brigade Bourdesoulle, and Pajol's detachment were still approaching. In addition, three regiments had been left behind, one each in Kovno, Vilna, and Minsk. Thus, the troops available to Davout included only 13,000 infantry and about 3000 to 4000 cavalry, divided as follows:

Battalions	Squadrons		
10		of Div. Desaix	
15		of Div. Compans	of I Corp.
	4	of Brig. Pajol	
—	16	of Div. Valence	of I Cav. Corps
25	20		

Chambray claims there were only 20 battalions.
3. Since two of Raievsky's battalions had been attached to Platov, his corps numbered 22 battalions and 8 squadrons of VII Infantry Corps and 16 squadrons of IV Cavalry Corps.
4. I Corps had only three divisions left, since two, as well as the light cavalry brigades, had gone with Davout. During his absence, the corps was commanded by Mouton-Lobau.
5. The strength of Tutshkov III's detachment was 4 battalions, 12 squadrons, and 1 Cossack regiment, with 6 guns.
6.

	Battalions	Squadrons
IV Inf. Corps	18	
From VI Inf. Corps		8
From I Cav. Corps		8
From II Cav. Corps	—	4
	18 (weak)	20

The troops absent from IV Corps (4 battalions and 8 squadrons) were at this time part of Dorochov's detachment.
7. Division Delzons had 17 battalions, and I Cavalry Corps had 44 squadrons. Division Valence of I Cavalry Corps was with Davout.
8. The strength of the troops at Napoleon's disposal on the 27th may be calculated as follows:

	Current Strength	Original Strength
The Guard (minus Vistula Legion and Colbert's brigade)	28,000	38,600
I Corps, 3 divisions	32,000	41,000
III Corps, 2 regiments in Vilna and Kovno	25,000	39,300
IV Corps, with Bavarian cavalry	37,000	47,600
I Cav. Corps (less Div. Valence)		8,500
II Cav. Corps	13,000	10,000
Total	135,000	185,000

The "Current" figures do not reflect the losses of the 25th, 26th, and 27th.

9. Konovnitzyn's rear guard consisted of his own 3rd Infantry Division (10 battalions), Ostermann's cavalry (20 squadrons), and the remainder of I Cavalry Corps (12 squadrons).

10. Pahlen's detachment was thrown together from troops of several corps and numbered 14 battalions, 32 squadrons, and 2 Cossack regiments, with 40 guns. The battalions, however, were so weak that the entire infantry numbered no more than 4000 men.

11.

	Battalions	Squadrons
Div. Delzons ⎱ of IV Corps	17	
Div. Broussier ⎰	18	
I Cav. Corps (less Div. Valence)	—	44
Total	35	44

12. Lesczynski, F., ed. *Kriegerleben des Johann von Borcke*. Berlin, 1888.

13. The Bavarian cavalry was not with the corps. It had been transferred to IV Corps, where it remained.

14. Ney's corps had suffered badly during the march to the Dvina, especially the Wuerttembergers, who had been constantly forced to march in the rear. Additionally, it had left behind seven battalions in Vilna and Kovno.

12. The Chase Resumes

"It would be foolish to go any further. Here we must halt and regain our strength." Some have attempted to interpret this remark, made by Napoleon at Vitebsk, as meaning that he had considered the idea of ending the campaign there, sitting out the winter, and going on in the next season. The order he dictated to Berthier, which called for the halt, says otherwise.

He had hoped to open the campaign with a damaging blow so that he might intimidate Alexander into suing for peace, but he had been unable to bring either about. Still, staying at Vitebsk was something other men might do. It would mean resorting to a kind of war that was light-years removed from the style of Napoleon, the master gunner, who brought his armies up in the fashion of horse artillery, unlimbered his guns in a flash, and let his cannonballs fly. What would they think in Vienna, Berlin, or London? In Paris?

Surely, the idea of calling a halt and sitting out the winter came up. Apart from the fact that it would have been more appropriate to do so in Smolensk than in Vitebsk, the idea had much to recommend it. Napoleon could have reorganized, cleared up his rear areas, and harnessed the resources of the formerly Polish provinces. He could have used the time to raise new forces, bring forward the reserves, and make all the necessary preparations to go not only after Moscow but St. Petersburg as well. That this respite would have benefited the Russians as well could hardly have bothered Napoleon, given the vast superiority of his resources.

But the idea also had its negative aspects, which Napoleon outlined to those around him at his headquarters. He saw the French army as an instrument for the offensive and believed it was not nearly so well suited for a defensive war, the waging of which would be further complicated when the rivers froze. He also did not think that the army would take kindly to wintering in a hostile country. Above all, however, he was concerned about the impression such a decision would make upon a Europe that had become accustomed to his lightning strokes. A halt in midstride would surely be interpreted as having been forced upon him by the actions rather than the passivity of the Russian army, and it would stir up all the enemies of France. "Nothing," said Napoleon, "is more dangerous to us than a prolonged war."

It was dangerous not merely for France but for the emperor himself. His position with the French nation demanded an early continuation of operations. This was the main consideration that drove him forward. If he were to postpone operations now, when misadventures had already occurred on both flanks, his decision would raise the specter of the Spanish campaign, which was already a serious drain on the empire. It would also raise the question of whether the French nation, already showing signs of war weariness, would be willing to support two such costly efforts. Not only was Napoleon's political opposition beginning to gain renewed impetus, but even his supporters were beginning to wonder if there would ever be an end to these wars.

These were the reasons that pointed toward the timely resumption of the advance. Such a course was also very much in line with Napoleon's character. He did not simply need new laurels—he craved them. He was so full of himself, his will to dominate was so boundless, that his overweening pride demanded the humiliation of his enemies and the quickest possible realization of his plans. Nothing that had happened so far could induce him to put all this off for another year.

Of course, at this point, his resources were such that he could still hope to force a timely conclusion of the war at a single grand stroke. Despite heavy losses, Napoleon still had command of 314,000 men.[1] Of these, 199,000 were under his own and Davout's command, and 115,000 were in the detached forces. Moreover, most of these men were the old soldiers, the fittest, who had survived the hardships and exertions and could be expected to hold up better under whatever was yet to come. That is, Napoleon expected that from here on the operational noncombat losses would not continue to run as high as they had.

In addition, Napoleon could count upon substantial new reinforcements. IX Corps, with about 31,000 men, was already across the Vistula and heading toward the Niemen. There were another 30,000 men in march formations that had come that far as well. At the same time, the new Polish-Lithuanian formations numbered about 23,000. Finally, about 2600 Wuerttembergers and Westphalians had been left behind in Koenigsberg and Danzig. All these added up to well over 86,000 additional men, and there were others. Under Augerau's command were another 55,000 men in Prussia and the bordering provinces; their own reinforcements, about 19,500 men, either were on their way or would soon be available. Thus, it was possible to bring up more than 28,000[2] of these as well. An additional 22,000 men were in march formations that were still on their way to Poland, and another 5800 Austrians were earmarked as replacements for Schwarzenberg's corps.

Given these circumstances, Napoleon could see no reason for halting his advance. Indeed, he felt the situation demanded that he continue. This, then, was exactly what he did, even though he was aware of the disgruntled mood of the army: From the generals on down into the rank and file, there were men who obviously had reservations about making a deeper penetration into the vast Russian expanses. Smarting from his lack of success so far and needing to justify himself, Napoleon had thrown open for discussion among his intimates the question of whether the campaign should be continued. He had asked for their opinion, and they gave it to him. There was, to say the least, no enthusiasm. It was unfortunate that Napoleon chose this time, when his luck appeared to have deserted him, to do something he had never done before. It was bound to undermine the confidence of his generals. "An expedition such as ours," he told them, "never succeeds unless it is done in a single move." They did not appear convinced.

The only direction a continuing advance could take was toward Smolensk and Moscow, the same direction the retreating Russian army had taken— and the Russian army itself, not some geographic point, had to be the objective. There would be no profit in secondary operations. A thrust at St. Petersburg instead would only lead through even more barren country than that which the army had just traversed. Indeed, it was to be hoped that the road to Smolensk and beyond would offer better resources than had been encountered so far. Therefore, the march to Smolensk was agreed upon.

But if a march to Moscow was to be accomplished within the year, then the army needed to be on its way soon. The weather could be counted upon for only another 2 months, and Moscow was still 350 miles away. Moreover, the Russian diplomatic success with Finland and Turkey now became known, making it all the more imperative that a military decision be forced before the effects of the agreement came into play. That is, Sweden could now be expected to shed its cloak of neutrality and step into the Russian camp. Also, the eventual intervention of the troops freed from the Swedish expedition, as well as the Danube Army (which had been operating against the Turks), would reinforce the Russian effort against the French. These events were bound to strengthen Alexander's resolve.

However, passing into a renewed attacking phase, Napoleon did not go straight for the enemy but, instead, opted for a wide strategic envelopment, such as those of Marengo, Ulm, Jena, and Regensburg. In a sweeping movement to his right, he intended to gain the left flank and rear of the Russians and thereby push them off the Moscow road. This made it necessary to cross the Dnieper twice.

Clausewitz calls this maneuver "the most incomprehensible event" of the entire campaign. The famed Prussian theorist was of the opinion that Napoleon should have gone straight for Smolensk via Rudnia—a direct approach, which would have taken him to his objective more quickly. St. Cyr, in his memoirs, thought Napoleon should have concentrated toward his left and gone around Barclay's right. Even though both alternatives would have spared Napoleon a twofold crossing of the Dnieper, each one was impractical. Clausewitz's proposal ignores the fact that on the basis of Napoleon's experience so far, the emperor could expect that Barclay would again avoid a confrontation (Napoleon could not possibly know of the conflicting crosscurrents at work in the Russian headquarters, which tended to force a fight on their commander in chief). St. Cyr's idea would have resulted in separating Napoleon even further from Davout and would have offered Barclay yet another opportunity to slip away.

To prepare for his wide strategic envelopment, Napoleon had already directed Eugene to extend himself to his left in order to attract Barclay's attention to his own right. At the same time, Davout made a move toward Dubrovna, attended by a great deal of commotion, to reinforce the suggestion that a concentration toward the Russian right was indeed under way. Junot and Poniatowski had instructions to remain quiet. In order to support this move across the Dnieper, the line of operations had to be changed as well. Instead of running via Glubkoye, it now led via Orsza, Borisov, and Minsk to Vilna, where the establishment of magazines was ordered, along with the strengthening of the defenses of these places.

As to the Russians, their two western armies were now united and numbered 113,119 men and 8000 Cossacks,[3] including Wintzingerode's reserve corps of 7000 men, which was broken up and distributed when it reached the armies. Of its 17 battalions, 10 went to First Army, which was now up to 77,712 men, while 7 went to Second Army, which now numbered 43,407 men. The cavalry of the reserve corps was sent to Miloradovitch in

Kaluga, where a reserve army was forming. Thus, in the course of the campaign, both armies had received about 20,000 replacements, while the losses came to about 30,000. Of these, about 7000 were combat losses; the remainder were due to illness and desertion, the latter particularly from the Polish-Lithuanian troops.

First Army stood on the right bank of the Dnieper, and the Second on the left. The latter had moved Division Neverovsky, reinforced with some cavalry, forward to Krasnoi to cover against Orsza, and its line of outposts ran, in an arc, from Katan by the Dnieper to Cholm on the road to Porietchie. On the extreme right, around Dukovtshina, stood Wintzingerode with a raiding detachment consisting of 1 dragoon and 3 Cossack regiments.

Now that the Russians were so closely concentrated, they were beginning to experience a serious supply pinch and a general lack of water. They had gone beyond the outer—or rather, the inner—perimeter of their magazines, which meant that far more supplies were destroyed than were used, although the French managed to lay their hands on some. Consequently, the Russians were forced to requisition. Being on their own ground, they had a great advantage over the French. Orders were issued for every household to furnish a fixed quantity of zwieback, grits, and oats, which were to be delivered to designated collecting points, where the army trains would take over. Supplies, however, were not the major problem.

The proximity of the two western armies brought Barclay and Bagration so close together that the air fairly bristled with electricity. Bagration indulged himself in a great deal of pompous and patriotic rhetoric, laden with innuendos and reproach, even while he made a grand gesture of subordinating himself to a man who had less seniority than he had. However, not even Alexander was deceived by this; the tsar laced his imperial authority with a large dose of diplomacy and forbearance to dampen the roar of the Russian bear.

Barclay managed to get in a few ripostes of his own in a duel of words that threatened to degenerate into a verbal brawl. Although he and Bagration met in an air that is best described as frigid, they did attempt to draw up some plans for united action. However, the differences between the two made it impossible for anything useful to emerge. The two western armies may have been united in body, but they were still as divided as ever in spirit. Barclay's quandary was exacerbated when Constantine, the tsar's brother, returned from St. Petersburg, providing a rallying point for all the troublemakers who continued to cling to headquarters.

The armies were united, but what should be done? In a letter to Barclay, Alexander expressed his hope for an offensive, but he failed to make this an order. The army wanted to fight as well, especially after news of Wittgenstein's and Tormassov's success began to circulate. Indeed, the occasion appeared auspicious. The extraordinary supply problems that had befallen the Grand Army were now known to the Russians, and the French were estimated to have no more than 150,000 men. Given the broad front Napoleon presented, it was thought that he could concentrate no more than about 75,000 men if an attack was made against his center—that is, in the direction of Rudnia-Vitebsk. If the action was successful, the Russians would hold the interior line and could then go after Napoleon's wings, which would be isolated and widely separated.

Toll made this proposal to Barclay but could not get him to agree. The general wanted to do no more than hold Smolensk with Second Army while First operated against Porietchie, where he assumed there were strong enemy forces. Only after these were beaten would he try for Rudnia.

Once Barclay expressed his opposition to Toll's plan, Constantine and Bagration were all for it. Constantine was so enthused by the plan that he called a war council on August 6, at which Toll's proposal was accepted. But it was not until evening, after the meeting had broken up, that Barclay finally gave in, with the proviso that the operation would be carried no farther than a day's march from Smolensk. However, Barclay agreed not because he was convinced that the plan was a good one but simply because he did not think that he could uphold his objections in the face of Constantine and Bagration, not to mention the aggressive mood of the army. Even if Barclay's worries about his right flank were unfounded and he should have been more worried about his left, it must be admitted that an offensive at that time was highly problematic. A resolute advance against the center of an apparently widely deployed enemy army might promise some success, but—especially against a Napoleon—it could not offer a lasting advantage. On the other hand, a defeat, even a mere setback, would put the Russian army into a critical position and bring Russia to the brink of disaster. Assuming that the Russian assessment of Napoleon's strength was correct—and it was not—he would still have had enough men to exploit a success. Thus, the possibilities of the little that might be gained were completely out of proportion to the magnitude of the risk.

However, the decision had been made, and on August 7 the Russians advanced in three columns into the country north of the Dnieper. The right, under Tutshkov I, went toward Kovalevskoie; the center, under Doctorov, toward Prikas-Vidra; and the left, under Bagration, toward Katan. To cover the road to Orsza against Davout, only Division Neverovsky[4] had been left at Krasnoi, an oversight that almost proved fatal.

The advance, however, soon bogged down. During the night of the 8th, Barclay received a report from Wintzingerode, who had advanced toward

Velish, that strengthened his belief that his right was in danger. It was an erroneous report that placed strong enemy forces at Porietchie. Tutshkov was turned around at once and sent back to Stabna before the night was out, while Doctorov waited at Prikas-Vidra for Bagration's arrival. While he was waiting, Doctorov's advance guard,[5] supported by Pahlen's III Cavalry Corps, had a smart action around Inkovo and Molevo-Boleto.

Sebastiani's division was still in its bivouacs, recovering from the marches, when it was again hit with a surprise attack at dawn. And, again, it seems that the French cavalry was caught unprepared. The diarists are unanimous in stating that it was Subverie's brigade, consisting of a Polish, a Prussian, and a Wuerttembergian regiment, that attempted to save what could be saved. Major von Werder, the commander of the Prussian Ulans, received the Officers' Cross of the Legion for covering the retreat with his lancers until Montbrun came up to restore the action. The Wuerttembergers, when roused from their bivouacs, had saddled up and gone off toward the sound of the trumpets without waiting to take down their picket lines. A while later, when some of them were being chased back, they ran into the pickets; several men (and their mounts) were brought crashing down and were taken prisoner by the Russians. During this same action, a Polish officer was hit in the thigh by an arrow, while a Wuerttemberger caught another in his clothes. Loosened by Kirgiz or Kalmuck horse archers, both arrows were saved as souvenirs and were great conversation pieces around the campfires for some time to come. Even though nobody mentions any particulars, the consensus in Subverie's brigade appears to have been that on that day, Sebastiani, a Corsican, lost what little love his foreign troopers had left for him.

Although the French cavalry had again suffered serious losses, Napoleon was pleased because the action gave him a clue as to what Barclay's intentions might be. The opposing armies had been completely out of touch with each other for several days, and Napoleon had received no information.

Meanwhile, on August 9, Tutshkov remained in place while Doctorov marched to Moszinki and Bagration to Prikas-Vidra. This change in direction, and Barclay's indecision, which it reflected, again elicited general displeasure and exasperation throughout the Russian army. Matters got worse when news of the successful cavalry action against Sebastiani got around, as this seemed to furnish clear proof of what might have been expected from a resolute offensive. When Barclay halted the advance altogether, a storm of protest arose. Voices were even heard loudly accusing him of treason.

But it was not until the 12th, after he had already lost 4 days on the road to Porietchie, that he could be induced to return to the road to Rudnia. By then, incoming reports no longer left any doubts that the enemy was massing between Babinoviczi and the Dnieper. Thus, on August 13 and 14, the army marched to Volkovaia, where Barclay was to meet the expected French offensive in an advantageous position. But the army was still in a foul mood and under the impression that it had been cheated out of a victorious offensive.

Bagration, who had taken it upon himself to return to Smolensk on the 12th, was ordered to get back into line and take part in the battle that was expected to take place on the 15th—Napoleon's Day (a French holiday). Bagration, however, took so much time complying that his main force had only gotten as far as Nadva on the 14th. Indeed, Raievsky had gotten no further than 10 miles from Smolensk. Bagration had no idea how fortuitous it was that he had not ordered Raievsky to march until that day.

The Russian advance forced Napoleon to move somewhat sooner than he had intended. However, during the time the army was in its quarters around Vitebsk, its condition had visibly improved. Indeed, drawing in various detachments, as well as many stragglers who were finding their way back to their units, had even increased the number of effectives. The improvement was partly due to the rest the forces had received but mostly to the better supply situation. Not only were the train columns catching up to the army again, but the windfalls of captured Russian magazines in Velish and Surash had placed valuable resources relatively close at hand. It even became possible to issue the troops 7 days' rations in advance when they resumed their march again.

As soon as Napoleon heard of Sebastiani's affair at Inkovo, he ordered Ney and Eugene, as well as the three divisions of Davout's I Corps, which had remained with the central army throughout operations so far, to concentrate at Liozna, along with Murat's reserve cavalry. But Eugene had to give up one of his cavalry brigades (Guyot's), which was reinforced with three Hessian battalions taken from the Guard Corps. They were to remain in Vitebsk to keep an eye on Wintzingerode.

Once more, heavy thunderstorms were dumping sheets of rain onto the countryside, and the artillery promptly got stuck again. But the infantry, no doubt relieved by the cooler temperatures, forged ahead, and the assembly was completed by August 11. Even though the Guard was still on its way, 100,000 men were already massed in the area where Barclay was expected to attack. This again furnishes proof of how little the Russians knew about the French positions or the strength of their forces, even at this advanced stage. At the same time, Davout was ordered to bring up Junot and Poniatowski as far as Liuboviczi, in the event the Russians were to press.

For Napoleon, this was a highly satisfactory development, to say the least. It appeared as if the Russians wanted to fight at last. Napoleon had long passed the point where strategic moves played a central role in his operations. As his military means had grown, so had his propensity to seek battle. He intended to cross the Dnieper on a front of about 15 miles near Orsza. However, the planned envelopment had now been reduced to a simple insurance policy to force the battle that had so far eluded him. A battle was the only thing that mattered any longer. If the Russians could be forced to fight, they would lose, and all of Napoleon's difficulties would evaporate. A victory would reanimate the army and free the way for an unopposed march to Moscow, presumably the final objective of the war.

The Russian offensive, however, had already ground to a halt, and this was the signal for Napoleon to pass to the attack himself. He intended to cross to the south side (left bank) of the Dnieper and capture Smolensk, thereby cutting the Russians off from a retreat to Moscow.

On August 13, Davout assembled his corps at Rasana, on the left bank of the Dnieper, covering the construction of four bridges there and at Chomino. Poniatowski came as far as Romanovo on that same day, with Junot, coming from Orsza, in tow. Latour-Maubourg was sent back to Mohilev on the 14th and was to follow the army via Mstislavl. Division Dombrowski, reinforced with a light cavalry brigade,[6] was to keep an eye on Bobruisk and Corps Oertel, which stood near Mozyr.

Meanwhile, the main army group marched off to the right, its movements screened against observation from Babinoviczi by the great forests running eastward from the Beresina. As additional insurance, Pajol's light cavalry division (he had taken over from Sebastiani) was left behind as well. On the 13th and 14th, the entire army group crossed the Dnieper. Minus IV Cavalry Corps (which did not depart from Rohaczev until the 14th) and Pajol's division, Napoleon now had about 186,000 men,[7] including 31,700 cavalry. The advance began on the 14th, again in a single, large column: Murat up front with the three cavalry corps, which still mustered about 15,000 sabers; then Ney, Davout, and Eugene; with the Guard bringing up a distant rear. Poniatowski and Junot were making a simultaneous advance from Romanovo.

THE ACTION AT KRASNOI

It will be recalled that Bagration had reinforced Neverovsky's division with some cavalry and left it at an advanced position around Krasnoi to cover in the direction of Orsza. Ney arrived in front of Krasnoi at about 3 p.m. When the points of Murat's cavalry were fired upon by Neverovsky's advance troops,

Ney sent forward infantry from Ledru's division; they had no trouble ejecting the Russians in short order, leaving the town in the hands of the victors.

Unfortunately, the Russians had demolished the bridge, so Murat's cavalry had to negotiate the stream through fords. Still, it was a small stream, and Murat was across in no time. He chased off the Russian cavalry and captured part of Neverovsky's artillery—the first trophies of the entire campaign. The Russian general then pulled together his two columns of about 6,000 men, most of them recruits; they assembled into a huge square, which drove Murat to distraction. Running his cavalry willy-nilly up against this infantry mass, by the squadron, by the regiment, he raged on and on without plan. This was despite the fact that the Russians were withdrawing through oat fields, where every dip in the ground obscured their vision and field of fire.

It was not until Neverovsky's men came up against a palisade fence when the real trouble began. While his rearmost elements maintained a murderous fusillade, the leading troops scaled the fence and spread out along the other side to give covering fire while the rear scrambled across. Wanting to seize the opportunity, Murat sent a Wuerttembergian regiment forward. But the fence, which had at first been an obstacle for Neverovsky's infantry, now served splendidly to keep the cavalry at bay. Although he left many of his men behind, Neverovsky was able to reform his columns undisturbed and make his getaway in good order.

It was only at this stage when a horse battery of the Wuerttembergers came up and laid some damaging fire on the retreating Russians, but it was too late. Neverovsky reached a defile ahead of Grouchy, and that was the end of the affair. The Russians had lost about 1500 men, the French barely 500. Murat was forced to give up the chase even before the Russians reached Korytnia because his horses were exhausted and could hardly walk. The *bon sabreur* had done it once again, and one must ask why he had not made timelier use of his numerous horse artillery.

Neverovsky was able to continue his retreat on the 15th without further mishap and was received in the afternoon by Raievsky's corps, which had come up at a run. In view of his own weakness, however—he had only sixteen battalions, roughly 13,000 men in all—Raievsky could not even consider making a stand in the open field. Thus, everyone returned to Smolensk during the night of the 15th without further disturbance, while Murat and Ney, who formed the head of Napoleon's huge column, had gotten as far as Lubna. Eugene, who had halted to allow the Guard to pass, reached Siniaki.

Neverovsky had informed both Barclay and Bagration of the French juggernaut heading their way during the night of August 14–15. However, despite their numerous light cavalry, they were still poorly informed about the whereabouts of the French and refused to give credence to the idea that the entire French army had crossed the Dnieper. As a result, they had sent only Raievsky's corps, which was just 10 miles away from Smolensk anyhow, to lend Neverovsky a hand. When further reports came in, confirming Neverovsky's information, an adventurous plan was hatched to send Bagration across the river at Katan on the 15th to block the enemy's march to Smolensk; Barclay was to follow, covering the area between the Dvina and the Dnieper while he supported Bagration. As a result, Bagration marched to Katan on the 15th and began to construct bridges. But new reports had Bagration as well as Barclay, who was still dawdling around Volkovaia, running toward Smolensk on the 16th.

NOTES

1. See Appendix VIII.
2. The exact figure was 28,249 men:
   11,592 men of Div. Durette (not counting 2,000 men left in Warsaw)
   14,090 men of Div. Loison, including Neapolitan detachment
   2,567 men of Brig. Coutard
3. The strength (in round numbers) of the two armies at this time was as follows:

First Army	*Men*	*Second Army*	*Men*
II Inf. Corps Baggehuffwudt	13,000	VII Inf. Corps Raievsky	13,000
III Inf. Corps Tutshkov I	13,500	VIII Inf. Corps Borosdin I	15,400
IV Inf. Corps Ostermann	9,500	27th Inf. Div. Neverovsky	7,000
V Inf. Corps Lavrov	17,500	IV Cav. Corps Sievers	4,000
VI Inf. Corps Doctorov	12,500	Cossacks	3,300
I Cav. Corps Uvarov	3,700	Total	42,700
II Cav. Corps Korff II	1,200		
III Cav. Corps Pahlen	2,100		
Platov's Cossacks	4,700		
Total	77,700		

In this table, I and IV Cavalry Corps appear quite strong and II quite weak, so it is possible that some subsequent shifts were made. But the overall totals would be unaffected.

4. Neverovsky's detachment included the 27th Infantry Division, 1 dragoon regiment, and 3 Cossack regiments, totaling 7000 men, and 14 guns. Since the 27th Division was composed entirely of reservists, two of its regiments were exchanged with the 26th Division.

5. In all there were 4 battalions, 32 squadrons, and 7 Cossack regiments.

6. Division Dombrowski of V Corps had 11 battalions, with 6000 men. Attached was the 28th Light Cavalry Brigade of IV Cavalry Corps, which had 12 squadrons, with 1000 men. The battalion that was absent from Dombrowski's division was still in Grodno, but it came up shortly.

7. The strength of the individual corps can be checked in Appendix VIII. However, the numbers of II Cavalry Corps, due to the losses suffered on the 8th, and of the detachment of Pajol's division, which had been hit hardest, must be revised downward by about 2000 men.

13. The Battle of Smolensk

From the heights surrounding the city in a wide semicircle, Smolensk presented a picturesque view that impressed all the diarists who saw it. Dominating the scene was the brick wall of the old fortress, appearing more forbidding than it actually was. Much of it was in such a poor state of repair that the wall varied from about 27 to 40 feet in height along its perimeter. Nearly 20 feet thick at the base, the wall tapered to about 10 feet in the sections where it still reached its full height. Only seventeen of its towers were left. At the foot of the wall, a shallow ditch and covered walkway ran along most of its length.

Access to the city within the walls was provided by three gates and two old breaches. A third, rather large breach was covered by a bastioned earthwork, which also served as a citadel. This was actually the weakest spot in the city's defenses, but the French didn't discover this until after the battle for the city was over. Just above and below the city, two deeply cut brooks flowed into the Dnieper. A wooden bridge led across the river to a bastioned bridgehead on the other side. Barclay had augmented this with two boat bridges. In front of the bridgehead was the St. Petersburg suburb, while five other suburbs were situated outside the old wall on the south side. The heights beyond the south side of the city were deeply cut through in places and thickly covered with birch growths, which did not facilitate an easy approach by large masses of troops.

Raievsky had about 17,000 men and 74 guns[1] available for the defense. While the infantry and artillery took its position in the suburbs, the cavalry remained out in the forefield.

Both Murat and Ney appeared on the heights in front of the city about 8 a.m. on August 16. Grouchy at once went forward and drove the Russian cavalry back into the city, while Ney deployed for an attack. By about 9 a.m., Napoleon himself appeared on the scene with Davout's corps. If Napoleon was intent on taking Smolensk—when he could see how weakly the city was defended—the time to advance energetically was now, before the Russian main force arrived. Instead, he limited himself to a useless cannonade and a few infantry attacks, which could hardly have accomplished more than making certain that the Russians meant to make a serious defense. Meanwhile, he awaited the arrival of the rest of the army.

By the 17th, 140,000 men were in place. Only Eugene and Junot were missing. The former, left behind as a rear guard at Siniaki, had come as far as Korytnia, where he took up another rear-guard position on the 16th. Junot was supposed to have arrived by 8 a.m. on the 17th, but letting himself be led astray by a "guide," he had gone in a circle and did not arrive until 5 p.m.

Napoleon's unfortunate hesitation on the 16th had afforded Barclay and Bagration the time they needed to bring up their armies. The first elements of Second Army moved into the city during the course of the day, and First Army arrived toward evening, after a forced march of 30 miles.

The terrain around Smolensk favored the Russians, since it was unlikely that Napoleon would attempt to force a river crossing in the immediate vicinity of the city. Even so, there remained the danger that he might do so further upriver, thus blocking the road to Moscow, which ran closely parallel to the right bank of the Dnieper for a bit more than a mile. It would have been wise for the Russians to march off at once and leave Smolensk defended by a rear guard. But the mood of the army precluded the idea that the "Holy City," which contained important relics of the Russian Orthodox church, should be yielded without a struggle. Besides, an old belief, dating from the Polish wars, maintained that "he who has Smolensk also has Moscow."

For once, Bagration and Barclay appeared to act in unison. The former was to occupy the city, and the latter was to deploy east of the city along the Kolodnia. However, if Bagration and the entire Russian army expected Barclay to accept a battle now, they were to be disappointed again. He had already decided to withdraw just as soon as the Moscow road was secured and the supplies in Smolensk were either removed or destroyed. Thus, the "battle" that took place on the 17th was in reality nothing more than a rear-guard action. Only VI Infantry Corps and the 3rd Division of III Infantry Corps joined the 27th Division, which was already in the city; there were about 20,000 men in all.[2] They were not even able to make use of their entire artillery because of the great difficulty of deploying the guns on the walls.

As noted, Barclay deployed outside the city, in front of the St. Petersburg suburb, by the road to Porietchie. His front faced south, toward the city. At 4 a.m. on the 17th, Bagration marched along the Moscow road and made a front behind the Kolodnia, facing west.

Napoleon was deployed in a wide semicircle at the foot of the heights surrounding the city. Ney was on the left; Davout was in the center, with the Guard behind him; and Murat and Poniatowski were on the right. Junot, once he arrived, was behind Poniatowski.

Doctorov began his defense with a sally, which drove the French points out of the suburbs. This was followed by a rather desultory cannonade, with neither side concentrating on anything specific. Apparently, Napoleon was hoping that the Russians would break forward out of the city and make a major attack, but this was even less likely now than it had been before. Thus, each side waited for the other to make a move, and they both ended up doing nothing.

Toward noon, Napoleon received reports of strong Russian columns marching away on the Moscow road. They were parts of Bagration's army. He rode off at once to see for himself and realized that, once again, Barclay did not intend to stand and fight. He then decided to do what Barclay had already half expected him to do: cross the river above Smolensk and attack the Russians on the other side.

However, due to the poor state of the French cavalry and the general lack of information from spies, valuable time passed before suitable fords were found. (The idea of constructing bridges in the face of the enemy appeared too chancy a proposition.) Worse, Napoleon had to expect that the Russians might break out of Smolensk and fall upon his rear right in the middle of a crossing. The only action that appeared feasible at the moment was to pin down the Russians by making a serious attack against the city. Napoleon had spent half the day hoping for something that wasn't about to happen, and it was 2 p.m. before he ordered the attack.

First, the weak Russian cavalry, which had come out of the city again, was driven back; then Ney, Davout, and Poniatowski launched simultaneous attacks against the suburbs. After 3 hours of stiff fighting, the suburbs were taken; some troops even succeeded in penetrating the covered walk in front of the city walls. There, the attack ground to a halt in the face of Russian reserves. Unfortunately, the attackers neither found the breaches in the wall nor recognized the weakness of the citadel.

Napoleon brought up more artillery, 150 guns in all, but they weren't able to put so much as a dent into the old brick wall, even though twenty-six 12-pounders tried to do just that. Repeated infantry attacks failed again, with heavy losses sustained, especially by the Poles. Napoleon then deployed a battery of sixty guns on the right flank in order to lay enfilading fire on the bridges in the city and thereby stem the flow of reinforcements from the north side of the river and silence a Russian battery on the opposite bank. At the same time, he had the howitzers throw grenades into the city to set its wooden buildings on fire. But the Russians refused to give way, and the fighting went on unabated until nightfall. The Russians lost about 6000 men, the French more than 9000.

Despite the fact that the French had been unable to penetrate the inner city, Barclay was justified in evacuating it once the Moscow road had been secured, because his strategic position was untenable. If Napoleon forced a crossing of the Dnieper above the city, the army would be in great danger. But once Barclay's decision to retreat became known, all the resentment stored up in the army broke out into the open. A number of generals, headed by an emotionally overwrought Constantine and also by Benningsen, confronted Barclay and attempted to force him to make a stand. A letter from Bagration expressed the same sentiments. It was a turbulent scene. Even if less than half of what has been written about these events at headquarters is true, then some weighty accusations flew through the air. But Barclay stood his ground. In doing so, he not only displayed an inordinate amount of intestinal fortitude but also saved the army and Russia.

The evacuation of Smolensk got under way during the night of August 17–18, while the bridges across the Dnieper were dismantled. Only the St. Petersburg suburb on the north side of the river continued to be occupied.

On the 18th, Barclay remained in his position on both sides of the Porietchie road because his troops—those who had fought as well as those who had made the forced march on the 16th—were in desperate need of a rest. The day passed relatively quietly. That is, it did for the armies at large. For Korff, who had been left in the bridgehead to defend against a French attempt to cross into the St. Petersburg suburb, and for Ney, who attempted to do just that, it was another hard day. Splashing through thigh-deep water, the Wuerttembergers and what was left of a Portuguese battalion succeeded in getting across, only to be blasted back by the withering musketry of Korff's jaegers. Many who thought they had survived the battle of Smolensk didn't.

The suburbs of Smolensk presented a gruesome sight, death having thrown together friend and foe with impartial finality. Inside the city, entire blocks had been turned into ashes, containing the carbonized remains of the wounded who had been unable to flee the flames. Everywhere in the streets were corpses that had been rolled flat by guns, caissons, and wagons. This, in brief, describes the horrific scenes painted at great length in so many diaries, both by the combatants and by those who entered the city after the fighting was over. As always, the street fighting had been a thankless sort of struggle where victory was measured in the taking of a building and defeat in its loss; where the respite after success lasted only until the drumbeat of approaching reserves was heard; where the enemy could be lurking behind every window, and a cannon, double-loaded with canister, could be waiting around every corner. All this, and more, is contained in the term "see-saw action," so often used in describing street or town fighting. Such action has little in common with a battle in the open field, where, by comparison, everything seems clear and uncomplicated.

For Barclay, it was now high time to leave. The march had to be made to the left. Although military historians never fail to make mention of whether a march was to be made to the right or to the left by a deployed army, the true significance of this escapes the vast majority of casual readers. Even though it has already been noted in Chapter 7, it is appropriate to repeat here that all formations, down to the last company, deployed dressing on their right guides. Thus, when an army reformed into columns again and the march was to go to the left, this was more difficult than simply going to the right, because every battalion, brigade, and division now had to turn back on, or enfilade, itself so that the head of the column would be up front, where it belonged.

The march was to be made in two columns. The northern column under Doctorov stepped off at 7 p.m. and took the Porietchie road. The southern column under Tutshkov took the St. Petersburg road around 9 p.m., leaving Korff II behind with a strong rear guard.[3] Both were to reunite at Solovieva-Pereprava. Bagration, in a rage over Barclay's decision to retreat, did not wait, but took off on the Moscow road during the morning hours. All he left behind to cover the road was General Karpov II with four Cossack regiments, who stood on the Pruditchevo Heights. Somewhat farther on, Prince Gortshakov was left with the rather weak 2nd Grenadier Division of VIII Infantry Corps, reinforced with some cavalry from VII Infantry Corps (10 battalions and 8 squadrons), in case the former had to be received. Bagration's unconscionable abandonment of the Moscow road was bound to put the First Army into grave danger.

.   .   .

Napoleon was not satisfied with the results of the 17th and intended to renew the assault against Smolensk on the 18th. He, too, was confronted with arguments and remonstrations from his generals, but again it seems improper to say much more than that, because it is quite difficult to determine how much of what has been written afterward about the conversations has been influenced by hindsight, self-justification, and posturing.

Still, the emperor's problems were real enough. He spent the day completing the assembly of the army for yet another crossing of the Dnieper. The supply situation also demanded his attention again. Since the last crossing of the river, thousands more stragglers had fallen behind. Napoleon's lack of operational activity—indeed, his entire behavior since his arrival at Smolensk—was most curious.

Upon resuming his offensive, he had assembled his forces with admirable speed. No matter what one might think of his plan, he had put it into execution with flawless precision. However, at the decisive moment, when he arrived at Smolensk and recognized that the enemy's measures, aided by local circumstances, had foiled his original intentions, he lapsed into inactivity when he should have redoubled his efforts. Neither the ignorance of local circumstances nor the inability to secure the services of local agents and spies, which presented his generals with great difficulties, can suffice to explain this failure any more than can the fact that the army had its own difficulties. Thus, there remains no recourse but to seek the explanation in Napoleon himself.

If his plan was to succeed, then speed was of the essence. Thus, when he found Smolensk occupied, he had to either do everything in his power to seize it quickly or, without waiting for the complete assembly of his army (i.e., on the 16th), take his main force across the river above the city. In view of the irresolution the Russians had exhibited so far, he might very well have taken such a risk. An immediate and thorough reconnaissance of the Dnieper, a little over 300 feet wide at this point, would have revealed that a crossing was possible even without the bridge train, which had apparently not yet arrived. As it turned out, there was a ford just above the city and two more at Pruditchevo. By the time they were eventually discovered, the time to capitalize on them had long passed.

Even if Napoleon had not thought it prudent to ford the river immediately above the city with a strong part of his army, the conditions at Pruditchevo were not merely advantageous but ideal. Not only was there a ford that was quite wide and usable by all arms, because the dry summer had resulted in a low water level, but all the raw materials for bridge construction were locally at hand as well. More than that, the location of both fords was obscured from the enemy's view. For the success of his plan, it was immaterial whether he crossed at Smolensk or Pruditchevo. The risk was acceptable, provided a sufficient rear guard was left to observe Smolensk.

It appears, however, that the emperor no longer had the quickness of eye and decision of times gone by. Indeed, it seems that the continued failure of his plans—first, his designs on Bagration; then those on Barclay; and now his advance against both—had stunted his taste for strategic maneuvers. There would be further indications of such lapses as the campaign progressed. Instead of adapting his operations to the changed conditions, Napoleon insisted on forcing a crossing through Smolensk. It almost appears as if he felt that his reputation in the eyes of the army, especially the allied contingents, was at stake. He had to enter Smolensk through the front door.

He might have done that with speed and resolution. Instead, he wasted the 16th waiting for the army to assemble, even though he must have known that even if he succeeded, crossing the river through Smolensk, in the face of the enemy's concentrated forces, would be difficult and costly. Then he wasted the 17th waiting for the enemy to make a virtually impossible move, for no better reason than the fact that it would have suited him splendidly if the enemy had indeed attempted the impossible. After the Russians evacuated Smolensk, he still might have scored a great success, but he let the 18th pass as well without doing anything.

Despite the fact that he saw parts of the Russian army withdrawing on the 17th, he still clung to the idea that Bagration and Barclay, now with all their forces in hand, would give him a battle. But the entire campaign had been pinned on such a hope. Instead, as at Vitebsk, he again allowed the strongly desired battle to drift off into the indeterminate future.

VALUTINO AND STRAGAN BROOK

By 3 a.m. on August 19, the bridges of Smolensk had been reconstructed. Ney crossed, positioning himself beyond the St. Petersburg suburb, between the St. Petersburg and Moscow roads. He remained there for several hours, because patrols had located Russian troops retreating along both roads. These were Korff's along the St. Petersburg road and Karpov's Cossacks on the Moscow road. Murat then forded the river with the reserve cavalry right behind Ney, sending Grouchy along the St. Petersburg road, while he himself took Nansouty's and Montbrun's corps along the Moscow road.

Tutshkov's southern column[4] of the First Army blundered into a difficult situation, due entirely to Bagration's high-handed action. During a very difficult night march through forested terrain, Tutshkov's column had separated. The rearmost part, all of II Infantry Corps and parts of IV Infantry Corps, had been late getting off the mark and went astray in the dark. By morning, between 5 and 6 a.m., it suddenly found itself only about a mile away from the St. Petersburg suburb. After three hours' march, the troops were almost back where they had started. The situation was critical. The entire column, still stuck on difficult forest paths, was in great confusion. Korff's rear guard was far off, and the enemy was in cannon range.

It was a stroke of good fortune that Barclay himself was present with the column. As always in difficult situations, he kept a cool head. Ordering the column to about-face, he left Duke Eugene of Wuerttemberg with a weak rear guard[5] at Gedeonovo while the column headed along the road to Gorbunovo, as originally ordered.

Fortune again militated in favor of the Russians when Ney and Murat, uncertain about the enemy's line of retreat, did not make immediate use of the time directly after their river crossing. As a result, the French were even more surprised than the Russians when the latter's column suddenly turned up so close to them, and it was nearly 8 a.m. before the French mounted any attacks with substantial strength. However, the timely arrival of four Russian hussar regiments enabled Duke Eugene, who had made a tenacious defense despite his lack of numbers, to fall back to Hapanovchina in good order. There, he was received by two battalions from II Infantry Corps. Soon after, Korff was able to get past the danger point as well, and he closed up without further mishap.

As soon as Napoleon heard of the action, he sent Davout across the river, where he took the same position that Ney had held after his crossing. Junot was ordered to cross at Pruditchevo, where the fords had at last been discovered. The Guard, Eugene, and Poniatowski remained on the left bank at Smolensk. Once aware of the presence of Russian forces on the Moscow road, Napoleon recalled Ney and sent him off in that direction. Napoleon himself, expecting nothing more than a rear-guard action, returned to Smolensk.

Meanwhile, Prince Gortshakov had withdrawn along the Moscow road, leaving only Karpov's Cossacks behind, as soon as the latter had been approached by the points of Tutshkov III's advance guard[6] of the First Army's southern column at about 8 a.m. Since it had taken Tutshkov nearly 12 hours to make this march of only about 15 miles over forest paths, it was hardly to be expected that the entire column would be able to pass the dangerous junction with the Moscow road before nightfall.

Recognizing the importance of this junction and informed of the enemy's approach, Tutschkov at once took his tired troops (3200 men, with 12 guns) back along the Moscow road toward the advancing French and took a position behind the Kolodnia. There, Ney attacked his position toward noon with Razout's division. Ney's troops, however, arrived only gradually, and Tutshkov was himself reinforced by another 2200 men and 6 guns.[7] These reinforcements had already gotten as far as Bredichino when Yermolov ordered Tutshkov I to send them back. As a result, Tutshkov III was able to maintain himself until only about 3 p.m., at which time he withdrew behind the Stragan Brook, where he was received by fresh forces.

A stiff action ensued along the banks of this brook. It is referred to as the Battle of Valutino-Gora or the Battle of Stragan Brook; Valutino-Gora is the place where the first encounter occurred. This action eventually involved all of III and IV Infantry Corps and I Cavalry Corps on the Russian side; not counting the Cossacks, 23,000 men[8] were involved. On the French side, Murat and Ney had, at first, 27,500 men, who were joined by another 8000 from Gudin's division from I Corps.[9]

While the action was in progress, Junot (who had crossed the Dnieper at Pruditchevo) stood by watching, figuratively speaking, with his hands in his pockets. At this point, one may no longer say that the man was merely mentally disturbed; he was an alcoholic in an advanced state of deterioration (within a year he went completely insane and killed himself). Regarding Stragan Brook, Junot states that he stood in a "superb position, in the rear of the enemy's left," but he fails to explain why he did nothing, despite the fact that he and Murat had heated exchanges over this. Again, the romances are fairly low key about the subject, but anyone who cares to look at the sources can learn all about it from the Westphalians—from the division commander, Ochs, right down into the rank and file.

Here, one is again struck by the fact that despite all the resentments and grievances, once the action was joined everything was forgotten and winning was more important than anything else. From his nearby battalions, Junot heard shouts that said, in effect, "Let's go . . . what are we waiting for?" He became so enraged over this that he started to curse and threatened to have anyone else who opened his mouth shot. Some claim that only the discipline of the Westphalians prevented an open mutiny. When Murat came galloping up, he was greeted with a thunderous "hurrah!" But nothing came of this, except a verbal battle between Murat and Junot, while the real one was raging in plain sight of the entire corps. The only thing Ochs could wring from Junot was permission to clear out a nearby patch of woods covering the Russian left flank. The most interesting footnote to this is that after his violent encounter with Murat, Junot left for a nearby manor, which had already been commandeered for him, and sat down to have breakfast.

After he had gone, the Westphalians did get to take some part in the action, and some of the cavalry went with Murat. But without central direction, their actions turned out to be chaotic and episodic. As a result of all this, Ney and Murat were reduced to making frontal assaults that were not worth the sacrifices they demanded. The fight, which reached its peak of intensity with the arrival of Gudin's division, burned itself out by nightfall.

II Russian Infantry Corps and Morand's division from I French Corps did not arrive on the battlefield until after the action was over. The Russians lost about 5000 men, the French 8768, including General Gudin, the first general officer to be killed in action during the Russian campaign. That the Russians did not suffer a total defeat is entirely due to the fact that Napoleon had returned to Smolensk instead of remaining with his corps up in the first line. As a result, given the well-known intransigence and insubordination of Napoleon's top-echelon commanders, there was no unified conduct of the action.

Despite the fact that Junot was one of Napoleon's old favorites, from the days of Toulon, the emperor was beside himself and, for a moment, contemplated relieving Junot of his command. He decided against this and, typically, transferred his ire to the hapless Westphalians, innocent bystanders in more ways than one, who were given the task of cleaning up the battlefield. It must, however, be kept in mind that Junot certainly was no longer in full possession of his faculties.

The Russians, who had bivouacked behind the Jarovenka, just beyond the battlefield, continued their retreat by 4 a.m. on the 20th, and the reunited First Army crossed the Dnieper on the next day. Bagration was already a day's march ahead at Michailevka. The losses of both sides during the fighting from the 14th to the 19th had been high. The Russians had lost more than 14,000 men, the French more than 19,000. Ney's corps had again been hit hardest.[10] But the French losses were not confined to the ones suffered in action. Because of renewed supply difficulties, thousands had again left the ranks. The net result was that the French army had been down by 30,000 since the 13th.

For the Russians, the days of Smolensk represented the critical point of the entire campaign. Had the army been beaten there, the results would have been far worse than those of Borodino. Given the direction of the attack and the still great superiority of the French, this could have led to a total destruction of the western armies, since there would have been no finite limit for a pursuit. But Barclay had remained steadfast against his fellow field marshal, the tsar's brother, and all the other noisemakers at his headquarters. He thereby saved the army, against its own will, from a catastrophe. His services in behalf of Russia cannot possibly be overestimated. His conduct was as commendable as Bagration's was deplorable.

In the history of Napoleon's brilliant career, the days of Smolensk brought no laurels. That the daring plan he had conceived and implemented so resolutely bore no fruit is due entirely to the fact that, at the decisive moment, his genius appeared to have deserted him. His conduct is another striking example of the fact that, in war, what one does is not so important as how one does it.

Possibly, he might have achieved greater results with fewer sacrifices had he displayed less genius in staging and executing a brilliant strategic envelopment and, instead, gone straight to Smolensk by the shortest route, and done so with resolution. Given the constant resistance against further retreats in the Russian army, such a course might have possibly given him the battle he so ardently desired and the opportunity to bring the war to a successful conclusion. In this respect, Clausewitz was correct in his contention that Napoleon should have gone straight ahead and confronted Barclay by the shortest possible route. Smolensk spelled the end of the chance to conclude the war victoriously, because Napoleon did not remain true to the spirit of his plan, which called for quick and decisive action.

NOTES

1. Entire VII Inf. Corps.   24 bns. ⎫   The detached regiments had rejoined.
   27th Inf. Div.   12 bns. ⎭
   Of IV Cav. Corps   16 sqns.
   Cossacks   3 regts.
2. Of First Army:
     VI Inf. Corps (7th and 24th Inf. Divs.)   24 bns.
     3rd Inf. Div. of III Inf. Corps   12 bns.
    Of Second Army:
     From 12th Inf. Div. of VII Inf. Corps   2 bns.
     27th Inf. Div.   12 bns.
    Plus 3 dragoon regiments
     In all, there were 50 battalions and 12 squadrons, comprising 20,000 men

and some Cossacks. In the course of the 17th, these were joined by the following:

From V (Guard) Corps	3 bns.
Of II Inf. Corps, 44th Inf. Div. with	12 bns.
From 17th Inf. Div.	4 bns.

These 19 battalions brought an additional 10,000 men.

3. 4 jaeger regiments of II Corps, 3 of
   IV Inf. Corps   14 bns.
   1 hussar regiment of VI Inf. Corps,
   1 of III Cav. Corps
   1 ulan regiment of II Cav. Corps   24 sqns.
   1 heavy battery and a few Cossack
   regiments

4. The order of march of this column was as follows:
   Advance guard: Tutshkov III
   Main force: I Cav. Corps
                   III Inf. Corps
                   IV Inf. Corps
                   II Inf. Corps
   Rear guard: Korff II

5. The rear guard consisted of 4 battalions of the 17th Infantry Division, 2 battalions of the 4th Infantry Division, and ½ squadron of hussars, with 4 guns.

6. In the advance guard were 6 battalions from the 3rd Infantry Division, III Infantry Corps; 8 squadrons of hussars of II Cavalry Corps; 3 Cossack regiments; and 1 battery. In all, there were 3200 men, with 12 guns. They were eventually joined by 3 Cossack regiments under Karpov I.

7. The reinforcements included 4 battalions from the 1st Grenadier Division, III Infantry Corps, and ½ battery.

8. According to documents cited by Buturlin, the Russians numbered:

	Men
III Inf. Corps	13,500
IV Inf. Corps	9,500
I Cav. Corps	3,700
Total	26,700

Duke Eugene, however, puts the strength at only 23,000.

9. III Corps accounted for 19,500 men, while I and II Cavalry Corps provided another 8000.

10. At the beginning of the campaign, Ney's corps had numbered 39,342 men. Now, exclusive of the seven battalions left in Kovno and Vilna, the corps had only 16,053 effectives; by September 3, it was further diminished to 11,278 men. The Wuerttembergian infantry, 8200 men in the beginning, lost only 555 men in the action; on 2 September, it was down to 1456 men, who were amalgamated into three composite battalions.

14. A Change in Command

Napoleon had departed from Vitebsk in the hope of catching up to the Russians, defeating them, and thus opening the road to Moscow. This hope had not been fulfilled. If he now halted at Smolensk, the border of the old Polish empire, then he had a good starting position for a continuation of the campaign the following spring. If the Russians were to undertake some offensive operations during the interim, all the better. He still had the means of meeting these with sufficient force. Things would be different if he continued his advance. When he had departed from Vitebsk, Napoleon still enjoyed massive superiority. He could have dealt the Russians a massive blow and still, or rather because of it, arrive in Moscow with sufficient strength to hold the city.

But the balance of power had shifted again. Unless one suffered from delusions, it was clear that the army could not reach Moscow with a force that could maintain itself there, even if no peace was made. Based on what had transpired so far, this eventuality had become a distinct possibility. Added to this must be the certainty that the enemy's powers of resistance had to increase substantially around Moscow, because to the south of the city were Russia's richest provinces, which offered the greatest resources.

The news from the army's wings was not encouraging either. Wittgenstein and Tormassov were making advances that gave clear warning signals. Although there had been no great concern over an envelopment so far, given the width of the front, an advance from Smolensk would take place on a much narrower operations base. This became all the more dangerous because a continued advance—the direct-line distance from Kovno to Moscow was about 575 miles—created so long line of communications that it would be impossible to effect a quick concentration of the army at any threatened point. If Napoleon continued his advance, he would surrender the tactical advantage he had enjoyed, as well as the security of his line of communications, which was doubly sensitive now, in view of the great distances involved. If the enemy capitalized on this Achilles' heel, the French army was doomed to grind itself down even without help from the Nordic winter.

However, regardless of the extent to which Napoleon overestimated his own strength and underestimated not only the enemy's strength but also the dangers that lay ahead, he could not quite ignore them. Thus, at Smolensk, he began to have his first doubts about the outcome of his undertaking.

As he began to waver, he drew his intimates into conversations, expressing his intention to halt the campaign. These men, who knew the mood of the army better than he did, at once agreed with him. The army desperately needed a rest, and not merely for a few days. The heat and the lack of food and water, which had also given the Russians a great deal of trouble at Smolensk, were unbearable.

Such second thoughts, however, could not really take firm root in Napoleon. General Bonaparte could have halted at Smolensk and postponed the conclusion of the campaign to the next year, but for the emperor this was next to impossible. The same political and personal considerations that had governed his decisions in Vitebsk were at work at Smolensk as well. They called for a continuation of his advance. It was the statesman who pushed the field marshal and caused him to stumble, and it was the field marshal's error that permitted the statesman to override him. If, and only if, the continued advance was a viable military proposition, it was also demanded. But the military decision had to be the governing factor.

At this point Napoleon received some good news. Schwarzenberg had beaten Tormassov at Gorodeczna; and St. Cyr, who had taken over from Oudinot, had beaten Wittgenstein at Polotsk. The new great dangers that would arise in these places were still latent. Above all, there was Murat's report that the Russians were withdrawing in good order and appeared resolved to fight a battle as soon as they found a good position. This possibility attracted Napoleon like a magnet. Deciding to go forward, the emperor met all objections with the comment "The wine has been poured, it must now be drunk."

•   •   •

The hope for a decisive battle was to pull Napoleon to the gates of Moscow; it carried with it the promise that peace would also be found there. This was despite the fact that Napoleon's hopes for a battle had already been dashed twice and his hopes for a peace in Moscow were entirely arbitrary. He might have thought differently had he not closed his eyes to the tenacious defense the Russians were making and the local enmity that met the French everywhere once the army entered into old-Russian territory.

What if the Russians did not retreat to Moscow but headed south, perhaps in the direction of Viasma or Kaluga? Could he then continue his advance against Moscow, or would he be forced to turn around, unless he was to follow them into indeterminate distances?

Surely, the decision to go on did not come easily to Napoleon. A mishap now would have far greater consequences than would an interruption of the campaign. That he was aware of this emerges from a letter outlining the use of Victor's corps as a reserve at Smolensk. It says: "If I can not find the peace I seek there, then my retreat, supported by a strong reserve, will be made secure and I will be forced to make haste." It was a high-stakes game, and Napoleon, spoiled by luck, like a true gambler, placed everything on one card without weighing the risks too much. However, Clausewitz warns that "the possibility of success is the first law of any undertaking." For Napoleon, this possibility had receded into a nebulous distance at this point. Things being as they were, Napoleon's decision to press on from Smolensk would prove to be the pivotal mistake of the entire war.

The means Napoleon had in hand for a continuance of his advance were not in any way sufficient for the task. The main army group (including Latour-Maubourg's cavalry corps, which was still coming up, and Pajol's division, but not Dombrowski's division) had numbered 286,000 men at the crossing of the Niemen and 191,500 at the departure from Vitebsk; now, on 23 August, it was down to only 161,475 men.[1] Yet no decisive victory had been won, and some stiff fighting would probably occur before Moscow, 270 miles from Smolensk, could be reached.

However, not even all of these forces were immediately available. Until the march formations from the reserve came up, Smolensk had to be garrisoned with first-line formations. It was also necessary to send a strong detachment back in the direction of Vitebsk because the covering force left there (3 Hessian battalions and 8 squadrons from IV Cavalry Corps), about

2000 men, was hardly able to contain Wintzingerode's raiding detachments. To deal with this situation, Division Laborde of the Young Guard (minus the battalions seconded for security duties at imperial headquarters), about 4500 men, with 400 cavalry from V Corps, was left in Smolensk. Meanwhile, Division Pino, Italians from IV Corps, and Division Pajol from II Cavalry Corps, about 6000 infantry and 1500 cavalry, were sent to Vitebsk. This left Napoleon with 115,278 infantry and 33,797 cavalry, a total of 149,075 men, of which Latour-Maubourg's 4000 cavalrymen were still to come up.

Given these circumstances, it was doubly necessary to have a strong reserve at Smolensk to fill the gap that would be left in the center by the advance against Moscow. At this point, however, only about 5000 to 6000 men in march formations were on their way there. Victor, who was already on his way to Kovno, was ordered to take his corps of 31,000 men[2] to Smolensk. He crossed the Niemen at Kovno on September 3 and arrived in Smolensk on the 27th with 25,000 men, after detaching a Saxon brigade and leaving some troops in Vitebsk and other places. His mission was to form a reserve for both the main army and the flanking corps, especially St. Cyr's by the Dvina. Napoleon was less concerned about Schwarzenberg.

Before leaving Smolensk, Napoleon again went to considerable pains to secure the supply situation. He ordered that magazines and hospitals be established, but again the French administration did not accomplish its assigned task even by half.

While Napoleon was still in Smolensk, Murat crossed the Dnieper at Solovieva-Pereprava on August 22 with the reserve cavalry, closely followed by Davout and Ney. This caused the Russian rear guard[3] under Platov and Rosen to draw back to Michailevka, where a brisk delaying action ensued in the afternoon that resulted in no advantages for the French.

Since the army had entered old Russia, the scene greeting the troops had undergone some changes. The march now led through fertile regions, where the rye stood tall in the fields. The roads were better as well, especially the Smolensk-Moscow road, which was grand in comparison to what had been seen so far. A three-lane avenue, lined with a double row of birch on both sides, it would have given pleasure had it not been for the blistering heat and the fact that it was largely off-limits for the infantry, who had to march along its sides. Worse, the dust churned up by the marching columns caused eyes and throats to burn, and water was still hard to find. As long as the Dnieper was near, water could be obtained; away from the river, it was back to the way things had been before. The men drank from every well and every puddle, no matter how revolting and odious the water might be—and no matter how sick they got. The entries in Mertens' diary for August 25, 26, 28, and 31 say that the air was so thick with dust that one could look into the blood-red sun without injury to the eyes and that a Westphalian saw men, even officers, attempting to slake their thirst by drinking their own urine. A Saxon dragoon observed that the sun had bleached out the skin of the horses: Horses that had left Saxony as dark bays had turned into isabellas; dark bays had become mouse-colored; and blacks were now light bays.

On the other hand, food was not a problem. "All the farms were full of harvest," writes Lossberg, a Westphalian major. "The regiments bake their own bread and if we can't find flour, we take the grain to the local mills, which are numerous hereabouts, to have it ground." Of course, Napoleon had wanted to equip the troops with hand mills from the start, but the first of these did not arrive until after the retreat had already gotten under way.

There was also a plentitude of livestock. However, this benefited only the troops at the head of the marching order, who quickly expropriated everything in sight and often deliberately ruined whatever they didn't use. Honey also became a problem. Apparently, it was harder on the weakened stomachs of the soldiers than were the stings of the angry bees. (Though the faces of some men were swollen beyond recognition, and a few who had been too careless even died.) But that, save for the bees, was the good side. Accounts by Chambray and other eyewitnesses also refer to the new character the war was now assuming. The Russians were becoming aroused, their fanaticism fanned by the barbaric behavior of the Grand Army. The pillaging army rolled forward, and what the soldiers couldn't use, they burned.

To return to the action: Grouchy's cavalry had reached Dukovtshina on the army's left, and Eugene took the same direction, joining him at Dorogobush. On the right, Poniatowski had gone through Belkino; further to the right, Latour-Maubourg was still several marches to the rear at Jelnia. The Guard left Smolensk on the 23rd, followed by Junot, who had remained on the battlefield of the 19th. Napoleon himself did not leave Smolensk until the night of the 25th, when he received news from Murat that the Russians stood in front of Dorogobush. It was time to assemble the army again.

Despite the fact that Barclay had retreated again on the 20th and 21st, he was firmly convinced that the time to offer a battle was at hand, even though he didn't expect to win. Indeed, he didn't even think he could wait for the arrival of Miloradovitch's reserves. Instead, Barclay ordered him to take a supporting position at Viasma as an insurance policy in the event of a defeat. He had already sent officers ahead from Smolensk to find suitable positions where a battle might be fought. They had come up with two possibilities: One was behind the Usha, west of Dorogobush; the other was southwest of Gshatsk. Both were along the great Moscow road.

The First Army occupied the Usha position on the 22nd. Bagration, who had already gone as far as Dorogobush, was summoned back. But the prince now denied his cooperation with all sorts of subterfuges. He ranted at Toll, who had selected both positions, and sent him packing. Thus, the First Army could do little else but retreat again on the 24th. By the time it got to Dorogobush, Bagration had already gone 15 miles farther to Brashino. This put an end to the adventurous plan of attempting to risk a battle with barely 90,000 men against Napoleon's 145,000.

What was one to make of Bagration's behavior? He constantly clamored for a battle, only to end up foiling every attempt to have one. He did this several times and, at least on one occasion, put Barclay into a serious position. But his reasons were really quite simple. The intrigues of his party to unseat Barclay had by now reached all the way to St. Petersburg. The very last thing Bagration wanted to do was to fight a battle on Barclay's initiative. This was bound to blunt the thrust of the conspiracy. At the same time, it was not sufficient for Bagration to think Barclay was wrong. The army had to think so as well. Hence, all the noise. The only thing that may be said of this in Bagration's behalf was that, unlike the connivers of Benningsen's and Yermolov's stripe, he sincerely believed that Barclay's ill will and incompetence would plunge Russia into disaster and ruin.

With Murat and Platov dueling on the 26th and 27th, Barclay and Bagration both made it to Viasma by the latter date. Again, Barclay wanted to make a stand; again, Bagration objected. When no suitable position offered itself anyhow, the retreat was continued on the 28th. On the evening of the 27th, by a special order from Alexander, General Konovnitzyn, one of the finest generals in the entire army, had been given charge of the rear guard, which was also strongly reinforced.[4] An immediate result of this was that the French advance was slowed up considerably.

On the 29th, at Zarevo-Saimishtshe, Barclay again wanted to fight and Bagration didn't. Not that the position there was any good. Contrary to popular belief, it was not behind the swamp, which could be crossed only over a single dam, but in front of it. Nor was there actually a swamp in existence at the time, because the hot weather had dried it up completely.

The two united armies numbered 95,734 men, not counting the Cossacks. In sharp contrast to the French, this force had sustained no losses other than those suffered in combat. This was despite the fact that the Russians had been little better off than the French, since no one had even remotely considered the possibility that operations would be carried so far into the interior. Adding to this total was the arrival of reinforcements, although these were not as numerous as had been expected. Miloradovitch had reached Gshatsk with 15,589 men; they were to remain there as a backup, underlining Barclay's lack of faith in the outcome of a battle.

Dependent upon the goodwill of his fellow army commander, lacking the confidence of his subordinates, threatened by overwhelmingly superior forces commanded by one of the greatest captains of all time, Barclay had conducted his operations to the best of his knowledge and abilities under the greatest difficulties imaginable. In doing so, he had by and large made the correct choices, even if he was not aware of having done so. His actions had not so much expressed any inner convictions as they had constantly betrayed timidity, frequently paired with irresolution, in the face of his grand opponent. As a result, Russian pride and conceit had been deeply wounded, making his position untenable. General opinion, blind to the improving situation, clamored for Barclay's replacement by a full-blooded Russian. Indeed, the lack of confidence and authority that had attached itself to his person demanded that, in the interests of the army, a change in supreme command be made at once.

All Alexander knew of the affair was what had been fed to him by Barclay's enemies. Barclay's reserve had prevented him from speaking for himself. The tsar could only give in and appoint a board of inquiry. Before he had even learned of the events at Smolensk, he had appointed Kutuzov, who had been made a prince just a few days before, to the post of commander in chief over all the Russian forces fighting against the French. It was neither confidence in his abilities nor respect for his character that prompted Alexander's choice. Just a few weeks earlier, he had relieved Kutuzov from his command over the Danube Army because of his political intrigues. Naming him to this post instead had become a political necessity, because he was the only man who could be considered for the post who was also a Slav.

Kutuzov was 67 at the time, but his body and spirit had already aged beyond his years. He was so obese that he could hardly ride a horse, and then it could only be at a walk. There was no fire left in his spirit. Added to this was a weakness of character, increasing with his age, that often made him dependent and irresolute. He was, of course, not lacking in military abilities, but these were geared more to the past than to Napoleon's new style of warfare. Not exactly of daring nature even in his younger years, his experience of Napoleon at Austerlitz had been so overwhelming that the very name exercised a paralyzing influence over him.

Although Kutuzov was hardly the man to be played against a Napoleon, general opinion, which hoped to see another Suvorov in him, had not erred after all when it demanded his appointment. He might not have been the great captain's equal, but he possessed the insights needed to play the role of a Fabius Cunctator (the man who had delayed Hannibal's march against Rome). Fully cognizant of his opponent's superiority, he sought—even more than he had in the past—to reach his objective not through risk and daring but by avoiding a direct confrontation and by simply outlasting Napoleon.

There can be little doubt that Kutuzov's greatest achievement was that he saw the change in the wind long before nearly everyone else did. He was already aware that, at worst, the winter would come to his aid in driving the French out of Russia. Thus, what Barclay had done because he could not do otherwise Kutuzov now did with deliberation. He had a strategy, and his implementation of this strategy was greatly eased by the fact that, unlike Barclay, he was in complete charge and had the confidence of the army. His second-greatest achievement was that he knew how to hold on to this confidence despite his shortcomings and weaknesses, even when things continued to go wrong for a time. Kutuzov had a natural shrewdness and knew exactly how to play the Russian character. A braggart by nature, he would brashly proclaim himself the victor even when he was beaten, and he never tired of telling those around him that the French were already finished, no matter what they did. And since he knew this to be true, he was able to give free rein to his braggadocio, no matter how he actually felt about facing Napoleon in a battle. Thus, nature had fully equipped him to reap without effort the harvest which Barclay had sown and which circumstances had ripened to become the savior of Russia.

With Kutuzov, Benningsen returned as chief of staff to the army he had just left. This was hardly a fortunate choice. But though his abilities were highly debatable, Benningsen knew how to win Kutuzov's approval, especially in the beginning. This was despite the fact that Kutuzov rightfully distrusted Benningsen, who was angling for an independent command. As a result, Kutuzov often left Benningsen in the dark about his intentions. Indeed, Kutuzov's paranoia generally prevented him from confiding in anyone. The fact that this did not result in a major disaster was largely due to the efforts of Colonel von Toll. Kutuzov had great confidence in him and brought him into his headquarters, where he soon exercised a decisive influence on the course of operations, something he had never been able to achieve while serving in Barclay's headquarters.

Alexander must have at last caught on to some of the ill wind that had been blowing Barclay's way, because he never entirely abandoned him. Barclay was left in command of First Army. However, Kutuzov's suspicious nature tried to constrict him even there. Totally misreading Barclay's character, he expected that the general would allow the slight he had received to reflect itself in his leadership of First Army. Therefore, the rear guard under Konovnitzyn was taken away from him, even though it consisted entirely of troops from First Army. But this could hardly be considered a bone of contention, because Kutuzov commanded both armies. Therefore, the rear guard became Kutuzov's business as well. But Kutuzov also meddled in Barclay's affairs in other ways.

Justice demands the recognition of Barclay's achievement in saving the army, actually against its will, and handing it over to his successor unimpaired. At the beginning of the war, the ratio of forces had stood at 3 to 1[5] against him. A battle at that time would have led to the destruction of both western armies because there was nothing to receive or protect them after such a disaster. All of Russia would have lain open before the invader, with nothing to impede the consolidation of his victory. Barclay had prevented this from happening by his continuing retreat, but in doing so, he had drawn upon himself the anger of the entire nation.

But the power ratio had been reduced and now stood at 5 to 4.[6] On top of this, the strategic situation of the Russian army was vastly superior. Even as the French had distanced themselves from their power bases, the Russians had drawn closer to their own. Winter was nearing, and the time gained had made it possible for the flanking armies to prepare a dramatic turnaround that would prove virtually fatal for the central army group. Barclay deserved to reap what he had sown. In time, the Russian army would realize that its harvest would have been richer had he remained in command, rather than being replaced by Kutuzov. Due to the infirmities of old age, crafty old Kutuzov turned out to be as unfit for the battlefield as he was for the pursuit of the retreating French. However, Barclay heard precious little of this laudatory assessment during his own lifetime.

On August 29, Kutuzov arrived at Zarevo-Saimishtshe, greeted by the thunderous cheers of the soldiers. His appearance alone raised the morale of the army at once. Although he pompously announced that the retreat had come to an end, he actually had no choice in the matter. As little as he relished a direct confrontation and as unnecessary as it was in reality, the mood of the army made such an event a necessary evil. He had to offer a battle, not only because an attempt had to be made at denying the French entry into Moscow but also because he had been appointed specifically to put an end to the retreat.

The fickleness of fate willed that his very arrival at Zarevo-Saimishtshe would once again postpone the battle Barclay had meant to fight there. Even though the position was not so good that Barclay's enemies would have found it difficult to persuade Kutuzov to abandon it, the very insinuation that Barclay might claim the credit for a victory because he had selected the site was enough to do so.

The retreat to Gshatsk was made in the afternoon of the 30th. A possible position had been located near Ivashkovo, but Kutusov did not stop there either. He let Benningsen induce him to go on to Borodino, where the army arrived on the 3rd of September. Even though the site there was not without its own shortcomings, Benningsen, who had ordered the search for a suitable position, pronounced it acceptable. But there was no longer any choice. Another position was not to be found forward of Moscow, and a battle had to be fought.

NOTES

1. See Appendix IX.
2. IX Corps was to number 54 battalions and 16 squadrons. Its present strength, however, was only 44 battalions and 15 squadrons—in all, 33,567 men. Of these, a further 4 battalions with 2600 men were to remain behind in Germany for the time being. Thus, on crossing the Niemen, there were only 40 battalions and 15 squadrons, with 28,000 infantry and 2000 cavalry, plus about 1000 artillery personnel. A further 3 Polish battalions, just formed, were already on the march to Smolensk, where they were to remain as part of the garrison.
3. The rear guard consisted of 12 jaeger battalions of II, IV, and VI Infantry Corps and 32 squadrons of hussars and ulans, as well as the greatest part of the Cossacks.
4. Added were 3rd Infantry Division, III Corps, and the remaining 4 dragoon regiments of II Cavalry Corps—in all, 14 battalions and 16 squadrons. Thus, the rear guard now totaled 26 battalions and 48 squadrons.
5. At the beginning of the campaign, Barclay and Bagration together had over 137,000 line troops. Napoleon, without Schwarzenberg, who was drawn off by Tormassov, had more than 415,000.
6. Including Miloradovitch, the two Russian armies now numbered 111,000 line troops. Napoleon still had about 140,000.

15. Borodino

As the Russians closed in on Borodino, where they would halt their retreat, the French kept up the pressure. Reinforced with additional cavalry, the Russian rear guard under Konovnitzyn[1] clashed with the French advance guard under Murat[2] and was driven back to Gshatsk. From there, it continued on to Gridnevo on September 3; there, it was again substantially reinforced with more cavalry, as the Russians made a determined effort to meet the French cavalry masses with masses of their own. Passing through Gshatsk, the Russians absorbed the reserves, totaling 15,589 men, that Miloradovitch had brought and reassigned them to the depleted formations of the two western armies. At Borodino, another 16,000 men[3] of the Moscow and Smolensk militias were waiting. These, however, were not at all usable, being for the greatest part only with pikes.

The Russian army massing at Borodino numbered 111,000 men and 7000 Cossacks, with 640 guns, not counting the militia of Wintzingerode's 3000-man raiding detachment and other detached Cossacks. Some organizational changes were put in place in preparation for the coming battle: The infantry corps lost their light cavalry, which was reassigned to the cavalry corps, which had been rather weak. A similar move was made with the artillery. The corps were to retain only about two batteries, on average. The rest was passed into the artillery reserve park.

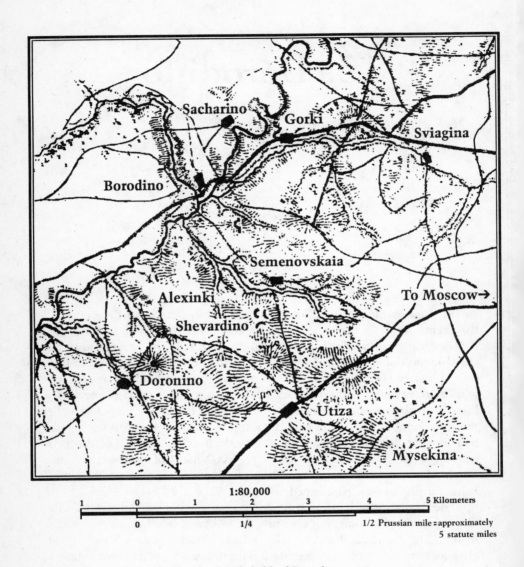

The Battlefield of Borodino

*   *   *

Murat and the French advance guard arrived in Gshatsk on September 1 and occupied the town after a light skirmish. Napoleon himself got there just a short while later, while the army was still a march behind.

Again, day after day, the densely packed columns were marching through dry stretches of country while the mercury topped the 90°F mark. The Russians had already stripped the countryside on their way through, so the French had to look far and wide to come up with anything. Napoleon made the infantry march alongside, not on the great Moscow road, so that the road itself would be open to facilitate the free movement of the artillery and train columns. However, given even this advantage, the commissariat still left virtually everything to be desired. There was meat but no salt or supplemental comestibles; there was flour but no bread. Above all, there was a general lack of water. Suicides were rampant again. On September 1, a heavy rain brought relief from the heat, but it was killing the army with kindness: It lasted for 3 days without letup. The bottom went out of the road once more. Thousands of horses faltered and collapsed, and the corps commanders again became insistent that it was impossible to advance further. The army, which on its departure from Smolensk had numbered 149,075 men, was down to 133,819, including Latour-Maubourg's cavalry and 7321 men who were detached on foraging expeditions. Most of the latter, however, were to return before the battle.

In little more than a week, the army had lost another 15,256 men, of which only a small fraction can be accounted for by the security detachments left behind and by the combat losses sustained in the advance guard. The vast majority were victims of the weather and the marching conditions it had brought about. However, the army was modestly reinforced by the return of Pajol's division, which still had 1400 troopers. Together with Pinot's Italian division and Guyon's brigade, coming from Vitebsk, Pajol's troopers had been sent after Wintzingerode and had actually pursued him as far as Ivanoviczy, at which point they had left off to return to the army. But Pajol was the only one to make it back in time for the battle; Pinot and Guyon did not arrive until afterward. In all, the central army group on September 2 numbered 90,507 infantry, 29,219 cavalry, and 15,493 artillerymen, with 587 guns.

Expecting that the new Russian commander would at last offer him the battle he desired, Napoleon let his army rest around Gshatsk on September 2 and 3. Only the Westphalians had to make a short march on the 3rd to close up with the rest of the army. In the meantime, the foraging detachments and as many stragglers as could be rounded up were brought in.

The sun came out again on the 4th, but the great heat had gone with the rain. It was a beautiful day. As if to give an early warning, however, a number of diarists make mention of the frosty touch in the breezes that wafted through the bivouacs at night. Napoleon was among the first to catch a cold, which was to bother him severely during the coming battle.

In the afternoon, Murat ran into Konovnitzyn near Gridnevo and a steady action ensued. It lasted until nightfall, when Konovnitzyn, his right flank threatened, withdrew to the Kolotzkoi cloister. The next day, September 5, brought a repeat performance, and Konovnitzyn withdrew again when Eugene appeared in his right flank. He made an unhindered getaway through Borodino into the Russian main position because Napoleon, who was present, ordered that he be left alone so that Gortshakov's detachment,[4] placed in front of the Russian main position's left wing, would get the undivided attention of the forces present. The detachment was deployed near the village of Shevardino, where a large earthwork had been thrown up in front of the Russian army's left wing. Napoleon saw at once that its guns would have created difficulties for a continuing pursuit of Konovnitzyn's detachment. This marked the beginning of the action of Shevardino, in which Davout was to commit Morand and Friant with their divisions to support Murat's advance guard.[5]

The Shevardino redoubt, of the usual pentagon shape, was an earthwork armed with a battery of twelve guns. As was to be the case in the upcoming Battle of Borodino, the redoubt served as a sort of citadel for Gortshakov's infantry, which was deployed around it at a distance of several hundred paces.

Napoleon ordered the cavalry to drive off their opposite numbers, which they did until they were brought up short by the Russian artillery. Then the infantry of Compans's division, who were part of Murat's advance guard, attacked and made their way into the redoubt. But this merely marked the beginning of the action. The earthwork changed hands several times before final possession was claimed by the Spanish regiment in Friant's division. Darkness was beginning to fall when Poniatowski[6] appeared on the old Smolensk road and threatened to envelop the Russian left. This marked the end of the action. The Russians withdrew into the darkness, leaving several guns behind.

Most sources claim that the French suffered only about 2000 casualties, which is not far from the truth, but this number includes only the ones sustained in the fighting for the redoubt at Shevardino. In contrast, the same sources cite about 7000 Russian casualties, but this is a count of the total casualties sustained in all the actions, including those against Konovnitzyn over the previous 2 days. Actually, the French casualties covering the same period came to about 4000 men.

That the affair at Shevardino almost became a battle was due entirely to Bagration's pugnacity. The Russian bear's fighting blood had been up and he kept on feeding reinforcements into the action until Poniatowski's arrival and the oncoming night put an end to it. He had fallen into the trap of defending an advanced position long after it had accomplished its purpose, which was to give the army time to occupy its main position.

The two western armies were now completely assembled, with the exception of a few Cossack regiments. Taking into account the losses of the last several days, their total came to 103,000 men, with 637 guns. In addition, there were about 7000 Cossacks, as well as the militia already mentioned, which was not to figure in the fighting.[7]

The present strength of the French army at Borodino, on the eve of the first general battle it was to fight in this campaign, may be realistically set at about 124,000 men, with 587 guns.[8] This was all that was left of this portion of the Grand Army, which had numbered 286,000 men[9] just 11 weeks before. Even though the French army was numerically stronger and even though the rigors of the campaign had trimmed away the weakest and left only the hardiest elements, the army was still at a disadvantage. This was largely because the horses of the cavalry and artillery were in poor condition and because the artillery included 160 three- and four-pounders, which left its broadside weight at a disadvantage of 3800 pounds to the Russians' 4800. A moment of virtual equilibrium had now arrived, in which the two forces were, at last, to take each other's measure in battle.

Benningsen, now Kutuzov's chief of staff, had sent Toll out to scout for a suitable position. This was not quite as simple as it sounds. Clausewitz, who was with the Russian headquarters throughout this phase of the campaign, points out that the Russian terrain in the operations area was not rich in the sort of features that make a good position, that is, ground features that favor a defense. The areas where the great swamps are found were also extensively forested. As a result, it was difficult to find clearings large enough to deploy substantial masses of troops. Where the forestation was less dense (e.g., between Smolensk and Moscow), the terrain was flat, lacking distinct heights or deeply cut valleys. The cultivated fields were not in any way fenced and thus could be crossed everywhere. Not even the villages offered good strongpoints, because they were composed entirely of wooden structures, which could be easily set on fire with grenades thrown from howitzers. The more open terrain in front of Moscow did not offer an unobstructed view in any direction, because small stands of trees and wooded patches dotted the ground everywhere. Thus, there was no great choice of positions available to Kutuzov. Indeed, at this point, it was Borodino or nothing.

There was no other place between there and Moscow that could have even pretended to offer the status of a "position."

The Russian position at Borodino ran in a shallow arc. Its right, extending almost to the Moskva, was covered in front by the Kalotsha, a tributary that flowed into the Moskva not far beyond the extreme right of the position. Its center receded back from the Kalotsha near the village of Borodino and extended via Semenovskoye toward Utiza.

Even though the right wing of this position was strongly favored by the terrain and virtually unassailable, Kutuzov packed First Army into this side and left the weak left, which hung in the air without anything to anchor it, to be defended by Bagration's far weaker Second Army. Both Bagration and Barclay had strongly argued against this, but Kutuzov was not to be budged. A large earthwork had been thrown up in front of the center, a short way upriver and across from Borodino. Since it was in front of Raievsky's division, it became known as the "Raievsky's redoubt" or the "great redoubt." Three more redoubts, thrown up in front of Bagration's position, are collectively known as "Bagration's redoubts." These were intended to give the left wing of the Russian position the strength that was lacking in the terrain. It was only when Poniatowski was seen approaching along the old Smolensk road during the night of September 5–6 that III Infantry Corps was taken out of the First Army's reserve and moved over to extend the Russian left as far as Utiza.

This is the way things remained, even though Kutuzov had received a sensible proposal to shift his army after dark on the 6th so that Bagration would have been massed around Utiza and the more powerful First Army would have been positioned between Bagration and Gorki. This would have resulted in the naturally strong right flank being covered by only a few line troops, the Cossacks, and the militia who, from a distance, would look like regulars in reserve, and thus would have freed the bulk of the First Army to reinforce the center and left. In all, the Russian position extended for about 11,000 paces. However, since the right was never attacked, all the action took place on a front of about 6500 paces, and most of the heavy fighting concentrated on a front of considerably less than 2 miles. As a result of this, the excellent Russian artillery, much of it massed with the First Army, voluntarily yielded its considerable superiority because a large portion of it never came into action. This allowed the weaker, but expertly handled, French artillery to become the decisive factor in the battle.

Although Davout had suggested an enveloping movement around the Russian left, Napoleon stuck to the frontal attack, both because he feared that the Russians might run again and because he did not want to take the two of Davout's five divisions assigned to Eugene's IV Corps away from there. This would have been necessary in order to act on Davout's plan. Thus, it was left to Poniatowski's weak corps to make the enveloping maneuver by itself. As a result, Eugene had more troops than he could effectively use, while neither Davout nor Poniatowski had enough to effectively carry out their assigned tasks.

The main attack was planned for the center, where Davout was to go against Bagration's redoubts with three divisions from his corps. Behind Davout's right, Murat was to support his attack with Nansouty's, Montbrun's, and Latour-Maubourg's cavalry corps and the light cavalry of I and II Army Corps. Behind his left, Ney was to do likewise with his own III Corps, as well as Junot's VIII Corps, which had been placed under his command on that day. Ney was supposed to keep an eye on its commander and to prevent another lapse such as the one that had occurred at Smolensk. However, Junot was to be quite his old self.

Simultaneously with Davout, Eugene was to deliver another main attack with his own IV Corps, the two remaining divisions of I Corps, and Grouchy's cavalry. He was to take Borodino, cross the Kalotsha, and then take on the Raievsky redoubt and keep the Russians busy there. Both attacks were to be supported by powerful batteries, with the guard held in reserve behind the center.

In order to fully understand Napoleon's intentions, it must be kept in mind that Napoleon had not been able to have a good look at the Russian position. He was under the impression that the Raievsky redoubt and Bagration's redoubts all stood on the same stretch of high ground.

THE BATTLE

Both commanders were up and about at the crack of dawn. Kutuzov, surrounded by a horde of priests and popes bearing the holy relics brought from Smolensk, had already made a religious procession through the bivouacs. His address to the troops spoke of the Holy Virgin, Heaven, tyrants, and the sword of St. Michael, making the defense of the homeland a religious duty. Napoleon could not even think of striking such notes in front of his erstwhile republicans. Instead, he spoke of glory, Austerlitz, the promise of winter quarters, and a happy return home. Thus, both sides accommodated the spiritual needs of their troops with something that seemed appropriate to the situation.

About 6 a.m. on September 7, 1812, three French batteries roared to life. With a 102-gun salute, they announced the opening of one of the bloodiest battles of the entire nineteenth century.

Compans's division was passing through the near side of the brush around Utiza to go up against the southernmost and strongest of the three Bagration redoubts. To its left, a little farther back, covered by the stands of trees and low growths for the time being, came Dessaix's division. Behind Compans came Friant's division in support. When Compans emerged from the woods, he was received with a murderous barrage of canister from the Russian artillery, which included a large number of 12-pounders. The French doggedly pushed forward, passing through the dried-up bed of the Kamenka Brook. As soon as the skirmishers of the leading brigade had pressed in, the columns came forward, but they quickly ran afoul of the Russian guns. Both Compans and Desaix were seriously wounded and down.

Davout, who was with General Sorbier, who directed the fire of the French artillery, saw the attack of Compans's leading brigade wavering. He went up to Compans's division, where he placed himself in front of the 57th Line Regiment (actually a brigade of five battalions) and went off in the wake of the brigade up front, whose columns had fallen apart in the withering fire from the redoubt. He did not get far before his horse was shot out from under him. Davout landed so hard that Sorbier thought he had been killed and sent a message to Napoleon informing him so. The emperor sent Rapp to replace Davout, but the latter was already back on his feet. Davout took the 57th (Teste's brigade) forward again when Teste was shot down in yet another failed attempt on the redoubt. All of this, however, reads a lot faster than it actually happened. Rapp had arrived in time to have another try with the 61st Line, a regiment he had once commanded in Egypt (and now also a brigade of five battalions). He renewed the assault only to receive his twenty-second wound around 7 a.m. By about 7:30 Davout had possession of the southern redoubt.

When Bagration, a good man up front, saw that the French were going after his redoubts in force, he seized hold of all troops that were close at hand and brought them up quickly, before the French in and around the redoubt could sort out and reform their broken formations. Out with the French, in with the Russians. However, Ney, never far from a good fight, came up with one of the brigades from Ledru's division, the 24th Light Infantry, and together with Davout's leading two divisions made a rush that drove the Russians from all three redoubts before they had a chance to reorganize.

Badly outnumbered, Bagration did what was, for him, a difficult thing to do: Not even bothering to ask Kutuzov, who stood on the height of Gorki with his glittering entourage of "do-nothings," Bagration went straight to Barclay for the help he desperately needed. He had come to the right address. Barclay at once sent 3 guard regiments, 8 grenadier battalions, and 24 twelve-pounders in the direction of Semenovskoye at the forced march pace. Baggehuffwudt's corps was sent to Tutshkov on the extreme left to replace Konovnitzyn's division. In the meanwhile, Bagration had a bad time. The French had thrown strong cavalry masses at his infantry after it had been thrown out of the redoubts. Duka's 2nd Cuirassier Division now broke forward with Neverovsky's infantry division in tow. Murat was in trouble at once and had to save himself by fleeing into a battalion of Wuerttembergers, who were holding the left redoubt. This was the point at which both Davout and Ney reported that Bagration's redoubts had been taken but that they would be unable to hold them without reinforcements. And this was also the point at which Napoleon refused to turn loose any of his guards.

All sorts of reasons—his cold, poor health, declining powers, and increasing weight—have been invoked to explain away Napoleon's failure to send in the guards. But his refusal may have simply been based on the fact that he was unwilling to commit his last ace in the hole so early in a battle, let alone 1000 miles from home. After briefly toying with the idea of sending in Claparede's division of Polish veterans from the Vistula Legion, he decided to commit Friant's division, which was still standing by the edge of the woods around Utiza in support of Compans and Dessaix.

However, even before Friant was able to come up, Bagration renewed the attack with the guards Barclay had sent from the right. General Pelet, who was probably with the 48th Line Regiment, a brigade in Friant's division, witnessed the Russian counterattack and wrote this description:

> As Bagration's supporting troops arrived, they were fed into the action, boldly advancing over the bodies of the fallen to retake the lost redoubts. The Russian columns moved in accurate response to the orders from their commanders and were, themselves, living bastions. As soon as they emerged into the open terrain, our canister knocked them down, but these brave warriors let nothing bother them and continued to come at us as before. It was during this attack, when Prince Bagration was mortally wounded.[10]

The Russian losses were enormous, as canister tore through their ranks again and again. Wolzogen, in his memoirs, relates running into a lieutenant with a troop of between thirty and forty men. When the colonel told the lieutenant somewhat testily to get back to his regiment, the lieutenant replied: "This is the regiment!" The Russian Regiment Lithuania had lost 956 men in about an hour.

About 11:30, Friant's division took a hand in the action, and the Bagration redoubts were taken for the fourth and last time. But the French could make no headway against the low ground around Semenovskoye.

Strong artillery was brought forward to support a massive cavalry attack by Murat. Nansouty's corps was to pass around the right of Semenovskoye, Latour-Maubourg's around the left. Here again, Murat proved himself to be a brave cavalryman but not even remotely a Seydlitz. The two corps were not committed in a coordinated attack, so only Latour-Maubourg was able to score some minor successes. However, the final taking of Bagration's redoubts had forced the entire Russian line back to the edge of the woods behind the Russian main line.

It was a stroke of good fortune for the Russians that due to the great clouds of dust and the powder smoke generated by hundreds of guns, neither Murat, Davout, nor Ney was aware of the fact that the Russians were in full disarray, with hardly any of their formations still intact. In view of their own losses and exhaustion, Davout and Ney did not believe that they could advance any farther without reinforcements.

But Napoleon had refused their request. He was not present at the decisive point, having remained behind, atop the redoubt of Shevardino, until about 4 p.m. Like Kutuzov, he was very far removed from the action and took practically no hand in the course of the battle. He had, however, given his army a better-than-even chance for success, while Kutuzov seems to have had little concern about its outcome except, perhaps, the hope that it wouldn't go too badly. The behavior of both men certainly lends credence to Tolstoy's tirade against the commanders in chief.

The events related so far, however, describe only half the battle. When Davout had advanced against Bagration's redoubts, about 6 a.m., Eugene had sent his columns against Borodino. Advancing with overwhelming force, Delzons' division soon ejected the Russian Guard Jaeger (light infantry) from the town. Following on the heels of the retreating Russians, those of Delzons' assault columns that had not broken up and turned into howling mobs going through Borodino now did so as they ran over the Kalotsha bridge, across the sunken road on the other side, and up the slope toward Gorki. The sight of these men so surprised a Russian battery halting on top of the hill that it took off without firing a shot.

However, as soon as the fleeing Russian defenders of Borodino were received and the front was cleared, the mass of French soldiers suddenly found themselves facing deployed Russian lines. The Russian columns came forward and drove the entire horde, which had been the first brigade Delzons had committed to action, back across the Kalotsha. However, the Russians following across the bridge were not able to reform to make a determined try at the village. Delzons had strongly established himself in Borodino and was not about to let go again.

In the meanwhile, Morand's division had crossed the dry bed of the

Semenovka Brook. The two battalions deployed at the foot of the rise, which was surmounted by the Raievsky redoubt, probably dissolved into a powerful skirmishing line. Eugene, seeing that an assault from the north side would be too difficult, had the remainder of his force cross the Kalotsha on three bridges and then advanced against the Raievsky redoubt from the south side. The redoubt was armed with cannon. At its foot stood light infantry. To the right and left, there were four infantry battalions on each side. Morand's skirmishers could make only slow headway against the Russian jaeger until Eugene deployed strong artillery. Between them, they slowly pushed the Russians back toward the redoubt.

The crossing of the Kalotsha, however, had delayed the main attack against the redoubt until about 10 a.m. At that time, Broussier and Morand advanced together, supported by a blistering artillery barrage. Bonami's brigade, the 30th French Line, spearheaded the French attack. At the critical point, the Russian guns ran short of ammunition. The gunfire abated, and the attackers were in. This resounding success could have had dire consequences for the Russians. If the attack was pressed on here, then the Russian line would have been pierced. It was around this time that Ney was wrestling with the Russian guards and Bagration was wounded.

This was to be Yermolov's moment. Barclay was busy attempting to rally the Paskevitch regiment, which was fleeing from the redoubt. When Kutuzov was informed that Ney had taken the Bagration redoubts for the third time and that Bagration had been carried off unconscious, he is said to have turned to Yermolov, the chief of staff of First Army, and said, "My dear fellow, see if something might be done there." Yermolov rode off at once in the direction of the left wing. On the way, he ran into Colonel Nikitin, the chief of the artillery reserve. "Take three horse batteries," he told him, "and don't lose sight of me!" Passing to the rear of the Raievsky redoubt, he saw that the Russian troops were flooding back in disorder and that the French had gotten in. Deciding that the most useful thing he could do would be to retake the redoubt, he had the horse artillery unlimber and fire into the open throat of the redoubt. Although Bonami's men had captured eighteen guns, there was no ammunition for them, so they could not reply. (It had not yet been possible to bring up any French guns.)

Once the Russian guns were firing, Yermolov seized upon any troops he could find. For the moment, this was only the 3rd Battalion, Ufa Regiment. With it, he gathered up what stragglers he could and mounted a vicious bayonet attack against the open throat of the redoubt; at that very moment, two jaeger regiments, brought personally by Barclay, arrived. Without firing a shot, the Russian columns came on. With no canister to impede their advance, they rolled into the rear of the redoubt, and what was left of

Bonami's brigade was either trampled underfoot or flattened against the embrasures. Barclay himself had been in the forefront of the attack. Bonami was down, bleeding from twenty wounds. The young Russian artillery chief, Kutaisov, who had accompanied Yermolov, met his end there. This was a fateful strike against the Russian artillery, which felt the loss of his skills throughout the rest of the day.

At this point, the Raievsky redoubt was back in Russian hands, but Ney and Davout held Semenovskoye and had deployed strong batteries on the heights there. Prince Eugene of Wuerttemberg was coming through the bush of Knaskovo with four line regiments, about 3600 men, to plug the gap in the center when the shot from the French batteries at Semenovskoye began to reach his ranks. The French Eugene's batteries also found the range of this Russian support column. The Russian Eugene had been about to deploy for an attack against the Raievsky redoubt, but Yermolov was already on his way in. Barclay, as cool and as level-headed as always, rode up to the prince and, while under the cross fire of the French batteries, calmly pointed out an alternate target, a strong French infantry column moving forward between Semenovskoye and the redoubt. If it succeeded in breaking through, then the center and left were finished. The prince said afterward:

> Actually, it was a walk into Hell. In front of us was a mass of indeterminate depth, even as its front was impressive enough. To the left, a battery, the full extent of which we could not determine, but which the French say contained 80 guns. And everywhere French cavalry, waiting to cut off our way back. To insure a retreat I attached a battalion from Tobolsk to both flanks of the deployed regiment Volhynia. Some distance to the rear, the second brigade followed in columns.
>
> In this order we went straight for the enemy mass, while the huge battery hurled its balls at us. The grisly cannonade claimed Generals Schroeder and Rossy. The two regiments in front, Volhynia and Tobolsk, lost several hundred men and I had three horses shot out from under me in a very short time.
>
> Despite these heavy losses, the division continued to advance and the enemy did not even await our arrival but withdrew again, even as our dragoons rushed past us to threaten their flank as well as the battery.[11]

While this was going on, the French Eugene was preparing for his second assault of the Raievsky redoubt. Miloradovitch, who was in charge of its defense, did not think he could face the assault without reinforcements. Therefore, Barclay again found his own Eugene, the Wuerttemberger who fought on the Russian side, and asked him to move his second brigade farther to the right so that it might support Miloradovitch in case he needed help.

In the meanwhile, Kutuzov's apathy had allowed a splendid opportunity to simply slip by. Quite early in the morning, Platov and his Cossacks had begun to search for a place where the Kalotsha might be forded. When they found a ford and crossed to the other side, they discovered to their astonishment that there were no French forces other than a weak cavalry brigade under Ornano in front of the Russian right. Platov immediately sent his adjutant off to Gorki to request the necessary support to make something of this unexpected windfall. Toll saw the point at once, but Kutuzov seemed totally disinterested. According to Clausewitz, he appeared to be in a trance, mumbling the same phrases over and over as he listened to Toll. In the end, all that was provided for the venture was Uvarov with about 2500 light cavalry of the Guard. By the time they and their twelve guns had crossed the river, it was almost noon. Two miles farther south, Eugene was just in the process of concentrating his masses for the second assault against the Raievsky when he was informed that Borodino and his left flank were threatened. Eugene at once took some of Grouchy's cavalry to see for himself and promptly ran into Uvarov's first attacks. But Uvarov could do little more than cause a few moments of anxiety. Without infantry and artillery, he could not even think of making a serious attack against Borodino or of crossing the Voina. As a result, the only thing that came of Platov's discovery was the delay of Eugene's attack to recapture the Raievsky redoubt. On the other hand, Kutuzov and the Russians may hardly be faulted for not having made more of this apparent windfall, because they simply could not afford to take sufficient troops out of the main line for such a venture once the French attacks had started. Moreover, Kutuzov knew that he had to fight a defensive battle, banking on the proverbial tenacity of his infantry to hold out. Trying to capitalize on Platov's discovery of the ford with sufficient force to cause serious trouble would have precipitated a liquid tactical situation, at which the French were far more adept than the Russians.

Because of this interlude, it was not until 2 p.m. when Napoleon ordered Eugene to renew his attack against the great redoubt. Broussier's, Morand's, and Gerard's divisions were to form the assault columns for a frontal attack against the Russian line, with Chastel's light cavalry division on the left. The right, facing the Raievsky redoubt, was left to the cavalry. While the redoubt was subjected to a withering fire from Ney's batteries near Semenovskoye, the cavalry opened the assault. Caulaincourt, who now commanded II Cavalry Corps in place of Montbrun (who had already fallen to the guns of the great redoubt) put Wathier's cuirassier division at the head of the assault that was about to take place.

Barclay had observed Eugene's preparations for the coming attack and had gathered whatever troops he could to defend against it. Ostermann was to bring forward the troops of IV Infantry Corps, but the French batteries at Semenovskoye were taking a heavy toll of them even as they were moving into the line. The last of the guards and everyone that could still sit on a horse was brought up. But the French artillery was the dominant factor, both by pouring its fire into these reserves and by acting as a counterbattery as well. Colonel Nikitin's horse batteries, which had taken a hand in the recapture of the great redoubt, had already lost 93 gunners and 113 horses and had seven of their gun carriages smashed.

Seeing the Russian infantry columns coming forward, Caulaincourt ordered Wathier's cuirassiers to charge, and he rode along with them. Passing to the right of the redoubt, before the columns were up, his cuirassiers succeeded in crashing through the open throat at its rear. The Russian infantry gave them musketry at short range. A musket ball severed Caulaincourt's jugular, killing him. But in the dense press, horses shot down and kicking were almost as lethal as the musketry. The cuirassiers were forced out.

Now Latour-Maubourg's heavies—Lorges cuirassiers, Saxons, Westphalians, and Poles—came up. The Marquise de Chambray, the author of the first important work on the Russian campaign, immortalized the Saxon Gardes du Corps by creating a controversy that went on for decades: He credited Caulaincourt's cuirassiers and not the Saxons with the final capture of the redoubt.

The Saxons had been in action before noon, in connection with Murat's and Ney's attacks against the ground in and around Semenovskoye. Since then, the Saxons and the rest of their brigade had spent some 2 to 3 hours coursing back and forth in a futile effort to escape the Russian artillery by making it difficult for the Russians to find the range. All the while they were roundly cursing Murat and Napoleon for leaving them sitting around and doing nothing better than furnishing a target for the Russian guns. About 2:30 p.m., they were ordered to support Eugene's attempt to retake the Raievsky redoubt.

Thielemann now took his brigade, 8 Saxon and 2 Polish squadrons, up against the redoubt, attacking it simultaneously from three sides. Again, the melee centered around the throat of the redoubt, where the troopers were driven back. But several officers and noncoms, superbly mounted, had managed to drive their horses up the steep face of the redoubt and get inside through the gun ports. Although they were no more than about ten men, they created such confusion inside the redoubt that the rest of the brigade renewed its attack by driving their mounts forward once more. The horses, however, could only be made to walk, since the charges ridden during the course of the day had left them thoroughly winded. But by then the infantry was up and able to help break into the redoubt as well, saving the handful of Gardes du Corps who were still swinging their sabers and engaging the attention of most of the Russian defenders inside.

This, the decisive part of the action, had been totally immersed in the legends woven about the death of Auguste Caulaincourt, beginning with Napoleon's 18th Bulletin, covering the battle and crediting Caulaincourt's cuirassiers with the taking of the Raievsky redoubt, and Chambray's account, repeating this assertion. Chambray's massive work on the campaign remained the prime and only comprehensive source on the Russian campaign until well past the middle of the nineteenth century. As its circulation spread, it was bound to gain the attention of the Saxons, as well as other participants, who knew differently. As a result, the ensuing controversy enhanced the reputation of the Saxon Gardes du Corps even further by publicizing an event that might otherwise have simply merged into the fabric of the battle. Still, the Caulaincourt legend exhibited a remarkable capacity for survival, as legends are wont to do.

The fight for the Raievsky redoubt and the Russian position around it lasted less than an hour. Even so, it is generally regarded as having been the fiercest struggle in a battle that saw a great many brutal encounters, thanks to the proverbial tenacity of the Russian soldier. By about 3 p.m., however, both sides were so exhausted that the fighting ceased; only the artillery of both sides continued to ply its trade.

Napoleon refused to commit the Guard; only Uvarov's unexpected sally into the French left had induced him to dispatch a few batteries of the Guard's artillery. Barclay, who was acutely aware of the Russian army's condition, was quite apprehensive that such an attack might come as a *coup de grace*. When none appeared, he sent Wolzogen to Kutuzov to ask for instructions. Barclay told Wolzogen: "Get the answer in writing. One has to be careful with Kutuzov." Wolzogen's description of his mission is laced with biting sarcasm:

I rode for a long time, before I found the prince. I finally located him by the Moscow road, about half an hour's ride behind the army, surrounded by a suite which seemed to be an entire auxiliary corps. It appeared to consist almost entirely of wealthy young Russian nobles, wallowing in all sorts of rich delicacies and who seemed to be totally unconcerned about the seriousness of what was taking place. Toll was among them as well and was in the process of devouring a capon.

When I reported the condition of the army and that, with the exception of the right, all important posts had been lost and that the regiments were exhausted and falling apart, Kutuzov shouted: "With what ruddy sutleress did you liquor yourself up that you make such a preposterous report? I myself know best the condition of the army! The attacks of the French have been victoriously turned back everywhere, so that I will place myself at the head of the army tomorrow. . . ."

All the while, his eyes traveled around, challenging his audience, who eagerly nodded their agreement. I was put out over this treatment. I had only reported what I had seen with my own eyes while I knew that he had spent the entire day in the rear of the army in the company of champagne bottles and delicacies. But as soon as I regained my composure, I saw through Kutuzov's sly subterfuge.

Those around him were to remain in ignorance of the true condition of the army, so that they might not brand the bulletin he was about to issue a lie. Moreover, he was aware that Napoleon had suspended the action after failing to win a complete victory in a fight that had lasted from 6 a.m. to 5 p.m. and that he would hardly start up again this late in the day. So Kutuzov still had the battlefield, at least until morning.[12]

So Barclay received his orders: Unless Napoleon decided otherwise, the Russians were to undertake nothing; Doctorov was to take Bagration's place; and all the necessary preparations should be made for Kutuzov to attack the French on the next day. Barclay, of course, had no idea how any of this was to be accomplished. The army had shot its bolt.

There had been a third focal point of action in the grand melee that was the Battle of Borodino. While the possession of the Bagration and Raievsky redoubts was being hotly contested, Poniatowski and his Poles had fought a battle of their own. He carried Utiza with his first assault, but by 8 a.m. he had already been ejected. Then Junot's Westphalians were sent in to fill the gap in the line; linking up with Poniatowski, they helped him retake the village. It was around this time that Tutshkov I had been forced to send Konovnitzyn's division to reinforce the position at Semenovskoye.

The forests and bush growths around Utiza gave Poniatowski a difficult time and greatly hindered his advance. Still, Tutshkov was in a difficult situation and in danger of being cut off. This was when Barclay had sent Baggehuffwudt (generally called Bagavout in the French and English literature) to his aid, along with Konovnitzyn, who was again shifted farther to the left.

Around 4 p.m., when fighting along the entire line was beginning to flag, Ochs led his Westphalian division forward to dislodge Baggehuffwudt, who stood atop the grave mound behind Utiza. As soon as Poniatowski took note of this, he renewed his attack as well. With the extreme Russian left also pushed back, the fighting flagged in this sector too. It was over.

The French artillery had fired 60,000 rounds[13] and the infantry had expended nearly 2 million cartridges.

The losses on both sides were enormous. The French had lost about 28,000 men, including 49 generals. The Russian losses ran to about 52,000, that is, half the line troops. This included not only about 1000 prisoners but also about 8000 men who had become separated from their formations during the fighting and who eventually found their way back to their units over the next several days. Four generals had been killed and another eighteen were wounded, including Bagration and Tutshkov I, both of whom were to die of their wounds.

That the French success obtained from the battle was not commensurate with the sacrifices it exacted was entirely Napoleon's fault. Had he been willing to commit his guard, the bulk of Eugene's forces (which had not been overtaxed), and Junot's Westphalians (who had seen relatively little fighting), the Russian army, severely shaken, would have been destroyed. Apart from a large number of batteries, which had never become engaged, it had no untapped reserves left. Worse, it was backed up against the Moskva in a line that ran parallel to its line of retreat. Thus, despite the fact that the "brass ring" was within his reach and despite the fact that he, better than anyone else, understood that success had to be exploited with every last ounce of strength, Napoleon had done nothing. He, who had until now given too little care to the preservation of his army, suddenly became excessively cautious.

Clausewitz maintains that Napoleon no longer felt wealthy enough (in terms of troops) to commit his guards. But what would he have risked? After the battle, his army still numbered 96,000 men, whereas the Russians had only 52,000, not counting the Cossacks and militia. Thus, even in the event of a mishap, the loss of another 5000 or 6000 men would not have weighed in the scales all that heavily. But in the event of a success and with the two western armies destroyed, it would have been totally beside the point if Napoleon arrived in Moscow with 6000 fewer men.

There has been much speculation about Napoleon's failure to act. Possibly because he had remained too far away from the action, he had failed to take note of the dissolution that had overtaken the Russian army. However, he did come forward to have a look for himself after the redoubts had been taken and his forces had established themselves in what had been the Russian main line of defense. By then, however, the Russians had drawn back to the next ridge line. Seen at a distance of several hundred yards, their densely packed masses probably looked more formidable than they actually were. It seems that even his marshals were not too certain about just how badly the Russians had been shaken, although they had been much closer to the action. The incessant movement of large masses of infantry and cavalry had raised a considerable amount of dust in the air, not to mention the powder smoke generated by the firing of hundreds of artillery pieces. The combined effects of dust, smoke, and battle fatigue probably impaired their vision as well. This appears to be borne out by the fact that when Napoleon did express the thought of sending in the Young Guard Division, Murat, who had been all over the battlefield, added his objections to Berthier's, claiming that nothing less than an all-out attack would do. In this way, the day ended with Napoleon half expecting to fight yet another battle on the following day.

Of the two salient ways in which a field marshal can exhibit his mastery on the battlefield—recognizing the most advantageous direction of the main thrust and properly using the reserves—Napoleon showed none at Borodino. Instead, he simply used superior masses to press the enemy's front, and he made no use whatever of his reserves, not even when his troop superiority had exhausted itself and the time had come to complete the success that had been achieved. Thus, it must be admitted that at Borodino, as at Smolensk, the great captain did not function at the peak of his capacity. Once again, Napoleon's indecision robbed him of the opportunity to destroy the enemy, a move which might have created the right climate for a peace. He would not receive another chance.

NOTES

1. The rear guard now included:

Battalions	Squadrons	
14		of 3rd Inf. Div., III Inf. Corps
12 (jaeger)		of II, IV, and VI Corps

Battalions	Squadrons	
	28	of II, III, IV, and VI Inf. Corps
	24	of II Cav. Corps
—	20	of III Cav. Corps
26	72	

Other sources place the totals at 25 battalions and 76 squadrons.

2. The French advance guard included the following:

Battalions	Squadrons	
20		Div. Compans of I Corps
	60	I Cav. Corps Nansouty
	32	II Cav. Corps Montbrun (minus Div. Pajol)
—	40	light cavalry of I and III Corps
20	132	

All the printed works list III Cavalry Corps in place of the light cavalry of I and III Army Corps. Thus, it is possible that the above may be incorrect in this respect. However, Pelet's (see note 10, below) arrangement suggests that the light cavalry of I and III Corps had been assigned to Murat before September 2 and that III Cavalry Corps was with Eugene.

3. Various sources place the figure at from 10,000 to 16,000. However, since about 14,000 men were actually ranked into the line troops after the battle, the larger figure has better claim to accuracy.

4. Gortshakov's detachment:

Battalions	Squadrons	
12		of 27th Inf. Div.
2		of 26th Inf. Div., VII Inf. Corps
2		of 2nd United Gren. Div., III Inf. Corps
	18	of IV Cav. Corps
	20	of 2nd Cuirassier Div.
16	38	

In the course of the action, these were joined by 12 battalions of the 2nd United Grenadier Division, bringing the total to 28 battalions and 38 squadrons, comprising about 20,000 men. (After the action, these troops numbered about 16,800 men.)

5.

	Battalions	Squadrons
Murat's advance guard (as in note 2, above)	20	132
Div. Morand (minus 1 battalion in Vitebsk)	16	
Div. Friant	17	—
Total	53	132

6. VIII Corps had 18 battalions and 12 squadrons.
7. See Appendix XI.
8. See Appendix XII.
9. The troops assembled here (minus Division Doumerc and the troops under Dombrowski) had numbered 286,000 men at the start of the campaign. Of these, about 22,000 (Divisions Laborde and Pinot, as well as Brigade Guyot and some minor rear-area postings) had been detached. About 40,000 had become combat casualties and 100,000 had absented themselves from the army.
10. Pelet, J. J. G. *Memoires sur les Guerres de Napoleon Depuis 1796 Jusqu'en 1815.* (no date)
11. Wuerttemberg, Herzog Eugen von. *Erinnerungen aus dem Feldzuge des Jahres 1812 in Russland.* Breslau, 1846.
12. Wolzogen, Ludwig Freiherr v. *Memoiren des Koeniglich Preussischen Generals der Rufanterie.* Leipzig, 1851.
13. The Russians, even though they failed to bring the full weight of their own artillery to bear, can be assumed to have fired at least 40,000 rounds, probably more.

16. Only 70 Miles
to Go

It was not because of Kutuzov that the battle had not been worse for the Russians. It was mainly Barclay, the man he had replaced in command, who had striven to keep some unified order in the conduct of the fighting. Back at Gorki, the old general seemed to have sunken into a trance, occasionally nodding and mumbling to himself to let, as Clausewitz quotes him, "those handle matters who had them in hand." But those who had them in hand were neither him nor his chief of staff, Benningsen. The heir of the battle was Barclay, who had appeared everywhere and had had three horses shot out from under him without sustaining so much as a scratch himself. Some observers thought he was deliberately trying to get himself killed.

This was not the case with Bagration, who had stood his ground in the sort of scramble at which he excelled. He received a leg wound that would hardly have been fatal in modern times. But in those days, gangrene still killed off thousands of men, often with comparatively light wounds, who thought they had survived a battle. Bagration lived long enough to hold out his hand to Barclay, whom he had considered his enemy, and made peace with him. Barclay also had the satisfaction of hearing the cheers of the troops, whenever he passed by—the same troops who had all but vilified him during the previous several weeks. Yet those who would meet Yermolov again a year later at Kulm would hardly recognize him as the man of resolution he had been at Borodino.

But it was Kutuzov who had told Wolzogen, "I am going to place myself at the head of the army and drive the enemy from Russia's sacred soil." The note he handed him to take back to Barclay spoke of renewing the battle with the enemy on the next day. Everyone, including Barclay, thought that Kutuzov could not possibly mean this, and even if he did mean it for only an instant, then it was only because he was so far to the rear that he had no idea what the world looked like half an hour's ride away. Or did he? It must be remembered that from the start he thought the battle was unnecessary. More than a century and a half has passed and the question is still raised in every discussion of the Russian campaign and the Battle of Borodino. The old fox indeed! He knew exactly what he was doing, and he knew exactly what he was saying. And subsequent events were to prove him right. Soon after, he did order the retreat, as he probably knew he would all along. It began before the hours of daylight on the morning of September 8. The troops marched in two columns, with Miloradovitch leading one via Moshaisk and Doctorov leading the other along the old Smolensk road.

Beyond Moshaisk, near Shukovo, the army halted and sorted out its shattered formations. Despite the heavy bloodletting, it had never lost its composure even during the retreat. This was possible mainly because the army did not consider itself to have been beaten. Partly, this was Napoleon's fault, not merely because he had failed to deliver the *coup de grace* but also because he had ordered his points back at nightfall in order to avoid disturbances during the hours of darkness. As a result, the average soldier, who had no encompassing view of the situation, was under the impression and ready to believe that the fight would be renewed at the next opportunity, as Kutuzov had indicated.

In view of all this, it is difficult to find fault with either Kutuzov's words or his actions. The wily old campaigner knew that no matter how bad the situation might look in the short run, his estimate would be correct in the long. The short and the long: These concepts serve splendidly in describing the difference between Napoleon and Kutuzov. Napoleon was the master of the short run, but Kutuzov understood the long. Campaigning by the shores of the Black Sea, Kutuzov had learned about distances, sparsely populated tracts, and the effects these exercised on the troops. Still, Napoleon's decision to pull back his outposts at nightfall gave Kutuzov the opportunity to claim victory in his initial report to the tsar. This was to have far-reaching consequences.

Reflecting the mood of the army, the resistance Platov's rear guard[1] offered was so determined that Napoleon, who had intended to be in Moshaisk on the 8th, had to remain at Borodino. For its part, Murat's reserve cavalry had suffered so badly in the battle that the horses could hardly be made to do more than walk. On the 9th as well, when the Russian army continued its withdrawal to Semolino, its reinforced rear guard maintained itself in Moshaisk until afternoon; at that time the rear guard was forced to evacuate, leaving behind about 10,000 wounded, who had been brought there after the battle. On that same evening, the rear guard was again reinforced and placed under Miloradovitch's command, because Kutuzov feared that the enemy might press too closely. Thus, the rear guard was so strong that on the 10th, when the main army withdrew behind the Nara at Krutiza, it was able to throw back the French advance guard at Krimskoye, each side losing about 2000 men in the encounter.

It was also on the 10th when the French army finally departed from the battlefield. Davout was in the lead, followed by Mortier with the Young Guard; then came Ney, with the Old Guard bringing up the rear. On the day after the battle, Pino's division and Guyon's brigade rejoined Eugene, who was to march on the left, toward Rusa. Poniatowski was to the right, on the Moscow-Kaluga road, marching toward Fominskoye. The entire army, not merely the cavalry of the advance guard, was bone-weary, its exhaustion exacerbated by hunger. Still, had there been any energy left, there would have been a spring in the steps of the troops. Few absented themselves from the army after the battle, because El Dorado, that is, Moscow, was just beyond the horizon; its promise of rest, plentitude, and loot was beckoning these tired soldiers onward like a magnet.

As at Smolensk, Junot's VIII Corps was left behind at Moshaisk, while some 5000 of his men cleaned up the battlefield. The dead had to be collected and, if possible, buried. Still serviceable weapons (left by the dead and wounded), especially the muskets, which were forever in short supply, had to be reclaimed. Napoleon had ordered extensive measures especially for the care of the wounded, but few of these were ever implemented because, as usual, there was a lack of everything—manpower as well as materials. The lot of the wounded, especially the Russians, was sad, and just as many died from starvation as died from a lack of care.

Napoleon was still ailing and stayed in Moshaisk until the 12th. Worried about arriving in Moscow with insufficient strength, he busied himself with ordering up all available forces. The great majority of detachments, large and small, from almost all the army corps with the central army were called in, and IX Corps, which had been left behind in Germany, was now brought up as well. Most of these troops arrived between October 8 and 15, even though a few small formations were diverted to other uses. The only troops remaining in Prussia and northern Germany were the Divisions Heudelet, Lagrange, and Destrees, Dragoon Brigade Cavaignac, and the six cohorts in Bremen, to which another six were to be added.

This was the measure of the Grand Army's second wind. Napoleon concentrated most of the troops into the communications line of the central army because his flanks did not trouble him unduly at this time. His lack of concern was based entirely on the assumption that the imminent occupation of Moscow would attract all the Russian forces to concentrate there. That, at least, is how he described the situation in a letter to Maret on September 10.

The losses sustained at Borodino were slowly being replaced. First to rejoin the army were Division Pinot and Brigade Guyot, which arrived right after the battle with 7000 men. Laborde's division of the Young Guard, another 4000 men, was on its way from Smolensk. Another 7600 men, march formations, and various security detachments were also ordered up from Smolensk. This came to more than 18,000 men, who either had arrived already or were due shortly. Victor's IX Corps had crossed the Niemen on September 3.

Minus some temporary detachments, Victor had 28,000 men, of whom a 3000-man Saxon brigade was left behind in Minsk to cover the magazines established there. Since Napoleon was convinced that he would have to draw upon this corps and even Dombrowski's division, an additional strong reserve was to be massed at Smolensk. Thus, that city became the objective of all the security detachments, march formations, and reserves called up from the rear areas and Germany. The rear-area garrisons were to be left entirely in the hands of the Lithuanians, who drew bitter complaints from Napoleon over their slowness in raising the new formations. As a result, some of the march formations continued to be absorbed in the rear areas, along with others entirely composed of stragglers who had been rounded up.

In the meanwhile, the Russians had continued their retreat without undue haste. The first extensive stage was a march to Vaseomo on the 11th, followed by marches to Mamonovo on the 12th and to Fili on the 13th. Wintzingerode's detachment[2] had accompanied these marches in the right flank of the army, withdrawing via Svenigorod. Due to heavy losses, many battalions and squadrons had to be amalgamated, and the combined grenadier formations were broken up. II and III Cavalry Corps were united into one.

At this time, the militia was also placed into the third ranks of the infantry battalions. In this connection, most sources dote on the idea that most of these men were armed only with pikes. Since the image lends itself nicely to the concepts of patriotism and heroism, even military men often repeated the story. They ought to have known better. Similar stories continue to persist about the Prussian Landwehr of 1813. There is, however, no concrete evidence that such weapons ever actually appeared in a mobile field unit.

As already noted, Kutuzov had declared that he would fight another battle in defense of Moscow. But the army was far too weak, and the position at Fili could hardly be called a position. A war council, which met on the 13th, decided to retreat through Moscow and on to Ryasan. This was a difficult decision for Kutuzov, who had already implied in his first report that the battle at Borodino had been won.

Here, for the first time, Toll apparently expressed a thought that should have been aired long before: to retreat not in an easterly direction but, rather, in a southerly one. It was an idea that was to yield great results later on. Only Benningsen, who had lost all of his influence since Borodino, spoke against a retreat and even suggested an offensive, but he apparently did this only after he was certain that Kutuzov had made up his mind and would stand firm. His suggestion, however, was obviously an attempt to get the tsar's attention and to recommend himself as a future commander in chief, just in case giving up Moscow might cost Kutuzov his job. There are, of course, nearly as many accounts of this conference as there were participants—and as many versions of what was said there, most of them self-serving. But the decision to retreat definitely emerged from the meeting, and beyond it stood the abandonment of Moscow.

Immediately after the army had passed through Moscow, taking almost all the population along with it, Rostopchin, the governor of the city, was ready to put his own plans into operation.

Moscow in 1812 was a sprawling city of about 250,000 inhabitants during the fall. Throughout the winter months, when the nobles and their serfs returned from their country estates, the population would increase by about 100,000. To the eyes of the western visitor, the city represented a curious, colorful, and exciting mix of east and west. Rising out of a sea of single-story wooden houses, many little better than huts, were the great stone palaces of the aristocracy (a legacy of Peter the Great's westernizing reforms) and the compact, multiturreted Orthodox churches, with their onion-shaped domes clustering atop narrow-shouldered arches (the legacy of traditional Russian architecture). The palaces, situated in large gardens, were not nearly so numerous as the six cathedrals and 1500 churches that tended to the souls of the Muscovites. As elsewhere in Russia, a citizen either had very much or very little or, as others would have it, either had everything or nothing. Everyone either was connected to the great families or served them. The small middle class consisted mainly of merchants and those who provided skilled services for the nobles or for the government. Many of these people were foreigners.

To describe the Russian aristocrats as "conspicuous consumers" would be something of an understatement. Apart from government employees, the bulk of Moscow's population in 1812 served the palaces in various capacities. This is underlined by the summer exodus of the nobility; when the nobles took their service entourages along, the population of the city was reduced by about 28 percent. Yet even this statistic does not include everyone connected with the palaces, because staffs remained behind to look after these empty "townhouses."

In addition to maintaining residences in St. Petersburg (because it was fashionable to be wherever the tsar was in residence), the great families duplicated their lavish domiciles in their summer residences outside Moscow and, often, on their vast agricultural domains. There, amid thousands of serfs, they lived in a grand style. To put it plainly, this very thin elite layer atop the Russian social strata was all that counted. The rest of the population was considered of little consequence. Indeed, the question has been raised as to why Napoleon didn't turn the entire campaign around by simply circulating a declaration emancipating the serfs. Many feel that he, himself the son of a revolution, shied away from this because he could not be certain of what might have come of such an action.

Once word of what had happened at Borodino got around, the nobles at once put their serfs to work stripping their Moscow residences of all valuables. Nobody believed that the French could be stopped at this point. By the time Kutuzov's troops had passed through the city, the rest of the Muscovites had taken their cue as well. The merchants, with their ears glued to the ground on which the aristocracy walked, had already gone. Thus, almost everything of consequence was already secured when Rostopchin opened the jails and had the fire-fighting equipment destroyed. About 10,000 Russian soldiers wounded in the battle needed to be moved, but there were no wagons or draft teams left because everything that had wheels had been used to transport the property of the wealthy.

That large quantities of foodstuffs were left behind is quite understandable because much of it was dispersed in many places. But that large amounts of military stores were abandoned instead of being secured for the militia is not so easily explainable. There was probably no transport available for these either.

Putting aside the moral aspects of the abandonment of Moscow, its material aspects, in terms of the only Muscovites who really counted, posed more of an inconvenience than a sacrifice. The brunt of the exodus fell, as ever, on the small middle class. The rest of the population, maintained largely on a subsistence economy, merely moved with their jobs. These people had gone out to the summer estates, along with whatever government there remained. This must be kept in mind if one is to understand why the spontaneous dislocation of nearly a quarter of a million people, even if it was only of a few weeks duration, did not devastate the city for a generation to come.

Miloradovitch's rear guard remained behind to cover the withdrawal of the Russian army. Since the French advance guard exhibited a noticeable reluctance to start any real fighting in the city, for fear that it would go the way of Smolensk (where only 350 of about 2250 buildings remained habitable after the fires had gotten started), arranging a truce had been easy. Under its cover, Miloradovitch made a clean getaway.

In the afternoon of September 14, just hours after the departure of the Russian rear guard, Napoleon arrived in the Moscow suburbs after having waited in vain for some sort of deputation to come out and meet him. Still hoping that one would eventually show up, he set up temporary quarters in Dorogomikov. The eleventh hour had already struck, as Napoleon himself admitted. Actually, however, it was already too late, since he could no longer hope to maintain himself in Moscow. But it was absolutely necessary to grant the troops an extensive rest, lest the army fall completely apart. Barely 100,000 strong, its open seams were showing everywhere as the bonds of discipline were visibly loosening even more than they had been.

The troops, however, no matter what their native language, were elated. *Moscou! Moskau! Moska!* Here were winter quarters, rest, food, and all the other things that make a soldier's heart beat faster at the end of a campaign. Every man had his own personal dream version of what the city held in store for him.

Napoleon halted by the side of the road as the regiments rolled by on their way into the city. When Claparede's division, the Vistula Legion, passed, Brandt noticed that the emperor's eyes constantly strayed toward the city, as if he was expecting something or someone from there. But a Polish captain next to him remarked: "He can wait there for a long time. The Russians would rather go to Siberia than make peace now." Still, after a while, a deputation of some merchants who had stayed behind in the city appeared. After all, some sort of pro forma showing could be made to protect sensibilities and imperial egos. Somewhat relieved, Napoleon made the best of it. These merchants weren't the government, but they were something. Thus, he received them with the grace and charm that was part of the other side of his character.

But no one was deceived. From the high ground on the near side of the city, endless processions could be observed, heading in an easterly direction along every road. They were hardly the Russian army, much less Milora-dovitch's rear guard. Roos, the regimental surgeon with the Wuerttemberg contingent in Ney's III Corps, described the scene as follows:

> As we marched through the streets leading to the Moskva, not a soul was to be seen. The bridge had been demolished, but we rode through the river, which was about axle-deep to the guns or a bit more than knee-deep for the horses. Once beyond the river, a few inhabitants could be spotted in doorways and windows, watching us, apparently without interest. Further on, we encountered some handsome buildings of stone and wood. Occa-sionally, there were ladies and gentlemen on the balconies and our officers gave friendly salutes, which were returned with equal grace. Still, we saw but few inhabitants and around the palaces only such who appeared to be servants.
>
> By nightfall, we also encountered a few tired Russians soldiers, stragglers on horse and foot, as well as baggage wagons which had fallen behind. We let them pass unhindered.
>
> Our march progressed slowly through winding streets, where the out-landish architecture of the churches, with their multiple turrets and exterior decorations caught our eyes, as did the palaces sitting amid gardens. We crossed a market place, where the stands were open, with the merchandise in disorder and scattered all over the street, as though looters had gotten there ahead of us.
>
> Often, our column ground to a halt. And soon, the sensitive noses of our troopers smelled out the fact that most of the Russian soldiers, fast asleep on the ground everywhere, had spirits in their canteens. Since no one was allowed to dismount, the troopers used their sabers to cut the straps tying the canteens to the soldiers' packs and hoisted them aboard with the small hooks most had filed into their sabertips. In this artful fashion, one obtained strong drink, which had been rare for some time.
>
> All the while, Murat rode up and down alongside our column and if he wasn't there, his eyes were. He was at the head of our column, when we arrived in front of the arsenal. Its gates were open and people were coming out, carrying arms while others were pushing past them to get in. An argument ensued at once, as soon as Murat's adjutants rode up, which got quite loud as soon as some rode into the arsenal.

At the same time, everyone became aware of a large crowd milling around in the square behind the arsenal, which became more agitated by the minute. This, together with the scene in front, caused Murat to order up some artillery. They unlimbered and three rounds was all that was required to disperse the mob and clear the square with unbelievable speed.[3]

There was no longer any mistaking the increasingly hostile mood of these crowds who were thought to be the inhabitants. They are described by the various diarists as being furtive, shaggy, ragtag, and defiant. They were actually mostly the sweepings of the Moscow jails, turned loose by Rostopchin. As one diarist described them, "These were Rostopchin's guards, which the noble Russian, next to Herostrat and Nero, the most famous arsonist of the world, had pulled from the city's dens of iniquity and the darkest chambers of the Muskovite jails to warm the enemy's stay in their fair city."

This, by and large, constituted the entry into Moscow. It was, to say the least, something completely beyond Napoleon's experience. There was not the faintest resemblance to the entries he had made elsewhere, as in Vienna and Berlin. That is, the martial show was there, but there was no one to admire it. His triumphal entry into Moscow had all the excitement of a troupe of actors playing to an empty house.

NOTES

1. The rear guard consisted of 4 jaeger regiments from II Corps, 1 Hussar regiment, the Cossacks, and 1 horse battery, with 12 guns. On the 9th, these were joined by Uvarov's I Cavalry Corps and then 6 infantry regiments and 1 battery from VI Corps. Division Dufour (ex-Friant) of I Corps had 17 battalions.

   Murat's advance guard included the entire reserve cavalry (194 squadrons) and possibly also the light cavalry of I and III Corps (40 squadrons), although the light cavalry is not mentioned elsewhere.

2. After sending a Cossack regiment to Wittgenstein, Wintzingerode's detachment had only 1 dragoon regiment and 2 Cossack regiments left. On September 10, however, it had been reinforced with 1 hussar regiment and 2 Cossack regiments, with 2 guns. Temporarily, there were also 500 infantrymen.

3. Holzhausen, Paul (ed.), *Mit Napoleon in Russland*. The memoirs of H. von Roos. Stuttgart, 1911.

17. The Flanking Forces

Until now, the French flanking forces, some operating more than a hundred miles away from the main army group, as well as Reynier's Saxons and Dombrowski's column, operating more or less independently, have received only passing mention in this narrative. However, as the main army group marched beyond Smolensk and toward Moscow, the operations of these forces steadily assumed greater importance, as the flanking forces the Russians had deployed gradually came into action and eventually closed in until they began to exercise a direct effect upon the events in the center and the main army's line of communications.

VOLHYNIA: THE SOUTHERN FLANK

Early in July, Schwarzenberg and his Austrian Auxiliary Corps had crossed the Bug at Drohiczyn. Operating just north of the great Pripet Marshes, which divided Volhynia to the south from the central theater of operations, the Austrians were to cover the right flank of the Grand Army. Schwarzenberg started this by positioning himself near Pruzany, pushing his points forward as far as the Muchavetz and Pina, and putting a detachment into Pinsk, which was about 70 miles toward the southeast. At his disposal were 34,000 men, with 60 guns. Unaware of the strength the Russians were

268

gathering in Volhynia, Napoleon soon decided to pull the Austrians in toward the main army; Reynier's Saxon VII Corps was to take their place. Schwarzenberg, instead of waiting for the Saxons, simply marched off, meeting up with them at Slonim on July 19.

Reynier's VII Corps had numbered over 17,000 men[1] at the beginning of the campaign, and the task Napoleon had set for Reynier was anything but simple. With a force of not quite 16,000 men and 50 guns,[2] he was expected to cover a line almost 300 miles long, stretching from Brest-Litovsk to Pinsk and Mozyr. To do this effectively, it would have been necessary for him to occupy all three places. Since Reynier did not think he was strong enough to do this, he decided, quite sensibly, to limit himself to the coverage of Brest, the point nearest to the operations base. Thus, like the Austrians, he would also deploy his main force at Pruzany and push two strong advance guards forward, one to Yanov and another via Kobryn to Brest-Litovsk.

On the Russian side, Tormassov had pulled together his widely scattered forces around Lutzk by July 14—about 38,000 men and 4000 Cossacks, with 161 guns. On the 17th, he moved in the direction of the grand duchy of Warsaw. At this time, however, orders from Alexander directed him into the rear of the French forces facing Bagration. This, then, caused him to turn against Reynier, who stood in the way.

Tormassov left Sacken's corps behind to keep an eye on the Galician border. But Sacken had to give up half his infantry to Oertel's corps (standing near Mozyr to guard the eastern edge of the Pripet Marshes), while Tormassov took along half his cavalry and artillery. This indicates that security of the Austrian-Galician border did not rate highly on the list of priorities. But Tormassov also had to leave a strong cavalry detachment under Crushtshev along the upper Bug to observe the Polish border. This left hardly more than 33,000 men at Tormassov's disposal.[3] However, he still had twice Reynier's strength.

Detaching a column in the direction of Janov and Pinsk, Tormassov was able to induce Reynier to advance his main force toward Autopol. He then took his own force toward Kobryn while a further two secondary columns went against Brest-Litovsk, which was quickly occupied on the 25th.

The Saxon Brigade Klengel,[4] from Reynier's corps, had been on its way to Brest but was pushed back in the direction of Kobryn. There, on the 27th, a sharp action took place; Tormassov's main column was also involved. Attacked from all sides, Klengel was overwhelmed.[5] Russian sources state that the brigade surrendered with 2458 men and 8 guns, which were left over after the action. But Funck states that there was no surrender as such, that there were only 1900 men, and that these had simply been overrun.

This latter figure seems more likely, since Funck places the strength of the Saxons after Kobryn at 14,700 men.

This incident was entirely the result of high-handed orders by Colonel von Langenau, the Saxon chief of staff of VII Corps. Issued without Reynier's knowledge, the orders led to disaster when Schwarzenberg departed from Brest before the Saxons were in place, leaving Klengel's brigade isolated and unsupported. The loss of Klengel's brigade left Reynier in a precarious position. He stood near Autopol, only 15 miles from Kobryn, with fewer than 15,000 men[6] and with his sole line of retreat threatened. Tormassov, however, made no further advance (he later claimed this was due to supply difficulties). As a result, Reynier was able to slip his head out of the noose with a forced march to Slonim.

Tormassov halted at Autopol and sent his raiding parties coursing widely, as far as Warsaw and Bialystok, sending waves of fear rippling across Poland. Indeed, the situation appeared so dangerous that Loison, then the governor of Koenigsberg, took 10,000 men to Rastenburg, poising them for a move against Bialystok, should it become necessary.

Reynier's accident caused Napoleon to drop the idea of bringing in Schwarzenberg, who had already turned around anyway to answer Reynier's call for help. Instead, the Austrian was placed in charge of the entire force, including the Saxons, which now came to about 43,000 men. Their mission was to operate against Tormassov and force a battle on him.

When Tormassov received news of their advance on August 11, he began to concentrate his troops. However, with another 13,000 men detached, in addition to Sacken's and Crushtshev's forces, all he could muster at the moment were 18,000 men.[7] But instead of evading a confrontation until some of his detachments came up, he thought he was strong enough to make a stand in a position near the village of Podubno, behind a marshy riverbed. While Schwarzenberg, who disposed of about 42,000 men,[8] spent the 12th standing before the Russians' unassailable front, Reynier was to cross the riverbed above, that is, in a direction west of the Russian left, to attack their flank.

During the night before the attack, the Saxons were suddenly roused by the sounds of a wild cavalcade heading toward their bivouacs. Drums rolled and bugles blared as the Saxons formed up in time to watch about forty horses careening past with a group of Austrian officers in hot pursuit. It turned out later that the horses, apparently frightened by wolves, had torn themselves loose from the picket lines of an Austrian hussar regiment and gone straight for the Saxon campfires. As the frenzied horses passed through the camp, some of the Saxon officers' horses joined their stampede. The next day, the Austrian regiment still listed a dismounted troop.

By 5 a.m. on the 12th, Reynier's attack was under way, but he ran into trouble at once because his weak corps had been reinforced with no more than a cavalry and an infantry brigade by Schwarzenberg. Brigade Sahr blundered into a dangerous swamp, where some men sank in up to their necks and had to be rescued. Its commander, Sahr, described by Funck as a man who went quite mad at the very sight of the enemy, had gone straight ahead, swamp or not, as soon as Schwarzenberg had asked him to support the Austrian Regiment Colloredo, which had come under heavy attack.

For 12 hours, the Saxons struggled in a swamp forest, much of which was negotiable only over stick dams, while the fight degenerated into a series of small actions that ended only with nightfall. Still, Tormassov was not able to maintain himself in the face of Schwarzenberg's strength. Also, the direction of Schwarzenberg's attack threatened his line of retreat. In view of this, he was indeed fortunate that Schwarzenberg's lack of resolution had built him a golden bridge to Kobryn. He had lost about 3000 men, Schwarzenberg about 2000—900 of them Saxons.

Just as Tormassov had failed to exploit his earlier success, so did Schwarzenberg now fail to make the most of his own. Even though Tormassov had to fight several actions, notably on the 16th at Divin and on the 25th at Vizva, he made his retreat without haste, pulling in his detachments as he went along. Behind the Styx, his army took a strong position at Lutzk on the 29th and awaited the approach of the Danube Army, which had left the Walachia (present-day southern Rumania) on July 31. Once these troops arrived, the Russian forces in the area would add up to about 66,000 men, not counting another 15,000 who either were part of Sacken's detachments or would come up later.

Schwarzenberg had stopped his pursuit at Vladimir because of a premature report of Tshitshagov's arrival with the Danube Army (which, in fact, did not come up until September 20). Sending his troops into cantonments, he failed to make use of his superior numbers before these Russian reinforcements arrived. Despite his losses, his force, joined by several detachments, still numbered 41,000 men, of which more might have been made. There now ensued a pause in the operations, which the Russians filled by actively pursuing a guerrilla war.

Schwarzenberg's lackadaisical conduct of operations did serious damage to Napoleon's interests. Of course, the emperor had an entirely false image of the Russian forces operating in Volhynia, thinking that they numbered no more than 20,000 men, mostly poor reservists. Thus, his vision toward the south was no better than it had been to the north. After Schwarzenberg's successful encounter with Tormassov, Napoleon had even considered having Schwarzenberg make an offensive into southern Russia in the direction of

Kiev and Kaluga. Napoleon thought this would be possible because he believed that Tshitshagov was still far from the scene.

DOMBROWSKI'S DETACHMENT

Apart from Tormassov's reserve army, there was still II Reserve Corps, under Oertel, which, since the beginning of the war, had stood near Mozyr by the Pripet, as noted above. Including some troops that had joined it since then, it numbered about 12,000 men, with 22 guns.[9] To keep an eye on this corps and the Russian 5000-man garrison of Bobruisk,[10] Division Dombrowski[11] of V (Polish) Corps, reinforced with a cavalry brigade from IV Cavalry Corps—in all, about 7000 men, with 24 guns—had been left behind. With such weak forces, Dombrowski was expected not only to cover the area between the Dnieper and the Beresina but also to protect Minsk against a possible coup by Oertel. At Minsk, now a main depot for the French, General Bronikowski had only a few march formations and depots, which were temporarily joined by detachments from I, III, and IX Corps, as well as the 1st Reserve Division. At a later date, some new Lithuanian formations appeared as well.

Leaving a strong detachment to cover Mohilev, Dombrowski took the rest of his troops to Sviszlocz on the Beresina. From there, he sent most of his cavalry to Glusk to cover the Minsk-Bobruisk road and to patrol as far as Mozyr.

To put an end to Dombrowski's activities and to suppress an insurrection the appearance of the Poles had caused in Glusk, Oertel took some of his troops[12] to make a sally against Glusk, while another detachment under Zapolsky[13] advanced against Pinsk. The intention, obviously, was to intimidate the Polish segments of the population in these areas.

Dombrowski had just sent strong reinforcements to Mohilev, because he thought his detachment there was threatened by a Russian insurrection. Thus, he went to the aid of his cavalry outposts at Glusk with what few troops remained, but he was forced to fall back to Sviszlocz in the face of Oertel's superior force. The Russian, however, showed little enterprise and returned to Mozyr, directing Zapolsky to go there as well.

That was the end of operations in this area for the time being. Dombrowski was too weak to effectively control and oversee an area of several hundred square miles, and Oertel was content to limit himself to guerrilla operations that kept the French exercised.

.   .   .

THE SIDESHOW IN THE NORTH: RIGA AND POLOTSK

On the extreme Russian right, the fortress of Riga and its fortified Baltic seaport facility at Dunamunde covered the Russian flank and denied French shipping access to the Dvina. The man in command there was Lieutenant General von Essen I, who had disposed of about 12,000 men at the beginning of the campaign. Lieutenant General Lewis, with about 6000 men, stood to the southwest of Riga at Mitau.

As already noted, Napoleon placed great value upon the capture of Riga, because this would have opened the Dvina to water transport, making it possible to carry massive quantities of supplies deeply into the operations area. In addition to securing the extreme northern flank, Macdonald had, above all, been charged with its capture.

Division Grandjean, which was composed mostly of Poles but also had a collection of Bavarians and Westphalians, had reached Smigli and Poniewicz on July 14 and Jakobstad by the 21st. From there, a regiment was sent to occupy Dunaburg in early August. This was done to secure the southern flank for the advance against Riga and to observe the Dvina line between Macdonald's own forces and those of Oudinot, who were operating to the south and on the left flank of the main army group. Graewert's Prussians, leaving various detachments along their route, were to make the actual advance against Riga itself.

On the 19th, the Prussians ran into Lewis's detachment at Eckau and sent it back to Riga. They then moved forward and positioned themselves on the left bank of the Dvina, in front of the fortress, on the Dahlenkirchen-Olai-Schlock line. The Russian garrison, supported by the fleet, made some sallies, which generally failed. Only on the 22nd did the Russians manage to gain a local success around Dahlenkirchen. At the very start of these operations, General Graewert, who had been ailing, handed his command over to General Hans David Ludwig von Yorck. This routine event was to have far-reaching consequences at the end of the campaign.

Given the weakness of the Prussian corps and the absence of the siege train, which did not arrive until September, the Prussians could do little more than observe the fortress from the left side of the river and conduct some guerrilla operations. At the same time, Macdonald, who was with Grandjean's division in Jakobstad, was suffering from a lack of initiative and of specific orders from Napoleon. Lapsing into apathy, he also failed to lend active support to Oudinot's operations against Wittgenstein.

Since the events with X Corps transpired in total isolation from the rest of the campaign, it may be noted at this time that only one major interruption

occurred in this area. It took place when, as a result of the Treaty of Abo
between Alexander and the crown prince of Sweden, the Finnish Corps
became freed for operations against the French. General Steinheil landed
in Reval on September 23 with 10,500 men. On their march to join Wittgenstein, Steinheil's troops passed through Essen's area of operations, and
Essen promptly secured their aid in mounting a major operation against the
Prussians. Essen now had about 27,000 men at his disposal against the
Prussians' 14,000, who, in their observatory role, were widely dispersed.
This presented him with a splendid opportunity to mount an offensive
operation against them and to throw them back across the Aa. He might
even be able to get his hands on the siege artillery park, which had arrived
at last, because the Prussians, going overland, might find it difficult to quickly
move its heavy artillery equipment out of harm's way.

The Russians assembled 22,200 men with 27 guns for the operation. Of
these, a secondary column was to go against Mitau, which the Prussians had
already vacated, while the main thrust was to be delivered in the direction
of Ruhenthal. This gave rise to a series of actions between September 26
and October 1 in the area around Bauske. The most important of these was
fought on the 29th, when the Prussians were joined by a detachment of
Grandjean's division,[14] which had been brought up on the double from
Friedrichstadt by Macdonald. As a result of these actions, the Russians were
driven back along the entire line. Their cumulative loss was about 5000
men, whereas the Prussian losses came to barely 1200 men. The Prussians
under Yorck had not yielded. On the other hand, Alexander had just cause
to be dissatisfied with Steinheil, especially over the fact that he had split
his forces and sent a column against Mitau instead of concentrating his
operations against the Prussians' main forces. In the wake of these actions,
everyone lapsed into inactivity once again. Macdonald, now at Eckau with
the Prussians, was content to stay behind the Aa, where he was temporarily
joined by one of Grandjean's brigades. And even though it hardly needed
it, the siege train was given a good rest as well. Macdonald did not even
attempt to lay siege to Riga.

The Russians were not unhappy about this lack of initiative on Macdonald's part. Steinheil brought his corps back up to 9500 men by syphoning
off replacements from the garrison of Riga. Then he continued his march
to Wittgenstein, leaving Paulucci, who had taken over from Essen, with
only about 8000 men to defend the fortress.[15] The guerrilla war now resumed.
It was interrupted only between September 16 and 19, when Macdonald
came out in force and threw the Russians, who had extended themselves as
far as Friedrichstadt, back into Riga.

WITTGENSTEIN

When the First Western Army left Drissa on July 16, going to Vitebsk, Barclay had left Wittgenstein behind. With his corps reinforced to 25,000 men, with 108 guns,[16] Wittgenstein was to place himself between the Druia and Drissa to cover the road to St. Petersburg against any secondary operations the French might mount in that direction. Wittgenstein might have lacked the ability to handle a large command under difficult circumstances, but he was well suited to handling an independent command such as this one. He was a daring soldier and had the insight to permit himself to be guided by the good advice of men like d'Auvray and Diebitsch II. The defenses of Dunaburg, intended to be a major strongpoint in the area, were nowhere near complete, and the city could not have withstood even the assault of a field army lacking siege equipment. Its Russian garrison consisted of about 3000 men in ten reserve battalions under General Hamen.

Napoleon had left Oudinot's II Corps behind to deal with Wittgenstein. Reinforced with Doumerc's cuirassier division, Oudinot's force numbered about 28,000 men, with 114 guns. The French marshal, whose numerous wounds furnished ample proof of his personal courage, was not exactly one of the coryphaei among the French marshals, but he was an excellent corps commander. That is, he functioned excellently under direction but lacked the resolution and enterprise necessary for an independent command.

Napoleon had grossly underestimated Wittgenstein's strength, assuming his infantry to number only about 10,000 men. Thus, he ordered Oudinot to take the offensive against him. As a result, Oudinot advanced from Polotsk along the St. Petersburg road toward the end of July, in total ignorance of Wittgenstein's whereabouts.

Wittgenstein had planned to cross the Dvina at Druia and fall on Oudinot's rear. In the meantime, however, he had learned that Macdonald was about to cross the river at Jakobstad. Apprehensive that Oudinot and Macdonald might mount a combined operation against him, Wittgenstein turned around and moved toward Sebesh. On his way there, he learned that Oudinot was headed in that direction as well. (The information had come out of an encounter his advance guard cavalry had with Corbineau's cavalry near Valnitzy on July 28.) Wittgenstein decided to attack at once to clear his own way to Sebesh.

Oudinot still had no idea where Wittgenstein was when he arrived in Jakabovo on the afternoon of the 30th with Legrand's infantry division and Castex's light cavalry brigade. There, he came under attack from Wittgenstein's advance guard under Kulnev, who had crossed the Svolna at Katerinovo. Promptly reinforced, Kulnev, a capable cavalry officer, was able to force his way out of the woods so that he might find the room to deploy. But the French, for their part reinforced by Verdier's division toward evening, were able to hold on in Jakabovo. On the following day, the 31st, the Russians renewed their attacks at 3 a.m. Wittgenstein had virtually his entire corps, about 23,000 men,[17] in hand, while Oudinot had only about 20,000.[18]

Since the terrain prevented Oudinot from deploying all of his artillery, his counterattacks collapsed in the face of the superior Russian artillery, and he was finally forced to give way to Wittgenstein. To cover his withdrawal across the Nishtsha, Oudinot positioned his reserves on a line of heights on the near side of the river, near Kliastitza. However, this village fell to the Russians as well by 8 a.m., sending the French back across the stream in considerable disorder. Fortunately for the French, the Russians were too exhausted to continue the pursuit. Oudinot continued his retreat across the Drissa and took a position behind the river at Oboiarszina. When Kulnev, supposedly reinforced to 12,000 men, attacked this position on August 1, he was badly beaten. This defeat was, in turn, partially redressed when Oudinot sent only Verdier's division across the Drissa to pursue the Russians. Pressing forward rashly, the French suffered a sharp reverse when they unexpectedly encountered Wittgenstein's main force at Golovshiza. There, Verdier, left without support, was severely mauled. This so intimidated Oudinot, who thought that Wittgenstein's numbers were vastly superior to his own, that he retreated back to Polotsk.

For the time being, Wittgenstein followed Oudinot as far as Sivoszina, but he withdrew to Rasizi when he was advised by General Hamen that Dunaburg had been occupied by strong enemy forces. Rasizi offered a good central position from whence he could act against either Macdonald or Oudinot. In 3 days of fighting, the Russians had lost 4300 men and 9 guns. The French losses were somewhat fewer. Wittgenstein's resolute behavior was to have far-reaching repercussions throughout the campaign. His boldness suggested a substantial numerical superiority and secured for him the initiative, which he would never again yield.

As a result of these actions, Napoleon sent VI (Bavarian) Corps[19] to reinforce Oudinot. Its commander, St. Cyr, was one of the most capable general officers of the entire army. Departing from Beszenkoviczi on the 4th, the Bavarians arrived in Polotsk on August 7. Both because it had been hit hard by disease (especially dysentery) and because its cavalry had been detached to IV Corps, the Bavarian corps numbered only about 13,000 effectives, despite the fact that it had yet to see the enemy. With St. Cyr's arrival, Oudinot's force increased to 36,000 men.

However, even now Oudinot's renewed offensive quickly ground to a halt again. With St. Cyr moving toward Valnitzy, Oudinot moved toward the Svolna, where he ran into the Russians. In the ensuing action, neither side gained a river crossing. The Russians lost 700 men; the French are said to have lost 1500, which seems a bit high for an inconclusive fight. Despite the fact that no decision was reached, Oudinot again went all the way back to an area behind the Drissa.

Now it was Wittgenstein's turn to attack again. Reinforced by Hamen's erstwhile garrison of Dunaburg, which had evacuated the place and left it to Macdonald, he now had 22,000 men.[20] He put these to use at once, spending the days from the 14th to the 16th pushing Oudinot back to Polotsk. The difficult withdrawal caused Oudinot substantial losses, not so much from the nearly constant rear-guard actions as from the fact that the night marches through forested terrain caused men to go astray by the hundreds (quite a few were picked up by the Russians). In 3 days, the Bavarians alone lost about 2000 effectives.

Finally, at Polotsk, a battle was fought. The city sat astride the Dvina at its confluence with the Polota, which was little more than a brook but flowed in a deeply cut bed, as did the Dvina at this point. Oudinot, who still believed Wittgenstein had superior forces, did not want to expose himself to the possibility of a defeat with the Dvina at his back, so the battle that eventually developed was merely a rear-guard action to cover his retreat. He had already sent part of his force across the river, so the opposing forces, 22,000 Russians and 19,000 French,[21] were almost equal.

With only about half the French forces remaining on the Russian side of the river, the Bavarians barricaded themselves in Spas and the farm complex of Prismenzia, which lay a few hundred paces in front of the village. The farm was only a collection of wooden structures, but Spas included a stone manor house and several other stout buildings that were suited for a strong defense. On the 17th, the Bavarians held on to the farm and village, thus preventing Wittgenstein from breaking out of the wooded terrain that encircled Polotsk, which was at the center of its approximately 1-mile radius.

Nothing had been gained or lost. Despite the fact that Oudinot had fought with one hand held behind him, the Bavarians had not budged and his own corps had hardly been engaged. Still, after wrangling with St. Cyr over how the action ought to be conducted, he decided to retreat anyway. He was the marshal, whereas St. Cyr was only a division general. It was at this point that fate intervened. Oudinot was wounded by a stray musket ball as he was supervising the preparations for the withdrawal.

The Russian who wounded Oudinot on the evening of the 17th did his country no service, because now St. Cyr was able to take charge. He was not a pleasant man, as far as the Bavarians were concerned, but he was far more talented than the *bon sabreur* he replaced. St. Cyr didn't retreat. Instead, he completely deceived Wittgenstein by sending back the baggage trains. The Russian did not consider himself to be nearly as superior as Oudinot thought he was. Thus, he never really intended to physically push the French back across the Dvina. Rather, he had hoped to accomplish this with demonstrations threatening an attack. He now thought his ruse had been successful when he saw the French baggage trains moving out on the morning of the 18th.

By afternoon, however, St. Cyr had quietly moved the bulk of II Corps back across the river, and he suddenly attacked with such force that Wittgenstein recoiled with heavy losses. But the success had required heavy fighting in which the Bavarians, already gravely depleted, were involved in heated, close combat in and around the fiercely contested farm complex of Prismenzia. There they found themselves repeatedly isolated when Legrand's division, to their left, yielded its ground to the Russians several times. Most of their field grade officers became casualties. The 9th Bavarian Infantry, now commanded by a captain, finally carried the complex with a bayonet attack.

But Wittgenstein did not go quietly. As a parting shot, to cover his getaway, he turned loose his cavalry. With darkness about to settle in, this achieved its desired effect. St. Cyr was suddenly in danger of being cut down in the ensuing confusion, and he saved himself only by diving into a ditch. In the end, Merle and his Swiss infantry, which made up the 9th Division, finally broke the Russian cavalry attack. On the flank of the Swiss, two Bavarian guns put on such a splendid exhibition of rapid fire that the Russians were deceived into thinking they were an entire battery. Wittgenstein, who had lost 5500 men, took his corps, now down to about 16,000, back into the fortified position of Sivoszina, only 20 miles from Polotsk.

St. Cyr, however, did not exploit his success. He had lost about 3000 men, which left him with about 29,000, but these were totally exhausted. He, too, believed Wittgenstein was much stronger than he actually was, so he limited himself to a short advance that was undertaken by VI Corps on the 22nd, 4 days after the battle. After that, he again united both corps at Polotsk and dug in for a determined defense.

Napoleon was quite pleased with the way things had gone at Polotsk and rewarded St. Cyr with a marshal's baton. Despite the fact that there was little love lost between St. Cyr and the Bavarians, he was nevertheless unsparing in his praise of their conduct in the battle, and Napoleon responded by sending sixty crosses of the Legion of Honor for them. Among the men who had not lived to enjoy the honor was old General Deroy, a veteran campaigner who had been popular with the rank and file. He was killed in action, and his elevation to the rank of a count of the empire and a donation of 30,000 francs reached him only posthumously.

This action led to a pause in operations that would last until mid-October, despite the fact that the two opponents were so near to each other. However, only Wittgenstein was to benefit from this hiatus, as substantial reinforcements were coming his way. These consisted mainly of elements from the Finnish Corps and the militias of St. Petersburg and Novgorod, which had been the first to achieve a reasonably mobile status. These new arrivals would gradually increase Wittgenstein's force to 50,000 men. Conversely, while Wittgenstein's situation improved from one day to the next, St. Cyr's deteriorated. The intense guerrilla war against constantly growing superior forces, coupled with the chronically disastrous shortage of supplies, steadily drained his forces.

However, it was the locale itself that would prove to be the undoing of St. Cyr's men, French and Bavarians alike. Mosquito ridden and fever infested, even the Russians had pulled their peacetime garrisons out of the area during the summer months. As everywhere in Lithuania, the water was brackish and contained all sorts of living organisms, so it couldn't even be used for cooking. All this was accompanied by thick swarms of flies. "One could hardly manage a spoonfull of soup without swallowing some of these pests," relates a diarist. The stories in a hundred other diaries and memoirs expounding upon the highly dubious virtues of downtown Polotsk and its surrounding recreational areas can still turn a modern reader's stomach. The filth was overwhelming: The human habitations showed evidence of having been shared with livestock and looked like unkempt stables. The careless disposal of human and animal excrement, as well as rotting garbage, attracted every sort of rodent and insect. It is not surprising that Wittgenstein left the French alone there. No doubt, he was familiar with the locale, but even if he was not, there certainly were men in his command who were. Wittgenstein could be content to sit back and let nature take its course.

However, St. Cyr now had an opportunity to show what he could do to create order out of chaos. Not only had his generalship provided his troops with some breathing space (never mind how bad the local air was), but he had also retarded the rate of defection among the troops by resorting to an organized requisitioning system. He divided his rear area into zones and had them systematically combed with positive results.

St. Cyr stated that in the beginning of October his two corps numbered only 17,000 men. This is probably not entirely accurate, because in mid-October—after the arrival of 5000 reinforcements, march troops, and convalescents—his force stood at 27,000 men again. By then, however, the consequences of his failure to consolidate the victory that had gained him his marshal's baton were making themselves felt. He might have done much greater damage to Wittgenstein had he continued to strike while the iron was hot and while he possessed the necessary strength to do so.

The lack of French success at the Dvina, despite the fact that the French had sufficient force there, must, for the most part, be traced back directly to Napoleon. On the one hand, the force he sent against Riga was too weak to do what it was expected to do and too strong to do what it ended up doing. On the other hand, and far more importantly, Napoleon had neglected to place II, VI, and X Corps under a single command. Had an army been formed out of these three corps, Riga could have been held under observation while joint operations against Wittgenstein would surely have achieved far-reaching results. At the very least, Napoleon's left flank would have been secure.

At the root of this problem, of course, was the proverbial lack of discipline among the marshals. These military and social parvenus had been catapulted into fame and fortune during the upheavals of the revolution. As a group, they were men of quite uneven talents. Years of having honors and adulation heaped upon them had done nothing to restrain their egos. Of course, they would readily subordinate themselves to Napoleon, the tap root of their existence. But as soon as they were expected to cooperate when the master was absent, they placed the jealous guardianship of their prerogatives above the tasks set for them and began to bicker among themselves. It took the musket ball of a Russian soldier to bring about the placement of II and VI Corps under a unified command, with positive, even if temporary results. But this did not bring Macdonald even an inch closer to supporting either Oudinot's or St. Cyr's operations, although there had been opportunities for him to do so. Thus, Macdonald's corps was totally switched out of operations against Wittgenstein, while St. Cyr did not get to do much of anything against the Russians either.

That Napoleon did not even attempt to put these corps under a unified command from the start may be explained by the fact that he had no clear idea of the extent of Wittgenstein's forces and had arbitrarily assumed that the Russian was weak. After the fight at Kliastitza, however, he should have recognized his error. There was still time to rectify the situation. It was an omission that was to cost him dearly.

As a whole, the commanders of the French flanking forces, uncoordinated and each acting as he saw fit, had failed to seize the initiative while they still had the combined superior strength to do so. Now the moment was approaching when Russian reinforcements would begin to balance, and then to tip, the scales in their own favor. When that happened, the flanking forces could hardly be expected to even continue to hold their own. This was bound to pose a grave danger for the main army group, which had been in Moscow since September 14, especially since the main army itself was now inferior to the enemy's numbers.

NOTES

1. The corps included 18 battalions and 16 squadrons, totaling 15,003 infantry and artillery and 2186 cavalry, with 50 guns. Thielemann's brigade of heavy cavalry had been detached before the campaign got under way.

2. It is noteworthy that until then, and unlike in the center, the corps had lost only a few hundred men, including a battalion left in Bialystok.

3. The reserve army included 54 battalions, 76 squadrons, 9 Cossack regiments, and 14 batteries, comprising 38,000 men and 4000 Cossacks, with 161 guns. Of these, 6 battalions, 12 squadrons, and 1 battery were with Sacken; 6 battalions were with Oertel; and 8 squadrons and 2 Cossack regiments were along the upper Bug with Crushtshev. Thus, Tormassov had available 42 battalions, 56 squadrons, 7 Cossack regiments, and 13 batteries, totaling 33,000 men, with 152 guns (possibly the 22 guns with Oertel must be subtracted from this as well).

4. The brigade had 4 battalions and 3 squadrons, which amounted to barely 3000 men, with 8 guns.

5. The Russians committed a total of 12 battalions, 36 squadrons, and 36 guns to action under General Lambert.

6. Included were detachments left behind by the field army and march troops of the 1st reserve division, as well as march cavalry and parts of Division Loison.

7. Present on the Russian side were 24 battalions, 36 squadrons, 3 Cossack regiments, and 8 (6?) batteries, 18,000 men. Chovanski's detachment of 6 battalions and 2 batteries.

   Tshaplitz's detachment of 8 battalions, 12 squadrons, and 4 Cossack regiments had been pushed aside in the direction of Chomsk. Another under Melissino of 4 battalions and 7 squadrons had been sent to Pinsk. This, together with another detached squadron, accounted for the absence of about 13,000 men.

8. The total figure includes 29,000 Austrians and 13,000 Saxons.

9. The corps originally consisted of 11 battalions and 14 squadrons. Added to this were 6 battalions from Sacken and 3 regiments, as well as a further 13 *sotnias* of Cossacks and 2 batteries.

10. After Bagration had taken 6 battalions into his army, the garrison of Bobruisk

still consisted of 12 reserve battalions and 1 *sotnia* of Cossacks—in all, about 3000 men—and a number of garrison troops, infantry, and artillery. The total is said to have come to about 5000 men under General Ignatiev.

11. Division Dombrowski with its attached cavalry brigade from IV Cavalry Corps had 11 battalions, 12 squadrons, and 3 batteries, numbering about 6000 infantry and 1000 horses. Another battalion was in Grodno.

12. Oertel had 7 battalions, 10 squadrons, and 2 Cossack regiments.

13. Zapolsky had 8 battalions and 2 Cossack regiments.

14. It included 3 battalions and 2 squadrons, with 4 guns.

15. The fortress was not reinforced again until additional parts of the Finnish Corps, which came up later, raised the number of men to between 12,000 and 13,000.

16. In the beginning, Wittgenstein's corps had consisted of 28 battalions, 16 squadrons, 3 Cossack regiments, and 9 batteries. Of these, 1 Cossack regiment had been detached to the First Western Army, and 1 Cossack regiment and 1 battalion had gone to the Riga garrison.

17. On the Russian side, 7 squadrons had been detached, so the Russians disposed of 36 battalions, 24 squadrons, 1 Cossack regiment, and 9 batteries, totaling about 23,000 men, with 108 guns.

18. On the French side, Merle's division (15 battalions and about 22 guns) and Corbineau's brigade (8 squadrons), about 8000 men, were absent. This left Oudinot with about 33 battalions and 28 squadrons, amounting to about 20,000 men, with 92 guns. Corbineau had been sent to Valnitzy; Merle was still coming up.

19. Disease, desertion, and the detachment of its cavalry to IV Corps had reduced the original strength of VI (Bavarian) Corps from 25,134 men to about 13,000.

20. Since Hamen had sent the heavy guns with a battalion to Pskov, he brought only 9 battalions to Wittgenstein, who now had 45 battalions, 23 squadrons, 1 Cossack regiment, and 9 batteries, comprising about 22,000 men, with 98 guns. The missing 8 squadrons observed Dunaburg and Macdonald.

21. Coming into action on the French side were Division Legrand and Brigade Corbineau with, in all, 7000 infantry and 700 cavalry and VI Corps with 11,000 infantry.

IV
The Futile Wait

18. Moscow

When Napoleon entered Moscow with his severely shaken army of about 100,000 men on September 14, he expected to attain the objective that had drawn him on like a magnet: a compliant Russia and an advantageous peace. The army, aspiring to no such lofty goals, was looking for a good rest and a life of plenty to counterbalance the nightmare of the previous several weeks of marching, seemingly to nowhere, which had come to a hair-raising climax at Borodino. Both the army and its commander were to be cruelly disappointed.

The air of expectation began to cloud over when the city was found to be deserted, though the several fires that broke out on that same evening were still thought to be accidental. Before another 24 hours had gone by, however, there was no longer any doubt that the fires were being set on purpose. Most of the city had already been put to the torch, and within another 24 hours, three-quarters of it was reduced to ashes.

In 1812, there had been approximately 4000 stone structures and 8000 wooden houses in Moscow. Of these, there remained after the fires only about 200 of the stone buildings and some 500 wooden houses along with about half of the 1600 churches, although nearly every church was damaged to some extent. As in Smolensk, the wounded who were left behind in many of the buildings died by the hundreds. The large number of churches that escaped total destruction by the flames is probably explained by the fact that the altar implements and other church paraphernalia were made of precious metals, which immediately attracted the attention of the looters. Indeed, Napoleon had a systematic sweep made for the church silver, which ended up in his war chest, the mobile treasury.

Napoleon had taken quarters in the Kremlin on the 15th. But by afternoon of the next day, he was forced to leave the inner city because the fires threatened to isolate him from his troops. He temporarily set up his headquarters in the Petrovski Palace, outside the city, but he did not remain there. Even before all the fires had burned themselves out, he made his way past the ashes and gutted buildings and back into the Kremlin, which had escaped the fires.

Not only the army's hopes had gone up in smoke. The energy, tenacity, and resolution radiating from the ruins of Moscow bore their own unmistakable messages, and none of these could be regarded as the harbingers of peace. Once hopes for peace were dashed, a timely retreat would have been in order. After failing to do so twice, at Smolensk and Borodino, Napoleon no longer had the means of destroying the enemy's power to resist, and wintering in Moscow was out of the question.

Indeed, time was now of the essence. A French emperor should not be sitting in the middle of a hostile Russia, 1000 miles from his power bases, with an army of only 100,000 men. The Russians, sitting atop their own resources, were bound to regain more than they had lost so far, and they would do so day by day. Only if he availed himself of their momentary weakness could Napoleon hope to lead what was left of his army into a more tenable position without suffering serious disturbances during his retreat.

This, however, would have been an admission of defeat. Napoleon, however, had spent the last several years making and unmaking kings and had altered the face of Europe. He was not yet ready to admit defeat to himself, much less to the world. No matter how high his self-esteem may have been and how grossly he may have misread the mood of nations, it was clear to him that a defeat would do serious damage to his reputation. Here, unlike in Spain, he was the man at the helm, and whatever came of the Russian campaign would attach itself to his person. That this posed an inherent danger to his fortunes was clear to him, even if he could not possibly predict how serious it would eventually become. For these reasons, he was bound to stay in Moscow as long as there was even a glimmer of hope that he might, after all, find some sort of accommodation that would make it possible for him to come away from this misadventure with no more than a black eye.

Of course, no modern psychoanalyst ever had the opportunity to pry into Napoleon's mind to find out what he really thought. However, his voluminous correspondence of 1813 clearly reveals a man who had already retreated into seeing the world around him not as what it was but as what he wanted it to be. He was trying to prop up himself as much as those to whom his correspondence was directed. Similarly, in 1812 he was already deceiving himself into believing that Alexander would come around after all; he rationalized that the tsar could not do otherwise because he, Napoleon, had taken Moscow.

Part and parcel of this self-delusion, of course, was the fact that he did not yet perceive his own situation to be quite as desperate as it would eventually become. It is one of the attributes of genius to see resources where ordinary men do not. A genius who is spoiled and blinded by success, however, will tend to see resources where, in fact, none exist. These non-existent resources, coupled with the emperor's overblown self-regard and underestimation of his opposition, probably explain Napoleon's entirely arbitrary assumptions about the strength and intentions of his adversaries and his increasingly consistent overestimation of his own strength. He places mass and numbers above their content. The Grand Army he brought into Russia underlines this; it contained as much chaff as it did wheat.

Vastly superior military resources had changed the artful master gunner turned general, who could handle his army as a skillful commander would handle a horse battery, into an ordinary gunner who simply relied on the weight of his ordnance to batter down whatever stood before him. This reliance on numerically superior force ("God is on the side of the biggest battalions") did not begin in 1812; it had been built into the Napoleonic concept from the start. However, as the means had increased, their application had become increasingly less artful.

Thus, Napoleon could still believe that his situation in Moscow was better than it actually was, especially since he still had superior numbers. At the end of September his strength reports showed 307,000 men (see Appendix XIII), of which 59,000 were still coming up; a further 43,000 would become available by the end of the year. Against this, he assumed that the Russians had only 120,000 men (50,000 under Kutuzov, 30,000 under Wittgenstein, and about 20,000 each under Tshitshagov and Tormassov). Actually, including the Cossacks and militia, they had 193,000 men (more than half again as many as Napoleon assumed), ignoring various garrisons. But those of Riga and Bobruisk alone came to about 21,000 men, and the whole would be joined by another 92,000 men in December.

In his scheme of things, Napoleon could see no danger where numbers were concerned. This, however, was not so when his decisions had to take into account the condition of his troops and the disadvantages of his strategic position, which offered numerous weak points to his opponents, who were consistently able to avoid his attacks. Thus, it was inevitable that even Napoleon would soon begin to experience a sense of insecurity that, in a manner of speaking, he had already brought with him. This was all the more inevitable as the burning of Moscow carried with it unmistakable messages from the Russians. With each passing day, the hope of an accommodation with the Russians dwindled, and it had to become clear to Napoleon that he would have to take the first step—to the rear—something against which every fiber in his being rebelled. Still, he continued to hope, because there was little else he could do.

Alexander, back in St. Petersburg, had no intention whatever of backing down, even though the mantle of rhetoric clothing this resolve was of a far more patriotic and uplifting nature than it was reflective of his personal antipathy against the French emperor. Alexander had been disenchanted with Napoleon for a long time, even before the war began. Now there was no reason on earth (except in Napoleon's mind) for the tsar to change his mind again, certainly not with the French emperor standing in Moscow at the head of a hostile army.

Indeed, when the situation of September 1812 is viewed in such elementary terms, one can only wonder about the mind-set of Napoleon, who believed he could simply let bygones be bygones with yet another treaty, written with the blood of 100,000 soldiers and dried with the ashes of two cities and a hundred towns and villages. If he expected this of Alexander, whose head was not on a block, with the sword hovering above his neck, then all the historians who have ever spoken of Napoleon's delusions of grandeur need no further proof of his intellectual and emotional derangement.

Prompted by Kutuzov's initial report, Alexander had at first thought that Borodino was a Russian victory. He had already rewarded the victor with a marshal's baton and was looking forward to a vigorous pursuit of the success gained. In order to give this pursuit direction, he had ordered that an operations plan be drawn up containing the following salient features:

- The flanking armies, together with the substantial reinforcements coming their way, were to press the French detachments that were in front of them back toward the border.

- Then Tormassov and the Finnish Corps, the latter reinforced by the Riga garrison, were to keep these detachments in check while Tshitshagov and Wittgenstein joined hands across the French line of communications.

- As this was being accomplished on the flanks, Kutuzov's main army was to drive the French central army group into their arms.

It has been claimed with justification that this plan was rather artificial and that it would have been more appropriate to send all reinforcements marching in the direction of Kutuzov's main army. But it must be kept in mind that Alexander was under the impression that Napoleon had been beaten and was already retreating. In such a case, it would have indeed been correct to bring all forces to bear by the most direct routes. Still, in the end the plan did succeed, even if its success did depend largely upon the enemy's mistakes. It would, of course, have produced even greater results had someone other than Kutuzov been in command.

However, the sobering truth about Borodino came to Alexander soon enough. In the midst of the celebrations, the news, first of the retreat and then of the loss of Moscow, arrived like a stroke of lightning. Following on the heels of the elation over the supposed victory, the depression over what was seen as a defeat was all the greater. The idea that the French had occupied Moscow overshadowed all else, including the more detailed accounts of the battle, as well as the news of the burning of the city.

The so-called French party, led by Chancellor Rumanzov, had been in favor of a peace treaty and now raised its head again. Even the dowager empress and the passionate Grand Duke Constantine, presumably Alexander's successor, both spoke of peace, though both were Napoleon haters. But Alexander was the one who counted, and he soon regained his composure, due in large part to von Stein's efforts. Replacing the tsar's initial distress was his firm resolve to wrest Moscow from the intruder as soon as possible and to exact revenge on Napoleon, the source of this great misfortune. By the time Colonel Michaud delivered Kutuzov's official report of the battle, Alexander had recovered so much that he is said to have exclaimed: "Napoleon or I, I or he!" His words reflected the attitude of the Russians, embittered by the burning of Moscow, for which the French were, of course, blamed.

At the same time, Alexander was annoyed about Kutuzov's machinations. Having already sent Prince Volkonski to the army to find out what was really going on, he now also ordered that a board of inquiry convene under Field Marshal Saltykov to look into Kutuzov's behavior. Yet whatever one may think of Kutuzov's actions, he had achieved one thing: Once the first excitement had passed, the loss of Moscow was less keenly felt and Borodino continued to be perceived as a victory, because the news of the loss of Moscow had blotted out all the reports of what had actually transpired at Borodino. As a result, Kutuzov, strange as it may seem, continued to retain the confidence of the nation. Indeed, the juxtaposition of Barclay and Kutuzov may hardly be improved upon as an example of how important and decisive it is for a commander in chief to have the confidence of both the army and the entire nation.

Alexander's resolve to stand firm, which might easily have been replaced by a depression had he known the truth about Borodino from the start, was entirely justified. An impartial assessment of the situation, as Volkonski was to receive from Toll, could hardly call for a different course of action. Despite the difficulties of the moment, the opportunity was too great not to be exploited to the full once it was accepted that there could be no peaceful coexistence with Napoleon, that nothing lasting would be gained by giving in to him. There could be no doubt whatever that the moment would soon come when Napoleon would be forced to retreat, despite his victory at Borodino. For this reason, Alexander held on to the operations plan he had adopted. The changed circumstances had not really changed the nature of the plan, merely the timing of its execution. There would be no appeasement.

With the decision made, the necessary measures were taken, especially the reinforcement of the main army with the recruits still available in the depots of the interior, as well as the strengthening of the flanking armies with the Danube Army and the Finnish Corps. All but a few of the detachments that were still abroad and the militias of St. Petersburg and Novgorod, which were already in sufficiently serviceable condition to be made mobile, were also called in. At the same time, a corps was assembled at Novgorod under General Novak. It was thought possible that, despite the distance, a move on St. Petersburg might develop from the direction of Moscow. All that stood at Novgorod at the moment was Wintzingerode's flying column, reinforced to 3200 cavalry, but it was impossible to scrape more than 6000 men together for Novak's corps. This, however, was not all. Since the reserves already assembled at the start of the war had nearly all been committed, the formation of new reserves[1] was ordered in the beginning of October (and again in December), although these men would not be available until spring. There was no shortage of manpower. The real difficulty was finding the necessary cadre and the arms and accoutrements to equip them.

After the evacuation of Moscow, the Russian main army had withdrawn along the road to Ryasan. The flight of the Muscovites had so clogged the roads that the army was forced to halt on September 15, despite the proximity of the enemy. Miloradovitch's rear guard was no more than 5 miles from the city; the army itself was no more than 10 miles away. Turning over the city to the enemy without a fight had made a bad impression on the troops and loosened the bonds of discipline, which had, until then, been exemplary. It was not until the army arrived in the camp of Tarutino that its composure was fully restored.

Kutuzov was quite aware that something should be done to wipe away the demoralizing effect the abandonment of the city had exercised upon the troops. Thus, he accepted Toll's recommendation that he turn southward, even if only to save the magazine stores around Kaluga. The fact that both the Moskva and the Oka usually spill over their banks in the fall and make crossings difficult also played an important part in the decision. The swollen rivers would make it that much more difficult for the French to follow if they should be of a mind to do so. Thus, the army recrossed the Moskva to its right (western) bank on the 16th and reached Podolsk on the 18th. On the 20th, the flank march was continued; Krasnaia-Pachra was reached on the 21st. Miloradovitch was pushed forward in the direction of Moscow as far as Desna. There, despite being only 15 miles from the city, he remained unobserved for quite a while. To cover the Moscow-Ryasan road leading past Kutuzov's flank, Raievsky's infantry took a position at Lukovkina, his cavalry at Podolsk. Strong cavalry detachments were now being sent forward against the Moscow-Smolensk road to interrupt Napoleon's line of communications. A flying column of 2000 cavalry[2] was formed under Dorochov, who set up his base at Shtshaparovo. From there, he sent raiding parties against the Moscow roads.

Even before Borodino, Kutuzov had ordered Tormassov to march into the rear of the main French army as soon as he was relieved by Tshitshagov. From Podolsk, he reversed these roles, which would have called for an extensive march by Tshitshagov. Now Tshernishev arrived with the tsar's operations plan, which Kutuzov was obliged to follow. Indeed, he did so gladly, because since Borodino he was even less inclined to have a confrontation with Napoleon than he had been before. Now he could hope that Wittgenstein's and Tshitshagov's operations would induce Napoleon to leave Moscow without any direct action on his part. The only change he recommended regarding the tsar's plan was that the date on which the two armies were to meet at the Beresina be pushed back from the 22nd to the 27th of October.

The plan had been drawn up when it was thought that the French had been beaten at Borodino. Under the circumstances, however, it was clear that Kutuzov's 50,000 men were hardly enough to drive Napoleon out of Moscow at once, but that's what Kutuzov would have been forced to accomplish were he to be at the Beresina by the 22nd. Despite the fact that the truth about Borodino was now out, he could hardly admit to the tsar that, at the moment, he still feared an attack from Napoleon and that he had, from the start, pinned all his hopes for victory on the coming of winter and the gradually cumulative effect of a vigorous guerrilla war. At least for the time being, he was not in a position to mount an offensive, nor did he intend to launch one any time soon.

The Russians had been able to make their flank march from Borovskoi to Krasnaia-Pachra (the Pachra is only 20 miles from Moscow) undisturbed, because the tired and worn-out French army had lost all contact with them and had halted in Moscow. Only Murat was sent along the Ryasan road to follow the Russians with a strong advance guard.[3] Murat, however, assumed that the war was as good as over. He even remained in Moscow at first, thinking the Russians had gone beyond the Oka, in the direction of Ryasan. Thus, despite the strong cavalry forces involved, the pursuit had been rather lax, and the pitiful condition of the horses contributed more than a little to the loss of contact with the Russians. There had been a lot of rain in the second half of September, and the tired horses had become bogged down again.

It was not until September 20 that Napoleon was advised by informants that the Russian army stood on the Tula road, near Podolsk. This was startling. He at once recognized the inherent danger of this new line of retreat the enemy was taking. Once his cavalry had confirmed the information, he decided to throw the Russians back across the Oka. On the 22nd a report arrived from Sebastiani, sent on the 21st, stating that the Russians were withdrawing along the road to Ryasan. To confuse matters further, news arrived that the Cossacks had captured a convoy on the Moshaisk road. It was high time to clarify the situation.

Napoleon ordered Murat, who had rejoined the advance guard on the 22nd, to take his main force along the Ryasan road, while Poniatowski was to investigate along the Tula road as far as Podolsk. A newly formed column under Bessieres[4] was to check out the old Kaluga road in the direction of Disna. Owing to the army's general exhaustion, none of these columns pursued their missions energetically. Bessieres reported only a weak Russian detachment near Disna on the 22nd; he occupied the place on the 25th. Poniatowski found Podolsk free of the enemy on the 24th. But Murat's news was the most important: He found nothing but Yefremov's Cossacks on the road to Ryasan. Then he continued to Podolsk to join Poniatowski. There was still no sign of the Russian army. Only the reports of informers placed it on its way to Kaluga.

At the same time, hordes of Cossacks appeared everywhere, and the French cavalry with its worn-out horses could not even begin to cope with them. At times, the Cossacks even interrupted communications with the outlying detachments and began to show up in the Moscow suburbs. On the 22nd, Napoleon had to send a detachment of 250 dragoons to the Beresky estate, 15 miles from Moscow, to secure communications with Moshaisk. On the 23rd, St. Sulpice had to follow with the guard dragoons because the situation was too dangerous to wait for the assembly of 1500 cavalry from the march squadrons, which were to eventually gather there. At the same time, Junot in Moshaisk and Baraquey d'Hilliers in Smolensk were ordered to cover all transports with strong escorts. The capture of further transports, including two march squadrons,[5] and an ambush of the guard dragoons on the 25th, which added nothing to their reputation, forced Napoleon to add 1000 infantry to his post.[6] At the same time, Ornano was placed halfway between Moscow and Beresky with Broussier's infantry division and strong cavalry.

The news of Murat's and Poniatowski's approach had caused Kutuzov to cover his right by also sending Ostermann-Tolstoy to Niemtshinino with IV Infantry and II Cavalry Corps. For the same reason, Raievsky, who, like Miloradovitch, had withdrawn a bit farther, had sent Paskevitch's division farther to the right, to the banks of the Motsha at Satino.

The opinion at the Russian headquarters was that a French attack would occur in the direction of Podolsk, so the detachments that had been sent against the Moshaisk road were recalled. To avoid such an attack, a war council was held on the 26th. Toll's recommendation to withdraw to Tarutino, behind the Nara, was accepted, despite the fact that this went against the tsar's operations plan. Again, Benningsen wanted to attack in the direction of Podolsk, while Barclay, who did not think a French attack would materialize, wanted to stand pat. Toll, however, prevailed with his idea that the army should avoid any and all confrontations with the enemy until the expected reinforcements arrived and that, above all, Kaluga, a main depot and the place where the reinforcements were assembling, should be covered.

On the same day, September 26, Murat confirmed that the Russian army stood on the Kaluga road. From this, Napoleon at once inferred that Kutuzov was awaiting Tshitshagov's approach via Kaluga, because this conformed with his notions. Bessieres's suggestion that the enemy might advance against the Moshaisk road was, to Napoleon, out of the question, because the emperor did not think the Russians were in any condition to make such an offensive. Still, he ordered Bessieres not only to support Murat but also to keep an eye on the Moshaisk road and to start the rumor that Napoleon himself was following.

Murat, now united with Poniatowski and with III Cavalry Corps (transferred to him from Bessieres's column), was to advance against the Russians. Hopefully, this action alone would induce the enemy to withdraw behind the Oka, and the French would not need to deploy strong forces. The main army was to follow only in the event that, against all expectations, the Russians made a stand by the Pachra. Napoleon had given up on going after them in force not only because his army was exhausted but also because he had no great desire to again follow them for indeterminate distances. Twice on the 28th, and once after that, he decided to take the entire army to the Motsha because he had received indications from Murat that the enemy meant to stand there. But he gave up on the idea as soon as the information was discovered to be inaccurate.

Once it had been decided to go behind the Nara, the Russians reached Babenkovo on the 27th. There they were joined by 7700 recruits. Miloradovitch, who had closed up to Raievsky, drew back to Tshirikovo after a stiff brush with Bessieres. There he got into another scrap on the 29th, this time with Poniatowski, but he stood his ground, as his cavalry showed a marked superiority over the French and their tired horses. Ostermann, who had crossed the Motsha on the previous day, also had a skirmish on the 29th.

The Russian army reached the camp of Tarutino on October 2. The rear guard under Miloradovitch had been joined by Ostermann on the 1st. It had another action on the 2nd and again on the 4th, when Miloradovitch was forced to evacuate his position near Spas-Kuplia but maintained himself behind the Tshernishnia near Vinkovo. By the 6th, the main army was concentrated in the camp, and only Miloradovitch remained on the left bank of the Nara with II/III and IV Cavalry Corps. Nearby, only about 5 miles from the Russians, Murat made camp with his advance guard. After the losses in the various engagements, he had about 23,000 to 24,000 troops left. Bessieres returned to Moscow with Colbert's lancer brigade. The rest of his troops,[7] who had been joined by what was left of the Bavarian cavalry, remained near Voronovo in support of Murat.

Napoleon made a serious mistake in permitting the Russians to remain in a position that was closer to Moshaisk and Gshatsk (both on his line of retreat) than was his own. The poor condition of his army was no excuse. An offensive was all the more indicated because of the expected approach, via Kaluga, of the Danube Army, which, however, he estimated at only 20,000 men. Until it arrived, Napoleon held the advantage in numbers. Even without Junot, he had 95,500 men at the end of September (see Appendix XIV), while the Russians had no more than 60,000, not counting Cossacks and militia. Napoleon even thought they had only 50,000. Also, toward the end of September, the weather improved again. It was clear, even if the nights were getting colder. One can only assume that his continued hopes for an accommodation with the Russians prevented him from taking advantage of the situation.

NOTES

1. By mid-October, after the field army had been reinforced, there were only 27 reserve battalions left. Of these, 9 battalions with 5100 men joined the main army in November, and another 15 battalions with 5000 men joined in December. The remaining 3 battalions were added to the new formations of October.

   In the beginning of October, 109 battalions, 104 squadrons, 5 guard cavalry depots, ½ guard horse battery, and 37 mobile (with draft teams) and 40 immobile batteries were formed. These were followed in December by another 64 battalions and 20 squadrons.

   This added 208,000 men to the organizational strength of the reserve formations. But the planned strength was not nearly achieved.

2. It consisted of 1 guard dragoon and hussar regiment from I Cavalry Corps and 3 Cossack regiments, totaling about 2000 men, with 2 guns.

3. The composition of the advance guard (as of the September 20 returns) was as follows:

Men
6,923 of V Corps
2,862 of Vistula Legion
4,967 of Div. Dufour (ex-Friant) and a light cavalry brigade
2,721 of I Cav. Corps
4,263 of II Cav. Corps and the light cavalry of III Corps
1,775 of IV Cav. Corps
23,511 (including 10,000 cavalry)

4. The column numbered 10,030 men:
   6,030 men of Div. Friedrichs and a light cavalry brigade
   3,000 men of III Cav. Corps
   1,000 men of Guard Lancer Brig. Colbert

5. The two squadrons were part of Lanusse's column, from which they had been detached.
6. Added was the IIth Infantry Regiment of 1000 men, with 2 guns.
7. The remaining troops, about 6500 men, included Division Friedrichs, a light cavalry brigade of I Corps, and 2 Bavarian cavalry brigades of IV Corps.

19. The Russians Regroup

When the Russian army arrived in the camp of Tarutino, it numbered 60,033 regulars, although 7690 were barely trained recruits. However, a steadily arriving stream of irregular cavalry soon brought the number of Cossacks past the 10,000 mark, and there was an influx of about 15,000 militiamen, who still stood in the third ranks of the line units. Finally, Wintzingerode's flying column accounted for another 3200 cavalry. The number of old soldiers was almost exactly the same as it had been on the eve of Borodino: about 52,343. That is, the losses that had been sustained since then had been covered by the return of stragglers.

Changes in the command structure had also occurred during the previous few days. Kutuzov implemented these in response to a secret letter in which Alexander informed him that he had given command of the Danube Army and reserve army to Admiral Tshitshagov, "who was especially fitted for this task because of his resolute character[!]" and had made Tormassov Bagration's successor. However, he left it to Kutuzov's discretion to make some other use of Tormassov if, due to the losses incurred, a further separation of the two erstwhile western armies was no longer justified. As a result, Kutuzov did away with the division on September 28 and redesignated the main army temporarily as the First Western Army and then as the *corps de bataille*[1] under Barclay and the reserve under Tormassov. Miloradovitch was to fill in until the latter's arrival.

It would have been better had Kutuzov limited himself to his role as commander in chief and left Barclay in charge of the new First Western Army. The continuing split of command, even after the division between the erstwhile two western armies had been eliminated, was disadvantageous. But it would have been entirely against Kutuzov's nature to have done anything else. Besides, even though he pretended otherwise, he wanted to rid himself of Barclay, and in this he succeeded. The reorganization, which became effective when the army reached Tarutino, stripped Barclay of his role as an army commander. This was more than he was willing to swallow, which is exactly what Kutuzov had hoped for. On October 4, tired of the incessant frictions, Barclay left the army, leaving Kutuzov in command of both the supreme headquarters and the *corps de bataille*. Yermolov remained as the chief of staff of the latter; Benningsen held the same post at supreme headquarters.

During the stay of nearly 3 weeks in the camp of Tarutino, the army received important reinforcements. First to arrive were about 10,000 Don Cossacks.[2] Then, 33,581 recruits arrived in several echelons, along with more Cossacks. By mid-October, the army again numbered about 94,000 men, including the militia, and about 20,000 Cossacks (see Appendix XIV). And these numbers would grow by several thousand more in the near future. Since it was impossible to bring all the battalions and squadrons up to operational strengths and useful standards, a substantial number of battalions and squadrons were stripped of all but their cadre and sent back to Kaluga, Tula, and other collecting points, where they were to be rebuilt.[3] The troops that had been pulled out of the formations sent back were used to replenish those remaining with the field army. Also broken up and redistributed to the line were twenty-one united grenadier battalions. Several other regiments saw themselves reduced to a single battalion. In the cavalry, no regiments were, as yet, sent back to be reconstructed, but most saw a reduction in the number of their squadrons.

As a whole, the troops were well provided for in the camp of Tarutino. There was plenty of food, and new issues of clothes arrived as well, including woolens and fur vests, which would stand the troops in good stead during the coming winter. The spirit of the army, flagging since the abandonment of Moscow, improved visibly. The arrival of the replacements and the successes of the light troops did much to raise morale, and the veterans succeeded in transplanting this higher morale into the recruits. The army was, in all respects, ready to have another go at the French. By the time of the departure from the camp of Tarutino, the army had increased to 97,000 men (including only 5500 militia) and 20,000 Cossacks, with 622 guns.[4] The army would again be reorganized when it marched. In place of the reserve, an advance guard was formed under Miloradovitch, as Tormassov took command of the *corps de bataille*. (See Appendix XVII.)

While the Russians made optimum use of the breathing spell allowed by Napoleon, the French let the time pass without taking advantage of the superior strength they still had. Napoleon allowed the rest of September to go by, hoping for an accommodation with Alexander. At the same time, his own situation deteriorated from one day to the next. He soon realized that he would need something more than the mere possession of Moscow to force a treaty. Thus, during the early days of October (the exact date is not known), he drew up plans for a massive demonstration against St. Petersburg.

- Victor and St. Cyr, reinforced to 70,000 men, with march troops and one of Macdonald's divisions, were to take a position along the lower Dvina.

- Napoleon, with another 70,000 men (the Guard, plus I and IV Corps), would operate against Veliki-Luki, while Ney and Murat were to cover his rear against Kutuzov.

- Should these maneuvers fail to yield the desired results, the army would winter between Smolensk and Riga (he counted on its capture by then) and would advance against St. Petersburg with 300,000 men the following spring.

Napoleon's stepson Eugene was the only one who thought the plan was workable. The remainder of the commanders declared that the army was still in dire need of rest and that Moscow still offered ample resources. Should a retreat become necessary, it would be more advantageous to proceed in a southerly direction. At the same time, it would still be possible to deliver damaging strokes against the Russians.

Even though he wasn't convinced, Napoleon gave in, remarking upon something he had not himself heeded, that "peace could hardly be expected from those who had set Moscow on fire." For this same reason, a move toward St. Petersburg, 250 miles from Veliki-Luki, would hardly have succeeded. Failure was all the more likely since the army would have to make another march of over 350 miles through poorly cultivated country and could hardly be expected to arrive there in good condition.

Having given up on the military front, Napoleon made a last-ditch effort on the diplomatic front when he sent General Lauriston off to the Russian headquarters on October 4. Lauriston did manage to meet with Kutuzov, but nothing came of it. The latter might have shied away from meeting Napoleon again on a battlefield, but he was far too shrewd not to see what stood behind Lauriston's mission. At the same time, he was quite aware of Alexander's desire to see the French expelled from Russian territory as quickly as possible. Negotiations could only delay Napoleon's expected withdrawal from Moscow, once he realized that no peace offers would be made and none accepted.

Thus, Kutuzov made certain that he left no doubt whatever in Lauriston's mind. Napoleon got the point and gave in to the inevitable. A letter written to Victor on October 6, the day of Lauriston's return, indicates that Napoleon was fully aware of the fact that his position had become untenable. He expressed the conviction that Tshitshagov and Tormassov would unite (which had already happened) and that Schwarzenberg would not be able to stand against them. He also feared that the tsar would reinforce Wittgenstein to such a point that Macdonald and St. Cyr would be forced back from the Dvina.

But it was not simply the situation on his flanks that was forcing Napoleon to retreat. The situation of the main army group was what Clausewitz has described as "strategically debilitated." Just as Napoleon had neglected to adequately secure his flanks in the wider sense, so too, contrary to his actions in the past, had he failed to pay careful heed to his own line of communications. Even if coverage of its entire length, 575 miles to Kovno, was not necessary, it would have been imperative to secure the line at least back to Smolensk, 270 miles away. Up to that city, at least, the width of his operational base, as well as the more favorable disposition of the civilian population, offered better security. But all this came to an end at Smolensk. All Napoleon had done to secure this critical stretch was to establish a stronger post at Moshaisk, 70 miles from Moscow, with Junot's weak Westphalian corps and to leave smaller garrisons in Gshatsk, Viasma, and Dorogobush. The smaller garrisons generally consisted of only a weak battalion and two guns. In between, there were only a few isolated posts that usually had no more than 100 men, who would dig in as best they could.

Now the consequences were making themselves felt. The enemy's light troops no longer confined themselves to swarming around the outposts of the French army. More than a dozen raiding detachments, most of them consisting of one or two Cossack regiments but some with regular light cavalry as well, operated around Viasma and Moshaisk; some even entered the Moscow suburbs from the north, east, and south. The French lines of communication were pierced everywhere. Small detachments were wiped out and captured; small transport columns and poorly secured magazines were taken. Even the smaller march formations suddenly found themselves under attack and defeated.

The Russian raiding parties were able to claim that they had brought in 15,000 prisoners by mid-October. Thousands more had been killed, not only by the Cossacks but also by the enraged peasantry, whose cruelty occasionally knew no bounds. Some men had been crucified; others had been buried alive or wrapped in straw and set on fire. As could be expected, these horrors were answered by the French with other horrors in moments of reprisal.

Since the cavalry had been run into the ground through Napoleon's own fault, it proved impossible to put an end to this sort of guerrilla warfare. The commandants in Moshaisk and Smolensk could only be warned not to let any transports march without a strong escort and not to send small detachments at all. Of course, since the middle of September, the number of troops along the Moscow-Smolensk road had steadily increased. Thus, on October 6, Baraquey d'Hilliers was ordered to hold on to twelve battalions of reinforcements coming up (see Appendix XV), which were to be deployed in Dorogobush, Viasma, and Gshatsk. However, it took time to implement even these belated measures, and none were ever completely carried out. As a result, the situation of the army, cut off from nearly all its communications, became ever more precarious. Few supply transports got through, and the troops in Moscow were reduced to foraging again. And this practice, in view of prevailing conditions, became ever more dangerous and costly.

Although there were rather large stocks of food in Moscow, the commissariat, in time-honored fashion, had failed to secure them and see to their orderly distribution. Again, abundance and waste walked hand in hand with opulence and privation. With the burning of Moscow and the looting that took place amid the flames, a lack of discipline was again rampant, causing some diarists to liken the situation to a "witches' sabbath."

In the beginning of October, Napoleon decided to expand the cantonments of the army, that is, to spread its quarters out over a larger area. This would facilitate the upkeep of the troops and make the Russians believe he was settling in for the winter. Of course, Napoleon had no such intentions, and Kutuzov was not taken in even for a moment. Still, the guard cavalry detachments were taken back into Moscow, while Ney's and Delzon's divisions of IV Corps were sent to Bogorodsk and Dmitriov, respectively, to set up housekeeping in those locations by October 10.

While the troops in Moscow were beginning to experience a shortage of supplies again, the situation was even worse outside the city. Murat was supposed to draw his rations from Moscow, but there was no transport to move them. Since the advance guard was also in constant friction with the Russians, it was down to about 20,000 men by October 18, despite the arrival of some replacements. The cavalry, in particular, was in a bad way. As a result of all this, and despite the arrival of 30,000 replacements and reinforcements (see Appendix XV), the army as a whole was only a few thousand men stronger on October 18 than it had been upon its arrival in Moscow. Including Junot's corps, it numbered only 108,000 men, with 569 guns. Worse, the condition of the army, rather than improving during its stay in Moscow, had only gotten worse. The cavalry and artillery horses, whose condition had been poor on arrival, were now useless.

As noted earlier, when Napoleon learned on October 6 that Lauriston's mission had failed, he immediately decided to retreat. At that time, he was thinking of making Smolensk his objective. He hoped to winter there and to augment his forces by drawing on the newly raised levies of the 1813 draft (ordered from Moscow) and by summoning his allies to the counter once again. With the army strengthened, he would renew his offensive in the spring. Preparations began at once. On the 6th, Napoleon ordered that the sick and wounded be sent back. A directive went out to Victor that ordered him to position himself between Smolensk and Orsza so that he could support either Schwarzenberg or St. Cyr, as needed. Baraquey d'Hilliers was ordered to assemble another 12,000 men in Smolensk, in addition to the garrison and the twelve battalions already mentioned. The object was to have a reserve for the army even if Victor had to go off in support of one or the other flanking force. On October 10, Baraquey d'Hilliers was advised to be ready to go forward to meet the army, but he was to do this along secondary roads, which would be scouted first, in order to avoid clogging the already overused main road.

However, the start of the withdrawal kept being postponed from one day to the next, partly because the preparations, which had been started too late, were not complete but also because Napoleon still clung to the hope that something might happen, after all, that would make the retreat unnecessary. For a man who had become accustomed to having his way for all too many years, the acceptance of the idea that the initiative had passed from his hands did not come easily. He still hoped to intimidate Alexander, to make him believe that he might stay in Moscow. Once he began his retreat, it would all be over. There could be no turning back.

When Napoleon circumvented Kutuzov by having a Russian noble, who had fallen into the hands of the French, hand-carry a letter to Alexander, he not only stripped himself naked but also exposed the sorry conditions that had prompted him to take this step. But Alexander needed no reassurance from Napoleon that the French were in a bad way. He simply did not reply.

Meanwhile, the French position continued to deteriorate. On October 10, Dorochov (5 battalions, 4 squadrons, and 2 Cossack regiments) took Vereia, which contained a French magazine and a Westphalian battalion, by storm. This marked the beginning of an all-out guerrilla war that turned the entire French army into a garrison under siege. It was no longer a matter of choice or even of time. Napoleon had tarried too long, and now he had to get out. Even his plan to winter at Smolensk was no longer feasible. How deeply Napoleon was depressed over his misfortune is reflected in his unusual vacillations concerning the choice of his line of retreat. He had three options at his disposal:

- Via Volaklamsk, Subtsov, and Bieloi toward Vitebsk

- Via Moshaisk, Viasma, and Dorogobush to Smolensk

- Via Kaluga, Yuhnov, and Yelnia, also to Smolensk

The first of these led through poorly cultivated tracts that had, however, been left untouched by the war. This route was also the most convenient and would have allowed a head start against a pursuit by Kutuzov. The second led along the way the army had come, through areas leached and stripped bare during the advance. The third led through relatively well cultivated regions that had also remained untouched by the war, but it was also the route that could most easily be blocked by the enemy. If Napoleon chose this option, he would have to be prepared to fight his way through. This would have been the most preferable route if, and only if, he still thought his army was capable of seeking another decision by force of arms. Ending the campaign with an offensive action would take the sting out of a failed campaign, raise the morale of the army, and lend credence to the claim that whatever was done afterward was done by design and not by the enemy's force of arms. The political value of this at home was not something to be overlooked. That Napoleon would opt for this route, rather than the first one, which would have saved his army but not his reputation, was to be expected. As long as he had a choice in the matter, the central route did not even enter into his considerations. Its exhausted countryside would have doomed the army.

But Napoleon vacillated. Having first decided on Kaluga, he changed his mind on the 14th, deciding on Bieloi instead, only to return to his original choice on the 15th. This, however, occasioned a delay of the retreat, which was to have started on that day. As soon as the final choice was made, however, preparations began. Broussier's division of IV Corps and the Italian cavalry, in Beresky until now, were to be the points along the new road to Kaluga. As an intermediate post, the Italian guard cavalry was deployed at Shtshaparovo, along the same road. Baraquey d'Hilliers was sent to Yelnia to collect supplies for the army.

Still, even though time was of the essence, another 2 days passed before, on the 18th, the retreat actually began. Two events made it impossible to put matters off any longer. The first snow had fallen on the 15th, and in the early morning of the 18th Murat had been attacked and beaten at Vinkovo. Winter was approaching, and the Russians had sent a warning.

As already noted, Murat had arrived in Vinkovo on October 4. There, the advance guard took a position only 5 miles from the Russians but about 50 miles from Moscow. Due to the incessant actions along the lines of the outposts and to the guerrilla war, not to mention the exhaustion of the troops and the logistical problems, Murat had only about 20,000 men left, with 187 guns.[5] However, the sorry condition of the horses meant that his cavalry and artillery were of only limited use. Indeed, the 187 guns were now nothing short of a burden. The only support he could possibly expect in his exposed position was from the detachment at Voronovo, 10 miles from Vinkovo, but that detachment was barely 6000 men strong.[6]

It would be an understatement to say that Murat's position in the immediate proximity of a fivefold superiority was dangerous. It was all the more so since his force stood on the left bank of the Tshernishnia and his left flank floated in the air. On top of this, despite the fact that the enemy was so near, and in the fashion typical of Napoleonic armies, security measures were careless and virtually nonexistent. Murat was quite aware of his precarious position, but he did nothing to improve it other than advising Napoleon of its shortcomings. In response, the emperor authorized Murat to withdraw beyond the defile of Voronovo, behind the Motsha, if he felt he couldn't maintain himself at Vinkovo until the 15th, at that time the projected date for the retreat.

Murat, however, did not avail himself of this opportunity to improve his position. Instead, he asked for permission to march to Borovsk, along the march route Napoleon had selected. On the 14th, however, Napoleon refused this request, because he thought that such a flank march was too dangerous for Murat and because he himself had just considered taking this road with the army.

·   ·   ·

At the Russian headquarters, Toll was just as aware of the French advance guard's precarious position as he was of the careless fashion in which the French handled their security. He had succeeded in getting Kutuzov to agree to a surprise attack. Even though the commander in chief still shied away from any tactical confrontations with the enemy, he knew that the tsar expected him to act energetically and that this was a comparatively safe opportunity to achieve something that would restore his somewhat tarnished reputation.

Indeed, a letter of October 16 indicates that Alexander was not entirely pleased with Kutuzov's lack of activity, which all the carefully worded phrases in his dispatches could not cover up. Above all, the tsar wanted the French out of Moscow, and yesterday would be a better time than tomorrow. Thus, time and circumstances were on Toll's side, and Kutuzov gave in.

The attack against Murat was to be launched on the 17th, but it was postponed to the 18th because Yermolov, the chief of staff of the army, was nowhere to be found and thus the issue of the necessary orders had not been made. Now Konovnitzyn was put in his place. Unfortunately, the attack of the 18th, while successful, fell considerably short of expectations.

According to the plan, the left wing (V, VI, VII, and VIII Corps with the two cuirassier divisions), accompanied by Kutuzov, was to place itself behind Miloradovitch's advance guard (II/III and IV Cavalry Corps) in two columns. The latter had been left in place to deceive the enemy. The advance guard was not to attack until the right wing, consisting of three columns under Benningsen (II, III, and IV Infantry Corps, I Cavalry Corps, and 10 Cossack regiments), had gone around Murat's free-floating left.

But Benningsen's movement failed because he lacked sufficient energy. The enemy was completely surprised at daybreak, so the first two of his columns (the cavalry with II and III Infantry Corps) gained some success. However, since IV Infantry Corps was late, Benningsen did not exploit his initial success but halted and settled for the ground he had taken, even after the third column at last arrived. This made Kutuzov cautious, not because he was jealous of a success that Benningsen might gain (as has often been maintained) but simply because he himself was not overburdened with energy. Thus, despite Miloradovitch's and Yermolov's pleas (Toll was with the right wing), Kutuzov halted his own advance. As a result, Murat got off lightly, with the loss of only 2000 men and 36 guns, and he wasn't even pursued. The Russians had lost about 500, far too many for what had been gained. Their infantry, stuffed with recruits, had shown itself to be still quite awkward.

The action brought about a total break between Kutuzov and Benningsen, who finally lost whatever influence he had had. True to form, Benningsen sent a letter to Alexander, blaming Kutuzov for the failure and stating that his (Benningsen's) being blamed instead was unjust and uncalled for. Of course, he did not neglect to extol his own role in the affair, laud his merits in general, and offer himself up for the post of commander in chief. But the experience of the previous several months was beginning to clear Alexander's vision. Instead of replying to Benningsen's letter, he simply forwarded it to Kutuzov. And that, for the time being, was the end of Benningsen. Toward the end of November, he quietly disappeared from the army.

Napoleon had been reviewing Ney's troops and had just returned from Bogorodsk when he was told of the action at Vinkovo, mere hours after it had taken place. He at once issued orders for the retreat. In the afternoon of the same day, the 18th, the greatest part of the army, I and IV Corps, was sent to bivouac in front of the city, along the road to Kaluga. The rest, the Guard and Ney's III Corps, remained in Moscow.

But Napoleon had waited too long. Now, just as he finally made up his mind to move, events on his flanks took a turn that brought into question whether he would still find the road to the rear open.

NOTES

1. The *corps de bataille* included II, III, IV, VII, and VIII Infantry Corps and I, II/III, and IV Cavalry Corps. The reserve included V (Guard) and VI Infantry Corps and the 1st and 2nd Cuirassier Divisions.
2. 26 regiments and ½ battery arrived.
3. Sent back were 2 regiments of the 23rd Infantry Division and 1 regiment each from the 4th, 7th, 11th, 12th, 17th, 24th, 26th, and 27th Divisions.
4. On October 23, the army numbered as follows:
   76,629 infantry, including 5498 militia
   10,711 cavalry
   8,859 artillery
   813 engineers
   In addition to these 97,012 men there were, as noted, 20,000 Cossacks. The 622 guns included 216 heavy guns and 294 light guns of the foot artillery and 112 light guns of the horse artillery.
5. The troops under Murat consisted of:
   Div. Claparede, Vistula Legion of the Guard

Div. Dufour and 1st Cav. Brig. of I Corps
Light cavalry of III Corps
V Corps
I, II, III, and IV Cav. Corps
6. The detachment included Division Friedrichs and the 1st Cavalry Brigade of I Corps and the two quite weak Bavarian cavalry brigades of IV Corps.

20. The Flanks Begin to Waver

THE TURNAROUND IN VOLHYNIA

Even as Napoleon's central army group was still massed at Smolensk and preparing for its continuing advance, which was to take it on to Borodino and Moscow, events in the distant flanks were already beginning to cast their shadows ahead.

Tormassov was last seen taking the Russian reserve army back behind the Styx, where he had taken a position near Lutzk on August 29, after the battle of Gorodeczna. There, he settled in to await the arrival of Admiral Tshitshagov and his Danube Army. This force had become available for disposition against Napoleon's invasion almost as soon as hostilities had gotten under way. However, stationed in Walachia in southern Romania, it had to make a long march before it arrived in its new area of operations. By then, toward the end of September, its force—about 30,000 after leaving some troops to continue observing the Turks and a few other detachments—loomed far more importantly than it had in the middle of July, when it first became available.

Tshitshagov was a good seaman and the tsar thought a great deal of him, even though the admiral had not as yet been able to display his qualities as a general. Alexander had originally appointed him to pursue the peace with the Turks after Kutuzov had dawdled and drawn out the negotiations in the hope that Alexander might seek an accommodation with Napoleon rather than risk a war that, he was convinced, Russia would lose. However, by the time the admiral arrived, the peace had been concluded (on May 28).

After the treaty had been ratified by Alexander on June 23 and by the sultan on July 15, and after it was decided that instead of operating in upper Italy, the Danube Army would join operations against Napoleon, Tshitshagov departed from the Danube on July 31. He arrived at the Styx in three echelons on September 19, 20, and 21. The forces now united there with Tormassov numbered 60,000 men, including about 6000 to 7000 Cossacks, with 223 guns.[1] Additionally, Osten-Sacken's corps, with only about 4000 men left after detachments and transfers, stood at Shitomir to watch the Austrian border, and General Lueders's column of 11,000 men was still coming up.

Against this force, Schwarzenberg could muster only 41,000 men, with 107 guns. His main force, including VII Corps, reinforced with Kosinsky's brigade (? battalions, 3 newly formed lancer squadrons, and 3 squadrons of the Warsaw militia—about 5000 men), stood in the area of Vladimir. Division Siegenthal and Brigade Mohr (in all about 5000 infantry and 900 cavalry) stood along the Kovel-Ratno road and at Pinsk, respectively. For the moment, Schwarzenberg could not count on any reinforcements. About 6000 Austrian reserves had been mobilized, and Durutte's division of XI Corps (13,600 men) had been ordered to march from Berlin to Warsaw. But none of these would arrive in Warsaw (Durutte) or Volhynia (Austrian reserves) before the end of October.

Kutuzov had ordered Tshitshagov to operate against Schwarzenberg and Tormassov to go against Napoleon's right flank even before Borodino. However, the two Russian commanders had decided instead to mount a joint offensive against Schwarzenberg. In doing so, the left wing, formed by the Danube Army, was to be taken forward to crowd Schwarzenberg away from the border and into the Pripet Marshes.

After mounting the operation, the Danube Army crossed the Styx on the 22nd of September, the reserve army on the 23rd. On their approach, Schwarzenberg withdrew to Liuboml. As the Russians continued to follow him, Kutuzov sent new orders from Podolsk. Tormassov was to remain facing Schwarzenberg, while Tshitshagov was to join the main army via Mozyr and Mohilev. However, even now the two generals did not think they should follow this order, since they expected Schwarzenberg to offer them a battle at Liuboml.

The Austrian had indeed intended to make a stand in this strong position. However, since the Poles (Kosinsky's brigade) had been pushed through Vladimir and were forced to withdraw to the weakly garrisoned fortress of Zamoscz and since Siegenthal's division and Mohr's brigade were absent as well, Schwarzenberg could not assemble even 30,000 men. Although he was able to turn back a feeble attempt by the Russians to cross the canal in front of his position, he thought it best to vacate his ground because Essen's and Langeron's corps threatened to envelop his right flank. Thus, on September 30, he marched to Opolin, only weakly pursued by the advance guard of the Danube Army and Essen's corps. Schwarzenberg continued his retreat. Crossing the Bug at Vlodava on October 1, he marched along its left (western) bank to Brest-Litovsk, where he recrossed to the right bank and took a position behind the Muchavets to wait for Siegenthal's division to close up again.

Even as Tormassov and Tshitshagov made ready to attack the position at Liuboml, Tshernishev arrived with the tsar's operations plan (drawn up after the Battle of Borodino). It recalled Tormassov and charged Tshitshagov with the task of pushing Schwarzenberg back into Poland, leaving Sacken to face him with the reserve army. The admiral was then to draw Oertel's corps into the Danube Army and march to the Beresina via Minsk.

Tshitshagov now took the new Third Western Army, formed from the combination of the two armies, and continued his offensive. Following through on the operations plan, he took his right wing, the erstwhile reserve army, forward to threaten Schwarzenberg's left and induce him to retreat into Poland, while he moved against Brest-Litovsk with full force.

This put Siegenthal's division and Mohr's brigade into difficulties, because Oertel had just ordered General Zapolsky to drive them out of Pinsk. The advanced Russian right wing threatened Siegenthal's communications just when he wanted to move from Ratno to the Bug. Siegenthal only barely succeeded, but Mohr was forced to go back through Pruzany to Bielove before he could make the connection again via Drohiczyn.

In the meanwhile, Tshitshagov had continued his advance to Brest-Litovsk, where he faced Schwarzenberg on October 10. He intended to make a frontal attack with his main force, while Lambert's and Voinov's corps were to envelop his left. Fearing he would be backed into the swamps, Schwarzenberg evaded this blow and crossed to the far side of the Liesna during the night of the 11th. There, he denied the Russians a crossing with a series of lively engagements. Still, Schwarzenberg wanted more of a safety margin. During the following night, he marched off again, recrossed the Bug, and took another position near Drohiczyn, where Mohr's brigade finally caught up as well. This brought the strength of Schwarzenberg's force, which had suffered substantial losses, back up to 33,000 men (24,000 Austrians and 9000 Saxons). In the Drohiczyn position, he thought he would be able to cover the grand duchy of Warsaw as well as the communications of the

French main army. He wanted to wait at that position for the arrival of his own reinforcements from Austria and Durutte's division.

Durutte's division was made up mostly of draft evaders, stockade inmates, and a solid sprinkling of Spanish and Portuguese prisoners of war. Although these regiments eventually received ordinal numbers, they were, at that time, known by their erstwhile island garrisons (Belle Isle, Walcheren, de Rhe). Funck says of them:

On 1 November . . . we were met by several battalions from Durutte's division. These were poor troops, scraped together, conscripts, 15 and 16 year olds [the Germans consistently underestimated the age of the French conscripts], totally lacking military training or discipline, the officers inexperienced, the better among them displeased with their assignment [to these regiments]. . . . And this, if I recall correctly . . . Regiment de Rhe, under Colonel Maury . . . was said to be the best of the lot.

The commanders were full of bluster and quite discourteous toward us . . . exhibiting their disdain of us at every opportunity. From the start, there was nothing but trouble with them and the only way to coexist was to be equally rude and let them know one was not intimidated.

The other regiments, one of which bore the title Mediterrane, were much worse, the dregs of the French army. Mostly Illyrians and Spaniards, who had been impressed. To them, the war was nothing but an opportunity to loot; and they did this openly, under the eyes of their officers and especially the Spaniards committed the worst excesses against women. Reynier always had them march in the center, between the two divisions . . . after midnight, they would come into the villages to loot. The sentries could no longer handle them, the central guard had to fall out every time. Restoration of order was possible only with a formal attack. And even though I prohibited my men from using their bayonets, I permitted the use of the musket butts.

A single battalion of Wuerzburgers, decent and proper men, were the sole exception. Durutte's division was said to number 6,000 men. There were but 4,000 of them before they had their first look at the enemy. They were only infantry and had no guns.[2]

These were the reinforcements with which the Saxons had been saddled—and that seems the only proper expression. They had to keep as much watch over them as over the Russians.

Fortunately, Tshitshagov did not think he could follow up on his success because this would have conflicted with Alexander's operations plan. Nor did he think he could start his march to the Beresina without first taking extensive logistical measures. Since this required some time, he had his troops go into cantonments around Brest-Litovsk without undertaking any action during the interim.

This brought on another hiatus filled with guerrilla actions in which the Russians were becoming increasingly aggressive. General Tshaplitz (4 battalions, 12 squadrons, 2½ Cossack regiments, and 1 battery) sent shock waves through Lithuania, disturbing even the formation of the militia there. On October 20, during a raid on Slonim, he scattered the lancers there, who were in the process of being formed up to become the 3rd Regiment Chevaulegers Lanciers of Napoleon's Imperial Guard. Tshernishev (7 squadrons and 3 Cossack regiments—about 1800 men with 4 guns) went into the French rear areas, as far as Vengrov and Siedlice, twice spreading terror through Warsaw. Indeed, he created so much commotion that Schwarzenberg was forced to attack Essen, who had been sent forward to receive Tshernishev. This brought on a sharp action between Reynier and Essen on October 18 near Biala, in which the Russians were brought up short. These raids, however, yielded an important bit of information for the Russians in that they exposed the fact that the Poles no longer exhibited a great urge to arm. The earlier enthusiasm was evaporating because Napoleon had shown himself to be insensitive to their national aspirations.

However, even as operations in the Grand Army's southern flank had confined themselves to the so-called little war (or, as the Spanish called it, the *guerillo*), renewed rumblings were heard in the north.

WITTGENSTEIN ENHANCES HIS REPUTATION

While Schwarzenberg was rooted into place on the left, the situation on the right flank was beginning to deteriorate. After Polotsk, Wittgenstein had stood back, barely a day's march from St. Cyr, without being in any way molested by the latter. With reinforcements constantly dribbling in, his army, barely 16,000 men, with 98 guns, after the lost battle, had grown to about 40,000, with 158 guns.[3] In addition, the Finnish Corps, at this time still coming up along the right bank of the Dvina with 9500 men and 18 guns under Steinheil, was also slated to join Wittgenstein. Thus, the latter soon had 50,000 men, with 176 guns. Against these, St. Cyr could muster little better than half that number. Despite reinforcements, the guerrilla war, supply difficulties, and disease (running to epidemic proportions among the Bavarians) had reduced his force to about 27,000 men.[4] This, and the danger of his position, caused St. Cyr to reinforce Polotsk with earthworks.

On October 16, close to the day Napoleon decided to leave Moscow, Wittgenstein passed to the attack again. The tsar's operations plan called upon him to drive the French in front of him toward the border and then to leave the enemy to the attention of Steinheil and the Riga garrison while he took his main force to the Beresina and the French main line of retreat. There, he and Tshitshagov were to block the enemy.

To carry out this plan, Wittgenstein formed his army into three columns.[5] The right, under Yashvil, was to go against Polotsk along the right bank of the Polota and keep St. Cyr occupied. Meanwhile, Wittgenstein would cross to the left bank of the river at Yurovitshi and move against Goryani, 15 miles above Polotsk, where he would cross the Dvina. To induce St. Cyr to cross to the left of the Dvina, Steinheil was to threaten his line of communications by crossing to the left of the Dvina himself at Pridruisk, 55 miles below Polotsk, and then marching toward the town. A bridge was laid at Disna to facilitate communications between Steinheil and Wittgenstein. To cover this bridge, two strong detachments were sent to Goryani and Disna. The one at Disna would become the advance guard for Steinheil's Finnish Corps.

As soon as the Russian advance became known, the French outposts were withdrawn toward Polotsk. This brought on some brushes on the 17th, when the Russians crossing at Yurovitshi were briefly delayed. St. Cyr was firmly resolved to hold on at Polotsk and to retreat only after the bulk of the enemy's forces had crossed the Dvina. To secure accurate information about what was afoot, St. Cyr sent all but five squadrons of his cavalry to the left side of the Dvina. Doumerc's division was to watch the river above Polotsk, while Corbineau's brigade, reinforced with three weak battalions, was to watch below. These were the opening moves leading to the second Battle of Polotsk.

While Yashvil advanced against Polotsk along the right of the Polota, Wittgenstein attacked along the left side. His initial objective went no further than securing the construction of the bridge at Goryani against a possible French sally, but when it proved impossible to build the bridge there, he decided to move on toward gaining a decision. However, his attacks failed in front of St. Cyr's field fortifications. Thus, he remained quiet on the 19th and waited for Steinheil's arrival.

On the 18th, Steinheil had gotten as far as Polyudoviczy, 20 miles from Polotsk, while his advance guard reached Uszacz. Corbineau lacked the strength to stop Steinheil's continuing advance on the 19th, and a column (1 infantry brigade and 1 cuirassier regiment) under Amey, which had been sent to support him, had no better luck. St. Cyr's situation was now getting serious. It was only 3 p.m. If he stood fast, he incurred the danger of being attacked from two sides. If he retreated, he could expect an immediate attack from Wittgenstein. He decided to hold on until nightfall. Fortunately for St. Cyr, a thick fog descended, which forced Steinheil, who was now only about 4 miles away, to halt. This, in turn, caused Yashvil, who could observe the action across the river, to delay his own attack, which had been just about to begin.

When darkness descended, St. Cyr began his withdrawal at once, first extracting his numerous artillery out of its positions. However, his attempt to make a quiet getaway failed when a French general committed the blunder of ordering that the huts of his division's encampment be set on fire. This aroused the attention of the Russians, who came forward at once.

Lieutenant Legler, a Swiss officer, claims that the fire which signaled the attack had been set by deserters, and he casts an interesting sidelight when he says that the Russians were full of vodka and that, during their attacks, they had their backs (read "courage") tickled by the Cossacks' pikes. The Swiss defended the town itself until past midnight. Apparently, the Bavarians were involved in the battle as well. Brutal house-to-house fighting ensued. The defenders held out as long as they could hear the rumble of the guns and caissons crossing the two boat bridges. Again, the wounded of both sides perished by the hundreds as Polotsk went up in flames.

But St. Cyr made good his retreat. The bridges were burned at about 3 a.m., but the Swiss rear guard held on until about 4 a.m., when the last of the men were ferried across the river in pontoons saved from the bridges. Even though St. Cyr had brought his army across the river, he was still in a precarious position. Not only did Steinheil threaten his continuing retreat, but St. Cyr had to expect that the victorious Wittgenstein, his crossing covered by Steinheil, would come roaring across the river to finish what he had started.

But Steinheil himself was in an exposed position. The destruction of the Polotsk bridges had left him isolated and, at least temporarily, cut off from support by Wittgenstein. It was imperative that St. Cyr avail himself of this opportunity. Since he was wounded, he charged the Bavarian Wrede, temporarily in command of VI Corps, with the task.[6] Wrede attacked before daybreak. Since Steinheil's advance guard had gone beyond the narrows of Yekimanya, where the road from Disna crosses the Uszacz, and had neglected to take any security measures, Wrede succeeded in surprising him at 5 a.m. on the 20th. The result was a total defeat, which cost the Russians at least 1800 prisoners alone. It would have gone even worse for the Russians but for Amey's ineptitude, which completely bungled his part of the attack. Steinheil, fearing that he was under attack from St. Cyr's entire force, ran

all the way back to Disna, where he recrossed the Dvina on the next day
and rejoined Wittgenstein.

Losses had been heavy on both sides: about 8000 for the French and
12,000 for the Russians. Unfortunately for the French, St. Cyr had been
wounded so badly that he had to turn over command to General Legrand,
but Wrede, who was a corps commander, refused to take orders from a
division general. As a result, Legrand, his pride wounded, passed command
on to Merle, who accepted with the proviso that he would not be required
to give orders to Wrede. St. Cyr, who had remained with the troops,
attempted to intercede without avail.

Despite their final success, the French were no longer able to hold the
Dvina line. II Corps, for the moment a formation in name only, as the
division commanders now emulated the marshals in bickering with each
other, withdrew to the Ula; its main force at Czasniki, Division Legrand,
which now also operated independently, because its commander did not
want to subordinate himself to Merle, his junior, went to Beszenkoviczi.
Wrede, "in order to preserve his troops from a catastrophe," contradicted
the orders which Legrand had given him and which had been confirmed by
St. Cyr. He took the 2000 to 3000 remaining Bavarians toward Glubkoye,
that is, in the direction of Vilna.

St. Cyr's wounding and the eccentric retreat precipitated by the indiscipline of the commanding generals reduced the forces facing Wittgenstein
by more than half. Wittgenstein, quite apart from the importance of his
victory, was able to redress his losses through his union with Steinheil and
the arrival of a few reinforcements. He still had command of 39,000 men.

Thus, at the very moment Napoleon began his retreat from Moscow,
the situation in the rear of the French main army took on a dangerous
complexion. On the right, Schwarzenberg had been pushed into a defensive
stance by forces nearly twice his own strength, while the enemy made ready
to turn part of this superiority against the French line of retreat. The situation
on the left had become just as bad. There, the fragments of St. Cyr's army
were also no longer able to keep the Russians away from the main line of
retreat.

Again, the lack of a unified command in the rear and on the flanks
exacted its punishment. Given the distance between these formations and
Napoleon's headquarters, it would have been imperative to conduct unified
operations at least on the left, where relatively substantial forces had been
deployed.

The situation called, above all, for ensuring the security of the main
line of retreat. Despite Schwarzenberg's faulty measures, this would still have

been possible had Macdonald been pulled in at the right time. The necessity of this deployment should have been obvious, especially since the capture of Riga was of only secondary importance at the time, but no one had the authority to order the move. Thus, the safety of the French army rested solely on Victor's IX Corps, the only major formation along the line of retreat. This corps, however, was far too weak to deal with the dual danger.

As a result, the catastrophe shaping up on the horizon was becoming inevitable, and it no longer allowed any margin for error. Napoleon had already lost the campaign. The only real question that remained was what price the Russians would exact. If the situation in the flanks deteriorated any further, only the Russians could cheat themselves out of a total victory.

NOTES

1. After detachments, Tormassov's reserve army had 48 battalions, 72 squadrons, 10 Cossack regiments, and 11 batteries. The Danube Army under Tshitshagov had 74 battalions, 64 squadrons, 14 Cossack regiments, and 20 batteries. These troops were organized into five corps: I (Langeron), II (Essen III), III (Voinov), IV (Bulatov), and the reserve corps (Sabaneyev).

    After various detachments and new arrivals, the Russian forces in Volhynia had the following strengths:

	Battalions	Squadrons	Cossack Regiments	Batteries	Men	Guns
Reserve army	42	56	9	10	30,000	115
Danube Army	47	56	8	9	36,000	108
Detached						
Sacken	6	16	2	1	4,000	12
Approaching: Lueders, etc.	20	8	2	4	11,000	48

When the two armies were amalgamated, the corps were reorganized and three new ones were added. The new corps were under Lambert, Markov (later Shtsherbatov and then Sacken), and Engelhardt. The corps were still of quite uneven size, and some were composed of units from both armies.

2. Brabaut, p. 167ff.

3. Wittgenstein's total strength by mid-October was 50 battalions, 15 *drushinas* (militia battalions), 38 squadrons, 2 Cossack regiments, and 14 batteries, totaling about 40,000 men, with 168 guns.

    After October 20 another 2 *drushinas* of the Novgorod militia arrived, joined in November by 2 more *drushinas* and 1 Cossack regiment of the Third Western Army.

4. At this time, St. Cyr's force consisted of II Corps with Division Doumerc (18,000 infantry and 4000 cavalry) and VI Corps (5000 infantry).

5.

Column	Battalions	Drushinas	Squadrons	Cossack Regiments	Men	Guns
Right	14	6	7	1	11,000	68
Center	18		16	1	12,000	50
Left	8	8	4	¼	9,000	18

    At the time of the battle, another 11 battalions and 11 squadrons were detached.

6. The troops under Wrede's orders were:
Corbineau's detachment: 1 Swiss regiment and 3 light cavalry regiments
Amey's detachment: 3 French infantry regiments and 1 cuirassier regiment
Stroehl's detachment: the remainder of the Bavarians
According to St. Cyr, Wrede's force included:
3 French regiments from Legrand's division
1 Swiss and 1 Bavarian infantry regiment
1 cuirassier regiment and Corbineau's brigade

V
The Retreat

21. The Retreat Begins: Moscow to Malo-Jaroslavets

When Napoleon received news of the mishap at Vinkovo, he knew that the time for deferring the decision any further had passed. It was time to go. It was, in fact, getting too late. Both the oncoming winter and the Russians had already stolen some marches from him. At 5 a.m. on the 19th, the retreat began in earnest. At the point was Eugene's corps, now the best one remaining, with 25,000 men still in the ranks. Eugene was followed by Ney, the Old Guard, two of Davout's divisions, and Roguet's division of the Young Guard with the trophies won in the campaign. The rear was brought up by Morand's division of Davout's corps, with Colbert's brigade of guard lancers. On the first day, the points reached Vatutinka, and Napoleon went to Troizkoye.

Remaining behind in Moscow, for the time being, were about 8500 men[1] under Mortier. Even though he had no intention of returning to the city, Napoleon wanted to keep up the pretense for as long as possible, even toward his marshals, that the exodus was just another of the army's operational moves against the Russians. "It is possible the emperor might return to Moscow," read the phrase contained in the operations order. However, nobody was deceived, least of all the rank and file.

Including the troops under Murat at Voronovo[2] and Junot's Westphalians in Moshaisk, the army still numbered 108,000 men, with 569 guns (see Appendix XVI). The men who remained with the colors were the survivors, the veterans, and those who had become veterans over the previous several months. The infantry still looked good, but the cavalry was in abominable condition. Four thousand unhorsed troopers had already been formed into infantry battalions. All that really remained usable were the 4600 men of the guard cavalry; they had not participated in Murat's follies and consequently were in fairly good condition. The horses of the remaining 10,700 cavalry and especially those of the artillery were of limited use, being largely on the point of collapse. This was all the worse since the Russians had many good cavalrymen, in the face of which the French were all but helpless. Napoleon now paid for Murat's reckless expenditure of the cavalry on the way in. Now, when they were needed most, the army no longer had any eyes and ears; it marched blindly toward its doom.

The artillery was even worse off than the cavalry. General Lariboissiere, the artillery chief, as well as other senior officers, had recommended that some of the artillery be left behind so that what was taken might be better equipped with the necessary draft teams and ammunition; there was only a single day's battle supply left for the entire artillery. Indeed, 569 guns for about 100,000 men was far too much artillery, especially in view of the condition of the horses, which were already exhausted when they crossed the Niemen in June. Of course, Napoleon scoffed at the notion, declaring it unworthy of the French army. On the one hand, this artilleryman was loathe to part with any of his guns. On the other, any guns left behind would become trophies, like captured colors and standards, for the Russians. Napoleon was not about to permit that to happen, no matter how useless the guns were to him. To leave them behind would have been another admission of defeat. Yet, as happens so often, he who wanted to save everything would end up saving nothing.

But worst of all was the alarming deterioration of discipline. Rather than regaining its posture during the extended stay in Moscow, the army had gotten worse. This was not exactly a new phenomenon. It had already occurred in 1806, when the stamina and the marching capacity of the army were greatly diminished after its prolonged stay in Berlin—and this was after a victorious campaign. Now, after marches of Herculean proportions and without the experience of even a sense of victory, the situation was even worse. No amount of disciplining, not even Davout's brand of summary justice, could halt the decay.

It has been noted that, of all the aspects of military history, the lessons it has to teach on the subject of troop psychology are the most important because they are of the most lasting value. It becomes obvious that although the weeks spent in Moscow might have enabled the troops to regain some of the physical energy they had expended on their march to Moscow, the time was not nearly sufficient to recharge the psychic batteries of the men, especially not when such a hiatus in action came deep inside hostile enemy territory. Nor were the conditions in Moscow conducive to such a moral reconstruction, especially since a large part of the troops there had been forced to see to their own needs in the ad hoc fashion of every man for himself (a policy that had long been typical of the French army on foreign soil). That this system had, even in relatively good times, reflected adversely on the discipline of the French troops has already been explored. In Moscow, this problem was exacerbated by the absence of the civilian population. It was, after all, much easier to loot an abandoned house than an occupied one, in which the plunderer might come face to face with the hapless owner. As a result, the population's abandonment of Moscow and its suburbs, coupled with the inevitable letdown experienced by the troops after what they thought was the conclusion of a difficult and strenuous campaign, had removed the last vestiges of restraint. Even the Old Guard, the soldiers among soldiers, had taken part in the looting. The situation had reached a point where not even Napoleon could halt the decay of discipline.

The men of Murat's advance guard had seen little of Moscow, and for them the previous several weeks had been only a continuation of the privations suffered since the beginning of the campaign. Thus, when some of them first laid eyes upon the columns coming out of Moscow, they could hardly believe what they saw. According to one diarist, the entire column took 30 hours to pass.

In three broad columns, on and alongside the old Kaluga road, the once mighty juggernaut rolled on, with the cavalry columns on the left, the infantry on the right, and the artillery, trains, and baggage in the center. Several observers thought that the spectacle resembled a giant Oriental caravan more than it did an army. Intermingling with the army and joining the retreat were the foreign merchants and their families, who could expect reprisals for having fraternized and even traded with the invaders. Every army vehicle was loaded down not only with foodstuffs but with loot as well, to such an extent that the axles threatened to give way. But that was only the half of it. The baggage trains of the ranking officers had taken on gargantuan proportions, and now many of the junior officers had some sort of cart in addition to their packhorses.

Even in ordinary times, most of the generals and staff officers had maintained sumptuous standards of housekeeping in the field—sumptuous, that is, at least in the eyes of the rank and file and even the junior officers. Now each general had several new carriages, hansoms, droshkys, four-wheelers, and two-wheelers, as well as two or more supply wagons to carry his personal gear, not to mention a string of saddle horses. All of this was presided over by a cook and one or more personal servants, as well as grooms and drivers, none of whom were military personnel. Including the refugees, among whom were several hundred women and children, these noncombatants have been estimated to have numbered about 32,000 people.

Even though restrictions had been set upon the baggage trains of the formations, none existed where the staffs were concerned. Thus, many of the staff officers, whose means were now augmented by what had been commandeered during the campaign, had retinues which rivaled those of the generals. Even the rank and file had commandeered every imaginable kind of conveyance to haul away anything that seemed to have some value. It is unlikely that even a single useful vehicle remained in Moscow or for several miles around.

Some of the officers had made an effort to see that their men obtained whatever clothing might prove useful for the coming winter. Most of the officers had acquired every conceivable kind of fur coats and capes, which were to be had for a pittance in and around Moscow. Unfortunately, the mass of the rank and file had rid themselves of almost all necessities in order to carry useless junk. Best off were those who had commandeered items of female apparel for their ladies at home. Although the ladies never got to see any of the clothes, they did get to see their men again: In a month's time, these garments provided life-giving warmth to the soldiers who donned them to keep out the biting cold. Other soldiers weren't as fortunate. One diarist tells of a Westphalian, for example, who was sitting by the roadside sometime in November or December offering a large chunk of silver, hammered into a cube, for a slice of bread. He found no takers.

Soon, the army began to take on the multicolored, unmilitary image that was to become engraved in the memories of those who witnessed its passing. As the trek rolled on to the south, more noncombatants and stragglers collected around the trains; they were joined by the sick and wounded who had been left behind on the way in. These would be among the first to perish, giving the army a dreadful preview of its own future.

Often, the wagons traveled in four columns abreast. Thus, at every bottleneck in the road, such as towns, villages, and bridges, they would jam into each other. And at these places, the field gendarmes of the army were waiting to weed out the unauthorized vehicles hauled along by the battalions. Naturally, the gendarmes were most effective at the bottom of the pecking order. The rank and file lost all their spoils, except, of course, what they could carry on their backs.

The entrepreneurs in the rank and file, getting wind of these checkpoints, stopped their carts by the roadside and opened shop, offering their goods at bargain prices. Some of these were rather successful and were probably the ones who much later, when hunger and cold set in, were able to pull rolls of gold coins from their pockets and thus achieve minor miracles wherever peasants were still to be found. Even in the worst of times, hard cash could generally secure at least some provisions in the villages and towns. Indeed, the question has been raised as to why the French commissariat didn't avail itself of the free purchase system, a tried and proven method. But that would have been asking the leopard to change his spots.

As great as the trains had become, they were completely inadequate to take care of the army's needs. There was not enough food, clothing, or, for that matter, ammunition. The foodstuffs found in Moscow had not been properly distributed. Instead, those who had direct access had wantonly ruined whatever they could not use themselves, while others had next to nothing.

All these were difficulties that no amount of leadership could surmount at this late date, because the foundations were lacking. The failings of the commissariat and the consequent erosive effects upon the discipline of the troops were problems that would not lend themselves to any quick remedies even in ordinary times. To have attempted to accomplish anything really effective in the middle of a campaign was completely out of the question. The only hope for survival rested with the fighting power of the army. Thus, it seems inconceivable that Napoleon had not done more to restore its strength at least to the extent that was still possible. Napoleon and his generals had habitually overlooked many of their soldiers' transgressions. If, even now, the emperor did not think he should insert a stronger hand because he did not want to compromise their loyalty and his own popularity, he should have at least sent off the trains well in advance of the army and by the direct route to Moshaisk. Then he could have reached Malo-Jaroslavets by the 21st or 22nd instead of on the 24th.

Since the army was thus hardly in a condition to weather a collision with the enemy, a fact that a man of Napoleon's experience could hardly have overlooked, the choice of the road via Kaluga-Yuhnov-Yelnia to Smolensk was decidedly wrong. It had to be clear to him from the start that this route would surely give rise to serious confrontations. If he did not deem his army in condition to weather heavy fighting, then he really had no choice at all. Only the road via Subtsov and Bieloi offered any hope of getting by without serious trouble.

To have any chance of success in taking the route he did, Napoleon would have had to rid the army of its trains and following, that is, to reduce it to its bare minimum. The question immediately arises of whether one should be more surprised by the emperor's powerlessness, the indiscipline that had taken hold of his troops, or his self-delusion, which appeared to see no danger in choosing the Kaluga road. Did he still hope to strike fear into his enemies by his name and reputation alone?

Napoleon had selected the new Kaluga road because he still hoped to slip past the Russians at Tarutino. On the 15th, he had placed Broussier's division of IV Corps at Fominskoye to become a sort of point for the army; but for the start of the march, Napoleon had taken the old Kaluga road, which led to Tarutino. Many critics have seen this as a manifestation of his uncertainty, but this view is not entirely correct. Rather, Napoleon did this so that the army would be ready quickly to receive Murat after he had been attacked by Kutuzov and so that it would be prepared if Kutuzov followed up on this and passed to the offensive. If the Russian commander meant to do this, then the advance to the Pachra offered the army the possibility of giving him a defensive battle under favorable conditions—and a defensive battle was all that could still be expected of the artillery. This could hardly have brought about a decisive turn, because the enemy could be destroyed only in an offensive battle. And that was no longer in the cards. But any kind of a win would certainly have been useful and would have given Napoleon at least some modest advantages.

But Kutuzov did not come forward. Thus, in view of the army's condition, Napoleon was entirely correct in deciding not to go farther in the direction of Tarutino but, instead, to turn aside and reach the new Kaluga road as quickly as possible. In keeping with this plan, Napoleon changed the direction of his march on October 20; covered by Murat and Ney, who had remained in place by the Motsha, he turned right to Fominskoye. The points arrived there on the 21st. Morand and the rear guard got as far as Desna.

Up to this point, the weather had been good. The nights were getting cold, but the days were still sunny and warm. On the 22nd, a light rain set in and the roads promptly became difficult again, sending the train and artillery horses to the brink of oblivion. Chambray thought that if the rain had lasted for 24 hours, the greatest part of the artillery and train would never have succeeded in getting beyond the secondary side roads that connected the Tarutino and Kaluga roads.

On the 22nd, the greatest part of the army was assembled at Fominskoye, where Murat and Morand closed up as well. To secure communications with Junot in Moshaisk, Poniatowski was sent to Vereia, upon the holding of which Napoleon placed great value. Ney, reinforced to 15,000 men and the disproportionately large number of 110 guns, stayed behind on the Motsha, near Tshirikovo. Remaining there on the 22nd, he was to screen the withdrawal and then assume the rear-guard duties. He did not march until 1 a.m. on the 23rd.

During the night of October 22–23, Mortier also left Moscow and marched to Vereia, where he was due on the 24th. In a fit of rage, Napoleon had ordered him to destroy the Kremlin and all public buildings in the city, with the exception of the orphanage. Mortier, or those charged with the execution of the order, seem to have had other things on their minds, because only superficial damage was done. (One is reminded here of Hitler's order to destroy Paris in 1944 and his generals' unwillingness to do so.)

But that order and another to shoot Russian prisoners who could not keep up with the army, plus the systematic destruction of every town and village the army passed through, offer a clear indication of Napoleon's mindset. The nature of such orders is far removed from the sober discussions of his operational decisions and the neatly compartmentalized descriptions of the horrors, the nonmilitary aspects, that necessarily mark all the accounts of the 1812 campaign. There certainly was a connection between the army's behavior and the violent reaction this begot from the Russian peasantry, but Napoleon may not himself be held blameless in all of this.

Right from the start of Napoleon's retreat, it became noticeable that the Russian cavalry, despite its great superiority, failed to keep its own high command advised of whatever moves the French made. This was to happen time and again. Funck, in an assessment of the Russian cavalry, says that the Cossacks had no skills at systematic reconnaissance. The light cavalry of the line, however, customarily left these matters to the Cossacks and, consequently, ended up developing no skills of its own in such matters.

Thus, it was only on the 19th that Kutuzov learned from Dorochov, who then stood at Katovo, that strong enemy formations were around Fominskoye. On the 21st, news followed that the French were advancing along the old Kaluga road. Dorochov had assumed that the French main force was around Voronovo. To clarify the situation, Doctorov, reinforced by Dorochov and the cavalry of VI Infantry Corps,[3] was sent to take Fominskoye on the 22nd, but he got only as far as Aristovo on that day. By 9 p.m., however, he learned from Dorochov and Seslavin, the capable raider, that the French were making a flank march from the old Kaluga road to the new one. On the basis of these reports, which arrived at Russian headquarters by 2 a.m. on the 23rd, Toll's recommendation that the French be intercepted at Malo-Jaroslavets was accepted because it was uncertain whether Borovsk could be reached in time.

Doctorov took off at once with four Cossack regiments galloping ahead of him, followed by Platov's Cossacks in the afternoon. By evening, the main army was on its way, after a reconnaissance in the direction of Voronovo found no French on the old Kaluga road.

The army now numbered 97,100 men and 20,000 Cossacks, with 622 guns (see Appendix XVIII). Among the line troops were 10,700 cavalry who, like the artillery, were quite good. It was, however, quite characteristic of Kutuzov that as soon as he heard of the French army's movement, he ordered the governor of Kaluga to take all the necessary precautions to prevent any of the supplies there from possibly falling into French hands.

MALO-JAROSLAVETS

On the French side, Eugene, who had also been assigned III Cavalry Corps, marched at 2 a.m. on the 23rd. His van, Delzons' division, reached Malo-Jaroslavets on the same day. Even though he found it occupied by Doctorov's Cossacks, Delzons was able to take the town easily; he had it occupied with two battalions. The rest of Eugene's troops did not go far beyond Borovsk, where Napoleon arrived on the same day.

Ney and the rear guard made a difficult night march over rain-soaked secondary roads to Buykassovo. Poniatowski occupied Vereia, with Mortier on his way there via Fominskoye. Junot was still in Moshaisk.

Napoleon did not think Kutuzov had marched from Tarutino; he assumed that the Russian had ordered the occupation of Aristovo because he feared a French envelopment. Thus, Napoleon hoped to get to Malo-Jaroslavets ahead of Kutuzov, secure the crossing of the Lusha there, and take the army across on the 24th. In this way, he hoped to reach Kaluga prepared to fight a battle for its possession so that he might base himself at Yelnia.

Assuming that his plan would be successful, he directed Junot in Moshaisk to send everything available there, by way of march formations and replacements to Vereia. General Teste, the governor of Viasma, was ordered to send Evers, with a detachment of 4000 march troops gathered in Viasma, to Yuhnov. Victor, informed of the evacuation of Moscow and the march to Kaluga, was assumed to be in Smolensk. He, too, was ordered on the 24th to take the Saxon-Polish Division Girard to Yelnia, where Baraquey d'Hilliers's division had collected large amounts of supplies. Napoleon, however, was to be bitterly disappointed.

Platov, speeding ahead of the main army, had already appeared in front of Malo-Jaroslavets, but he had immediately turned aside to cross the Lusha. Doctorov followed, arriving around 5 a.m. on the 24th. He had made it despite getting a late start from Aristovo, where he had had to wait for orders, and then being further delayed by having to throw two bridges across the Provta near Spaskoye. Doctorov attacked at once and threw out the two French battalions there. This marked the start of a bitter fight in which the French attempted to hold on despite the Russians' great superiority. At last, between 10 and 11 a.m., the viceroy arrived with the rest of his troops and engaged at once. Again, a seesaw ensued, with neither side gaining a lasting advantage.

By afternoon, the Guard and Davout arrived. Napoleon, who had sped ahead, placed them to the north of the town, across the road to Borovsk, and sent Gerard's (ex-Gudin's) and Compans's divisions to support Eugene.

Somewhat later, the Russian main army arrived. Raievsky, who was on the scene first, attacked at once, while the rest of the army placed itself south of the town, across the Kaluga road. Finally, Miloradovitch arrived as well. After the reconnaissance, he had been forced to make a long march to arrive on the battlefield, where he took his place on the extreme right of the Russian army. There can be little doubt that Kutuzov could have arrived much sooner, but he had still hoped to avoid a direct confrontation. Attempting to do so without being obvious, he had allowed the troops to take a long rest at Spaskoye.

The fight for the burning town lasted until 11 p.m., that is, 18 hours. On the Russian side, two additional divisions had been fed into the action, but the French eventually succeeded in expelling them. Although the French managed to turn back a final Russian attack, the possibility of a further French advance, beyond Malo-Jaroslavets, was now out of the question. The total number of troops committed to action came to about 24,000 on each side.[4] The losses had been heavy: about 8000 for the Russians, including General Dorochov, and about 6000 for the French, including General Delzons.

The Russian infantry, more than half of it consisting of recruits, had fought well but had been awkward in its tactical movements. Likewise, the Russian high command had not shown any skill whatever in making use of the favorable terrain. During the night, Kutuzov drew back a couple of miles and left only his advance guard in front of Malo-Jaroslavets. Although a tactical success may have eluded him, he had nevertheless achieved his purpose by blocking the road to Kaluga.

Napoleon, who had returned to Gorodnia with his guards, was now in a very difficult position. With the road to Kaluga closed, he could either fight his way through or retreat. But while Kutuzov had regained the numbers he had lost at Borodino, the French cavalry and artillery, the decisive factors there, could no longer be counted upon. Under these circumstances, the idea of a battle was risky, to say the least. If, as Clausewitz puts it, Napoleon had not believed that he was sufficiently wealthy to commit his guards at Borodino, then now, after hundreds of thousands had been sacrificed to the march on Moscow, he no longer had the wherewithal to risk a battle with the Russian main army. Nor was the idea of a retreat all that attractive. Now it would be necessary to march to Smolensk via Moshaisk, but that route led through country that had been stripped bare on the way in. In addition, no preparations whatever had been made for the army to pass that way. The few magazines there were totally inadequate. With Moshaisk 50 miles away, and Smolensk 240 miles beyond Moshaisk, such a march would precipitate the most serious losses imaginable.

It was a difficult decision. At first, Napoleon appeared ready to try his luck with another attack—possibly in the hope that Kutuzov would draw back voluntarily—because Ney had arrived in Fominskoye and was ordered to move to Borovsk. There, he was to leave the Vistula Legion and the Wuerttembergers to cover the parks and the baggage and place himself between Malo-Jaroslavets and Borovsk. This plan lasted only until 5 p.m. on the 25th, when Gourgaud advised the emperor that the Russians had not budged. Now Napoleon became uncertain and sought the advice of Murat, Bessieres, and Mouton-Lobau, the latter known throughout the army for his cold-nosed courage. Murat and Ney, expectedly, held out a hope for victory, but they also feared the consequences of even a success and thus recommended a retreat. Lobau bluntly told Napoleon to retreat at once, via Moshaisk, and not only to Smolensk but all the way back to the Niemen.

Napoleon was still not convinced. At daybreak he went up to the outposts to have a look for himself. There, only the timely appearance of the four duty squadrons—as usual, the emperor had raced off without waiting for anybody—saved him from falling into the hands of Kaisarov's Cossacks, who had gone around the French right during the night, capturing eleven guns. Armand de Caulaincourt, Napoleon's master of horse and brother of Auguste Caulaincourt (who had been killed at the Raievsky redoubt at Borodino), painted a vivid, if somewhat less "colorful," picture of the incident.

Once Napoleon had decided to have a look for himself, he wanted to take off at once into the predawn darkness, without giving those who were charged with the security of his person a chance to react. Fortunately, Berthier and Bessieres arrived just in time to help Caulaincourt persuade the emperor to wait until dawn, because the Guard had arrived in its bivouacs after dark and no one was certain just where the other corps were. But after a message arrived advising that some peasants and prisoners had brought news that the Cossacks had withdrawn, there was no holding him any longer. Accompanied by only a few officers and his customary picket of ten or twelve chasseurs, who guarded his person around the clock, the emperor took off in his coach. Caulaincourt relates:

> It was hardly dawn when, three-quarters of a mile from headquarters we found ourselves face to face with some Cossacks. . . .

It was still so dark that we were alerted only by their shouts, and were almost upon them before we could see them. It was so unexpected to find them inside the lines where our Guard were bivouacked that (I must admit) we paid little heed to the first shouts. It was only when the shouting increased and closed in around the emperor that General Rapp . . . came back to the emperor and said "Halt, Sire! The Cossacks!" . . . Only the clash of arms and the shouts of men fighting indicated the direction of the skirmish, or even that we had fallen in with the enemy.

The emperor was left alone with the Prince of Neuchatel [Berthier] and myself. All three of us [dismounted and] held our swords drawn. As the fighting was near and shifting closer towards him, the emperor decided to move on several yards, to the crest of the rise, so as to see better. At this moment, the remaining chasseurs of the picket caught up with us; and the squadrons in attendance . . . came up immediately after.[5]

There must have been quite a few Cossacks, because Caulaincourt goes on to state that the four duty squadrons had a hard fight on their hands before it was over. Worst of all, it had apparently all happened inside the French pickets—if, indeed, there had been any. Such lapses on the part of the French were quite common. Caulaincourt had good cause to complain, as he continues:

If these details had not the testimony of the army and of so many trustworthy men to confirm them, they might be called in question. And how, indeed, can anyone believe that a man of such foresight, a sovereign, and the greatest captain of all time, could have been in danger of capture five hundred yards from his headquarters?[6]

After this incident, Napoleon spent the rest of the day scouting around and did not return to Gorodnia until 5 p.m. There, another conference with his intimates resulted in the same conclusion: Retreat to Moshaisk. Only Davout expressed a preference for going to Medyn. But the Russians blocked the direct route there, so it could have been reached only by a detour via Vereia. However, the Russian cavalry was known to be on the Vereia road as well, not to mention that this route called for the crossing of several rivers. And perhaps Kutuzov would again get to Medyn ahead of him. So, on the 26th, the decision was made to march to Moshaisk. This decision, one of the most fateful of Napoleon's entire career, would send his army to its doom.

Kutuzov also decided to withdraw on the same day. Even though he had made up his mind to have a battle and had written the tsar of his resolve on the evening of the 24th, the stress of the previous few days had been too much for him. The immediate presence of Napoleon continued to intimidate him, and the threat of an attack, which had hung over his head all day long, had finally brought the scales down on the side of caution again. Since he was still unaware that Moscow had been abandoned by the French, he did not see Napoleon's movements as the beginning of a retreat, as Toll did; rather, he thought they were the start of an offensive against Kaluga. This idea was reinforced when, in the course of the day, news came in of an action fought near Medyn. The Cossacks had attacked a detachment sent forward by Poniatowski, and it was thrown back with the loss of five guns. Again, he saw in this the opening move of yet another French envelopment.

Thus, against Toll's pleas to attack or, at least, to stay in place, Kutuzov opted to retire to Gontsharevo and Detshino, where he intended to take his next position covering Kaluga. This move was under way by 5 a.m. on the 26th. Only Miloradovitch, who had returned on the 25th, reinforced with fourteen Cossack regiments, remained in contact with the French.

Napoleon, who had gone forward again on the morning of the 26th to have another look, received news of the enemy's withdrawal even before the army had started on its retreat. Once more, fortune opened its arms to him by removing the obstacle that had blocked his way to Medyn. If he took the mass of the army along the road to Yuhnov via Medyn, while the trains were placed on the main road with the necessary escort, then it was still possible to save the army, especially if he could see his way clear to getting rid of part of his artillery to facilitate the movement of the rest.

The fact that he did not do this raises the question of whether his mind was fixed on the idea that Yuhnov could be reached only via Kaluga or whether he shrank away from executing a flank march to Medyn because the Russian advance guard was so near. Had Napoleon, contrary to his usual habit, not underestimated the power of his own reputation and, perhaps, overestimated the enemy, the Russians might have continued their withdrawal. Even if Kutuzov did not abandon Kaluga, Napoleon might still have been able to execute his flank march without being disturbed by the enemy.

Although explanations can be found for Napoleon's decision not to attack, less evident are reasons for the unfortunate march to Malo-Jaroslavets. It had been made on the assumption that Kutuzov had not marched from Tarutino and that he had ordered the occupation of Aristovo simply because he had feared a French envelopment. The detour had cost the French far too much. The supplies hauled along from Moscow, and what had been consumed on the way, would have sufficed the army as far as Viasma, and the supplies now being hauled from Dorogobush to Yelnia could have remained in place. Added to this must be the fact that until Malo-Jaroslavets the army had advanced; its confidence in its leadership had been intact, and the army had still perceived itself to be invincible. Now, however, it turned its back on the enemy, and with this move came the loss of self-confidence. The final deterioration would soon follow.

Thus, when Napoleon finally began his retreat to Moshaisk, the march was bound to be far more destructive than it would have been had he gone that way in the first place. Not only had he robbed himself of what he had hoped to gain by going to Malo-Jaroslavets, but he had also failed to seize the opportunity the enemy had offered him at the last moment. His genius had dimmed under the pressure of his first major failure, which was so overwhelming to him that it was impossible to restore the confidence of those around him. This, in turn, had reinfected him. Thus, he fell into using the sort of half measures he had always punished his adversaries for using. As at Vitebsk, Smolensk, and Borodino, his power of decision had deserted him. These lapses, following each other at ever-shortening intervals, mark the decline of the genius. Although he was still lacking an energetic opponent who would exploit these lapses, he had to cope with the disadvantages of his own situation, disadvantages that he had brought upon himself. In this campaign, the great captain was not to be defeated by the enemy but by his very own mistakes.

NOTES

1. Left behind were about 3500 to 4000 men of Young Guard Division Laborde, 4000 dismounted cavalry men, and 500 men of mounted cavalry brigade, an artillery company and two engineer companies.
2. These included:
   The Vistula Legion
   2 divisions and the light cavalry of I Corps
   The light cavalry of III Corps
   2 Bavarian cavalry brigades of IV Corps
   V Corps
   I, II, III, and IV Cav. Corps
3. The reinforcements were as follows:
   VI Inf. Corps (7th and 27th Inf. Div.)
   Dorochov's detachment: 51 battalions, 4 squadrons, and 3 Cossack regiments, with 8 guns

      3 light guard cavalry regiments of I Cav. Corps
      Several Cossack regiments
4. The troops involved in the action were as follows:
    On the French side:
      The infantry of IV Corps
      Div. Gerard and Compans of I Corps
    On the Russian side:
      VI Inf. Corps
      VIII Inf. Corps
      3rd Div. of III Inf. Corps
      27th Div. of VIII Inf. Corps
      Dorochov's detachment
5. Caulaincourt, Armand Augustin. *Memoires du General de Caulaincourt, Duc de Vincence, Grand Ecuyer de l'Empereur.* Paris 1933. 3 Vols.
6. Ibid.

22. Back to Smolensk

In order to give the army and its still endless train a good head start, Davout delayed the departure of his own troops, as well as I and III Cavalry Corps, from Malo-Jaroslavets. They remained behind until 9 p.m., observing the enemy with a strong forward detachment. To secure the flank of the retreat, Napoleon sent Poniatowski to Yegorievskoye and ordered Junot to withdraw to Viasma as soon as the army came up. Evers's detachment was directed to Viasma as well. The supplies that had just been hauled from Dorogobush to Yelnia (on the assumption that the army would retreat in that direction) had to be sent back, as was Baraquey d'Hilliers's division, because the army was now marching toward Moshaisk.

Napoleon reached Vereia on the 27th with the Guard and II and III Cavalry Corps; there, he was reunited with the Young Guard. The remaining corps either stayed in place or made only short marches. On the 28th, the bulk of the army was collected between Kolotzkoi, Vereia, and Moshaisk. Since Davout was still as far back as Borovsk, the entire column was 60 miles long. Poniatowski was on his way from Yegorievskoye to Gshatsk, where he inserted himself into the column.

On the afternoon of the 28th, Davout sent Napoleon a report stating that he had only Cossacks left in front of him; along with the report he sent a captured Russian officer who said that Kutuzov was on his way to Smolensk. Even though Napoleon thought the information about Kutuzov was false, he was nevertheless so disquieted by the idea that he went to the van of the army and henceforth remained there.

Napoleon's personal behavior, which had given way to complete passivity, caused even Thiers, the architect of the Napoleonic legend, to remark:

> In the midst of his guard, which marched at the point, consuming what little food there was, leaving only dead horses for those who came behind, Napoleon saw nothing of the retreat and wanted to see nothing because that would have forced him to see the terrible results of his errors. He preferred to refute them and insisted instead—[5 statute] miles distant and without admitting to its plight—on complaining about the rear guard instead of leading it.[1]

On October 29 and 30, the greatest part of the army passed over the battlefield of Borodino. It still presented a frightful sight and had a depressing effect on the doomed army. Cadavers, both equine and human, were visible in quantity everywhere. Half decomposed, then dried out and mummified by the fall winds, their density marked the spots where the action had been especially heavy. The redoubts themselves were ringed by walls of bodies. The graves of some who had been buried were already overblown by mounds of drifting leaves and could hardly be identified. Only the rough-hewn monument Ney had ordered erected for his friend Montbrun still stood. Among the allied soldiers, a bitterness against the man who had plunged them into this colossal folly began to rise to the surface.

In the days following, the entire army was back on the main road, marching in a single column that, even though it had shortened, was still 40 miles long. The maneuvering had come to an end; from here onward engagements would be mainly artless confrontations. They have military interest only because they show how much resistance desperate men can put up when fighting for survival. Soon, the first harbinger of the horrors to come manifested itself. The winter, long overdue, at last checked in during the night of October 27–28, when the thermometer sank to 23°F (-4°R).

As yet, there were only isolated instances of shortage and want, but the supplies the troops had carried along were beginning to run out. The ambulatory sick and wounded, who had dragged themselves along as best they could, began to be abandoned by the hundreds (along with vehicles that had either broken down or lost their draft teams). There had been neither the necessary transport nor the personnel to look after these men. Indeed, their chances for survival would have been far better had they remained behind, but that was something no one had been prepared to do. Thus, even though the retreat was only a few days under way, the wreckage, both human and material, was already beginning to mark the path of the army. It started to poison the morale of the troops, and the loose bonds of discipline began to weaken even further.

Fighting broke out between the Westphalians and the Young Guard when the latter attempted to help themselves to supplies that had spilled out of an overturned wagon belonging to the former. Also, the tail of the army, the stragglers, began to grow in alarming proportions as more and more men dropped out of their formations. But as the privations intensified, the ranks of the stragglers began to thin out again.

On top of everything, the Cossacks were pressing in from all sides, and there was no longer any cavalry to hold them back. If not for their pathological fear of musketry, they would have gone after the formations. However, for the time being, there were plenty of stragglers to hold their attention, and it was these men who first suffered at the hands of the Cossacks.

The numbers of these unfortunates will never be known. Many met with horrible deaths by torture, although this was done not so much by the Cossacks as by the enraged peasants, who were beginning to reemerge from their hiding places. But all, Cossack and peasant, were greatly embittered, especially over the murder of hundreds of Russian prisoners, who were being shot in droves on Napoleon's orders when they could no longer keep up with the marching columns. The reason advanced for this atrocity was to prevent the Russians from learning about the condition of the French army. This, and Napoleon's order that the rear guard was to burn every village and town along the way, leaving desolation in its wake, helped ensure that the French who fell behind met with little compassion or sympathy.

On the Russian side, the pursuit continued to be mainly in the hands of the Cossacks. Kutuzov, still not fully convinced that the ogre was actually retreating, kept his army at a prudent distance. Not until the 29th did he receive confirmed news indicating that Moscow had indeed been evacuated and that the French were in full retreat to the west.

Understandably, the Russians believed that the retreat would go toward Subtsov and Bieloi, the northern route, which would have posed no obstacles for the French. The pursuit was to take the Russian army on a parallel course. Only Platov was to stay directly on the heels of the French. For this purpose, his Cossack corps was reinforced with some infantry.[1] Another column was formed under Ozarovski[2] to go toward Yelnia.

Thus, when the Russian army finally marched on the afternoon of the 29th, the direction it took did not put it on a collision course with the French. Instead of heading for Viasma, it went to Moshaisk. On the 30th, when Kutuzov reached Kremenskoye, the Russian headquarters at last obtained a clear image. It was long overdue. Typically, Platov was totally lacking in his discharge of light cavalry duties and almost always limited himself to doing whatever the moment suggested; he sent reports only in exceptional circumstances. However, on the basis of his last report, the army was finally aimed in the proper direction, that is, toward Viasma. Platov now tacked himself directly onto Davout's heels, picking up twenty guns, most of which had been left behind because there were not enough horses left to haul them.

In the meanwhile, Napoleon continued his drive to the west. The head of the column, the Young Guard and Westphalians, reached Viasma on the 31st. There, the army was joined by the local garrison and Evers's column, which was now broken up. The troops were returned to their respective corps, and the Hessians were incorporated into the Guard. Davout's rear guard had gotten only as far as Gridnevo, 60 miles to the rear. Constantly scrapping with the Cossacks, he had been forced to leave behind the guns mentioned above, as well as many vehicles. A large number of ammunition caissons were blown up, so that they would not fall into the hands of the Russians; the thunder and flashes of the explosions sent shock waves of fear through the stragglers, who were unaware of what was going on. Still, even now, Napoleon brushed off Ney's repeated suggestion that they leave some of the superfluous artillery behind and use the draft horses that would thus be redundant to make the rest of the column more mobile.

In Viasma, Napoleon received more disconcerting news. Tshitshagov had driven Schwarzenberg to Brest and St. Cyr had vacated Polotsk, forcing Victor to come to his aid. This put the line of retreat in great danger, with no help in the offing. Even worse was the news that due to Victor's departure from Smolensk, Baraquey d'Hilliers had not received his change of orders and was still in Yelnia, along with the supplies that were to have been moved back to Dorogobush. Of course, Victor's departure put an end to all notions about wintering in Smolensk and ending the retreat there.

Since Eugene made contact with Miloradovitch on November 1, while passing through Zarevo-Saimishtshe, it became necessary to slow down and give Davout a chance to close up. While the army made short marches, Davout had to make a 30-mile forced march, fighting an engagement with Platov along the way. Despite Miloradovitch's immediate proximity and a necessary halt to do some bridge construction, the ingenious Davout succeeded in passing through the defile of Zarevo-Saimishtshe in the dead of night. Miloradovitch had missed a splendid opportunity to do some serious damage.

Napoleon spent November 1 in Viasma. There, he ordered that henceforth the troops were to march in closed squares, as they had once done in

Egypt, in order to minimize losses to the Cossacks, who were everywhere, day and night. On the 2nd, the points got to just beyond Semlevo. Ney, who was now to assume rear-guard duties, remained in Viasma. He was to relieve Davout because Napoleon was dissatisfied with the latter's performance, complaining that he halted every time the Cossacks made an attack, thus holding up the main force. The viceroy and Poniatowski hung back, halting in Federovskoie to receive Davout, who was still far to the rear.

The French army was in a precarious position. Only Napoleon, with the Guard and the Westphalians, had a head start. Ney, still in Viasma, had the Russian main army only 20 miles away on his flank. If the Russians were to go straight on to the city, it could hardly be expected that either Eugene, Poniatowski, or Davout, the latter accompanied by Miloradovitch on his flank, could get there in time to help him. Even though this dangerous situation called for Napoleon's presence and even though the emperor was very much aware of the plight of his rearward corps, he continued his forward march on November 3. Murat and the Guard reached Slavkovo, while Junot got to Dorogobush.

Meanwhile, Miloradovitch advanced against the main road from the south. His cavalry encountered Davout's points between 8 and 9 a.m. near Maximovo, just as Davout's main force, under severe pressure from Platov, was emerging from Federovskoie. Since Eugene and Poniatowski had already marched off, Davout was in serious trouble. Fortunately, Eugene noticed, and he ordered an about-face at once. Thus, when the Russian infantry approached from the south around 10 a.m., Davout had already passed behind Eugene's receiving position. Eugene made a right turn and faced the Russians, but he was pressed back via Myasoyedova. Since Napoleon was not present, the French generals, none of whom would willingly subordinate themselves to another, held a council and decided that the situation called for a continued retreat.[3]

Eugene and Poniatowski were the first to depart, around 2 p.m. Since they were under constant attack from the Russians, their retreat was not made in the best of order. However, Ney was ready to receive them at Viasma. Davout followed, but the posture of his troops had steadily diminished during the time they had spent as the rear guard. Now, under pressure from the enemy, they fell apart altogether and streamed through Viasma in great disorder. After nightfall, when the last of them had gone, Ney also evacuated the burning city, but the disengagement was bought only at the cost of another stiff fight. To Napoleon, a complaining Ney wrote later, "Better measures would have led to better results." Once again, three commanders had held a council and come up with nothing better than the realization that they would have to continue their retreat. Typically, the retreat was conducted by three separate commanders rather than permitting one to coordinate the movements of all.

Of the 37,500 French still under arms, including about 3000 cavalry hardly worthy of the description, about two-thirds had been engaged. Of these, about 4000 had been killed or wounded. In addition, the Russians had picked up several thousand prisoners, nearly all of them stragglers, and three guns. The strength of the Russians, who had lost about 1800 men, was placed at 23,500 men and 3000 Cossacks by Bogdanovich. This includes the two cuirassier divisions, which had been sent forward from the main army but which did not take part in these combats. Other sources place the number of Cossacks at 10,000. However, given the poor value of the Cossacks in formal actions, their actual number was immaterial. Still, Bogdanovich's numbers appear somewhat low.

While the action was in progress, Kutuzov had taken the Russian main army, about 60,000 men, from Dubrovna, barely 20 miles from Viasma, to Bykovo. Despite being urged by Yermolov, Konovnitzyn, and Toll to take the army to the scene of the action, Kutuzov had sent only the cuirassiers. Had Napoleon been in Kutuzov's place, he would hardly have missed the opportunity to deliver an annihilating stroke to the enemy. He would have sent his entire cavalry to Viasma early in the morning, with the infantry moving in its wake as fast as it could be driven. Kutuzov's failure can be explained only by the fact that despite the Cossacks who were swarming around the French on all sides, it was only after the action at Viasma when he learned of the state of dissolution prevailing among the French. How suddenly this dissolution had set in is best illustrated by the fact that these same corps, which had mustered 73,283 men when they departed from Moscow just 2 weeks earlier, were down to about 37,500 effectives at Viasma. The combat losses sustained during this period, however, hardly came to more than 6000 men.

On November 4, Eugene, Poniatowski, and Davout got as far as Semlevo. Ney's rear guard, which was the only corps apart from the Guard that still maintained a semblance of order, was somewhat farther back. Indeed, the continued existence of I, IV, and V Corps was in dire peril due to the pervasive disorder that had taken hold in those corps. Fezensac, an eye-witness, reports that only the men in the Italian Guard still maintained order. The rest were dispirited and worn out, and most of them had thrown away their arms after their formations had dissolved.

Napoleon, who had learned of the events of the 3rd but did not as yet know much about the details, halted at Slavkovo; the Westphalians were at Dorogobush. Thinking it was time to put a damper on the offensive-mindedness of the Russians, he formulated the somewhat adventurous plan of laying an ambush for them between those two towns. Soon, however, he realized the impossibility of this as he learned of the true condition of the forces that were still to the rear, and he returned to Dorogobush on November 5 with Murat and the Guard. The other corps got to Slavkovo. Ney, who was not to permit himself unnecessary delays, as Davout had done, got as far as Semlevo, where he had another brush with the Russians. The army was still stretched out in a column 25 miles long.

During the following days, the army pressed on toward Smolensk, 65 miles away from Dorogobush. Now hunger began to set in. The Westphalians had drawn their last meager rations on the 4th, and they, being at the head of the column, fared much better than those in the rear. The fact that they were devastated at a rate faster than the rest of the troops is most likely due in large part to Junot. There have been claims made (and not only by Westphalians) that his troops, instead of being allowed to find what little shelter was to be had, were forced to bivouac out in the open, night after night, to protect their French commander's private caravan loaded with loot.

Horse and dog meat had already become staples of the soldiers' diet. The men would pounce on fallen artillery or train horses almost the instant they were down and sometimes would cut them up without bothering to first give them the *coup de grace*. Only the Guard had still received a little flour in Gshatsk, Viasma, and Dorogobush. The condition of the army now became extreme because the Cossacks, swarming everywhere, made it impossible to spread out in quest of forage. Starvation began to reap a grim harvest at an ever-accelerating rate. To leave the columns in quest of food was a daring undertaking, but the overwhelming need again and again pushed men into attempting it.

Away from the columns, a gruesome death awaited most of them. As in Spain, the worst excesses had overtones of religious fanaticism. Invoking the name of God, the aroused peasants committed unspeakable cruelties and almost every kind of torture imaginable to prolong the agony of their victims. In this they were morally abetted by the fact that the average Russian believed that all west Europeans were unbaptized heathens who had been led into holy Russia by the anti-Christ. This is the way the situation had been presented to the uneducated population; from St. Petersburg, Moscow, and the Russian army headquarters, manifestos attesting to these "facts" were circulated in every market square.

As the French columns moved on, the deterioration of the weather steadily added its effect to the hunger. The winter had been rather late in coming, but the temperature dropped to 23°F during the night of October 27–28 and to 14°F on November 1. On the 4th the temperature began to drop in earnest, down to 5°F (-12°R), and with this cold wave came the snow, causing the roads to ice over. The horses were weak and had not been sharp-shod, which would have given them traction on the ice, so they again fell by the hundreds. Once they were down, whether from exhaustion or just a plain slip, there was no getting up from the ice.

In the days following, the weather became milder again, but on the 7th the temperatures began to drop once more. This time, the cold was intensified by the rise of a sharp north wind, which sent the wind-chill factor plummeting even as the continuing snowfall covered man and horse with a crust of ice. During the night of November 8–9, when the thermometer registered 5°F again, 300 men froze to death in a single bivouac. Desperate men who fled to the campfires of the Russians were generally accepted with compassion—not all, but a great many. The Russian soldiers paid little attention to them and usually marched off in the morning, leaving them behind. Then the peasants came and began their gruesome work.

Even though the winter of 1806–1807 had been colder and had lasted longer in many areas than that of 1812–1813, the troops had been far better equipped and supplied in that earlier campaign. Now they lacked everything. Inadequately protected against the cold, with their immune systems and powers of resistance weakened by hunger and exertions, they continued marching day after day and bivouacking night after night. Even the strong became weak, the healthy sick.

Since the action at Viasma, Platov, with Miloradovitch just behind him, had followed the French along the main road. At Semlevo, Platov turned off to the right, leaving Miloradovitch directly behind the French. The Russian main army rested at Bykovo on the 4th. There, Toll's recommendation that the army march to Orsza via Yelnia and Krasnoi was accepted. This move would prevent the French from taking the southernmost road to Smolensk, which led through relatively untouched countryside. At the same time, Tshitshagov, Wittgenstein, and Oertel were ordered to coordinate their movements with those of the main army. On the 5th, the army started on its way toward Yelnia.

On the 6th, Napoleon reached Michailevka, where troublesome news awaited him, from Paris as well as from Victor. In Paris, a conspiracy led by General Malet had broken out during the night of October 22–23. Even though it had been put down after only a few hours, it once again exposed the shaky underpinnings of Napoleon's rule at home. It also filled him with dire forebodings concerning the future of his dynasty if something were to happen to him. It was probably at this point when the idea of leaving the army and speeding on ahead to Paris began to occupy his thoughts.

Of more immediate concern was the report from Victor. He had suffered

a reverse against Wittgenstein at Czasniki on October 31 and had withdrawn
to Senno, only 30 miles from the main army's line of retreat. On November
7, Victor was ordered to recapture Polotsk without delay. In order to impress
upon him the need to do so, Napoleon even gave him a hint of the army's
condition. "The emperor and the army will be in Smolensk tomorrow, worn
out by a march of 120 road hours . . . the army's cavalry is on foot."
Closemouthed as Napoleon now was (in contrast to normal times) in order
to hide his feelings, this was the only admission of the army's dire straits
that he could wring from himself. Macdonald and Schwarzenberg were left
completely in the dark about the true condition of the central army group,
which was an extremely serious error considering the general lack of initiative
on the part of these commanders on the flanks.

On this day, when the first stragglers from the Guard were observed,
the greatest part of the French army crossed the Dnieper at Solovieva-
Pereprava. Eugene, who was to link up with Victor via Dukovtshina and
Vitebsk, had already crossed at Dorogobush. Ney was overtaken by Miloradovitch along the Osma and pushed to Dorogobush. There, he made a
stand to give the army the time it needed to cross the Dnieper, but he was
finally forced to retreat, leaving six guns behind. After this action, Miloradovitch left the main road when he was ordered to close up to the main
army by marching left toward Liaskova. Since Platov[4] was already following
the viceroy toward Dukovtshina, all that remained on the main road was
Grekov I[5] with part of the Cossacks and Yurkovski with some regulars from
Miloradovitch's advance guard.

Napoleon reached Smolensk on November 9. There, he received news
of the Russian occupation of Vitebsk. In Smolensk, the army was reinforced
by about 7500 men[6] from the city's garrison and from Baraquey d'Hilliers's
division, which was still arriving from Yelnia. The last echelon of this
division, Brigade Augerau (Jean Pierre Augerau, a brigadier; not the marshal), was unable to close up in time and was surrounded in Liaskova on
the 9th, where its 1740 men had to lay down their arms. While the Guard
remained in Smolensk on the 10th, Junot's Westphalians and the Poles
under Zaionczek (who commanded in place of Poniatowski, who had been
taken ill) were pushed about 5 and 7 miles, respectively, along the roads to
Yelnia and Mstislavl. Unfortunately, they were unable to prevent Russian
raiders from taking several magazines near Smolensk and about 1500 cattle,
which had been gathered there for the army. Several transports coming from
Mstislavl were also captured. Only a single transport of 200 oxen reached
Smolensk.

Ney's rear guard, which was now faced by only weak forces under Grekov
and Karpenkov,[7] still stood at Solovieva-Pereprava on the 10th, with Davout

in support near Tsuginovo. From there, Ney was ordered to make a short march in order to give Eugene a chance to close up. The viceroy had been forced to ford the Wop under the most difficult conditions on the 9th (his rear guard crossed on the 10th) while on his way to Dukovtshina. The ford was becoming unusable when Platov arrived. This gave rise to a panic that caused thousands of stragglers, thirty-seven guns, and all the baggage to fall into the hands of the Russians. In the ensuing pursuit, Platov captured another twenty-three guns. With only 6000 men and 12 guns left, Eugene continued his march to Dukovtshina and arrived there on the 10th. To do this, however, he first had to fight his way past the advance guard of Count Kutuzov's raiding corps, which had left Moscow on November 3. This action cost Eugene another 500 men and 2 guns. Hearing of the loss of Vitebsk, Eugene departed for Smolensk during the night of November 11–12 and arrived there on the 12th, after being surrounded by swarms of Cossacks and losing another two guns along the way. Ney, who had spent the 12th at Tsuginovo, had a sharp action with Karpenkov. Over the next 2 days, he fell back into the St. Petersburg suburb of Smolensk, where he replaced Davout. These actions resulted in the loss of another twenty-nine guns.

The losses the army had suffered since leaving Moscow were frightful. Numbering 107,955 men, with 569 guns, on October 18, it had been joined by another 15,000 men, with 18 guns.[8] Of this total, 44,000 men had been lost. Of these losses, only a small fraction were combat losses, sustained in the actions of Malo-Jaroslavets, Viasma, and several lesser scrapes. More than two-thirds of the men lost had either been captured or fallen victim to starvation and cold. Of the remainder of the army group, about 35,000 had left the ranks and become stragglers. Most of these had thrown away their arms and mingled with the noncombatants and refugees, who had attached themselves mostly to the baggage trains. They followed the army, encumbering its movements and exacerbating the supply difficulties without adding anything to its fighting power. Even greater was the loss of horses. In addition, 138 guns[9] had been lost so far, and another 140 would soon be left behind in Smolensk.

In Smolensk, Napoleon expended considerable energy in an attempt to get the army back into some sort of condition. With the help of the supplies and reinforcements there and by pressing several thousand stragglers back into the ranks, he achieved some reconstructive work. He reorganized the remainders of formations into temporary units, issued fifty rounds of ammunition for every musket, and provided each corps with 6 days' rations (and the Guard with 14 days' worth). The corps, however, received only meat, flour, rye and liquor—no bread, zwieback, salt, or other comestibles. Distribution of supplies was made only upon the presentation of a *bon en regle*, duly executed by an officer. But it was far too late for such measures. The stragglers, who no longer had any officers to issue them with these *bons*, came up empty and were driven to commit the worst excesses, which ended up in bloody riots. For example, 300 entirely useful horses, who had hauled the supplies into Smolensk, were slaughtered in the streets for their meat. Warehouses still containing stores went up in flames, while the stores of others were spilled into the streets and trampled underfoot by rioters.

Still, the attempts to restore the army did bring the number of combatants back up to about 49,000 men[10] (37,000 infantry, about 5100 cavalry, and 7000 artillery personnel). Despite the 140 guns that had to be left behind, the army still had 300; this was far too many, in terms of both available ammunition and draft teams. For this reason, another 112 guns would have to be abandoned on the very next march.

The Guard and I, II, and IV Corps (the latter had been reissued new guns to replace those that had been lost) were still in passable condition. On the other hand, the Poles and Westphalians, the latter now joined by the dismounted cavalry, numbered only a few hundred men. The cavalry was in particularly bad condition. What was left of the Polish and German cavalry was formed into a cavalry corps under Latour-Maubourg. Over the next few days it shrank from 1900 to about 400. The rest of the cavalry, that is, the troopers who still had horses, were with the corps.

This was the extent of the repairs Napoleon had been able to make during the brief stay at Smolensk. Of course, the material damage suffered during the previous several weeks was far too great to be undone with the resources Smolensk had to offer. But had the reorganization revitalized the moral strength of what was left of the central army group? Only time would tell.

NOTES

1. Thiers, L.A. *Histoire du consulat et de l'Empire*. Paris 1845–1869.
2. The column included 1 jaeger regiment, 1 hussar regiment, and 4 Cossack regiments, with 6 guns.
3. The Russians' strength at Viasma was as follows:

	Men
II Inf. Corps	7,000
IV Inf. Corp	7,000

	Men	
II and III Cav. Corps	3,500	
		17,500	under Miloradovitch
26th Inf. Div., VII Corps	4,000	
Cossacks	3,000	
		7,000	under Platov
Others (the cuirassiers, 1 Cossack regiment)	2,000	
Total	26,500	

The French strength at Viasma was as follows:

	Men (current)	*Men on Oct. 18*
I Corps	13,000	27,499
III Corps	6,000	9,597
IV Corps	12,000	23,963
V Corps	3,500	4,844
I and III Cav. Corps and the light cavalry of the above	3,000	7,430
Total	37,500	73,283

4. Under Platov were 1 jaeger regiment, 6 Cossack regiments, and 1 Cossack battery.
5. Grekov I had 5 Cossack regiments; Yurkovski had 1 jaeger regiment, 2 dragoon regiments, and Cossacks, with 4 guns.
6. Joining in Smolensk were about 1500 men:
   3 Polish third battalions of IX Corps
   1 Polish cavalry regiment of V Corps

Baraquey d'Hilliers's troops, 6000 men in all, consisted of:

1000 march infantry of the Guard

1565 march infantry of I Corps and 500 march infantry of III Corps (probably the 1st and 2nd March Half-Brigades)

2500 infantry of III Corps, 129th Line, and an Illyrian regiment

3 march squadrons

1 battery, several artillery, and 1 engineer company

Brigade Augerau, probably the 4th March Half-Brigade, had 1740 men on the day of its destruction.

7. Yurkovski had returned to Miloradovitch with some of his Cossacks and had left behind only Colonel Karpenkov with a regiment of jaegers, one of dragoons, and one of Cossacks, with four guns. The other dragoon regiment had been left with Grekov.

8. The 15,000 men consisted of the following:

7500 men under Baraquey d'Hilliers and Charpentier in Smolensk

1740 men of Brig. Augerau (lost before coming up)

4,000 men under Evers in Viasma

700 men from the garrison of Gshatsk

500 men from the garrison of Viasma

500 men from the garrison of Dorogobush

The garrison of Viasma was possibly stronger and Evers's column a bit weaker than the figures presented, but the total number of men is probably correct.

These troops were earmarked for use, or had already been used, to reinforce the corps. Only the disposition of the men from the Smolensk garrison remains in doubt. Consisting of about 1500 Poles (3 battalions and 3 squadrons), these men did not join V Corps. Possibly, the infantry was temporarily assigned to the Guard and the cavalry to the cavalry reserve.

9. The French gun losses to date were:

5 at Medyn

11 at Malo-Jaroslavets

20 at Kolotzkoi and Zarevo-Saimishtshe

3 at Viasma

6 at Dorogobush

29 during the further rear-guard actions under Ney

64 at the crossing of the Wop and the actions following

140 left behind in Smolensk.

Kutuzov's report arrives at the same total (278) but adds:

8 from Borodino (actually Shevardino)

26 found in Moscow

37 from Vinkovo

Thus, the grand total comes to 349.

10. The combatants consisted of the following:

	Infantry	Cavalry	Artillery
The Guard	14,000	2,000	
I Corps	10,000		
III Corps	6,000		
IV Corps	5,000	1,200	7,000
V Corps	800		
VIII Corps	700		
Dismounted cavalry	500		
Cavalry reserve		1,900	

There were approximately 300 guns.

23. Krasnoi

Napoleon had given up hope of wintering in Smolensk even before he got there. When Victor reported on November 9 that he was standing at Czereia, with Wittgenstein at Czasniki, Napoleon responded on the 11th that it might be possible to let the army go into winter cantonments behind the Dvina and Dnieper. This was another forlorn hope. Could he really be serious about the idea after he had been informed in Smolensk that Tshit-shagov had arrived in Slonim on November 6, possibly on his way to Minsk, with nothing to stop him from placing himself squarely across the French lines of communication? Regardless of Napoleon's illusions about the ca-pacities of the Russian main army, seriously considering such an idea had to be out of the question.

In his letter to Victor, he expressed the thought that the Russians were just as tired and worn out as his own troops and just as incapable of fighting another battle—an assumption for which there was no justification what-soever. Since Viasma, there had been no contact with the Russian regulars, as only Cossacks had come into action. Yet similar contentions appear again in his correspondence during 1813, in which his phrases have the ring of a man who is trying to convince himself as much as those whom he is ad-dressing.

But Victor needed a spur. Given the circumspection of the Russian high command, there was always the possibility that if Victor was pushed into action and succeeded in handing Wittgenstein a reverse, this would surely make a suitable impression on the Russians and bring them up short. And, of course, it was also imperative that Wittgenstein be pushed away from Napoleon's threatened line of retreat. Thus, in the letter of the 11th, the emperor informed Victor that the army's march to Orsza could only proceed slowly, but he also directed him to push Wittgenstein into a retreat. It was made clear to Victor that the army's continued progress hinged on his offensive, and while the condition of the army could not pass without mention, this was attenuated by presenting the Russians as being no better off. The letter contains another interesting aspect. In spurring Victor to make haste, Napoleon implies that Kutuzov might join Wittgenstein via Vitebsk and that, if this were to happen, they could be mastered only in a main battle, which, in view of the advanced season, was no longer possible. Chambray is quite justified in wondering whether Napoleon was misled by the situation or whether he deliberately suggested this possibility to urge Victor to act.

It seems, however, that Napoleon had drawn the wrong conclusion from the capture of Vitebsk. Perhaps he thought at first that Kutuzov had crossed the main road to join Wittgenstein and that only raiders had remained to· the south of Smolensk. But then Kutuzov's movements and the statements of prisoners, which no longer left any doubt about Kutuzov's approach, caused Napoleon to assume that Kutuzov was merely awaiting the evacuation of Smolensk to go to Vitebsk from there.

Napoleon's dispositions for the continuance of the retreat make it clear that he did not believe the road to Krasnoi was threatened. Otherwise, he would have marched on the right (northern) side of the Dnieper and kept his army closer together. Soon, he was to be robbed of this illusion as well as the one concerning his estimate of the condition of the Russian army.

Napoleon wanted to make the stay at Smolensk as short as possible once it became clear that the city could not serve as a center for winter quarters. He wanted to be off by the 11th but had to wait for Eugene to catch up. Thus, only the Poles stepped off on that day, followed by Junot with the Westphalians, the dismounted cavalry, and the artillery park. On the 13th the Vistula Legion departed, followed on the 14th by the emperor with the Guard and the cavalry. Eugene, Davout, and Ney, the latter reinforced with one of Davout's divisions, were to follow at 1-day intervals. Again, Ney was to destroy whatever could be destroyed. The intention was that retreating in echelons would ease the march, which had been made more difficult by the large numbers of stragglers and vehicles and by the new cold wave that had set in. (On November 13, the thermometer had descended to $-6°F$, or $-17°R$.) Of course, given the weakness of the leading echelons, the retreat would be possible only if the main road were not threatened by the enemy. However, since this was not the case, the order of march, with each corps separated from the next by a day's march, was an open invitation to disaster.

The Russian main army, on its march to Krasnoi via Yelnia, reached Tshelkanov, a place along the Smolensk-Mstislavl road, on the 13th. To cover against the direction of Smolensk, Ostermann took a position at Lutshniki, while Miloradovitch, preceded by Ozarovski's flying column, went as far forward as Tshervonnoie in the direction of Krasnoi. There, Orlov-Dennisov had already intercepted a large French convoy and taken 1000 prisoners. A detachment from V Corps, which had departed on the 11th, was on its way to Mohilev to reorganize there with march troops when it was ambushed. After losing several hundred men, Zaionczek was forced to continue his march via Krasnoi to reach Orsza. On the right bank of the Dnieper Platov stood in front of Smolensk, where Ney had been pushed by Grekov and Karpenkov. Count Kutuzov's column reached Dukovtshina.

Even at this stage of the French retreat, Russian headquarters continued to be poorly informed about the enemy. On the basis of reports in hand, the French were thought to be retreating in three columns, one via Kasplia to Vitebsk, another via Liuboviczi to Babinoviczi, and a third via Krasnoi to Orsza. Under these circumstances, it was believed that the Russians would become involved with only a third of the enemy, and without Napoleon's personal presence at that. Thus, Toll had been able to talk Kutuzov into making an attack against what was thought to be the southernmost column. Once this was destroyed, the enemy's main force was to be annihilated between the Dvina, Dnieper, and Beresina in an action in conjunction with Wittgenstein. Tshitshagov, whose slow movements had evoked displeasure at headquarters, was not counted upon.

Rolling toward Krasnoi, Miloradovitch reached Grigorkovo, while Oza-rovski drove the weak French garrison out of Krasnoi. Now, except for a few detachments, the entire Russian army was on the right bank of the Dnieper, quite close to the main road, where the separate echelons of the French army were passing after again having suffered heavy losses from the bitter cold. However, over the previous few days the Russians themselves had not been immune to the weather, despite the fact that materially they were considerably better off. Still, without the Cossacks, they numbered 60,000 men (other sources place them at about 50,000). But these men were in excellent condition with a large cavalry and 500 guns.

On the French side, Claparede and his Vistula Legion had overtaken Junot and now formed the head of the column with the rest of the Poles. When Claparede reached Krasnoi, he had no trouble expelling Ozarovski's

Cossacks, but he was too late to save the magazines there. Junot arrived later on the 14th.

Kutuzov could have been in Krasnoi by the 16th. Instead, he took his time about it and ordered a day of rest for the troops. Only the advance guard (16,000 men) under Miloradovitch was sent to Rshavka, which was on the main road. The Russians got there just as Napoleon's Guard was passing. Miloradovitch was again not at all informed about the enemy, and the resolute posture of the guards, who might have been nearly as strong as the Russians, filled him with caution. He left the road open and made do with a cannonade. Still, he got his hands on about 2000 stragglers and 11 guns, which had been left behind.

On the French side, Zaionczek reached Liady while Napoleon with the Guard met the Vistula Legion and Junot's troops in Krasnoi. Davout and Ney were still in Smolensk, where some lively fighting took place in the St. Petersburg suburb with Platov's Cossacks. Finally, the French withdrew into the city, leaving another eight guns behind.

On November 16, Napoleon learned from a prisoner that Kutuzov was nearby. He recognized the danger at once. Trusting in the Russian's irresolution, he instantly made a decision that would have been sheer madness in the face of any other opponent but offered the only possible solution under the circumstances, unless he wanted to abandon Eugene, Davout, and Ney, whose arrival he was awaiting. Thus, he had Zaionczek and Junot continue their retreat to Dubrovna and Liady, respectively, while he, aided by improving weather conditions since the 14th, deployed the Guard, the Vistula Legion, and the reserve cavalry (all 400 members of it that remained). In all, he had about 14,000 infantry and 2200 cavalry, with 50 guns.

Kutuzov was not to disappoint him. The Russian had been made even more cautious by Ozarovski's summary ejection from Krasnoi; now the knowledge of Napoleon's personal presence totally paralyzed him. Despite his overwhelming strength—even without Ostermann (who had been left behind) and Miloradovitch, he still had 35,000 men, including an excellent cavalry and artillery—he did no more than take his army forward to Shilova, which was barely 5 miles away.[1] However, even this appeared too dangerous to him, so he ordered Miloradovitch, reinforced to about 17,000 men with some of Ostermann's cavalry, to close up to his right at Merlino. In addition, Miloradovitch was ordered not to become embroiled in any serious fighting. No action took place on this day until late afternoon, when Eugene's depleted column (only about 5000 men, not counting stragglers, with 17 guns) approached from Korytnia. But then the action heated up and continued until after nightfall. It was only thanks to Miloradovitch's all-too-scrupulous adherence to Kutuzov's orders, which held back his own commanders, especially the pugnacious Eugene of Wuerttemberg, that the action was broken off at nightfall and Eugene the viceroy was able to reach Krasnoi without being pursued. Still, apart from another several thousand stragglers, the French had lost 1500 men and Eugene had to leave the rest of his guns behind. Of the corps remaining behind, Davout and four of his divisions had marched as far as Korytnia, bivouacking nearby. Ney and Division Ricard (ex-Friant) from I Corps were still in Smolensk.

On November 17, Kutuzov believed that Napoleon had gone, so he allowed Konovnitzyn and Toll to talk him into at least another attack against the rear guard of the French. Tormassov, with the bulk of the army,[2] was to envelop the French right via Putkova and to block the road to Orsza. Gallitzin was then to go against Krasnoi via Uvarovo. Miloradovitch was to take a position at Larinovo, let Davout pass, and then also advance against Krasnoi. For the time being, Ostermann was directed against Korytnia, but he was then ordered to march to Tolstiki along the Yrove-Krasnoi road.

Napoleon, however, was still there. Only Eugene's corps, hardly fit for another action, had gone. But Napoleon sensed that the situation called for something more than just standing and waiting. If he attacked, he would draw Miloradovitch in, thus clearing the road for Davout. And thanks to Kutuzov's supine measures, Davout's corps, 7500 men with 15 guns, not counting stragglers, also got past the Russians and joined Napoleon. Realizing his dangerous position, Davout had taken his corps from its bivouac at 5 a.m. and had to endure only Miloradovitch's long-range cannonade.

By then, Napoleon had already engaged Kutuzov's weak center under Gallitzin. Also marching at 5 a.m., the emperor had anticipated the Russians with his thrust at Uvarovo. By a stroke of luck Kutuzov learned of Napoleon's continuing presence and at once ordered a halt of Tormassov's enveloping movement. Miloradovitch, who might yet have made something of this affair, did not press either. As a result, Napoleon, who soon learned of Tormassov's interrupted envelopment, was able to continue his retreat. It would have been altogether too daring to wait for Ney's arrival.

The Young Guard battalions suffered heavy casualties when they withdrew from Uvarovo, where they had spent hours standing in the midst of the Russian artillery fire. It was almost noon when Miloradovitch was finally allowed to follow—after there was no longer any doubt of the French withdrawal. Three hours later, all he found was the rear guard, Friedrichs's division of Davout's corps, which was totally destroyed.

Ozarovski, unable to block Napoleon's path by himself, had to stand aside and let him pass. Reaching Liady on the same day, Napoleon is said to have exclaimed "*Oh, mon etoile!*" when he realized that he, the Guard, and Davout were all safe. But the half dozen actions, which have become collectively known as the Battle of Krasnoi, had been costly. The Russians had taken 6000 prisoners, again mostly stragglers, and 45 guns, some say as many as 70, had been left behind. In addition, the Guard is said to have buried twelve of its guns in Krasnoi.

The number of stragglers taken prisoner might have been greater if not for an episode that, despite its seriousness, was not without humor. Observing a column of stragglers at the tail end of the Guard who were being singled out and brought to bay by a horde of Cossacks, General von Stockmayer rode back and whipped them into a semblance of formation. As the line was forming, perhaps 300 more stragglers were gathering, most of them unarmed. They shouldered ramrods and sticks, and the few who still had muskets acted out the role of skirmishers and fired them off while the officers among them, and others who had ridden up as well, discharged their pistols. The Cossacks were so intimidated by this apparent show of force that they rode off and allowed the stragglers to catch up to the columns of the Guard again.

Also coming into the foreground around this time is the mysterious fate of Hiller's Saxon horse battery, which became something of a misty legend. On September 30, the Saxons had the misfortune of shooting down the highly unpopular Colonel Serron, Latour-Maubourg's chief of staff. Although it was proved to have been an accident, they incurred Latour-Maubourg's ire until they regained his confidence at Voronovo. After the Saxon cavalry, in dire straits itself, had been forced to give up twenty-two of its horses to keep the battery rolling, it was last seen in the area around Krasnoi. At that time, all the crews were on foot and there were only two horses left for each gun, so the drivers and gunners stepped into the harnesses as well to give the horses a hand. As a result, the battery always fell behind at every march stage. Roth von Schreckenstein, one of the most frequently quoted diarists, especially on the taking of the Raievsky redoubt, thought he overheard Captain Hiller reporting to Thielemann, the Saxon brigadier, that he had been forced to give up trying to save the guns; Hiller emphasized that the Russians would not have an easy time finding them, because after ruining the guns, he had ordered them thrown into a pit. But Schreckenstein is not certain, and an air of mystery continues to hang over the demise of this intrepid troop. Another report claims that on November 18 the entire battery disappeared into a swamp and was never seen again. A third story claims that the last of its gunners had died in a blazing barn. There was, however, not a single soul left of the battery's personnel to deny or confirm any of these stories. As Holzhausen put it, Battery Hiller, like a ship in a storm, was lost with all hands aboard.

In the meanwhile, Kutuzov, unaware that Ney was still behind, pulled Ostermann in to Tolstiki and had Tormassov advance to Dobroie. Gallitzin was left in Krasnoi, where Miloradovitch joined him by evening. Instead of mounting a pursuit, Kutuzov busied himself with reorganizing the infantry corps. The tsar wished to have the two grenadier divisions combined into a grenadier corps, and this gave Kutuzov a splendid excuse for allowing more distance to come between himself and Napoleon. Thus, with the exception of Ney's Corps, all the French troops had gotten past the Russians, although a great many stragglers had been lost. In the end, even Ney managed to save a small part of his corps. When he at last left Smolensk during the night of November 16–17, his corps, including Ricard's division, numbered 8000 infantry and 300 cavalry, with 12 guns; it was followed by about 7000 stragglers. Two Wuerttembergian battalions with a few guns had already gone ahead with the foremost echelon and were following the Guard when the episode with General Stockmayer occurred. Ney reached Korytnia on the 17th.

Platov, who had picked up another 2000 stragglers and 2000 more men in the hospitals of Smolensk, not to mention the 140 guns left behind there, sent Grekov[3] after Ney with some of the Cossacks. Platov then crossed the Dnieper in order to reach Orsza ahead of Napoleon.

Even though Davout had informed Ney of Eugene's defeat before he left Smolensk, Ney continued his march on the 18th, still expecting to find Napoleon in Krasnoi. There, at 3 p.m., instead of meeting the emperor, he ran into Miloradovitch. In the dim light of a gray day, he came upon the Russians quite unexpectedly, and they were no less surprised than he was. Once again, Platov had failed to report. After a brief initial success, Ney had to give way with heavy losses. With only 3000 men left, he drew back in the direction of Smolensk. The Russians failed to pursue and soon lost sight of him. Thus, after a few hours' rest in a deserted village, Ney turned toward the Dnieper and found a spot near Syrokorenie where the ice seemed just thick enough to allow a crossing during the night. But the ice gave out when the vehicles attempted to cross. Only 1500 men collected on the other bank. The rest, as well as all the vehicles and guns, remained behind.

After an adventurous march and constant scrappings with the Cossacks, Ney reached Jakabovo on the 20th. From there he marched on at 9 p.m., after only a few hours rest, to the Vitebsk-Orsza road. There, shortly after midnight, he found Eugene waiting for him (a courier had managed to slip through the Cossacks to advise the viceroy of Ney's coming). He had 900 men left; together with the 300 Wuerttembergers, who had gone ahead, his corps was now reduced to only 1200 men. But for both Ney and the French,

his escape was a moral success. The Russians would not be able to claim
the annihilation of an entire army corps and the capture of a French marshal,
one of the most famous of all at that.

The actions around Krasnoi had cost the Russians no more than 2000
men. Against this, about 6000 French had been killed and 26,000 captured.[4]
The prisoners, with the exception of those from Ney's corps, were almost
entirely stragglers. More than 200 guns had been lost, including 112 abandoned during the first march. The rest had been saved only thanks to
Kutuzov's aversion to facing Napoleon. The Russian commander's behavior
speaks for itself, so no further words need be lost on the subject. Despite
the fact that he had daily evidence of the French army's state of dissolution,
he refused to believe it and also wanted to avoid driving Napoleon to the
point of desperation. But what were the risks, had he gone at the emperor
offensively? At worst, a few thousand French might have broken through.
Now he began to sense that the army's mood was turning against him, just
as it had against Barclay. His teacher, Suvorov, whom he could imitate only
superficially, made the final judgment when he said, "A powerful stroke
would have saved three years of spilled blood." And, indeed, if Napoleon
had not brought 2000 officers out of Russia, who would command the cadre
for the new formations of 1813, the Russians and their allies would have
been spared 3 more years of war.

Yet it is extremely doubtful that Kutuzov's vision extended as far as that
of many of his critics, who viewed the situation from the advantageous
perspective of hindsight. He had been against the war from the start because
he feared it would be lost. However, when he was recalled to assume command, he was one of the very first, among those whose opinion counted,
to see that Napoleon was already holding a losing hand. The rank and file
could easily forgive him for not flogging them into combats he thought
unnecessary. With the coming of winter, the mere presence of the Russian
army was grinding up the French war machine in a manner previously unseen.

At the same time, he had been charged with driving the French out of
Russia and certainly perceived this as his mission. And that was exactly
what was happening—with or without his help. It was also obvious to him,
even if it was not to others, that Napoleon would not be coming back soon.

That Russia would eventually carry the war beyond its own borders and
expend as much energy as it had in the country's defense was far beyond
the old general's expectations in 1812. This was a new element that began
to gather momentum only when Yorck's independent action indicated that
Prussia would be driven into the war, whether the Prussian king wished it
or not. Russia might defend itself effectively by waging a war of attrition,
but thoughts of offensive action could be fostered only with outside help.

Kutuzov, mentally and physically exhausted and fragile, had only a few months of life left. Even as late as December 1812, he could not possibly have imagined how much weight Russia would bring to bear in a continuing war against Napoleon in 1813. Thus, no matter how much truth there may be in all the criticisms posterity has heaped upon Kutuzov's head, his own views were, within the context of his own time, not without merit. Here, one is again reminded of Clausewitz, who maintains that the outcome of an event may indeed provide the basis for a critique but that judgment may be made only on the basis of information that was, or should have been, available at the time the event transpired.

As for Napoleon, credit must be given where credit is due. As soon as he recognized the error of his measures during the retreat, he wasted not a moment in correcting what he could. On the 17th, he was once again the great captain. It is nothing short of amazing that, having been shaken to the very marrow of his existence, he was able to rise to the occasion once more. So, too, did his generals, the viceroy, Davout, and especially Ney show themselves worthy of the honors he had heaped upon them.

It was a grand stroke of good fortune, within the framework of the greater disaster that had descended upon Napoleon, that Kutuzov did not exploit his victory at Krasnoi. Instead of pursuing vigorously, he remained in place on the 18th and 19th, keeping only his raiding detachments on the heels of the French. Kutuzov wanted to go in the direction of Kopys with the main army because he thought Napoleon was headed for Minsk and would turn farther south if he saw that his road to Minsk was blocked. Kutuzov wanted to prevent this with a parallel march.

Thus, Tshitshagov was directed on the 18th to link his communications with the main army via Minsk and Kopys; Wittgenstein was ordered to withdraw behind the Uszacz, at worst even behind the Dvina(!) should he be threatened by the French main force. But drawing Tshitshagov in toward the main army and authorizing Wittgenstein to withdraw behind the Dvina would have meant a clearing of the road for the retreating French. Was this to be the result of the victory of Krasnoi? What had become of the soaring phrases of the tsar's plan, which spoke of trapping Napoleon inside Russia? Fortunately, the situation of the Russians had been far too advantageous for Kutuzov to be able to spoil it entirely. Thus, Tshitshagov did not withdraw to Kopys, nor did Wittgenstein go and hide behind the Dvina.

At last, on the 21st, the main army marched; but on the 22nd Kutuzov had it rest again. Reports coming in from Platov showed that Napoleon had made good use of time, so it was no longer possible for the main army to catch him. For once, however, Kutuzov underestimated the French. He no longer thought that their main army had any fighting power left, despite its imminent union with Victor. Thus, he decided that only Miloradovitch and the detachments already sent ahead would continue the pursuit, while the main army would continue its march to the lower Beresina. He wrote to Tshitshagov on the 22nd, assuring him that with Oertel's and Lueders's columns, he would be strong enough even without Wittgenstein to confront Napoleon. He emphasized that Tshitshagov was to make certain that Napoleon did not evade him via Igumen. This stands in curious contradiction to Kutuzov's instructions of the 18th. Perhaps the truth had at last dawned on him when he learned of the condition of Napoleon's forces from the French prisoners and as their increasing head counts were coming into headquarters. At any rate, this left only Miloradovitch on Napoleon's heels. In all, he had about 32,000 men, including the Cossacks (see Appendix XIX). The main army now made a slow march in the direction of the lower Beresina and did not cross the Dnieper until November 26, at Kopys. There, 3 light cavalry regiments (those of the guard) and 12 batteries were left behind to replace themselves, while the bulk of their manpower was distributed to the remaining formations.

Kutuzov's vision of the situation emerges from a letter he sent to Tshitshagov on the 25th. In it, he says: "Napoleon would probably go toward Bobr and draw in Victor and Oudinot, who were to be followed by Wittgenstein, and then attempt to reach Vilna via Borisov. For this reason Tshitshagov was to occupy the defile of Zembin. The main army would go to Beresino, as much for logistical reasons as to forestall an enemy move toward the south."

That Kutuzov failed to be up front with his leading elements turned out to be a serious error. That Napoleon would be able to make yet another getaway at the Beresina was very much due to the absence of a unified Russian command.

NOTES

1.

   Kutuzov: III, V, VI, and VIII Inf. Corps and cuirassier corps.
   Miloradovitch: II and VII Inf. Corps and I Cav. Corps
   Ostermann: IV Inf. Corps and II/III and IV Cav. Corps

2.

   Ostermann: IV Inf. Corps and IV Cav. Corps

Miloradovitch: II and VII Inf. Corps, I and II Cav. Corps, and Borosdin's column.

Gallitzin: III Inf. Corps and the 2nd Cuirassier Div.

Tormassov: V, VI, and VIII Inf. Corps, the 1st Cuirassier Div., and Ozarovski's column

3.

Platov: 1 jaeger regiment and 12 Cossack regiments, with 12 guns

Grekov: 6 dragoon squadrons and 6 Cossack regiments, with 4 guns

Left behind in Smolensk: 1 jaeger regiment

4. The prisoners taken during these November days were:

5,170 by Miloradovitch on the 15th, 16th, and 17th

12,000 by Miloradovitch on the 18th

4,000 by Tormassov on the 17th

4,000 by Ostermann on the 17th

1,000 collected on the 19th and 20th

24. The Flanks Cave In

WITTGENSTEIN

The loss of the second battle of Polotsk made it impossible for the French to maintain the Dvina line. After St. Cyr had been put out of action, three generals each went their own way. Going behind the Ula, Legrand took his division to Beszenkoviczi; Wrede took what was left of Bavarian VI Corps to Glubkoye; while the remainder of II Corps, Cuirassier Division Doumerc, and Light Cavalry Brigade Castex, as well as the two remaining divisions, Maison (ex-Verdier) and Merle, the latter in pro forma command, went to Czasniki.

When Victor heard of these events, he marched toward the Ula at once, sending Daendels' division to Beszenkoviczi while he himself went to Czasniki.[1] With Victor on the scene, there was no longer any question about who was in command. When the two corps united between October 29 and 31, Victor had 36,000 men at his disposal, including 4000 cavalry. Of these, 14,000 were from II Corps and 22,000 from IX Corps, slightly weakened by detachments.

After repairing the bridges at Polotsk on the 23rd, Wittgenstein crossed the Dvina on the 24th. Since he had failed to push St. Cyr away from the French line of retreat, as called for in the tsar's operations plan, but had, instead, pushed him toward it, he decided to compensate for this by attacking again in an attempt to destroy St. Cyr's force. Leaving about 4000 men in

Polotsk and sending a column of about 5000 men under Vlastov to keep an eye on Macdonald, Wittgenstein took up the pursuit with 30,000 men. Taking his time about it, he didn't arrive in front of Czasniki until October 31.

There, Victor had assembled 30,000 men. Legrand's division of 4000 was not present because it had been accidentally misdirected to Boiszikova. Also absent was Fournier with the IX Corps cavalry, some 2000 men. Victor knew he had to engage Wittgenstein, but he wanted to do so with full strength, so he decided to postpone his attack to the next day. Wittgenstein, however, unaware of Victor's presence, attacked II Corps, which was only 10,000 strong due to Legrand's absence. The Corps stood in an advanced position on the left bank of the Lukomlia at Czasniki, but it was driven back toward Victor. As Wittgenstein came up, he became aware of Victor's presence and settled for limited success, making do with a cannonade across the river, which continued until nightfall. The French had lost 800 men, the Russians about 400.

Victor was no less impressed by Wittgenstein's brass than Oudinot and St. Cyr had been. Thus, despite the fact that it was urgent to push the Russian back, Victor withdrew to Senno early in the morning on November 1. In doing so, he unwittingly stepped aside to let Wittgenstein and Tshitshagov unite across the French main line of retreat.

St. Cyr, who was still with his corps despite his wounding, was so disgusted with Victor's action that he left the army so that he could convalesce as far away as possible from the fools who seemed to be all around him. Victor soon did see the error of his ways. On the 4th and 5th, he marched to Czereia, but the opportunity to thrash Wittgenstein with a superior force had passed once and for all. Wittgenstein spent the next several days conducting harassing operations with various columns. However, the sharp cold had set in again, forcing everybody to seek shelter. The French also began to feel logistical pressure again. By November 10, Victor and Oudinot (the latter had resumed command of his corps even though his wound had not yet healed) were down to 25,000 effectives.

Wittgenstein also began to experience the effects of the cold, but not quite on the scale of the French. Not only were the Russians better supplied, but they were more accustomed to the climate and its hardships. At the same time, Wittgenstein was able to make good on his losses. Thanks to Macdonald's inactivity, he had been able to recall Vlastov's detachment. Novak's detachment, which had been forming up at Pskov, was now also on its way to Vitebsk.

Napoleon at once saw the danger of Victor's mishap at Czasniki. Thus, he had Berthier send him an order on the 7th directing him to keep Wittgenstein at arm's length. "The safety of the army depends upon it, every day's delay is a disaster. Forward!" These were the words that reached Victor on November 10. The marshal didn't hesitate for a moment. The next day saw him marching against Wittgenstein. Victor knew that the position behind the Lukomlia was strong, and he wanted to envelop it via Boiszikova with IX Corps while Oudinot made a frontal attack, pinning Wittgenstein in place. Oudinot disagreed; he wanted to forego the flanking movement and rely entirely on a frontal assault. Despite Napoleon's order, which had precisely spelled out the kind of maneuver he wanted to make, Victor gave in to Oudinot, partly because he was worried about leaving the Orsza road open and partly because Oudinot's subordination was loosely defined. It was a stroke of misfortune for the French that Oudinot had not remained on the sick list for a few more days.

Wittgenstein concentrated as soon as he learned of Victor's advance. Near the small village of Axenzi, his advance guard ran into the entire cavalry of IX Corps and was thrown back to Smoliany, despite being reinforced. There, a greater clash took place. Victor had only reluctantly given in to Oudinot and did not think that much would come of a frontal attack. Moreover, since he was apprehensive over the possible consequences of a setback, he did not pursue the assault with great energy. Thus, although his infantry succeeded in taking Smoliany, the attack against the Russian right was turned back. In the end, the Russians even recaptured the town.

Oudinot, who could have forced the decision by enveloping the Russian right, allowed himself to be bogged down at Poczavizi by a weak Russian detachment and limited himself to an artillery duel. Each side ended up losing about 3000 men. On the next day, Victor withdrew; II Corps went toward Czereia, while IX Corps marched toward Krasnogura, where it halted on the 17th.

Wittgenstein had fared no better. Impressed by the French attack, he failed to pursue his own success and sat still at Czasniki. The situation offers yet another proof of how initiative can deceive the enemy and obscure a difficult situation. From this point onward, the operations of the French main army became interlocked with those of Victor and Wittgenstein, so they may no longer be discussed separately.

Despite his repeated successes, Wittgenstein has been accused of not having understood the task that was set for him in the tsar's plan of operations. He was to have pushed the enemy toward the west, leaving the Finnish Corps to face it while he took his main force to meet Tshitshagov in the rear of the French main army. Since he had not succeeded with the first part of the plan, he could not now block Napoleon's way to Borisov because he could not possibly know in what condition the wreckage of the main army would arrive at the Beresina. If Napoleon was now joined by Victor and Oudinot, Wittgenstein stood in danger of being overrun and thrown into the swamps of the Beresina. Thus, Tshitshagov was left to his own devices, while Wittgenstein had to limit himself to following the enemy he was supposed to have blocked so that he might cut off and isolate some of its elements.

Even if this critique of Wittgenstein's actions is partially justified, one must not overlook the factors that speak in his favor. To begin with, it would have been very difficult for him to push St. Cyr toward the border because of the direction of the Finnish Corps' approach, which virtually demanded an envelopment of the French left. On the other hand, going in the opposite direction would have taken him away from this reinforcement. Finally, it had proved to be impossible to lay a bridge above Polotsk, and the Finnish Corps had become so weak after various detachments that it could no longer carry out the part assigned to it in the operations plan. For the Finnish Corps to succeed, it would have been necessary for Wittgenstein to detach some of his own forces to flesh the corps out again, and this would have presumably left him with insufficient force to face Victor's IX Corps. Once these points are taken into consideration, it is difficult to deny Wittgenstein his due. In part, his failures lay beyond the reach of his abilities, but he at least attempted to redress this with resolute actions.

Viewing Wittgenstein's performance within the context of the whole, Clausewitz summed it up in the clearest terms. When Clausewitz arrived at Wittgenstein's headquarters during those very days, he found a sense of self-confidence and proud accomplishment, which stood in stark contrast to the mood at Kutuzov's headquarters. He believed that Wittgenstein and the men around him were morally equal and often superior to the enemy and that the general had more than merely discharged his duty in this theater of operations. He says:

> If one added up the three French corps which had been deployed against Wittgenstein, these came to represent a mass of 98,000 men. All that had, until then, fought under Wittgenstein hardly exceeded 75,000 men (including several thousand militia).
>
> Thus he had, in fact, neutralized a superior mass of the enemy from the actual offensive, had yielded no terrain and had, quite to the contrary, gained such a preponderance that he was prepared to take part in the plan developed in St. Petersburg. Such a result against French troops and Bonapartist generals deserves the aura of a glorious campaign.[2]

Wittgenstein's opponent, Victor, deserves no such praise. His withdrawal from Czasniki has been excused on the ground that he had not been aware of the main army's condition at the time. In army jargon, that is a reason, not an excuse. A victory has far-reaching consequences, and for this reason alone he could not unnecessarily leave a victory in the hands of the enemy. Also, the better he thought the situation of the main army to be, the more ready he should have been to risk a reverse. That he desisted from executing an envelopment via Boiszikova at Smoliany underlines his weakness when it came to facing Oudinot. This is especially damning since Napoleon himself had pointed out to him that executing the envelopment was the only possible way to succeed. The frontal attack offered no such promise and was thus a mistake. He demonstrated his awareness of this in his uncertainty regarding the point of attack. Contrary to many narratives, which make light of this action, the extent of his losses indicates that some serious fighting must have taken place. That he did not continue his costly and useless efforts in a situation in which he had to avoid a defeat at all costs (in contrast to his behavior at Czasniki) is entirely understandable. Oudinot's behavior, however, stands convicted on its own merits. His untimely return to the army was decidedly a misfortune.

Victor's offensive against Smoliany was to be supported by Wrede, whose Bavarian corps had shrunk to 2600 men but was reinforced by a few march troops. In the beginning of November, he had withdrawn to Daniloviczi. So that Wrede might support Victor vigorously, Maret, Napoleon's deputy in Vilna, assigned to him Brigade Coutard, which had been held back from IX Corps, and Brigade Franceschi, which had been assembled from march troops. This brought his corps back to 12,400 men,[3] but these troops did not come together until November 13. At that time, Wrede advanced to Dokszitzi, but it was already too late. There, he remained in place not only because he wanted to avoid falling into the middle of the victorious army but also because the extreme cold caused his troops so much trouble that he feared for their continued existence. Only Brigade Corbineau was sent back to II Corps.

The number of forces under Oudinot, Victor, Wrede, and Macdonald that were still present in this operations area gives rise to the question of what turn events might have taken had these men been in the hands of an energetic commander in chief. Even if the tsar's operations plan did not become fully operational, mainly because of its inherent artifice (Clausewitz called it curious and impractical), Napoleon's situation was bad enough. But no matter how great the threat was from Wittgenstein's position at Czasniki, the threat posed by Tshitshagov was far more serious.

*   *   *

TSHITSHAGOV

The admiral was last observed preparing for his march to the Beresina. Once his logistical preparations were complete, he started out for Minsk on October 29 at the head of 29,000 men, most of them from the erstwhile reserve army. Along the way, he was joined by another 9000 men, the last echelon of troops from the Danube Army, which swelled his force to 38,000 (including the Cossacks) with 180 guns.

Oertel, whose force numbered about 15,000, had been ordered to join Tshitshagov at Minsk. Instead, he sent only a 3000-man detachment and remained standing at Mozyr, doing absolutely nothing. He was soon fired and replaced by Tutshkov II. Tshitshagov had also ordered Sacken, who was to remain behind to face Schwarzenberg, to send Essen's column, but it did not come up in time. To carry out his task against Schwarzenberg, Sacken had been given 27,000 men, with 92 guns. The Ukrainian Cossacks and other reinforcements, coming to about 5000 men, with 60 guns, were sent to him as well. This was thought sufficient to keep Schwarzenberg away.

In southern Volhynia, Muffin-Pushkin had taken over from Sacken. His troops consisted of Repninski's and Witte's detachments. The former detachment, reinforced with troops from Lueders, had about 4500 men and was delegated to keep an eye on the upper Bug and the grand duchy of Warsaw. Witte, with about 2500 Cossacks, observed the Galician border.

Tshitshagov reached Slonim on November 6. There, he learned of Napoleon's departure from Moscow and the capture of Polotsk by Wittgenstein. The extreme cold made him halt on the 7th, but he marched again on the 8th and sent Tshernishev forward with his Cossacks to get in touch with Wittgenstein. Raising havoc among the Lithuanians, capturing couriers, freeing prisoners, and disturbing the arming of the insurgency, Tshernishev did far more than merely get in touch with Wittgenstein. When Schwarzenberg heard of Tshitshagov's departure on October 29, he marched on the same day, following him. The orders given to Schwarzenberg amounted to "See to it that the Russians in front of you will be unable to march against me." After leaving Drohiczyn, he failed to catch up to Tshitshagov, despite the fact that the Russian had taken his time and did not arrive in Slonim until the 14th. Reynier's VII Corps had been left behind near Volkovisk to cover against Sacken's approach. With the arrival of the 5800 Austrians and the 9000 men of Durutte's division (sent by Maret), which were attached to Reynier, Schwarzenberg now had 47,000 men.

Learning that Schwarzenberg had crossed the Bug at Drohiczyn, Sacken followed at once, even though he knew he lacked the strength to engage him. Leaving a small detachment at Brest, he reached Yzabelin on the 14th and faced Reynier, who held Volkovisk, while the outposts skirmished. Sacken took Reynier by surprise and captured the town in a night attack, but he was unable to dislodge Reynier from his main position on the high ground north of Volkovisk. Renewing his attack on the 15th, Sacken suddenly realized that he was in a precarious position.

As soon as Schwarzenberg learned of Sacken's attack on the 15th, he turned around to lend a hand, leaving only 6500 men to cover Slonim toward the direction of Minsk. When the Austrians appeared in Sacken's flank and rear on the 16th, the Russians were in trouble. Attacked on three sides, they were able to extricate themselves only thanks to Reynier's lack of energy. Sacken now withdrew toward Brest with Reynier following on his heels and Schwarzenberg attempting to get ahead of him along the main road to Pruzany. But Sacken made good his escape after a sharp action in front of Brest on the 25th. This was the end of the pursuit, because orders from Maret directed Schwarzenberg to continue on to Minsk at once. But the Austrian did not "speed" to his objective until the 29th. Sacken had gotten away, supposedly with a loss of 10,000 men and parts of his artillery and baggage. Now Essen started his march to join Tshitshagov. But the Austrian presence in Pinsk forced him to detour around the southern edge of the Pripet Marshes, thus precluding any possibility of his still taking a timely part in this campaign.

That Schwarzenberg did not continue his march to Minsk, sending at the most only part of his cavalry to Reynier's aid, was a major error. Instead of tying down Tshitshagov, he permitted himself to be tied down by Sacken. Even if he had turned around at once after the action of Volkovisk, he still would have been unable to appear at the point of decision by the 27th. The 225 miles from Volkovisk to Borisov led through poor country, and additional difficulties were posed by the increasingly deteriorating weather. Even so, his very approach might have sufficed to paralyze Tshitshagov. Certainly, he could have prevented at least part of the disaster at the Beresina. Following Sacken with his entire force robbed him of any possibility of taking a hand, or even making his influence felt, in the decisive actions. In this way, Napoleon was denied the presence of more than 40,000 men who might have taken events on the Beresina onto a different course.

In behalf of Schwarzenberg, it has been said that he could not possibly have predicted the consequences of his absence, since Napoleon had left him in the dark about the condition of the main army. This is entirely true. For this reason, Napoleon bears part of the blame for Schwarzenberg's failure to appear. Even so, the Austrian knew the emperor well enough to be able to discern some of the truth between the lines of his rounded phrases.

Schwarzenberg's continuing behavior, however, makes it doubtful that he would have acted differently even if he had known the whole truth.

In addition, the true situation continues to be obscured by the fact that the Austrians, unwilling allies of Napoleon from the start, were playing a double game. The Russian and Austrian courts never really lost touch with each other throughout the campaign. Thus, it is certain that Schwarzenberg had directives from Vienna in addition to his orders from Napoleon.

Unmolested by Schwarzenberg, Tshitshagov made his march to the Beresina without encountering resistance, because Victor's departure left the entire center unprotected. Napoleon was now paying the price for having consistently underestimated the strength of the Russian forces on his flanks. Thus, he thought it sufficient to send Durutte's and Loison's divisions to help the forces already present to keep Volhynia and Lithuania in check. Now, with Tshitshagov approaching Minsk, all that was left in the center were a few weak garrisons and Dombrowski's division.[4]

Minsk, which had been made into a depot, was held by 5700 men under General Bronikowski. Most of these were raw Lithuanian troops and a collection of depot formations. With Vilna now bare of troops, and with Coutard's and Franceschi's brigades in transit to Wrede and the foremost echelon of Loison's division not arriving until the 21st, Dombrowski's division was Bronikowski's only hope for support.

Due to the arrival of some replacements, Dombrowski had about 6500 men, in addition to the garrisons of Mohilev and Borisov, at that time. When Victor marched off to St. Cyr, Dombrowski was ordered to call in his detachments and to concentrate by the Beresina. He received this order on October 28 and was making ready to comply when another order directed him to Minsk at once. He departed with the troops he had in hand, 2300 infantry and 300 cavalry, with 12 guns, and reached Smeloviczi on November 15. He had ordered the remainder of his detachments to follow him there.

The news of the Russian approach had created a great deal of activity in Minsk. Bronikowski asked Maret for help (he had none to give) and sent General Kosezki with a French battalion and Lithuanian troops (said to have numbered 3000 infantry and 500 cavalry) to Novi-Sverzen where they were to cover the crossing of the Niemen. On November 13, Lambert showed up there with the advance guard of the Third Western Army. Kosezki had made the error of positioning himself in front of the defile, and his raw Lithuanian recruits were summarily chased off with heavy losses. Lambert did not settle for this but mounted an energetic pursuit, catching up to Kosezki at Keidarov, where he destroyed the entire detachment. Only Kosezki and about 100 of his cavalry escaped back to Minsk. Bronikowski evacuated Minsk at once. With only about 1000 men left to him, including 484 men of the 7th Wuerttembergian Infantry, he withdrew to Borisóv. A number of civilians of the administration and commissariat, along with many soldiers, supposedly 1000 in all, fled to Vilna, where their arrival caused a panic because the Russians were thought to be on their heels.

Dombrowski, who had sped ahead of his troops, would have landed himself in a difficult situation had Oertel been roused from his languor long enough to advance against Minsk as well. But Dombrowski made an about-face and with forced marches took his troops to Borisov, where he joined Bronikowski on November 20. Including the Borisov garrison, Dombrowski now had about 5500 men,[5] with 20 guns; some of these men were still coming up. Leaving most of the artillery and all of his cavalry in Borisov, he took his infantry across the river to occupy the bridgehead on the right (western) bank. Unfortunately for the French, the Russians had neglected to finish the earthworks there, although they had been started before the war. They were intended to cover not only the bridge but also a defile, about 1000 paces long, leading through swampy bottomland. The work that had been done had been allowed to fall into disrepair. What was Dombrowski to do in the face of Tshitshagov's approach?

Tshitshagov's advance guard occupied Minsk on the 16th. Large stockpiles of supplies and about 6000 men, almost all of them sick, wounded, and stragglers, fell into its hands. For the time being, he halted there because of Schwarzenberg's advance against Volkovisk as well as exaggerated reports about Victor's strength. This made Oertel's failure all the more vexing. By the 18th, however, more reassuring news arrived, including that from Kutuzov about the disorderly retreat of the French army. In addition, a letter from the tsar arrived that summoned the admiral to become more active. The advance guard departed on November 19, followed by the admiral, whose troops marched in two columns on the 20th. Only a weak detachment was left behind in Minsk. There appeared to be nothing that would prevent Tshitshagov from arriving at the Beresina with his army (still 35,000 strong), as called for in the operations plan.

Back in the center and along the French main army group's line of retreat toward the Beresina, the situation had become quite dangerous for Napoleon. At Czasniki stood Wittgenstein with more than 30,000 men against the 22,000 under Oudinot and Victor, who stood at Czereia and Krasnogura. Coming toward Borisov was Tshitshagov with 35,000 men. He intended to wrest Borisov, the most important crossing point of the Beresina, from Dombrowski, who was attempting to hold it with about 5500 men. The remainder of the French forces—the army detachments under Schwarzenberg, Wrede, Loison, and Macdonald, altogether more than 90,000 men—

were, apart from Sacken, not faced with equal force. However, they were all too far away to exercise any influence on the main events that were about to take place at the Beresina.

While the artificial plan put together at Russian imperial headquarters (not Kutuzov's) succeeded in bringing almost all the available forces into concentric action at the decisive point, the greatest captain of his time could meet these with only a fraction of the forces still available to him. The fault for this lies mainly with Napoleon. This is partly because he failed to inform his most distant commanders, even his deputy, Maret, about his true situation and partly because he could not bring himself to cut his losses (since this might—only *might*—have been unnecessary). Young General Bonaparte, with a keen eye for what was possible, did not hesitate to give up the siege of Mantua. But Emperor Napoleon, blinded by so much success, could not bring himself to give up on Riga even after his campaign had already become a failure. By this time, however, it was too late. The time for strategic moves had passed, as events were progressing toward an inevitable conclusion. Even another flash of the Napoleon of old at the Beresina could not stave off the ultimate disaster.

NOTES

1. IX Corps consisted of the following:

	Battalions	Squadrons
Div. Partouneaux (French)	17	
Div. Daendels (Badensians and Bergers)	13	
Div. Girard (Saxons and Poles)	10	
Brig. Delatre (Bergers and Hessians)		7
Brig. Fournier (Saxons and Badensians)		8
Brig. Coutard (Westphalians and Hessians in Vilna)	4	
In Smolensk (Poles)	3	

2. Clausewitz, Carl von. *Der Russische Feldzug von 1812*, p. 146. Essen, no date.
3. The troops under Wrede consisted of:
   Remainders of VI Bavarian Corps (3405 infantry and 92 cavalry, with 16 guns, plus march troops)

Light Cav. Brig. Corbineau of II Corps

Brig. Coutard of IX Corps (1 Westphalian and 1 Hessian infantry regiment)

Brig. Franceschi (1 French march infantry regiment and 1 Lithuanian Cavalry regiment)

In all, there were 9525 infantry and artillery and 1895 cavalry, for a total of 12,420 men, with 26 guns.

4. Division Dombrowski had been reinforced by a battalion taken out of Grodno and by new Polish formations. It numbered 5500 men at the end of October.

5. Dombrowski's troops included 4000 men of Division Dombrowski, 1000 men of the garrison of Minsk, and 500 men of the Borisov garrison.

25. The Beresina

What was left of Napoleon's army, now drawing close to the Beresina, amounted to no more than 25,000 men still in the ranks, with virtually no cavalry and artillery. What little cavalry there was consisted almost entirely of Napoleon's own escort. The artillery still had nearly 100 guns, but many of these were useless because adequate draft teams, crews, and ammunition were lacking. Ney's corps and two of Davout's divisions had ceased to exist altogether. The remaining men in Davout's and Eugene's corps had dwindled to such a point that the regiments could no longer form even a single battalion.

It was now Napoleon's intention to join Schwarzenberg via Minsk. Thus, everything was directed toward Borisov. The emperor still hoped he could then go into winter quarters behind the Beresina. But the bad news kept on coming. Victor had failed at Smoliany, and Minsk had been occupied by Tshitshagov on the 16th. Napoleon's situation was desperate and permitted no hesitation. Dombrowski was ordered to occupy the bridgehead at Borisov. Oudinot was directed there as well, from Czereia, so that Minsk could eventually be retaken. For this operation Oudinot had, at best, no more than 13,500 men, including Dombrowski's 5500. During the night of November 18–19, Victor was ordered to take the 12,000 men he had remaining and close up sufficiently to cover Oudinot's march. But Victor was also to make Wittgenstein believe that Napoleon intended to attack him.

On the 19th, all but Davout had crossed the Dnieper at Orsza. Davout,

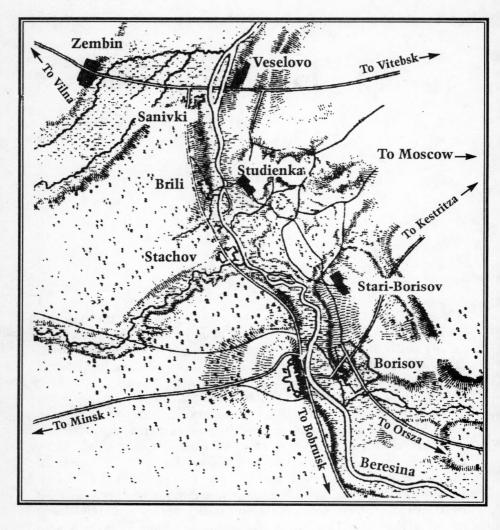

The Beresina crossing at Studienka

whose rear guard had been attacked by Borosdin in Liady, was to remain in Dubrovna; there, he was to receive Ney, who was known to have turned toward the Dnieper after failing to break through at Krasnoi. The losses sustained during these days, despite the fact that only the Russian raiders were on the heels of the main army, were extraordinary. Arriving in Orsza, the army, without Ney, had only 18,300 men[1] in the ranks. Even so, the state of the troops—starving, dressed in rags, and bone-weary—was such that the worst was to be expected. Even the Guard, upon whose cohesion all else hinged, had fallen into disarray and was beginning to feel demoralized. Hour by hour, day by day, its columns were getting longer as more and more men slowed down or took a break from the endless marching whenever they were of a mind to do so. Orders were carried out reluctantly—if at all. Indeed, things got so bad that Napoleon addressed the Guard with a speech, reminding the men of their past glories and of the fact that they were the Guard and should therefore set the example for the rest of the army. It made the desired impression, even if the effects were only temporary. While at Orsza, Napoleon had some of the regimental colors burned; although some of their eagle capitals were saved, some would be lost later. In all, twelve regimental eagles are said to have been lost during the Russian campaign, but the scorekeeping in this matter has always remained open to argument.

The army's stay at Orsza lasted only a couple of days, more or less, depending on the order in which the columns arrived. During that time an attempt was made to restore some semblance of order among what was left of the troops. The magazines there were well stocked, so the troops in the ranks were fed and even received some foodstuffs to take along on the march to the Beresina. At the same time, the fragments of the remaining infantry formations were amalgamated to form at least a few combat-worthy battalions.[2] As for the cavalry, there was not much left to reorganize. To ensure draft teams for the few guns that remained, the baggage train, already greatly depleted, was further reduced. Two pontoon trains, which had been left behind in Orsza during the advance, were burned because Napoleon thought that the crossing at Borisov was secure. It was to prove a stroke of good fortune that General Eblé[3] did not feel nearly so assured and therefore saved two field forges, two wagonloads of coal, and another six wagonloads of tools and iron fittings. He even made each of his pontoniers carry some spikes, clamps, and at least one tool.

However, the efforts at halting the continuing decay of the army proved futile. Despite the fact that the country now being traversed had been neither depleted nor deserted by its population, that the troops had drawn supplies from the magazines in Dubrovna and Orsza, and that the weather had become mild again, the ranks continued to thin. And even though a thaw had set in, the rain on the 20th did not help the situation. The rate of dropouts increased even further, and it was now due principally to an increasing loss of morale: The troops had lost hope that the endless marches would ever come to an end.

The wet bivouacs made everything even worse. Serious illness claimed numerous victims. Others simply collapsed from exhaustion and stayed down, their adrenaline refusing to flow any longer. Still others, driven to desperation, committed suicide or suffered complete nervous breakdowns. What the troops needed the most—a long rest—they could not have. The Russians and the winter did not permit it. Even the stay in Moscow had not nearly sufficed to restore the army either physically or morally. No one rested securely hundreds of miles within hostile territory. The march back from Moscow had been even worse. On the advance through Russia, the alternating spells of intense heat and heavy rain and of plenty and starvation had been debilitating. However, the ultimate horror came now, on the retreat, with the cold and with the knowledge that when the body began to feel comfortable, death was only a short while away. The cold that struck on the way out of Russia was a far more effective killer than the heat and rain had been on the way in.

It was among the stragglers where the misery struck first. The men who dropped out of their formations also abandoned what little help they could have received had they pushed on. In the magazines they came up empty time and again. The commissaires of the supply administration mulishly stuck to regulations made at another time, in another place. Orders were orders, and they have always provided a haven for the nonentity. But neither the commissaires nor the stragglers should be judged too harshly. Long before the army got to Smolensk, life had already become a matter of survival of the fittest and every man for himself. Thus, when the stragglers began to take matters into their own hands, the resulting riots often saved the men from the commissariat the trouble of destroying the stores. And when stragglers did manage to lay their hands on some supplies, they spoiled more than they took and cared little about others who came up empty.

It would be fruitless to seek a common denominator among the men who dropped out of the ranks. Some were exhausted and unwilling to continue carrying their packs and muskets, which was the price of staying in the formations, if indeed they still merited being called formations. Others were angry. Still others no longer cared. The psychological surrender exercised an even greater effect than the physical. If the fittest at the heads of the columns stepped out strongly, the columns would stretch out even under normal conditions, forcing those at the end to run every so often in order to catch up. Now the time for running was past, and the columns just got longer. In this fashion, many men became stragglers quite unwittingly, and the psychological surrender eventually prevented them from hanging on. At first, they might be an hour or two late getting to the bivouacs. Then they would arrive after nightfall and fail to find their units. Finally, they would give up even trying to reach the bivouacs; they would simply plod on as best they could. But when the cold came, it struck with impartial finality. Disease might bring down the weak and debilitated, but hypothermia could bring down even the strongest.

Despite the constant attrition among the hordes of stragglers who followed every column, their numbers did not diminish, because being a straggler was a sort of halfway stage for the men destined for oblivion. As stragglers were lost at the tail end, falling victim to the privations, the Cossacks, or the peasantry, their numbers were constantly replenished by other men who continued to fall out of the ranks of the formations. The formations had been reduced by another third by the time the army reached the Beresina.[4]

For a while, the hordes of stragglers increased. All the way to the Vistula, numerous men (actually *maraudeurs*, i.e., deserters) who had left the army in June and July were congregating along the line of retreat. There had been 50,000 in Lithuania alone. When they heard that the army was retreating, they began returning by the thousands.

On the 20th, Napoleon reached Barami, where he learned of Ney's escape. Davout, who had waited 24 hours to receive Ney, withdrew to Orsza before the approach of the Russian raiders. There, he crossed the Dnieper on the same day and destroyed the town's two bridges. Since his corps of 4500 men was still the largest at that time, he continued to perform rear-guard duties. Even though the entire army was now back across the Dnieper, it was still in great danger. Not only was it pursued by a superior and victorious enemy, but two other hostile armies, insufficiently contained, threatened the line of retreat and a difficult river crossing was yet to be made under the eyes of the enemy.

Napoleon had misgivings about the crossing at Borisov. In Kamionka, he thought that if Borisov was lost and no other usable crossing point was found, the army should march toward Lepel. How justified his misgivings were would be quickly revealed. On the very next day, news of the loss of Borisov was received. Lambert had made his move on the morning of the 21st before Oudinot could come up. Apparently, the sentries posted by Bronikowski had fallen asleep and were ambushed. Dombrowski had only about 2000 men left. The Russians had lost about 2000 as well, including Lambert, who had been mortally wounded. However, on the 22nd, Oudinot got as far as Losnitza, where Corbineau's brigade, which had been carried off by Wrede, rejoined him. They forded the Beresina at Studienka.

Tshitshagov, carrying out his part of the operations plan, took the greatest part of his army across the Beresina at Borisov and pushed his advance guard to Losnitza. The advance guard failed to reconnoiter and instead attacked Oudinot without waiting to be reinforced. As a result, it received a good thrashing. Deciding to exploit the moment, Oudinot made for Borisov, where he caught the Russians unaware and summarily ejected them. Unfortunately for the French, the Russians had destroyed the bridge at Borisov, and since they held the far bank in force, there could be no thought of repairing it. Still, Oudinot had deflated Tshitshagov's self-confidence and reduced him to a passive role.

The loss of the Borisov bridge heightened the danger facing the French. Wedged between three hostile armies, the French could not attempt a breakthrough against any of them. Only some adroit maneuvering offered a chance for survival. And this depended on the quick construction of a bridge—one for which no material had been gathered and one that the enemy, holding the opposite bank, was sure to disturb.

As soon as he heard of the loss of Borisov, Napoleon ordered Oudinot to provide a crossing above or, better yet, below Borisov. This soon turned out to be impossible due to terrain difficulties. At the same time, a review of the tactical situation indicated that the army's best chance was to march in the direction of Vilna, via Zembin, slipping through between Tshitshagov and Kutuzov. Thus, during the night of November 22–23, Napoleon ordered Oudinot to construct bridges and a bridgehead near Veselovo, where the road to Zembin crossed the Beresina. Although the bridge there had been destroyed, a ford was said to be nearby.

On November 23, Napoleon reached Bobr with the Guard. On arriving there, he directed Victor to occupy the road to Lepel and prevent Wittgenstein from going against Oudinot. At the same time, Oudinot reported the recapture of Borisov, the destruction of the bridge there, and the fact that Corbineau's brigade had forded the river at Studienka, finding it to have little depth there. Therefore, on the morning of the 24th, Generals Eble and Chasseloup,[5] as well as all the pontoniers and engineers, were dispatched to Oudinot with the equipment Eble had wisely saved.

Around this time, a new corps was formed for Ney. It was composed of the remaining men of his own corps, V Polish Corps, and the garrison of Mohilev; they were soon joined by the Vistula Legion. With this corps, Ney was to support Davout and Eugene (who had again suffered serious losses against Kutuzov) in order to give Napoleon time to have the bridge laid. In the meanwhile, Victor, who had barely 12,000 men left after Oudinot's departure, had withdrawn to Baturi. Wittgenstein followed him to Czereia but sent his advance guard to Kolopeniczi. There, a lively action developed, which Victor broke off as soon as he noted the presence of stronger forces. He then went to Dokutshin, leaving only Margrave William of Baden at Baturi with an infantry and cavalry brigade. This was contrary to Napoleon's orders, which arrived during the night of the 24th and which would have sent him to Baran. Victor thought that going there was too dangerous; unaware of Napoleon's intention to cross at Veselovo, he marched instead to Losnitza and then withdrew to Shavry. There, he was joined by the margrave, who had been pushed out of Baturi by Vlastov, who commanded Wittgenstein's advance guard.

Through the union with Victor, Oudinot, and Dombrowski, the main army's strength rose to 35,000 effectives again (not counting a similar number of stragglers) with 250 guns. Napoleon did his best to keep the core of his army at this level. Two battalions were formed with unhorsed cavalry troopers, and two squadrons were formed with cavalry officers who still had horses but no commands. They were combined with the 150 cavalrymen who were still left to Latour-Maubourg. Part of Oudinot's excess artillery was parceled out to the other corps. The trains were again reduced in order to keep the guns rolling and to increase the mobility of the army.

Still, Napoleon could not stem the ongoing disintegration, which had again cost the army several thousand men without an action being fought. On the 24th, after 5 days of thaw, the cold returned, with the temperature dropping to 14°F (-8°R). On the 26th, the first day of the crossing, the army numbered only 31,000 men, with 250 guns (see Appendix XX), and there were about 36,000 stragglers. The sight of the pitiful remnants of the once huge central army group had a terrible effect upon the morale of Victor's and Oudinot's troops, who were still in relatively good condition but who were now also becoming infected by the general demoralization.

With this ragtag army, Napoleon had to make his way past an enemy that was surrounding him on three sides. Tshitshagov still had 31,500 men; Wittgenstein had more than 30,000; and Miloradovitch had more than 25,000. The main army itself accounted for another 39,000 under Kutuzov and Tormassov. Slipping past the enemy was one of the most difficult tasks Napoleon ever faced. He accomplished it mainly because his proverbial luck favored him once more with a grand gesture and also because his very presence visibly intimidated the Russian commanders, who had no inkling of just how badly the French army had fallen apart.

Miloradovitch didn't cross the Dnieper until the 23rd; he reached To-loczin, 35 miles from Borisov, on the 25th, the eve of the Beresina crossing. Yermolov, who had crossed the Dubrovna on the 21st, got only as far as Maljevka, that is, about 8 miles, by the 25th. Platov, too, had not been very active. He was about 12 miles from Borisov on the 25th. Since all of these advanced only about 7 or 8 miles on the 26th, only Yermolov, Platov, and the tireless Seslavin, who had been sent to establish communications with Tshitshagov, could take part in the actions fought by the Beresina. Even so, they were still too far off to take a hand during the first day of the crossing and did not arrive until the second.

Wittgenstein, who obviously overestimated Napoleon's strength, was so intimidated as to be hardly recognizable. Having fallen short of the task set for him in the operations plan, he now hesitated to risk his newly won reputation. Since he was somewhat better informed about the general state of affairs, he would have been the best man to oversee the situation. Yet, despite his numerous cavalry, he was not aware of just how bad the state of the French really was. At the same time, the action at Losnitza had made him cautious. Also, the direction of Oudinot's departure misled him into thinking that the emperor intended to cross south of Borisov. (Wittgenstein, of course, was unaware that Oudinot's move had been made in contradiction to Napoleon's orders.) Thus, he failed to thrust his victorious army into the center of the French army's wreckage. On the 25th, both he and his advance guard arrived in Baran, barely 10 miles from the crossing site chosen by Napoleon and the road left open by Victor, who had continued his retreat to Losnitza that morning. Even so, Wittgenstein did not go to Studienka on the 26th but only to Kostritza, barely 5 miles away and not even in the right direction, because he still thought Napoleon would cross south of Borisov. He, too, did not arrive at Studienka until the 27th.

Thus, for the time being, Tshitshagov was on his own, and he, too, cleared the road for the enemy at the decisive moment. Since his precipitate surrender of Borisov had made it impossible to join hands with Wittgenstein in the rear of the French, he partially corrected Wittgenstein's error by standing on the far bank of the Beresina, across from Borisov. Upriver, across from Studienka, stood Tshaplitz.[6] Below, near Gury-Uczevzy, stood a cavalry detachment under Orurk[7] that was reconnoitering as far as Beresino. After assuming that the French were in a total state of dissolution (which had caused Tshitshagov to issue a handbill with a reward on Napoleon's head) Tshitshagov received a sharp jolt on the 23rd when Oudinot retook Borisov, and it caused him to swing to the opposite extreme. Estimating the French at 70,000 (the raw number was not off the mark), he thought it possible that Napoleon would attempt a forced crossing at Borisov in order to go to Minsk. And this possibility, then, stood at the bottom of his measures.

In the meanwhile, circumstances arose that made Tshitshagov believe that Napoleon would attempt a crossing below Borisov—which was Napoleon's actual intention for a short while. He received a report from downriver that Oudinot, who was creating a diversion there, was preparing to lay a bridge (not true) and that the Austrians were advancing against Minsk (also not true). On top of this, Wittgenstein had remarked that Napoleon might turn south. (Similar suggestions from Kutuzov did not arrive until the 26th.) Thus, on the 25th, Tshitshagov took his main force south to Szabaszeviki in order to be at the center of a 55-mile stretch that he thought would contain the likely crossing site. Only Langeron's weak corps[8] remained across from Borisov. Tshaplitz was still at Studienka but was soon to join Langeron, leaving only some pickets behind.

But on the same day, Tshitshagov, who seemed to be glad to have any excuse for avoiding a confrontation with Napoleon, received other news that made him uncertain again. He was told that Schwarzenberg had been beaten by Sacken and was retreating to Vilna. Also, Wittgenstein informed him of Victor's and Oudinot's movement and stated that he himself was going to Kolopeniczi and accelerating his march to the Beresina. Tshitshagov now became cautious; he ordered Tshaplitz to stay at Studienka, with Langeron to support him if necessary.

Langeron, however, was not informed of these new orders, and as he could observe numerous campfires around Borisov, he repeated the orders for Tshaplitz to join him. Although Tshaplitz was also observing numerous campfires around Studienka, he nevertheless obeyed Langeron's orders on the 26th. He had also seen the French scouting the banks, obviously in search of a crossing site, and he reported this at once to Tshitshagov and Langeron. Still, all that remained at Studienka was a weak detachment under Kornilov.[9] Even if Tshitshagov bore the responsibility for all this, part of the blame must be laid at Tshaplitz's feet for not having disobeyed Langeron and stood his ground on the basis of what he had seen. His behavior indicates, at the very least, a serious lack of initiative.

Oudinot wanted to march to Studienka, his chosen bridge site, on the evening of the 23rd. But General Aubry, who had scouted the site himself, did not think the terrain there was suitable in the face of the enemy observed across the river at Brili. Thus, Oudinot faked preparations above and below Borisov, but he had the preparations at Studienka proceed at a far too leisurely pace. Napoleon, who had hoped Oudinot would cross on the 24th, became apprehensive and sent him a stern note on that day, telling him it was imperative that he should cross before the day was out. However, even here, the error of a subordinate commander, General Aubry, turned out to be fortunate. A crossing would have been exceedingly difficult on the 24th or even the 25th, since the enemy had not yet departed.

Bridge construction at Studienka started in earnest on the 25th, when Eble and Chasseloup returned from their diversionary operations. On their arrival, they found that practically no preparations had been made and hurriedly started to collect the necessary construction materials. Trees were cut down and the abandoned village of Studienka was dismantled to provide the necessary lumber.

During the night of the 24th, while he was still in Losnitza, Napoleon received word from Victor stating that he himself was withdrawing there. This would mean giving up the road to Studienka. Angry, Napoleon ordered Victor to leave only a rear guard on the Kolopeniczi-Losnitza road and to take two divisions to Kostritza, on the road from Lepel to Borisov. There, Victor was to attack the enemy in case the Russians did not attack first.

When he issued this order, Napoleon expected that Victor would occupy Kostritza by afternoon. This would enable Napoleon, during the following night, to force a crossing with the Guard, II, and IX Corps and thereby close his campaign with a successful operation. But before he arrived at Borisov at 2 p.m. on the 25th, he received more unwelcome news from Victor. The marshal claimed that the new orders had not reached him until he was already on his way to Losnitza and that by then he considered them impossible to execute, so he was therefore continuing his march to Losnitza. Victor now received orders, couched in unmistakable terms, that at least held him in place at Ratuliczi. But the road to the bridge still remained open to Wittgenstein.

In the meanwhile, the rest of the army was drawing near the crossing site. On the evening of the 25th, Davout and Eugene were still in or east of Losnitza, Victor was at Ratuliczi, and Napoleon and the Guard were in and around Borisov, with Ney and Junot on their way there. After nightfall, Oudinot took his corps from Borisov to Studienka, where the bridge construction was to start around 10 p.m. However, even this deadline could not be met because, despite their labors, Eble and Chasseloup had been unable to complete their preparations. The situation appeared all the more desperate because the road was open for Wittgenstein to go straight to Studienka, which he could reach at any time. Also, numerous campfires observed across the river appeared to indicate Tshitshagov's presence. The French also had to expect that Kutuzov would arrive sooner or later. It seemed totally beyond reason that, in fact, the Guard and II Corps held a ten-to-one superiority at this, the decisive, crossing point.

At the moment, the chances for escape appeared dim. Murat suggested that Napoleon slip out during the night in disguise and try to make a getaway under the escort of some loyal Poles. Everyone saw the danger of the situation: The army might be trapped, and Napoleon along with it. Just in case an attack might materialize, Oudinot's entire artillery (40 guns) was deployed on the heights of Studienka and reinforced with parts of the Guard artillery by morning. But Napoleon's star had not yet dimmed. Daybreak on November 26 revealed that the opposite bank of the Beresina had been virtually deserted by the enemy. Thus, around 8 a.m., forty cavalry troopers, each with a voltigeur mounted behind him, crossed over to form a skirmishing line on the far side. Under its cover, another 400 men from Dombrowski's division were ferried across in three small boats. Supported by the fire of the grand battery on the heights of Studienka, this small detachment pushed Kornilov's weak column toward the south.

It was another grand stroke of good fortune for the French that the Cossacks had not destroyed the three successive wooden bridges that led the Zembin road across the Gaina Swamp on the far side of the Beresina. Had they done so, the crossing of the Beresina at Studienka would have been useless, because without those bridges the swamp could not be crossed, despite its ice cover.

Two bridges were laid across the Beresina simultaneously, the one to the north being merely a footbridge. The larger one, about 200 yards to the south, could accommodate the vehicles and guns. Each was supported by 23 trestles, or horses, which required just about all the stout lumber available. Only sticks, thin boards, and straw were to be had for the bridges' covering. Neither of the bridges had a railing, and the larger one was just wide enough to accommodate the wheels of a gun carriage.

Colonel Chapelle, a French engineer officer, compiled a detailed report about the construction of the bridge. According to the reports, the Beresina was 354 feet wide at the crossing site, with its depth varying from about 7 to 8 feet in the center. Thanks to the frost, the ground was hard, so it was possible to get across the marshy banks, which were about 100 paces wide. Otherwise, the vehicles would have been unable to reach the water's edge. The 23 trestles constructed for each bridge varied in height from 3 to 9 feet, which gives a good indication of the depth of the muddy bottom, into which the trestles sank quite deeply. With the trestles set at about 14-foot intervals, the lumber used for the stretchers, about 16 to 17 feet long, had a diameter of between 5 and 6 inches, and there had not been enough time to hew them square. The covering consisted mainly of sticks, 15 to 16 feet long and about 3 to four inches in diameter. For the smaller bridge, the roofing boards of the houses in Studienka had been used in a triple layer, since they were less than an inch thick. They were so weak that their surfaces were awash when they bent under the load of troops passing over. The construction of a third bridge had to be dispensed with because there was not sufficient lumber.

The smaller bridge was completed by 1 p.m., and Oudinot was sent across first with 5600 infantry and 1400 cavalry. By exercising great care, a cannon and a howitzer were brought across, along with a few ammunition caissons. By 4 p.m. the rest of Oudinot's artillery and that of the Guard came across the larger bridge. The guns and wagons bumping over the round-log covering of the bridge shook it so badly that some of the supporting trestles began to settle more deeply into the mud bottom, causing its cover to undulate. After Oudinot was safely across, Napoleon was reluctant to follow because he expected Wittgenstein to appear at any moment. At nightfall, however, he sent Ney across with his 3700 infantry and 300 cavalry.

The first crisis came at 8 p.m. when two of the trestles under the large bridge gave way. Eble was worried about getting enough of the exhausted engineers together to do the repair job, but he was in luck. He found them all bivouacking nearby. But he roused only half of them and left the rest sleeping. At 2 a.m. on the 27th came the next crisis: Another three trestles collapsed, and these were in the deepest part of the river. Now the other half of the engineers, whom Eble had wisely left sleeping, were called in to make repairs. It was 6 a.m. when the bridge was once again open to traffic, but it continued to be a shaky structure that threatened to give way again at any time. Eugene reached Niemanitza on the 26th; Davout made it to Losnitza by nightfall. Victor marched to Borisov, leaving Division Partou-neaux and Delaitre's cavalry brigade behind near Losnitza to form a new rear guard.

During the early morning hours of the 27th, the first stragglers pressed their way across the bridges in considerable disorder. The disarray caused many of them to be pushed into the Beresina, which was not very deep but was ice cold. Then they had to stand aside, as Napoleon took the Guard across—about 5000 infantry and 1400 cavalry—and established his head-quarters in Sanivki. Still on the eastern side of the river were Victor, with about 10,000 infantry and 800 cavalry; Davout and Eugene, each with about 1200 men; and the bulk of the stragglers, intermingled with the baggage train. Only now did the Russians appear at the crossing site in some force.

On the right (western) bank, Tshaplitz had turned around as soon as he heard of the crossing, but he took his time about it. Meeting Kornilov's troops between Stachov and Brili, and some reinforcements sent by Lan-geron, he now had 5000 men together. But they included only about 2800 infantry, which was hardly sufficient to make any headway against Oudinot's 7000, who had gone as far as Stachov. (Langeron himself did not show up until nightfall had put an end to the fighting.) Tshitshagov, learning from Orurk that nothing was going on to the south, had turned around as well, but he got only as far as Borisov. He refused Tshaplitz's suggestion that he attack with everything on hand, because he could assemble only about 20,000 men at that time.

On the eastern bank, Victor had deployed Girard's infantry division and Fournier's cavalry brigade near Studienka to meet a possible attack from Wittgenstein. To deceive the Russian, Napoleon specifically ordered Victor to leave Partouneaux's 4000 infantry and Delaitre's 400 cavalry at Stary-Borisov. But instead of going against Victor, Wittgenstein continued his march to Borisov, even though the sound of gunfire told him where the action was. Afterward, he claimed that bad roads had dictated his course. Thus, on the 27th, he settled for pushing Partouneaux, who had lost his way, in the direction of Borisov. The ever-industrious Seslavin had already arrived there, so Partouneaux was caught in the middle and had to lay down his arms. Only his rearmost element, 1 battalion, with 4 guns, managed to get away.

Back at the crossing, the stragglers began to pour across again, but at 4 p.m. two more trestles of the large bridge gave out. It took 2 hours to repair them, and the number of stragglers began to pile up, creating an impenetrable chaos. Eble and the other officers at the crossing attempted to maintain order, but their efforts were in vain. The stragglers, long bereft of discipline, became an increasingly desperate and ugly mob. At sundown on the 27th, the approaches to the bridges had become totally clogged with vehicles facing every which way. Curiously, however, by nightfall the stragglers became totally disinterested in the bridges, lit their campfires, and settled down for the night. They could not be moved and did not make use of the bridges even when they were repaired and empty.

During the night of the 27th, the rest of I and IV Corps crossed the river and went on at once toward Zembin. But in the morning, on the 28th, Napoleon sent Division Daendels back to the left bank because he had decided to hold the bridges open for another day. Considering the fact that apart from Victor only stragglers remained on the eastern bank, it would have been better for all concerned had Napoleon ordered him across, burned the bridges, and continued his march on the morning of the 28th. Given the situation, Napoleon could no longer expect a lasting success. Indeed, the only success he could achieve at this point would be the saving of that which he still had in hand. Thus, he should have avoided taking any risks with the troops still remaining in the ranks simply to save some more stragglers. Of course, like any soldier, and that's what he still was at heart, he had a deeply seated aversion to leaving anything behind, be it men or guns. And this aversion had both psychological and material roots. On the one hand, like any commander, Napoleon was loathe to leave his men behind; on the other, he was well aware that many, no matter what their present state, could become useful soldiers again. Soon, however, it became impossible to save many more of the stragglers anyway. Had he cut his losses at the right time, the Guard, Oudinot, Victor, and Ney would have still retained their combat-worthiness, and the consequences for all, including the stragglers, would have probably been somewhat milder. At this point, the stragglers were responsible for their own predicament. Remaining deaf to the pleas of the officers who had tried their best to move them, the stragglers had refused to make use of the bridges when they were unused during the hours of darkness.

After Tshitshagov had laid a pontoon bridge during the night of the 27th and had had a conference with Wittgenstein, both of them finally made a simultaneous attack, the latter reinforced by Yermolov's and Platov's troops. Despite the bitter cold and a strong north wind, the entire day was filled with heavy fighting. On the French side, the Poles and Germans, who now constituted the mass of the infantry, surpassed themselves, especially on the right (western) bank, where the favorable terrain prevented the Russians from bringing much artillery into action. Victor and Ney fully lived up to their reputations as combat commanders, conducting their actions with skill and resolution. Here, where the fighting was heaviest, the French success was also the greatest. Since light stands of timber covered most of the ground, only the Borisov-Zembin road offered the Russians a good field of fire, but for no more than two guns. The French, on the other hand, commanded a rise where nine guns could be deployed.

Tshaplitz, reinforced by the infantry of the advance guard, attacked the French forward positions, took Stachov by noon, and advanced against the main position. There, a standing firefight ensued that lasted until about 2 p.m., when Tshitshagov sent Sabaneyev forward with two more divisions. Oudinot's infantry began to waver, even as Oudinot himself was wounded again, and fell back. But the infantrymen were received by Ney, who stood behind.

The Russian infantry, dissolving into great skirmishing swarms in the overgrown terrain, suddenly found itself charged by Doumerc's cuirassiers and 1500 men were taken prisoner. The Russian cavalry waded in to restore the action, but the advance had come to a halt, even though the firefight lasted into the night. A simultaneous attempt by Platov to make for the Gaina bridges, which Tshaplitz's detachment had failed to destroy on the 26th, became bogged down in the swamp.

On the French side, only 10,000 men had come into action. It had not been necessary to use the Guard. The Russians had eventually committed

15,000 men and lost nearly 7000, a testimony to the bitterness of the fighting and the staying power of the Russian infantry.

On the left, Victor's 6000 men occupied a line of heights that ran behind a stretch of bottomland, about 700 paces wide. Wittgenstein's advance guard attacked the points by 5 a.m. and threw them back, but it was 10 a.m. before he was ready to attack the main position. Here, too, the action wore on and took a dangerous turn for the French only when Berg's and Fock's corps entered the fight.

Toward 1 p.m., the Russians at last succeeded in taking a small but strategic patch of woods, from whence they could envelop the French left, while their artillery could fire at the bridges. However, the weak French cavalry, composed of barely 350 German troopers, made Wittgenstein's attack falter. The Russians had brought 14,000 men into the action on this side of the river (Steinheil was still busy disarming Partouneaux's division), and these suffered severely. Here, too, the action eventually abated into a cannonade that lasted into the night.

While the fight was raging on both sides of the river, the scene at the bridgeheads defied description. As soon as the battle had started, hundreds of vehicles and thousands of panic-stricken stragglers had again created an impenetrable maze, described by Colonel Chapelle as being about 1500 meters wide and about 400 meters deep. Radiating from the large bridge like a starburst, more than a dozen columns of vehicles had telescoped into each other, creating a massive blockage, with horses and wagons facing this way and that. Many drivers, attempting to wheel out of their columns, had only made matters worse. Pressing into this mass were thousands of stragglers, terrifying the horses even as solid shot and grenades from the Russian artillery landed among them again and again. The cannonballs left particularly bloody trails as they smashed through men, horses, and vehicles, the latter sending razor-sharp wood splinters flying off in all directions.

IX Corps, which was covering this mass of humanity, stood fast, but its frontage was insufficient to prevent the Russians from deploying even more guns to fire at the bridges and into the melee at the bridgehead. Had Napoleon burned the bridges and marched in the morning, none of this would have happened—and he would not have lost thousands more of his remaining good troops.

Men, and even women and children, who had survived until now were being trampled underfoot. Hundreds drowned while trying to swim across the Beresina. Others managed to cross, but their wet clothing marked them for serious illness and even death in the freezing temperatures. Many drivers had run their horses and wagons into the river, but the vehicles became stuck in the mud of the riverbed before they had gone very far. The drivers abandoned their charges, thereby creating new barriers against which the floating ice floes piled up.

Around 5 p.m. the shooting abated, but the unraveling of the press at the bridgehead progressed at a painfully slow pace. General Eble put his 150 engineers to work to create a path for IX Corps so that it might get across. Selecting a line of approach, they overturned the wagons nearest the bridge and then, one by one, extricated the others along the path. The wagons that still had serviceable teams were sent across; those that didn't were manhandled onto the bridge and dumped into the river. The horses that were still harnessed to broken wagons were cut loose and run across, a small number at a time, to prevent any further traffic jams. On both sides of the avenue thus created, openings were made to permit the movement of people and vehicles. Occasionally, the crack of a pistol or musket was heard, calling the mob to order. Most, but not all, of these shots were fired into the air. It had not been possible to move all the horse cadavers out of the way, so some were literally rolled flat and stamped into the ground, adding to the grisliness of the scene.

Finally, toward 10 p.m., IX Corps made its own crossing in good order, taking along all its artillery. By 1 a.m. all the troops were across, and the bridges were empty again. As soon as the gunfire had stopped, the stragglers had again lit their campfires and settled in for the night. An hour or so after the struggles to get onto the bridges, nobody seemed interested at all. This, of course, had been all the better for IX Corps, which did not have to fight any crowds. After his corps had crossed, Victor spent half the night moving among the campfires, attempting to rouse the stragglers, urging them to cross the river. Eble even had some of the wagons set on fire to induce those around them to move, but he had no better luck than Victor. At 6:30 a.m., the marshal pulled in the last of his pickets and took them across the bridge. This, at last, stirred the stragglers to activity. In no time at all, the press of the day before repeated itself. Eble had been ordered to burn the bridges at 7 a.m., but not until 8:30 could he finally bring himself to do it. Thousands were left behind on the eastern bank of the Beresina. In the long run, however, this was to be a kinder fate than what awaited those who had managed to cross.

On the 29th, Napoleon marched at 6 a.m. with the Guard, followed by Victor, who had crossed between 6:30 and 7 a.m., bringing up the rear of the French. The losses had been extraordinary. Wittgenstein alone had taken about 13,000 prisoners, mostly stragglers, some 5000 of whom were waiting at the bridgehead after they had been cut off by the burning bridges. The number of those killed in action, from starvation, or by the icy cold cannot be calculated. The Guard, for example, which had not come into action at all, lost about 1500 men out of 3500. The total of French losses can only be estimated as being about 30,000. Only twenty-four guns had been taken by the Russians, but a number of others had been thrown into the river.

Still, no matter how great the losses, much had been saved. Napoleon, his generals, and thousands of officers and veteran soldiers had escaped oblivion. Without this cadre, Napoleon could not have rebuilt the Grand Army in 1813. The number of those saved is generally estimated at nearly 40,000, of whom about 12,000 infantry and 2000 cavalry had maintained order right up to the end. Also saved, at least for the time being, were 200 guns, the war chest, and a large part of the baggage.

That this had been at all possible is explained by Clausewitz as follows:

Chance certainly favored Napoleon somewhat, but in the main it had been done by the reputation of his arms. Wittgenstein and Tshitshagov were both afraid of him, his army and his guards, just as Kutuzov had feared them at Krasnoi. Kutuzov thought he could gain his ends without fighting, Wittgenstein did not want to place his newly gained reputation on the line and Tshitshagov did not want to expose himself to another check. These were the moral powers which armed Napoleon when he extricated himself from one of the most difficult situations a general had ever faced. Of course, it was not the moral potential alone. The strength of his spirit, the martial virtues of his army, which not even the most destructive elements could fully overcome, were to show themselves once more in all their lustre.[10]

There is little, if anything, that might be added to Clausewitz's assessment of the events that had transpired during the march from Krasnoi to the Beresina. To do so would simply add up to rephrasing what the great military philosopher has already said.

If anything, the tracing of events during this period has always been difficult. Napoleon himself had ordered that many of his documents be burned during the brief stay in Orsza, and more were lost on the way to the Beresina, as well as during the crossing.

As for Napoleon, he once again lapsed into the passive depression from which he had only briefly, albeit brilliantly, emerged during the days of Krasnoi. That this mood continued to keep hold of him until his departure from the army cannot be denied. Also, it must be regarded as a serious, even if entirely understandable, error that he did not depart with his army on the morning of the 28th, no matter what one might think of it subjectively. As a direct result of the delay, many men who had remained with the colors either died or were wounded and taken prisoner by the Russians; these men deserved a better fate. Their loss was especially tragic since the great majority of the stragglers at the Beresina were men who had deliberately abandoned the colors in July and August and who, on top of this, had refused to make the most of the chances that were offered to them.

NOTES

1. The troops remaining were as follows:

	Men
The Guard	8,000 (including 1500 cavalry)
Davout	4,500
Eugene	2,200
Zaionczek	600
Junot	500
Vistula Legion	1,800
Cavalry reserve	400
Wuerttembergers from Ney's corps (They had gone ahead.)	307
Total	18,307
Plus:	
Remainder of Ney	900
Garrison of Mohilev	1,200
Garrison of Orsza, Cav. Depot Gorki	?

2. Davout's and Eugene's infantry were each formed into 3 battalions with 2 batteries; another 2 batteries were earmarked for Ney. The remainder of the Westphalians were formed into 3 companies and 4 platoons of cavalry, about 300 men in all.
3. Eble was the commander of the bridge train.
4. On its arrival at the Beresina, the Grand Army had the following left in the ranks:

	Men
Old and Young Guard	5,000
Guard cavalry	1,400
Corps Davout	1,200
Corps Ney	1,000
Corps Eugene	1,200
Poles	500
Westphalians	100
Reserve cavalry	100
Vistula Legion	1,500
Total	12,000

5. Chasseloup commanded the engineers.
6. Tshaplitz had 4 battalions, 12 squadrons, 3 Cossack regiments, and 1 battery, totaling 3000 men, with 12 guns. On the 27th, he was joined by another 4 battalions from Corps Langeron, which added about 1500 to 2000 men.
7. There were 8 squadrons and 1 Cossack regiment, with 12 guns.
8. The corps consisted of 10 battalions of the 15th Division, 8 squadrons of dragoons and the light artillery of the 15th Division, with 8 heavy guns.
9. Kornilov had 1 infantry regiment and 2 Cossack regiments, with 4 guns.
10. Clausewitz, Carl von. *Der Russische Feldzug von 1812.* Stuttgart, n.d.

26. The Final Curtain

The crossing of the Beresina marked the end of the Grand Army of 1812. Hunger and cold broke up what was left. There were no magazines between the Beresina and Oszmiana, which was reached on December 6. But by the 3rd, winter had already reasserted itself, and the thermometer dropped to $-4°F$ ($-16°R$); it then plunged to $-29°F$ ($-27°R$) on the 8th. The Cossacks, constantly on the heels of the retreating army, rounded up prisoners by the hundreds and by the thousands every day. In all, 36,000 prisoners and 311 abandoned guns were taken by the Russians between December 1 and 14. The march to the Niemen had become a flight.

Three days after the crossing of the Beresina, only 8823 men remained in the ranks.[1] There was no hope for an end to the pursuit, because the army no longer had the strength to stem it. Nor were there any noteworthy reinforcements waiting to receive the army. In the beginning Ney (and then Victor, who relieved Ney from his rear-guard duties) attempted to delay the pursuers. This brought on several actions, which usually ended with the French continuing their flight. However, even this came to an end, because soon the only troops left in the ranks were those guarding the emperor's person. As a result, the Russians no longer needed to commit infantry to the pursuit and left it almost entirely in the hands of the light cavalry, which was entirely sufficient to break whatever resistance was left.

Wittgenstein and Tshitshagov remained by the Beresina on November

29 and 30 to reorganize their shaken troops. Kutuzov, who did not cross the Dnieper until the 26th, pretended to be upset and feigned disbelief when told of Napoleon's crossing of the Beresina. However, he remained true to his character to the last, again interrupting his march until he received confirmation of the news that Napoleon had continued his retreat.

While the Russians lumbered forward, Napoleon spent most of his time spinning plans that were bound to come to naught. At first, he still hoped to halt the flight ahead of Vilna with Loison's division of 14,000 men, which had assembled there between November 21 and 23, and with Wrede's corps, which still had 5000 men (although Napoleon thought there were more). Schwarzenberg, who had been told only about Ney's and Victor's success of the 28th but nothing of the army's condition, was directed by Maret to draw close. Macdonald was told nothing.

But all of Napoleon's hopes had already been dashed by December 3, when Molodeczno was reached. At the same time, Napoleon's decision to leave the army was ripening. The conspiracy in Paris, even though it had been quickly suppressed, required his presence there, and better sooner than later. A bulletin was issued from Molodeczno on the 3rd to prepare the world for what had happened. It blamed the winter for the disaster, and an astonished Europe readily believed it. How could it have been otherwise? After that, the mold was quickly cast. On the 5th, in Smorgoni, Napoleon advised those around him that he would dash ahead to Paris and raise an army of 300,000 men. Murat was to be in charge of the army, and Berthier, very much against his will, was directed to collect what was left of it at Vilna. The army was to maintain itself there and withdraw across the Niemen only if it became necessary.

Although he could hardly have believed that Vilna could be held at this point in time, Napoleon did hope that Murat, with the help of what was left of the flanking armies, could maintain himself on the Russian side of the Niemen until he would return with a new Grand Army. Napoleon placed great value upon this. If Murat could keep the front that far east, it would be possible to prevent the full extent of the debacle from becoming all too obvious and, at the same time, to retain the resources of Poland and Prussia. Finally, it was important to have a forward staging area for the new campaign. Napoleon was firmly resolved to redress his defeat and have another try at the Russians come spring.

That the Russians would beat him to the punch and pass to the offensive was completely beyond his expectations, especially since he had grossly overestimated the losses they had suffered in the campaign. Nor did it occur to him even for a moment that his vassals were on the point of rebellion.

Napoleon left the army on December 5. Via the waystations of Vilna,

Warsaw, Glogau, Dresden, Erfurt, and Mainz, he galloped into Paris on the night of December 18–19. In passing through Warsaw, he halted just long enough to cast about for more troops, but the gloss of the Polish romance had worn thin. From Dresden, he demanded another 30,000 men from the Austrians and 10,000 from the Prussians. But the time had passed when he could simply raise a finger to gain compliance.

Napoleon has been roundly criticized for leaving the army. While this may be a valid criticism of Napoleon the general, Napoleon the emperor and head of state also had other concerns that demanded his attention. For one thing, his throne had been threatened by the conspiracy. Also, his personal presence in Paris would be helpful when the bulletin of Molodeczno arrived, whereas his presence among the troops could no longer help the army.

St. Cyr put it best when he wrote later that a Napoleon on the defensive did not possess the superiority of a Napoleon on the offensive and that, at this point, the emperor's potential for raising reinforcements was of far greater importance for the army. He ended his dissertation by pointing out how many men Napoleon had succeeded in mobilizing in just 3 weeks after his arrival in Paris, thereby making his departure from the army quite beneficial for the army. Indeed, the need to raise new troops alone justified his departure. Everything had been lost, so everything had to be replaced: officers, soldiers, horses, arms, accoutrements, uniforms, and the money to pay for all these essentials. But now Napoleon also had to pay the price for not having taken any precautions whatever for the event of a failure. Never had France been in so dire need of an army as it was now.

Another factor complicating Napoleon's position was the fact that the entire foundation of his political power in France rested on his military renown. Thus, it was essential that he recover his military status as quickly as possible, despite the catastrophe he had just suffered. And this is where the winter, late but devastating, came to his rescue. The bone-chilling cold was the final, and strongest, impression brought back by the survivors; the debacles suffered by the army in the heat, thirst, and hunger of July and August were relegated to the realm of ancient history, privations only dimly remembered. The frigid winter enabled the general, who had thrown away an army of hundreds of thousands, to claim that only God and the elements were stronger than he. More importantly, for the reasons just stated, this claim found an echo among the survivors.

Although in military circles the truth circulated soon enough, the general public did not perceive even a glimmer of the realities until the Napoleonic era was no longer a topic of current interest. The glory of the capture of

Moscow and the inconclusive bloodbath of Borodino, which was now touted as a grand victory, completely obscured the catastrophe of the Beresina. Thus, Napoleon came away from the Russian disaster with his reputation enhanced rather than diminished.

If, however, Napoleon may be exonerated of the charges leveled against him for leaving the army, he may be seriously faulted for his appointment of Murat as commander of the army during his absence. Murat would make an excellent "spanking boy" if things continued to go wrong, but he was ill-suited for heading the attempt to salvage what could be saved. Murat was a *bon sabreur*. His flamboyance made him popular with the troops, a useful attribute for a leader of men. Brave to the point of recklessness, he was a good man at the head of a charge. But he was not a commander in chief, not even an ideal cavalry commander. His range of excellence and ability was far too narrow for that. Off the battlefield he lacked any of the talents of a commander. Eugene, who was to relieve him, was also not the right man for the post. He had already shown in 1809 that he lacked the necessary attributes of a commander in chief. But with the marshals perpetually bickering among themselves in the absence of their master, Napoleon could not put Davout in charge, even though he would have been the best man for the job. With Davout at the helm, Napoleon might have had a better starting position in 1813.

As Napoleon headed for Paris, the flight of what remained of the central army group continued. However, his departure caused such a loss of posture that even the men of the Old Guard began to throw away their muskets. Barely 2000 of its men were still together. All else had dissolved. It was no longer possible to form even a rear guard. When Loison, Wrede, and a few of the rear-area garrisons joined the column, they were at once caught up in the dissolution of the rest. Loison's division, 14,000 strong on its departure from Vilna, lost 3000 men on the way to Oszmiana. Taking over the rear guard from December 6 to 8, the division lost another 7000 men when the thermometer bottomed out at $-29°F$ ($-27°R$). Even the remaining 4000 diminished by the hour. Wrede fared no better. The 2000 men who joined the column on the 9th disappeared altogether. Hunger, cold, and Cossacks took them all. But, above all, the enemy was the cold. Thus, Napoleon had no trouble whatever throwing its cloak over the real disaster of the Russian campaign.

On the 8th, Murat reached Vilna. Macdonald and Schwarzenberg were finally ordered to withdraw from Vilna to Tilsit and Bialystok, respectively. There was no longer any possibility of holding anything. All in all, the army had only 4300 men[2] left in the ranks. Thus, the mere appearance of Cossacks sufficed to send it flying toward Kovno on the 10th. Only what was left of the Poles had been ordered by Napoleon to go via Olita to Warsaw so that their formations might be rebuilt there. While Murat, accompanied by the rest of the marshals, ran on ahead under the protection of the Guard, Ney attempted to hold back the Cossacks with the remainder of Loison's and Wrede's troops. This ended with their total destruction at Ponari. Whatever the French had succeeded in bringing this far—the guns, baggage, and trophies—was all lost there.

On the same day, the 10th, the Russians occupied Vilna, where they found 15,000 stragglers, including 5000 sick and wounded, as well as 141 guns. Of the guns, 41 were found in the arsenal and 100 were collected from the streets of the city and from the foot of the heights at Ponari. Kutuzov and the main army also arrived in Vilna on the 10th. The misery the Russians found in Vilna again defies description, contrasting starkly with the festive air and the good life that had prevailed in the city just a few days earlier.

The entire diplomatic following of the Grand Army had remained in Vilna, and their presence had also attracted most of the Polish high aris-tocracy, who whiled away their days in endless rounds of receptions, dinners, and balls. Napoleon had been so successful at concealing the true condition of the army that the news of the disaster arrived only with the first refugees. And then it had the effect of a bombshell.

When the Russians arrived, nearly all the houses were filled with the sick and wounded; the yards served as repositories for the dead bodies. The walking dead, wrapped in rags, wandered through the streets. At one church-yard alone, 8000 cadavers were said to have been piled up and covered with snow, which the cold soon turned into a shroud of ice.

From Vilna onward, the Russian cavalry again sufficed to chase the French across the Niemen. Ney attempted to hold the bridge at Kovno, but this turned out to be a futile gesture because both the Niemen and the Vilia were frozen over. The Russians entered the city on the 14th. Upon reaching the Niemen, the Russian pursuit, which had lasted nearly 2 months and had covered about 575 miles, came to an end. The French losses had been enormous; the army was destroyed.

The rest of the French, including the Poles and Lithuanians, who crossed the Niemen numbered somewhere between 40,000 and 45,000. On their way to the Vistula, they were joined by a few thousand more who had not participated in the campaign. However, all that remained in the ranks were 400 men of the Old Guard and 600 of the Guard cavalry. All else was dissolved. What had once been corps, numbering in the tens of thousands, were now only bands of 50 or 60 men. In a final manifestation of martial spirit, they gathered around the eagles, colors, and standards that had been collected at what was left of the corps headquarters. The entire artillery came to nine guns, hauled along from Kovno. The stragglers who had managed to come this far wound their way through the countryside in groups of tens and twenties, most of them already marked by death or permanent disabilities. Still, among these remnants were about 2000 officers and some 10,000 trained cavalrymen who would soon become cadres for new formations. For the moment, however, they were only promissory notes.

The only real troops left were those of the flanking forces: 43,000 men under Schwarzenberg (25,000 Austrians, 8000 French, 8000 Saxons, and 2000 Poles) and 23,000 under Macdonald (15,000 Prussians and 8000 Poles, Bavarians, and Westphalians). These 66,000 men plus the more than 40,000 stragglers from the central army group, totaling no more than 110,000 men, were all that was left of the army of 612,000 men (including reinforcements) that Napoleon had taken against the Russians. About half a million men, 150,000 army horses, and an even greater number of commandeered and privately owned horses of the officers were missing. Of the men, no more than 100,000 had become prisoners. Some of the others filled the hospitals; most of the missing, however, were dead. The Russians reported the burial or burning of 243,612 bodies during the early months of 1813. Thousands more, already disposed of before then, remain uncounted.

Still, no matter how grave his losses, Napoleon's hope of ending the campaign along the Niemen was not entirely without foundation. The two flanking armies still numbered 66,000 men between them and reinforcements were coming up. Division Heudelet, plus garrison and march troops, numbered 26,700 men (see Appendix XXI). Division Grenier and other march troops, accounting for another 24,500, could follow shortly. In addition, Napoleon, who still underestimated his own losses, continued to count on a large fraction of the main army. Indeed, after only a few weeks, 15,800 men were again usable. There were also nearly 10,000 cavalry troopers who had to be remounted and another 12,400 who could be used only for new formations. Among the latter totals, however, were several thousand officers and noncommissioned officers who had been wounded and were sent back long before the retreat began.

Notwithstanding their disenchantment, the Poles provided another 17,000 men in the following weeks. The other allies could also be asked to step up to the counter again, notably the Austrians and Prussians, whose potentials were second only to that of France itself.

Thus, there was the theoretical possibility of amassing 190,000 men within a few weeks, even without new formations and without weakening the French presence in Prussia and adjoining territories. Given the heavy losses the Russians had themselves suffered, they would never have been able to carry the war into Germany in the face of these forces. The Russian losses may be placed at 250,000 men. Although 40,000 of these eventually returned to the army, the forces the Russians had available in mid-December (see Appendix XXII) were rather weak. As a result, there was little inclination to continue the war.

The three Russian armies were now gathered in Lithuania. The main army had numbered 97,112 men and 20,000 Cossacks, with 622 guns, on its departure from Tarutino; it had been joined by 5142 recruits during the interim (according to the returns of December 4). It now had 38,944 men and about 10,000 Cossacks, with 272 guns. Thus, apart from the Cossacks, it was down by 63,310 men. Of these, about 12,000 were dead and 48,355 were in the hospitals. Thus, the battalions remaining, despite the amalgamations, had only company strength, while the cavalry regiments consisted of only 120 to 150 men each. The Cossack regiments were down to an average of about 150 men as well.

The Third Western Army had suffered no less. Tshitshagov had 31,150 men, with 180 guns, at the Beresina. On December 19, excluding Knorring's detachment in Minsk, he had only 17,454 men, with 156 guns. Also under Tshitshagov and coming up was II Reserve Corps, which, with Knorring's column, came to about 10,000 men.

Relatively strongest was Wittgenstein. Including some reinforcements on the way, he had 33,783 men and 3000 Cossacks with 191 guns. Added to these must be the Bobruisk garrison of 2000 men.

In Volhynia stood Sacken, whose losses had been partially replaced by reinforcements. With Essen's corps coming up, as well as other detachments, he had 19,000 men, with 96 guns. There were other detachments, too, such as that of Repninski, which had 4200 men and 700 Cossacks, with 16 guns.

Thus, the total strength of the Russians in mid-December came to about 128,000 men and 21,800 Cossacks, with 804 guns. Of reinforcements, only about 8000 were to be expected any time soon. The training and equipping of the reserve troops took time, and none could be expected on the Niemen before early May. That was not enough to conduct a war against Napoleon, who was still believed to have enormous resources. Furthermore, the internal condition of the Russian army left much to be desired. Although in infinitely better shape than the remnants of the French army, the troops were so exhausted that it became necessary to halt operations. This was all the more problematic, since an advance into Germany would have required leaving substantial forces behind in Poland and in front of Danzig. At the same time, Kutuzov, who now wielded considerable clout, had his own personal reasons (in addition to his physical infirmities) for not wanting to put his newly won glory on the line. Thus, he was resolved to settle for pushing the French back across the Niemen. This is what he had been charged with, and he had done it.

Since matters with the central army group had settled themselves for the time being, all that still needed to be done was to eject Macdonald and Schwarzenberg. The latter had sufficient strength to maintain himself at Slonim, where he arrived on December 7. Indeed, he still might have achieved considerable results. However, on the 14th, he retreated voluntarily after being accurately informed about conditions in the center and after being advised about the true attitudes of the cabinet in Vienna. Thus, he placed no value whatever on winning any success for Napoleon but sought only to retrieve his corps in good condition. He was already on his way when Murat's order directing him to Bialystok arrived. He made it there by the 21st. However, acting on orders from Vienna, he had already entered into confidential negotiations with the Russian generals in front of him, so he did not stay in Bialystok. Contrary to Murat's orders, he went to Pultusk, arriving there on the 29th. He remained in Poltusk with his Austrians, while Reynier was sent to Czarnoglov to cover Warsaw.

Metternich had already embarked upon his politics of mediation, which, for the moment, came to no more than a tacit armistice between the Austrians and the Russians. The idea was to induce Napoleon to give in and make peace should his military position deteriorate further. This secret defection, which left the Austrians with a foot in both camps, was the first step in this direction.

Meanwhile, the Russians in the southern sector, like those in the center, had gone into winter quarters. But in the north, the Russian high command planned a last major stroke against Macdonald. He had refused to lend credence to the news coming from the center and had not dared to take it upon himself to withdraw without orders. Thus, he had remained in the area around Mitau and did not even begin to draw back until December 18 and 19. The Russians now wanted to avail themselves of this opportunity.

Wittgenstein was to march from Czervonny-Dwor and Niemenczin on the 17th, via Keidany and Yurborg, to block Macdonald's retreat. Meanwhile, Lewis and Paulucci were to follow Wittgenstein with columns formed from the Riga garrison. Unfortunately for the French, Macdonald's corps, upon which the possibility of holding the Niemen line rested, contained the least trustworthy elements of all, the Prussians, who made up two-thirds of the force. Yorck, one of the more noteworthy generals in the allied camp, was a fiery patriot and Napoleon hater. Although he had repeatedly turned back overtures from the Russians since the retreat began, he now saw that the time had come to do something that might lead toward casting off the yoke Napoleon had placed upon his nation. Since he could not possibly get his king's approval to seek any kind of accommodation with the Russians, he took it upon himself to act. Macdonald's faulty disposition for the retreat had left Yorck trailing behind the leading echelons of X Corps with most of his troops. Availing himself of this opportunity, Yorck unilaterally concluded what has since become known as the Convention of Tauroggen with General von Diebitsch from Wittgenstein's corps. In doing so, he detached his corps from the Napoleonic juggernaut and declared himself neutral.

The Russians had placed great store in the possibility that this would happen, and Alexander had long prompted Essen and Paulucci to get in touch with Yorck for reasons that were as much political as they were military. Now it had finally happened, after the Prussian general received confirmed news of what had occurred in the center. Most French historians, taking the Napoleonic party line, have regarded this event as simply an act of Prussian treachery. Others have tended to treat it as a local matter. But it was, in effect, a pivotal incident that went far beyond the immediate military consequences. The defection of the Prussian corps reduced Macdonald's force to only a few thousand men, Poles, Bavarians, and Westphalians, with whom Macdonald himself barely managed to escape.

With the passing of X Corps, all chances for holding on to the Niemen line were gone. All the French could do was retreat to the Vistula. But this was only the immediate result of Yorck's action. Now it also became evident how daring it had been of Napoleon to leave the Prussians, embittered by years of French exactions, armed and in his rear. He had not been unaware of the Prussian potential. The severe military restrictions he had placed upon the Prussians in the Treaty of Tilsit and the watchdogs he had put in place to guard its provisions speak for themselves. Napoleon had also read Frederick William quite correctly. He was certain that there would be no daring moves from him. But now this obscure Prussian general had dared to do what his king would not, thereby igniting a spark that was to inflame anti-Napoleonic passions across the whole of northern Germany.

These passions had been there, however, burning beneath the surface, even before news of the Russian debacle began to circulate. For example, in Hanover the police commissioner observed most of the congregation walking out of a church before a *te deum* was offered for the Battle of Borodino; nor had the commissioner himself liked the sermon. On October 1, his follow-up report indicated that in the other churches, the reaction had been even more pointed. In several places, most of the congregation had clapped their hymnbooks shut with a bang and walked out in the middle of the *te deum*, visibly demonstrating their displeasure.[3] But if public opinion in Westphalia was smoldering, it was beginning to boil in Prussia. It was only a question of time before it found an echo in Russia.

Tsar Alexander had long recognized that he would have to beat Napoleon to the punch rather than sit still and wait for the next assault from a wiser and more prudent Napoleon. Thus, he resolved to carry the war to Napoleon until the emperor was thoroughly defeated and overthrown. At this point, however, this intention was mostly a personal matter. Neither the army nor the nation were greatly excited over any such prospect. Nevertheless, Alexander forged ahead with his preparations. On December 12, he ordered a new and extensive draft call, 8 men from every 500 souls, as well as the creation of numerous new reserve formations and a substantial expansion of the line cavalry.

Until now, Alexander had been reluctant to break the resistance of those around him against carrying the war beyond the borders of Russia. This had been due mainly to his lack of success in winning support for, and backing of, his own insufficient resources through positive responses from Berlin and Vienna. Now Prussian participation had become a distinct possibility. Yorck's action had incited a popular response that King Frederick William could neither ignore nor suppress. At first, the Prussian king had repudiated Yorck's high-handed action. After all, there were still French garrisons all over Prussia. But after the first dust had settled on the matter, it had to be clear to him that he no longer had any choice at all. Yorck's defection was sufficient to bring Napoleon's ire down on the heads of the Prussians again, even if the king were to repudiate the Convention of Tauroggen. Thus, for better or worse, the Prussians would have to prepare to defend themselves. But first, the French presence in Prussia had to be reduced.

Alexander had now succeeded halfway. Austria would need more convincing, because Metternich would allow no hostile moves until Austria was adequately rearmed. But the tsar was already on the move. His vision was clear. However, even modern historians occasionally still allude to the idea that his sole motivation was his vanity and his self-perception as the savior of Europe. But in the face of the underlying hard realities of the continuing Napoleonic presence in Europe, such a view may hardly be upheld. Despite all of his posturing, Alexander did what he knew had to be done.

Tshitshagov and Platov had already been ordered to join Wittgenstein in pursuit of Macdonald. On the Russian New Year's Day of 1813, the Russian main army also crossed the Niemen. The Wars of Liberation had begun, and their military events would eclipse even those of 1812.

NOTES

1. Remaining in the ranks were the following:

	Infantry	Cavalry
Old Guard	2000	
Young Guard	800	
Guard cavalry		1200
Victor	2000	100
Davout and Eugene	400	
Under Ney:		
Vistula Legion	200	
Dombrowski	800	
V Corps	323	500
II Corps	500	____
Total	7023	1800

2. On December 10, departing from Vilna, the troops still in the ranks were as follows:

	Infantry	Cavalry
Old Guard	600	800
Young Guard	100	
Ney, Wrede, Loison	2300	200
I, II, III, IV, and IX Corps	300	____
Total	3300	1000

3. Kleinschmidt. Kassel 1970.

Epilogue

In our modern society, the parameters of distance and time have changed. Having breakfast in Paris and lunch in New York on the same day is commonplace. Few people pause to consider that an automobile trip from Boston to New York, a matter of only a few hours today, once involved six 18-hour stages by coach and 5 nights spent at inns along the Boston Post Road. For these reasons, modern readers are apt to accept the enormous distances of the marches executed by Napoleon's armies with an equanimity that is completely misplaced. Even for the modern soldier, a 50-mile forced march is an experience shared by comparatively few—though forgotten by none who ever participated in one. The thought of stringing together several such marches is an idea light-years away from modern realities, in which such massive overland displacements are undertaken by truck or railroad. As a result, to the tabletop strategist who has never experienced even one such march, ten of them strung together are simply twice as many as five, without their implications being fully thought through. One might just as well ask a runner to do another 10 miles on the day after he has finished a marathon race.

When it comes to the magnitude of the distances the Russian theater of operations offered to Napoleon's infantry, it is helpful to remember that even today most westerners, especially Americans, generally know very little about eastern Europe and north Asia. Even places like Iran, so much in the news in recent years, are generally viewed on large-scale maps, where the span of a hand may cover a thousand miles and telescope vast distances into insignificance. Numbers such as 300, 400, or 500 miles are likely to become abstractions unless they are translated into more meaningful terms. For example, the distance from Berlin to Moscow, 998 miles as the bird flies, is roughly equal to the 1100 road miles from New York City to Omaha, Nebraska. However, even this comparison will have meaning only to those who have covered such a distance by automobile, not by airplane or railroad.

Even those who remember from their school days that Russia covers about one-sixth of the earth's land surface are still apt to be at a loss when the Russian landmass is measured by more familiar parameters. Few, for example, are aware of the fact that the distance from Berlin to Vladivostok, the Russian seaport on the Sea of Japan, is equal to the distance (in the opposite direction) from Berlin to San Francisco.

It must be obvious that even Napoleon and the men around him could have had only a vague notion about such distances and that only those who had traveled extensively inside Russia would have had even an inkling of the practical problems the movement of troops on such a vast scale would present. Surely, Napoleon could calculate how many marches would take his army to Moscow, and his envoys and ambassadors to the Russian court in St. Petersburg certainly knew the roads there as well as any western traveler. As to the rest of Russia, that remained largely *terra incognita*, illuminated by secondhand hearsay. Although Napoleon had gathered a considerable amount of intelligence about Russia, the realities were something else again. Even though he had gotten a taste of the east European winter in 1806–1807, he could hardly predict what the Continental summer might hold in store for his troops.

Of course, it was the emperor's fondest wish that the Russians would come to meet him somewhere near their western frontier so that he might smash their armies with one or two of his patented master strokes. Had they not done so, twice before, when their own country wasn't even in immediate danger? But anything that happened beyond that had to be three parts gamble to one part certainty. This appears to be contradicted by the great care Napoleon took in laying the logistical foundations for his Russian venture. However, massive though his logistical preparations were, they were intended to feed an army of equally massive proportions. Thus, for a while, even after the campaign had gotten under way, he must have expected to make most of the march to Moscow as the conqueror of a nation already defeated and bowing before him.

From the start, it was obviously impossible to overrun so much Russian territory that a substantial portion of the Russian army would be effectively separated from its depots and the resources it needed to continue waging war. All Napoleon could do was drive a wedge deeply into Russia. Even at that, the wedge aimed in the direction of Moscow would cover only some of the poorest tracts of Russia in Europe, not by any means its most fertile and populated provinces. And once this wedge was driven so deeply that its point reached Moscow (which Napoleon had correctly recognized as the national and spiritual hub of Russia), then the invader was bound to present the defender with a pair of enormous and correspondingly sensitive flanks. Indeed, most critics agree that once Napoleon ventured beyond Smolensk, the base of the wedge he had driven was already too narrow and an open invitation to disaster.

In light of these considerations, the idea advanced by Osten-Sacken offered a far better chance for a military success: Napoleon ought to have taken his right shoulder forward in an attempt to throw the two Russian armies into each other and then pin them against the Baltic. As matters stood, however, Napoleon's best hope for such a success was that the Russians would stand and fight it out on their western frontier. Failing in this, the next order of business, according to Osten-Sacken, would have been to arrive in Moscow with sufficient strength to continue holding the initiative and to dictate the further course of events. Interestingly, the Prussian, who reflected the thinking of the Prussian general staff around the turn of the century, thought that Napoleon should have succeeded in this had he paid better heed to the condition of his army and desisted from driving it into the ground.

This poses a deliciously Clausewitzian dilemma about the nature of political and military objectives in war. Modern historians dote on the Prussian military philosopher's maxim that political objectives should, at all times, govern military considerations. But how does one distinguish one from the other? Clearly, the motivations that drove Napoleon onward beyond the point of military prudence were political rather than military. Yet, in the end, the military failure that sprang from this brought political failure in its wake.

Osten-Sacken pointed out that a more methodical approach should have enabled Napoleon to reach Moscow with his army still numbering about 400,000 effectives. He thought that about half of these would have sufficed to control Moscow and its surrounding tracts, while the other half, after subtracting about 20,000 men to garrison the line of communications, should have been divided into three roughly equal parts. Of these, one should have covered Smolensk, another should have covered Volhynia, while the third should have kept Wittgenstein in check, ignoring Riga altogether.

However, this would have called for the sort of methodical campaigning that ran totally contrary to Napoleon's nature, and it would have demanded at least two campaign seasons, which was politically unacceptable. Europe was expecting another lightning stroke in the grand Napoleonic style, and the nymbus of Napoleon's military invincibility stood at the very foundation of the pax Napoleon, such as it was.

In all of this, it must be patently clear that all plans for bringing Russia to heel were based on the premise that Alexander's resolve to continue fighting would collapse as soon as his forces suffered a serious defeat. There can be no other sensible conclusion.

Looking back upon the events of 1812 with the benefit of hindsight and the experiences of more recent times, it appears unrealistic in the extreme to envision a takeover of the Russian giant by military means alone. Even if the scheme advanced by Osten-Sacken succeeded in full measure, how long could Napoleon sustain a force of 400,000 men 1000 miles from its support bases if the Russians continued to resist? Was he to fight a war of attrition under such circumstances? Hardly. Again, an arrival in Moscow with sufficient force to implement Osten-Sacken's scheme could aim only at inducing Alexander to seek a political accommodation. It could not possibly have imposed a military solution.

Everything hinged on the Russian resolve to hold out. If the Russians gave up, then all things were possible. If they did not, then no military solution was to be had. This then, the misreading of the Russian resolve, was the source of Napoleon's greatest miscalculation.

There remains the idea, advanced by some, that Napoleon might have put Russia into turmoil with a declaration of emancipation for the Russian serfs. But that would have precipitated a situation not unlike the one France had experienced during its own revolution. There was no telling where that would lead.

As stated earlier, Clausewitz thought it quite appropriate to judge an event by its outcome, but he also said that it could be critiqued only on the basis of information that was available at the time the event transpired. That is, second thoughts based on hindsight can never provide a fair and accurate basis for criticism.

On a geographic basis alone, and with the Spanish experience in mind, surely Napoleon's topographical engineers could advise him that Russia in Europe alone was about six times the size of the Iberian Peninsula or metropolitan France and thus was capable of swallowing even an army as large as the one he was proposing to lead into Russia. And just as surely, Napoleon's military experience must have made him acutely aware of the military implications of driving a wedge so deeply into a hostile Russia that its apex reached all the way to Moscow.

In short, anything that might have made a Russian campaign feasible had to be based on the idea that the Russians would give up the fight long before the army reached Moscow. If they did not, then there was nothing that could make an invasion work. As it was, Napoleon, his blood up for the kill after his unchecked advances, failed to read these fundamental signs, which ought to have given him pause. Quite probably, the continuing withdrawals of the Russians misled him into thinking that they lacked the stomach to face him. Even today, Napoleon's cheering section sees nothing but victory in his advances into Russia and hails every inconclusive brush with the Russians' rear guards as yet another glorious victory. Time and again, it must have seemed to Napoleon that the moment of decision was just another leap ahead—from Vilna to Vitebsk to Smolensk, pushing him onward beyond the point of no return. When he did finally awaken to the fact that the worst might happen, the situation had become very much a matter of "in for a penny, in for a pound." This concept was already evident at Smolensk, where Napoleon exhibited an unmistakable lack of his customary decisiveness, as if he already believed that what was happening was inevitable anyway. This must have come as a tremendous shock to him, he who had made all Europe bend before him like reeds in a wind. His self-confidence severely shaken, other lapses were soon to follow: first in Moscow; then during the retreat, when only the desperate situation at Krasnoi briefly revived him; and again after the first day of the Battle of Leipzig in October 1813. It has become conventional to say that his genius had deserted him during those moments, but perhaps the opposite was true. Perhaps his genius saw the future all too clearly, and this caused the emperor, who had been so favored by his "lucky star," to experience despair and hold on in the desperate hope that somehow a solution might offer itself, that the enemy might yet make some incredible blunder. Above all, however, he might have simply refused to accept the truth, because the next move would entail an admission of failure. This could hardly come easily to a man like Napoleon.

As for the Russians, their greatest stroke of good fortune reposed in the fact that the plans they had formulated for the defense of Russia proved unworkable even before they were put into execution. The greatest feat of the Russian high command during the French offensive was that Barclay, no matter what he did or did not do, never lost his head, even in the face of vociferous critics at his own headquarters. He was able to hand over to

Kutuzov an army that was still in combat-worthy condition. Barclay received very little credit for this accomplishment or for his stellar performance at Borodino during his lifetime. If he received any satisfaction at all, it came from Bagration's deathbed admission that he had been wrong and that Barclay had done the right thing after all.

As the Grand Army rolled on toward Moscow, it was only a matter of time before the Russians became fully aware of its internal state of dissolution. But not everybody in command on the Russian side truly appreciated the significance of this. That was left to Kutuzov. This crafty old campaigner also had a thorough understanding of the elements of time and distance, even if his perceptions were totally different from those of Napoleon. Napoleon translated these elements into force and energy, whereas Kutuzov translated them into difficulties and problems. And just as Napoleon's views were entirely appropriate for the blitzkriegs he had become accustomed to waging, so, too, were Kutuzov's views quite appropriate for the conditions prevailing in the Russian theater of operations. Campaigning on the southern frontiers of the Russian empire had made him acutely aware of the importance of adequate logistics and the difficulties they posed. Thus, he was among the very first of those in positions of authority to see clearly that Napoleon was destined to run back out of Russia faster than he had come in, even if not a single battle was fought.

The stand the Russian army made at Borodino had been forced upon him by those who failed to see the situation as clearly as he did. It was a mere gesture of appeasement toward the hawks in the Russian high command, serving the psychological rather than the military needs of the moment. This clear perception of the realities of the situation must always be invoked in assessing Kutuzov's subsequent behavior, even if his apprehensions about facing Napoleon in battle ruled his actions. Borodino did nothing to lessen the experience of Austerlitz. The real arguments against Kutuzov center largely on his failure to completely destroy Napoleon's central army group and possibly make Napoleon himself a prisoner of war. This would have indeed precluded the necessity of renewing the war against him in 1813 at further enormous cost in human lives and misery.

A completely different set of arguments centers on the idea that Napoleon might have come back to Russia for a second attempt if Murat or Eugene had displayed better generalship, if Yorck and the Prussians hadn't defected, if the Austrians had been loyal to the cause, and so on. However, such "what ifs" tend to negate the other side's responses. Everyone agrees that the Russians were tenacious fighters. They had faced the ogre at Borodino and come away bloodied but unbowed. By the end of the campaign they had tasted the sweet smell of success, even of outright victory. And the fact that this had not been due to the men who commanded them was completely beside the point.

It is also doubtful that the Grand Army Napoleon assembled in Saxony in 1813 would have fared any better in Russia than had the juggernaut of 1812, even as the Russians of 1813 performed better than those of 1812. And the massive logistical support the British threw into the Prussian Baltic ports in 1813 could just as easily have gone a bit farther up into Russian ports. Also, the difficulties and obstacles posed by the Russian expanses would not have been any different from those of 1812, except that the Russians might have capitalized on them from the start.

The military machine Napoleon the artilleryman had created was perfectly suited to fight short, violent campaigns, but whenever a long-term sustained effort was in the offing, it tended to expose feet of clay. Napoleon had virtually invented mass armies. However, even though he knew how to wield these masses better than any man of his time, learning how to effectively support them in the field did not come nearly so easily. In the end, the logistics of the French military machine proved wholly inadequate. The experiences of short campaigns had left the French supply services completely unprepared for what they were to face in Russia, and this was despite the precautions Napoleon had taken. There was no quick remedy in the offing that might have repaired these inadequacies from one campaign to the next. Even in 1813, when another campaign was fought out in a far more limited space and when massive depots along the Elbe River were never more than a few marches distant, the Napoleonic armies often went hungry and operational noncombat losses continued to be enormous. The limitations of horse-drawn transport and the road networks to support it were simply not up to the task.

Indeed, modern militaires have long been in agreement that Napoleon's military machine at its apex, and the scale on which he attempted to operate with it in 1812 and 1813, had become an anachronism that could succeed only with the use of railroads and the telegraph. And these had not yet been invented.

Glossary

cadre This term refers to the skilled key personnel who form the skeleton of a unit. Around it a formation can be fleshed out with recruits and trained to become a useful military unit.

cavalry Throughout the eighteenth century, only the cuirassiers or regiments of horse were considered line cavalry, i.e., the cavalry that would deliver the charge in closed order—in the line.

commissariat Often simply referred to as the "administration" or the "intendance," this was the equivalent of the modern quartermaster services. The term "commissariat" was chosen deliberately for use in this book because every American who has served in the armed services is familiar with the "commissary."

The French intendance, or commissariat, was divided into five separate departments, of which only three played a major role during the Russian campaign: *vivres-pain* (responsible for the supply of bread, dried vegetables, salt, wine, vinegar, brandy, and rice—the latter highly unpopular with French troops), *vivres-viande* (responsible for meats), and *fourrages* (responsible for feed, fodder, and straw for the horses). It was presided over by a hierarchy of quasi-military officials (much like our modern-day civil service employees of the defense department), ranking from the intendant general and *commissaires-ordonnateurs* down to the butchers, bakers, and other specialized tradesmen. All of them, especially the ranking echelons of the intendance, were held in thoroughly ill repute by the French soldier—and deservedly so. However, the idea that the poor reputation of Napoleon's armies, which resulted from foraging and requisitioning, can be blamed entirely on the intendance alone, must be regarded as a half-truth at best.

Cossacks These were irregular tribal cavalrymen who, in the Russian army, fulfilled the role hussars played in central Europe. By the time of the 1812 campaign, the hussars had long been "regulars," but the Cossacks continued to be listed separately on army returns. This practice reflected their irregular status.

dragoons These were considered mounted infantrymen throughout most of the eighteenth century, and rode horses of inferior quality. However, as they were increasingly used in the line by the end of the century, they came to be regarded as line cavalry in their own right. Curiously, Napoleon reversed the general trend, in progress elsewhere in Europe, toward a standard, all-purpose cavalry by reemphasizing the differences among the various branches of the mounted arm.

flying column Generally a raiding party of unspecified size, a flying column could run to several thousand men. Operating only on general directives, it did not have a fixed base of operations and was not responsible to any intermediate headquarters; i.e., it was detached and hence "flying."

grenadiers It is thought that grenadiers originated in the Swedish army during the Thirty Years' War, when Regensburg (Ratisbon) was under siege in 1634. On that occasion, a special volunteer force was culled from the infantry to hurl grenades during the siege operations. Since the hand grenades were heavy, fickle, and thus dangerous to handle, their manipulation called for strong daredevils. Eventually, every company added several such extra-pay elites to its roster. They were eventually brigaded into companies and battalions, retaining both their title and elite status long after the throwing of grenades had ceased to be their primary function. The cognomen had become honorific.

hussars Originating in Hungary, hussars first appeared in Continental military establishments as irregular cavalrymen, designated primarily for the little, minor, or guerrilla war, i.e., for raiding, scouting, and security services. Reflecting their irregular status, they were, throughout much of the eighteenth century, listed separately on all army returns.

jaeger Derived from the German word for "hunter," this cognomen entered military parlance during the Thirty Years' War, when a formation of 300 sharpshooters was raised among the Hessian game wardens and forest rangers, who were collectively termed *Jaeger* (as they continue to be to this day). From that time onward, the term "jaeger" almost invariably described elite light infantry of the regular military establishment. These infantrymen generally dressed in green coats or otherwise displayed some green uniform elements; above all, they displayed the hunting horn, which became emblematic of such formations. The term "jaeger" thus came into general use in the Teutonic language orbit, as well as in Russia, while it entered the Romanic languages as *chasseurs* (French) and *cacciatores* (Italian) in its various forms.

light   This term refers to all those troops who were primarily intended to fight in open order. In contrast, line troops, in the sense of the linear order, were intended to fight in line formation.

line   In a generic sense, this term refers to all those troops who, in contrast to irregular formations, were part of the regular military establishment. The term, however, originated during the linear era, when formal tactics centered on the linear formations, which could be properly employed only by regular, well-trained professional troops.

points   These are the most forward elements of a military formation. They act as scouts and lookouts to prevent ambushes or surprises.

tirailleurs   These were skirmishers who fought in open order.

trains   As the transportation services of the army, the trains were charged with the hauling of all supplies.

ulans   These were cavalrymen armed with lances. The term is thought to have derived from the *oghlani*, the bodyguards of the khans of the Krim Tatars; the *oghlani* were young Tatar nobles who were armed with lances. The term "ulan" entered the European language orbit through the Poles, who excelled in the use of the lance.

voltigeurs   From the French *voltiger* (to flit, to fly, to flutter about), this term refers to the regular French light infantry soldiers of the line, who were specifically trained to fight in open order. A company of such voltigeurs eventually became an organic part of each line infantry battalion; it was designed to perform light infantry tasks detached from the column or line, in conjunction with the grenadier company. Thus, the voltigeurs began to represent a sort of halfway point on the road toward a standard infantry, trained to conduct all types of infantry combat.

With the institution of these light companies, the French light infantry regiments, originally designed to perform all light infantry tasks for the line regiments, lost their purpose. Thus, after the 1808 reorganizations, the light regiments lost their special status, retaining only their traditions, uniform distinctions, and titles: Their grenadiers were called *carabiniers*, and as they now had voltigeur companies of their own, the center or line companies retained the title of *chasseurs*.

Appendices

NOTE ON ARMY STRENGTH REPORTS

The numbers cited in the various strength reports at a given date usually represent an amalgam of actual numbers and estimates. This is due to the fact that the strength reports did not usually arrive at the headquarters on the same day (some units might be one or more days' marches distant). Thus, the aggregate strength of an army, as it was known at headquarters on any given day, always consisted in part of estimates. And, being transitory, that is, of use only until the next series of carnets or reports came in, many ended up being at least in part misplaced or lost. This was true especially at French Imperial Headquarters, where much was deliberately destroyed when Napoleon ordered a great many records to be burned at Orsza, when the central army group prepared for its march to the Beresina.

Due to researches made in the course of the nineteenth century, we are today more accurately informed about details relating to exact strengths at any specific point in time than were Napoleon or the Russian commanders in chief. Still, what was lost in 1812 remained lost, and researchers had to resort to interpolations gleaned from surviving reports of earlier and later dates and from ancillary sources, such as notations made in the memoirs of some corps and division commanders. This accounts for the "slippage" encountered in attempting to reconcile some detailed numbers with aggregates. And it is for this reason that most of the researchers generally give round numbers when citing aggregate strengths. Armies were, after all, living organisms and their numbers fluctuated by the day, even by the hour.

NOTE ON GENERAL COMMAND POSTINGS

Whenever, in the lists that follow, the name of the officer appointed to a command post is not given, it is because: a) the brigade or unit was operationally split so that no official appointment was made; b) the officer appointed to the post changed often; or c) the name of the officer is no longer ascertainable. Generally, whenever such a brigade acted as a unit, the ranking officer present would exercise the command function.

A Brief Demographic Survey of Europe, 1809

Area	Population
France (i.e., all the territories administered by the central government in Paris, including the territories to the right of the Rhine— Wesel, Kehl, Kastel, and Kostheim— incorporated by the senate resolution of January 21, 1808.)	36,559,000
Italy (a kingdom tied to France by personal union)	6,389,000
Rhine Confederation (German states that had declared themselves independent of the German empire under the protectorate of Napoleon)	
Signing on July 12, 1806:	
Bavaria, a kingdom	3,231,000
Wuerttemberg, a kingdom	1,211,000
Baden, a grand duchy	924,000
Berg, a grand duchy	931,000
Hesse-Darmstadt, a grand duchy	541,000
Prince Primate State (Frankfurt and Loewenstein-Wertheim)	170,000
Nassau, a duchy	272,000
Hohenzollern-Hechingen, a principality	14,000
Hohenzollern-Sigmaringen, a principality	36,000
Salm-Salm, a principality	30,000
Salm-Kyrburg, a principality	19,000
Isenburg-Bierstein, a principality	43,000
Aremberg, a principality	58,600
Liechtenstein, a principality	5,000
Hohengeroldseck, a principality	4,500
Signing on September 25, 1806:	
Wuerzburg, a grand duchy	285,000
Signing on December 11, 1806:	
Saxony, a kingdom	1,987,000

Area	*Population*
Signing on December 15, 1806:	
Saxe-Weimar, a Saxon duchy	109,000
Saxe-Gotha-Altenburg, a Saxon duchy	180,000
Saxe-Meiningen, a Saxon duchy	48,000
Saxe-Hildburghausen, a Saxon duchy	33,000
Saxe-Coburg-Saalfeld, a Saxon duchy	59,000
Signing on April 18, 1807:	
Anhalt-Bernburg, a duchy	35,000
Anhalt-Dessau, a duchy	53,000
Anhalt-Koethen, a duchy	28,800
Schwarzburg-Sondershausen, a duchy	45,000
Schwarzburg-Rudolstadt, a duchy	52,000
Waldeck, a duchy	47,800
Lippe-Detmold, a duchy	70,500
Schaumburg-Lippe, a duchy	20,000
Reuss (elder line), a duchy	26,000
Reuss (junior line), a duchy	56,000
Westphalia, a kingdom	1,942,000
Signing between February 18 and October 10, 1808:	
Mecklenburg-Strelitz, a duchy	70,000
Mecklenburg-Schwerin, a duchy	328,600
Oldenburg, a duchy	159,500
Total, upon completion of Rhine Confederation	14,537,000
Miscellaneous German Territories under French administration	1,411,300
Client states:	
Naples, a kingdom	4,963,000
Holland, a kingdom	2,011,000
Spain, a kingdom (in rebellion)	10,369,000
Other states:	
Austrian empire:	
German territories	8,735,000
Hungary and associated territories	10,366,000
Galicia (with Western Galicia)	3,900,000
Russian empire in Europe	30,000,000
Prussia, a kingdom	4,987,000
Denmark, a kingdom (with Norway)	3,367,000
Sweden, a kingdom	2,227,800
Warsaw, a duchy	2,277,000

Area	Population
Portugal, a kingdom	3,200,000
Helvetia, a republic (closely tied to France by constitution)	1,638,000
Wallis, a republic (same as above)	100,000
San Marino, a republic	7,000
Papal State (as of April 2, 1808)	668,000
Sardinia, a kingdom	520,000
Teutonic Order, sovereign territory of commandery	25,000
Danzig, a free Hanseatic City	84,000
Montenegro, a principality	196,000
Ottoman empire in Europe	10,725,000

APPENDIX II

The French Military
Establishment, 1812

THE GUARD CORPS

The Guard Corps consisted of the following:

3 grenadier regiments of the Old Guard (1 Dutch)
2 chasseur regiments of the Old Guard
1 fusilier grenadier regiment
1 fusilier chasseur regiment
1 flanqueur chasseur regiment
7 voltigeur regiments of the Young Guard
7 tirailleur regiments of the Young Guard
1 battalion velites of Turin
1 battalion velites of Florence

2 squadrons elite gendarmes
1 squadron mamelukes
1 regiment mounted grenadiers (grenadiers *a cheval*)
1 regiment dragoons
1 regiment light horse (chasseurs *a cheval*)
2 regiments lancers (1st Polish, 2nd Dutch)
2 companies honor guards (one of Turin, one of Florence)

1 regiment foot artillery (9 companies)
1 regiment horse artillery (6 companies)
2 battalions artillery train
Engineer troops (genie)

In the course of the 1812 campaign, a third regiment of Guard lancers was raised in Lithuania, but it never became operational.

The infantry regiments of the Guard Corps consisted of only 2 battalions, each of 4 companies. Since they were elites themselves, they had no elite (grenadier or voltigeur) companies. Nor did the Guard have any depots. It replenished itself by levying the line. This, however, can have held true only for the Old and so-called Middle Guard (the fusilier guards), because the voltigeurs and tirailleurs of the Young Guard were being expanded on such a scale that the pick of the recruits was directly

418

introduced into these regiments. This, of course, necessitated depot facilities to process, train, and equip the inductees.

The standard complement of the Guard cavalry regiments was 5 squadrons, with the exception of the chasseurs, who, together with the attached Mameluke squadron, numbered 10 squadrons.

The reason the chasseurs of the Guard had such a large complement was that they were, by designation, the emperor's escort; a squad of chasseurs accompanied him wherever he went. This picket, which consisted of an officer and twenty troopers, was always saddled and bridled, 24 hours a day. The men were drawn from the duty squadron, which was rotated daily. Owing to the special circumstances of the Russian campaign, the strength of this escort in attendance was increased to four squadrons, two each from the light and heavy cavalry, which rotated every other day.[1]

In time, the remainder of the Guard cavalry regiments took on extra squadrons as well; the regiments that had so-called Middle Guard squadrons by 1813 were the first to do so. These squadrons must have begun life as depot formations at a time, after 1809, when it was no longer prudent to denude the line cavalry of veteran troopers.

THE LINE INFANTRY

The line consisted of 107 line regiments and 31 light regiments, as well as 5 penal regiments. Even though there were only 107 line and 31 light, the ordinal numbers identifying these units ran to 130 and 34, respectively, because the shuffles during the reorganizations had left vacant 23 numbers in the line and 3 in the light. Eventually, the penal regiments were assigned numbers as well.

By 1812, the organizational structure of the infantry regiments already represented a compromise because of the growing lack of adequate overhead staffs and regimental depot facilities. That is, since the regiment no longer fulfilled a role in the tactical structure of the brigade, whose basic units of maneuver were the battalions, the regiment had become an administrative entity, responsible for collecting, equipping, and training the replacements. Thus, it was more convenient to have the depots raise extra battalions rather than to attempt to create new regimental overheads. As a result, the increases in the number of regiments during the years leading to the buildup for 1812, and again in 1813, were not at all representative of the increases in the French infantry's manpower, much of which went into the extra battalions of the existing regiments. Many of the new regimental numbers that did come into being originated with the incorporation of the Dutch and the annexed territories, the so-called neo-Frankish units.

The reduction of the number of companies per battalion in 1808, from 10 to 6 companies (4 fusilier, 1 grenadier, and 1 voltigeur company), had freed many noncoms and company officers for new formations, even though the strength of the battalions actually increased. Whereas the old fusilier company had placed 25 files (6 corporals and 69 fusiliers) into the line, the post-1808 table of organization called, instead, for 50 files (6 corporals and 144 fusiliers) in the deployed line. That is, the old companies had become platoons, of which the new companies had two.

Even though under the new establishment each regiment was to have 1 depot and 3 field battalions, this was nowhere uniform. The Spanish venture had already required the mobilization of the depots of many regiments, although the depots were reformed after their departure for Spain. When the army prepared for the Russian campaign, the table of organization of most French regiments designated to participate was raised to five field battalions each. This measure was bound to further dilute the veteran cadre of these units (most of which were assigned to I and II Corps). The situation was further exacerbated when the remaining cadre of the center companies was called upon to man the elite companies of all the new battalions with the best of the available manpower.

THE LINE CAVALRY

The line cavalry consisted of:

  2 carabinier regiments
 14 cuirassier regiments
 24 dragoon regiments
  9 lancer regiments
 12 hussar regiments
 28 light horse regiments (chasseurs *a cheval*)

The normal complement of a cavalry regiment was 5 squadrons, each consisting of 202 horses in the heavy cavalry and 256 horses in the light (lancers, hussars, chasseurs). Compared to the other Continental military establishments, these French squadrons were rather large and divided into two companies each. Elsewhere in Europe, the company formation had been abolished as a subunit of the squadron, but the latter remained somewhat larger, having about 150 horses on average. Only in the British cavalry did the troop (the equivalent of the company) continue to play a role. Unlike the situation with the ad hoc formations of the infantry that marched into Spain with 1000-man battalions, bloated with green conscripts, things were never so simple with the cavalry. Thus, the Spanish venture gave rise to combined cavalry formations. These consisted, on the one hand, of companies gleaned from the depots of several regiments and, on the other, of larger formations split away from their parent units to form so-called second formations, which were identified by the designation *bis* following the unit's ordinal number.

Generally, the cuirassier regiments were considered the best among the French cavalry, with the exception of the low-numbered hussar regiments, which had maintained an eighteenth-century mercenary character and still attracted the cream of the volunteers from all corners of Europe. On the whole, however, the French cavalry was not held in great respect by its adversaries. Most of its celebrated feats can be credited to the "foreigners" who served under its colors.

According to Pelet-Narbonne, who puts it rather blandly, the bulk of the French cavalry was mounted on cold-blooded stock (this situation improved somewhat when the depots of the cuirassiers were moved to the north German lowlands) and its greatest virtue reposed in the fact that it was accustomed to operate in very large formations.[2] Taking the analysis a step further, Friederich says that there was nothing wrong with the French cavalry troopers' courage but states that the men lacked the innate sense of care necessary to keep their horses in serviceable condition on campaign.[3] But it is Napoleon himself who informs us that *"Le Francais n'est pas homme de cheval."*

THE ARTILLERY

The French artillery was organized into:

  9 foot artillery regiments, each of 22 companies
  7 horse artillery regiments, each of 6 companies
12 artillery train battalions

The complement of the foot companies was 120 men; that of the mounted and train companies was somewhat less.

At this time, almost none of the European military establishments manned the batteries until the army mobilized; at that point, the guns and their associated equipment were drawn from the depots. In peacetime, only a few drill batteries were kept in hand to train the recruits.

Unlike the infantry and cavalry, which gradually fell victim to the drains and dilutions occasioned by incessant campaigning and expansions, the artillery remained a constant throughout, never yielding its high standards of quality and performance. This branch, from which Napoleon himself sprang, was excellently officered at all levels of command and was well trained. This, of course, was also due to the fact that the artillery was hardly ever subjected to the, at times, crippling losses that were the lot of the infantry. Additionally, the artilleryman generally traveled light, off-loading his pack onto the battery vehicles at every opportunity. Thus, notwithstanding the grinding marches, which might debilitate the draft horses, the artillery personnel was hardly ever subjected to excessive operational noncombat losses.

The foot batteries generally consisted of 8 pieces (6 guns and 2 howitzers). The horse batteries usually had only 6 pieces. The gun crews were drawn from the artillery regiments, while the artillery train provided the teams and drivers. The battalions of the artillery train were also commanded by artillery officers.

Also part of the artillery were:

   3 pontoon battalions, totaling 28 companies
147 companies Coast Guard (*gardes cotes*)
 33 companies fortress artillery (*canoniers sedentaires*)
 19 companies artificers
  6 companies armorers

Even though they were nominally part of the navy, mention must be made here of 4 marine artillery regiments, totaling 16,000 men in 12 battalions. Because of the inactivity of the fleet, they were available for artillery duties and, indeed, became part of the Grand Army of 1813—as infantry. On occasion, even military writers have characterized these troops as being of secondary quality, which is completely inaccurate. These men were excellently drilled veterans, a fact that Marmont appreciated the moment he first laid eyes on them. The troubles they ultimately encountered were due entirely to the lack of experienced infantry officers who had commensurate abilities to command them in combat, men who would have known how to make the most of these fine soldiers.

TECHNICAL TROOPS

These consisted of:

7 engineer battalions
2 miner battalions (*mineurs*, i.e., siege specialists)
2 squadrons engineer train

MISCELLANEA

In addition to all the units discussed above, there were the following:

22 army train battalions, each of 6 companies (The 18th was devoted entirely to the ambulance services.)
Veterans, who were organized into 75 fusilier companies and 25 gunners' companies
Military police
Municipal Guard of Paris
Departmental reserve companies

THE AUXILIARIES

A large number of foreign troops served under the eagles of the empire. (They must not be confused with the allied foreign contingents.) Apart from major uniform distinctions (where they existed), these auxiliaries were recognizable by the French national *tricolore* cockade they wore on their headgear. They included:

4 foreign regiments (*regiments etrangere*)
4 Swiss regiments, each of 4 battalions
1 Battalion Neufchatel
The Vistula Legion (Polish), consisting of 4 infantry regiments, each of 4 battalions

The Portuguese Legion, consisting of 3 infantry regiments, each of 3 battalions
2 Spanish infantry regiments, each of 2 battalions

There were also a Spanish Engineer Battalion and a Portuguese one. These, however, are better described as labor battalions, as they were made up of prisoners of war. Only the supervisory personnel bore arms.

Not included above are the two lancer regiments of the Vistula Legion (they had been incorporated into the French national military establishment as the 7th and 8th Lancer Regiments of the Line) or the three Polish infantry regiments (which, although in French pay, remained part of the Polish army). Similarly excluded are the troops of the kingdom of Italy, the Illyrian provinces, and the Ionian Islands, as well as Joseph Napoleon's Spanish troops.

THE NATIONAL GUARD

Garrison duties were to be performed primarily by the National Guard, which had been resurrected by Napoleon. It was equipped like the regular line infantry and came under the jurisdiction of military justice. Its use beyond the borders of metropolitan France, however, was prohibited by law. In March 1811, 88 cohorts of the National Guard, each with a complement of 6 fusilier companies of 140 men, were mobilized. Each cohort was to include a depot as well as an artillery company of 100 men. None of these units, however, were anywhere near up to strength.

NOTES

1. Caulaincourt, Armand de. *With Napoleon in Russia.* New York, 1935.
2. Pelet-Narbonne, G. von. *Geschichte der Brandenburgisch-Preussischen Reiterei.* Berlin, 1905. 2 vols.
3. Friederich, R. *Geschichte des Herbstfeldzuges 1813.* Berlin, 1903. 3 vols.

APPENDIX III

The Army of Spain

In 1812, the total number of troops in Spain came to about 220,000 men. The army included:

    4 regiments Young Guard
   84 line and light regiments and 3 foreign regiments, mostly of only 2 and 3 battalions each
    ? independant battalions (Their number was few and constantly changing.)
    1 provisional Swiss regiment
    1 Spanish regiment
   40 cavalry regiments or parts thereof
   92 artillery companies

Added to these must be another 30,000 allied troops, mostly Italian, German, and Spanish.

APPENDIX IV

Troops Remaining in France and Italy, 1812

These consisted of:

    2 regiments Young Guard
    8 infantry regiments, four with 4 battalions, four with 2 battalions
  104 single line battalions
   52 single light battalions
    1 foreign regiment with 4 battalions
    4 battalions from the other three foreign regiments
    8 supernumerary cavalry squadrons
   48 artillery companies
    ? Coastal guards, depots, Marine gunners, veterans, and cohorts of the National Guard

The actual present strength of these troops barely exceeded 275,000 men.

APPENDIX V

The Grand Army, 1812

HEADQUARTERS AND STAFF:
BERTHIER, CHIEF OF STAFF

The staff consisted of about 400 officers, headed by 21 general officers in charge of the various departments of Napoleon's headquarters—the general staff, general army administration, commissariat, general artillery staff, hospital administration—as well as the area and post commanders in the rear of the army. In addition, there were a large number of civilian government officials. An indeterminate number of secretaries, servants, grooms, and drivers—those of Napoleon's own household staff as well as those affiliated with the staff officers—collectively numbered in the thousands.

Headquarters Troops

Although the emperor generally set up housekeeping amid the bivouacs of the Old Guard, security of the general headquarters was in the hands of troops specifically designated for this purpose. These included:

Batallion Neufchatel	1 bn.
Guides of the chief of staff	1 co.
I Battalion, 2nd Infantry (Baden)	1 bn.
Gensdarmes d'Elite	2 sqns.
Squadrons in attendance	4 sqns.

The squadrons in attendance were furnished by the Guard cavalry. They were rotated approximately every other day, with each set consisting of two heavy and two light squadrons.

THE TROOPS

IMPERIAL GUARD

YOUNG GUARD: Mortier

1st Division: Delaborde

Brig. Berthezene	4th Tirailleurs	2 bns.
	4th Voltigeurs	2 bns.
	5th Voltigeurs	2 bns.
Brig. Lanusse	5th Tirailleurs	2 bns.
	6th Tirailleurs	2 bns.
	6th Voltigeurs	2 bns.

2nd Division: Rouguet

Brig. Lanabeze	1st Voltigeurs	2 bns.
	1st Tirailleurs	2 bns.
	Leibgarde (Hessian)	2 bns.
Brig. Boyeldieu:	Fusilier chasseurs	2 bns.
	Fusilier grenadiers	2 bns.
	Flanqueurs	2 bns.

OLD GUARD: Lefebvre

3rd Division: Dorsenne

Brig. Boyer	1st Chasseurs, O.G.	2 bns.
	2nd Chasseurs, O.G.	2 bns.
Brig. Curial	1st Grenadiers, O.G.	2 bns.
	2nd Grenadiers, O.G.	2 bns.
	3rd Grenadiers, O.G. (Dutch)	2 bns.

CAVALRY OF THE GUARD: Bessieres

Walther	Grenadiers a cheval	5 sqns.
St. Sulpice*	Dragoons	5 sqns.
Guyot	Chasseurs a cheval	5 sqns.
	Mamelukes	1 co.
Kraczinsky	1st Lancers (Polish)	4 sqns.
Colbert*	2nd Lancers (Dutch)	4 sqns.

ATTACHED TROOPS

Division Claparede (ex-Vistula Legion)		
Brig. Chlopiki*	1st Vistula Regt.	3 bns.†
	2nd Vistula Regt.	3 bns.†
Brig. Bronikowski:	3rd Vistula Regt.	3 bns.†
	4th Vistula Regt.	3 bns.‡

Velites du Prince Borghese (Italian)	1 bn.§
Velites of the Tuscan Guards (Italian)	1 bn.§
Engineers (Spanish)	1 bn.
7th Lancers of the Line (ex-1st Vistula Lancers)	4 sqns.
Prussian artillery	2 cos.

*Also functioned as brigadier.
†The 3rd Battalions came up later in the campaign.
‡The regiment came up later in the campaign.
§Came up in September.

I CORPS: Davout

1st Division: Morand		
Brig. d'Alton	13 Light Inf.	5 bns.
Brig. Gratien	17th Line Inf.	5 bns.
Brig. Bonami	30th Line Inf.	5 bns.

2nd Division: Friant (later Dufour, then Ricard)		
Brig. Dufour	15th Light Inf.	5 bns.
Brig. Vendedem	33rd Line Inf.	5 bns.
Brig. Grandeau	48th Line Inf.	5 bns.
	Regt. Joseph Napoleon (Spanish)	2 bns.

3rd Division: Gudin (then Gerard)		
Brig. Gerard	7th Light Inf.	5 bns.
Brig. Dessailly	12th Line Inf.	5 bns.
Brig. Leclerc	127th Line Inf.	2 bns.
	8th Rhine Conf. Regt. (Mecklenb.-Strel.)	1 bn.

I CORPS: Davout (*cont'd.*)

4th Division: Desaix
  (then Friedrichs)

Brig. Barbanegre	33th Light Inf.	4 bns.
Brig. Friedrichs	85th Line Inf.	5 bns.
Brig. Leguay	108th Line Inf.	5 bns.

5th Division:
  Compans

Brig. Duppelin	25th Line Inf.	5 bns.
Brig. Teste	57th Line Inf.	5 bns.
Brig. Guyardet	61st Line Inf.	5 bns.
Brig. (?)	11th Line Inf.	5 bns.

Corps cavalry:
  Girardin

Brig. Pajol	2nd Chass. a cheval	4 sqns.
	9th Lancers (Polish)	4 sqns.
Brig. Bourdesoulle	1st Chass. a cheval	4 sqns.
	3rd Chass. a cheval	4 sqns.

II CORPS: Oudinot

6th Division: Legrand

Brig. Albert	26th Light Inf.	4 bns.
Brig. Moreau	26th Line Inf.	4 bns.
Brig. Maison	19th Line Inf.	4 bns.
Brig. Pamplona	128th Line Inf.	2 bns.
	3rd Line Inf. (Portuguese)	2 bns.

8th Division: Verdier
  (then Maison)

Brig. Raymond-Vivies	11th Light Inf.	4 bns.
	2nd Line Inf.	5 bns.
Brig. Pouget	37th Line Inf.	4 bns.
	124th Line Inf.	3 bns.

9th Division: Merle

Brig. Amey	3rd Prov. Regt. (Croatian)	2 bns.
	4th Line Inf. (Swiss)	3 bns.
Brig. Condras	1st Line Inf. (Swiss)	2 bns.
	2nd Line Inf. (Swiss)	3 bns.
Brig. Coutard	3rd Line Inf. (Swiss)	3 bns.
	123rd Line Inf.	4 bns.

II CORPS: Oudinot (*cont'd.*)

Corps cavalry* (not certain)		
Brig. Castex	23rd Chass. a cheval	4 sqns.
	24th Chass. a cheval	4 sqns.
Brig. Corbineau	7th Chass. a cheval	4 sqns.
	20th Chass. a cheval	4 sqns.
	8th Lancers (Polish)	4 sqns.

*The four French cavalry regiments were barely up to half of their establishments even at the outset of the campaign.

III CORPS: Ney

10th Division: Ledru		
Brig. Gengoult	24th Light Inf.	4 bns.
	1st Line Inf. (Portuguese)	2 bns.
Brig. Morion	46th Line Inf.	4 bns.
Brig. Bruny	72nd Line Inf.	4 bns.
	129th Line Inf.	2 bns.
11th Division: Razout		
Brig. Joubert	4th Line Inf.	4 bns.
	18th Line Inf.	4 bns.
Brig. Compere	Illyrian Regt.	4 bns.
	2nd Line Inf. (Portuguese)	2 bns.
Brig. d'Henin	93rd Line Inf.	4 bns.
25th Division: Marchand		
Brig. von Hugel	1st Inf., "Prinz Paul" (Wuerttembg.)	2 bns.
	4th Inf. (Wuerttembg.)	2 bns.
Brig. von Koch	2nd Inf., "Herzog Wilhelm" (Wuerttembg.)	2 bns.
	6th Inf., "Kronprinz" (Wuerttembg.)	2 bns.
Brig. von Brusselle	1st Jaeger Bn., "Koenig" (Wuerttembg.)	1 bn.
	2nd Jaeger Bn. (Wuerttembg.)	1 bn.
	1st Light Inf. Bn. (Wuerttembg.)	1 bn.
	2nd Light Inf. Bn. (Wuerttembg.)	1 bn.
	7th Inf. (Wuerttembg.)*	2 bns.
Corps cavalry: Woellwarth		
Brig. Mouriez	11th Hussars	4 sqns.
	6th Lancers of the Line	3 sqns.
	4th Mtd. Jaeger Regt. (Wuerttembg.)	4 sqns.

III CORPS: Ney (cont'd.)

Brig. Beurmann	4th Chass. a cheval[†]	4 sqns.
	28th Chass. a cheval[†]	4 sqns.
	1st Mtd. Jaeger Regt. (Wuerttembg.)	4 sqns.
	2nd Mtd. Jaeger Regt. (Wuerttembg.)	4 sqns.

[*]In Danzig until September; joined division in November.
[†]As most of the French chasseur regiments, the present strength was quite weak.

IV CORPS: Eugene de Beauharnais

Italian Guard: Lecchi		
Honor guards[*]		1 co.
Royal velites[*]		2 bns.
Line elites		2 bns.
Conscripts of the guard		2 bns.
Guard cavalry: Triaire		
Dragoon guards		2 sqns.
Queen's Dragoons		4 sqns.
13th Division: Delzons (then Guilleminot)		
Brig. Huard	8th Light Inf.	2 bns.
	84th Line Inf.	4 bns.
Brig. Roussel	1st Prov. Regt. (Croatian)	2 bns.
	92nd Line Inf.	4 bns.
Brig. Ferrier	106th Line Inf.	4 bns.
14th Division: Broussier		
Brig. de Sivray	18th Light Inf.	2 bns.
	9th Line Inf.	4 bns.
Brig. Almeras	35th Line Inf.	4 bns.
	Regt. Joseph Napoleon (Spanish)[†]	2 bns.
Brig. Pastol	53rd Line Inf.	4 bns.
15th Division: Pino		
Brig. Fontana	1st Light Inf. (Italian)	1 bn.
	2nd Line Inf. (Italian)	4 bns.
Brig. Guillaume	Dalmatian Regt. (Italian)	3 bns.
	3rd Light Inf. (Italian)	4 bns.
Brig. Dembowski	3rd Line Inf. (Italian)	4 bns.
Corps cavalry: Ornano		
Brig. Guyot	9th Chass. a cheval	3 sqns.
	19th Chass. a cheval	3 sqns.

IV CORPS: Eugene de Beauharnais (*cont'd.*)

Brig. Villata	1st Chass. a cheval (Italian)	4 sqns.
	2nd Chass. a cheval (Italian)	4 sqns.

*Still in Berlin on September 19; then went to Warsaw.
†This is still questionable. The sources are conflicting.

V CORPS: Poniatowski (*Polish troops throughout*)

16th Division: Zaionczek		
Brig. Mielzynski	3rd Inf. Regt.	3 bns.
	15th Inf. Regt.	3 bns.
Brig. Paszkowski	16th Inf. Regt.	3 bns.
	13th Inf. Regt.	3 bns.
17th Division: Dombrowski		
Brig. Zoktowski	1st Inf. Regt.	3 bns.
	6th Inf. Regt.	3 bns.
Brig. Pakosz	14th Inf. Regt.	3 bns.
	17th Inf. Regt.	3 bns.
18th Division: Kamieniecki (then Knieaziewicz)		
Brig. Grabowski	2nd Inf. Regt.	3 bns.
	8th Inf. Regt.	3 bns.
Brig. Wierzbinski	12th Inf. Regt.	3 bns.
Corps cavalry: Kaminski		
Brig. Tyszkiewicz	4th Chass. a cheval	4 sqns.
Brig. Kaminski	1st Chass. a cheval	4 sqns.
	12th Lancers	4 sqns.
Brig. Sulkowski	5th Chass. a cheval	4 sqns.
	13th Hussars	4 sqns.

VI CORPS: St. Cyr (*Bavarian troops throughout*)

19th Division: Deroy		
Brig. Siebern	1st Light Inf.	2 bns.
	9th Line Inf.	2 bns.
	1st Light Inf.	1 bn.
Brig. Raglowicz	4th Line Inf.	2 bns.
	10th Line Inf.	2 bns.
	3rd Light Inf.	1 bn.

VI CORPS: St. Cyr (*Bavarian troops throughout*) (*cont'd.*)

Brig. Rechberg	8th Line Inf.	2 bns.
	6th Light Inf.	1 bn.

20th Division: Wrede

Brig. Vincenti	2nd Line Inf.	2 bns.
	6th Line Inf.	2 bns.
	2nd Light Inf.	1 bn.
Brig. Beckers	3rd Line Inf.	2 bns.
	7th Line Inf.	2 bns.
	4th Light Inf.	1 bn.
Brig. Habermann	5th Line Inf.	2 bns.
	11th Line Inf.	2 bns.
	5th Light Inf.	1 bn.

Corps cavalry: (No appointment made)

Brig. Seydewitz	3rd Chevaulegers	4 sqns.
	6th Chevaulegers	4 sqns.
Brig. Preysing	4th Chevaulegers	4 sqns.
	5th Chevaulegers	4 sqns.

VII CORPS: Reynier (*Saxon troops throughout*)

21st Division: Lecoq

Brig. Steindel	Gen. Bn. Liebenau	1 bn.
	Inf. Regt. Prinz Friedrich	2 bns.
	Inf. Regt. Prinz Clemens	2 bns.
Brig. Nostiz	Inf. Regt. Prinz Anton	2 bns.
	1st Light Inf. Regt.	2 bns.

22nd Division: Gutschmidt (then Funck)

Brig. von Sahr	Gren. Bn. von Anger	1 bn.
	Gren. Bn. von Spiegel	1 bn.
	2nd Light Inf. Regt.	2 bns.
Brig. von Klengel	Inf. Regt. Koenig	2 bns.
	Inf. Regt. Niesemeuschel	2 bns.
	Gren. Bn. Eychelberg	1 bn.

Corps cavalry: (?)

Brig. Gablentz	Hussar regiment	8 sqns.
	Drag. Regt. Polenz	4 sqns.
	Lancer Regt. Prinz Clemens	4 sqns.

VIII CORPS: Vandamme, later Tharreau, then Junot (*Westphalian troops throughout*)

23rd Division: Tharreau		
Brig. Damas	3rd Light Bn.	1 bn.
	2nd Line Inf.	3 bns.
	6th Line Inf.	2 bns.
Brig. Wickenberg	2nd Light Bn.	1 bn.
	3rd Line Inf.	2 bns.
	7th Line Inf.	3 bns.
24th Division: von Ochs*		
Brig. Legras	Elite chasseur carabiniers	1 bn.
	Chasser guards	1 bn.
	Grenadier guards	1 bn.
	1st Light Bn.	1 bn.
	5th Line Inf.	2 bns.
Corps cavalry: von Hammerstein		
Brig. von Hammerstein	1st Hussars	4 sqns.
	2nd Hussars	4 sqns.
Brig. Wolff†	Gardes du Corps	1 co.
	Chevauleger Guard lancers	4 sqns.

*Brigade Danloup-Verdun, originally part of Ochs's division, stayed behind in Danzig during the opening stages of the campaign and never entered Russia as an operational unit. It was eventually broken up. The 1st Line Inf. (2 battalions) was assigned to Grandjean's 7th Division; the 4th Line Inf. (2 batallions) was first assigned to Loison's 34th Division, then, during the late stages of the retreat, to the remainders of VI (Bavarian) Corps. The 8th Line Inf. (2 battalions) was sent into the central operations area at its own request. The exact times when these units passed from one jurisdiction to another may no longer be determined, but it is known that these dislocations took place between September and November.
†When Jerome left the army with his Gardes du Corps, the Guard lancers were assigned to Hammerstein.

IX CORPS: Victor

12th Division: Partouneaux		
Brig. Billiard	10th Light Inf.	1 bn.
	29th Light Inf.	4 bns.
Brig. Camus	Prov. Line Regt. (1 battalion each from 36th, 51st, and 55th Line)	3 bns.
	44th Line Inf.	2 bns.
Brig. Blammont	125th Line Inf.	3 bns.
	126th Line Inf.	4 bns.

IX CORPS: Victor (*cont'd.*)

26th Division: Daendels		
Brig. Damas	1st Line Inf. (Berg)	2 bns.
	2nd Line Inf. (Berg)	2 bns.
	3rd Line Inf. (Berg)	1 bn.
	4th Line Inf. (Berg)	2 bns.
Brig. Hochberg	1st Line Inf. (Baden)	2 bns.
	2nd Line Inf. (Baden)	1 bn.
	3rd Line Inf. (Baden)	2 bns.
	Light battalion	1 bn.
Brig. Prinz Emil*	Leibregiment (Hessian)	2 bns.
	Garde Fuesiliere (Hessian)	2 bns.
28th Division: Girard		
Brig.†	4th Inf. Regt. (Polish)	3 bns.
	7th Inf. Regt. (Polish)	3 bns.
	9th Inf. Regt. (Polish)	3 bns.
Brig. (?)	Inf. Regt. von Low (Saxon)	2 bns.
	Inf. Regt. von Rechten (Saxon)	2 bns.
Corps cavalry: Fournier		
Brig. Delatre	2nd Lancer Regt. (Berg)	3 sqns.
	Chevauleger regiment (Hessian)	3 sqns.
Brig. Fournier	Dragoon Regt. Prinz Johann (Saxon)	4 sqns.
	Hussar regiment (Baden)	4 sqns.

*The Hessian brigade did not serve as a field brigade but came up as single regiments from the Danzig garrison.
†The 3rd Battalions of these regiments joined the army on September 28 in Smolensk.

X CORPS: Macdonald

7th Division: Grandjean		
Brig. Bachelu	5th Inf. Regt. (Polish)	4 bns.
Brig. Radziwill	10th Inf. Regt. (Polish)	4 bns.
	11th Inf. Regt. (Polish)	4 bns.
Brig. Ricard	13th Inf. Regt. (Bavarian)	2 bns.
	1st Line Inf. (Westphalian)	2 bns.
27th Division: Graewert (then Yorck)		
Brig. Below	1st Combined Inf. (Prussian)	
	II/1st Eastpruss. Inf. ⎫	
	I/2nd Eastpruss. Inf. ⎬	3 bns.
	Fus./1st Eastpruss. Inf. ⎭	

X CORPS: Macdonald (*cont'd.*)

	2nd Combined Inf. (Prussian)	
	I/3d Eastpruss. Inf.	
	I/4th Eastpruss. Inf. } 3 bns.	
	Fus./4th Eastpruss. Inf.	
	Fus./2nd Eastpruss. Inf. *	1 bn.
Brig. Horn	3rd Combined Inf. (Prussian)	
	II/1st Pommeranian Inf.	
	I/Kolberg Inf. } 3 bns.	
	Fus./1st Pommeranian Inf.	
	4th (Combined) Inf. (Prussian)	
	I, II, and Fus./Leibregiment (King's Own)	3 bns.
Brig. Raumer	5th Combined Inf. (Prussian)	
	I/1st Westpruss. Inf.	
	I/2nd Westpruss. Inf. } 3 bns.	
	Fus./2nd Westpruss. Inf.	
	6th Combined Inf. (Prussian)	
	II/1st Silesian Inf.	
	II/2nd Silesian Inf. } 3 bns.	
	Fus./2nd Silesian Inf.	
Unattached	Eastprussian jaeger battalion	1 bn.
Corps cavalry: (?)		
Brig. Jeanneret	3rd Combined Hussars (Prussian)	
	1st and 3rd Sqns., 1st Silesian Huss.	
	1st and 2nd Sqns., 2nd Silesian Huss. } 4 sqns.	
	1st Combined Hussars (Prussian)	
	3rd and 4th Sqns., 1st Leib-Huss.	
	2nd and 3rd Sqns., 2 Leib-Huss. } 4 sqns.	
Brig. Huenerbein	1st Combined Dragoons (Prussian)	
	1st and 2nd Sqns., 2nd Westpruss. Drag.	
	2nd and 4th Sqns., Lithuanian Drag. } 4 sqns.	
	2nd Combined Dragoons (Prussian)	
	1st and 3rd Sqns., 1st Westpruss. Drag.	
	1st and 3rd Sqns., Brandenbg. Drag. } 4 sqns.	

*Was not mobilized until June 1812.

XI CORPS: Augerau

30th Division: Heudelet[a]
Brig. (?)	1st Prov. Regt.	3 bns.
Brig. (?)	6th Prov. Regt.	4 bns.
Brig. (?)	7th Prov. Regt.	3 bns.
	8th Prov. Regt.	4 bns.
	9th Prov. Regt.	4 bns.
	17th Prov. Regt.	4 bns.

31st Division: Lagrange[b]
Brig. (?)	10th Prov. Regt.	4 bns.
	11th Prov. Regt.	3 bns.
Brig. (?)	12th Prov. Regt.	4 bns.
	13th Prov. Regt.	3 bns.

32nd Division: Durutte[c]
Brig. Antheiny	36th Light Inf. (penal regiment)	3 bns.
	131st Line Inf. (penal regiment)	3 bns.
	7th Rhine Conf. Regt. (Wuerzburg)	3 bns.
	Chevaulegers de Wuerzbourg	1 sqn.
Brig. Maury	132nd Line Inf. (penal regiment)	3 bns.
	1st Mediterranean Regt. (Italian)	3 bns.
	2nd Mediterranean Regt. (Italian)	3 bns.

33rd Division: Destres[d]
Brig. Rossaroli	Marines and velites (Neapolitan)	4 bns.
Brig. Ambrosio	5th Line Inf. (Neapolitan)	2 bns.
	6th Line Inf. (Neapolitan)	2 bns.
	7th Line Inf. (Neapolitan)	2 bns.
Brig. (?)	Honor guards and velites (Neapolitan)	4 sqns.

34th Division: Morand (then Loison)[e]
Brig. (?)	22nd Light Inf.	2 bns.
Brig. Lacroix	3rd Line Inf.	
	29th Line Inf.	
	105th Line Inf.	
	113th Line Inf. (Erfurt brigade)	7 bns.
Brig. Anthing	Regt. Frankfurt	2 bns.
	4th Rhine Conf. Regt. (Dukes of Saxony)	3 bns.
	5th Rhine Conf. Regt. (Anhalt/Lippe)	3 bns.
	6th Rhine Conf. Regt. (Schwarzburg/ Waldeck/Reuss)	3 bns.

XI CORPS: Augerau (*cont'd.*)

Cav. Brig. Cavaignac:	1 company from each of the 2nd, 5th, 12th , 13th, 14th, 17th, 19th, and 20th Dragoon Regts.	4 sqns.
Brig. Coutard*f*	Leibregiment (Hessian)	2 bns.
	4th Line Inf. (Westphalian)	2 bns.
Unattached*g*	8th Line Inf. (Westphalian)	2 bns.

*a*This was the 2nd Reserve Division from Holstein and Mecklenburg. It went to Danzig in November, and from there two brigades went to Koenigsberg.

*b*This division formed the garrisons of the Prussian fortresses.

*c*Joined VII Corps (Reynier) in November. One regiment remained in Warsaw and did not join until December.

*d*Arrived in Danzig in September and stayed there, except for 2 battalions and 4 squadrons that were sent to Loison (34th Division).

*e*This division joined the wrecked Grand Army in December and took over rear-guard duties.

*f*The garrison of Ruegen; it later joined the remainder of VI Corps.

*g*This regiment was made mobile and sent to VIII Corps at its own request. It departed from Koenigsberg in October.

I CAVALRY CORPS: Nansouty

1st Light Cavalry Division: Bruyers

Brig. Jaquinot	7th Hussars	4 sqns.
	9th Lancers	4 sqns.
Brig. Pire	16th Chass. a cheval	4 sqns.
	8th Hussars	4 sqns.
Brig. Niemojewski	6th Lancers (Polish)	4 sqns.
	8th Lancers (Polish)	4 sqns.
	2nd Combined Hussars (Prussian) 1st and 3rd Sqns., Pomm. Huss. 3rd and 4th Sqns., Brandenbg. Huss. }	4 sqns.

1st Heavy Cavalry Division: St. Germain

Brig. Bessieres	2nd Cuirassiers	4 sqns.
Brig. Bruno	3rd Cuirassiers	4 sqns.
Brig. Queunot	9th Cuirassiers	4 sqns.
	1st Lancers of the Line	3 sqns.

5th Heavy Cavalry Division: Valence

Brig. Reynaud	6th Cuirassiers	4 sqns.
Brig. Dejean	11th Cuirassiers	4 sqns.
Brig. de la Grange	12th Cuirassiers	4 sqns.
	5th Lancers of the Line	3 sqns.

II CAVALRY CORPS: Montbrun, later Caulaincourt, then Sebastiani

2nd Light Cavalry Division: Sebastiani (then Pajol)
Brig. St. Geniez	11th Chass. a cheval	4 sqns.
	12th Chass. a cheval	4 sqns.
Brig. Burthe	5th Hussars	4 sqns.
	9th Hussars	4 sqns.
Brig. Subverie	10th Hussars (Polish)	3 sqns.
	Combined lancers (Prussian)	
	3rd and 4th Sqns., Brandenbg. Ulans	
	3rd and 4th Sqns., Silesian Ulans	4 sqns.
	3rd Mtd. Jaeger Regt. (Wuerttembg.)	4 sqns.

2nd Heavy Cavalry Division: Wathier
Brig. Caulaincourt	5th Cuirassiers	4 sqns.
Brig. Richter	8th Cuirassiers	4 sqns.
Brig. Dornez	10th Cuirassiers	4 sqns.
	2nd Lancers of the Line	3 sqns.

4th Heavy Cavalry Division: Defrance
Brig. Berkheim	1st Carabiniers	4 sqns.
Brig. le Heritier	2nd Carabiniers	4 sqns.
Brig. Ornano	1st Cuirassiers	3 sqns.

III CAVALRY CORPS: Grouchy

3rd Light Cavalry Division: Castel
Brig. Gauthrin	8th Chass. a cheval	4 sqns.
	6th Hussars	4 sqns.
Brig. Gerard	6th Chass. a cheval	4 sqns.
	25th Chass. a cheval	4 sqns.
Brig. Dommanget	1st Chevaulegers (Bavarian)	4 sqns.
	2nd Chevaulegers (Bavarian)	4 sqns.
	Prinz Albert Dragoons (Saxon)	4 sqns.

3rd Heavy Cavalry Division: Daumerc
Brig. Berkheim	4th Cuirassiers	4 sqns.
Brig. le Heritier	7th Cuirassiers	4 sqns.
Brig. Doullemboug	14th Cuirassiers	4 sqns.
	3rd Lancers of the Line	3 sqns.

III CAVALRY CORPS: Grouchy (*cont'd.*)

6th Heavy Cavalry Division: Lahoussaye
Brig. Thiry	7th Dragoons	4 sqns.
	23rd Dragoons	4 sqns.
Brig. Serou	28th Dragoons	4 sqns.
	30th Dragoons	4 sqns.

IV CAVALRY CORPS: Latour-Maubourg

4th Light Cavalry Division: Rozniecki
Brig.	2nd Lancers (Polish)	3 sqns.
Dziewanowski	7th Lancers (Polish)	3 sqns.
	11th Lancers (Polish)	3 sqns.
Brig. Turno	3rd Lancers (Polish)	3 sqns.
	15th Lancers (Polish)	3 sqns.
	16th Lancers (Polish)	3 sqns.

7th Heavy Cavalry Division: Lorge
Brig. Thielemann	Garde du Corps (Saxon)	4 sqns.
	Zastrow Cuirassiers (Saxon)	4 sqns.
	14th Cuirassiers (Polish)	2 sqns.
Brig. Lepel	1st Cuirassiers (Westphalian)	4 sqns.
	2nd Cuirassiers (Westphalian)	4 sqns.

AUSTRIAN AUXILIARY CORPS: Schwarzenberg

Division Bianchi:
Brig. Hesse Homburg	Inf. Regt. Hiller	2 bns.
	Inf. Regt. Colloredo-Mansfeld	2 bns.
	Gren. Bn. Kirchenbetter	1 bn.
Brig. Lilienberg	Inf. Regt. Simbchen	2 bns.
	Inf. Regt. Alvinzy	2 bns.
	Gren. Bn. Brezinski	1 bn.

Division Siegenthal:
Brig. Bolza	7th Jaeger Bn.	1 bn.
	Warasdiner Border Inf.	2 bns.
Brig. Mohr	Inf. Regt. Prinz de Ligne	2 bns.
	Inf. Regt. Czatoryski	2 bns.
Brig. Lichtenstein	Inf. Regt. Davidovich	2 bns.
	Inf. Regt. Sottulinski	2 bns.

AUSTRIAN AUXILIARY CORPS: Schwarzenberg (*cont'd.*)

Division Trautenberg:		
Brig. Pflacher	5th Jaeger Bn.	1 bn.
	Sankt Georger Border Inf.	2 bns.
Brig. Mayer	Inf. Regt. Wuertzburg	3 bns.
Cavalry Division Frimont:		
Brig. Schmelzer	Erzherzog Johann Dragoons	6 sqns.
	Hohenzollern Dragoons	6 sqns.
	O'Reilly Dragoons	6 sqns.
Brig. Frolich	Kaiser Hussars	8 sqns.
	Hessen-Homburg Hussars	8 sqns.
Brig. Zechmeister	Blankenstein Hussars	8 sqns.
	Kienmayer Hussars	

The total strength of the troops crossing the border was as follows:

265 French battalions
291 foreign battalions
219 French squadrons
261 foreign squadrons

These troops consisted of:

513,479 infantry and foot artillery
 98,379 cavalry and horse artillery
611,858 men

They brought with them 1242 field artillery pieces, 130 siege pieces, 32,700 miscellaneous army vehicles, and 183,911 army horses.

Added to these numbers must be about 25,000 civilians, officials, servants, and artisans. A probably even greater number of grooms and drivers were summarily commandeered, along with about 150,000 draft horses, in Germany. Most of these grooms and drivers either escaped or were turned loose in Poland (not their horses, though); some never returned. There are no statistics on any of these civilians, as they were not included on the strength reports.

Toward the end of the year, reinforcements became available, most of whom were used as receiving forces for the shattered remnants of the Grand Army. These included the following:

	Units	Men	Location
Guards	2 bns. Young Guard	1,800	To Stettin
I Corps	3 march bns.	2,000	End of Dec. in Thorn
VI Corps	? bns., 3 sqns.	4,500	End of Dec. in Poland
VIII Corps	3 bns.	1,500	End of Dec. in Thorn
	1 bn.	450	Mid-Feb. on the Oder
IX Corps	2 bns. and 1 sqn. Badensians	1,050	Infantry in Glogau in Feb.; cavalry on the lower Vistula in late Dec.
	Ships' companies	1,440	Early Jan. in Stettin
		1,800	Early Feb. in Berlin
		567	Jan. in Glogau
35th Div. Grenier	16 bns. French troops		
	7 bns. and 4 sqns. Italians	19,331	Mid-Jan. in the Kurmark in Prussia

The reinforcements totaled 32,918 foot troops and 1520 cavalry, with 40 guns.

Preparing an accurate compilation of the ·order of battle for the Grand Army of 1812—with all the formations that were organically assigned to it—as well as following many of its constituent units through their reassignments, was and will continue to remain a Sisyphean labor. The information presented here is based largely on Andrew Zaremba's work, which first appeared in *Adjutant's Call*, the journal of the Military Historical Society, and is based mainly on "Les effectives de la Grand-armee pour la campagne de Russe de 1812," by Robert Villatee des Prugnes. Published in *Revue des etudes historiques*, vol. 79, pages 245–287 (Paris, 1913), this article represents the first and most serious effort at a reconstruction of the Grand Army, based on the *livrets* or *carnets de situation* of July 1812.

Most of the modifications of this important work have centered almost entirely on the troops of the foreign contingents, especially the smaller ones, which were strewn all over the army. Many of these details emerge in the footnotes of the text. It must, however, be understood that the main order of battle, as given above, renders the status as of June 1812 and that, for the sake of clarity, some subsequent reassignments have been anticipated, especially where they do not involve operations. This is especially true of IX and XI Corps, which present an almost impenetrable maze.

The problem of the Spanish and Portuguese formations remains vexing. The *correspondance* mentions a Spanish regiment both with I and IV Corps and two Portuguese regiments with III Corps. Plotho places another Portuguese regiment with II Corps, but St. Cyr does not mention it. Also turning up like a bad penny is a Portuguese cavalry regiment, attached to the Guard, but this regiment had been disbanded in 1811. At the same time, there were only two Spanish regiments carried on the French establishment; the second of these was raised in 1812, and it fought and met its end at Salamanca. But there were three Portuguese regiments in the Grand Army.

APPENDIX VI

The Russian Military Establishment, June 1812

THE INFANTRY

The infantry consisted of:

- 6 Guard regiments
- 1 Guard battalion
- Ships' equipage
- 164 infantry regiments:
    - 14 grenadier regiments
    - 96 musketeer regiments
    - 50 jaeger regiments
    - 4 marine regiments

Each regiment had 3 field battalions, and each of the battalions consisted of 1 grenadier and 3 musketeer or jaeger companies.

The establishments called for 764 men at full strength in the guards and 738 men in the line. The effective numbers, however, came nowhere near the planned strength. These shortfalls were already chronic before the war and remained so all the way up to 1813–1814.

Like the French light infantry after 1808, the jaeger regiments in the Russian army did not receive any specially selected recruits, nor did their modus operandi vary from that of the line. However, as with the French, and as later with the hussars, regimental titles and traditions seemed to call for that extra measure of dash and daring, which continued to maintain the inherited reputations of these troops. The guards, however, were elite formations in every sense of the word.

The entire infantry, with the exception of a single marine regiment, was organized into 1 Guard and 27 infantry divisions. The 1st and 2nd Divisions each consisted of 6 grenadier regiments. The remaining divisions each consisted of 2 jaeger and 4 musketeer regiments, subdivided into 1 jaeger and 2 musketeer brigades. The only deviations from this norm were the 23rd Division, which had only 1 jaeger and 3 musketeer regiments, and the 25th, which consisted of 1 musketeer, 1 jaeger, and 3 marine regiments. The 19th and 20th Divisions, forming the Grusinian Corps in the Caucasus, were not organized into brigades; between them, they had 2 grenadier, 8 musketeer, and 5 jaeger regiments.

THE CAVALRY

The 6 Guard regiments of the cavalry consisted of:

2 cuirassier regiments
1 dragoon regiment
1 hussar regiment
1 ulan (lancer) regiment
1 Cossack regiment
2 independent sotnias (squadrons)

The 60 line cavalry regiments comprised

8 cuirassier regiments
36 dragoon regiments
11 hussar regiments
5 ulan regiments

The hussar and ulan regiments of the line each numbered 10 squadrons; the remaining regiments, including those of the Guard, each had 5 squadrons. The Guard squadron had a planned complement of 160 horses; the squadrons of the line, 159. All the cuirassiers, including those of the Guard, were massed into two cuirassier divisions, of which the 1st Cuirassier Division included both Guard regiments.

The remaining cavalry was organized into 1 Guard and 8 army cavalry divisions; the latter generally consisted of 4 dragoon and 2 hussar or ulan regiments. Of the 5 dragoon regiments not assigned to a division, 2 stood in Finland and 3 in the Caucasian border provinces.

THE ARTILLERY

Included in the artillery were the following:

1 Guard brigade of 4 foot and 2 horse companies
27 artillery brigades, each with 3 foot companies
10 reserve artillery brigades, totaling 21 foot and 22 horse companies
4 depot artillery brigades, totaling 29 companies

Each company was intended to man a battery, and 124⅓ batteries were actually formed in 1812. As a rule, the companies of each brigade were to form 1 heavy (position) battery and 2 light batteries. The reserve brigades together manned 17 heavy, 4 light, and 2 horse batteries.

Each battery was to have 12 guns. However, from the start, a number of batteries had only 10 guns, and each of the two Guard horse batteries had only 8 guns. The pieces of the batteries were to have the following calibers:

The heavy battery: 8 twelve-pounders and 4 twenty-pound unicorns
The light battery: 8 six-pounders and 4 ten-pound unicorns
The horse battery: 8 six-pounders and 4 ten-pound unicorns

The unicorns were a Russian specialty. So-called gun-howitzers, they were intended to be dual-purpose weapons, since their barrels were somewhat longer than a howitzer's barrel but shorter than a gun's. Their performance fell short in the smaller calibers but proved quite serviceable in the heavier calibers. Thus, unicorns with a shot weight of 10 pounds and above continued in service for quite some time.

Also attached to the artillery was the artillery pontonier regiment, consisting of 2 battalions, each of 4 companies, and totaling 2063 men.

TECHNICAL TROOPS

The technical troops consisted of 2 pioneer or engineer regiments, each with 2313 men in 3 battalions.

GARRISON AND LOCAL TROOPS

Included in this category were a large number of troops designated for service in the interior and Asian border districts.

The Inner Guard, in 40 companies located in 40 district capitals, numbered about 17,000 men. Not part of the Inner Guard were:

10 garrison regiments
20 garrison battalions (in all about 30,000 men)
84 invalid companies

The invalid companies fell into three categories:

Mobile invalids. Totaling 6204 men in 35 companies, the mobile invalids were distributed to the Guard, palaces, factories, hospitals, and arms depots to perform various duties.
Serving invalids. These invalids were still on active duty.
Nonserving invalids. Divided into 535 commands, the nonserving invalids were distributed to the garrison battalions and the Inner Guard, the district capitals and the fortresses. These commands averaged 2 officers and about 46 men each.

The siege artillery, laid up in the arsenals of St. Petersburg, Riga, and Kiev, numbered 180 guns.

In addition to these artillery depots and the garrison infantry, there was also an engineer corps and 57 fortress engineer commands (about 2000 men), as well as the cadet training facilities and 3 instructional grenadier battalions.

THE COSSACK ARMY

The Cossack regiments bore the names of their districts. Numerous at the outset of the campaign, even more regiments were formed after the commencement of hostilities, as shown below:

| | Regiments | | |
Cossacks	At Outset of Hostilities	Formed after June 12	Batteries
Don*	60	26	2½
Bug	3		
Ural	4	1	
Teptiarsky	1	1	
Orenburg		2	
Meshtshiarsky		2	
Minor Russian		15	
Black Sea	6		

*Of the Don Cossacks, 20 regiments stood in the Caucasus.

In addition to the Cossacks, there were:
  4 Tatar regiments
  2 Kalmuck regiments, with 2 more formed later
  1 Tshetshenzy regiment
  2 Backshir regiments, with 18 more formed later

Generally, each of these regiments was to consist of 500 men, formed into 5 sotnias (troops). Such planned strength, however, was rarely achieved.

MILITIA CAVALRY

A number of other irregular cavalry formations, even though not of Cossack origin, were styled in the Cossack fashion and eventually served in a way similar to that of the Cossack. Although there were many more such formations than those itemized below, the ones listed were known to have become mobile and to have been used in the operations area.

  Cossack volunteers:
  2 St. Petersburg regiments
  1 Livonian regiment

   4 Ukrainian regiments
Militia Cossacks:
   2 Poltava regiments
   2 Tula regiments
   1 Tversh or Yamstshik regiment (from the postal service)

These 12 regiments totaled about 7000 men.

The total strength of the irregular cavalry (not counting the Siberian Cossacks) came to 57 regiments, with 79 added, in Europe and 26 regiments in the Caucasus. Since most sources on this subject are conflicting, it is doubtful that these figures are really definitive. Most of the gray areas involve the question of which formations did or did not become operational before the campaign ran its course.

The same problem applies to the militia, which was already touched upon in the main text. However, with the exception of the formations specifically mentioned in the narrative covering the campaign—notably the ones ranked into the army after Borodino and the few under Wittgenstein—none exercised any influence on the conduct of operations.

The Russian Army, June 1812

THE FIRST WESTERN ARMY: BARCLAY DE TOLLY

I INFANTRY CORPS:* Wittgenstein

5th Infantry Division:
1st Brig.	Sjevski Gren. Regt.	2 bns.
	Kaluga Regt.	2 bns.
2nd Brig.	Perm Regt.	2 bns.
	Mohilev Regt.	2 bns.
3rd Brig.	23rd Jaeger Regt.	2 bns.
	24th Jaeger Regt.	2 bns.

14th Infantry Division:
1st Brig.	Tula Regt.	2 bns.
	Navaginski Regt.	2 bns.
2nd Brig.	Estonian Regt.	2 bns.
	Teginski Regt.	2 bns.
3rd Brig.	25th Jaeger Regt.	2 bns.
	26th Jaeger Regt.	2 bns.
	Combined grenadiers	4 bns.

Corps cavalry:	Riga Dragoons	4 sqns.
	Yamburg Dragoons	4 sqns.
	Grodno Hussars	8 sqns.
	3 Cossack regiments	

---

*The composition of this corps underwent numerous changes throughout the campaign, which may readily be traced through the footnotes in the text. The disposition of 11 reserve battalions that joined this corps in December remains obscure. Apparently, 5 went into the garrison of Riga. The remaining 6 might be identical with those under Colonel Shemtshushnikov, who joined the corps on January 5, 1813.

II INFANTRY CORPS: Baggehufftwudt (generally gallicized as Bagavout), later Dolgoroky, then Duke Eugene

4th Infantry Division:
1st Brig.	Kremtshuk Regt.	2 bns.
	Minsk Regt.	2 bns.
2nd Brig.	Tobol Regt.	2 bns.
	Volhynian Regt.	2 bns.
3rd Brig.	4th Jaeger Regt.	2 bns.
	34th Jaeger Regt.	2 bns.

17th Infantry Division:
1st Brig.	Ryazan Regt.	2 bns.
	Byeloserk Regt.	2 bns.
2nd Brig.	Willmannstrand Regt.	2 bns.
	Brest Regt.	2 bns.
3rd Brig.	30th Jaeger Regt.	2 bns.
	48th Jaeger Regt.	2 bns.

Corps cavalry:	Yellissavethgrad Hussars	8 sqns.

*After November 17, this corps consisted of the 3rd and 4th Infantry Divisions.

III INFANTRY CORPS: Tutshkov I, then Stroganov

1st (Grenadier) Division:
1st Brig.	Life Guard Grenadiers	2 bns.
	Araktsheyev Grenadiers	2 bns.
2nd Brig.	Pavlov Grenadiers	2 bns.
	Yekaterinoslav Grenadiers	2 bns.
3rd Brig.	St. Petersburg Grenadiers	2 bns.
	Tavrishesk Grenadiers	2 bns.
	Combined grenadiers	2 bns.

3rd Infantry Division:
1st Brig.	Reval Regt.	2 bns.
	Murom Regt.	2 bns.
2nd Brig.	Koporye Regt.	2 bns.
	Tshernigov Regt.	2 bns.

III INFANTRY CORPS: Tutshkov I, then Stroganov (*cont'd.*)

3rd Brig.	20th Jaeger Regt.	2 bns.
	21st Jaeger Regt.	2 bns.
Corps cavalry:	Life Guard Cossacks	4 sqns. *

*The Life Guard Cossacks had an establishment of only 3 squadrons. However, a fourth was added upon mobilization.

IV INFANTRY CORPS: Shuvalov, then Oster-mann-Tolstoy

11th Infantry Division:

1st Brig.	Kexholm Regt.	2 bns.
	Pernau Regt.	2 bns.
2nd Brig.	Polotsk Regt.	2 bns.
	Yelets Regt.	2 bns.
3rd Brig.	1st Jaeger Regt.	2 bns.
	33rd Jaeger Regt.	2 bns.

23rd Infantry Division:

1st Brig.	Rylsk Regt.	2 bns.
	Yekaterinburg Regt.	2 bns.
2nd Brig.	Szelenginsk Regt.	2 bns.
	18th Jaeger Regt.	2 bns.
	Combined grenadiers	2 bns.
Corps cavalry:	Ysyumsk Hussars	8 sqns.

V (GUARD) INFANTRY CORPS: Grand Duke Constantine

Guard Infantry Division:

1st Brig.	Preobrashenski Regt.	2 bns. *
	Semenovski Regt.	2 bns.
2nd Brig.	Ismailovski Regt.	2 bns.
	Lithuanian Regt.	2 bns.
3rd Brig.	Lifeguard Jaeger Regt.	2 bns.
	Finnish Lifeguard Jaeger Regt.	2 bns.

1st Combined Grenadier Division:
Corps cavalry—1st Cuirassier Division:

V (GUARD) INFANTRY CORPS: Grand Duke Constantine (*cont'd.*)

Guards	Horse Guards Regt.	4 sqns. *
1st Brig.	Emperor's Cuirassier Regt.	4 sqns.
	Empress's Cuirassier Regt.	4 sqns.
	Astrachan Cuirassiers	4 sqns.

*Bogdanovitch, Stein (who quotes him), Bernhardi, etc., appear to quote the planned number of battalion and squadron cadres per regiment here, the actual strength there. It is known that the infantry mobilized only its 1st and 3rd Battalions, the cavalry only the first 4 squadrons, and the light cavalry 8 of its 10 squadrons in each regiment. The depots remaining behind were used for new formations. However, it is doubtful that the Guard formations remaining behind were used in such fashion, since all sources later put the Guard infantry division at 19 battalions (including the Guard Equipage, a naval unit), which indicates that the 2nd Battalions of the Guard eventually joined their parent formations in the field. The same appears true for the 5th Squadrons in the Guard cavalry.

VI INFANTRY CORPS:* Doctorov

7th Infantry Division:

1st Brig.	Pskow Regt.	2 bns.
	Moscow Regt.	2 bns.
2nd Brig.	Libau Regt.	2 bns.
	Sophia Regt.	2 bns.
3rd Brig.	11th Jaeger Regt.	2 bns.
	36th Jaeger Regt.	2 bns.

24th Infantry Division:

1st Brig.	Ufa Regt.	2 bns.
	Shirvan Regt.	2 bns.
2nd Brig.	Butyrk Regt.	2 bns.
	Tomsk Regt.	2 bns.
3rd Brig.	19th Jaeger Regt.	2 bns.
	40th Jaeger Regt.	2 bns.

Corps cavalry:	Sumy Hussars	8 sqns.

*Before the Battle of Borodino, four combined grenadier battalions from VIII Corps were added.

THE CAVALRY[*]

I Cavalry Corps: Uvarov (then Moeller-Sakomelsky)

4th Cavalry Brig.	Kazan Dragoons	4 sqns.
	Nyeshin Dragoons	4 sqns.
	Polish Ulans (Lancers)	8 sqns.

II Cavalry Corps: Korff II

6th Cavalry Brig.	Pskow Dragoons	4 sqns.
	Moscow Dragoons	4 sqns.
7th Cavalry Brig.	Kargopol Dragoons	4 sqns.
	Ingermanland Dragoons	4 sqns.

III Cavalry Corps: Pahlen III (then Kreutz)

10th Cavalry Brig.	Sibirsk Dragoons	4 sqns.
	Irkutsk Dragoons	4 sqns.
	Orenburg Dragoons	4 sqns.
	Mariampol Hussars	8 sqns.

The Cossacks: Platov
14 regiments

[*]This force was also subject to repeated changes, receiving an additional regiment from I and III Corps, as well as from Second Army, but detaching three to Wintzingerode, etc. The changes can be traced in the text as they occur.

Added to all of the above must be the following reserve forces:

Drissa: Parts of I Reserve Corps (See "Drissa and Beyond," note 1.)
Smolensk: Parts of Wintzingerode's corps (See "The Chase Resumes," note 2.)
Gshatsk: Parts of Miloradovitch's troops (See "Borodino.")

The reserve formations were broken up and distributed to the line units.

THE SECOND WESTERN ARMY: BAGRATION

VII INFANTRY CORPS: Raievsky

12th Infantry Division:

1st Brig.	Smolensk Regt.	2 bns.
	Narva Regt.	2 bns.
2nd Brig.	Alexopol Regt.	2 bns.
	New Ingermanland Regt.	2 bns.
3rd Brig.	6th Jaeger Regt.	2 bns.
	41st Jaeger Regt.	2 bns.

VII INFANTRY CORPS: Raievsky (*cont'd.*)

16th Infantry Division:

1st Brig.	Ocholtsk Regt.	2 bns.
	Neuschlot Regt.	2 bns.
2nd Brig.	Kamtshatka Regt.	2 bns.
	Mingrel Regt.	2 bns.
3rd Brig.	27th Jaeger Regt.	2 bns.
	43rd Jaeger Regt.	2 bns.
Corps cavalry:	Achtyrka Hussars	8 sqns.

VIII INFANTRY CORPS:*   Borodin I then Dolgoruky

2nd Grenadier Division:

1st Brig.	Krim Grenadiers	2 bns.
	Moscow Grenadiers	2 bns.
2nd Brig.	Astrachan Grenadiers	2 bns.
	Phangor Grenadiers	2 bns.
3rd Brig.	Siberian Grenadiers	2 bns.
	Minor Russian Grenadiers	10 bns.

2nd Combined Grenadier Division:

Corps cavalry—2nd Cuirassier Division:

2nd Brig.	Yekaterinoslav Cuirassiers	4 sqns.
	Military Order Cuirassiers	4 sqns.
3rd Brig.	Glushov Cuirassiers	4 sqns.
	Minor Russian Cuirassiers	4 sqns.
	Novgorod Cuirassiers	4 sqns.

*At Borodino, the corps was composed of the 2nd and 27th Infantry Divisions; from November 17, it consisted of the 17th and 27th Infantry Divisions.

THE CAVALRY

IV Cavalry Corps: Sievers

12th Cavalry Brig.	Charkov Dragoons	4 sqns.
	Tshernikov Dragoons	4 sqns.
13th Cavalry Brig.	Kiev Dragoons	4 sqns.
	New Russian Dragoons	4 sqns.
	Lithuanian Hussars	8 sqns.

The Cossacks: Ilovaisky
    9 regiments

REINFORCEMENTS FOR SECOND ARMY*

27th Infantry Division:†

1st Brig.	Odessa Regt.	2 bns.
	Shitomir Regt.	2 bns.
2nd Brig.	Vilna Regt.	2 bns.
	Ssimbirsk Regt.	2 bns.
3rd Brig.	49th Jaeger Regt.	2 bns.
	50th Jaeger Regt.	2 bns.
Borisov Garrison:		3 bns.‡
Bobruisk Garrison:		6 bns.‡

*For information on the reserves joining at Gshatsk, see "Borodino."
†On July 3.
‡Placed under Second Army jurisdiction.

THE MAIN ARMY

For the strength and composition of the combined armies at Borodino, see Appendix XI. The organizational changes made after Borodino and in the camp at Tarutino are shown in Appendixes XVIII ans XIX, as well as in the appropriate sections of the text.

During the final phases of the campaign, the reinforcements received were:

	Men	*Phase*
Reserves from the disbanded recruit depots	7,690	During the retreat along the Motsha
	33,581	In the camp of Tarutino
	5,142	During the pursuit
	ca. 5,000	In Vilna, on Dec. 27
Cossacks (26 regiments)*	10,000	In Tarutino

*Several other irregular regiments arrived in Tarutino, as well as during the course of the pursuit.

THE THIRD (RESERVE) ARMY: TORMASSOV

IX INFANTRY CORPS: Kamensky

18th Infantry Division:

1st Brig.	Vladimir Regt.	2 bns.
	Tambow Regt.	2 bns.

IX INFANTRY CORPS: Kamensky (*cont'd.*)

2nd Brig.	Kostroma Regt.	2 bns.
	Dnieprovsk Regt.	2 bns.
3rd Brig.	28th Jaeger Regt.	2 bns.
	32nd Jaeger Regt.	2 bns.
Combined Gren. Brig.		6 bns.
Corps cavalry:	Pavlograd Hussars	8 sqns.

X INFANTRY CORPS: Markov

9th Infantry Division:		
1st Brig.	Nasheburg Regt.	2 bns.
	Yakutsk Regt.	2 bns.
2nd Brig.	Apsheron Regt.	2 bns.
	Ryaski Regt.	2 bns.
3rd Brig.	10th Jaeger Regt.	2 bns.
	38th Jaeger Regt.	2 bns.
15th Infantry Division:		
1st Brig.	Koslov Regt.	2 bns.
	Vitebsk Regt.	2 bns.
2nd. Brig.	Kura Regt.	2 bns.
	Kolyvan Regt.	2 bns.
3rd Brig.	13th Jaeger Regt.	2 bns.
	14th Jaeger Regt.	2 bns.
Corps cavalry:	Alexandria Hussars	8 sqns.

CORPS OSTEN-SACKEN*

36th Infantry Division:		
2nd (Depot) Battalions of 12th and 15th Inf. Divs.		12 bns.
Corps cavalry—11th Cavalry Division: 5th (Depot) Squadrons of 5th and 6th Cav. Divs.		16 sqns.
	Lubny Hussars	8 sqns.

*The Hussar regiment was transferred to IX Infantry Corps; 6 battalions went to II Reserve Corps, and they were followed later by another 2 battalions and 8 squadrons.

RESERVE CAVALRY CORPS: Lambert

5th Cavalry Division:

15th Brig.	Starodus Dragoons	4 sqns.
	Twer Dragoons	4 sqns.
16th Brig.	Shitomir Dragoons	4 sqns.
	Arsamass Dragoons	4 sqns.

From 8th Cavalry Division:

24th Brig.	Vladimir Dragoons	4 sqns.
	Taganrok Dragoons	4 sqns.
	Sserpuchov Dragoons	4 sqns.
	Tatar Ulans	8 sqns.

Cossacks	9 regiments	

THE DANUBE ARMY: Tshitshagov

8th Infantry Division:

1st Brig.	Ukrainian Regt.	3 bns.
	Archangelsk Regt.	3 bns.
2nd Brig.	Schluesselburg Regt.	3 bns.
	Old Ingermanland Regt.	3 bns.
3rd Brig.	7th Jaeger Regt.	3 bns.
	37th Jaeger Regt.	3 bns.

10th Infantry Division:

1st Brig.	Bialystok Regt.	3 bns.
	Krim Regt.	3 bns.
2nd Brig.	Kursk Regt.	3 bns.
	Yaroslav Regt.	3 bns.
3rd Brig.	8th Jaeger Regt.	3 bns.
	29th Jaeger Regt.	3 bns.

16th Infantry Division:

1st Brig.	Ocholtsk Regt.	3 bns.
	Neuschlot Regt.	3 bns.
2nd Brig.	Kamtshatka Regt.	3 bns.
	Mingrel Regt.	3 bns.
3rd Brig.	27th Jaeger Regt.	3 bns.
	43rd Jaeger Regt.	3 bns.

22nd Infantry Division:

1st Brig.	Vyatka Regt.	3 bns.
	Stavropol Regt.	3 bns.

THE DANUBE ARMY: Tshitshagov (*cont'd.*)

2nd Brig.	Olomez Regt.	3 bns.
	Wyborg Regt.	3 bns.
3rd Brig.	29th Jaeger Regt.	3 bns.
	45th Jaeger Regt.	3 bns.
From 13th Infantry Division:		2 bns.
6th Cavalry Division:		
18th Cav. Brig.	St. Petersburg Dragoons	5 sqns.
	Livonian Dragoons	5 sqns.
19th Cav. Brig.	Syeversk Dragoons	5 sqns.
	Kinburn Dragoons	5 sqns.
20th Cav. Brig.	White Russian Hussars	10 sqns.
	Volhynian Ulans	10 sqns.
7th Cavalry Division:		
21st Cav. Brig.	Smolensk Dragoons	5 sqns.
	Pereyaslav Dragoons	5 sqns.
22nd Cav. Brig.	Tiraspol Dragoons	5 sqns.
	Dorpat Dragoons	5 sqns.
23rd Cav. Brig.	Olviopol Hussars	10 sqns.
	Tshuguyex Ulans	10 sqns.
Reserves from the recruit depots in Oct.:		5 bns.

When the Danube Army was recalled to the central operations area, it was officially redesignated the "Third Western Army," even though many sources continued to refer to it as the Danube Army. It left only a few troops behind to observe the Turks; these troops appear to have consisted of a few cadre battalions and some cavalry formations.

The sources place the strength of the forces that went into Third Army at 74 battalions and 64 squadrons. This indicates that these formations originally went into the field with their full complements, because only in that case can the aggregate numbers be reconciled. Thus, during the general mobilization of 1811, the regiments of the Danube Army, unlike the rest of the army, stood in the field with 3 battalions or 5 (10) squadrons.

TROOPS IN THE CRIMEA AND ODESSA

13th Infantry Division:[*]

1st Brig.	Galitsh Regt.	3 bns.
	Veliki-Luki Regt.	3 bns.
2nd Brig.	Pensa Regt.	3 bns.
	Saratov Regt.	3 bns.
3rd Brig.	12th Jaeger Regt.	3 bns.
	22nd Jaeger Regt.	3 bns.

[*]Of this division, 2 battalions were with the Danube Army, and 8 futher battalions followed in two echelons; 8 battalions remained in southern Russia. However, 2 battalions were sent after the others listed above in January.

The new Third Western Army under Vice Admiral Tshitshagov moved toward the Beresina. Its strength and organization when it arrived on the scene is described in the text. After crossing the Beresina, some formations (3 battalions, 8 squadrons, 6 Cossack regiments, and 1½ batteries) remained there; others were left behind in the further course of the pursuit.

Colonel von Knorring's detachment (2 battalions, 8 squadrons, and ½ battery) joined by another 2 gun section from the main army, marched into the Minsk area.

When departing for the Beresina, Tshitshagov left behind Corps Osten-Sacken, which continued to watch the border. It was eventually joined by the Ukrainian Cossacks under Witte. Repninski's detachment was formed from these elements.

THE FINNISH CORPS: Steinheil

6th Infantry Division:

1st Brig.	Bryansk Regt.	3 bns.
	Nisov Regt.	3 bns.
2nd Brig.	Uglitsh Regt.	3 bns.
	35th Jaeger Regt.	3 bns.
3rd Brig.	Asov Regt.	3 bns.
	3rd Jaeger Regt.	3 bns.

21st Infantry Division:

1st Brig.	Petrovsk Regt.	3 bns.
	Podol Regt.	3 bns.
2nd Brig.	Neva Regt.	3 bns.
	Lithuanian Regt.	3 bns.
3rd Brig.	2nd Jaeger Regt.	3 bns.
	44th Jaeger Regt.	3 bns.

THE FINNISH CORPS: Steinheil (*cont'd.*)

25th Infantry Division:

1st Brig.	1st Marine Regt.	3 bns.
	2nd Marine Regt.	3 bns.
2nd Brig.	3rd Marine Regt.	3 bns.
	Voronesh Regt.	3 bns.
3rd Brig.	31st Jaeger Regt.	3 bns.
	47th Jaeger Regt.	3 bns.
Corps cavalry:	2 Dragoon regiments	10 sqns.
The Cossacks:	2 regiments	

The disposition of these troops was as follows:

	Battalions	Squadrons	Batteries	Cossack Regiments
To Wittgenstein	4	4	2	
To Reval*	16	4	2	1
To Corps Novak	2		1	
To Riga	4		1	
Remaining in north Russia	10		1	1
Not traceable (broken up?)	18†			

*September 23.
†These were possibly the 2nd Reserve Battalions.

RESERVE TROOPS

These consisted of the 2nd (Reserve) Battalions and the 5th (or 9th and 10th) Squadrons of the line and light cavalry, respectively, of all the regiments that took part in the general mobilization of 1811. The battalions had only 3 companies, because their grenadier companies had been used to form the 31 United Grenadier Battalions, which were among the troops of the first line. The three dragoon regiments in the Caucasus retained all their squadrons.

The total strength of the reserve troops has been placed at 100 battalions and 78 squadrons. Of these,

12 battalions and 16 squadrons were assigned to Sacken.
87 battalions and 54 squadrons (about 34,000 men) were accounted for.
 1 battalion and 8 squadrons could not be traced.

These reserve troops went into the making of the following major formations:

I Reserve Corps:* Moeller-Sakomelsky

32 Inf. Div.	From reserve battalions of 1st, 11th, and 23rd Inf. Divs.	
34th Inf. Div.	From reserve battalions of 24th and 26th Inf. Divs.	23 bns.†
9th Cav. Div.	From depot squadrons of 1st and 2nd Cav. Divs.	20 sqns.

II Reserve Corps: Oertel

33rd Inf. Div.	From 3rd and 7th Inf. Divs.	⎫
35th Inf. Div.	From 2nd and 18th Inf. Divs.	⎬ 11 bns.
10th Cav. Div.	From 3rd and 4th Cav. Divs.	14 sqns.

Garrisons of Riga and
Dunamunde: Essen I
(then Paulucci)

30th and 31st Inf. Divs.	From depots of 4th, 5th, 14th and 17th Inf. Divs.	20 bns.‡
Cavalry		4 sqns.

---

*This corps was disbanded at Drissa, where 11 battalions and 5 squadrons (5700 men) were broken up and distributed into the line units of the First Western Army. Another 8 battalions and 15 squadrons went to Wittgenstein, but they remained together as formations.

†Including 4 battalions in Dunaburg.

‡Some sources put this at 30 battalions, but that figure must include the garrison of Dunaburg, because the Riga garrison did not reach such a strength until December.

Reinforcements reached Riga as follows:

	Battalions	Squadrons	Cossack Regiments	Batteries
From Wittgenstein	5	1	1	2
Finnish Corps	4			1
Newly formed artillery				1⅓
From recruit depots	4			*
Local militia	2		3	

*Some were disbanded and distributed.

When the siege of Riga was raised, the following columns were formed from the garrison:

Detachment Lewis: 12 battalions, 4 squadrons, 3 Cossack regiments, 3 batteries, and 1 free corps.

Detachment Paulucci: 7 battalions, 1 Cossack regiment, 1⅓ batteries, and 1 free corps.

GARRISONS

The garrisons were as follows:

Dunaburg*	10 bns.
Borisov†	3 bns.
Bobruisk‡	18 bns.
Kiev	6 bns.§
In southern Russia, 12th Cav. Div.	16 sqns.¶

*When Dunaburg was evacuated, the garrison joined Wittgenstein.

†When Borisov was evacuated, the battalions went to Bagration's Second Army, where they were disbanded and distributed.

‡When Bobruisk was evacuated, 6 battalions went to Bagration's Second Army, where they were disbanded and distributed. The remainder were formed into a column near the end of the campaign.

§The 6 battalions joined II Reserve Corps in November and were replaced with 6 recruit battalions.

¶The use of these squadrons is not documented. They apparently represent the difference between the full establishment strength (80 squadrons) of the 6th and 7th Cavalry Divisions and the 64 squadrons the erstwhile Danube Army brought into the central operations area.

TROOPS OF THE THIRD LINE

Depots

The number of recruit depots cited in the sources varies from 33 to 41. The number of men these processed, however, is well set at about 95,000.

These depots contained the fall 1811 levy, which was used to form the 4th Battalions and 5th or 11th and 12th Squadrons, respectively. A few battalions were formed into reserve regiments. However, with only a few exceptions (Danube Army, Sacken, Wittgenstein, and II Reserve Corps), they were eventually disbanded and used to replenish the line units already in the field.

The following troops can be shown to have come from the depots:

76,002 men to the main army (First and Second Western)
2,925 men to Wittgenstein
2,000 men to Riga

8,000 men {
4 recruit battalions to II Reserve Corps.
6 recruit battalions to Kiev
5 (8?) recruit battalions to Sacken.

The total, 88,927 men, does not include 5 battalions with the Danube Army that were formed from its own depot cadres. (Remember, the army had its full establishments in the field.)

The Militia

In accordance with the General Armament under the Ukasa of 13 July/1 July, 1812 *
This list includes only those portions that actually found some operational use.

St. Petersburg and Novgorod	15,000 men in 25 drushinas (battalions) and 4 sotnias (troops); went to Wittgenstein.
Moscow and Smolensk	16,000 men, most of them armed with pikes; temporarily ranked into the line infantry after Borodino.
Militia cavalry and Cossacks	7000 men in 7 regiments and 2 free corps.
Regular formations	About 4000 militiamen were utilized in the formation of a new jaeger regiment (3 battalions) (3 bns.) as well as a ulan and hussar regiment.
Contingents of the Cossack tribes	24,000 men in 67 regiments.

*Dual date given to reflect both the Gregorian and the Julian calendars.

TROOPS OF THE FOURTH LINE

The Fourth Line included the following:

	Men

Troops in the Caucasian borderlands:
  19th and 20th Infantry Divisions:
    2 grenadier regiments
    8 musketeer regiments
    5 jaeger regiments
    2 artillery brigades
    3 garrison regiments

TROOPS OF THE FOURTH LINE (cont'd.)

	Men
Troops in the Caucasian borderlands:	
19th and 20th Infantry Divisions:	
1 garrison battalion	
3 dragoon regiments	
26 Cossack regiments	
3 (?) horse batteries	
Total	33,673*
Garrisons:	
1 Guard battalion	
32½ garrison regiments (86 battalions)†	
Fortress artillery	
Invalid companies	
Total	69,166
Local troops:	ca. 32,000
Inner Guard (96 battalions)	
Siberian Cossacks:	?
Remainder of militia:	ca. 230,000

*With 108 (?) guns.
†Parts of these formed the 28th and 29th Infantry Divisions.

TOTAL STRENGTH OF THE RUSSIAN ARMY, 1812

	Men	Cossacks	Militiamen	Total
First Line	175,000	15,000	—	190,000
Second Line	129,000	8,000	—	137,000
Third Line	99,000	31,000	31,000	161,000
Fourth Line	125,000	10,000	—	135,000
Total	528,000	64,000	31,000*	623,000

*An additional 230,000 militiamen were unusable.

APPENDIX VIII

The Strength of the French Army, Beginning of August

TROOPS UNDER NAPOLEON'S DIRECT COMMAND

Units		August	June	Left Behind
Guard Corps:*				
Old Guard	6,850			
Young Guard	10,000			
Guard cavalry†	4,250			
Guard artillery‡	3,500			
Total		24,600	40,373	2 Hessian bns. in Vitebsk
1st, 2nd, and 3rd Divs. of				
I Corps		30,113	41,051	1 Hessian bn. in Vitebsk
III Corps		22,282	39,342	3 bns. 129th Line Inf. in Vilna; 4 Illyrian bns. in Kovno
IV Corps (+ Bavarian cavalry)		33,823	47,704	2 sqns. from Guyot's brig. in Vitebsk
I Cav. Corps (− Div. Valence)		5,413	8,577	
II Cav. Corps		6,029§	10,436	
III Cav. Corps (− Div. Doumerc)		5,030	6,876	
Total		127,290	194,359	

*Excluding the Vistula Legion.
†Including Brig. Colbert.
‡Including 1000 men of the line artillery.
§Before the action of Inkovo.

TROOPS UNDER DAVOUT'S COMMAND

Units	August	June	Left Behind
4th and 5th Divs. and light cavalry of I Corps*	29,958	31,000	3 bns. 33rd Light Inf. in Minsk; 3 bns. Mecklenburg in Vilna
Vistula Legion†		7,000	1 bn. in Dubrovna
Div. Valence of I Cav. Corps		3,500	
V Corps (− Div. Dombrowski)	16,738	36,311	1 bn. ?
Div. Dombrowski	6,000		1 bn. in Grodno 1 detachment in Mohilev
VIII Corps	14,000	17,935	1 bn. in Orsza
IV Cav. Corps‡	5,000	7,994	
Total	71,696	103,740	

*Including Pajol's detachment, which had returned.
†Three new battalions (1800 men) still coming up.
‡One brigade (1000 men) detached to Dombrowski.

The total number of troops under Napoleon and Davout came to 198,986 in August, as compared with 298,099 in June.

DETACHED FORCES

Units	August	June	Left Behind
II Corps (+ Div. Doumerc)	23,000*	39,939	
VI Corps (− Cavalry)	13,000*	23,228	
X Corps	26,000	32,497	1 bn. in Bialystok
VII Corps	13,000	17,182	
Austrian Auxiliary Corps	30,000	34,448	
Troops left behind	10,000†	0	
Total	115,000	146,994	

*As of August 7.
†This is the aggregate of the formations listed in the fourth column (of the preceding table).

REINFORCEMENTS TO BE EXPECTED

IX Corps	31,000*	Between the Vistula and the Niemen
March formations (including 1st Res. Div.)	30,000	Approaching the Niemen; a small part already across
Lithuanian troops	14,000	Still forming
Polish troops†	9,000	Still forming
Part of III and VIII Corps	2,600	2 Wuerttembergian bns. in Danzig; 2 Westphalian bns. in Koenigsberg and Pillau
Total	86,600	
Plus	27,800	Additionally becoming available: 22,000 march troops, 5800 Austrians, etc.
Grand total	114,400	

*Excluding 3 battalions still forming and 4 battalions of Hessians and Westphalians of Brigade Coutard (2567 men) on the island of Ruegen.
†3 battalions of IX Corps, Brigade Kosinsky, militia, etc.

TROOPS IN PRUSSIA AND NORTHERN GERMANY

XI Corps:*		
30th Div. Heudelet	15,604	Near Hamburg
31st Div. Lagrange	9,128	In Stettin
32nd Div. Durutte	10,162	In Berlin
34th Div. Morand, then Loison†	10,142	In Stralsund and on Ruegen Island
6 cohorts	3,834	In Bremen
Combined Drag. Brig. Cavaignac	1,105	In Hanover
Artillery‡	5,000	In Danzig, the Prussian fortresses, and Magdeburg
Total	54,975	
Plus:		
33rd (Neapolitan) Div.§	7,599	On the way to Danzig
Troops of the Imperial Guard¶	3,200	2 bns. velites and 2 cos. Honor Guards on the march to Berlin, from there to Warsaw; 3 bns. of the Vistula Legion in Warsaw
Reinforcements for the above	9,700	Still approaching, including Erfurt Brig., which joined 34th Div.
Total	29,499	
Grand total	74,474	

*According to the *carnet* of July 15.
†The contingents from the small German states and the Hessian-Westphalian Brig. Coutard, which actually belonged to IX Corps and followed it.
‡Not listed in the *carnet*.
§This division is included in the report, even though it did not depart from Naples until May 2 and reach Danzig only toward the end of September. For the time being, there were in Danzig parts of the 1st Reserve Division, 2 battalions of Wuerttembergers, who joined Loison's Division.
¶Also not listed in this report.

Added to this list must be the troops that were assigned directly to imperial headquarters. Of the troops listed in the table, Division Durutte (minus 1 regiment), Division Loison, and Brigade Coutard (28,249 men in all) followed the army into Russia, and 1 regiment from Division Durutte (2000 men) went to Poland.

The numbers of the troops under Napoleon's and Davout's command are taken from Chambray, who lists them for August 3. His figures were based partly on *livrets de situation* and partly on estimates. The only numbers deviating from his figures are those given for IV Army Corps and II Cavalry Corps.

For IV Corps, Chambray cites a strength of only 30,445 men for August 3 and 32,823 for the 23rd. However, apart from some stragglers who found their way back, this corps received no reinforcements during that period but certainly suffered more losses. Thus, either the first number is too low or the second is too high. Chambray attributes the difference to returning troops; if this were the case, the report of August 3 should have indicated that at least some men were detached or left behind. For II Cavalry Corps, Chambray calculates 4029 men for August 3. However, for 23 August, after the corps had suffered substantial losses, he cites 3859 men, and this number apparently does not even include Division Pajol (erstwhile Sebastiani). Probably, data on this division is also missing from the August 3 report.

It has not been possible to ascertain whether there were additional garrisons left in the rear areas in Russia. Probably, several places—Smorgoni, Borisov, etc.— were already occupied by march formations that had come up or by provisional formations composed of rounded-up stragglers.

APPENDIX IX

The Strength of the French Main Army, August 23

The Guard:		
Old Guard	6,812	
Young Guard (+ Vistula Legion)	12,925	
Guard cavalry	4,208	
Foot artillery	2,500	
Horse artillery	1,000	
Total		27,445
I Corps		40,622*
III Corps		16,053*
IV Corps (+ Bavarian Cavalry)		32,823*
V Corps (− Div. Dombrowski)		11,857*
VIII Corps		12,686
I Cav. Corps		5,700
II Cav. Corps (+ Div. Pajol)		5,359
III Cav. Corps (− Div. Doumerc)		4,930
IV Cav. Corps (− 28th Light Brig. with Dombrowski)		4,000
Total		161,475

*The figures for I, III, IV, and V Corps include a total of 10,500 corps cavalry.

The total figure consists of 125,778 infantry and 35,697 cavalry. Chambray, arriving at the same overall totals, estimates the cavalry in the army corps at only 8000. This can't be, however, because the reports of September 2, which include detachments, place it at 9528 men, even though no replacements had been received and a light regiment from V Corps (400 men) had been left behind. Thus, the figure of 10,500, allowing for the loss of about 550 men, seems more realistic.

Chambray also cites the strength of II Cavalry Corps at only 3859 men by not taking into account Division Pajol. Since this division still numbered 1400 men when it rejoined the army just before the Battle of Borodino, placing its strength at about 1500 men on August 23 is a fair assessment.

Of the troops in the preceding table, the following remained behind for the time being:

Division Laborde of the Young Guard (− 2 battalions, with headquarters)	4500 men
1 light cavalry regiment of V Corps stayed in Smolensk.	400 men
Division Pino of IV Corps	6000 men
Division Pajol of II Cavalry Corps	1500 men
(Both were to operate in the direction of Vitebsk.)	
1 battalion of collected stragglers in Krasnoi	?

In all, approximately 10,500 infantry and 1900 cavalry remained behind. Pino's division consisted of 13 Italian and 3 Dalmatian battalions, totaling about 6000 men. In the Vitebsk area, he was joined by Guyot's light cavalry brigade, which had been left behind there and in the area of Surash (1000 men in 8 squadrons).

Thus, the advance was continued with only:

115,278 infantry
 33,797 cavalry
149,075 men

APPENDIX X

The French Army, September 2

Units	Present				Detached but expected in 5 days		
	Infantry	Cavalry	Artillery	Guns	Infantry	Cavalry	Artillery
Guard Corps:							
Old Guard	5,305		1,038	32			
Young Guard	3,649		463	16			
Vistula Legion	2,608		251	12			
Guard cavalry		4,000	351	12			
Guard artillery			1,184	37			
Total	11,562	4,000	3,287	109			
I Corps	33,241		3,161	147	2,784		
I Corps cavalry[a]		1,108				196	
III Corps cavalry[a]		1,810	89	6			
III Corps	8,867		1,447	69	964		

IV Corps[b]	17,287	3,465	2,776	88	1,466	27	
V Corps[c]	6,636	1,638	1,794	50	260	259	
VIII Corps[d]	6,911	936	1,021	30	529	160	
I Cav. Corps		4,314	685	25			
II Cav. Corps (− Div. Pajol)[e]		3,260	683	29	1,400		
III Cav. Corps[f]		2,770	137	10	676		
IV Cav. Corps[g]					6,003	5,200	400[h]
Total	84,504	23,301	14,991	563	14,321	7,918	400
Combined total (infantry & cavalry & artillery)	122,796						

[a] Under Murat's command.
[b] Without Division Pino and Brigade Guyot, but with the Bavarian cavalry.
[c] Without Division Dombrowski.
[d] Without 1 battalion left in Viasma and Dorogobush.
[e] Still coming up.
[f] Without Division Doumerc.
[g] Without the 28th Light Brigade, still coming up.
[h] With 24 guns.

The foregoing is based on Chambray and Pelet. They agree on the figures in "Present" columns, except that Chambray does not separate the artillery troops. Pelet does not list the detached troops, nor does he include IV Corps or Division Pajol. He does include the 764 men of the engineer park, but no numbers are cited for the artillery park, so his "present" figures total 123,662 men. Chambray, who counts the detached troops and IV Cavalry Corps but not Pajol's division, arrives at a total of 133,819.

Chambray and Pelet both took their numbers from the *livrets*. Only the strengths of IV Corps are based on estimates. Noteworthy about these numbers is the fact that all the corps, including the Guard, show substantial decreases since August 23, averaging from 2000 to 3000 for each army corps. For I Corps, however, a loss of only 230 men is indicated, while II Cavalry Corps is listed with the exact same strength as it had on August 23.

The Russian Army at Borodino

FIRST WESTERN ARMY: Barclay

	Battalion	Squadrons	Cossack Regiments	Batteries	Men
Right Wing: Miloradovitch					
II Corps: 4th and 17th Inf. Divs.	24			2	10,300
IV Corps: 11th and 23rd Inf. Divs.	23			2	9,500
I Cav. Corps		28		1	2,500
II Cav. Corps		32		1	3,500
Total	47	60		6	25,800
Center: Doctorov					
VI Corps: 7th and 24th Inf. Divs.[a]	28			2	9,900
III Cav. Corps		32		1	3,700
Total	28	32		3	13,600
Reserve of the right and center:					
III Corps: 1st Gren., 3rd Inf. Div.[b]	24			6	8,000
V Corps: Guard infantry, 1st United Gren. Div.	27				13,000
1st Cuirassier Div.		20			2,400
Platov's Cossacks[c]			14	2	5,500
Reserve artillery[d]				26	8,400
Total	51	20	14	34	37,300
Strength of First Western Army	126	112	14	43	76,700

SECOND WESTERN ARMY: Bagration

	Battalion	Squadrons	Cossack Regiments	Batteries	Men
Left Wing:					
Gortshakov					
VII Corps: 12th and 26th Inf. Divs.[e]	24			2	10,800
VIII Corps: 2nd Gren., 27th Inf. Div.	24			2	11,200
IV Cav. Corps		32		1	3,800
Total	48	32		5	25,800
Reserve of the left wing:					
2nd United Gren. Div.[f]	6				2,100
2nd Cuirassier Div.		20			2,300
Karpov's Cossacks			6		1,500
Reserve artillery[g]				7	2,400
Total	6	20	6	7	8,300
Strength of Second Western Army	54	52	6	12	34,100

FIRST AND SECOND WESTERN ARMIES

	Battalion	Squadrons	Cossack Regiments	Batteries	Men
Combined strength at Borodino	180	164	20	55	103,800

[a]Four united grenadier battalions had been added from the 2nd United Grenadier Division.
[b]Used to extend the left wing before the start of the battle.
[c]Including 1 battery and 1 regiment from the Second Army.
[d]Including 5 batteries of the Second Army, as well as 1 engineer and 2 pontoon companies.
[e]This corps first appears here in its new composition.
[f]Four battalions had been detached to VI Corps. (See note a, above.)
[g]Including 1 pontoon company.

The total Russian army at Borodino included 72,000 infantry, 17,300 cavalry, and 14,500 artillery, with 637 guns. The number of guns is generally given as 640, but those lost at Shevardino on September 5 must be subtracted.

At the beginning of the campaign, the Russian armies had numbered as follows:

	Battalions	Squadrons	Cossack Regiments	Batteries
First Western Army	150	132	18	49
Second Western Army	46	52	9	18
27th Inf. Div.	12	—	—	—
Total	208	184	27	67

The reserve troops that had been added were entirely broken up and distributed among the regular formations, that is, no new formations were raised.

Of the above aggregate at the beginning of the campaign, the following troops were detached at this time:

	Battalions	Squadrons	Cossack Regiments	Batteries
Corps Wittgenstein	28	16	1	9
To Riga			1	1
Wintzingerode's detachment		4	3	
Otherwise detached	—	—	2	—
Total	28	20	7	10

Two batteries cannot be accounted for. Probably, as was frequently the case on campaign, they were sent back for replenishment or were disbanded to bring others up to establishment. The troops sent to Riga had been part of Wittgenstein's corps.

APPENDIX XII

The French Army at Borodino

THE STRENGTH OF THE ARMY [a]

Corps	Battalions	Squadrons	Infantry	Cavalry	Artillery	Total Men	Guns
Guard	30	27[b]	11,200 (11,500)	4,000	3,300 (3,200)	18,500 (18,700)	109
I Corps	81[c]	—[d]	32,000	—[d]	3,100	35,100	147
III Corps	33	—[d]	8,600 (8,500)	—[d]	1,400 (1,500)	10,000	69
IV Corps	39	32[e]	17,000 (17,500)	3,000	2,700 (2,800)	23,300	88

Unit	Battalions	Squadrons	Infantry	Cavalry	Artillery	Total	Guns
V Corps	18	12	6,500	1,500	1,500	9,500	50
VIII Corps	13[f]	12	6,500	1,000	1,000	8,500	30
			(6,000)			(8,000)	
From I Corps		16					
From III Corps		24					6
I Cav. Corps		60					25
II Cav. Corps		60		14,200	1,800	16,000	29
				(14,000)	(2,000)		
IV Cav. Corps		30					24
III Cav. Corps		44		3,000	130	3,130	10
				(2,599)		(2,500)	
Total	214	317	82,400	26,700	14,900	124,000	587
			(82,000)	(26,000)	(15,000)	(123,000)	

[a] The numbers listed are generally those given by Bernhardi. Deviations from Bernhardi's numbers appear in parentheses.

[b] According to some sources, there were 32 squadrons.

[c] There were 84 according to some sources, 79 according to another. The latter would indicate that the Portuguese regiment was left behind in Mohilev.

[d] With Murat. (See below.)

[e] Including the Bavarian cavalry.

[f] According to other sources, there were 14 battalions.

Bernhardi's numbers are slightly lower than those of most other authors, who generally repeat Pelet's numbers for September 2, that is, without detachments. For the total, Bogdanovitch cites 130,000, Thiers 127,000, Pelet 126,000, Chambray 120,000, and so on. (A brief discussion of the deviations as they apply to the artillery is presented in Appendix X.) Regarding the deviations, the following points should be noted.

From the Guard strength, a battalion from the Vistula Legion—about 360 men—has been subtracted, since it was left in Gshatsk. Bernhardi ignores this. III Cavalry Corps apparently had not taken part in the actions of the 4th and 5th, as it was in reserve on the latter date. Thus, allowing for the arrival of detachments, the corps must have been stronger.

Bernhardi's assessment of the Westphalian infantry is too weak, because he omitted 2 battalions of the 8th regiment, which were supposedly left behind in Gshatsk. This fallacy is based on a strength report from the commandant in Gshatsk, but the report must be of a later date. The regiment in question did not arrive from Koenigsberg until the end of October. The corps had left two battalions behind, one each in Viasma and Dorogobush, but these were already accounted for in the September 2 report (see Appendix X). Apparently, the garrison of Gshatsk consisted, for the time being, of only a single battalion from the Vistula Legion and two depots of "light-duty" troops (footsore, etc.), one each from I and III Corps.

The troops left behind since crossing the Niemen were as follows:

From the Guard	10 battalions of Division Laborde, coming up from Smolensk; a further 2 battalions from the Legion had already followed the army—they were replaced by another as well as a march battalion, also from the Vistula Legion; a further Vistula battalion in Gshatsk and 2 Hessian battalions in Vitebsk.
From I Corps	2 battalions of the 33rd Light Infantry in Smolensk (they had moved up from Minsk)—a third battalion from this regiment remained in Minsk; 1 Hessian battalion in Vitebsk; 3 Mecklenburg battalions in Vilna.
From III Corps	4 Illyrian battalions in Kovno—these soon went on to Smolensk, along with 3 battalions of the 129th Line Regiment from Vilna; 9 Wuerttembergian battalions had been disbanded because of heavy losses.
From IV Corps	16 battalions of Division Pino and 8 squadrons of Brigade Guyot coming up; 1 battalion in Krasnoi (?).
From V Corps	12 battalions of Division Dombrowski; 2 battalions in Inkovo; 1 battalion (?) and 4 squadrons in Smolensk.
From VIII Corps	1 battalion in Orsza; 1 in Dorogobush; 1 in Viasma; 1 company of Gardes du Corps returned to Kassel.
From III Cav. Corps	16 squadrons and 12 guns of Division Doumerc.
From IV Cav. Corps	12 squadrons with Dombrowski's division.

THE ORDER OF BATTLE OF THE FRENCH ARMY AT BORODINO

	Battalions	Squadrons	Infantry	Cavalry	Artillery	Total Men	Guns
Right wing:							
V Corps: Poniatowski	18	12	6,500	1,500	1,500	9,500	50
Center:							
Davout:							
I Corps, Divs. Friant, Desaix, Compans	47		21,000		2,300	23,300	93
Ney:							
III Corps	33		8,600		1,400	10,000	69
VIII Corps	13	12	6,500	1,000	1,000	8,500	30
Murat:							
I and III Corps cavalry		40					
I Cav. Corps		60					
II Cav. Corps		60		14,200	1,800	16,000	84
IV Cav. Corps		30					
Total	93	202	36,100	15,200	6,500	57,800	276
Reserve:							
The Guard	30	27	11,200	4,000	3,300	18,500	109
The left: Eugene							
Divs. Morand and Gerard of I Corps	34		11,000		800	11,800	54
IV Corps	39	32	17,600	3,000	2,700	23,300	88
III Cav. Corps		44		3,000	100	3,100	10
Total	73	76	28,600	6,000	3,600	38,600	152
Army total	214	317	82,400	26,700	14,900	124,000	587

APPENDIX XIII

Opposing Forces, End of September

THE FRENCH

1. THE MAIN ARMY

Corps in and around Moscow[a]	95,000[b]	
VIII Corps Junot	5,000	
		100,000
Further reinforcements reaching the army in Moscow	28,000[c]	
Troops joining the main army during the retreat	17,000[d]	
		45,000[e]
Total		145,000

2. TROOPS IN THE CENTRAL AREA

Corps Victor (including detachments)	29,000	
Garrison of Smolensk	2,000	
Div. Dombrowski	6,000	
Lithuanian troops (used mostly in rear-area garrisons)	7,000	
Others[f]	ca. 15,000[g]	
		ca. 59,000[h]
Lithuanian troops still forming		7,000
Total		ca. 66,000

3. TROOPS IN POLAND AND VOLHYNIA

Austrian Corps	26,000
VII Corps Reynier	9,500[i]
Brig. Kosinsky	5,500
Total	41,000

THE FRENCH (*cont'd.*)

4. TROOPS IN THE NORTHERN THEATER OF OPERATIONS

X Corps (Macdonald)	24,000	
II and VI Corps under St. Cyr	24,000[j]	
		48,000
Reinforcements coming up for:		
Macdonald	2,000[k]	
St. Cyr	5,000	
		7,000
Total		55,000

5. FURTHER REINFORCEMENTS ADDED LATER

Divs. Durutte and Loison	25,682[l]
Brig. Coutard of IX Corps	2,567
Austrians	5,800
March troops: French,[m] Poles, 1000 Bavarians, 900 Saxons, 1360 Wuerttembergers	9,000
Total	43,039

[a]Including about 2000 reinforcements already arrived but excluding reinforcements after September 25.

[b]See Appendix XIV.

[c]See Appendix XV.

[d]See Appendix XVI.

[e]At that time, probably somewhat more numerous.

[f]Additional rear-area troops, portions of the 1st Reserve Division left behind, march troops, depots, battalions of rounded-up stragglers, etc.

[g]This number may be on the high side, since many of the troops left behind had already been brought up and may be accounted for with the main army. However, many isolated stragglers were still all over the rear areas; they eventually found their way back to the army during the retreat.

[h]At this time, many of the troops listed in section 1 were either near Smolensk or on the way there.

[i]Excluding 1 battalion in Bialystok, accounted for in section 2.

[j]According to St. Cyr, there were only 17,000 men. This, however, is contradicted by the fact that by mid-October, after more losses had been incurred but only 5000 reinforcements had been received, his troops numbered 27,000 men.

[k]Convalescents and reinforcements.

[l]A further 5200 men (2000 of Division Durutte and 3200 Poles and Italians of the Guard)

remained in Warsaw with an additional 8000 march troops of I, VI, and VIII Corps in
Poland and East Prussia, which joined the wreckage of the Grand Army after it came
out of Russia.

ᵐThe greatest part of the French march troops and 1 Lithuanian cavalry regiment were
used to form Brigade Franceski.

THE RUSSIANS

1. THE MAIN ARMY

Present on Oct. 2:
Regulars	60,000	
Militia	5,400*	
Cossacks	10,000	
		75,400

Coming up:
Recruits	33,600	
Cossacks	10,000	
		43,600
Total		119,000

2. TROOPS BETWEEN THE DNIEPER AND THE BERESINA

Corps Oertel	12,000	
Garrison of Bobruisk	5,000	
		17,000
Reinforcements for Oertel		2,000
Total		19,000

3. TROOPS IN VOLHYNIA

Reserve army under Tormassov	30,000	
Danube Army under Tshitshagov	36,000	
Corps Sacken	4,000	
		70,000
Further troops of the Danube Army coming up		11,000
Total		81,000

4. TROOPS IN THE NORTHERN THEATER OF OPERATIONS

Corps Wittgenstein	25,000

THE RUSSIANS (*cont'd.*)

4. TROOPS IN THE NORTHERN THEATER OF OPERATIONS (*cont'd.*)

Garrison of Riga†	16,700	
Finnish Corps†	10,500	
		52,200
Reinforcements for Wittgenstein, to mid-Oct.		15,000
Total		67,200

5. FURTHER REINFORCEMENTS

Reinforcements for Wittgenstein after Oct. 20	2,000
Corps Novak, forming	6,000
Reinforcements of Riga garrison‡	2,900
Recruits joining the main army during pursuit	5,100
Ukrainian Cossacks	ca. 2,000
Reinforcements for Sacken	3,000
	ca. 21,000

*Excluding the militiamen that had been ranked after Borodino but were withdrawn again after the arrival of the recruits.
†Before the actions of Bauske.
‡These consisted of 2600 men from the Finnish Corps and 300 artillerymen.

SUMMARY OF FRENCH AND RUSSIAN TROOPS

	Present	*Coming Up*	*Available Later*
THE FRENCH			
Main army	100,000	45,000	
In the center	59,000	7,000	
Poland and Volhynia	41,000		
Along the Dvina	48,000	7,000	
Further reinforcements	———	———	43,039
Total	248,000	59,000	43,039
Grand total		350,039	

SUMMARY OF FRENCH AND RUSSIAN TROOPS (*cont'd.*)

	Present	Coming Up	Available Later
THE RUSSIANS			
Main army	75,400	43,600	
Between Dnieper and Beresina	17,000	2,000	
In Volhynia	70,000	11,000	
Along the Dvina	52,200	15,000	
Further reinforcements	_____	_____	21,000
Total	214,600*	71,600	21,000
Grand total		318,200	

*Field troops: 192,900 men; garrisons: 21,700.

The French Main Army, End of September*

THE FRENCH MAIN ARMY, END OF SEPTEMBER*

		Infantry	Cavalry
The Guard:			
Old Guard	4,831		
Young Guard	9,875		
Cavalry	4,000		
Total		14,706	4,000
I Corps: 1st, 3rd, and 5th Divs.;		13,821	
2nd and 4th Divs. and Corps cavalry		9,756	1,241
III Corps, without Corps cavalry		6,243	
IV Corps		27,326	
V Corps		6,923†	
I Cav. Corps			2,721
II Cav. Corps, including III Corps cavalry			4,263
III Cav. Corps			3,000
IV Cav. Corps			1,775
Total		76,275	19,500

*Status as of September 20; Young Guard as of December 26.
†Including about 2500 cavalry between IV and V corps.

Regarding the table above, several points should be noted:

1. The numbers deviate from Chambray only in that he does not extrapolate the strength of the Cavalry for IV and V Corps and thus comes up with an extra 2500 infantry and correspondingly fewer cavalry.

2. The artillery, as of October 7, had 571 guns and 2325 artillery vehicles.

3. VIII Corps, at this time, numbered about 5000 men, with 34 guns.

4. Chambray reports that at the end of September, the hospitals in Moscow contained a further 15,000 sick and wounded. This appears debatable for the following reasons: First, it is not clear from whence these men would have come. It cannot be assumed that the French would have taken any men other than the lightly wounded, who had not left the ranks, along from Borodino to Moscow, and few casualties had been sustained since Borodino. On the other hand, one often notes that after a prolonged period of great exertion, considerable numbers of men take ill when a long rest period finally sets in.

Second, arguing most against Chambray's statement is the strength of the army. Nowhere does there exist an exact strength report of the army upon its arrival in Moscow. All statements to this effect rest on Chambray's numbers (cited above), which are not those of September 14, but those of September 20. These numbers cannot be reconciled with the strength of the army on its departure from Moscow.

APPENDIX XV

Reinforcements Received in Moscow and During the First Stage of the Retreat

Infantry	Cavalry	Units	Time
	2,000	Miscellaneous formations, apparently 1st, 2nd, 3rd, and 4th March Cav. Regts.*	Before Sept. 20
3,500		1 march regt., 1 bn. Guard, 1 regt. of III Corps, under Lanusse	Toward Sept. 20
	1,455	5th, 6th, and 7th March Cav. Regts. and 1 march sqn., also under Lanusse	Toward Sept. 20
1,300		Of I Corps, 3 bns. 33rd Light Inf. from Minsk; 1 Hessian bn. from Vitebsk	End of Sept.
	700	March cavalry	End of Sept.
2,000		2 march bns. from Vitebsk	In Oct.
3,000	500	March troops from Minsk, at first intended to garrison Smolensk	In Oct.
4,000		3 bns. of VIII Corps, left behind in Orsza, Dorogobush, and Viasma; also from Orsza, 3 bns. of V Corps; 2 from Yurovo; 1 (source unknown); 1 Vistula bn. from Gshatsk; 1 Vistula march bn.	In Oct.
ca. 11,500		1st, 2nd, and 3rd March Inf. Regts. 8th, 9th, 10th, and 11th March Cav. Regts. Various small detachments Convalescents, notably 1000	
ca. 30,000 men‡		Wuerttembergers†	In Oct.

489

*The strength of these formations is firmly established. However, it cannot be determined if one or the other of these was diverted to II Corps.

†The number of the other convalescents was modest, as most were held back for rear-area services; those who did not return to their units should be accounted for in the march regiments.

‡With 52 guns, including the guns of Divisions Laborde and Pino. The French artillery, which had had 587 guns at Borodino, had lost 8 at that battle and 36 at Vinkovo and had left another 26 in Moscow. Thus, with the additional guns, it had 569 on leaving Moscow.

The troops used as garrisons between Smolensk and Moscow were as follows:

Of the Guard	2 Hessian battalions (from Vitebsk) and 3 battalions of the Vistula Legion (from Smolensk)
Of I Corps	1 battalion, 33rd Light Infantry; 2, possibly all 3, battalions of the Mecklenburg Regiment (from Vilna)
Of VIII Corps	2 battalions of the 8th Westphalian Infantry (from Koenigsberg and Pillau)
Total	10 battalions, about 4000 men, with 12 guns

The troops of Division General Baraquey d'Hilliers consisted of:

3 battalions of the 129th Line Infantry from III Corps
3 battalions of the Illyrian Regiment of III Corps
9 battalions of the 1st, 2nd, and 4th March Half-Brigades of the 1st Reserve Division. 4th and 5th March Regiments
1 combined march cavalry regiment

The column of Brigadier General Evers consisted of about 4000 men from the units presented in the two lists above. However, the exact composition of this column is not known.

Some additional troops reached the army in Smolensk. These were 1000 men in march formations of the Guard, as well as several artillery companies.

APPENDIX XVI

The French Army, Mid-October

1. THE MAIN ARMY ON OCT. 18, AFTER THE ACTION OF VINKOVO

	Infantry*	Cavalry*	Guns	Artillery Vehicles
Guard	17,871	4,609	112	275
I Corps	27,449	1,500	144	633
III Corps	9,597	901	71	186
IV Corps	23,963	1,661	92	450
V Corps	4,844	868	49	239
VIII Corps	4,916	775	34	130
Dismounted cavalry	ca. 4,000			
I, II, III, and IV Cav. corps	_____	ca. 5,000	67	157
Total	92,640	15,314	569	2,070
Combined total (infantry & cavalry)				107,954

2. TROOPS ON THE MAIN ARMY'S LINES OF COMMUNICATION

See Appendix XV.   ca. 19,000

3. TROOPS IN THE CENTER

IX Corps (including detached troops in Vitebsk)	27,000
Div. Dombrowski (including some Polish and Lithuanian new formations and the garrisons of Mohilev and Borisov)	6,500
Garrison of Minsk, Wuerttemberger, and Lithuanian new formations and depots	5,700
Others,[†] forming the garrisons of: Krasnoi, Dubrovna, Gorki, Orsza	ca. 2,500

3. TROOPS IN THE CENTER (*cont'd.*)

Kovno, Vilna, Miedniki, Oszmiana, Smorgoni, and ?[‡]	ca. 12,000
Total	ca. 54,000

4. THE CORPS ON THE LEFT WING

X Corps	24,000[§]
II Corps (including Div. Doumerc)	22,00
VI Corps (minus its cavalry)	5,000
Total	51,000

5. THE CORPS ON THE LEFT WING

Austrian Auxiliary Corps	24,000
VII Corps	8,500
Brig. Kosinsky	4,500
Garrisons in Bialystok (1 Saxon battalion), Slonim (3rd Guard Lancers),[¶] and Grodno (formerly Dombrowski, now Lithuanians)	2,000
Total	39,000

6. REINFORCEMENTS COMING

See section 5 in the table "The French" in Appendix XIII.	ca. 43,000

[*]The numbers cited include the foot and horse artillery but not about 7000 men in the army administration, trains, and parks personnel.

[†]Troops left behind, march formations, reformed battalions of stragglers, depots, and Lithuanian new formations. It should be noted that the stragglers have not been taken into account either here or in section 2 of the table "The French" in Appendix XIII.

[‡]The places cited here were known to have garrisons, but it is certain that there were garrisons in numerous other places as well. It is not possible to give the exact strengths of most of them because there are virtually no records. The estimate for Kovno, etc., is not too high, since these garrisons included most of the Lithuanian new formations.

[§]Including some replacements, soon to arrive.

[¶]This regiment was disbanded again on October 20 in Tshaplitz.

Thus, the total number of French troops at this time was approximately 314,000 men.

APPENDIX XVII

The Russian Army, Mid-October

1. THE MAIN ARMY (before the action of Vinkovo)

II Inf. Corps: Baggehuffwudt	9,199
III Inf. Corps: Stroganov	12,526
IV Inf. Corps: Ostermann-Tolstoy	9,308
V (Guard) Inf. Corps: Lavrov*	8,562
VI Inf. Corps: Doctorov	9,542
VII Inf. Corps: Raievsky	10,813
VIII Inf. Corps: Borosdin I	9,476
I Cav. Corps: Moeller-Sakomelsky	2,413
II (and III) Cav. Corps: Korff II	2,205
IV Cav. Corps: Vassilchikov	1,641
Cuirassier corps: Gallitzin	2,785

		78,470†
Remainder of militia, artillery, engineers		15,000‡
		93,470
Cossacks		20,000
Reinforcements added to the above:		113,470§
Before the departure for Tarutino	ca. 11,000	
Coming up during the pursuit	ca. 5,000	
		ca. 16,000
Total		ca. 129,470

2. TROOPS IN THE NORTHERN OPERATIONS AREA

I Inf. Corps and attached troops: Wittgenstein	40,000
Finnish Corps	9,500
Garrison of Riga	10,000

2. TROOPS IN THE NORTHERN OPERATIONS AREA (*cont'd.*)

Reinforcements becoming available:		59,500
Militias, 1 Cossack regiment, and		
1 battery joining Wittgenstein after Oct. 20	2,000	
Corps Novak, still forming	6,000	
Parts of the Finnish Corps going to Riga	3,000	
		11,000
Total		70,500

3. TROOPS IN THE SOUTHERN OPERATIONS AREA (prior to Tshitshagov's departure to the Beresina)

Third Western Army: Vice Admiral Tshitshagov (including, in part, reinforcements under Lueders and those that formed Repinski's detachment)	66,200	
Corps Oertel	15,000	
Ukrainian Cossacks under Witte	2,000	
Garrison of Bobruisk	5,000	
		88,200
Reinforcements becoming available:		
Further troops from Danube Army and 13th Div. and reserves joining Sacken's detached corps in Dec.	3,000[¶]	
Total		91,200

*Now only the 19 Guard battalions.

†There were 69,426 infantry, including about 6000 militiamen, and 9414 cavalry, including Wintzingerode's raiding detachments.

‡The total of militia, including the 6000 still ranked with the line units, came to about 13,500 men, of which about 8000 were soon withdrawn and replaced with recruits.

§With 622 guns.

¶In all, after the action of Volkovich, about 500 men joined Sacken's corps, not counting the Ukrainian Cossacks. Some of these, apparently, did not arrive until December or early January.

Thus, the total number of Russian troops at this time was 253,500 men present, with an additional 32,142 men coming up. The present strength excludes 8000 militiamen who were soon to be withdrawn from the line, but it includes 15,000 men who garrisoned Riga and Bobruisk. The strength of those coming up excludes 11,000 men who no longer found use, but it includes 3000 men who went to Riga.

APPENDIX XVIII

The Russian Main Army During the Initial Stages of the Pursuit

- *Raiders:*
    Col. Kaisarov: 3 Cossack regiments
    Col. Kudashev: 2 Cossack regiments
    Col. Yefremov: 2 Cossack regiments
    Lt. Col. Davidov: 80 hussars and 150 Cossacks from diverse regiments and 2 Cossack regiments
    Staff Capt. (later Col.) Seslavin: Diverse detachments and 1 Cossack regiment, with 4 guns
    Capt. Figner: Diverse detachments and 1 Cossack regiment

- *Flying columns:*
    Maj. Gen. Count Kutuzov: 1 Guard Cossack, 1 dragoon, 1 hussar, and 6 Cossack regiments and 1 sotnia of Cossacks, with 2 guns
    Maj. Gen. Orlov-Denisov: 6 Cossack regiments, with 6 guns
    Gen. of Cavalry and Cossacks Platov: 1 jaeger regiment (from the 3rd Infantry Division) and 13 Cossack regiments, with 12 guns
    Maj. Gen. Karpov II: 7 Cossack regiments
    Maj. Gen. Ozarovski: (Not formed until November 29) 1 jaeger regiment (from the 24th Infantry Division) and 1 hussar and 4 Cossack regiments, with 6 guns.

The composition of Platov's and Karpov's detachments changed repeatedly, and other detachments were formed temporarily.

- *Advance guard:* Gen. of Infantry Miloradovitch
    II Infantry Corps—Lt. Gen. Dolgoruky: 4th Infantry Division (5 regiments) and 17th Infantry Division (5 regiments)
    IV Infantry Corps—Lt. Gen. Ostermann-Tolstoy: 11th Infantry Division (5 regiments) and 23rd Infantry Division (2 regiments)
    II (and III) Cavalry Corps—Lt. Gen. Korff II: 8 dragoon regiments and 1 hussar and 1 ulan regiment
    IV Cavalry Corps—Lt. Gen. Vassilchikov: 4 dragoon regiments and 1 hussar and 1 ulan regiment
    Cossacks: 4 regiments
    Artillery: 84 guns

- *Corps de bataille*: Gen. of Cavalry Tormassov

    III Infantry Corps—Lt. Gen. Stroganov: 1st Grenadier Division (6 regiments) and 3rd Infantry Division (5 regiments)

    V (Guard) Infantry Corps—Lt. Gen. Lavrov: Guard infantry (6 regiments plus 1 battalion, totaling 19 battalions)

    VI Infantry Corps—Gen. of Infantry Doctorov: 7th Infantry Division (5 regiments) and 24th Infantry Division (4 regiments)

    VII Infantry Corps—Lt. Gen. Raievsky: 12th Infantry Division (5 regiments) and 26th Infantry Division (5 regiments)

    VIII Infantry Corps—Lt. Gen. Borosdin: 2nd Grenadier Division (6 regiments) and 27th Infantry Division (5 regiments)

    I Cavalry Corps—Lt. Gen. Moeller-Sakomelsky: 3 Guard Cavalry regiments and 1 dragoon and 1 hussar regiment

    Cuirassier corps: Lt. Gen. Gallitzin V: 1st Cuirassier Division (5 regiments) and 2nd Cuirassier Division (5 regiments)

    Cossacks: Approximately 10 regiments

    Artillery: 508 guns

The total strength of the main army was as follows:

Units	*Men*	*Guns*
137 bns.	76,629*	
144 sqns.	10,711	
55 btrys.	8,959	622
Engineer troops	813	
	97,112	
57 (?) Cossack regts.	20,000	—
Total	117,112	622

It is next to impossible to get an accurate count of the battalion cadres at this time, since the number of battalions that were dissolved, that is, combined with others, is uncertain. It is known, however, that 21 united grenadier battalions had been dissolved and that 20 line battalions were in the process of reforming.

At Borodino, the army had numbered 180 battalions and 164 squadrons. Since that time, no others were formed and only 4 squadrons were detached. The number of Cossack regiments varied from one day to the next; new ones arrived daily, as others were left behind, detached, or disbanded.

APPENDIX XIX

The Russian Main Army During the Final Stages of the Pursuit

THE TROOPS UNDER MILORADOVITCH

- *Raiders:*
  As in Appendix XVIII, but without Davidov's detachment

- *Flying columns:*
  As in Appendix XVIII, but without Karpov's and Ozarovski's detachments)

- *Detachment of Lt. Gen. Yermolov:*
  12 jaeger battalions, 2 Cossack regiments, and 1 horse battery

- *Advance guard: Under Miloradovitch's direct command*
  II Infantry Corps—Lt. Gen Duke Eugene of Wuerttemberg: 3rd Infantry Division (5 regiments) and 4th Infantry Division (5 regiments)
  VII Infantry Corps—Lt. Gen. Raievsky: 12th Infantry Division (5 regiments) and 26th Infantry Division (5 regiments)
  II (and III) Cavalry Corps: Korff II: 8 dragoon regiments and 1 hussar and 1 ulan regiment
  Cossacks: 4 regiments
  Artillery: 60 guns

SUMMARY OF TROOPS UNDER MILORADOVITCH

	Battalions	Squadrons	Cossack Regiments	Guns	Men
Raiders			9	4	ca. 3,700
Borosdin II			6	6	
Kutuzov		14	6	2	3,300
Platov	2		15	12	10,000*
Yermolov	12		2	12	

SUMMARY OF TROOPS UNDER MILORADOVITCH (cont'd.)

	Battalions	Squadrons	Cossack Regiments	Guns	Men
Advance guard	<u>40</u>	<u>20</u>	<u>4</u>	<u>60</u>	<u>15,000</u>
Total	54	34	42	96	ca. 32,000

*Including Seslavin.

Bogdanovich places Miloradovitch's strength at only 25,000, since he counts only Seslavin's, Kutuzov's, and Borosdin's flying columns. However, since the others also followed the French army, they are included here.

His numbers differ further in that he calculates Platov's and Yermolov's infantry at 16 battalions, probably by including Platov's jaeger regiment, which was left behind in Smolensk. He also puts the advance guard at 54 battalions, but does not show from where the extra 14 battalions came. Possibly they were reserve battalions that arrived during the pursuit and were not broken up.

THE MAIN ARMY UNDER KUTUZOV

- *Flying Column Ozarovski:*
  1 jaeger regiment from 24th Division
  1 hussar regiment from III Cavalry Corps
  Cossacks: 4 regiments
  Artillery: 6 guns

- *Detachment Davidov:*
  Cossacks: 2 regiments, various detachments of unknown composition.

- *Advance guard: Vassilchikov*
  1 jaeger regiment from 11th Division
  IV Cavalry Corps: 4 dragoon regiments and 1 hussar and 1 ulan regiment

- *Corps de bataille: Tormassov*
  III (Grenadier) Infantry Corps—Stroganov: 1st Grenadier Division (6 regiments) and 2nd Grenadier Division (6 regiments) (For the time being, the 2nd Grenadier Division and 1 Cossack regiment remained behind in Syrokorenie.)
  IV Infantry Corps—Ostermann-Tolstoy: 11th Infantry Division (3 regiments) and 23rd Infantry Division (2 regiments)
  V (Guard) Corps—Lavrov: 4 Guard regiments and 1 Guard battalion, totaling 13 battalions
  VI Infantry Corps—Doctorov: 7th Infantry Division (3 regiments) and 24th Infantry Division (3 regiments)

VIII Infantry Corps—Dolgoruky: 17th Infantry Division (5 regiments)
and 27th Infantry Division (5 regiments) (For the time being, the 27th
Infantry Division and 1 Cossack regiment remained behind in Krasnoi.)
From I Cavalry Corps: 1 dragoon and 1 hussar regiment
Cuirassier corps—Gallitzin: 1st Cuirassier Division (5 regiments) and 2nd
Cuirassier Division (5 regiments)
Cossacks: 8 (?) regiments
Artillery: 182 guns

SUMMARY OF TROOPS WITH THE MAIN ARMY

	Battalions	Squadrons	Cossack Regiments	Guns	Men
Ozarovski	2	4	4	6	
Davidov			2		
Vassilchikov	2	12	1	6	
Corps de bataille	77	44	8 (?)	182	
Total	81	60	15	194	ca. 38,000

The troops left behind were:

1 jaeger regiment (from the 3rd Division of II Infantry Corps) of Platov's corps
in Smolensk
3 light cavalry regiments of the Guard (of I Cavalry Corps), which remained
at the Dnieper
12 heavy batteries
Parts of most light cavalry regiments, many batteries, and an indeterminate
number of Cossack regiments, some of which were replaced by newly arrived
formations

Thus, the total strength of the main army after the actions at Krasnoi was 135
battalions, 94 squadrons, 57 Cossack regiments, and an undetermined number of
batteries, comprising 70,000 men in all, with 250 guns.

This head count, which includes Kutuzov's flying column and the Cossacks,
reflects the estimates after the actions of Krasnoi. (The numbers dropped substantially
soon afterward.) At this time, the battalions generally consisted of 300 to 350 men,
the cavalry regiments generally had no more than 200 men, and the Cossack regiments still averaged about 200.

APPENDIX XX

The French Army at the Beresina

The term "estimate" looms large for the French army at the Beresina. Fezensac puts the number of men still in the ranks at 50,000, including about 5000 cavalry. Thiers places the number at 40,000. Fain speaks of 40,780 on November 28, that is, 3 days after the crossing of the Beresina and after the heavy losses sustained on the previous day by Victor's corps. About 45,000 to 50,000 stragglers should be added to all of these numbers.

Chambray cites the lowest figures for the troops still in the ranks, placing their number at 26,700 infantry and 4000 cavalry. However, when the following facts are taken into consideration, Chambray's numbers again appear to be closest to the truth:

The remainder of the main army numbered only 12,000 men when it arrived at the Beresina.

Victor had only 12,000 men on November 20.

On the 23rd, Oudinot had only 9500 men (including the troops attached to him) before the action at Borisov.

The garrison of Mohilev, 1200 men, had arrived.

Perhaps, one might add a few hundred Westphalians, the dismounted cavalry troopers, and the two squadrons made up of officers without commands. Thus, the French army at the Beresina probably numbered 27,000 infantry and 4200 cavalry, with 250 guns. The stragglers may have numbered about 35,000.

The numbers for the different corps, as cited by Chambray and Fain, are as follows:

| | Chambray | | Fain |
	Infantry	Cavalry	Men
Corps			
Old Guard	3,500		4,500
Young Guard	1,500		2,200
Guard cavalry		1,400	200
Oudinot	5,600	1,400	9,300*
Ney	3,700	300	5,400†

Appendix XX

	Chambray		Fain
Corps	Infantry	Cavalry	Men
Victor	10,000	800	10,000
Davout	1,200		
Eugene	1,200		9,000
Latour-Maubourg		100	
Dismounted cavalry	_____	_____	180
Total	26,700	4,000	40,780

*II Corps with Divisions Doumerc and Dombrowski and the garrisons of Minsk
and Borisov.
†III and V Corps, the Vistula Legion, and the garrison of Mohilev.

APPENDIX XXI

Survey of French Forces, Mid-December 1812

	Men	Guns	Men	Guns
1. TROOPS IN THE VISTULA PROVINCES				
First-line forces:				
Austrian Auxiliary Corps	25,000	59		
VII Corps	16,000	62		
Miscellaneous Polish Detachments	2,000	6		
			43,000	127
X Corps			23,000	84
Total			66,000	211
2. REINFORCEMENTS IMMEDIATELY AT HAND				
In Warsaw:				
Guard, Italians, Poles	3,200	2		
Lithuanian Horse battery	100	6		
			3,300	8
In Danzig and Marienburg:				
Div. Heudelet (− 2 battalions)	13,439	24		
Drag. Brig. Cavaignac	1,400	—		
			14,839	24
In Plock or on the way there:				
3 Bavarian march columns	4,500			
VI Corps artillery, left behind	400	20	4,900	

	Men	Guns	Men	Guns
2. REINFORCEMENTS IMMEDIATELY AT HAND (*cont'd.*)				
Marching to Thorn:				
3 French march battalions of I Corps	2,000	—		
3 Westphalian march battalions	1,500	2	6,900	20
1 Badensian march squadron	150	—		
			3,650	2
Total			26,689	54
3. REMAINDERS OF THE GRAND ARMY AVAILABLE FOR SERVICE BY EARLY JANUARY				
In Koenigsberg:				
Of the Guard	1,200	4		
Div. Marchand (ex-Loison)	3,000	5		
			4,200	9
In Plock:				
From VI Bavarian Corps			1,600	—
Total			5,800	9
Combined total (sections 1, 2, and 3)			98,489	274
4. TROOPS BECOMING AVAILABLE BY MID-FEBRUARY 1813				
On the Warthe and Oder:				
Remainders of the Grand Army			10,000	10
At Warsaw and Modlin:				
Remainder of Polish army and new formations*			13,500	20
At Posen			1,360	
At Zamosz and Czenstochau			2,200	—
			27,060	30

	Men	Guns	Men	Guns
5. FORTRESS GARRISONS†				
Pillau:				
March troops, French,				
Poles, artillery			1,800	
Danzig:				
Neapolitan Div.				
Destrees, depots,				
artillery			8,000	8
Thorn:				
March troops, French,				
artillery			700	
Modlin:				
Poles, depots, artillery			1,000	
Zamosz:				
Poles, depots, new				
formations, artillery			2,000	
Czenstochau: (?)				8
Total			13,500	8
6. AVAILABLE FOR NEW FORMATIONS				
Redundant French cadre of				
the Grand Army			9,000	
Dismounted French cavalry			10,000	
From allied troops of the				
Grand Army			3,400	
Polish recruits (raw, or yet				
to be raised):				
Kalish	3,000			
Pacen	2,350			
			5,350	
Total			27,750	
Combined total (sections 1–6)			166,799‡	312

*The Polish recruits were yet to be drafted.
†The defense plans for these places called for about 30,000 men.
‡Another 8500 men of the Grand Army who were in the area had been stricken from the records as either deceased or disabled.

	Men	Guns	Men	Guns

1. TROOPS IN THE ODER PROVINCES

	Men	Guns	Men	Guns
In Berlin and the Prussian fortresses:				
2 battalions of the Young Guard	1,800	8		
Div. Lagrange	10,150	16		
2 battalions of Div. Heudelet	1,500			
Artillery	3,700	—		
			17,150	24
In Swedish Pommerania:				
Brig. Morand, French and Saxons			3,000	10
Total			20,150	34

2. MARCHING TOWARD THE ELBE

	Men	Guns	Men	Guns
Div. Grenier (French and Italian) in the Kurmark by mid-Jan.			19,331	30
March companies made up of ships' companies:				
1 battalion in Glogau in Jan.	567			
3 battalions in Stettin in Jan.	1,440			
4 battalions in Berlin, beginning of Feb.	1,800			
			3,807	
Badensian march troops, 2 battalions in Glogau by Feb.			900	
Westphalians, 2 battalions in Kuestrin by mid-Feb.			450	—
Total			24,488	30
Combined total (sections 1 and 2)			44,638	64

Thus, the total forces available in the Vistula and Oder provinces were 211,437 men, with 376 guns.

APPENDIX XXII

Russian Forces Available, Mid-December

THE MAIN ARMY: Kutuzov*

II Inf. Corps: Duke Eugene of Wuerttemberg	2,283
III (Gren.) Inf. Corps: Stroganov	8,531
IV Inf. Corps: Ostermann-Tolstoy	2,722
V (Guard) Inf. Corps: Lavrov	5,320
VI Inf. Corps: Doctorov	2,994
VII Inf. Corps: Raievsky	6,583
VIII Inf. Corps: Dolgoruky	3,711
I Cav. Corps:	692
II (and III) Cav. Corps: Korff II	2,662
IV Cav. Corps: Gallitzin	1,969
	38,944[†]
Cossacks	ca. 10,000
Total	48,944

*As of December 4. The numbers include all detachments, except Count Kutuzov's.
[†]Including 1515 militia and 5142 recruits who had just arrived.
[‡]And 272 guns.

Bogdanovich cites the strength of the main army (including Count Kutuzov's column, which has been set at about 3000 men and deducted from the totals below) as follows:

Corps de bataille: III, IV, V, VI, and VIII Infantry Corps, IV Cavalry Corps, and cuirassier corps	27,464 men	200 guns
Advance guard: II and VII Infantry Corps and II Cavalry Corps	6,500 men	} 74 guns
Detached, left behind, with raiding detachments, etc.	8,000 men	

507

The detached formations include 11 regiments and 1½ battalions of infantry; 2 cuirassier, 6 dragoon, and 3 hussar regiments; 1 uhlan regiment; and 1 hussar and 1 uhlan squadron. Bogdanovich does not list the Cossacks.

THE THIRD WESTERN ARMY: Vice Admiral Tshitshagov[*]

	Strength	
	Current	*On 1st Day of Beresina crossing*
Infantry	8,215	19,750
Cavalry	5,208	
Cossacks	1,690	8,800
Artillery	2,341	3,000
Total	17,454[†]	31,550

[*]As of December 19.
[†]With 156 guns, as opposed to 180 on the first day of crossing the Beresina.

Not included in this table are the troops left behind in the course of the pursuit:

3 battalions, 8 squadrons, 6 Cossack regiments, and 1½ batteries, totaling 1800 men, with 18 guns

Colonel Knorring's detachment: 2 battalions, 8 squadrons, and ½ battery, totaling 1200 men, with 6 guns

Even taking into account these troops as well as further detachments left behind in Lithuania and artillery transferred to the main army, the Third Western Army still could not have entered East Prussia at the end of December with about 15,800 men and 122 guns unless it received another 4000 reinforcements, which seems out of the question. The actual reinforcements appear to have been only 1 Cossack regiment, 3 batteries, and a few hundred convalescents, in all no more than 1400 to 1500 men, with 36 guns. If this is not accepted, then the reinforcements listed at the end of this appendix must be correspondingly increased.

II Reserve Corps, under Tutshkov (also under Tshitshagov's orders) numbered 10,000 men, with 33 guns, as of December 23. The men included 1123 Cossacks as well as Knorring's detachment. Bogdanovich puts the strength of this corps at only 7034 men, with 24 guns, but he ignores the cavalry, the Cossacks, and Knorring's detachment. Including these troops, the corps numbered 7858 men and 1123 Cossacks, with 21 guns, on January 5, 1813, after leaving further detachments behind.

Wittgenstein's corps, including detachments as well as reinforcements (Corps Novak and Colonel Pahlen's detachment), numbered:

Infantry	26,257
Cavalry (including Cossacks)	7,344
Artillery	3,182
	36,783* with 191 guns

*Including about 10,500 militia and 3000 Cossacks.

Bogdanovich gives the strength of the cavalry and Cossacks at 2300 and lists the artillery as having 14 guns less, because he does not include Count Kutuzov's raiding column and 1 battery that was coming up.

Corps Osten-Sacken consisted of 19,000 men (including about 4000 Cossacks), with 96 guns. This is the aggregate strength of the main corps and the detached force under Essen, as well as 7000 reinforcements, which include the Ukrainian Cossacks arriving in December and early January. It is not possible to determine the strength during mid-December.

The other detachments were as follows:

	Men	Cossacks	Guns
Count Muffin-Pushkin	4,200	700	16
von Ratt	2,000		
von Lewis	8,000	1,100	36
Marquis Paulucci	2,500		4
Total	16,700	1,800	56

Thus, the available Russian forces in mid-December were 116,800 line troops, 12,000 militiamen, and 21,800 Cossacks, totaling 150,600 men in all.

In addition, the following reinforcements were soon to come up:

15 reserve battalions of Prince Urusov (to main army
   on December 27)   5,000 men

Cossacks (to main army)	ca. 1,000 to 2,000 men
6 reserve battalions under Shemtshushnikov (to Wittgenstein on January 5)	6,000 men
2 battalions of the 13th Division (returning to Sacken, end of January)	} 1,600 men
2 battalions of the 13th Division, which had been left behind by the Third Western Army	
1 Cossack regiment, 3 batteries, and convalescents (returning to the Third Army, end of December)	1,400 men

In all, the reinforcements amounted to 12,000 to 13,000 men, with 36 guns.

Bibliography

Barraclough, G. *The Origins of Modern Germany*. New York, 1963.

Bernhardi, Theodor v. *Denkwuerdigkeiten aud dem Leben des kaiserl. russ. Generals von der Infanterie Carl Friedrich von Toll*. Leipzig, 1865.

Bleckwenn, H. *Das Altrpeussische Heer, 1713–1807*. Osnabrueck, 1970–.

Bogdanovich, Modest I. *Geschichte des Feldzuges im Jahre 1812*. Leipzig, 1861–1863. 3 vols.

Brabant, Arthur. *In Russland und Sachsen*. From the papers of Saxon Lt. Gen. Ferdinand von Funck. Dresden, 1930.

Brandt, H. v. *Aus dem Leben des Generals Heinrich v. Brandt*. Berlin, 1868.

Camon, Hubert. *Quand et Comment Napoleon a Concu son Systeme de Bataille*. Paris, 1935.

Cate, Curtis. *The War of the Two Emperors*. New York, 1985.

Chambray, Georges de. *Histoire de l'Expedition an Russie*. Paris, 1823. 2 vols.

Chandler, David G. *The Campaigns of Napoleon*. New York, 1966.

Clausewitz, Carl von. *Der Russische Feldzug von 1812*. Essen, no date. Repr.

——— *On War*. Howard and Paret trans. Princeton, 1976.

Connelli, Owen. *Blundering to Glory*. Wilmington, 1987.

Du Casse, Albert (ed.). *Les Rois Freres de Napoleon Ier*. Paris, 1883.

Esposito, V. J. and Elting, J. R. *A Military History and Atlas of the Napoleonic Wars*. New York, 1964.

Fain, Baron A. J. F. *Manuscrit de l'an 1812, contenant le precis des evenements de cette annee*. 2 vols. Paris, 1827.

Fiedler, Siegfried. *Grundriss der Militaer und Kriegsgeschichte*. Vol. II. Munich, 1976.

Fieffe, Eugene. *Histoire des Troupes Etrangeres au Service de France*. Paris, 1854.

Hildebrand, Bernhard (ed.). *Drei Schwaben unter Napoleon*. Stuttgart, 1987.

Holzhausen, Paul. *Die Deutschen in Russland 1812*. Berlin, 1912. 2 vols.

Kleinschmidt, Arthur. *Geschichte des Koenigreichs Westfalen*. Kassel, 1970. Repr.

Kraft, Heinz. *Die Wuerttemberger in den Napoleonischen Kriegen*. Stuttgart, no date. [1952].

Loewenstern, W. H. von. *Denkwuerdigkeiten eines Livlaenders*. Vol. I. (F. von Smitt, ed.) Leipzig and Heidelberg, 1858.

Maendler, Friedrich. *Erinnnerungen aus meinen Feldzuegen*. Nuremberg, 1854.

Martens, Christian von. *Vor Fuenfzig Jahren*. Stuttgart and Oehringen, 1862.

Martinien, A. *Tableaux par Corps et par Baitailles des Officiers Tues et Blesses*. Paris, no date. Repr. of 1899 edition.

Montesquiou-Fezensac, R. A. P. J. *Souvenirs Militaires de 1804 à 1814*. Paris, 1863.

[Morvan, Jean] Capitaine M. Tixier. *Le Soldat Imperial*. Paris, 1904. 2 vols.

Osten-Sacken und von Rhein, Freiherr von der. *Der Feldzug von 1812*. Berlin, 1901.

Pelet-Narbonne, G. von. *Geschichte der Brandenburg-Preussischen Reiterei*. Vol. II. Berlin, 1905.

Pfister, N. *Aus dem Lager des Rheinbundes 1812 und 1813*. Stuttgart and Leipzig, 1897.

Prussia. General Staff. *Militaer-Wochenblatt, Beihefte 8 und 9*. Berlin, 1894:
　　Krahmer, Maj. Gen. von. *Die Operationen der Russischen und Franzoesischen Armee im Kriege 1812 von der Schlacht von Krasnoi bis zur Beresina*.
　　Chapelle, Col. *Der Uebergang ueber die Beresina*.
———*Truppenfuehrung und Heereskunde*. (Quarterlies.) Berlin, 1904–1912:
　　Freytag-Loringhoven, v. *Ueber das Anwachsen der Heere*. 1906/1.
———*Die Armeen des ersten Kaiserreichs*. 1908/2.
　　Renner. *Wechselwirkung zwischen Heereszucht und Verpflegung*. 1909/3.

Rapp, Comte. *Die Memoiren des General Rapp*. H. Schmidt and C. Guenther (eds.) Leipzig, 1902.

Roeder, Helen (ed.). *The Ordeal of Captain Roeder, being the memoirs of Franz Roeder*. New York, 1961.

Sachs, Karl. *Erinnnerungs-Blaetter aus dem Russischen Feldzug*. Ulm, 1987.

Sauzey, Camile. *Les Allemagnes sous les Aigles Francaise*. 6 vols. Paris, 1902–1912.

Schauroth, Alex von. *Im Rheinbundregiment*. Berlin, 1905.

Schehl, Karl. *Vom Rhein zur Moskwa 1812*. Krefeld, 1957.

Schenk, Carl Christian Ludwig. *Mitteilungen aud dem Leben eines franzoesischen Oberstlieutenants*. Celle, 1829.

Schreckenstein, Roth von. *Die Kavallerie in der Schlacht an der Moskwa.* Muenster, 1858.

Schwarz, Herbert. *Gefechtsformen der Infanterie in Europa.* Munich, 1977.

Stein, F. von. *Geschichte des Russischen Heeres.* Krefeld, 1975. Repr.

Strachan, Hew. *European Armies and the Conduct of War.* London, 1983.

Thiers, L. A. *Histoire du consulat et de l'empire.* 20 vols. Paris, 1845–1869.

Wedel, K. A. von. *Geschichte eines Offiziers im Kriege gegen Russland.* Berlin, 1897.

Wesemann, H. D. (ed.). *Kanonier des Kaisers. Kriegstagebuch des Heinrich Wesemann, 1808–1814.* Koeln, 1971.

Wrangell, G. (ed.). *Mit Graf Pahlen's Reiterei gegen Napoleon.* Berlin, 1910.

Index